A Companion to Europe 1900-

BLACKWELL COMPANIONS TO HISTORY

This series provides sophisticated and authoritative overviews of the scholarship that has shaped our current understanding of the past. Defined by theme, period and/or region, each volume comprises between twenty-five and forty concise essays written by individual scholars within their area of specialization. The aim of each contribution is to synthesize the current state of scholarship from a variety of historical perspectives and to provide a statement on where the field is heading. The essays are written in a clear, provocative, and lively manner, designed for an international audience of scholars, students, and general readers.

BLACKWELL COMPANIONS TO EUROPEAN HISTORY

BLACKWELL COMPANIONS TO BRITISH HISTORY

BLACKWELL COMPANIONS TO AMERICAN HISTORY

BLACKWELL COMPANIONS TO WORLD HISTORY

A COMPANION TO EUROPE
1900–1945

Edited by

Gordon Martel

A John Wiley & Sons, Ltd., Publication

This paperback edition first published 2011
© 2011 Blackwell Publishing Ltd

Edition history: Blackwell Publishing Ltd (hardback, 2006)

Blackwell Publishing was acquired by John Wiley & Sons in February 2007. Blackwell's publishing program has been merged with Wiley's global Scientific, Technical, and Medical business to form Wiley-Blackwell.

Registered Office
John Wiley & Sons Ltd, The Atrium, Southern Gate, Chichester, West Sussex, PO19 8SQ, United Kingdom

Editorial Offices
350 Main Street, Malden, MA 02148-5020, USA
9600 Garsington Road, Oxford, OX4 2DQ, UK
The Atrium, Southern Gate, Chichester, West Sussex, PO19 8SQ, UK

For details of our global editorial offices, for customer services, and for information about how to apply for permission to reuse the copyright material in this book please see our website at www.wiley.com/wiley-blackwell.

The right of Gordon Martel to be identified as the author of the editorial material in this work has been asserted in accordance with the UK Copyright, Designs and Patents Act 1988.

Wiley also publishes its books in a variety of electronic formats. Some content that appears in print may not be available in electronic books.

Designations used by companies to distinguish their products are often claimed as trademarks. All brand names and product names used in this book are trade names, service marks, trademarks or registered trademarks of their respective owners. The publisher is not associated with any product or vendor mentioned in this book. This publication is designed to provide accurate and authoritative information in regard to the subject matter covered. It is sold on the understanding that the publisher is not engaged in rendering professional services. If professional advice or other expert assistance is required, the services of a competent professional should be sought.

Library of Congress Cataloging-in-Publication Data

A companion to Europe: 1900–1945 / edited by Gordon Martel.
    p. cm. — (Blackwell companions to European history)
  Includes bibliographical references and index.
  ISBN: 978-1-4051-0664-1 (hardcover : alk. paper)
  ISBN: 978-1-4443-3840-9 (pbk.: alk. paper)
  1. Europe—History—20th century. I. Martel, Gordon. II. Series.
  D424.C66 2005
  940.5—dc22

                                    2005013772

A catalogue record for this book is available from the British Library.

Set in 10/12 pt Galliard by Toppan Best-set Premedia Limited
Printed in Malaysia by Ho Printing (M) Sdn Bhd

1 2011

Contents

Contributors

Nicholas Atkin was Professor of Modern European History at the University of Reading. He has written extensively on France under Nazi rule and has authored *Church and Schools in Vichy France* (New York, Garland, 1991), *Pétain* (London, Longman, 1997), *The French at War, 1934–1944* (London, Longman, 2001), *The Forgotten French: Exiles in the British Isles, 1940–1944* (Manchester, MUP, 2003), *The Fifth French Republic* (Basingstoke, Palgrave, 2004) and, with Frank Tallett, *Priests, Prelates and People: A History European Catholicism since 1750* (London, Tauris, 2003). Professor Atkin died in 2009.

Mark Baker is Lecturer in Eastern European History at California State University, Bakersfield. His book manuscript, "Peasants, Power and Revolution in the Village: A Social History of Kharkiv Province, 1914–1921," is currently under review for publication. He has published several articles on the revolutionary period, the most pertinent of which is "Rampaging *Soldatki*, Cowering Police, Bazaar Riots and Moral Economy: The Social Impact of the Great War in Kharkiv Province," *Canadian–American Slavic Studies* 35, Nos. 2–3 (Summer–Fall 2001).

Tami Davis Biddle is George C. Marshall Chair of Military Studies at the US Army War College. Her research focus is on twentieth-century warfare, and she is the author of *Rhetoric and Reality in Air Warfare: The Evolution of British and American Ideas about Strategic Bombing, 1914–1945* (2002), which was a *Choice* Outstanding Academic Book for 2002. She has also written many articles on various aspects of air warfare, and the history of the Cold War. From 1992 to 2001 she taught military and diplomatic history at Duke University and was a core faculty member of the Duke–University of North Carolina Joint Program in Military History.

Martin Blinkhorn is Professor of Modern European History at Lancaster University. He is the author and editor of numerous works on the Spanish and Portuguese right, Italian fascism, and European fascism from a comparative perspective. This last category includes the edited volume *Fascists and Conservatives: The Radical Right and the Establishment in Twentieth-Century Europe* (1990) and his *Fascism and the Right in Europe, 1919–1945* (2000).

Michael Jabara Carley is Chair and Professor of History at the Université de Montréal, interested in early Soviet-western relations, the author of *1939: The Alliance that Never Was and the Coming of World War II* (1999), which has been translated into French (2001) and Russian (2005), and

Revolution & Intervention: The French Government and the Russian Civil War, 1917–1919 (1983), and a great many articles and review articles (1976 to the present) in learned journals in Canada, the United Kingdom, France, and the United States.

Cathryn Carson is Associate Professor of History at the University of California, Berkeley, where she directs the Office for History of Science and Technology. She has published on the history of quantum physics, the politics of science in Germany, and the cultural and philosophical lessons scientists have drawn from their work. Her forthcoming book is titled Heisenberg in the Atomic Age: Science and the Public Sphere.

William J. Chase is a Professor of History at the University of Pittsburgh. He is the author of Workers, Society, and the Soviet State: Labor and Life in Moscow, 1918–1929 (1987) and Enemies Within the Gates? The Comintern and the Stalinist Repression, 1934–1939 (1999). He is a co-director and co-editor of the Russian Archive Series, a Russian–American collaborative project that has published guides to central Russian archives.

James M. Diehl has recently retired as Professor of History at Indiana University, Bloomington. His main publications are Paramilitary Politics in Weimar Germany (1977) and The Thanks of the Fatherland: German Veterans after the Second World War (1993). He is currently working on a study of the emergence of a democratic political culture in western Germany after 1945.

David Engel is Maurice R. and Corinne P. Greenberg Professor of Holocaust Studies, Professor of History, and Professor of Hebrew and Judaic Studies at New York University and a fellow of the Goldstein-Goren Diaspora Research Center at Tel Aviv University. His books include In the Shadow of Auschwitz: The Polish Government-in-Exile and the Jews 1939–1942 (1987), Facing a Holocaust: The Polish Government-in-Exile and the Jews 1943–1945 (1993), Between Liberation and Flight: Holocaust Survivors in Poland and the Struggle for Leadership 1944–1946 (Hebrew, 1996),

The Holocaust: The Third Reich and the Jews (2000), and "A Truly Overwhelming Picture": The Holocaust and the Writing of Jewish History (Hebrew, forthcoming).

Carole Fink is Distinguished Humanities Professor in History at Ohio State University. She is the author of Defending the Rights of Others: The Great Powers, the Jews, and International Minority Protection, 1878–1938 (2004), Marc Bloch: A Life in History (1989), which has been translated into six languages, and The Genoa Conference (1984), which was awarded the George Louis Beer prize of the American Historical Association. She is the editor of five volumes: Human Rights in Europe since 1945 (2003), 1968: The World Transformed (1998), The Establishment of European Frontiers after Two World Wars (1996), European Reconstruction in 1921–1922 (1991), and German Nationalism and the European Response, 1890–1945 (1985).

David French is Professor of History at University College London. His book Raising Churchill's Army: The British Army and the War against Germany, 1919–1945 (2000) was awarded the Templer Medal by the Society for Army Historical Research and the Arthur Goodzeit Prize by the New York Military Affairs Symposium. He is now completing a study of the place of the regimental system in British military culture since 1870.

Dick Geary taught at the University of Lancaster from 1973 to 1989, then moved to the Chair of Modern History at Nottingham. His research concerned itself until recently with comparative labor history, the social history of modern Germany, and the history of Marxism. Recently, he has been working on comparisons between Brazilian slavery and free labor in Europe. His books include European Labour Protest, 1848–1939 (1981), Karl Kautsky (1987), The German Unemployed, edited with Richard J. Evans, (1987), Labour and Socialist Movements in Europe before 1914 (1989), European Labour Politics from 1900 to the Depression (1991), and Hitler and Nazism (1993, 2000).

Lesley A. Hall is Senior Archivist at the Wellcome Library for the History and Understanding of Medicine in London, and Honorary Lecturer in History of Medicine at the University of London. She has written several books and numerous articles and chapters on sexuality and gender in the nineteenth and twentieth centuries. She co-edited (with Franz Eder and Gert Hekma) *Sexual Cultures in Europe: National Histories* and *Sexual Cultures in Europe: Themes in Sexuality* (1998) and (with Roger Davidson) *Sex, Sin and Suffering: Venereal Disease and European Society since 1870* (2001).

June Hannam is Reader in History and Associate Dean (research and staff development) in the Faculty of Humanities, Languages and Social Science at the University of the West of England, Bristol. Her publications include *Isabella Ford, 1855–1924* (Blackwell, 1989), *Socialist Women: Britain, c. 1880s to 1920s* (2001) (with Karen Hunt), and *International Encyclopaedia of Women's Suffrage* (2000) (with Mitzi Auchterlonie and Katherine Holden). She has also written numerous articles on feminist and socialist politics in the late nineteenth and early twentieth centuries.

Elizabeth Harvey is Professor of History at the University of Nottingham, the author of *Women and the Nazi East: Agents and Witnesses of Germanization* (2003) and *Youth and the Welfare State in Weimar Germany* (1993), and the co-editor of *Zwischen Kriegen: Nationen, Nationalismen und Geschlechterverhältnisse in Mittel- und Osteuropa 1918–1939* (2004) (with Johanna Gehmacher and Sophia Kemlein), *Gender Relations in German History: Power, Agency and Experience from the Sixteenth to the Twentieth Century* (1996) (with Lynn Abrams), and *Determined Women: Studies in the Construction of the Female Subject 1900–1990* (1991) (with Jennifer Birkett).

Paul Lawrence is Lecturer in European History at the Open University, where he helps to run the European Centre for the Study of Policing. His publications include *Nationalism: History and Theory* (2004) and articles on various aspects of immigration, crime, and policing. He is currently working on a history of the relationship between the police and the poor in France and England.

Harold Marcuse is a Professor of History at the University of California, Santa Barbara. His publications include *Steine des Anstosses* (Stones of Contention), the catalog of an exhibition surveying monuments and memorials for events during World War II from around the world (1985), and *Legacies of Dachau: The Uses and Abuses of a Concentration Camp, 1933–2001* (2001).

Gordon Martel is Emeritus Professor of History at the University of Northern British Columbia and Adjunct Professor at the University of Victoria. He is the author of *Imperial Diplomacy* (1986) and *The Origins of the First World War* (3rd edn, 2003). Among his edited works are: *The World War Two Reader* (2004); *The Times & Appeasement: The Journals of A. L. Kennedy* (2000); *The Origins of the Second World War Reconsidered: A. J. P. Taylor and the Historians* (2nd edn, 1999); and *Modern Germany Reconsidered* (1992). He is Editor-in-Chief of the forthcoming *Encyclopedia of War* (Wiley-Blackwell).

Annika Mombauer is Senior Lecturer in Modern European History at the Open University. Her publications include *Helmuth von Moltke and the Origins of the First World War* (2001) and *The Origins of the First World War: Controversies and Consensus* (2002). She has co-edited (with Wilhelm Deist) *The Kaiser: New Research on Wilhelm II's Role in Imperial Germany* (2003).

Anita J. Prazmowska is a Senior Lecturer at the Department of International History, London School of Economics. She has published two monographs on Polish–British relations prior to and during World War II: *Britain, Poland and the Eastern Front, 1939* (1987) and *Britain and Poland 1939–1943: The Betrayed Ally* (1995). More recently she has published a book on origins of communism in Poland entitled

Civil War in Poland, 1942–48 (2004). Her next project is a wide-ranging analysis of the events of 1956 in eastern Europe.

Michael Richards lectures in contemporary European history at the University of the West of England, Bristol. He is author of *A Time of Silence: Civil War and the Culture of Repression in Franco's Spain, 1936–45* (1998) and co-editor of *The Splintering of Spain: Cultural History and the Spanish Civil War, 1936–39* (2005). He has published many articles on aspects of the cultural history of the Spanish Civil War with particular reference to collective memory, religiosity, ritual and mourning, and psychiatry and identity. Current projects include collaborative and comparative work on Spanish public health and epidemics, memory and migration in twentieth-century Europe, and a social history of the post-civil war years in Spain.

Thomas J. Saunders is Associate Professor of History at the University of Victoria in British Columbia. He is the author of *Hollywood in Berlin: American Cinema and Weimar Germany* (1994) and articles on interwar European cinema and fascism and popular culture. He is currently researching the political and popular dimensions of financial scandals in 1920s Germany.

Alan Sharp was Professor of International Studies and Head of the School of History and International Affairs at the University of Ulster prior to his retirement in 2009. His research interests are in British foreign policy after the First World War, on which he has published widely. His books include *The Versailles Settlement* (1991) and (with Glyn Stone) *Anglo-French Relations in the Twentieth Century* (2000).

Angela K. Smith is a Senior Lecturer in English Literature at the University of Plymouth. Her publications include *The Second Battlefield: Women, Modernism and the First World War* (2000) and *Suffrage Discourse in Britain During the First World War* (2005). She is the editor of *Women's Writing of the First World War: An Anthology* (2000) and *Gender and Warfare in the Twentieth Century: Textual Representations* (2004).

Woodruff D. Smith is Professor of History at the University of Massachusetts. He is the author of several books and articles on the history of imperialism, including *The Ideological Origins of Nazi Imperialism* (1986). He also studies the history of cultural science and the economic and cultural history of the Atlantic world. He is the author of *Consumption and the Making of Respectability, 1600–1800* (2002).

Gary P. Steenson has taught in the History Department at California Polytechnic State University since 1998. His major publications include *Karl Kautsky, 1854–1938: Marxism in the Classical Year* (1978), *Not One Man! Not One Penny: German Social Democracy, 1863–1914* (1981), and *After Marx, Before Lenin: Marxism and Socialist Working-Class Parties, 1884–1914* (1991).

Matthew Stibbe is Senior Lecturer in History at Sheffield Hallam University. His publications include *German Anglophobia and the Great War, 1914–1918* (2001) and *Women in the Third Reich* (2003). He is currently writing a book on civilian POWs during World War I, with special reference to the Ruhleben camp for British nationals interned in Germany.

Tim Travers became Professor Emeritus of the University of Calgary in 2004. He is the author of *The Killing Ground: The British Army, the Western Front, and the Emergence of Modern Warfare, 1900–1918* (1987) and *How the War Was Won: Command and Technology in the British Army on the Western Front, 1917–1918* (1992), *Gallipoli 1915* (2001), and co-author of *World History of Warfare* (2002). Currently, he is working on a history of piracy.

Peter Waldron is Professor of Modern History at the University of East Anglia. His publications include *The End of Imperial Russia* (1997), *Between Two Revolutions* (1998) and *Governing Tsarist Russia* (2007).

Robin Walz is Associate Professor of History at the University of Alaska Southeast. A specialist in the history of popular culture in modern France, he is the author of *Pulp Surrealism: Insolent Popular Culture in Early Twentieth-Century Paris* (2000).

Peter Wardley is Principal Lecturer in Modern Economic and Business History at the University of the West of England, Bristol. He was Information Technology Editor of the *Economic History Review*, has written several articles on historical computing, and edited the *Bristol Historical Resource* CD. His ongoing research project, which has resulted in a number of publications, investigates the emergence and consolidation of "Big Business" in the first half of the twentieth century.

David Welch is Professor of Modern History and Director of the Centre for the Study of Propaganda at the University of Kent at Canterbury. His books include *Germany, Propaganda and Total War 1914–1918: The Sins of Omission* (2000), *Modern European History 1871–2000: A Documentary Reader* (2000), *The Third Reich: Politics and Propaganda* (2nd edn 2002), *Hitler: Profile of a Dictator* (2001), and (with N. Cull and D. Culbert) *Propaganda and Mass Persuasion: A Historical Encyclopedia, 1500 to the Present* (2003). He is the editor of Routledge's *Sources in History* series.

Preface

I wish to thank Andrew MacLennan for suggesting this project to me during his short tour of duty at Blackwell Publishing; his zeal for making books is infectious. Since its initial inception, Tessa Harvey has been responsible for seeing the project through to completion and during this process her intelligence and humor have provided invaluable support. In its final stages, Angela Cohen has given helpful and timely guidance. I sincerely thank them all for their encouragement and their assistance.

My greatest debt is to the contributors. The challenge of covering such enormous and complicated ground in such a short space is a daunting one – but they have been brave enough to try. I believe that they have succeeded in writing essays that are thoughtful, informative, and based on vast reading and careful reflection. They are also clear and engagingly written and will, I believe, be helpful to any and all students of the subject. I sincerely thank them for their efforts and for their willingness to put up with a demanding and overbearing editor.

Map 1 Europe 1900–1914

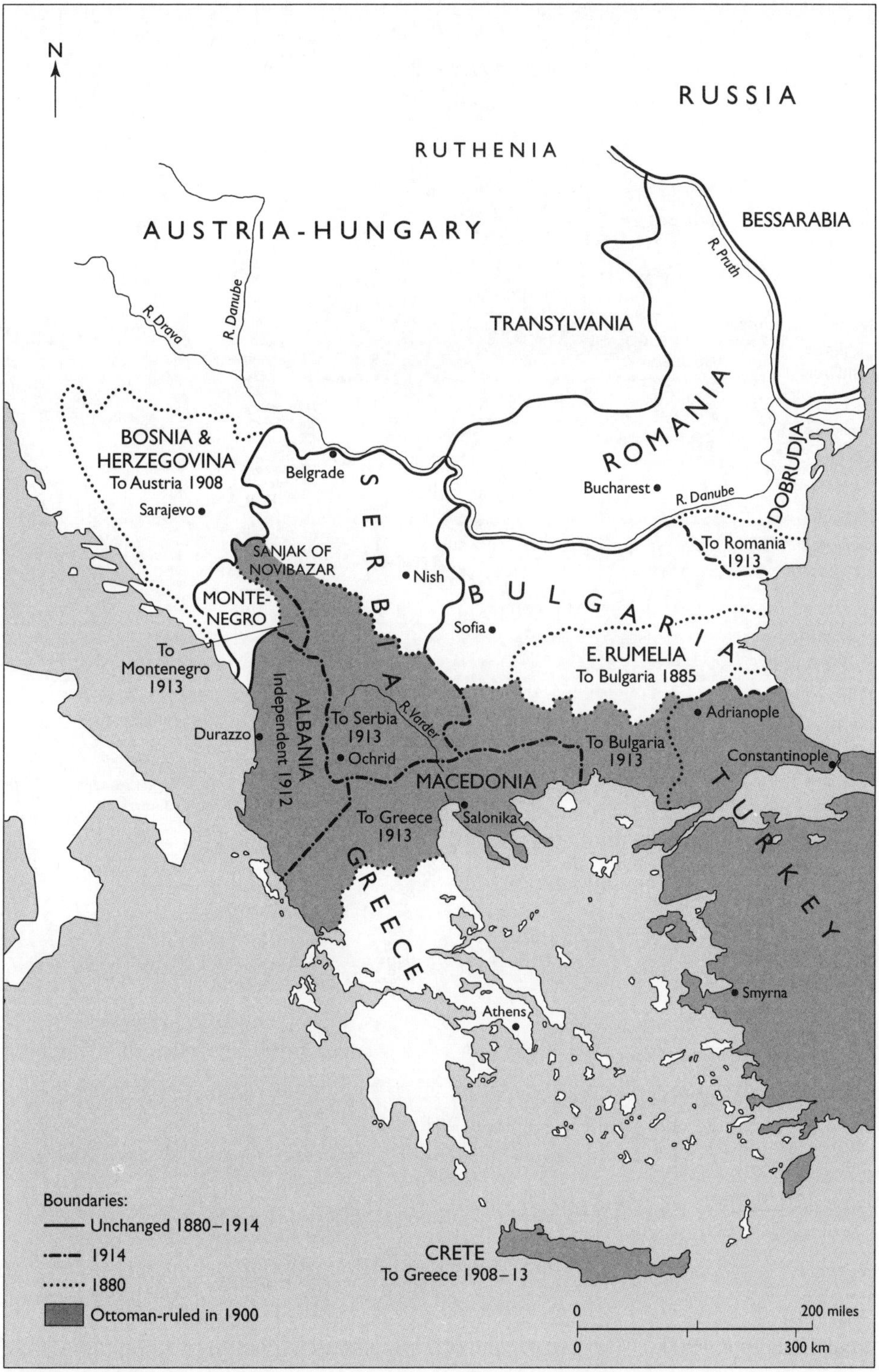
N
RUSSIA
RUTHENIA
AUSTRIA-HUNGARY
BESSARABIA
R. Pruth
R. Drava
R. Danube
TRANSYLVANIA
ROMANIA
DOBRUDJA
BOSNIA & HERZEGOVINA
To Austria 1908
Belgrade
Bucharest
R. Danube
Sarajevo
SERBIA
To Romania 1913
SANJAK OF NOVIBAZAR
Nish
MONTE-NEGRO
BULGARIA
Sofia
To Montenegro 1913
E. RUMELIA
To Bulgaria 1885
ALBANIA
Independent 1912
R. Varder
Adrianople
To Serbia 1913
Durazzo
Ochrid
To Bulgaria 1913
Constantinople
MACEDONIA
Salonika
To Greece 1913
TURKEY
GREECE
Smyrna
Athens
Boundaries:
Unchanged 1880–1914
1914
1880
Ottoman-ruled in 1900
CRETE
To Greece 1908–13
0
200 miles
0
300 km

Map 2 The Balkans 1880–1914

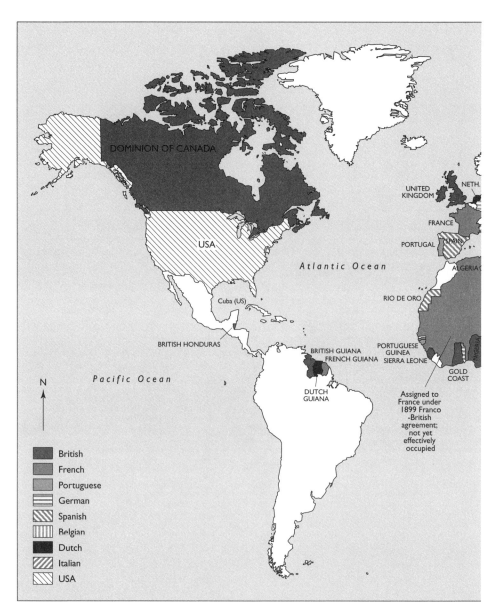

Map 3 European and American empires 1901

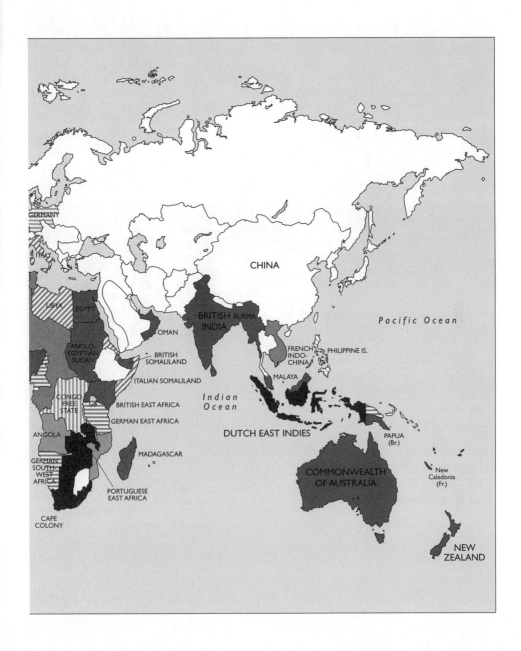

GERMANY

ITALY

LIBYA

EGYPT

OMAN

ANGLO-
EGYPTIAN
SUDAN

BRITISH
SOMALILAND

ITALIAN SOMALILAND

CONGO
FREE
STATE

BRITISH EAST AFRICA

GERMAN EAST AFRICA

ANGOLA

MADAGASCAR

GERMAN
SOUTH
WEST
AFRICA

PORTUGUESE
EAST AFRICA

CAPE
COLONY

CHINA

BRITISH BURMA
INDIA

FRENCH
INDO-
CHINA

PHILIPPINE IS.

MALAYA

*Indian
Ocean*

Pacific Ocean

DUTCH EAST INDIES

PAPUA
(Br.)

COMMONWEALTH
OF AUSTRALIA

New
Caledonia
(Fr.)

NEW
ZEALAND

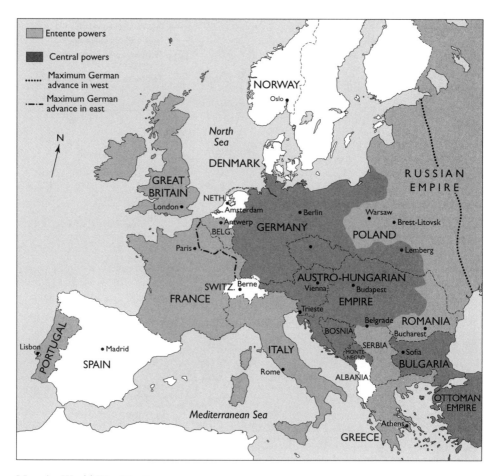

Map 4 World War I in Europe

Map 5 The settlement of central and eastern Europe 1917–1922

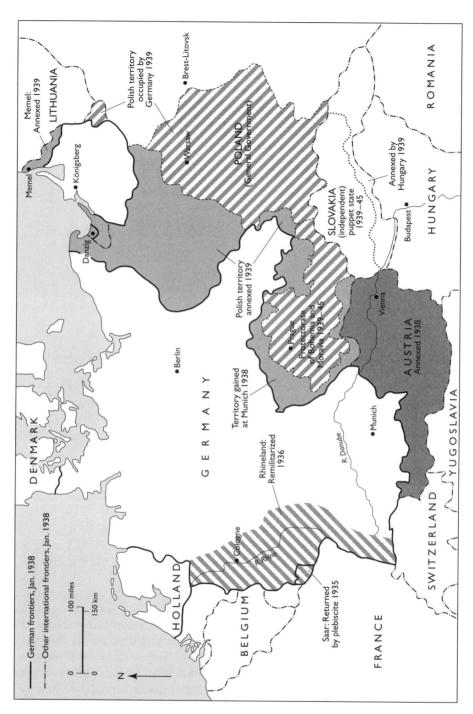

Map 6 Greater Germany 1933–1945

Introduction

Europe in Agony, 1900–1945

GORDON MARTEL

Europe, over the course of the first half of the twentieth century, was transformed, and its transformation was caused primarily, if not entirely, by the experience of war. The geopolitical map, politics, society, and culture were reshaped, rethought, and reconstructed, and it is impossible to understand Europe at the beginning of the twenty-first century without coming to grips with the sufferings endured by Europeans between 1914 and 1945. This is not what people had expected in 1900. Viewed from the vantage points of London and Paris, Berlin and Vienna – even St. Petersburg and Rome – the twentieth century was expected to be Europe's finest. The "world" was European: controlled by Europeans and their descendants, or becoming "European" by accepting its political institutions, its economic model, and its values. The wars of religion that had beleaguered the continent were distant memories, of interest only to antiquarians; the last great war of ideology – that waged against the French revolutionaries – was now remembered as a triumph over Napoleon. Secular societies aimed not to impose their vision on other Europeans, but to improve the health and welfare of their own people. Governments were coming to regard it as their duty to eradicate crime, promote education, protect the sick, and sustain the elderly. The sciences – both physical and social – promised to find ways of achieving these lofty goals: technology was producing undreamed-of prosperity and creature comforts; research into the minds and bodies of human beings was unraveling the mysteries of behavior and disease. Civilization was European, and the twentieth century would be the most civilized, humane, and progressive in the history of humanity. Europeans could believe in this future in spite of problems that were evident – particularly to critics – in 1900: poverty, prejudice, racism, and violence, both within Europe itself and within the European empires in Africa and Asia. But even Europe's harshest critics believed that Europe could overcome these problems; indeed, that it was Europe's duty to humanity as a whole to do so.

By 1945 these expectations seemed naive at best, wicked at worst. The nineteenth century, reviled by the "modernists" of 1900–14, seemed peaceful, comfortable, and civilized in comparison with what Europeans suffered between 1914 and 1945. The world wars, the civil wars, the influenza pandemic, and the Holocaust had killed something like 100 million people. The wars waged in Europe since 1815 had resulted in the deaths of not much more than a million; the "potato famine" in mid-century Ireland and central Europe paled in comparison with the influenza pandemic; there was nothing like the deliberate extermination of a European people such as occurred in the Holocaust or was perpetrated against the Armenians during World War I. By the end of World War II and in its aftermath the remembrance of suffering and horror had inscribed itself onto the European psyche; after 1919, memorials to the dead had replaced the triumphalist art and architecture, iconography and statuary of previous postwar eras. Even the victors looked back on their victories as the triumph of endurance over horror; shrines to unknown soldiers and tours of battle-field graveyards after 1918 and of extermination camps after 1945 replaced the glorification of war and warriors located at the Brandenburg Gate, the Arc d'Triomphe, and Trafalgar Square.

Emotionally, the Europe of 1945 was a vastly different place than the Europe of 1900. France had suffered a shattering defeat, then physically divided and occupied, which led to national self-doubt, soul searching, and internecine conflict. The bombing of Britain and the imminent prospect of invasion had destroyed forever the sense of insular invulnerability. In central and eastern Europe Czechoslovakia, Yugoslavia, and Poland had been pillaged and brutalized; the USSR had almost collapsed and suffered the most devastating human losses of any of the combatant states. But the differences between 1900 and 1945 were not only emotional, not merely in the minds of Europeans. At the end of World War II Germany was conquered, divided, and occupied. The streets of Weimar, Frankfurt, and Hamburg were patrolled by Russian, American, and British soldiers and, in the case of Berlin, by all three with the addition of the French. Within a year of Adolf Hitler's suicide in his Berlin bunker, Winston Churchill was declaring that an "iron curtain" had descended and divided Europe between east and west. Russian troops were stationed throughout eastern Europe; American troops throughout western. No one had foreseen such things a half-century before, not even the wildest prophet could have envisioned such a fundamental reshaping of European geopolitics.

The United States had been of no consequence in European affairs in 1900. Russia was, of course, a European power with a vast Asian empire – but, while the tsarist autocracy was reviled by the liberals and democrats of western Europe, few feared that this power would be used to impose an ideological system on its neighbors, and the revolution of 1905 encouraged them to believe that the tide of history had already turned against it. European liberals believed that backward political structures would be shattered and that the autocrats and aristocrats who benefited from them would disappear. The politics of 1945 appeared to be of a fundamentally different order than those of 1900: the contest between the communists and the "free world" was central to all debates; there seemed to be little or no middle ground; every issue was ideological. Such a simplistic, philosophical division would have been unrecognizable to the politicians of 1900. From Vienna and Berlin to Paris and London, politics at the turn of the century centered on issues of constitutional reform: extension of the suffrage farther down the socioeconomic scale; extending the franchise to women; electoral reform; parliamentary control over budgets; civilian control over the military; where there was no constitution – as in Russia – reformers and revolutionaries demanded one. The positions taken on these issues were variegated and complicated within each of the countries of Europe – and Europeans would have been astonished at the notion that their politics would, a half-century later, have become internationalized and polarized.

Popular culture mirrored the transformation in political culture. The radio, motion pictures, and record players had created new forms of mass entertainment that transcended political boundaries and polarized masses and elites. Traditionalists sneered at "the pictures" and reviled "jazz" and the latest dance crazes at the same time that they worried that these activities would erode the foundations of European civilization. The authorities attempted to control them: states took responsibility for broadcasting and established codes of conduct and imposed censorship in order to prevent these mass pursuits from undermining conventional values and acceptable forms of behavior. The fact that so much of the new culture was "American" also meant that it introduced foreign ideas into realms that were previously the domain of the national state; the fact that some of this new culture was "Afro-American" threatened to undermine the foundations of European civilization itself. While the established authorities of Europe sought to contain and control these new pastimes of the masses, "modern" politicians arose – usually from the masses – who saw the opportunity to create a new kind of politics from them.

By 1945 the reality of mass culture was widely accepted as a permanent feature of modern European life. The experience of 1900–45 had demonstrated that the forces behind it were irreversible, but that the fears of its effects had not been exaggerated: it had transformed more than the way people entertained themselves – it was altering their behavior and their beliefs. Everyone in a position of authority in 1945 recognized that the world had changed dramatically in half a century. Along with movies and music, dancing and the radio came new sensibilities concerning youth and adolescence, women and sexuality. There had been no "youth culture" to speak of in the Europe of 1900: adolescents were not regarded as a group, as a thing apart from their parents; they did not have an identity, an ethos of their own; they were expected to inherit the places and the property of their elders and – depending on what this inheritance consisted of – to be trained or educated in a manner that fit the places they would inevitably come to occupy. But with masses of "teenagers" congregating together in state-run schools where they spent their days with others of almost exactly the same age, they had come to regard themselves as sharing more with their peers than their parents. And one of the things they shared (and their parents feared) was a growing fascination with sex – which, given the proximity of girls or boys of their own age and class – they were able to act on in ways unimagined before the twentieth century.

By 1945 Europeans had come to accept the idea that sex was, if not the primary driving force behind their behavior, certainly one of the most important. This was partly because of the vibrant sexuality of the new popular culture, but also because of the efforts of psychoanalysts, psychologists, and social scientists to comprehend and explain where this drive came from, how it operated, and how it might be contained or at least channeled in directions where it might do less harm. The new sciences of the mind that paid less attention to the physical functioning of the brain and more to the emotional dynamics of the psyche revolutionized the way that Europeans understood themselves. Although this was fiercely contested ground, few doubted that comprehending the power of sexual drives was fundamental to an understanding of human behavior. And nowhere was this revelation more profound in its impact than on the "high culture" of art and literature. In 1900 the number of artists and writers whose work was informed by an interest in sexuality was tiny; by mid-century many – critics of modernism and postmodernism, especially – believed they were mesmerized by it. The gulf between high culture and popular grew throughout the first half of the century. Those on the borderlines of "acceptable" art around the turn of the century – the impressionists, the avant-garde in literature – had achieved iconic status. Unheard-of prices were paid for Monets and Gauguins, Van Goghs and Picassos; Eliot and Woolf, Schnitzler and Mann were coming to be regarded as modern classics, published in cheap editions and taught as texts in schools. Fifty, even twenty, years earlier they had been regarded as renegades unworthy of serious consideration.

The new sensibility that penetrated the canon of European art, literature, and music over the first half of the century perplexed those who puzzled over its meaning. What were those lines in a Mondrian painting meant to *be*? Could there really be a "found" art as the surrealists claimed? What was poetry if it had no rhyme and perhaps no meter? What was music without a melody? Was it still music? The fact that these paintings found their way into the most important galleries, that the rebel modernists of the early century were anthologized and lionized, that Stravinsky and Schoenberg were performed in the leading concert halls certainly indicated that there had been a seismic shift in sensibilities.

At least as confusing to those untutored in modernist tastes, however, was the revolution that occurred in science. Like the eruption of new insights in psychoanalysis and the invention of new techniques in the arts, the revolution in science began around the turn of the century and seemed the domain of a few maverick thinkers who could be dismissed by those in the mainstream as frivolous and insignificant theorists. The dropping of atomic bombs on Hiroshima and Nagasaki obliterated any remaining skepticism that these theories were nonsensical and impractical.

Concepts like relativity, that time was not fixed, that subatomic particles existed that could not be seen but whose presence could be theorized, were extremely difficult to grasp. The new science of the twentieth century, unlike that of the nineteenth, was not something to be played with, and it seemed as remote from reality as the metaphysical questions posed by medieval theologians. The technological consequences, in spite of the atomic bomb, were largely unknown, unpredictable, and lay in the future. In some ways the manner in which life was lived in the Europe of 1945 was not fundamentally different than that of Europe in 1900: using airplanes as a form of mass transportation was still a dream; ownership of an automobile was still confined to a privileged elite; the television sets, computers, and mobile telephones that would transform leisure, work, and entertainment were unknown, unimagined, or dismissed as gimmicks that no one would want or could need.

The technology that was gradually transforming the lives of Europeans in the first half of the twentieth century was largely the consequence of nineteenth-century science. *Alltagsgeschichte*, everyday life, continued to be shaped by mechanical innovations that gradually found their way into homes: sewing machines, washing machines, and vacuum cleaners were altering the domestic lives of Europeans. Servants were gradually displaced from middle-class homes; the drudgery of cleaning and cooking was gradually giving way to time for leisure activities or work outside the home –

trends that were slowly changing the lives of women in particular. Where people lived and how they worked were changing as well: subway systems, electric trams, and automobiles encouraged the movement of people away from city centers and to the "suburbs"; and when people got to work they were more and more likely to perform "white collar" jobs in offices, or to become more technological themselves, more mechanized, becoming a cog in a complicated industrial machine. Dramatic events such as the world wars seem to turn lives upside-down, but do they do so fundamentally or permanently? Or are they temporary aberrations? This is a perplexing question that is not easily answered: millions of women performed the work traditionally done by men during World War I – but most of them returned to their homes or customary roles when the war ended, and it is at least arguable that more enduring changes in the lives of women were produced by a mechanized workplace that placed less emphasis on size and strength. The typewriter and the telephone – although less dramatic than war or revolution – may ultimately have produced changes that were more profound.

The recognition that many, if not most, of the ways in which people live their lives changes very slowly is one of the frustrating conclusions of much historical research. Whereas journalists and social scientists are inclined to announce a revolution of some kind almost weekly, historians are disinclined to agree and more likely to argue in some way or another that *plus ça change, plus c'est la meme chôse*. Whether one sees sudden, seismic changes or gradually changing patterns of life depends largely on who, what, and where is being studied. The events of 1900–45 certainly changed some lives in dramatic (and often deadly) ways. Take, for example, a German boy born in 1900, sent off to the western front to fight as a 17-year-old in World War I and who, after the armistice of November, returning home to find no job, decides to keep his rifle, stay in uniform, and join paramilitary forces fighting against social revolutionaries within Germany; when the revolution is quashed and the Weimar republic stabilizes he remains unemployed and uprooted and joins the *Sturmabteilung*; after a decade or so of upheavals he flourishes under the Nazis and is elevated to a position of importance in the *Schutzstaffel*; he ends his days leading an assassination squad in the Soviet Union, where he is killed at the age of 44. Such a life (led, in fact, not by hundreds, but thousands of such men in Germany) did not fit the well-established patterns of a nineteenth-century existence. It was a life that was unpredicted and unpredictable – governed largely by the singular events of the century.

Nor was the life and death of a man caught up in the phenomenon of Nazism the only one dramatically altered by events that had not been foreseen in 1900. Almost forgotten are the hundreds of thousands of young women whose young husbands did not survive the carnage of World War I. Their stories were undramatic, their response to their situation unpolitical: no new ideology or mass movement grew from them – they suffered in silence. Living in dire poverty, some with minuscule pensions, some without even this support, they survived for decades on the margins of existence; most, with little education or training (and little prospect of gainful employment even if they did) had expected to live on the earnings of a male partner. With such a proportion of Europe's young manhood dead between the wars (and especially – contrary to myth – working-class men), the shape of demography changed dramatically, making it extremely difficult for younger women without property or prospects to find a male partner. It might be argued that their lives were as tragic as the deaths of their young men, yet no memorials were erected to their endurance and they have practically disappeared from the landscape of memory. Why do we choose to remember some lives and forget others? Is there a political economy of death as there is for life? While thousands of books and articles have been written on almost every aspect of Nazism and fascism, anyone seeking to understand the disrupted and devastated lives of young, working-class European women between the wars will have to look very hard indeed.

Whether remembered or forgotten, memorialized or disappeared, these are lives that changed dramatically as the result of forces largely beyond their control. And there were millions of other lives, fitting different social categories, occupying different spaces, which were also twisted out of recognition by events. Nevertheless, millions of others continued to live in ways that, judging by appearances, remained unaltered. The numbers of men who did not die, did not fight, vastly outnumbered those who did; the numbers of women who did not lose their young men, who did not work in munitions factories, did not go off to nurse the wounded at the front, vastly outnumbered those who did. Although tradesmen and teachers, laborers and lawyers saw their living standards alter with the changing circumstances of war and peace, the fundamentals of their existence remained unchanged: they occupied the same place in the social hierarchy; they dwelt in the same houses in the same neighborhoods in the same cities, towns, and villages of Europe; they followed the same religion they had always done, attended the same schools and married within the same circle of friends and acquaintances. Quite possibly they continued to identify with the same nation-state, share the values of the same social class, and support the same political party as they had done at the beginning of the century. A social scientist in 1900, predicting what their place, their behavior, and their beliefs were likely to be a half-century later, could have done so with surprising accuracy.

Trying to understand how much changed and how much remained the same, then accounting for why they did or did not change, is a puzzle that always confronts historians. There was nothing entirely "new" in the Europe of 1945 – nothing that had not been present in some form in 1900. The two most obvious sociopolitical innovations – fascism and communism – did not spring from nothing. Communism owed its philosophical essence to the writings of Marx and Engels, and they took much of their inspiration from the experience of the French revolution. Fascism, which disdained philosophical systematizing, owed its appeal to the rabid nationalism, aggressive imperialism, and "scientific" racism of the nineteenth century. It is arguable that neither would have succeeded in taking hold of the apparatus of the state in Russia, Italy, and Germany without the shattering experience of World War I. The tsarist autocracy in Russia, the most powerful conservative force throughout most of the nineteenth century, fell to pieces because of its inability to withstand the demands imposed upon it by fighting Germany, Austria-Hungary, Bulgaria, and the Ottoman Empire. The Bolsheviks saw and seized the opportunity that the war presented to them. This was, in essence, what occurred in Italy and Germany as well. The Italians, convinced that they had been cheated out of the gains that were properly theirs for having chosen to fight on the side of the Entente, were persuaded that "liberal" Italy could not grow and prosper in the postwar world, that something more daring, more dynamic, would have to take its place. Mussolini, marshaling his blackshirts, offered them an alternative to the bourgeois politics of the past half-century. The Germans, persuaded to give "social democracy" a try in the aftermath of defeat, were more gradually disillusioned, convinced that they had not really lost the war, that the *Diktat* of Versailles imposed upon them a kind of perpetual servitude. Hitler, evoking hatred and suspicion of all things un-German – including German Jews, communists, socialists, and bourgeois democrats – offered them an alternative to defeat and second-rate status in Europe.

Insofar as the most dynamic, innovative political systems were concerned, the experience of war and the impact of its outcome were instrumental in altering how people thought and how they behaved – but their thinking and their behavior were rooted in the prewar world. Similarly, the structure of the European state system itself was shaken by the war and the peace: frontiers were moved; some states disappeared while others were created – but these changes were firmly rooted in the ambitions and fears demonstrated by nations and empires before World War I.

Each of the great powers of Europe believed that the war would determine their destiny: Austria-Hungary initiated the crisis that precipitated the war in order to "solve" the problem of Serbian nationalism that was threatening to dissolve the multinational Habsburg Empire; Germany was prepared to support this initiative because failing to do so would ultimately reduce its ability to grow and prosper – and power and influence in the twentieth century would, the Germans believed, go to the great empires of the world: Russia, Britain, the United States; their only chance to compete on an equal footing was to establish a great central European entity stretching from the Baltic to the Mediterranean. The Russians feared that if this Habsburg/Hohenzollern vision were realized, they would lose their influence over the western borderlands stretching from Finland and Poland to Serbia and Turkey; Germanic influence in the old Ottoman Empire would imperil Russia's standing in the Black Sea, the Caucasus, and the Persian Gulf. The French feared that without a strong Russia and an effective alliance they would be overwhelmed by German power and that their empire in Africa and Asia would not save them from being reduced to satellite status. Britain was satisfied with the balance that competition between the competing alliance systems produced in Europe; it was only when it appeared likely that the central powers might succeed in overwhelming France and Russia that the British reluctantly attempted to redress the balance by coming into the war on the side of the Entente. The thinking behind these calculations was firmly rooted in the experience of the nineteenth century, during which states grappled with the consequences of nationalism and imperialism and calculated how to withstand their destructive capabilities or utilize their constructive possibilities.

The "new" Europe that was created in 1919 was founded upon two guiding principles of nineteenth-century liberal idealism: that it was the desire and the destiny of "nations" to be free, and that peace and progress could only be achieved when these nations were governed by representative, constitutional regimes. Ideologically, the Entente was hampered by the reality of the tsarist autocracy, and once that regime collapsed, a consistent position on the future shape of Europe was easier to arrive at. Thus, while the possibility of dismantling the "national" German state was never entertained seriously at Paris in 1919, the Habsburg Empire appeared to have disintegrated on its own accord, largely along "national" lines and therefore could be – needed to be – restructured on the basis of the principle of nationality. Poland is the most important example of this thinking: created (or recreated) from territories formerly ruled from Vienna, Berlin, and St. Petersburg, it was assumed that linguistic, religious, and historical forces would combine to establish a coherent, stable, and constitutional state; it would not be aggressive or expansionist because the goal of national unity would have been achieved. The same principle was, in essence, applied to Czechoslovakia, Finland, Latvia, Lithuania, and Estonia – as well as to Austria and Hungary. Everywhere in Europe the nationalists had claimed that ruthless autocratic regimes had prevented them from realizing their dreams of establishing nations based upon the will of the people through the instrument of representative governments. Thus was the new Europe designed to endure for as far into the future as anyone could foresee; sorting out the frontiers between the national states was difficult and messy, but with good will to guide those who drew the boundaries, and with a new League of *Nations* to assist in resolving disagreements, the grievances and instability that had plagued the old Europe would gradually disappear. Thus was the Europe of the interwar years simultaneously old and new. The peacemakers of 1919 had recognized both the complexities of national identities and ambitions and the power that nationalism had to undo their efforts – and had created a new international code of behavior in the form of "Minority treaties" which sought to give rights to minorities that had been created by their frontier adjustments and to protect them from the majority.

The victorious powers who had conceived of and then created the new Europe laid themselves open to the charge of cynical self-interest. The most compelling case against them could be made by looking at the map outside of Europe. Here there was no more than lip-service paid to the principle of national self-determination: the empires of the British and French were expanded to an unprecedented extent; those of the Germans and the Turks dismantled. The British succeeded in limiting the old tsarist threat to their empire in Asia; the French succeeded in limiting the German threat in Europe through the imposition of demilitarization, punishing reparations and recapturing Alsace and Lorraine. The peace of enlightened progress could be dismissed by its critics as one of hypocrisy; Germans and Russians could agree that it was not national self-determination that established its foundations, but acquisitive imperialism. The complaints of Poles, Hungarians, and Italians concerning this or that frontier arrangement were petty in comparison with those of Germans and Russians who argued that the French and the British were seeking to keep them forever in chains.

And thus was the new Europe of 1919 beleaguered by attacks on its very essence. According to its critics, the only thing that had changed since 1900 was the Machiavellian realization of the goals of western imperialism. And the way to reverse the judgment imposed by the French and the British was to restore those elements of imperial might that had enabled their opponents to succeed: they must rebuild their armies and navies. Indeed, in order to succeed where they had previously failed they needed to go further: they would have to build political and social systems that were more cohesive and dynamic than those that had collapsed under the weight of war. Thus, in Soviet Russia, then fascist Italy, and finally in Nazi Germany, there was little nostalgic yearning to restore the world of 1900; instead, they promoted a "futurist" vision of a new society that would harness the power of modernity to overcome the limitations imposed by history and tradition. Mass communications and massive assemblies would allow a charismatic leader to mobilize his nation, race, or class to an unparalleled extent; individuals and groups, customs and laws that stood in the way would be, had to be, marginalized, removed, or destroyed.

In this way were the foundations of the new Europe, grounded in the principles of nineteenth-century idealism, eroded and assaulted by forces that regarded these ideals as backward, as bourgeois, as decadent. While they attacked the adherents of the old order as hypocrites, they had no wish to force them to live up to the promises of their rhetoric: the fascists, Nazis, and communists of the interwar years had no interest in creating a system of limited national states with mechanisms for mediating or arbitrating the inevitable disputes that arose over this or that bit of frontier. They strove for higher ideals than the bourgeois complacency of liberal democracy: a new imperial Rome, a third reich, a proletarian paradise. The divisive tendencies of the prewar years became violent ideological confrontations between the wars. Everywhere in Europe people took to the streets: marches, demonstrations, and strikes were the order of the day. The temperature of political culture became feverish; every issue was hotly contested because it seemed part of a much larger struggle for the shape of the future for nation, race, or class.

Against the assaults of the new ambitions the proponents of the old order seemed fumbling and powerless. The charges of hypocrisy and decadence stuck because the liberals and conservatives, the bourgeoisie and the aristocrats, the democrats and constitutionalists looked like old-fashioned fuddy-duddies next to their modern, militarized opponents; top hats, tails, furled umbrellas, and patent-leather shoes were no match for blackshirts and brownshirts, for jackboots and holstered revolvers. Between the wars the tide of history seemed to be moving in another direction. Areas of life that were previously immune from (or at least remote from) politics – painting, music, sport, leisure – were now part of a wider political culture, where their relative decadence or purity were debated as if the future of civilization depended upon them.

No doubt the realities of life after 1919, the poverty, the unemployment, the upheavals of inflation and deflation, the loss of husbands, fathers, and sons, accounts for much of the ideological confrontation in Europe between the wars. And yet different cultures responded differently to these realities. While there were communist and fascist parties everywhere, they did not all succeed in overcoming the old order. And when, in 1939, Nazi Germany rolled the dice and attacked Poland, the old democracies of the west decided that they could not stand by on the sidelines and watch. And in this decision they were generally supported by their own people who were, in spite of the horrific memories of 1914–18, prepared to go to war once again.

But this war was different, both in the manner of its fighting and in the nature of the issues involved. New strategies, tactics, and weapons were employed to escape another war of attrition like that of 1914–18. Blitzkrieg, the rapid deployment of troops using armored personnel carriers supported by tanks and fighter planes and dive bombers, was the kind of war designed by those strategists horrified by trench warfare and fixed fronts. Compared with World War I, World War II was one of movement, of shifting fronts, of stunning victories and crushing defeats. And this time civilians were involved to an unparalleled extent. Those who had fought in the trenches the first time around believed that the war would not have been allowed to continue as it did if the older generation – safe and comfortable at home – had to endure the same horrors they faced. Concurrent with the tactical innovations of blitzkrieg, then, was the strategy of terrifying civilians by bombing their cities from the skies. The consequence of the strategy was ironic: instead of eroding the will to fight, the bombing intensified the will to resist. And thus World War II became a "total war" in a way that World War I had not been.

As with World War I, World War II altered the course of European history. Before the war, few were prepared to face the horrors of another war. Unlike 1914, there was no rejoicing, no spontaneous demonstrations in the streets in 1939. Everyone expected that this war would be even more devastating: there was little or no popular enthusiasm for the war even in Nazi Germany, Soviet Russia, or fascist Italy. Nevertheless, the "totalitarian" regimes were able to mobilize sufficient support to fight the war – but so were the old regimes of the parliamentary democracies. The stunning defeat of France in 1940, followed by the battle of Britain and the invasion of the Soviet Union, brought the Axis states to the brink of total victory. By 1941 they controlled, directly or through compliant, puppet regimes all of continental Europe. And it was at that point that the tide, both strategically and culturally, began to change. The consequences of a Europe under Nazi domination quickly became clear: political opposition would not be tolerated, economies would be pillaged for the sake of Germany, racist ideals would be fulfilled. The conquered, the occupied, or the controlled could choose either to submit and obey or to resist. Where World War I had, in retrospect, seemed to have been fought for nothing more than the dynastic or imperial ambitions of the great powers, World War II seemed to live up to the promises of the propaganda that surrounded it: it did seem to be about the future of civilization – and it soon seemed impossible to be indifferent to it. The outcome of this war would determine how people lived their lives every day, and for as far into the future as anyone could foresee.

The memory of that struggle has changed over the course of time, but in a manner that has produced even starker contrasts and more vivid lessons. No one went to war in 1939, 1940, or 1941 in order to save the Jews of Europe from annihilation. But the horrors of the extermination camps, the gas chambers, and the killing squads have, in the twenty-first century, worked themselves into the consciousness of Europe and the west. Those who believe that the war was unnecessary and immoral have rarely been heard from. Unlike the debates and the disillusionment that followed 1919, the controversy surrounding World War II consists largely of debating when and where Hitler and Mussolini should have been stopped – not whether their demands were reasonable or whether they were susceptible to policies of moderation. Despite the even greater horrors of World War II it has come to be regarded as a just and necessary war.

The agony suffered by Europe between 1900 and 1945 changed fundamentally the way Europeans regarded themselves, their past, and their future. Fundamental beliefs in what it means to be European, what Europeans can and cannot tolerate, changed dramatically as a result of the two world wars, revolutions, civil wars, the experience of totalitarianism, the purges and the holocaust. Few periods in history were as dramatic, as important, as painful, and as heartbreaking as this half century.

PART I

Continuity and Change; Forces and Movements

Chapter One

Urbanization, Poverty, and Crime

Paul Lawrence

Thus on every side the strange and artificial growth of our cities confronts us . . . We cannot but observe the evil effects of the enforced severance from natural conditions of life. (C. F. G. Masterman, *The Heart of the Empire*, 1901)

It is relatively easy to construct a portrait of Europe during the first half of the twentieth century as intrinsically "modern." After all, the "metropolis" – blazing with electric light, crowded with commuters, flanked by suburbs – was already an established feature of European society by World War I. The growth of fledgling welfare state initiatives across Europe revolutionized living conditions for many during the period. Paid holidays, slum clearances, town planning, and improving educational provision – all seem indicative of early "progress" towards the comfortable present of twenty-first century Europe. Similarly, the period can also be viewed as a "Golden Age" of policing in some countries. The lack of public legitimacy and problems with professional conduct which had beset crime control institutions for much of the nineteenth century were subsiding, and the advent of early forensic science and the development of international institutions such as Interpol (set up in 1923) again seem indicative of a Europe not dissimilar to our own. It is tempting, therefore, in looking back on the first half of the twentieth century, to discern in retrospect *only* our current Europe in its nascent form.

However, caution must be exercised. It is inadvisable to look back from the vantage point of twenty-first century Europe and perceive only its smooth genesis. Rather than a history of progress, even the most cursory study of the Europe of the first half of the twentieth century also throws up startling incongruities. In the first place, significant regional and temporal variations are apparent when any single vector of change is considered. For example, while more than half of all Britons had been classed as living in urban areas by the mid-nineteenth century, it took until the 1930s for this proportion to be reached just across the Channel in France. Equally, welfare provision and the amelioration of poverty varied widely across time and place. While Germany, Denmark, and Norway all pioneered the introduction of welfare legislation, as late as 1931 barely 40 percent of houses in Moscow had running water. In the field of crime and policing, too, while there is certainly some evidence of growing public acceptance of increasingly professional policing, a "revisionist" history of crime and policing might also be presented, which might highlight the London Metropolitan Police baton charging Hunger Marchers in 1932 or the disturbing uses to which the police were put in Nazi Germany (and, to a lesser extent, in Nazi-occupied nations).

Perhaps even more significantly, however, not only were there wide variations in social conditions across Europe, in patterns of urbanization, and in the nature of crime and policing, but there were also big divergences in the ways in which these topics were perceived by contemporaries. The nature of modern urban life and "the city" were often hotly debated. Some, like the German art critic August Endell, believed that the urban environment was "a marvel of beauty and poetry . . . a fairy tale, brighter, more colorful, more diverse than anything ever invented by a poet."[1] Others, however, believed that the city was primarily a degenerating, enervating, and unnatural environment, marked by a divisive "urban morality" which glorified the most egoistic, inconsiderate, and destructive traits of human nature. Similarly divergent views and fierce debates concerning poverty (or, more specifically, the poor) and criminality can also be identified. What is also particularly striking is how these three themes – the urban environment, poverty, and criminality – were continually intertwined. One of most obvious vehicles via which these conceptual links were made were the Eugenics movements which existed in most European countries during the period and which (despite postwar efforts to indicate the contrary in Britain and France) were a seriously considered response to the issues of poverty, welfare costs, and criminality.

Care must be taken, therefore, not to underplay either the extent of regional and temporal diversity in Europe in the period 1900–45, or the extent to which ways of thinking about urbanization, poverty, and crime may have differed from our own contemporary views. With this in mind, this chapter will provide an overview of these three themes – urbanization, poverty and welfare, and crime and policing – and will illustrate the diversity of developments across Europe during the period. In addition, it will highlight the range of intertwined perceptions, debates, and opinions which these issues aroused.

Urbanization and the "Metropolis"

While urbanization in Europe was a long process (most of the major cities we know today were founded before 1300), *rapid* urbanization is usually associated with the nineteenth century and with the rise of industrial societies. During the period 1800–1910, the urban population of Europe grew about six-fold, partly because of a growth in overall population sizes and partly because of a shift towards urban living. It might be assumed, therefore, that this process was largely tailing off by 1900. In fact, Europe as a whole remained more rural than urban up until 1914, and even until after World War II if the Soviet Union is included. This is because the trend towards urbanization before 1900 disguised considerable regional variations. Thus, while England had a predominantly urban population by 1871, Russia had barely begun to urbanize by World War I. While almost 80 percent of the Welsh population and

57 percent of Belgians were classed as urban in 1920, this figure was only 46 percent for the French, and 30 percent for Swedes and Norwegians.[2] Clearly, urbanization was neither an even process, nor largely complete by 1900. Variations between countries were marked, and even within individual nations processes of urbanization could vary considerably. London was by far the biggest city in Europe at the turn of the century – twice the size of Paris and almost five times as populous as Moscow. However, Paris in 1911 (together with its suburbs), dominated urban life in France to a greater extent than London did England, and had more inhabitants than all other French cities with more than 50,000 inhabitants put together. In Germany, the landscape of the west was dominated by the Ruhr conurbation. While described as a "city of cities," this huge industrial sprawl in fact had no unified direction of any form until 1920.

Thus, diverse urban contexts could be found across Europe in the period before World War I. And yet, by 1950, almost all of the countries of Europe could be described as industrial and urban. The period 1900–45 was therefore certainly still one marked by the significant expansion of major towns and cities, often into suburban hinterlands. Unlike the factory industrialization of the nineteenth century, however, which had concentrated people near coalfields and water sources, the capitalism of the twentieth century favored large capital cities and commercial centers. Concerns generated by this continued urbanization led, in many countries, to the development of town planning – something relatively unknown during the chaotic first wave of nineteenth-century urbanization. While moves towards planning had begun around the turn of the century, interest (and indeed a new profession of "town planning") grew rapidly. Authors like Patrick Geddes, the Scottish biologist and pioneer of town planning, argued that only a "new association of civic and social action with architectural and artistic effort" could counter slums and "the mean ugliness of our towns."[3] While some gains were made, the results of town planning were very mixed. Municipal planners sometimes struggled to cope with the rapid development of existing major cities and the infrastructure demands this created. An official report on Paris, for example, noted in 1908 that the suburbs were "not sufficiently prepared to receive such a large and a rapid addition of new inhabitants" and that "old villages, scattered here and there, have become in a few years large centers of population, which in an uninterrupted chain meet to form a disorderly mass like a single city."[4] The Parisian *banlieue* (suburbs) had few effective building regulations between the wars. Despite this, however, public funds contributed to 77,000 of the 320,000 dwellings built in Paris between 1920 and 1938 and similar successes can be found elsewhere. In Vienna, Social Democrats managed to house 1/8 of the population in *Gemeindebauten* and British local councils helped to demolish many slums and build 1.5 million out of 4 million new homes.

Centralized planning in regard to cities perhaps reached its peak under the communist and fascist regimes of the interwar period, yet even here results were mixed. In Russia, socialism had an immediate impact after the revolution, as it authorized the subdivision of large houses owned by the middle classes, and their occupation by workers. Thus, the pre-revolutionary spatial distinctions of class and income were swept away. However, low priority was given to housing in the early five-year plans from 1928 onwards, and the 1935 "General Plan for the Reconstruction of Moscow" was deprived of funding. This meant that urban conditions in many Russian cities remained among the worst in Europe until the 1950s. In Germany the National Socialist approach to urban issues suffered from inherent contradictions. While fascist propaganda scorned the decadent morality of urban populations, the Nazis also invested heavily in grandiose urban redevelopment schemes during the period before World War II, particularly in Berlin.

The impact of the two world wars themselves should also not be neglected when considering the major factors influencing urban development during the first half of the century. World War I had a considerable impact on the urban infrastructure (housing stock, transport networks, municipal services) of most of Europe. Lack of investment during the war created complications for planners throughout the 1920s and 1930s. However, the destruction wrought by World War II was of another magnitude altogether. Aerial bombardment quickly became the weapon of choice for strategists. This had grave implications for the cities of most combatant nations and for Germany in particular. Fifty percent of the built-up areas of German cities with more than 100,000 inhabitants in 1939 had been destroyed by 1945. Equally, conflict on the ground could have similarly grave consequences for cities, as in the case of Stalingrad. Destruction wrought by retreating troops also reduced parts of many cities (including much of Rotterdam and a staggering 80 percent of Warsaw) to rubble.

The spread and nature of urbanization thus varied greatly across Europe during the period 1900–45. However, there is no doubt that this period saw the rise of the "metropolis," in the modern sense of the word. Indeed, it was at the start of the century that statisticians first began to distinguish between normal cities, big cities (*grandes villes* or *Grossstädte*), and metropolises (*Weltstädte*). In 1900 there were only eight cities in Europe with over a million inhabitants. By 1950 this number had risen to 22. These vast new agglomerations were closely linked to modernity and the notion of progress, and in many senses this faith was justified. Paris, London, Berlin, and Moscow were all early pioneers of the futuristic novelty of underground train systems. All major cities were associated with the excitement generated by electric light, seen as one of the crucial attributes of modern metropolitan life. In October 1928, for example, the "Berlin in the Light" festival celebrated just this – the practical aspects of electric lighting (in terms of safer travel and leisure) as well as its symbolic relationship with progress and modernity. However, as was the case with urbanization in general, contrasts and incongruities abound where metropolitan life is considered. In Moscow between the wars, for example, a metropolis of well over a million inhabitants, overcrowding was such that an average small apartment was home to nine individuals. Water was in such short supply that it was frequently rationed, and diseases such as cholera remained widespread. This was hardly an exemplar of modernity and progress. Even in London, Paris, and Berlin, the "success stories" of urban development, the veneer of modernity was often perilously thin. Stepping away from the renovated central districts, visitors still encountered slum conditions of the worst sort. Even the prized features of electricity and electric light could initially only be found in certain central districts. A visitor to Berlin in 1930 remarked that "a step into the side streets, and you felt set back by centuries."[5] In London before World War I, competition between boroughs meant that there were 65 electricity suppliers, 49 different supply systems, 10 frequencies, and 24 voltage levels. And, presumably, frequent interruptions to supply.

While inevitably impressionistic, these examples indicate that, while the period 1900–40 was marked by continued urbanization and the growth of large cities, experiences of these processes varied widely due to geography and social status. In other words, who and where you were determined your impressions of urban life. Hence it is perhaps unsurprising that a great diversity of opinion (and often heated debate) existed concerning urbanization and urban life. Specific debates about "urban man" and a specifically "urban" mode of living were already becoming entrenched in the social sciences by the turn of the century. Theorists such as Emile Durkheim and Max Weber came to posit a distinction between urban life (characterized by formal, rationalized, social organizations which nonetheless give the individual great freedom of action) and rural life (which they saw as dominated by spontaneous, informal social organizations founded upon tradition and kinship). Such notions were further elaborated on. Georg Simmel, for example, sought to delineate in more detail a specifically "metropolitan type of man." He admitted that variants of this type existed, but felt that the basic distinction between city and rural life would eventually produce a new type of human. As he noted: "With each crossing of the street, with the tempo and multiplicity of economic, occupational and social life, the city sets up a deep contrast with small town and rural life with reference to the sensory foundations of psychic life."[6] The work on these issues of American sociologists of the Chicago School, such as Robert Parks and Louis Wirth, was also widely debated in Europe.

Obviously, the concept of a specifically "urban" way of life also generated discussion well beyond the academic sphere. Most commentators had mixed views, but among some, in the artistic field for example, primarily positive views prevailed. Avant-garde artists in particular were captivated before World War I by the modernity which the city represented. The Italian futurist Filippo Tommaso Marinetti aimed at an art that would "sing of the great crowds in the excitement of labor, pleasure, and rebellion, of the multi-colored and polyphonic surf of revolutions in modern capital cities; of the nocturnal vibrations of arsenals and workshops beneath their violent electrical moons."[7] The author Ford Madox Hueffer (later Ford Madox Ford) similarly praised the diversity and freedom which the big city represented, writing of London that it had "as it were on show . . . the best products of the cook, of the painter, of the flower-gardener, of the engineer, of the religious and of the scientists."[8]

Inevitably, there were plenty who disagreed, and who viewed urbanization and city life in a much more sinister light. Adverse critiques often tended to focus on the putative problematic attributes of city dwellers (both physical and moral). C. F. G. Masterman, for example, writing in the context of England, claimed to have identified "a new race, hitherto unreckoned and of incalculable action." Physically deficient and morally weak, this new type of "City Man" was "ineffective, battered into futility by the ceaseless struggle of life."[9] Other authors also focused on the detrimental effects of cities on their surroundings and on the national society. These critiques often focused on demographics and the birth rate (a subject of almost universal concern in Europe at the time). City dwellers were seen as inherently unlikely (either for physical or moral reasons) to have large families. Hence cities were seen as a drain on the surrounding countryside and on the vigor of the population of the nation as a whole. Oswald Spengler, in his widely read 1922 essay "The Soul of the City," argued that the *Weltstädt* would "suck the country dry," until it grew weary and died "in the midst of an almost uninhabited waste."[10] Finally, it was also common for critics to focus on the horrendous living conditions which still prevailed in many cities, especially in the early part of the century. Slum areas were seen as a haven for criminals, but many religious figures and social reformers were also genuinely moved and concerned by the plight of the lower classes.

The city during the first half of the twentieth century was thus often simultaneously a symbolic figurehead of progress and light, and a contested terrain wherein the problems of health, housing, degeneration, and crime (among others) were debated. Of all the problems associated with city life, however, the degenerating nature of the urban environment and its effect on poorer, weaker citizens was seen to be the most imperative. The "problem of the poor" was still unsolved in Europe at the turn of the century, and it is to this sphere that we now turn our attention.

Poverty, Welfare, and Eugenics

The problems of poverty and the persistence of "the poor" had been widely discussed across Europe as the nineteenth century drew to a close. Many studies of major cities had investigated the living conditions of the working classes and the urban poor. During the 1880s, for example, the French politician and writer Othenin D'Haussonville published a long series of articles on Parisian poverty in the respected *Revue des deux mondes*. In Germany, impressive empirical social research was conducted under the aegis of the *Verein für Sozialpolitik* (Association for Social Policy). It was in England, however, that the most detailed studies were produced. The social investigator Charles Booth published his 17-volume *Life and Labour of the People in London* between 1889 and 1903, with detailed color-coded maps showing the extent of poverty in the capital, street by street. This tradition of social investigation and public concern continued in England well into the twentieth century. Indeed, the century opened with the "thunder-clap" of another such survey – Seebohm Rowntree's study of the outwardly prosperous city of York, which concluded that over 27 percent of the inhabitants were in fact living in poverty. Further research, conducted in the interwar period by social scientists, appeared to confirm the persistence of poverty despite widespread improvements in standards of living for many. Llewellyn Smith's *New Survey of London Life and Labour 1930–1935* argued that 500,000 Londoners were still living below a poverty line fixed in accordance with that used by Booth forty years earlier.

The empirical social survey was probably most common in England during the early twentieth century, which is interesting in itself given that the measurement of per capita income shows that Britain was clearly the richest country in Europe at the time. Elsewhere, however, concern over the condition of the lowest social strata was also in evidence. In Germany, housing provision and the problems of overcrowding were particular issues. In 1907, for example, the socialist Rosa Luxemburg was prompted to write "In the Shelter" to criticize the Berlin authorities (and even her own party) for their neglect of the homeless. In France the work of the human geographer Alfred Sauvy demonstrated for the *Revue d'économie politique* that, even during the 1930s when urban populations became a majority in France, poor standards of living were the norm even for many with jobs. Of course, the studies of poverty undertaken in the first half of the twentieth century were usually not conducted to the exacting standards of today's social scientists. The research of Booth and Rowntree in particular has been subjected to considerable scrutiny, and the validity of their findings often questioned. What is important, however, is that the problem of poverty was one which remained noticeable enough, even during the 1930s, to provoke concern, investigation, and action. In particular, it is interesting to note the early growth of nascent welfare state systems across much of Europe. The exact forms of state-sponsored initiatives varied, of course, but the growth of government intervention in the social sphere was common across Europe during the period 1900–45.

Germany was in many ways a pioneer of this process. Compulsory insurance schemes had been introduced under Bismarck, including schemes covering sickness (1883), accidents (1884), and invalidity and old age (1889). However, these schemes only applied initially to industrial workers. Although they were extended in 1911 to include salaried workers, the poor remained excluded. The Weimar republic introduced an ambitious program of welfare after World War I – including a constitutional guarantee of a range of social rights for all citizens. However, the implementation of social welfare initiatives was hampered by the economic and political turmoil of the interwar period. Compulsory unemployment insurance, for example, was introduced in 1927 but collapsed under the pressure of mass unemployment in 1928.

Other countries also began to instigate a diverse range of welfare initiatives. In England, the involvement of non-governmental agencies (including both the philanthropic organizations set up by the middle classes and the mutual assistance schemes set up by workers themselves) remained crucial at the turn of the century. However, while a mix of state/private agencies continued to administer welfare, state provision gradually rose to the fore. Britain introduced the first compulsory unemployment insurance scheme in 1911, pensions were administered by the government from their introduction in 1908, and local authorities were empowered to build and manage council housing. By 1939, 12 percent of housing stock was owned by the government, whereas the comparable figure for Germany and France was less than 1 percent. In Italy, although technically under central direction by a totalitarian regime from 1922, the influence of the Catholic church (especially in the areas of education and social assistance) ensured a continued mix of state/private welfare here too. France has traditionally been seen as a laggard in relation to welfare policy, partly perhaps because the slow pace of urbanization and industrialization made such initiatives less urgent. While France was a pioneer in the area of family policy, relief to the able-bodied remained meager until after World War I (and even, some argue, until the 1930s). The situation in the USSR is harder to determine, partly because accurate data is usually unavailable. However, it is clear that (as in Germany) industrial workers remained the primary focus of welfare initiatives during the early part of the century. Accident and sickness insurance was provided in 1912, but was restricted to workers in key firms which were important to the government's plans for industrial advancement.

Clearly, then, broadly analogous moves towards greater state intervention in the social welfare of citizens can be traced across Europe. It is somewhat harder, however, to assess the causes of this process. It might be argued, of course, that the rise of state welfare was an inevitable and desirable consequence of urbanization and industrialization. Only the state had the resources to attempt to manage the rapid change and economic vagaries of industrial society. However, this assessment does not fully explain why rural, non-industrial nations witnessed similar trends in the period. Sweden, for example, a primarily agrarian nation with a strong monarchy until 1917, introduced compulsory universal pensions in 1913. Equally, it might be contended that industrial labor used its growing political influence to secure improvements for workers. However, this does not explain why contemporary industrial nations like the USA and Japan have still not introduced full welfare systems. World War I could be cited as setting a precedent for increasing state intervention in everyday life, but many welfare initiatives had begun long before 1914. National politics also certainly had a role to play in determining the timing of welfare reforms. In Germany, for example, Bismarck clearly intended his social insurance legislation to allay socialist unrest. In England, the burst of reforms introduced by the Liberal government between 1906 and 1914 coincided precisely with the rise of the Labour Party. It is likely, therefore (as with all historical processes), that a wide range of factors led to the adoption of welfare policies across Europe in the period 1900–45. Concern for the plight of the poor may have been one variable but, given that most state welfare was initially aimed at those in work, was arguably not the most significant. Despite this, however, most available evidence suggests that the new welfare policies were efficacious in ameliorating the lives of the poorest. Welfare, combined with the economic recovery prompted by the end of World War II, meant that absolute poverty was much less widespread in 1950 than at the start of the century, and that standards of living throughout Europe had generally improved.

However, this cozy tale of progress is not the whole story. While, as noted above, many commentators had been moved and shocked by the plight of the poor, and had argued successfully for state intervention and political solutions, there were other strands of thought. Welfare itself, for example, was not universally seen as progressive. Some believed that permanent systems of welfare would only lead to inertia on the part of the poor. Many agreed with a German commentator writing in Germany in 1914, who debated "whether the extraordinarily extensive welfare system provided here for the sick and the weak truly benefits the health of the people, and whether the system of the old Spartans, in which the inferior were banished and abandoned, would not be more suitable."[11] Even those generally amenable to the working class, such as the French commentator Édouard Cormouls-Houlès (who wrote an 800-page study of welfare and unemployment – *L'Assistance par le travail*), believed that permanent programs of relief would stifle initiative and institutionalize dependency. A proportion of those who were opposed to state and political interventions in the sphere of social welfare turned instead to the collectivist social policies proposed by science and medicine.

Notions of degeneration in connection with urban life were not new to the twentieth century. A diffuse and nebulous concept, the term "degeneration" was common in medical and criminological writings, in fiction, in scientific texts, and in works of philosophy at the turn of the century. Essentially, degeneration was a negation of confidence in universal progress and of Darwin's theory of evolution. Far from species evolving into ever more sophisticated forms over time, the concept implied that some people were "degenerating" into lower, more animalistic forms of being. While degeneration could affect the effete aristocrats of the upper classes, it was far more commonly linked to urban environments and particularly the slum areas where the very poor lived. The filthy, squalid existence of the poor was seen to have a detrimental effect on their physical, mental, and moral health. Alarmingly, degenerative changes were seen to be hereditary, thus threatening the very future of developed nations.

Such ideas remained persistent well into the twentieth century. Taking England as an example, early twentieth-century concerns were often focused on the degenerate physical and moral condition of the urban poor. Masterman, writing in the wake of the shock revelation of the poor health of the urban working class during recruitment of soldiers for the Boer War, described the characteristic physical type of a town dweller as "Stunted, narrow-chested, easily wearied; yet voluble, excitable, with little ballast, stamina, or endurance – seeking stimulus in drink."[12]

This theme of actual *physical* difference declined as the century progressed, but was replaced by a focus on the poor standard of mental health of the lowest segment of the population, and on the social problems (alcoholism, vagrancy, petty criminality) seen to be associated with this. The Report of the Women's Group on Public Welfare, from as late as 1943, identified a putative "submerged tenth" – a strata of "problem families" at the bottom end of the social spectrum – "always at the edge of pauperism and crime, riddled with mental and physical defects, in and out of the courts for child neglect."[13] Such views of the very poorest remained relatively common across Europe during the period until after World War II.

Concerns over the moral and physical health of the poor collided with another set of fears in the interwar period: fears of demographic decline and the reproductive health of nations. Put simply, while the period 1750–1850 had been one of rapid population growth, the period 1850–1950 witnessed a shift towards decreasing fertility. This shift was becoming apparent by the turn of the century, and became a source of increasing consternation to many middle-class observers. Many believed that the fertility of the poorer classes had remained robust, while the urban elites were becoming increasingly less likely to have children. Hence, societies were in danger of being "swamped" by the offspring of the poor. Such concerns were particularly pronounced in France, where the birth rate was especially low in the interwar period. Dr Henri Sicard predicted in 1932 that "the increased swamping of superior classes of society by the lower classes will certainly resort in the complete bankruptcy of the nation in gifted, capable and energetic individuals."[14]

Similar concerns were voiced across Europe. In Italy, Mussolini himself sought to counter those who cited Malthusian claims that declining population sizes would lead to increased standards of living. In an essay entitled "Numbers as force," first published in 1928, he branded this contention "absurd." Italy, and many other states, introduced policies designed to encourage women to remain in the domestic sphere and to bear larger families. Government campaigns with slogans such as "equality in difference" and "motherhood is a social function" were designed to encourage this.

Ideas about degeneration and the hereditary transmission of problematic social traits, and fears over the reproductive health of nations, all primarily focused on the poorest elements of society as weak, unproductive, and sick. In many nations eugenics societies were formed which aimed to tackle the problem not by welfarist policies, but via medical and scientific interventions, including sterilization projects and selective breeding plans. In many ways, the eugenics movement is most closely associated with Germany under National Socialism. Certainly it was here during the 1930s that it assumed its most extreme form, but it had a long genesis. At the same time as the welfare legislation of the 1880s was being introduced, a vociferous lobby argued that the biological laws of natural selection should be allowed to function freely. Between 1890 and 1930 the influence of those advocating biological purity – *Rassenhygiene* – grew. The defeat of World War I arguably provided a turning point, with eugenics henceforth seen as a promising means via which to reinvigorate the German people, and the economic crisis of 1929 bolstered the view that the existing welfare apparatus was unsustainable. The Nazis introduced a heightened focus on race as an issue in eugenics, but also in many ways merely enforced, *in extremis*, pre-existing ideas.

Given some of the horrific eugenic programs implemented in Nazi Germany (including the systematic murder of up to 200,000 mentally ill or physically disabled people) it would be reassuring to believe that eugenic theories were largely confined to Germany. This was not the case. Eugenics societies were set up in many countries. England's, for example, was instigated in 1907, just two years after that of Germany. It has often been argued that British eugenics focused more on issues of "class" than on "issues" of race, as in the German case. However, such distinctions have recently been called into question as primarily a postwar claim. Moreover, even after World War II, liberal intellectuals such as Aldous Huxley, while deploring the Nazi practices, still advocated "humane" and "scientific" ways of genetically improving the human race. In France, too, a eugenics society was set up in 1912, which involved itself heavily in natalist policies. However, there was a harder edge to French eugenics, too, which has often been ignored. A key figure, Charles Richet, for example, argued that "no sentimental ranting will make me acknowledge the right of unfortunate individuals to bring into the world children as unfortunate as they: epileptics, alcoholics, degenerates, neurasthenics, criminals."[15] In Scandinavia a focus on mental health issues led to sterilization legislation in Denmark (1929) and in Sweden (1934 and 1941). In Finland, 2,000 people were compulsorily sterilized between 1935 and 1955.

It can be seen, therefore, that social conditions and public responses to social problems were very mixed in Europe during the period 1900–45. While welfare initiatives undoubtedly ameliorated living conditions for many of the working class, concerns over city life, persistent poverty, and demographic decline all coalesced in an enduring image of a degenerate, feckless "underclass." This non-productive residuum, and indeed the urban poor in general, were routinely linked to crime in this period, and developments in the area of crime and policing form the subject of the next section.

Crime and Policing

Even the most cursory glance at trends in crime and policing during the first half of the twentieth century shows the extent to which they were intertwined with the themes of urban life and poverty discussed above. In the first instance, crime and criminality remained closely associated with the urban environment by both popular and academic writers. In the academic milieu, the distinction made by Weber,

Durkheim, and others between rural and urban life has already been noted. It remained common to associate the transformation from one to the other with "modernization" – the rise of modern, industrial societies. However, during the interwar period a number of sociologists sought to highlight specific links between facets of this modernization process and rising levels of criminality. Robert Parks, for example, working within the School of Urban Studies at the University of Chicago, noted that certain sections of cities were characterized by high levels of residential mobility, by poverty, and by a dearth of community organizations. This led, he posited, to a lack of "social organization." The same areas displayed high rates of prostitution, drunkenness, and crime. Hence, he postulated that a lack of "social organization" – typically absent in periods or areas of rapid urbanization – could be causally linked to rising levels of criminality. In other words, the breakdown of stable, face-to-face rural communities and the rise of urban environments characterized by high mobility and anonymity were seen to lead inevitably to higher rates of crime.

Parks' work built on Durkheim's concept of "anomie" – the breakdown of rules and norms of expected behavior during periods of social change. Another sociologist, Robert Merton, added to this work in 1938 with a more subtle analysis of anomie as the disjunction between goals valued by society and the ability of individuals to attain these goals. It was the mismatch between what individuals were socialized to desire and what they were actually able to attain that led to crime. Thus it was not necessarily the dislocation of social values produced by rapid urbanization which made cities centers of crime, but rather the juxtapositioning of poverty and wealth in a society which valued material prosperity and attributed status accordingly. While many of the theorists contributing to this debate worked in the United States, it was highly influential in perceptions of cities and crime in Europe during the interwar period and remained so for many years.

However, while the causal chain of "rapid social change–poor urban living conditions–the breakdown of social norms and restraints–crime" might seem logical enough, many historians have recently sought empirically to challenge the assumptions implicit in this type of theory. Howard Zehr, for example, studying France and Germany, claimed that, rather than a rise in crime overall, modernization and urbanization caused a shift from violent crimes like assault to acquisitive crimes such as theft. Eric Johnson, however, has looked at Germany in detail and finds the reverse – that property offenses were declining in some urban areas during industrialization while violent crime was rising. No clear connection between patterns of urbanization and crime trends emerges. Moreover, many of the debates over urbanization and crime revolve around methodological issues. The nature of the data used to arrive at conclusions about crime trends is necessarily problematic (in that it only measures *recorded* crime rather than actual crime) and hence it is hard to make comprehensive statements about cities and crime. Suffice it to say, however, that enough historical evidence has now been presented to undermine the clumsy structural theories of the interwar period, and the notion that the urban setting *necessarily* leads to criminality. Indeed, recent research has challenged the idea that it is possible even to make a clear rural/urban distinction, arguing that the boundaries between city and countryside are much more ambiguous than previously assumed.

However, to return to the period 1900–45, the significant point is that, regardless of sociological debates, a "commonsense" connection was often made between cities and crime. What is also often apparent is that criminality was not located uniformly throughout the city. Crime was closely associated with the poorer areas of the urban environment, and criminality was usually located in the lowest social strata. At the start of the twentieth century, the criminal justice systems of Europe were thus over-whelmingly focused downwards. Partly, of course, this was due to a lack of recognition of the involvement of the middle and upper classes in criminal activities. The term "white collar crime" was only coined in the pioneering work of Edwin Sutherland in 1939, and the insurance and share frauds perpetrated by office workers and company directors were customarily marginalized in contemporary discussions of criminality. Despite the fact that a single case of insider dealing (a form of share fraud) could have a greater economic impact than thousands of petty burglaries and thefts, the police were often ill-prepared for the investigation of such complex crimes. It was not until World War II, with the advent of rationing and a black market (especially in gasoline or petrol), that the middle classes came into regular contact with the police at all.

Thus, criminality was primarily seen to reside among the lower classes, and there were a number of ways in which this connection was made. In the first instance, concerns over the degenerating effects of slum living on the poor often overlapped with debates about crime. Eugenics movements routinely associated race (or rather, foreigners) with crime, but also considered issues of class and social status as significant. In fascist Italy, for example, youngsters from deprived backgrounds were seen as inherently predisposed to criminality, and hence the fascist police often used their increased powers to put "suspicious" youths into custody. Even among those who did not perceive explicit physical or hereditary links between the poor and criminality, distaste for the overcrowded and unsanitary conditions in which many of the poorest still lived meant that the morality of the poor was tainted by association. Richard Jervis, a senior police officer in the north of England, believed that "slums, drunkenness and crime are inseparable. How can it be otherwise?"[16] Neither of these mechanisms for associating the poor with crime (physical and moral deficiency) was new to the twentieth century, but they proved persistent. However, it might be argued that the emergent academic discipline of criminology also served to perpetuate the association of the poor and criminality.

The early twentieth century was marked in many European nations by an expanding franchise, by a growth in the power of organized labor, and by a better-educated and more vocal working class. Hence, it became increasingly less easy for social elites to adopt openly repressive policies towards the poor (as had arguably been the case in the nineteenth century). However, it might be contended that the new pseudoscience of criminology helped to enable the continued regulation of the poor. Because early criminology sought the identification of a new *type* of person – the criminal (as separate from any criminal acts which he/she might commit) – it provided an explanation (and perhaps a justification) for a criminal justice system targeted on a specific section of the population. By viewing crime as "an inevitable outcome of a particular kind of character or constitution," criminology provided an explanation not only for the existence of a class which was constantly criminalized, but also for the very existence of an impoverished sector of the population.[17] By shifting attention away from specific *criminal acts* (which might be explained by environmental factors such as poverty) to criminals themselves, and by claiming a competence beyond the legal sphere (for example by analyzing vagrants, the "feeble-minded," and inebriates as *potential* criminals), criminology was thus conceivably another mechanism which enabled the continued association of the poor with crime.

While this particular reading of the emergence of criminology is by no means uncontroversial, it is certainly likely that the links perceived between criminality and the poor during the first half of the twentieth century may have had a role to play in the maintenance of power and influence within societies. However, it does seem apparent that there was a gradual shift during the period to 1945 from an undifferentiated view of the mass of the urban poor as suspect and potentially criminal to a perception that criminality was located within a few, closely defined groups of the poor. While the bulk of the working class was no longer viewed with suspicion by elites (as at the end of the nineteenth century), very visible groups such as gypsies and vagrants were increasingly targeted. The distinctive dress and lifestyle of traveling peoples such as Sinti and Roma, for example, often came to appear increasingly incongruous in European societies typified by urban milieux and fixed working patterns. Gypsies were thus seen by many as inherently criminal, and increasing efforts were made to observe and regulate their movements. In France, an official circular noted that gypsy caravans were "all too often composed of criminals" and from 1912 all such individuals had to carry a *carnet anthropometrique* – an identity card giving details of their family tree. Similar initiatives can be traced through much of Europe.[18] Thus, while perceptions of the link between the poor and crime changed significantly in the first half of the century (and were arguably eroded to some extent) cities, poverty, and crime remained conceptually linked up until World War II.

Any discussion of perceptions and patterns of crime, however, requires at least a brief mention of the mechanism of enforcement: the police. If the poor and their environs were seen to harbor criminality, what did this mean in terms of policing? Developments in policing during this period were diverse and are hard to characterize succinctly. Certainly, there were clear moves towards the police we know today. For example, professional training was developed. At the start of the period, training for most officers consisted of a few weeks at best, or an afternoon with a handbook at worst. By the end, training academies and professional development were the norm. Equally, the period was also marked by the growing use of technology by the police. Most forces gradually adopted motorized transport and progressive police chiefs (such as Dr Wilhelm Abegg, of the Police Section of the Prussian Interior Ministry) urged the deployment of forensic science. There were also early experiments with radio technology, although the sets were initially so cumbersome that an officer was required to strap the apparatus to his back. In the liberal democracies, at least, declining statistics for attacks on police officers appear indicative of growing public acceptance of the functions they performed. However, there is clearly another side to this story. As touched upon above, most police forces were closely involved in the regulation of the poor. While some were sympathetic, many officers displayed harsh attitudes towards vagrants, gypsies, and others on the margins of society. Also, more obviously, in day-to-day beat policing most officers still spent much of their time traversing the poorer areas of towns and cities. Given this, it is likely that perceptions of the involvement of the poor with crime became self-fulfilling. The greater scrutiny given to slum areas may have meant that more crime was detected there in proportion to other areas, thus reinforcing public perceptions and leading the police to concentrate even more of their efforts there, which in turn led again to yet more crime being detected.

Police forces across Europe were also routinely involved in the often violent suppression of political and economic protest during the period. Hunger Marchers in London in 1932, unemployed demonstrators at the Paris Bourse in 1903, socialist protestors in Berlin's Tiergarten in 1910 – all were on the receiving end of police brutality. While there was arguably an increasing divergence between the police in totalitarian regimes and in liberal democracies during the interwar period, even here firm distinctions are hard to draw. World War II certainly provided ample evidence of police heroism in the service of their citizenry. In Italy, for example, the *carabiniere* Salvo D'Aquisto gave his life in place of 22 civilian hostages who were scheduled to be shot in German reprisals on September 23, 1943. In Denmark just fewer than 2,000 police officers were transported to Buchenwald in September 1944 for non-compliance with the occupying Nazi authorities. Equally, however, forces in France and Holland have been judged at least partially complicit in the implementation of the genocide programs of National Socialism. Clearly, then, while the police were in many ways instrumental in the social control of the poor and working class, simplistic generalizations of their duties and functions must be avoided.

Conclusion

Looking back on Europe during the first half of the twentieth century, it is easy to discern much that seems familiar. Major cities were assuming the topographical forms they still bear today; the state was beginning to adopt greater responsibility for the social welfare of its citizens; the police were increasingly being seen less as an unwarranted intrusion into daily life and more as the arbiters of security for all. However, large cities were still new enough to warrant debate over their merits during the period, there were wide discrepancies across Europe in the amelioration of poverty, and the police were closely involved at times in the repression of the poor and the working class. Thus, while it might seem relatively easy to construct an image of this period as intrinsically "modern," a nuanced approach to the intertwined themes of urbanization, poverty, and crime reveals significant incongruities alongside the familiar.

NOTES

1 Cited in Andrew Lees, *Cities Perceived: Urban Society in European and American Thought, 1820–1940* (Manchester: Manchester University Press), p. 207.
2 Peter Hall, *The World Cities* (London: Wiedenfeld, 1966), p. 18.
3 Patrick Geddes, *Cities in Evolution: An Introduction to the Town Planning Movement and to the Study of Civics* (London: Ernest Benn, 1915), p. 220.
4 Cited in Anthony Sutcliffe, ed., *Metropolis 1890–1940* (London: Mansell, 1984), p. 266.
5 Cited in Joachim Schlör, *Nights in the Big City* (London: Reaktion, 1998), p. 66.
6 Georg Simmel, "The Metropolis and Mental Life" (1903) in *The Sociology of Georg Simmel*, Kurt H. Wolff, ed. (Glencoe IL: Free Press, 1950), p. 410.

7   Paul Hohenberg and Lynn Hollen Lees, *The Making of Urban Europe, 1000–1994* (Cambridge MA: Harvard University Press, 1995), p. 332.
8   Lees, *Cities Perceived*, p. 208.
9   C. F. G. Masterman, *The Heart of the Empire: Discussions of Problems of Modern City Life in England* (London: Fisher Unwin, 1901), p. 17.
10 Lees, *Cities Perceived*, p. 277.
11 J. Fleming, "Night Life in the Great German Cities" (1914), cited in Schlör, *Nights*, p. 207.
12 Masterman, *Heart of the Empire*, p. 8
13 Cited in John Macnicol, "In Pursuit of the Underclass," *Journal of Social Policy* 16/3 (1987): 297.
14 William H. Schnieder, *Quality and Quantity: The Quest for Biological Regeneration in Twentieth-Century France* (Cambridge: Cambridge University Press, 1990), p. 113.
15 Ibid, p. 181.
16 Cited in Paul Lawrence, "Images of Poverty and Crime: Police Memoirs in England and France," *Crime, History and Societies* 3/1 (2000): 70.
17 For this argument, see David Garland, "The Criminal and his Science," *British Journal of Criminology* 25/2 (1985): 131.
18 See Annemarie Cottaar and Wim Willems, "Justice or Injustice? A Survey of Government Policy towards Gypsies and Caravan Dwellers in Western Europe in the 19th and 20th Centuries," *Immigrants and Minorities* 11/1 (1992): 42–66.

GUIDE TO FURTHER READING

Peter Baldwin, *The Politics of Social Solidarity: Class Bases of the European Welfare State 1875–1975* (Cambridge: Cambridge University Press, 1990). An interesting conceptual analysis of the rise of welfare states.

Clive Emsley, Eric Johnson, and Pieter Spierenburg, *Social Control in Europe 1800–2000* (Columbus: Ohio State University Press, 2004). Part two of this volume contains a range of essays addressing the theme of policing during the period 1900–60.

V. A. C. Gatrell, "Crime, Authority and the Policeman-State," in *The Cambridge Social History of Britain 1750–1950*, vol. 3, F. M. L. Thompson, ed. (Cambridge: Cambridge University Press, 1990). An elegant piece which argues for an interpretation of the English police as a mechanism enabling elite control of the working class. Applicable more widely.

Paul Hohenberg and Lynn Hollen Lees, *The Making of Urban Europe, 1000–1994* (Cambridge, MA: Harvard University Press, 1995). A comprehensive overview of the rise of urban Europe.

Andrew Lees, *Cities Perceived: Urban Society in European and American Thought, 1820–1940* (Manchester: Manchester University Press, 1995). An excellent guide to the multifarious opinions generated by urbanization.

Anthony McElligott, *The German Urban Experience, 1900–1945: Modernity and Crisis* (London: Routledge, 2001). A useful reader containing a range of primary and secondary source extracts pertaining to German cities during the period 1900–45.

Gerard Oram, ed., *Conflict and Legality: Policing Mid-Twentieth Century Europe* (London: Francis Boutle, 2003). A collection of essays addressing the nature of policing in a range of countries.

Daniel Pick, *Faces of Degeneration: A European Disorder, c.1848–c.1918* (Cambridge: Cambridge University Press, 1989). An extremely readable discussion of the rise of notions of degeneration.

Maria Quine, *Population Politics in Twentieth-Century Europe* (London: Routledge, 1996). A consideration of fears of demographic decline and proposed remedies in Italy, France, and Germany.

Joachim Schlör, *Nights in the Big City* (London: Reaktion, 1998). An innovative exploration of changes in the perception of night in Paris, London, and Berlin.

William H. Schnieder, *Quality and Quantity: The Quest for Biological Regeneration in Twentieth-Century France* (Cambridge: Cambridge University Press, 1990). An investigation of the development of the eugenics movements in France.

Dan Stone, *Breeding Superman: Nietzsche, Race and Eugenics in Edwardian and Interwar Britain* (Liverpool: Liverpool University Press, 2002). A consideration of the British eugenics movements.

Anthony Sutcliffe, ed., *Metropolis 1890–1940* (London: Mansell, 1984). A useful guide to the rise of the metropolis, with essays on a range of cities.

Pat Thane, *The Foundations of the Welfare State* (Harlow: Longman, 1982). An informative consideration of the subject in Britain, with a section of international comparisons.

Paul Weindling, *Health, Race and German Politics Between National Unification and Nazism, 1870–1945* (Cambridge: Cambridge University Press, 1989). Locates eugenics and social Darwinism in Germany in its wider social and political context.

CHAPTER TWO

The Revolution in Science

CATHRYN CARSON

The age in which we live menaces with its unrest and its misfortune the values that formerly seemed to us secure; and if we take the political disorder as a measure for movements in the foundations of thought, then the catastrophes of these decades suggest that the weights of human thought are shifting and displacing the foundations. (Werner Heisenberg, manuscript of 1942)[1]

When Werner Heisenberg wrote these lines, he was looking back over one of modern science's most turbulent periods. In the space of a few decades beginning around 1900, the landscape of European science was transformed. Scientists and laymen alike remarked on the change. In fact, many were inclined to call it a revolution. When contemporary observers spoke of revolution, however, they knew what that meant from experience outside of science. "After the catastrophe of the First World War," Heisenberg observed, "we recognized outside of science, too, that there were no firm foundations for our existence, secure for all time."[2]

Like other revolutions, the revolution in early twentieth-century science was prepared by a longer period of change. Its consequences carried forward past its nominal end. Still, in exactly its flux, it had a coherence stretching from the turn of the century to the end of World War II. This chapter takes up three aspects of the upheaval. First is the content of science. These decades saw one revolutionary development after another: in physics, Heisenberg's own discipline; in the sciences of life; and in many other scientific fields. This intellectual effervescence was fostered, secondly, by changed social circumstances. The scientific enterprise had taken on its modern form only in the half-century preceding; now it found itself expanded, intensified, and unsettled. Thirdly, its consequences ramified – in industry, medicine, and warfare; in popular consciousness; and in the ideological realm. As Heisenberg implied, the changes in science were often tied into larger changes in the world around it. True, scientific training was growing ever more specialized, and much research ever more incomprehensible to outsiders. Yet manifold connections between science and society were increasingly on display. No longer a small, esoteric venture, but a professional, institutionalized, and powerful force, science depended on its surroundings for intellectual and material stimulation. It simultaneously drove change in a world ever more dependent on it.

Ideas

When contemporaries spoke of revolutions in science, physics was often first in their mind. In the space of two or three decades, an entirely new physics was erected, superseding "classical" physics in a host of domains. First, just before the turn of the century, wholly new forms of radiation were discovered. X-rays and radioactivity were mysterious. Where did these rays come from, and what was their energy source? At practically the same time, the electron, the first subatomic particle, was identified. If the atom was previously assumed to be literally "uncuttable," that could no longer be true. Along with opening up new realms for experiment – the atom's interior, and within it the nucleus – these discoveries revealed that there were many more things in the physical world than scientists had thought. They also raised an important possibility: would the familiar theories of nineteenth-century physics fail to describe the new domains of experience?

While experimenters were preoccupied with these discoveries, their theoretical colleagues were confronting equally radical change. In 1905 the young Albert Einstein proposed his theory of relativity, reconstructing basic intuitions about space and time. Ordinary experience suggested that space and time were separate, and all physics to date was built on that assumption. However, using some fairly simple reasoning, Einstein hypothesized that bodies moving at great velocity (near light speed) encountered the two woven together. Four-dimensional spacetime had counterintuitive consequences: moving clocks should run slow, moving objects get shorter and heavier, and the temporal order of events could change depending on how they were observed. Yet these strange effects were seen to hold true in sensitive experiments. The theory also showed that mass and energy were not stable quantities, but, just like space and time, could be converted into one another according to the famous equation $E = mc^2$. This was not the end of the road, either. In 1915 Einstein pushed the theory further by adding gravity. His general theory of relativity (building on the "special" theory of 1905) suggested that the gravitational pull of heavy bodies deformed the structure of spacetime itself. Compared with special relativity, the new theory was mathematically much more complex. Testing its consequences was even more subtle and difficult, involving tiny effects (such as the minute bending of a light beam) due to extremely massive bodies like stars.

Other scientists were going beyond the old physics in a different way. Beginning in 1900, physicists analyzing the light emitted by ordinary bodies revealed it to have a characteristic particle-like chunkiness. Such a "quantum" aspect of light, as its discoverer Max Planck called it, caught scientists by surprise. It conflicted directly with the extraordinarily successful theory of electromagnetism, which described it as a continuous wave. As explored by other scientists, led by Niels Bohr, the matter also had deep ramifications for the physics of the atom. It was from atoms, after all, that light was emitted as electrons jumped between energy levels. If only certain particle-like packets of light could be emitted, then only certain electron energy levels were allowed. As reasonable as this might seem, it went against the grain of previous physics

THE REVOLUTION IN SCIENCE

– supposing one imagined an atom as a miniature solar system, with a nucleus at the center and electrons orbiting around. But perhaps extending the quantum hypothesis to the atom could explain some of its mysterious features. For example, Bohr suggested, it might eventually account for chemical regularities in the periodic table of elements, observationally secure but completely unexplained.

The argument also ran in the other direction: if light had particle-like aspects, particles might have wave-like features as well. So an electron, rather than being best described as a particle, might be most appropriately captured by a "wave function" instead. By the mid-1920s an entirely new mechanics had been developed out of these ideas. In fact, two different versions were proposed within a few months, by Werner Heisenberg and Erwin Schrödinger. Once the confusion was sorted out, the result was properly named quantum mechanics. As construed by the "Copenhagen Interpretation" (named after its Danish architect, Bohr), the wave function of quantum mechanics never gave deterministic predictions for the future, but only probabilistic ones. The theory was also fundamentally characterized by Heisenberg's uncertainty principle. That is, in quantum mechanics it proved impossible to pin down certain things (say, where a particle was located) without interfering with knowledge of others (how fast it was moving). In a well-defined way, what an experimenter went looking for determined what he would find: if his apparatus was suited to measure certain characteristics of a system, he would get definite values for those features, but wash out other "complementary" aspects ordinarily presumed to exist.

Not all physicists agreed with this interpretation, which made the quantum world seem a very strange place. In fact, some of the theory's own creators – Planck, Einstein, and Schrödinger – rejected the view. However, the bulk of their colleagues went along with the "Copenhagen" stance. Viewed together, relativity and quantum mechanics then came to be seen as making up "modern physics," in contrast to the previous "classical" theories. Although those previous theories were not discarded, just constrained in their validity, the changes certainly looked revolutionary. Philosophically, they went to the core of what counted as science. Could science legitimately give up determinism, the basis of causality, and with it the assumption that known causes lead to certain effects? Could it restrict objectivity, the deep principle that observations are independent of who is making the measurement? Many physicists felt that they had to say yes.

Scientists might take or leave philosophy; they could not take or leave success. Whatever the debate over its foundations, quantum mechanics proved marvelously applicable in use. It was put to work in studies of the atom and ordinary matter (the solid state). Then it was naturally applied to that exciting domain, nuclear physics, as new experimental techniques blew it wide open in the 1930s. Understanding how nuclei were held together, however, proved harder than understanding how they fell apart. At least, this was the case after the discovery and explanation of nuclear fission in 1939. That remarkable and unexpected finding was the ultimate result of a long-term partnership between the nuclear chemist Otto Hahn and the nuclear physicist Lise Meitner.

In the burgeoning life sciences, too, stunning developments also gave the impression of a domain on the march – even if, unlike in physics, there was no coherent group of leaders or single, unifying story of revolutionary change. To start, an invisible world, too fine for human vision, was opened to scrutiny on several different fronts. While a dizzying array of details remained to be explicated, it seemed that microscopic explanations of the very processes of life were coming into view. By 1900, bacteriology and microbiology (the study of microorganisms) had already moved into high gear. Cell biology had picked out many constituents and substructures of the basic unit of the organism, looking to connect them with cell function and with organismal development. Cell biologists were now matched by a new breed of biochemists, who used methods from organic chemistry to investigate the substances and processes that kept organisms alive. In the post-1900 biochemical ferment, a string of enzymes (biological catalysts) were isolated. Metabolic pathways were described, culminating in the Krebs (citric acid) cycle, the final step of the processes by which organisms break down their foodstuffs. The structure of proteins was clarified, too, revealing that these all-important molecules were not special colloidal agglomerations, but simply very large molecules with definite compositions.

Over and against advances in the microworld, and initially quite separate, was the wide domain of macroscopic biological change. After Charles Darwin published *The Origin of Species* in 1859, broadly evolutionary accounts of species change found nearly universal acceptance in science. In that sense, Darwin's work became the foundation for practically everything that followed in a wide range of natural history fields. Paleontologists used descent through modification to make sense of the fossil record, while field naturalists studied the adaptation and geographical distribution of species. Far more contentious, however, than the general notion of evolution was Darwin's specific explanation in terms of natural selection operating differentially upon chance variations. In fact, around 1900, Darwinism in this strict sense was rejected by the bulk of expert opinion. Doubting its adequacy to explain the observed phenomena, many biologists hypothesized other mechanisms of evolutionary change. Exactly because evolutionary explanations operated over a long time scale and were founded on observation as much as experiment, the field was open for all sorts of ideas. This made the study of heredity, adaptation, and species change exciting but highly contentious.

Beginning in 1900, the rediscovery of Gregor Mendel's long-forgotten experiments on inheritance in pea plants gave a new impulse to these debates. By the 1910s, breeding experiments paired with cell biology to establish a material basis for heredity. When the American biologist Thomas Hunt Morgan identified chromosomes as the genetic material, fully responsible for an organism's palette of traits, a materialistic explanation of variation and inheritance was enthroned, even if the path to the expression of visible traits was unknown. For some European scientists, this was a great triumph; for others, a reductionistic diversion from the real questions of biological interest (e.g., organismal development). Still, as interest in evolution revived and strictly Darwinian explanations gained ground, the results suggested at just what level any evolutionary process would ultimately have to operate. Over the next decades, though not without controversy, that picture was filled out. The 1930s saw the rise of mathematical population genetics, which analyzed gene frequencies in a variable environment. This work gave tantalizing suggestions how macro and micro approaches might ultimately be fused. By the early 1940s the grandly and appropriately named "modern synthesis" was on offer. That theory finally linked large-scale evolution to molecular genetics through a revitalized Darwinian natural selection.

These developments touched some of science's deepest questions. How do we make sense of organic life's striking regularities – or its remarkable diversity at all of its scales? Indeed, how do we explain what it means to be living? A final frontier in the life sciences pushed these questions one step further: how can we understand human beings themselves as biological beings? As early twentieth-century biochemistry, endocrinology, and neurophysiology moved ahead, they took on deeply human matters as topics of naturalistic research. Accounts of sensation, mind, or emotion on a biological basis captured the imagination of many contemporaries. They claimed territory over which humanistic disciplines had once held sway. As in anthropology or experimental psychology (two fields outside the scope of this chapter), the life sciences brought human beings under the microscope. They gave yet another occasion for commentators to hymn science's transformative results.

Science's reach extended well beyond the most familiar examples. In these decades, for instance, chemistry gained its hoped-for quantum foundation, and with it a new account of bonds and valence. Why were certain combinations of atoms stable and others not? The answer came nearly painlessly from their electrons' behavior under quantum mechanics. Reaction mechanisms were subjected to systematization, and novel materials – the soon-to-be omnipresent plastics, artificial polymers like nylon – were synthesized. On the grand scale, astronomy and cosmology took up the challenge posed by mathematical physics in Einstein's field equations of 1915. Could the origin and large-scale structure of the universe be described? The decades between the two world wars found it newly possible to take on this issue, pairing Einstein's challenge with Edwin Hubble's telescopic observations of a universe that was not remotely static, but expanding at a rapid clip. With advances in nuclear physics in the 1930s, the life processes of stars also became fair game. The source of stellar energy was identified in nuclear fusion, finally bringing an answer to an age-old question: what makes the stars shine?

A scientist or a layman, surveying these fields and others, would have been impressed by the depth and breadth of contemporary research. New fields found their footing, as in ethology (the study of patterns in animal behavior in its natural setting) or ecology (the science of the relationships between organisms and their environment). At the interfaces between disciplines, hybrid fields sprang up, with new coinages like oceanography and biophysics leading the way. And in the bread-and-butter of scientific practice, in specialized research, enormous quantities of details were filled in. For some observers, the rapid growth of knowledge and wild proliferation of specialties generated a feeling of crisis. How could a single person grasp it all? How could a scientist stay abreast of developments outside a narrow subfield? Even as interdisciplinarity was celebrated, fears of fragmentation were floated – though not always, it bears remembering, by science's yeoman practitioners who did the bulk of the day-to-day research.

The Scientific Enterprise

If we want to understand why these decades were so phenomenally fruitful, we need to look beyond individual advances. By the start of the twentieth century, no scientist worked in isolation. Every intellectual accomplishment was enabled by a much larger enterprise, whose structures and functioning have attracted increasing attention from historians. This enterprise of science – the people, institutions, and relationships supporting it – was no more static than the ideas it sustained. Of course, something we could timelessly call "science" was evident as far back as the Renaissance – but at that time "scientists" (a term coined in the nineteenth century) were scarce on the ground. Indeed, the foundations of the professional scientific enterprise, as we know it today, were laid only in the half-century before 1900. The twentieth century's first decades took off from those beginnings – and built on them, strengthened them, sometimes turned them upside down. We can trace these changes in the community of scientific researchers, that community's support system, and the national settings that conditioned them both.

For the scientific community, to start, this was an era of consolidation and growth. Good statistics are hard to come by, as no one thought to count scientists back then. However, in 1900 a discipline like physics probably had a few thousand practitioners worldwide.[3] Other fields' figures are probably comparable, and the numbers would increase substantially over the next decades. The larger proportion of these scientists were located in Europe. Here, however, the pattern was changing. The major scientific powers of 1900 – Germany and Britain, to a lesser degree France – were joined by up-and-coming nations on the periphery – by Russia, the United States, and Japan. In the early decades of the century, most of the latter countries' scientists still got their training in one of the big three. By the 1930s, they were giving their erstwhile teachers a run for their money.

Already by this period, the career path to becoming a scientist was well-institutionalized and formalized. It required graduate education in a university or higher technical school, leading to an academic degree roughly comparable to the German PhD (doctorate). A budding researcher would necessarily choose a specialty and an established scientist to train with, completing a thesis on a project of independent research. Thereafter three main options were open: employment in an industrial laboratory, in government service, or back in higher education. The age of the amateur, the self-trained, or the polymath was nearly over; science was now a credentialed profession. That is not to say that it was as socially established as, say, medicine or the law. However, if scientists as everyday figures were still somewhat exotic, they became increasingly less so as their numbers grew.

One thing was constant: the scientific community of the early twentieth century remained overwhelmingly male. Until sometime around the turn of the century, women were officially barred from studying in many European universities; they could only audit courses with male professors' forbearance. Then when women did gain scientific education and employment, they were often subjected to discrimination or relegated to a technician's rank. There were exceptions, however. Women found more acceptance in some fields, though often less established and prestigious ones. The career of Marie Curie (née Sklodowska), Polish-born and Paris-trained, told of both the hardships and achievements of women in science.[4] For her work on radioactivity Marie Curie was celebrated as the world's first double Nobel laureate, recognized in 1903 and 1911. Curie's daughter, Irène Joliot-Curie, split a Nobel Prize with her husband in 1935. Ironically, nuclear physics was exactly the kind of marginal field where women could prosper.

The scientific community did not flourish in a vacuum, of course. It drew its strength from a support system reaching outside its bounds. This support system, too, deserves our attention, as it displays the fine mesh of threads tying science to the society surrounding it. In its practical existence, for instance, science could now count on a nascent commercial network specialized to its needs. That network extended from publishers of specialist journals (the main venue of scientific publication) to suppliers of test tubes and laboratory rats. There was money to be made in stocking research laboratories. In the same way, science's reward system was publicly crowned by titles, peerages, and prizes. Along with the internal forms of recognition, scientific fame was partially enacted in the modern mass media.

Most important among ways in which science drew upon external resources, of course, were investments by outside parties who expected returns. The institutions of science were scarcely built by scientists alone; and in institutional terms, especially, this period was a watershed for European science. The later nineteenth century had nurtured three main sites: research universities, government bureaus, and industrial labs. The twentieth century's first decades not only intensified those trends, but experimented with alternative institutions as well. The model of the day was the extra-university research institute, typically established at some distance from state and private interests, usually informally serving both. Europe's prime examples were the Pasteur Institutes in microbiology, established in 1888 and by now spreading throughout France (and its colonies); and the network of Kaiser Wilhelm Institutes, created beginning in 1911, the incarnation of late imperial Germany's scientific ambitions, passed on to the Weimar republic and then to the Third Reich.[5] Still more radical experiments were tried in the Soviet Union. By the 1930s, the old tsarist Academy of Sciences had been Bolshevized and reconstructed in the service of socialist science. Eventually built into a vast network of institutes in a wide spectrum of fields, the Academy was made over as the crucial institution of research. Its structure mirrored the Communist Party's centralizing ambitions and facilitated its centralized control.[6]

As the examples suggest, the role of the state here was central. Except for industrial research, most science was carried out in the public sector – for across Europe, with the historic exception of Britain, universities, too, were largely state-run. However, outside of the science-enthused Soviet Union, governmental attitudes toward financially supporting science remained mixed. For reasons of national prestige, competition, and power, Europe's scientific powers tried out new ways to invest in research: for instance, funding bodies were erected with budgets provided mainly by the central government, as in Germany or in France, or research councils and even a Department of Scientific and Industrial Research, as in Britain.[7] In practice, state support for science rarely satisfied their researchers, who publicly deplored the small fraction of government expenditures devoted to science. The cause of the situation was not so much disrespect for science, however, as other, more pressing obligations. Also involved was a more limited construal of the state's responsibility to underwrite technical innovation. The era of huge R&D budgets had not yet arrived.

These considerations have finally led historians to ask how science was shaped by its national context. This may seem odd, as science is conventionally understood to be international. However, a highly nationalistic era of European history highlighted science's rootedness in its national settings. The Nobel Prizes, first awarded in 1901, provided a perfect occasion.[8] From the start, the prizes were treated as tokens in an international contest. (Indeed, some countries' nominators caucused privately to coordinate the suggestions they were sending to Stockholm.) The naming of a new laureate was cause for national self-congratulation, and the press kept running tallies of their countries of origin. To no one's surprise (and the dismay of the French), Germany and Britain took top honors. In this way the prizes became a ready metric for a nation's scientific standing. They could also cause international furor. When the Nobel Foundation saw fit immediately after World War I to recognize the German chemist Fritz Haber, it honored a man who stood on the Allies' list for war crimes prosecution. The inverse problem arose in the late 1930s: after the Peace Prize was bestowed on the concentration camp inmate Carl von Ossietzky, several German scientists were compelled by Hitler to reject their prizes in science.

Clearly, science could not escape international tensions, nor could it avoid the effects of the continent's political convulsions. As in Europe as a whole, World War I deeply divided its scientists, as the atmosphere for international cooperation was poisoned by manifestos and charges of partisanship. A few pacifists, like Einstein, deplored the developments, but they were isolated from their peers. Again, after the armistice and the peace settlement, new international scientific organizations were founded, paralleling political bodies like the League of Nations. However, scientists from the former Central Powers were excluded until 1926. Tensions escalated again after 1933. The Nazis' rise to power had enormous consequences for German science. Some scientists emphatically supported the new regime, a small number opposed it, and many simply went ahead with their business. The latter option was unavailable to Germany's Jewish scientists, however. Because so many research institutions were subject to civil service rules, huge numbers of Jewish researchers were fired or fled. The resultant emigration drew away many of the country's leading minds – including such luminaries as Lise Meitner, Fritz Haber, and Hans Krebs; Albert Einstein had already left early in 1933 in disgust. The transfer of scientific talent gave a great boost to other countries, feeding in the greatest numbers into an American scientific community already on the rise. Through the Third Reich, some fields of research in Germany suffered greatly, while others flourished, depending on how adeptly their representatives wangled support. Giving the political repression an ideological edge, a few Nazi scientists – two Nobel laureates among them – even advocated an "Aryan" science in opposition to "Jewish" (abstract, theoretical) thinking.[9] On the whole, the German case made plain just how tightly science's fate could be tied to the national political setting. Other examples made the same point. From exuberant celebration in the Soviet Union's first years to blunt-minded demands for a dialectical materialist physics, even to arrests and murders in the Great Terror, science could not be much of a refuge from the era's political storms.

Even in far more peaceful domains, the national conditioning of science sometimes made itself felt. As any scientist might notice, and as historians have investigated with much curiosity, particular research traditions flourished in some countries, but found few advocates elsewhere. Before World War II, population genetics had only a scattered European audience outside of Britain; the philosophical excursions of quantum physicists, by contrast, carried much further in German-speaking central Europe than elsewhere. These differences, historians typically argue, are best under-stood not as national bias, but as a side-effect, at least in part, of how the scientific enterprise works. Recruitment and training of young scientists, mechanisms of professional advancement, fora in which conjectures were stamped as promising or bizarre

– each of these played out within national contexts, leaving their mark on the ideas of science.

Impact and Implications

The history of science is also the history of its ramifications in society. Those ramifications can take many forms. For the twentieth century, they have been conceived first of all as practical applications: in technology and industry, public health and medicine, and a multiplicity of regulatory and governmental tasks. Ideas from and about science also radiated into popular consciousness, educated discourse, cultural commentary, and ideological debate. Indeed, interwar Europe produced some of the century's most influential intellectual interpretations of science. While the venues varied, these different forms of impact were not disconnected. That is, scientists' technical usefulness provoked contemporary comment; so did their intellectual daring. Responsible for both was the manner in which they upset familiar ways of thinking and acting, presenting themselves as the heralds of the new. Science's boosters claimed to represent the up-to-date, modern, and (sometimes) solely legitimate way of doing things; their calls for transformation were frequently strident and shrill. That aggressive stance certainly mirrored their views of their venture. Along with admirers, however, it earned them critics as well.

In the visibility of its effects, the second industrial revolution of the later nineteenth century was the starting point for the wider impact of science. Around the 1870s, industrial research laboratories began to appear in large corporations. After the turn of the century, systematically scientized innovation spread to smaller firms, while the interwar economic boom swelled the ranks of scientists in huge enterprises like Siemens, Phillips, ICI (Imperial Chemical Industries), and I. G. Farben (formed from the merger of BASF, Bayer, Hoechst, and three other companies) into the thousands.[10] The main motive for the expensive commitment to research was the patent system, and the extent of investment in science-based innovation tracked different countries' patent protections. Key fields where scientists made a difference were electrotechnology, including telephony and wireless (radio) as well as lighting and power; and fine chemicals, starting from dyestuffs and moving into pharmaceuticals, photochemicals, and pesticides. Fortunes and industries were built on these discoveries. So was science's reputation as a revolutionary force. Yet incremental scientific changes may have been just as significant, in less spectacular fields from textile manufacture to brewing. Behind the advertising triumphalism stood also the idealizing hope that scientific inventiveness would make human life easier, happier, and more rewarding. Whether the link understood to exist between science and technology always worked in science's favor can be doubted, however. Anti-industrial screeds of the early twentieth century took aim at science as part of the package; and the world economic crisis of the late 1920s and 1930s called into question the dream of leisure and prosperity founded on capitalist production.

Similar tendencies were evident in medicine and public health – both in perceptions of science's efficacy, and in many cases its actual results. Building on the bacteriological revolution of the later nineteenth century, the germ theory of disease traced illnesses to specific microorganisms rather than general health or environmental conditions. The discoveries of the bacilli responsible for tuberculosis, cholera, typhoid fever, tetanus, and diphtheria set in motion several changes at once. First, they brought bench scientists into the game of diagnosis. Even more than a physician's assessment of symptoms, now cultures or serological tests would be definitive, and laboratories became universal in hospitals and municipal health authorities.[11] At the same time, the practice of public hygiene was changing. Along with progressive campaigns to clean up filthy habitations and workplaces, the vaccines, antitoxins, and antisera developed by medical scientists and now produced in mass quantities became standard immunological weapons in campaigns against disease. Chemotherapy – chemical "magic bullets" which could be used to kill disease-causing agents selectively without damaging the host – was given a celebrated boost with Paul Ehrlich's discovery of the arsenic compound Salvarsan against syphilis in 1907. While drug therapy continued to raise hopes, its promise was only gradually fulfilled in the sulfa drugs in the 1930s and antibiotics, first manufactured in bulk during World War II. Still, few critics found much to object to in the progress of medical science. The advancement of human health was less ambivalent, perhaps, than the advancement of purely material welfare.

Public health measures pointed to something broader as well. In a multitude of unremarkable ways, science's practical uses were being integrated into the tasks of the state. That is, as national, regional, and municipal authorities promulgated regulations and expanded services, scientists infiltrated the bureaucracy and staffed the new technical offices. Science came to be seen as a regular part of the governing apparatus. At the same time, certain domains of political action became technicized. While the process was gradual and more complete in some countries than others – scientific spokespersons complained about civil service rules that favored non-scientists, especially in Britain and Germany – scientists nonetheless made inroads at the lower levels. Many state functions today taken for granted had their origins in this early twentieth-century movement: food inspection, drug testing, physical standards, and testing bureaux. Even leaving aside the empirical social sciences, whose rapid ascent was directly tied to this circumstance, wide domains of scientific application contributed to the creeping expansion of the modern bureaucratic state. Historians are beginning to study the creation of scientific careers and the mobilization of expertise in resource conservation, mining, agriculture, or fisheries management. The same is true of colonial administration, in whose framework the "mission civilisatrice" and the "white man's burden" were imbued with the claim to be bringing the fruits of western science to colonized peoples.

Of course, states had one other overriding interest in science: its use for the conduct of war. It was for good reason that World War I was styled the "chemists' war." Under the supervision of Fritz Haber and his Allied counterparts, an array of poison gases were developed and deployed, starting with chlorine at Ypres in 1915.[12] Though ineffective as a military strategy, chemical warfare vividly symbolized the conflict's horrors. At the same time, it stirred up a wave of revulsion against science – though some found it difficult to understand why death or injury through cutting-edge chemistry was worse than death or injury by a bullet. In any case, the main lessons were the capacity of scientists (not only chemists) to take their place among modern warfare's combatants, and their willingness to do so in just about any national cause, without asking questions about ethical issues. Militarized or quasi-militarized science – German aeronautics research or investigations of synthetic rubber, Soviet studies of tank armor, or British air defense – became part of the interwar scene. Against some resistance within the armed services, scientific warfare began winning converts. Then all that was needed when war came again was full-scale mobilization of the scientific community. On all sides, scientists responded in strength. If Heisenberg wrote ruefully in 1942 of unrest, misfortune, and political disorder, he did so while engaged in applied fission research for the German war effort. In general, interwar investments proved to be good preparation for the great technical advances of World War II: short-wavelength radar, operations research, rocketry, and, of course, the Anglo-American project leading to the atomic bomb. Interestingly, the much-feared German technical community came up short in delivering radical new weapons.[13] That had as much to do with limitations of industrial production and Nazi demands for short-term results as with the decline of German science. It nonetheless bears noting how absolutely central a role in the Manhattan Project was played by refugees from German persecution. The director of Los Alamos's key Theoretical Division was Hans Bethe, whose Nobel-winning work lay in the future when the Nazis stripped him of his post. Under him worked an international crew including Edward Teller, a Hungarian Jew and a student of Heisenberg who had presciently seen that his prospects in Germany were nil.

With all this in the background, it is hardly surprising that attitudes toward science were contradictory and polarized. In the mass media and popular culture, as historians have begun to analyze them, the pure spectacle of science was celebrated often enough. Groundbreaking medical researchers were featured in breathless magazine articles. The mysterious fascination of radioactivity made its way into musical revues and medical tonics, and celebrity scientists like Marie Curie capitalized on their fame to the advantage of their research. The prime example of scientific celebrity was Albert Einstein, of course. Einstein was thrust onto the public stage immediately after World War I, in 1919, when a British-led expedition to exotic lands found confirmation of the German theorist's abstractions in starlight's minute deviation in a total solar eclipse. As a relativity craze spread around the world, the unconventional genius with the incomprehensible theory became a public icon. Einstein's opinions on every subject were solicited by newsmen and children.[14] But alongside tongue-in-cheek celebrations of unintelligibility, earnest writers (not least Einstein himself) tried to boil down the theory in terms the public could understand. Older national traditions of scientific popularization continued in strength. During these years they expanded from the classic didactic forms (the short book or magazine article, the popular science library, the illustrated lecture) into new media like radio and film (for instance, the newsreel or nature documentary).

Intellectuals, too, took up scientific ideas as touchstones for modernist projects in the arts and philosophy. Salvador Dali's 1931 painting "The Persistence of Memory," for instance, has commonly been interpreted as playing off Einsteinian spacetime, splaying fluidly surrealist clocks across a vaguely disquieting dreamscape. For some philosophers, following the lead of physicists like Heisenberg and Bohr, the shifting bases of natural science were indicative of a larger transformation at work. Talk of revolution reached from epistemology all the way to social theory. At the start of the 1930s, a young Max Horkheimer was the first director of the Frankfurt Institute for Social Research. Soon to emerge as a leading light of "critical theory," he went so far as to observe:

Since around the turn of the century scientists and philosophers have pointed out the
insufficiencies and unsuitability of purely mechanistic methods. The criticism has led to
discussion of the principles involved in the main foundations on which research rests,
so that today we may speak of a crisis within science. This inner crisis is now added to
the external dissatisfaction with science as a means of production which has not been
able to meet expectations in alleviating the general need. Modern physics has in large
measure overcome within its own field the deficiencies of the traditional method and
has revised its critical foundations.[15]

The admiration implicit in Horkheimer's comment on "critical" physics reveals the
extraordinary hopes that were placed in science. Operating at another level was the
Vienna Circle of logical empiricist philosophers, who advanced a "scientific worldview" in the late 1920s and early 1930s. Occupying themselves with logic, epistemology, and the philosophy of science, they developed an antimetaphysical critique that
put its faith in empirical science as the model of inquiry.

Programs like those of the Vienna Circle often had political overtones – quite
frequently of the left or Marxist variety. Their desire to put human affairs on a rational, empirical foundation carried forward Enlightenment impulses, questioning tradition and authority in the name of critical thought. Faith in science had more purchase
in some societies than others – in France, for instance, where Enlightenment rationalism still had admirers and high-caliber technical men had long been respected in state
service; and in the Soviet Union, where the cult of scientific Marxism-Leninism and
the drive for industrialization spilled over to hopes for science at large. In Britain,
too, the interwar "social relations of science movement" stood clearly on the left. It
was led by active scientists, some of them very influential, who argued that science's
capacity to improve human life was constrained by its subjugation to the capitalist
order.[16] As common as it was in the 1930s, however, science's alliance with leftist
politics was not universal. In Germany, for instance, no such movement ever came
close to arising. Many scientists argued, by contrast, that their discipline's great virtue
was that it was *un*political, standing above the partisan fray. That cut scientists' political choices free from their intellectual commitments, leaving nationalism as the
determining theme.

And on the other side, scientists could harness their own science in the service of
politically precarious goals. What we might call the "biologization" of social life –
understanding human communities in biomedical terms – was widespread by the turn
of the century. Urban poverty, for instance, was widely viewed as a problem of evolutionary degeneration, at least by the well-off and educated classes. In the 1920s
especially, fascination with genetics carried over to groups that advocated eugenics.
Transferring breeding ideas to the human species, eugenics set up biological scales
of human worth: one type of human being was intrinsically more valuable than
another, meaning better equipped to contribute to evolutionary advance. The ultimate subject of concern was not the individual, but the species as a whole. To the
eugenicist's mind, this was simply clear-eyed rationalism, against which sentimental
objections could have no force. Then social problems, such as endemic pauperism,
required scientific solutions, such as the differential regulation of reproduction.
Eugenics not only borrowed its vocabulary from science, but also found its leadership
there. Scientists and physicians were in the forefront of the movement, and they

offered their expertise for its implementation. Eugenics has typically been remembered as a project of Nazi Germany, where the biologization of social life in terms of the *Volk* reached its peak. The Third Reich encouraged procreation by sound Aryan couples, as confirmed by genetic health courts, and set harsh penalties for breaches of "racial hygiene," such as intercourse with Jews. Starting in 1934, the Nazis also sterilized more than 200,000 Germans for poor genetic constitutions, moving on to murder a roughly equal number of the mentally or physically disabled.[17] As a rehearsal for mass executions of Jews and other biologically "lower races," Nazi eugenic measures in all their ghastly consistency have come to stand for the eugenic movement as a whole. It is nonetheless essential to remember that eugenics was not solely a fascist venture, nor one confined to Germany. Into the 1930s it found advocates across Europe; the Scandinavian countries passed their own sterilization laws nearly simultaneously with Germany. In its political allegiance eugenics was at least as much a project of the progressive left. However, the energy with which the Nazis presented themselves, in this respect, as "scientific" made the Nazis' critics ask just what could be expected from science.

These various stripes of scientism did not lack for detractors. Among academics, resentment of imperialistic claims for science flowed together with reassertions of the priority of the humanities. In an aesthetic mode, they merged with calls for romantic reenchantment of nature and disgust at the industrial landscape, hatred of modern material culture, and horror at World War I's scientific destruction. This questioning strain in interwar culture was not a unified movement, but it consistently dissented from naive celebrations of progress. Along with various motions of withdrawal, it found expression in pointed intellectual critique. Science was rigidly mechanical and aridly analytic, unable to do justice to life and experience. If it claimed to bring human beings under its purview, it worked with an impoverished notion of the human. Uncritically wedded to an out-of-date positivism, it refused to scrutinize its own procedures of knowing. Above all, through its demand for lawful regularity and its elevation of experiment, it was structurally constituted as a tool to dominate the natural world. The critique of science was especially well articulated in Germany, where it was voiced in sophisticated form by philosophers such as Edmund Husserl (*The Crisis of European Sciences*, 1936) and Martin Heidegger ("The Age of the World Picture," 1938), as well as the famous Frankfurt School partners in exile, Max Horkheimer and Theodor Adorno (*Dialectic of Enlightenment*, 1944).

Interestingly, historians have shown how some of these criticisms finally found their way back into science. For instance, certain life scientists wholeheartedly agreed that reductionistic mechanical strategies were unlikely to succeed in their domain. When critics insisted that mechanism was the very essence of explanation, they responded that this was passé, a cramped notion of science. Understanding mind-body interactions, sense perception, or organismic functioning required a broader, more integrated frame.[18] Such proposals, even when they came labeled with the now suspicious word "holism," were intrinsically no more unscientific than quantum theorists' suggestion that science could be carried forward without rigid cause and effect. In fact, some historians have argued quantum mechanics itself responded to contemporary cultural pronouncements on the bankruptcy of mechanistic physics.[19] While the case is subtle and has not been universally accepted, the creators of the theory might have seen something in it. For some interwar scientists, the notion that science could fruitfully draw from its cultural environment was less controversial than many people find it today. Revolutionary science for a revolutionary age?

Conclusion

In its own terrible way, World War II marked the end of an era in European science. The atomic bombing of Hiroshima and Nagasaki encapsulated the deep ambivalence with which science would henceforth be viewed. Carrying pre-1945 experiences to their fullest conclusion, it brought scientists' relations with political power to a culminating point. And it sealed the ascendancy of American science, of whose postwar dominance there could be no doubt. Still, the processes and factors that made the atomic bombs possible were grounded in pre-1945 Europe. These included technical knowledge, of course, but also the sustenance of a large and professional scientific community. That scientific community could boast of social and epistemic authority and of close integration with industry and the state. The process of scientization that European society underwent between 1900 and 1945 was the hallmark of global things to come.

Scientization means science's permeation into a host of domains of our life. In post-World War II experience it has been pervasively plain. But if science was equally conspicuous to early twentieth-century observers, in our telling of that history it has too often been put to the side. In a sense, we perpetuate the period's own ambivalence about science when we sequester it from other historical forces. That cannot suffice, however, if we want to do justice to a remarkable and transformative era.

NOTES

1 Published posthumously as Werner Heisenberg, *Ordnung der Wirklichkeit* (Munich: R. Piper, 1989), p. 171.

2 Werner Heisenberg, "Die Beziehungen zwischen Physik und Chemie in den letzten 75 Jahren," in *Gesammelte Werke / Collected Works*, Walter Blum, Hans-Peter Dürr, and Helmut Rechenberg, eds, vol. C.1, p. 389.

3 Paul Forman, John L. Heilbron, and Spencer Weart, "Physics circa 1900: Personnel, Funding, and Productivity of the Academic Establishments," *Historical Studies in the Physical Sciences* 5 (1975): 12, with a rough correction factor to account for non-academic personnel.

4 Susan Quinn, *Marie Curie: A Life* (New York: Simon and Schuster, 1995).

5 An excellent institutional study is Rudolf Vierhaus and Bernhard vom Brocke, eds, *Forschung im Spannungsfeld von Politik und Gesellschaft: Geschichte und Struktur der Kaiser-Wilhelm-/Max-Planck-Gesellschaft* (Stuttgart: Deutsche Verlags-Anstalt, 1990). Unfortunately, nothing comparable exists for the Pasteur Institute; a starting point is *L'Institut Pasteur: contributions à son histoire* (Paris: Editions de la Découverte, 1991).

6 Nikolai Krementsov, *Stalinist Science* (Princeton NJ: Princeton University Press, 1997), pp. 37–9.

7 Ian Varcoe, "Scientists, Government and Organised Research in Great Britain 1914–1916: The Early History of the DSIR," *Minerva* 8 (1970): 192–216; Roy M. MacLeod and E. Kay Andrews, "The Origins of the D.S.I.R.: Reflections on Ideas and Men, 1915–1916," *Public Administration* 48 (1970): 23–48.

8 Elisabeth Crawford, *Nationalism and Internationalism in Science, 1880–1939: Four Studies of the Nobel Population* (Cambridge: Cambridge University Press, 1992).

9 The classic study is Alan Beyerchen, *Scientists under Hitler: Politics and the Physics Community in the Third Reich* (New Haven CT: Yale University Press, 1977).

10 The vast literature is reviewed in Robert Fox and Anna Guagnini, *Laboratories, Workshops, and Sites: Concepts and Practices of Research in Industrial Europe, 1800–1914* (Berkeley CA: Office for History of Science and Technology, 1999); and Ulrich Marsch, *Zwischen Wissenschaft und Wirtschaft: Industrieforschung in Deutschland und Großbritannien 1880– 1936* (Paderborn: Ferdinand Schöningh, 2000).

11 Andrew Cunningham and Perry Williams, eds, *The Laboratory Revolution in Medicine* (New York: Cambridge University Press, 1992).

12 Roy MacLeod, "The Chemists Go to War: The Mobilization of Civilian Chemists and the British War Effort, 1914–1918," *Annals of Science* 50 (1993): 455–81.

13 While the V-2 was technologically advanced, it was still next to useless as a practical weapon. See Michael Neufeld, *The Rocket and the Reich: Peenemünde and the Coming of the Ballistic Missile Era* (New York: Free Press, 1995); on nuclear weapons, Mark Walker, *German National Socialism and the Quest for Nuclear Power, 1939–1949* (Cambridge: Cambridge University Press, 1989).

14 Michel Biezunski, *Einstein à Paris: Le temps n'est plus . . .* (Saint-Denis: Presses Universitaires de Vincennes, 1991); Thomas Glick, *Einstein in Spain: Relativity and the Recovery of Science* (Princeton NJ: Princeton University Press, 1998).

15 Max Horkheimer, "Notes on Science and the Crisis," in *Critical Theory: Selected Essays*, Matthew J. O'Connell, trans. (New York: Continuum, 1999), p. 6.

16 For example, P. M. S. Blackett, "The Frustration of Science," in *The Frustration of Science* (New York: W. W. Norton, 1935), pp. 129–44.

17 The still unexcelled treatment is Robert Proctor, *Racial Hygiene: Medicine under the Nazis* (Cambridge MA: Harvard University Press, 1988).

18 Mitchell G. Ash, *Gestalt Psychology in German Culture, 1890–1967: Holism and the Quest for Objectivity* (Cambridge: Cambridge University Press, 1995); Anne Harrington, *Reenchanted Science: Holism in German Culture from Wilhelm II to Hitler* (Princeton NJ: Princeton University Press, 1996).

19 Paul Forman, "Weimar Culture, Causality, and Quantum Theory, 1918–1927: Adaptation by German Physicists and Mathematicians to a Hostile Intellectual Environment," *Historical Studies in the Physical Sciences* 3 (1971): 1–115.

GUIDE TO FURTHER READING

Alan Beyerchen, "On the Stimulation of Excellence in Wilhelmian Science," in *Another Germany: A Reconsideration of the Imperial Era*, Jack R. Dukes and Joachim Remak, eds (Boulder CO: Westview, 1988), pp. 139–68. Best short introduction to Germany before World War I.

William R. Everdell, *The First Moderns: Profiles in the Origins of Twentieth-Century Thought* (Chicago: University of Chicago Press, 1997). Sweeping attempt to integrate science with other realms of intellectual endeavor.

Loren Graham, *Science in Russia and the Soviet Union: A Short History* (Cambridge: Cambridge University Press, 1993). Accessible introductory text by the field's leading scholar.

Jonathan Harwood, *Styles of Scientific Thought: The German Genetics Community, 1900–1933* (Chicago: University of Chicago Press, 1993). Exemplary study integrating science with the sociology and politics of the scientific community.

J. L. Heilbron, ed.-in-chief, *The Oxford Companion to the History of Modern Science* (New York: Oxford University Press, 2003). Comprehensive encyclopedia-style coverage from the Renaissance to the present.

Arne Hessenbruch, *Reader's Guide to the History of Science* (London: Fitzroy Dearborn, 2000). Critical assessments of the secondary literature of the history of science, arranged by topic.

John Krige and Dominique Pestre, eds, *Science in the Twentieth Century* (Amsterdam: Harwood Academic, 1997). Longer essays on more scattershot topics, some quite specialized.

Mary Jo Nye, ed., *The Cambridge History of Science*, vol. 5: *The Modern Physical and Mathematical Sciences* (Cambridge: Cambridge University Press, 2003). Essays at a high introductory level; other topical volumes forthcoming.

R. C. Olby, G. N. Cantor, J. R. R. Christie, and M. J. S. Hodge, eds, *Companion to the History of Modern Science* (London: Routledge, 1990). Excellent short essays on both scientific and historiographic topics, though concentrated before 1900.

Harry W. Paul, *From Knowledge to Power: The Rise of the Science Empire in France, 1860–1939* (Cambridge: Cambridge University Press, 1985). Good example of a detailed national study.

Dorothy Ross, ed., *Modernist Impulses in the Human Sciences, 1870–1930* (Baltimore MD: Johns Hopkins University Press, 1994). Provocative essays covering more than the human sciences.

Margit Szöllosi-Janze, ed., *Science in the Third Reich* (Oxford: Berg, 2001). Exemplifies recent trends in the subject, highlighting the ordinary conduct of scientific research rather than persecution or pseudoscience.

Paul Weindling, *Health, Race and German Politics Between National Unification and Nazism, 1870–1945* (Cambridge: Cambridge University Press, 1989). Rich exploration of the interface between biology and politics.

CHAPTER THREE

Feminism: Women, Work, and Politics

JUNE HANNAM

Feminism as a social movement and as a set of ideas has played a prominent part in the political and social development of most countries of the world during the twentieth century. The term itself first appeared in France during the 1890s, but was not used widely in Europe until after World War I. Suffrage campaigners, for example, referred to themselves as suffragists, suffragettes, or advocates of women's rights rather than as feminists. Feminism posed a challenge to the status quo and therefore provoked a very negative reaction from its critics. Feminists were described as a "shrieking sisterhood," as "mannish" and unattractive in appearance, and as neglecting homes and children. They were characterized as extreme in their attitudes – waging a war against men or seeking to undermine "traditional" sex roles within the family. It is little wonder, therefore, that even those who explicitly sought to challenge women's subordinate social position could be reluctant to describe themselves as feminists.

This poses something of a dilemma for historians. Should the term feminism or feminist be used to describe organizations and individuals who did not use this word themselves? In general historians have employed the term as a useful shorthand. It conveys a set of meanings that are widely recognized and enables links to be made, and comparisons to be drawn, between individuals and organizations operating in very diverse contexts. Although feminist theorists and historians differ in what they see as lying at the heart of "modern feminism," it is possible to adopt a broad working definition that is flexible and inclusive.[1] At the heart of being a feminist is the recognition that there is an imbalance of power between the sexes and an intention to do something about it. Central to feminist arguments is the belief that women's condition is socially constructed, rather than rooted in biology, and therefore is open to change. Thus feminists question conventional wisdoms about the roles played by men and women and contest the assumption that there is a boundary between "private" issues (sexuality, the family, marital relationships) and the public concerns of work and politics. They emphasize that women's voices need to be heard – that they should represent themselves and achieve autonomy in their lives.

Any definition of feminism is inextricably linked to the ways in which its history is written and understood and there have been shifts over time in the interpretation of its main features. Members of the Women's Liberation Movement of the late 1960s and 1970s played a key role in developing a framework for analyzing the history of feminism. They were keen to trace the origins of their movement and to establish themselves in a feminist tradition and therefore tended to focus on well-organized women's movements that espoused explicit feminist goals. Reflecting divisions in contemporary feminist theory, historians identified distinct strands in the nineteenth and early twentieth-century women's movement and emphasized the tensions between ideas based on equality and those on difference.[2] They highlighted a key period of activism: "first wave" feminism ca. 1860s–1914, in particular the highly visible suffrage campaigns in Europe and North America in the immediate prewar years, when solidarity among women appeared to be at its height. In contrast the interwar years were seen as a time of fragmentation in feminist politics and of setback for women as they faced war, fascism, and unemployment. Indeed, it was assumed that feminism as a movement only revived with "second wave feminism" in the 1960s and 1970s.

More recently, however, the interpretive framework for understanding feminist history has shifted. Changes in feminist theory and politics, and the publication of a number of histories of feminism that compare different European countries, have drawn attention to the diversity of the movement. Thus historians are far more likely now to write about feminisms rather than feminism and to point to the interconnections between ideas and movements that were once seen as "separate" and distinct.[3] Emphasis is placed on the complex ways in which women developed a political identity. Studies of women's involvement in imperialism and colonialism, for example, have highlighted the different meanings of women's citizenship and the difficulties in constructing a "universal sisterhood." They point to the ethnocentrism and racism of white, European feminists who saw themselves as having a "civilizing mission."[4] Thus suffrage campaigners argued that if women had the vote they could use this to push forward women's emancipation in the colonies and to introduce social reforms for women and children that would in turn strengthen the empire.

Differences between women, whether of class, race, nation, or religion, were a central feature of the histories of feminism written in the 1970s and 1980s. Now, however, historians are less likely to write about these in terms of binary oppositions, such as sex versus class, but to look instead at how individual women and their organizations juggled between conflicting loyalties and at how the boundaries between them were shifting and permeable. In her challenging study, Denise Riley raised doubts about how far it was possible to talk about "woman" as a political category at all.[5] Thus historians have questioned women's attempts to create a "universal sisterhood" and have emphasized the class and race dimensions of European feminists' claims to speak for all women. An approach that emphasizes complexity has led to a reassessment of the extent to which feminists were active in periods that fell outside the two "waves" of high profile campaigning. It has been argued that a focus on "ebbs and flows" means that we can "miss the variety of ways in which feminisms can flourish," for example the "pragmatic feminism of women fighting for survival" in the hostile climate of the interwar years.[6] It has been recognized, too, that women pursued their feminist objectives in a variety of spaces and not just in overtly feminist organizations.

It is clearly important that women's attempts to challenge gender inequalities in "quieter" periods should be rescued from obscurity and be seen as part of feminist history. Nonetheless, there is a danger that the core of what it means to be a feminist can be lost if we stray too far from a definition that includes an explicit challenge to gender roles and inequalities. By acting together in a collective campaign, whether from the basis of a women-only group or from within mixed-sex political parties, women could develop a feminist consciousness that had the potential to affect the ways in which women and men thought about themselves and their place in the world.

It is impossible in a short chapter to provide an overview of the history of feminism in Europe in the first half of the twentieth century. Instead, the approaches and issues raised here will be examined through a focus on three areas: the women's suffrage movement; feminism, peace, and war; and the relationship between work, family, and politics in the interwar years. Throughout, attention will be drawn to key themes. Firstly, whenever women challenged gender inequalities they faced a dilemma: should they be seeking equality with men or should they seek to value "feminine" characteristics and roles and to celebrate difference, or indeed to look for a way of bringing the two together? These questions were made explicit when feminists debated the complex interrelationship between women's economic independence, their position within the family and the workplace, and their involvement in public life. Secondly, it is important to explore how far women's campaigns had an impact on their social position and how far change has come from other directions. In examining these questions it is crucial to make comparisons between European countries. These can reveal the complexity of feminist ideas, methods, and strategies and highlight the changes that took place over time.

Women's Suffrage

The women's suffrage movement has, understandably, received a great deal of attention both from contemporaries and from historians. In most European countries sex was a key factor in deciding who was able to exercise the vote. Women's exclusion from the franchise, therefore, highlighted the extent to which they shared common interests that could cut across class, religious, and political differences. It was the one issue that brought women together from very varied backgrounds in highly public campaigns that challenged conventional notions of a "woman's place" and contested the separation of the private and public spheres. In no country did women have the right to vote before men and when they finally achieved the franchise it was usually on a more restricted basis than their male counterparts. The one exception was Finland, where universal suffrage was introduced in 1906.

In most European countries the demand for women's enfranchisement was first made during the nineteenth century, but it was until the decade before World War I that suffrage movements increased the range of their activities and had a greater impact on national politics. New organizations were formed, the basis of support began to widen, and women developed different tactics and methods of campaigning. In this period the British movement took center stage as "militant" actions caught the imagination of women throughout Europe. Militancy was initiated by members of the Women's Social and Political Union (WSPU), formed in 1903 under the leadership of Emmeline and Christabel Pankhurst. At the same time the "constitutionalist" organization, the National Union of Women's Suffrage Societies (NUWSS), established in 1897, was also inspired to develop different forms of campaigning and began to organize demonstrations and processions. Support grew rapidly. By 1913 the WSPU had 88 branches and its newspaper had a circulation of 30,000–40,000, while the NUWSS had 380 affiliated societies and over 53,000 members.

The size and flamboyance of the British movement has tended to overshadow women's struggle for the franchise elsewhere, but this should not be underestimated. In Germany, France, Denmark, and Sweden new suffrage groups were formed and membership increased. In Denmark, for example, the two largest groups had 23,000 members by 1910, a significant proportion of the small female population of 1.5 million. The German Union for Women's Suffrage grew slowly and had only 2,500 members in 1908 but, when the ban on women's participation in politics was lifted in that year, membership expanded rapidly and reached 9,000 by 1913. Individual women engaged in acts of militancy. In France Hubertine Auclert entered a polling booth and smashed the ballot box which led to her arrest, while Madeleine Pelletier received a fine for breaking a window. In general, however, in countries where there was a strong emphasis on women's role as wife and mother, moderate suffrage campaigners were reluctant to take unconventional actions that could be seen as a challenge to traditional notions of "femininity." The German Union for Women's Suffrage, for example, held only one street demonstration in which women stayed in their carriages rather than walking. In contrast, the women's section of the Social Democratic Party organized demonstrations in favor of women's suffrage on the first International Proletarian Women's Day in 1911, when women walked through the streets carrying placards and banners.

The continuing fascination that the suffrage movement has had for historians means that there is a vast historiography on the subject, in particular on the British campaign.[7] Recent texts have raised new questions and have reinterpreted familiar narratives. For example, attention has been drawn to the importance of culture and propaganda, including suffrage plays, novels, poems, and art in the conduct of the campaign. In her pioneering study of the striking imagery of the movement, Lisa Tickner has argued that posters, banners, and other visual material were not just a "footnote" to the "real political history going on elsewhere, but an integral part of the struggle to shape thought, focus debates and stimulate action."[8] She has suggested that it promoted the image of the suffrage activist as a new type of political woman who was "womanly," well dressed, attractive, and caring, but also brave, intelligent, and prepared to suffer for her cause. The ways in which the "new political woman" was depicted varied in different countries and across organizations. In Austria and Germany, for instance, where mainstream suffragists were anxious to counter arguments that women would become too masculine if they entered politics, the images reflected a more "traditional view of femininity," although socialist women were prepared to use women of strength in their propaganda.

Historians are far more likely now to point to the complex ways in which women took part in suffrage politics and to challenge the view that there were rigid distinctions between organizations or between "constitutionalists" and "militants." Biographies of a wide range of participants and detailed local studies, for instance, have shown the extent to which suffragists made different political choices over the course of the campaign, moved from one organization to another, and in many cases continued to belong to a number of different organizations at once. Even in

Germany, where there was hostility between socialist women and the moderate suffrage movement, cooperation took place between them at a local level. Militancy itself has also been the subject of extensive reinterpretation. Hilda Kean and Laura Nym Mayhall have drawn attention to the way in which suffragettes, through their own histories of the campaign and through their autobiographies published in the interwar years, constructed a particular view of militancy.[9] Suffragettes emphasized the destruction of property, imprisonment, and hunger striking as the hallmarks of militancy and this view had a long lasting influence on historians. Sandra Holton and Krista Cowman, however, have pointed to the diverse nature of militancy and to the changes that took place over time.[10] Even in an overtly militant organization such as the WSPU not all members engaged in actions that would lead to arrest and women could choose to confine their activities to disrupting meetings or to raising money. Moreover the Women's Freedom League, which described itself as a militant group, carried out less violent acts such as tax resistance or refusal to fill in the 1911 Census forms.

Recent texts on the suffrage movement in Europe focus on the complexity of the ideas put forward during the campaign and explore what citizenship meant to women.[11] Suffragists had long expressed the view that women should be able to exercise the vote as a natural right based on their ability to reason and on their common humanity with men. They also argued that exclusion from the franchise reinforced women's subordinate status in other areas of their lives, including the workplace and the home, as well as denying them a voice in legislation that affected their lives. At the same time they suggested that women's enfranchisement would benefit the community, since they would bring different qualities to politics because of their role within the home. This argument was reinforced after the turn of the century. In a context in which motherhood was seen as vital for the strength of the nation, suffragists increasingly used their position within the family, and the qualities associated with domesticity and motherhood, as the basis for their claims to citizenship. They suggested that women, as active citizens, would contribute to a moral regeneration of society, would purify politics, and would support social reforms to improve the lives of women and children.

The demand for the vote, therefore, was never just about the principle of women's right to formal equality with men. It was also about challenging male-defined priorities and values and was always linked to broader debates about the meaning of women's emancipation. Suffragists agreed that women acting together as women could make a difference, but they disagreed about what they hoped to achieve and in their analysis of the causes of women's oppression. For example, for Christabel Pankhurst and many other members of the WSPU, the campaign for the vote highlighted the significance of male power over women and therefore the importance of women's solidarity with members of their sex. Christabel argued that women were economically, politically, and sexually subordinate to men and drew a link between their exclusion from political power and forms of social degradation such as prostitution and venereal disease. Indeed, she claimed there was a parallel between women's economic dependence on men within marriage and prostitution and coined the famous slogan, "Votes for Women and Chastity for Men."

Other committed suffrage activists, however, continued to work with men within mixed-sex political parties, although they might also be involved in all-female suffrage groups. They often suffered real tensions between their pursuit of sexual equality and their support for party political causes and in specific contexts might choose not to prioritize women's suffrage if it threatened party unity. Socialist women, for example, focused on class as well as sex oppression. This led some to question the importance of the vote for working-class women, in particular if they were likely to be excluded from proposals for a "limited" franchise where the demand was for votes for women on the same terms as men. Others argued that the principle was all-important and that women could only take a full part in the struggle for socialism, and in shaping a new society, if they were on an equal footing with men.[12] A cause of conflict within the socialist movement was over the basis on which the vote should be demanded. At the Second International meeting in Stuttgart in 1907 a resolution was passed calling on members to "struggle energetically" for women's suffrage as part of a general demand for universal suffrage. This caused difficulties in two directions. In some countries, such as Austria, it was argued that the demand for an adult male franchise should be pursued before that of women as the only realistic course in the context of that country's politics. This position was supported by Adelheid Popp, leader of the country's socialist women. When manhood suffrage was introduced in 1907, however, women formed a separate organization within the Social Democratic Party and campaigned for their own inclusion in the franchise. In countries such as Britain, where not all men could vote, socialist women feared that the demand for adult suffrage was both unrealistic and might also disguise a commitment to manhood suffrage. One socialist group, the Independent Labour Party, was unusual in supporting the demand for a limited franchise, that is votes for women on the same terms as men. It led to a fierce debate between those who prioritized the demand for "adult suffrage" and those who campaigned, on the grounds both of principle and political expediency, for a "limited franchise" as a first step to universal suffrage. Disagreements about which demand to support could divide the suffrage movement itself. In Germany, for example, the Women's Suffrage League supported socialist women in their call for a universal franchise, whereas the right-wing German Alliance for Women's Suffrage and the older, moderate group, the German Union for Women's Suffrage, supported a propertied franchise.

Despite differences between them – whether of religion, class, party politics, or nationality – exclusion from the franchise did prompt women to work together both within their own countries and also across national boundaries. International friendships developed after women met each other at conferences and were sustained through copious letter writing. The establishment of new transnational organizations provided more formal international links. A key group was the International Woman Suffrage Alliance. Based largely in countries in Europe and North America, its moderate, well-educated, middle-class membership held conferences every two years and kept in touch through their journal, *Jus Suffragii*. They were committed to the concept of internationalism, while at the same time having a strong sense of identification with their own nation-state. Before 1914 members of the IWSA saw their demands for suffrage and for peace as universal issues that could transcend differences between women, but their notions of "sisterhood" and female solidarity were harder to sustain when the outbreak of World War I raised different questions about what it meant to be an active citizen and placed a greater emphasis on loyalty to nation.

Feminism, Peace, and War

By the outbreak of war women had achieved the vote in only two European countries, Finland and Norway. Elsewhere, prewar suffrage organizations diverted their energies into activities related to war, although suffrage campaigning did not cease altogether. The war itself raised important new questions about the meaning of women's citizenship – whether or not they had the vote, women were increasingly called upon to "serve" their nation, either as paid workers or as volunteers to deal with the social problems faced by the community. Women took part in employment directly related to war, in particular the production of munitions and the nursing of wounded soldiers either at home or at the front. In the latter they shared to some extent the physical dangers and discomforts of soldiers themselves. It has been suggested that women's extensive participation in the war effort of their respective countries led to lasting gains in their social and economic position and that they developed self-confidence and new expectations. Recent studies, however, have modified this view by highlighting the complex and paradoxical impact of the war. Gail Braybon and Penny Summerfield suggest that we must be careful to look at the different ways in which women experienced the war according to their age, class, and marital status. They also note the ambivalence of the British government to women's war efforts and argue that prewar assumptions about women's responsibilities for the domestic sphere affected the nature and extent of women's participation in the war, as well as the possibility of long-term change.[13] This was certainly the case in Germany, where prewar patterns of employment coupled with the resistance of trade unions ensured that the proportion of women in factory work during the war was the lowest in Europe.

The state's need for women to contribute to the war effort, which opened a range of possibilities for women, sat uneasily alongside a competing narrative that emphasized the importance of motherhood for the future of the nation and that could simultaneously curtail their activities. These contradictory messages were reflected in the complex ways in which women were represented. They were praised for their bravery and heroism, in particular in famous cases such as the execution of Nurse Edith Cavell, and also for their contribution and flexibility as paid workers. And yet these portrayals could go hand in hand with more traditional images of women as caring, self-sacrificing, or in need of protection. The entry of women, in particular middle-class women, into unfamiliar areas of work, and the increased pay and freedom enjoyed by many working-class girls, created anxieties about an increase in sexual immorality and the threat that this posed to stable family lives. Susan Grayzel argues that this affected notions of citizenship and placed a new emphasis on gender differences, since motherhood was seen as the prime patriotic role for women in the way soldiering was for men.[14]

Where did feminists at the time stand on these questions? In most European countries they were divided in their attitudes towards the war and disagreed about the role that feminist organizations ought to play. The situation was complicated in countries such as Ireland where nationalism was also a consideration and where there were tensions about whether nationalist demands should take precedence over gender issues. The main prewar suffrage organizations in Britain, France, and Germany gave support to the war effort, although individual leaders and members of the rank and file had varied reasons for doing so. Many were of course patriotic and wished to do all they could to support their respective governments, but they also saw the potential for women to play a different public role and were hopeful that if women demonstrated their capacity to serve the nation as responsible citizens this would help their claims to enfranchisement. A minority, however, saw the core of their feminism as lying in a commitment to solve disputes by peaceful means – for them, the whole point of having the suffrage was so that women could advocate moral, rather than physical, force. These differing views came to a head in 1915 when the Dutch suffragist, Dr Aletta Jacobs, convened a meeting of the IWSA at The Hague with the aim of rallying women to seek a peaceful end to the conflict and reawakening a sense of internationalism.

Mainstream feminist organizations refused to send representatives, but individual members supported the initiative. Not all of them were able to attend the Congress – in Britain, for example, the government at first refused to issue passports and then cancelled shipping in the North Sea. Nonetheless, the Congress led to the formation of a new organization, the Women's International League (WIL), which provided a focus for peace campaigning. Supporters included women who had expressed radical views about suffrage and other political causes before the war, including the German activists Anita Augspurg and Lida Gustava Heymann, Gabrielle Duchêne from France, and Rosika Schwimmer from Hungary. In Britain members were drawn from all the suffrage groups and included Helena Swanwick, Maude Royden, and the ILP socialist Isabella Ford, as well as many activists from the labor movement. Approximately half of the executive of the NUWSS resigned over the issue. Peace campaigners used arguments that had been prevalent before the war and mixed equal rights issues with notions of women's difference. They pointed out that women, as non-voters, bore no responsibility for the outbreak of war. They also assumed that women's caring roles within the family, in particular as mothers, meant that they were naturally inclined towards peace and felt solidarity with other women that crossed national boundaries. Isabella Ford, for example, claimed that "the destruction of the race is felt more bitterly and more deeply by those who through suffering and anguish have brought the race into the world" and suggested that "as the mothers and the educators of the human race, the bond which unites us is deeper than any bond which at present unites men."[15]

The WIL aimed to bring the war to a speedy end through a negotiated peace settlement that would not contain the seeds of future wars. Members held numerous meetings and also disseminated their propaganda through publications such as newspapers and pamphlets. A group of WIL leaders also visited the heads of neutral states in an effort to persuade them to put their weight behind a negotiated peace. All peace activists came under criticism for their views, but those socialist and revolutionary women who took a more radical stand in opposition to the war were labeled as subversive and faced arrest and imprisonment. Clara Zetkin and Rosa Luxemburg from Germany, the French schoolteacher Hélène Brion and Nellie Best, who was associated with the British suffragette and revolutionary Sylvia Pankhurst, were all imprisoned for their anti-war activities.

The war, therefore, highlighted differences between women who disagreed about what active citizenship meant for feminists in a context of international conflict. Both supporters and opponents of war, however, saw opportunities for women to take part in, and to make an impact on, public life, while also emphasizing women's difference from men. As Grayzel notes, peace campaigners used gender stereotypes that depicted women as non-aggressive and caring for others for their own purposes, since it was easier for them as non-combatants to speak out against the war.[16]

During the war itself, therefore, feminist campaigning was diverted away from the suffrage cause either to the peace movement or else towards voluntary committee work to safeguard the interests of women as workers and as mothers. Feminists sought improved healthcare and protection from high prices and food shortages and were also at the forefront of caring for refugees. And yet during and after the war many European countries enfranchised women for the first time, including Denmark and Iceland in 1915, and Austria, Germany, and Britain in 1918, followed by Czechoslovakia and the Netherlands in 1919, Sweden in 1921, and Ireland in 1922. How important was the war in explaining women's achievement of the vote? A commonly held assumption is that women achieved the vote as a reward for their war services, but this is no longer regarded as a convincing explanation, in particular when comparisons are made between different countries. In France and Italy women were not enfranchised until the 1940s despite their contribution to the war effort, while in Britain politicians were at first reluctant to include women in their plans for extending the franchise. Those who did gain the vote in 1918 were aged over 30 and had been far less involved in war services than their younger counterparts. In some countries, including Germany, Austria, and Czechoslovakia, the upheavals brought by war led to the downfall of authoritarian regimes and the introduction of liberal democracies. Here it was the changed political context that favored the enfranchisement of women, since they were seen as a bulwark against extremism from the left and the right. Gisela Bock suggests that the timing of women's enfranchisement was linked to the "various national paths to manhood suffrage."[17] Thus, she argues that women had to wait so long for the vote in France and Switzerland because all men had enjoyed the franchise since the early nineteenth century and did not need women's support to get the suffrage for themselves.

But where does this leave women's agency and the long campaigns that had preceded enfranchisement? Clearly, on its own the existence of a strong suffrage movement was not enough, in particular when, as in France, the political context was unfavorable. On the other hand highly visible suffrage campaigns did keep the issue to the forefront of politics and helped to ensure that women would be included when changes were made to the franchise. Sandra Holton, for example, suggests that the continuation of suffrage activity during the war, which has often been overlooked, made it difficult for the British government to leave women out of the Representation of the People Act (1918), despite their continuing reservations.[18]

Work, Family, and Politics in the Interwar Years

In the postwar world the feminist movement appeared to be much more fragmented. In countries where women had gained the franchise, feminists differed among themselves about their goals, their priorities, and about how best to achieve their aims. It was difficult to agree on a common outlook and to act together. This was exacerbated as women pursued their feminist goals through a variety of different organizations, including prewar suffrage groups, many of which had changed their name to reflect their broader agenda, single-issue organizations, and mixed-sex political parties. Although the war had provided opportunities for women to become involved in public life, Susan Kingsley Kent suggests that fears about the disruption of gender relationships led to a desire to get back to normal in the interwar years and to an emphasis on an ideology of domesticity in which women were once again primarily identified with the home.[19] This was reinforced by a widespread economic depression and the development of conservative and fascist governments that created a context that was not conducive to feminist demands. Thus, women's role as wives and mothers was thought to be the basis from which they would engage as active citizens. Feminists themselves were affected by these changes and began to focus on women's role within the home. In the interwar years, therefore, they debated the relationship between women's role within the family and their economic and personal independence that raised broader questions about the nature of their citizenship.

Throughout Europe feminists continued to demand equal rights for women. In France, for instance, the campaign for the vote grew in strength and by 1929 the French Union for Women's Suffrage had 100,000 members. Many governments passed equal rights legislation after women had been enfranchised – the new constitutions of the Weimar republic in 1919 and the Irish Free State in 1922, for instance, declared that all citizens were equal under the law regardless of sex. Nonetheless, in the absence of a strong, united feminist movement, and in the climate of economic depression, it was difficult to ensure that formal equality would be put into practice. In Ireland, for example, the Catholic church opposed women's employment outside the home and legislation was introduced to restrict female work opportunities in 1935. This provides a useful reminder that gains for women could also be lost – in Spain, for example, women were successful in their campaign to ensure that the new constitution of the Second Republic would include women's enfranchisement, and other reforms were introduced that benefited women, including a secularized marriage law and civil divorce. But when Franco came to power in 1936, women were disenfranchised and emphasis was placed on their role within the home that was reinforced by legislative changes that made divorce illegal and restored male authority within marriage.

Alongside the continuing campaigns for equal rights many feminists also turned their attention to improving women's position within the home through social welfare reforms. This was a controversial issue for feminists since it raised questions about the meaning of women's emancipation. It led in particular to a consideration about the relationship between work, family, and the nature of women's citizenship, both within feminist groups and also among feminists who pursued their goals through mixed-sex political parties. In Britain, for example, members of the Six Points Group, led by Lady Rhondda, emphasized the importance of equal rights and women's common humanity with men as the basis of their citizenship. In contrast, many members of the National Union of Societies for Equal Citizenship, successor to the NUWSS and led by Eleanor Rathbone, argued that women could never achieve equality unless the economic independence of married women, and the special needs of mothers, were addressed. In recent years historians have suggested that differences between these groups should not be exaggerated, since they all supported equal rights legislation and sought to improve women's social and economic position.[20] Nonetheless there were differences of emphasis. Those who focused on social welfare reforms referred to maternity as "the most important of women's occupations," whereas "equality" feminists expressed the fear that a focus on motherhood would make it difficult for women to escape from traditional roles.

Conflicts arose over specific demands, in particular protective legislation at the workplace. On one side it was argued that women's role in the family meant that they needed protection at the workplace, whereas on the other it was contended that if barriers were removed to women's employment they would no longer be seen as marginal workers and changes in the family would follow. Conflicts over protective legislation spilled over into international feminist organizations as laws regulating women's labor became an international issue. It divided feminist organizations from each other and also drove a wedge between them and feminists within socialist and labor groups who generally supported protective legislation. This issue was particularly contentious because it raised the difficult question of whether women and men should be treated differently. In the case of other social welfare measures disagreements arose about the form that they should take rather than over whether they should be introduced at all.

Feminists who campaigned for social welfare reforms were working within a general context in which governments, pressure groups, and health professionals were all concerned with the health and welfare of the population. This raises the question, therefore, of what was distinctively feminist about their demands and whether there was a danger that their feminist perspective would be lost within general reform campaigns. Welfare feminism could provide a means to challenge women's subordinate position in the home and to give women more choices about what to do with their lives. Two demands in particular, for family allowances and access to birth control, appeared to have a radical potential for contesting traditional structures since they raised issues about women's autonomy and personal freedom. Feminists in several countries, including Britain, Germany, and Scandinavia, added their voices to a general demand for economic assistance to mothers.[21] They were not just concerned to alleviate poverty, but also argued that allowances should be set high enough to give married women greater independence. They disagreed among themselves, however, about how such reforms should be financed and what they hoped to achieve by their introduction. In Norway, for example, liberal feminists thought child allowances would enable women to pay for childcare and therefore to continue with paid employment, whereas socialist feminists saw it as a means to free women from work outside the home, enabling them to spend more time with their children.

After World War I there was a change in attitudes towards sex and morality that made it easier for feminists to raise the importance of birth control. Nonetheless, its association with "free love" in the early days of the Bolshevik revolution and the emphasis of many governments on the need for an increased population meant that feminists played down the importance of women's sexual autonomy and freedom. Instead, they stressed the health and welfare aspects of birth control, with socialist women arguing from a class perspective that working-class women needed local authority clinics to provide free contraceptive advice that was only available otherwise to wealthy women who could consult private doctors.

Feminists found it difficult to have an influence on social policy unless their aims coincided with those of the party in power. In Scandinavian countries, for example, where social democratic parties were in power during the 1930s, women played an important part in shaping the social welfare measures that were introduced. In Sweden these included job protection for married women, the legalization of contraception, and maternity benefits paid to mothers, while in Denmark and Sweden abortion based on a restricted set of criteria was also made legal. Elsewhere it was difficult to achieve reforms and the measures that were introduced did not necessarily shift the power relationships between men and women or challenge gender divisions. For example, when family allowances were introduced in Britain at the end of World War II, the intention was to reduce wage inflation and the amount paid was far too small to ensure the economic independence of married women.

The involvement of feminists in international issues, in particular the movement for peace, also raised concerns that feminist goals could become subsumed within a broader movement. Within the International Alliance of Women (successor of the IWSA) Nina Boyle argued that pacifism and social reform diverted feminists away from a focus on women's legal and material subordination to men, whereas the veteran American campaigner Carrie Chapman Catt claimed that she had moved on since achieving the vote and had become a humanist, but that she still wanted to protest against women's wrongs. Offen argues, however, that as feminists increasingly put their energies into working to protect democracy in the interests of both sexes, so campaigns around women's subordination became more marginal.[22] For these reasons too, feminism could appear to be more fragmented and diffuse than in the prewar years.

Nonetheless if the interwar years are looked at in their own right, rather than through the lens of very active periods of high-profile campaigning, then it can be seen that feminists did continue to make an effort to challenge gender inequalities. In a hostile political and economic climate it was difficult for them to make their voices heard and to develop a feminist consciousness, but they worked across multiple sites, including single-sex feminist organizations and mixed-sex political parties. This has drawn attention to the importance of exploring what is meant by feminist activity. Many women campaigned for social and political reforms from within women's organizations that refused to accept the label "feminist," and yet in several ways their work coincided with feminist goals.[23] In Denmark, for example, housewives' associations and women's sections in political parties drew an increasing number of women into political activity and some of their members supported demands for contraceptive advice. This was also the case in the British-based National Council of Women. In countries where women had the vote, feminists debated what it meant to be a citizen and began to address the issue of how women could benefit from equal rights when their social and economic position was different from that of men. They generally supported women's right to work, but the emphasis of the period was on women's role within the home as the basis for their active citizenship, rather than their waged labor.

Conclusion

Throughout the first half of the twentieth century feminism, as a theory and a practice, has been a key feature of European politics. It has been argued here that at the heart of any definition of feminism is the recognition of an unequal power relationship between the sexes and the desire to challenge this and to change it. Nonetheless, it should be recognized that the goals and strategies of feminists varied in different countries, and also over time, and that it is important not to exclude the activities of many women from a history of feminism through the use of prescriptive or narrow definitions. The suffrage movement has received a great deal of attention because it provided an opportunity for women to work together and to develop a sense of solidarity that was difficult to sustain once they left that environment. And yet women were rarely concerned only with improvements in the social position of their sex. In some contexts they prioritized the peace movement, party political issues, or the needs of the working class even if this meant that it was difficult to sustain a sense of their own autonomy.

To what extent was an active women's movement responsible for changes in women's lives? Feminist campaigns were crucial for ensuring that women's needs were not neglected, and also, in some periods, for raising consciousness of gender inequalities. On the other hand it was difficult to make headway in political and social contexts that were not conducive to radical politics and in these periods women's own demands and priorities could shift – for example in the interwar years, when a social welfare agenda came to the fore. The strength of the ideology of separate spheres and women's identification with domesticity was so embedded that it remained a central feature of social and economic life and social policy, despite the upheavals of two world wars. After World War II, for example, married women were expected to give a full-time commitment to family life and their domestic position was then reinforced by social policies, government propaganda, and popular magazines. Nonetheless, the restrictions on their lives after a period of raised expectations provided fertile ground for a continuing debate about gender roles and about the complex relationship between equality and difference. Women's organizations also persisted in their efforts to achieve equal rights and welfare reforms. It was from this ferment of ideas and activities that feminists in the 1960s and 1970s were able to make a sustained challenge to women's identification with the home and to put to the test contemporary assumptions about appropriate male and female roles.

NOTES

1 For a discussion of "modern feminism" see Barbara Caine, *English Feminism, 1780–1980* (Oxford: Oxford University Press, 1997); Jane Rendall, *The Origins of Modern Feminism: Women in Britain, France and the United States, 1780–1860* (Basingstoke: Macmillan, 1985); and Karen Offen, *European Feminisms, 1700–1950: A Political History* (Stanford CA: Stanford University Press, 2000).

2 For example, see Olive Banks, *Faces of Feminism: A Study of Feminism as a Social Movement* (Oxford: Martin Robertson, 1981).

3 For example, see Offen, *European Feminisms*; Caroline Daley and Melanie Nolan, eds, *Suffrage and Beyond: International Feminist Perspectives* (Auckland: Auckland University Press, 1994).

4 Ian C. Fletcher, Laura E. Nym Mayhall, and Philippa Levine, eds, *Women's Suffrage in the British Empire: Citizenship, Nation and Race* (London: Routledge, 2002).

5 Denise Riley, *"Am I That Name?" Feminism and the Category of "Women" in History* (Basingstoke: Macmillan, 1988).

6 Marlene Legates, *In Their Time: A History of Feminism in Western Society* (London: Routledge, 2001), p. 282.

7   For a useful overview of the literature, see Harold L. Smith, *The British Women's Suffrage Campaign, 1866–1928* (London: Addison Wesley Longman, 1998).

8   Lisa Tickner, *The Spectacle of Women: Imagery of the Suffrage Campaign, 1907–1914* (London: Chatto and Windus, 1987), p. lx.

9   Hilda Kean, "'Searching for the Past in Present Defeat': The Construction of Historical and Political Identity in British Feminism in the 1920s and 1930s," *Women's History Review* 3/1 (1994): 57–80; Laura E. Nym Mayhall, "Creating the 'Suffragette' Spirit: British Feminism and the Historical Imagination," *Women's History Review* 4/3 (1995): 319–44.

10 Sandra S. Holton, "Women and the Vote," in *Women's History: Britain, 1850–1945*, June Purvis, ed. (London: UCL Press, 1995) and Krista Cowman, "Crossing the Great Divide: Inter-Organisational Suffrage Relationships on Merseyside, 1895–1914," in *A Suffrage Reader: Charting Directions in British Suffrage History*, Claire Eustance, Joan Ryan, and Laura Ugolini, eds (London, 2000), pp. 37–52.

11 For example, see Offen, *European Feminisms.*

12 The involvement of socialist women in the suffrage campaign and the debates that ensued are discussed in Ellen C. DuBois, "Woman Suffrage and the Left: An International Socialist Feminist Perspective," *New Left Review* 186 (1991): 20–45, and June Hannam and Karen Hunt, *Socialist Women: Britain 1880s to 1920s* (London: Routledge, 2001).

13 Gail Braybon and Penny Summerfield, *Out of the Cage: Women's Experiences in Two World Wars* (London: Pandora, 1987) and Penny Summerfield, "Women and War in the Twentieth Century," in Purvis, *Women's History.*

14 Susan Grayzel, *Women's Identities at War: Gender, Motherhood and Politics in Britain and France during the First World War* (Chapel Hill: University of North Carolina Press, 1999).

15 *Leeds Weekly Citizen,* March 12, 1915 and May 28, 1915. The arguments of peace campaigners are discussed in Leila Rupp, *Worlds of Women: The Making of an International Women's Movement* (Princeton NJ: Princeton University Press, 1997).

16 Susan Grayzel, *Women and the First World War* (London: Longman, 2002).

17 Gisela Bock, *Women in European History* (Oxford: Blackwell, 2002), pp. 146–7.

18 Sandra S. Holton, *Feminism and Democracy: Women's Suffrage and Reform Politics in Britain, 1900–1918* (Cambridge: Cambridge University Press, 1986).

19 Susan K. Kent, *Making Peace: The Reconstruction of Gender in Interwar Britain* (Princeton NJ: Princeton University Press, 1993).

20 Harold L. Smith, ed., *British Feminism in the Twentieth Century* (Aldershot: Edward Elgar, 1990).

21 Helmut Gruber and Pamela Graves, eds, *Women and Socialism, Socialism and Women: Europe between the Two World Wars* (Oxford: Berghahn, 1998).

22 Offen, *European Feminisms,* pp. 371–5.

23 See the discussion in Caitriona Beaumont, "Citizens not Feminists: The Boundary Negotiated between Citizenship and Feminism by Mainstream Women's Organisations in England, 1928–39," *Women's History Review* 9/2 (2000): 411–29.

GUIDE TO FURTHER READING

Gisela Bock, *Women in European History* (Oxford: Blackwell, 2002). Explores debates over the "woman question" from the middle ages to the present; a thought-provoking section on the interwar years.

Caroline Daley and Melanie Nolan, eds, *Suffrage and Beyond: International Feminist Perspectives* (Auckland: Auckland University Press, 1994). A pioneering collection of essays that compares the suffrage movement in a variety of countries throughout the world. Critical of using an Anglo-American model as a lens through which to view suffrage elsewhere.

Ian C. Fletcher, Laura E. Nym Mayhall, and Philippa Levine, eds, *Women's Suffrage in the British Empire: Citizenship, Nation and Race* (London: Routledge, 2002). A stimulating collection of essays on feminist involvement in the project of Empire that reveals the multiple ways in which the local, the global, and the international intersect.

Susan Grayzel, *Women and the First World War* (London: Longman, 2002). A useful comparative text that provides an overview of the literature on the impact of war on women in Europe.

Gabrielle Griffin and Rosie Braidotti, eds, *Thinking Differently: A Reader in European Women's Studies* (London: Zed Books, 2002). One section has essays on the women's movement in various European countries.

Helmut Gruber and Pamela Graves, eds, *Women and Socialism, Socialism and Women: Europe between the Two World Wars* (Oxford: Berghahn, 1998). An important collection of essays exploring socialism, feminism, and the politics of welfare in several European countries.

June Hannam and Karen Hunt, *Socialist Women: Britain c. 1880s to 1920s* (London: Routledge, 2001). A study of the complex relationship between socialism and feminism in Britain.

Sandra S. Holton, *Suffrage Days: Stories from the Women's Suffrage Movement* (London: Routledge, 1996). A pathbreaking study that explores the link between a radical strand in the nineteenth-century women's movement and militancy.

Laura E. Nym Mayhall, *The Militant Suffrage Movement: Citizenship and Resistance in Britain, 1860–1930* (Oxford: Oxford University Press, 2003). A provocative text arguing for a new way of looking at suffrage militancy.

Karen Offen, *European Feminisms, 1700–1950: A Political History* (Stanford CA: Stanford University Press), 2000. A key text providing a comparison of feminist ideas and movements in a wide range of European countries.

June Purvis, ed., *Women's History: Britain, 1850–1945* (London: UCL Press, 1995). A collection of essays providing an overview of aspects of feminist history, including race and empire, war in the twentieth century, and the vote.

Leila Rupp, *Worlds of Women: The Making of an International Women's Movement* (Princeton NJ: Princeton University Press, 1997). A key text on the international links and organizations established by women in Europe and North America.

Harold L. Smith, *British Feminism in the Twentieth Century* (Aldershot: Edward Elgar, 1990). Important collection of essays on the complex aims and ideas of British feminists between the wars.

CHAPTER FOUR

Modernism

ROBIN WALZ

In the early twentieth century, a cultural revolution occurred in Europe across the fields of art, literature, and music, as well as in architecture, theater, and film. A century later, a familiar cast of figures from this cultural moment have achieved nearly canonical status: Henri Matisse, Wassily Kandinsky, and Pablo Picasso in painting; James Joyce, Virginia Woolf, T. S. Eliot, Gertrude Stein, Thomas Mann, and Franz Kafka in literature; Guillaume Apollinaire, F. T. Marinetti, and Vladimir Mayakovsky in poetry; Arnold Schoenberg and Igor Stravinsky in music; Le Corbusier and Walter Gropius in architecture; Bertolt Brecht and Luigi Pirandello in theater; Sergei Eisenstein and Dziga Vertov in film. Multiple radical avant-garde movements crossing artistic media – futurism, constructivism, dada, and surrealism – emerged during this era as well. Taken together, the fundamental reorientation in European culture produced by these artists and movements is known as modernism.

Today, the notion of modernism has passed into general parlance. Museums exhibit modernist art retrospectives, academics critically reinterpret canonical modernist works, students learn about modernism through textbooks. Yet familiarity should not yield to complacence. A historical approach to the topic can help recover what was culturally vital and revolutionary about modernism. The general term is derived from the root stem "modern." It is also closely related to the concepts of modernization and modernity. Yet, while sharing affinities with these other ideas, modernism should not be equated with or subsumed by them. Modernism does not describe a historical period, large-scale transformations in political economy, or even a mentality that favors contemporary values over traditional ones. Rather, modernism marks a radical break in European aesthetics (what is considered artistically valid or beautiful) to produce what art critic Harold Rosenberg has called "the tradition of the new." Artists, as both creative producers and intellectual critics, constituted the vanguard, or avant-garde, of modernism. Rejecting the aesthetic values of their nineteenth-century romantic and realist forebears, the modernist avant-garde sought to set European civilization upon a new path in the twentieth century.

Yet the aesthetic challenge expressed by modernism did not necessarily translate directly into political radicalism; modernist artists and writers can be found across

the political spectrum in Europe before 1940. Neither can modernism be characterized as a distinctive style, unlike late nineteenth-century movements in art such as
impressionism, naturalism, symbolism, or art nouveau. The aims of modernist movements such as expressionism, cubism, futurism, dada, surrealism, constructivism,
functionalism, and neoclassicism were diverse, and even antithetical to one another.
Still, viewed from a comparative perspective, general features may be established.
Foremost, there is a strong impulse toward experimentation in modernist art, to
examine, alter, and transform basic forms. Such experimentation places a high value
on innovation and novelty, to make art "new."

In addition to this basic orientation, the intellectual historian Eugene Lunn has
articulated four broad dimensions to the modernist aesthetic: self-reflexivity, simultaneity, uncertainty of meaning, and dehumanization.[1] Through *self-reflexivity*,
modernist art simultaneously draws attention to both the work itself – its media
materials, as well as the rules and form of its construction – and to the artist who
created it. By doing so, artists self-consciously emphasize the direct relationship
between the work of art and its creator. One can instantly recognize, for example, a
painting as "a Picasso" or a short story as "Kafkaesque." In this regard, modernist
art and literature are often more about the material expression of the subjective reality
of the artist, than a description of the objective world. Interestingly, modernists
tended to believe this process is reproduced within the consumer of the work of art
as well. The viewer, reader, or audience is encouraged to find meaning through a
direct, subjective response to the work of art, rather than through judging whether
the piece conforms to some set of external aesthetic standards.

The second dimension of modernist aesthetics concerns *simultaneity* in the construction of the work of art. Rather than seeking mimesis or naturalistic representation, the work of art becomes a kind of montage in which form is achieved through
the juxtaposition of media elements, images, words, and objects within the same
space. Three-dimensional perspective and linear development in time give way to a
sense of saturated, synchronic time (i.e., the arrangement of multiple things at the
same time, or a rapid succession of images or words through time). While the effect
of the work of art may produce a sense or feeling of unity, in fact the elements have
only been placed together (the way, for example, an overwhelming number of still
images are imprinted upon celluloid film, juxtaposed through montage editing, and
threaded through a projector to produce the unifying illusion of "moving pictures").
Dreams are perhaps the best lived experience of this (Freud's *The Interpretation of
Dreams* inspired many modernist artists and writers). "Stream of consciousness" in
literature, cubism and collage in visual art, and atonality and multitonality in music,
are common examples of simultaneity in modernism.

The third dimension of modernist aesthetics emphasizes the *uncertainty of meaning*.
In contrast to nineteenth-century positivism – the optimistic belief that scientific
knowledge and social progress would produce a more enlightened humanity – modernists were attuned to the paradoxes, ambiguities, and uncertainties of contemporary
life. Such a "revolt against positivism" had already been in preparation by such
prominent intellectuals as Darwin, Nietzsche, and Freud, and was fueled by more
widespread fears about "the masses," biological regression, and moral decadence at
the end of the nineteenth century. Modernists, in various ways, tended to be "against
nature." One of the goals of modernism became to "defamiliarize" the world, to

draw attention to the realization that modern life is not "natural," but is historically constructed and is continually undergoing transformation. Rather than systematically build up knowledge in methodical fashion, the modernist project was to reassemble the fundamental elements of art, literature, and music in ways that demanded the active participation of viewers, readers, and audiences – who would be provoked to reexamine the world and to perceive it differently.

The final dimension in modernist aesthetics proposed by Lunn is *dehumanization*, meaning that man is no longer the measure of all things, but that human identity is the composite effect of a tremendous number of external forces upon a fragile human psyche. For modernists, personality is not integrated and human nature is not fixed or natural. Rather, humans experience the world subjectively through a "psychic field" of external sensations, perceptions, images, and objects. The depiction of humans in modernist visual art is often expressed through distortions of the human body, or simply by treating disembodied body parts as montage elements in some larger image. In modernism, humans have characteristics, but no longer an organic core. It was precisely this belief in the constructed and composite view of human identity that led modernists to believe they possessed a mission as an elite avant-garde. A modernist civilization of their creation, they held, could transform human nature itself. Modernist art was not only about aesthetics, it offered a path toward social engineering.

The Perceptual Revolution

While modernism specifically refers to a reorientation in aesthetics, it is useful to situate it among an array of cultural and intellectual innovations from the opening decade of the twentieth century that changed the fundamental worldview of Europeans. Economic and technological developments at the turn of the century were rapidly transforming everyday life, and the impact of World War I upon European society and politics was cataclysmic. With a backward glance from the postwar perspective of the 1920s, poet William Butler Yeats lamented, "Things fall apart; the centre cannot hold." For Yeats, the rapidity of change in combination with the loss of traditional moorings had produced a kind of cultural anarchy. Yet, as the literary critic James McFarlane has countered, "the defining thing in the Modernist mode is not so much that things fall *apart* but that they fall *together*."[2] Revolutionary changes in ideology, society, and politics at the dawn of the twentieth century had superseded the imperial order of the late nineteenth-century *ancien régime*. Reality had not disintegrated, but had been multiplied and collapsed in upon itself. As McFarlane emphasizes, the modernist challenge was not to bring order to chaos, but to sort out and redefine the contours of a contemporary civilization whose inertia of material and intellectual abundance overwhelmed outmoded categories. Viewed historically, modernism was not the cause of radical change, but rode a wave of rapid transformations and gave them expression.

This shift had been in preparation for at least half a century. At its base was the second industrial revolution in petroleum, chemicals, transportation, electricity, and communications media. These changes in the industrial base were accompanied by the shift to consumer capitalism as well. As the average standard of living rose across western Europe, people as a whole literally "bought into" this new era of manufacture, quintessentially represented in the dream world of the department store. Large-scale urban renovations – construction of boulevards, underground gas, water, and sewers, electrification, city parks – transformed large cities into alluring environments. The modern metropolises of Paris, Berlin, London, Vienna, St Petersburg, Prague, and Budapest became both the artistic hubs of Europe and the sites of vast commercial spectacles for urban inhabitants and tourists. Steamship transport, passenger rail, commuter lines, subways, the bicycle, and finally the automobile made it possible for individuals to traverse the globe in a matter of days, one's country in a few hours, the city within minutes. The mass-circulation newspaper connected readers across the social spectrum by the tens and hundreds of thousands on a daily basis, creating a montage of modern life decades before any cubist collage. In tandem with the telegraph, daily news became instantaneous, collapsing together international and local events, high politics and sensational crimes, factual reportage and entertainment stories. Such technological and commercial transformations combined to establish the conditions for what the intellectual historian Stephen Kern has identified as an entirely new "culture of time and space." Clock time and geographic distance were becoming less meaningful as objective categories, now being registered instead as a subjective psychological reality within the multiple and diverse experiences of daily modern life.

For some Europeans, such transformations in modern life constituted a *belle époque* or "beautiful age." However, other turn-of-the-century European intellectuals were less sanguine about what modernization heralded for the human condition. Pessimistic philosophers Arthur Schopenhauer and Friedrich Nietzsche had viewed the shift toward technology and mass society in terms of cultural nihilism, the exhaustion of vital force in human beings and within western civilization overall. Negative assessments about the human condition emanated from the fields of social science as well. When applied as social theory, Darwin's ideas about the evolutionary descent of humanity fueled fears that Europeans were actually degenerating and regressing. In the emerging field of depth psychology, Freud pitted an individual's fragile ego against two overwhelming and antithetical forces, a biological unconscious demanding satisfaction on the one hand, and an increasingly large constellation of laws, morality, and social conventions constraining human behavior on the other. The assessments of more even-minded sociologists were mixed. For Emile Durkheim, the contemporary transition from traditional to modern ways of living had generated anomie, or "social anxiety," as evidenced by increasing rates of suicide and crime. The vibrancy of the city, Georg Simmel judged, was accompanied by a heightened awareness of anonymity and alienation inherent in modern urban life. For Max Weber, the efficiency gained through technical knowledge and bureaucratic administration also yielded a disenchanted "iron cage of reality" that left humans spiritually impoverished. Far from a *belle époque*, the modernization of European society could as easily be construed as the *fin de siècle*, literally the "end of the century."

Yet even from within such a pessimistic assessment, certain writers and aesthetes had caught glimpses of an exciting new dynamic within modern art as early as the mid-nineteenth century. In "The Painter of Modern Life" (1863) poet Charles Baudelaire articulated a novel approach to art in the newly urbanized and commercialized world. The task of the modern artist, for Baudelaire, was to capture an image of eternal beauty in the ephemera of a modern world undergoing continual transformation. An important formal dimension of such art was "synesthesia," a blurring of perceptions that evokes unanticipated correspondences ("feeling" colors, "hearing" sensations, "seeing" sounds). Impressionism in French painting became the first artistic movement to realize this type of agenda. But it was foremost through the symbolist movement in poetry, particularly under the guidance of Stéphane Mallarmé, that artists became fully self-reflexive about their own creative processes. Through bohemian clubs, literary circles, and the small journals they produced, writers and artists became critics as well. In Mallarmé's case, his critical commentary was not limited to poetry, but extended to art and music criticism. Widespread discussions about the music and ideas of German composer Richard Wagner, proponent of the "total union of the arts" (*Gesamtkunstwerk*) as the foundation of a modern mythology, were particularly spirited throughout turn-of-the-century Europe. From the depths of an exhausted Europe, prescient writers and critics heralded new arts for the modern age.

Europe was, in fact, on the verge of a vast reorientation in perception and knowledge. The intellectual historian Donald M. Lowe has defined a perceptual revolution in a shift in epistemology from linearity to multi-perspectivity in the critical decade 1905–15, and he has charted key moments in that epistemic break across a variety of intellectual disciplines. In a new realm of psychology known as phenomenology, Edmond Husserl explored how the subjective, internal experience of the flow of time and memory had a greater effect upon human consciousness than external, objective measures of time. In linguistics Ferdinand de Saussure proposed that the deep grammar of language itself rested upon arbitrary foundations, and linguistic philosopher Ludwig Wittgenstein soon pursued the implications of the indeterminacy of language even further. The stable Newtonian worldview was disrupted by innovations in mathematics and physics advanced by Herman Minkowski, Albert Einstein, Ernest Rutherford, and Neils Bohr, each of whom contributed in various ways to the notion that time and space are relational, rather than fixed, categories. In addition, some of these physicists noted that the inclusion of the investigator at the level of subatomic physics altered the outcome of experiments, an insight shortly thereafter articulated by Werner Heisenberg as the "uncertainty principle." In the modern world, therefore, knowledge was no longer the cumulative project of cataloging an objective world, but a subjective, creative, and ever-shifting process of construction and self-reflection. Nowhere would this perceptual revolution become more apparent and well developed than in modernist art and literature.

The Early Avant-Garde

As modernist literary critic Astradur Eysteinsson has observed, "Most of us do not experience modernity as a mode of disruption, however many disruptive historical events we may be aware of." In this light, he continues, it is perhaps best to understand "modernism as an attempt to *interrupt* the modernity that we live and understand as a social, if not 'normal,' way of life."[3] It would become the task of the artistic avant-garde to wake up a slumbering population, to open their eyes to the effects of the rapidly changing world, and inspire them to live a new reality. For most of the nineteenth century, with rare exceptions such as the Paris Commune of 1871 and Emile Zola's defense of the wrongfully accused Captain Dreyfus in 1898, political revolutionaries and the artistic elite had largely inhabited different intellectual and political spheres. In the early twentieth century, though, modernism became a revolutionary project. The artist-as-revolutionary would change modern culture, thereby transforming human consciousness and revitalizing society.

Few modernists at the beginning of the twentieth century were the kinds of cultural iconoclasts and political revolutionaries commonly associated with the radical avant-garde that later emerged in the wake of the Great War and Russian revolution. Many early avant-garde artists and writers viewed themselves as working within their artistic, literary, and musical traditions. At the same time, the impulse to innovate and revitalize their craft ran deeply among them. Through experimenting with the forms of their artistic practice, and then critically reflecting upon what was being accomplished by doing so, this early avant-garde began to develop the techniques and language of the modernist idiom. By the eve of the war, the aesthetic innovations of the avant-garde had become highly developed, and some of its artistic production and manifesto declarations quite bold and jarring. The development of this early avant-garde is perhaps best reconstructed by charting the emergence of ideas through representative and influential individuals across artistic disciplines.

In the field of painting, Henri Matisse is emblematic of the kind of avant-garde artist who was an innovator while remaining respectful of the traditions of his craft. A leading member of the *Fauves* ("wild beasts") group of Parisian painters, Matisse had followed in the footsteps of the impressionists and neoimpressionists, and specifically the painting of Paul Cézanne. Working broadly within a representational approach – where human figures, home interiors, and exterior landscapes, if not "naturalistic," are nonetheless easily recognizable – Matisse's aesthetic shifted to the abstract elements of the painting medium itself and the expressive impact the work of art made upon a viewer. For Matisse, what was most foundational to painting were the elements of the medium itself: the size and strength of the brushstroke, the boldness and luster of paint colors, the harmony of elements upon the canvas. The purpose for putting paint to canvas was less to reproduce reality than to evoke a strong response in the viewer that would resonate with the inner world of the artist. As Matisse articulated in *Notes of a Painter* (1908), "The entire arrangement of my picture is expressive: the place occupied by the figure, the empty spaces around them, the proportions, everything has its share. Composition is the art of arranging in a decorative manner the diverse elements at the painter's command to express his feelings."[4] Such expressionism, the external representation of an artist's or writer's inner reality, became a dominant modernist aesthetic and would be particularly influential among both visual artists and writers, particularly in central and northern Europe, well into the 1920s.

Matisse had a profound impact upon Wassily Kandinsky, the Russian-born painter who, together with Franz Marc and Paul Klee, was one of the founding collaborators of the *Blaue Reiter* ("Blue Rider") group of artists. Kandinsky pushed ideas about abstraction and expressionism further than Matisse, articulating his theory about the language of color and form in painting in *Concerning the Spiritual in Art* (1911). For Kandinsky, art not only expressed the inner feelings of the artist, it also constituted an actual depiction of the human soul. Colors, lines, and shapes, he believed, invoked sympathetic vibrations with the human spirit: the more abstract the work of art, the more directly it corresponded to the "inner need" of the viewer. Kandinsky cast the artist into an avant-garde role by charging him with no less than the spiritual care of humanity. Drawing upon the form of an ascending triangle, an important composition element in the history of art that Kandinsky traced from Renaissance art through Cézanne's "Bathing Women," he established a correspondence between the soul of the artist and the collective spirit of humanity itself (Kandinsky was influenced by the theosophy of Madame Blavatsky at the time). Only the true artist, Kandinsky claimed, occupied the pinnacle of the triangle, and thus only he had the capacity to lead humanity to a greater spiritual reality. This would be accomplished by degrees, Kandinsky believed, with the artist moving from simpler "melodic" paintings to more complex "symphonic" ones. These symphonic paintings, in turn, would resonate in viewers through a series of ascending stages, first as "impressions," then "improvisations," and finally as complex "compositions" (all three terms used as series titles for paintings by Kandinsky). The avant-garde task of the artist, then, was to give exterior expression of the inner needs of the soul.

The language of music was not accidental in Kandinsky, for in addition to the realm of painting he was strongly influenced by the music and ideas of Austrian composer Arnold Schoenberg. A pioneer in the field of atonal music – the infinitesimal division and saturation of dissonant tones between the conventional notes in the tempered scale – for Schoenberg, music amounted to phenomenological philosophy in a different form. The project was to realize a new language of music, to turn a composition into a "text" constructed of musical "sentences." The structure of such atonal musical compositions would express an inherent logic radically different from the standard forms of music theory. The goal was to move beyond the comforts of melody and harmony and to provoke strong, conflicting, deep emotional responses in the listener. Dissonance was therefore the foremost element, the musical unleashing of the "logic of the unconscious" as Schoenberg understood it. Consciousness equaled the "emancipation" of dissonance, measured by the listener's capacity to withstand a nearly unbearable saturation of varied, juxtaposed, non-repetitious sounds. And it became the obligation of the composer to construct, objectively, musical pieces designed to invoke such a self-consciously subjective response in listeners.

Many of the foregoing ideas were brought together in one the most provocative early avant-garde forms in the visual arts: cubism. The birth of cubism is often marked by Pablo Picasso's *Les Demoiselles d'Avignon* (1907), a painting recognized at the time as simultaneously "primitive" (of roughly drawn female nudes, some wearing "savage" African masks) and multi-perspectival (in that multiple views on the figures had been combined and flattened out upon the two-dimensional canvas surface). The art critic John Golding has summarized the basic aesthetic of cubism as "the construction of a painting in terms of a linear grid or framework, the fusion of objects with their surroundings, the combination of several views of an object within a single image, and of abstract and representational elements in the same picture."[5] In collaboration with painter Georges Braque, Picasso pioneered this cubist aesthetic, working from semi-recognizable still life paintings to entirely abstract and non-representational works. Cubism also moved beyond the constraints of the paint medium, to juxtapose images and words in a montage, and further to combine wood, metal, newspaper clippings, wallpaper, and painted surfaces into multimedia collages. While the cubist style itself would not endure beyond World War I, it exerted a foundational influence upon a great number of subsequent modernist painters, such as Fernand Léger, Robert Delaunay, and Piet Mondrian, among others.

As a historical caveat, it is important to bear in mind in this brief summation of early modernism that the examples of aesthetic innovation provided by these early avant-garde figures are by no means exclusive or authoritative. While important and influential modernists in their own right, they were not alone and do not necessarily deserve some heroic status over their artistic, literary, and musical contemporaries. Rather, what even this relatively small cast of artists, writers, and musicians reveals is a dynamic of cross-influences within and between artistic movements. Few of these modernists lived in isolation. Most lived and worked in the capital cities of Europe – Paris, London, Vienna, Berlin, St Petersburg, Prague, Budapest – and their immediate circles included networks of artists, writers, and intellectuals. Further, aesthetic innovations in one artistic field were sometimes transferred to another. At the dawn of the century, Claude Debussy and Maurice Ravel turned impressionism into musical form, and Erik Satie composed music for the first cubist ballet, *Parade* (1917). Literary modernism particularly thrived on experimentation across cultural boundaries. Franz Kafka turned expressionism into a fantastic literary form in short stories such as *Metamorphosis* (1912) and novels like *The Trial* (1914). In poetry, Guillaume Apollinaire joined the sonorous and visual in *Calligrammes* (1918), a collection of pieces in which words were assembled into the visual form of the poetic image. As Schoenberg sought to unleash the "logic" of the unconscious through atonal music, writers such as Thomas Mann, James Joyce, and Virginia Woolf penned "stream of consciousness" into literature (influenced as much by the American psychologist William James as by Freud). Mann and Joyce were also exemplars of the transgeographic dimension of literary modernism, as authors who wrote in their native languages while living in exile in foreign terrains. This condition of cultural and geographic displacement was shared by American literary modernists living in Europe, such as Gertrude Stein, Ezra Pound, and T. S. Eliot (as well as by subsequent authors of the American "Lost Generation" and Harlem Renaissance living in postwar Paris).

The full flowering of this modernist cross-fertilization of the arts would become most apparent in the various radical avant-garde movements after World War I. It was on the eve of the war, however, that the radical avant-garde first emerged. The "Manifesto of Futurism" by Italian poet Filippo Tommaso Marinetti, as much a *provocateur* as a man of letters, appeared in the Parisian daily newspaper *Le Figaro* on February 20, 1909. Art, Marinetti proclaimed, should be revolutionary – bold, energetic, fervent, destructive, violently sweeping away the old world with the newest technologies to hurl humanity into a chaotically beautiful future. Artists of the future, he declared, value action over thought, speed over stasis, aggression over contemplation, ecstasy over repose, masculinity over femininity. The futurist embraces a total image of the modern world in dynamic terms:

> We shall sing of the great crowds in the excitement of labour, pleasure and rebellion; of the multi-coloured and polyphonic surf of revolutions in modern capital cities; of the nocturnal vibration of arsenals and workshops beneath their violent electric moons; of the greedy stations swallowing smoking snakes; of factories suspended from the clouds by their strings of smoke; of bridges leaping like gymnasts over the diabolical cutlery of

sunbathed rivers; of adventurous liners scenting the horizon; of broad-chested locomotives prancing on the rails, like huge steel horses bridled with long tubes; and of the
gliding flight of aeroplanes, the sound of whose screw is like the flapping of flags and
the applause of an enthusiastic crowd.[6]

Marinetti's rant might have simply remained just that, had it not been for the
convergence of a number of historical factors. First, in terms of modernist aesthetics,
futurism was not the idea of a solitary man, but quickly developed into a multifaceted
artistic movement in Italian literature, poetry, painting, and music – a movement so
strong that it was one of the few early avant-gardes to survive the Great War of 1914
(Marinetti became a supporter of Mussolini's fascist Italy in the 1920s). Second,
futurism influenced the development of other radical avant-garde movements during
and after the war, directly upon Bolshevik constructivism through Russian poet and
playwright Vladimir Mayakovsky, and indirectly upon the dada and surrealist movements. But perhaps the most difficult and disturbing historical dimension of futurism
lay in its prescience about the near future. Barely five years after the appearance of
the manifesto, the conflagration of technological warfare would engulf Europe and
traumatize millions of ordinary people. The terrible beauty of the modern world no
longer remained an image fashioned by a futurist avant-garde, but would become
the subjective reality of the masses.

From Radical Avant-Garde to the New Sobriety

The traumatic effects of World War I upon the European economy, politics, society,
and culture were overwhelming. This applies no less to modernism than to any other
realm. In the immediate aftermath of the war, a radicalized avant-garde emerged,
survivors of the "Generation of 1914" who were ready to scrap the values of their
fathers and to construct an entirely new culture and society out of the wreckage of
industrial warfare and empire. Many of the influential figures from the radical avant-
garde belonged to the revolutionary communist left, or at least their political sympathies lay in that direction. Other avant-garde artists and writers, however, moved
to the political right, and the most extreme of them became supporters of fascism.
Within a decade after the end of the Great War, modernism also began to become
domesticated into the service of corporate business and government-sponsored public
works projects. Yet the war itself was the crucible from which these developments in
modernism emerged.

As trench warfare settled into stalemate on the western front, an assortment of
nonconformists and pacifists who refused to take part in patriotic slaughter took
refuge in the Swiss city of Zurich. There, in May 1915, German expressionist writer
Hugo Ball opened the "Cabaret Voltaire," featuring chanteuse Emmy Hennings
singing popular songs from Munich and Paris. Within a few months, the cabaret had
developed into a bohemian club, attracting a refugee clientele of artists and the
curious from Germany, France, Italy, Hungary, and Romania. Abstract and primitivist
art by Hans Arp and Augusto Giacometti adorned the walls of the Cabaret Voltaire.
"Simultaneous poetry" in multiple broken languages was performed by Tristan Tzara,
Marcel Janco, and Richard Huelsenbeck. Backed by a "brutist" musical accompaniment on piano, banjos, and drums, dancers in primitive masks designed by Janco

hopped around the stage and shouted "negro" chants. By the time the landlord closed down the club in July 1916, because of its utter commercial failure, the performances of the Cabaret Voltaire had a name: dada.

The birth of dada marked a crucial turning point for modernism as an anti-art movement. Convinced that European art, literature, philosophy, and religion had produced the kind of nationalistic jingoism responsible for the war, the avant-garde project begun in the Cabaret Voltaire amounted to no less than the total rejection of the aesthetics and values of western civilization and their replacement by dada, or baby blather ("dada" is a child's word for hobbyhorse in French). Deemed preferable to the discontents of civilization, dada sought a direct connection between the objective world and subjective human experience by reducing art, language, and music to their most primitive elements and endlessly recombining them into novel images, poetry, and performances. Dada constituted an intellectual avant-garde as well. "DADA MEANS NOTHING," Tristan Tzara proclaimed in the *Dada Manifesto* of 1918. "Freedom: Dada Dada Dada, a roaring of tense colors, an interlacing of opposites and of all contradictions, grotesques, inconsistencies: LIFE."[7] Provocation and irony were the critical tools of the anarchistic Zurich Dada movement.

Dadaist Richard Huelsenbeck returned to Berlin and linked up with leftist artists Georg Grosz, Wieland Herzfelde, and John Heartfield to form Club Dada in January 1918. Continuing with the anti-art agenda from Zurich, the early impulse in Berlin Dada was one of "bluff and counter-bluff, bewilderment, and parody."[8] Club Dada chose writer and artist Raoul Hausmann as the movement's "Dadasopher" and heralded an apocalyptic Christian prophet named Joannes Baader as their "Superdada." Yet with the collapse of imperial Germany in November 1918, the subsequent communist uprisings in Berlin and Bavaria, and the slaughter of communists by the roving paramilitary *Freikorps*, Berlin Dada quickly moved in a revolutionary political direction. With disdain for the newly established Weimar Republic and admiration for the Bolshevik revolution in Russia, Berlin Dada produced deliberately provocative political art from the ephemeral materials of mass media. Montages from newspaper print and magazine images emphasized dehumanization within the chaos of postwar life; photomontage posters criticized the government and military; advertising parodies attacked the values of capitalism and the decadent lifestyles of the bourgeoisie. The culmination of the movement was realized in the Dada Fair of June 5, 1920, accompanied by the publishing of the *Dada Almanach*. By the mid-1920s, the antics of Berlin Dada had been largely supplanted by the even more politically committed *Neue Sachlichkeit* or "New Objectivity" movement. Leading artists in the movement included Georg Grosz and Otto Dix, who politically adhered to the German Communist Party and painted unflinchingly critical depictions of middle-class greed, commodified sexuality, and military and political corruption into their works. *Neue Sachlichkeit* was expressed through politically engaged theatrical productions as well, such as in *Man Equals Man* by Bertolt Brecht and adaptations of films and novels staged by Edwin Piscator.

In the newly established Soviet Union, the modernist avant-garde was put directly into the service of the Bolshevik revolution. Following the October Revolution of 1917 and after a bitterly fought civil war, Russian artists, poets, actors, and filmmakers were organized by Anatoly Lunarcharsky, the Bolshevik Commissar of Enlightenment, into the Prolekult ("proletarian culture") movement to proselytize the people about the virtues of communism. Many participants adhered to the leading radical avant-garde movement of the era, constructivism, and were more than willing to participate in the utopian political project of building a new communist society from scratch. The *Constructivist Manifesto* of 1921 stated: "We consider self-sufficient studio art and our activity as mere painters to be useless . . . We declare industrial art absolute and Constructivism its only form of expression."[9] Constructivists utterly rejected the nineteenth-century notion of "art for art's sake" and gave art an immediate and applied function, fusing technology with modern design toward solving practical problems in everyday life. For example, Russian futurist poet Vladimir Mayakovsky collaborated with painter and photographer Alexander Rodchenko to design posters, advertising copy, and product logos for Soviet consumer goods. Motion pictures represent perhaps the supreme expression of the constructivist fusion of technology and art. Whether or not Lenin actually said, "Of all the arts, for us the cinema is the most important," there is no doubt that the Soviets seized upon film's propaganda potential. Constructivist techniques in film montage, in both feature films and documentaries, pioneered by Sergei Eisenstein in *Battleship Potemkin* (1925), Vsevolod Pudovkin in *Mother* (1926), and Dziga Vertov in *Man with a Movie Camera* (1929), had lasting impacts upon the development of cinema, not only in the Soviet Union but also internationally. In the early 1920s, during the experimental years of the New Economic Policy (NEP), the constructivist avant-garde aspired to mold new Soviet men and women through artistically directed modern technologies, a cultural revolution that resonated with the more utopian aspects of the Bolshevik revolution.

In postwar France, the cultural and political situation was altogether different. Unlike defeated imperialist Germany or tsarist Russia, the victorious French Third Republic had survived the Great War. But French victory had been achieved at the cost of more than one and a half million French soldiers killed, and more than double that number permanently maimed and psychologically traumatized. In homage, war memorials were constructed across northern France, the site of the western front. Soon, though, the mood of the country shifted toward a desire to "return to normalcy." Some members of the prewar avant-garde retreated from some of their more radical modernist experiments, such as Picasso who gave up cubism for a more humanist "neoclassical" period of portraiture and paintings based on classical themes. Others sought to forget the immediate past in the frivolities of *les années folles*, the "crazy years" of the jazz age. This superficially lighthearted mood permeated Paul Colin's *Le Tumulte noir* (1927), a portfolio of color lithographs celebrating the exotic and erotic energy of African-American entertainer Josephine Baker, the sensation of *La Revue Nègre*. Popular entertainment was preferable to dwelling upon war trauma.

For other young Frenchmen of the "Generation of 1914," such as André Breton, Louis Aragon, Paul Éluard, Benjamin Péret, and Philippe Soupault, the war was not something to be commemorated or forgotten, but served as the impetus to revolutionize art and consciousness. These young men initially embraced the provocative tactics of dada as their mode of expression, a choice reinforced by Tristan Tzara's move from Zurich to Paris in 1920, and by the inclusion of artists Marcel Duchamp, Max Ernst, and Francis Picabia in the group. Within a few years, however, Breton in particular became dissatisfied with the anti-art stance of dada, and he proposed a new movement: surrealism. Where dada dismantled art, surrealism would create a new reality, a *sur*-reality that would embrace the modern world at a higher level of consciousness. In the *Manifesto of Surrealism* (1924) Breton declared: "Surrealism is based on the belief in the superior reality of certain forms of associations hitherto neglected, in the omnipotence of dream, in the disinterested play of thought."[10] The goal was to reconfigure consciousness by breaking old patterns of thought, what Breton called the "paucity of reality," and then forming entirely new, richer, and more complex images of modern life based upon juxtapositions between seemingly dissimilar elements. Surrealist art would not be based upon preconceived ideas or aesthetics, but would be drawn from the vast terrain of "found" objects (*la trouvaille*) littering the modern cultural landscape, as well as from the biological unconscious. The direct encounter with such unbounded material was, the surrealists believed, a shocking experience to the human psyche, and the art yielded by such an encounter expressed a "convulsive beauty." The surrealists developed a range of techniques to invoke the kinds of uncanny, disturbing experiences that would enhance surreal perceptions, from word-and-image "exquisite corpse" games to "automatic writing" from semi-trance dream states. While many of the early surrealists were poets and writers, it was later through painting that surrealism became most widely known through the work of such artists as André Masson, Yves Tanguy, Salvador Dalí, and René Magritte.

Like Berlin Dada and Russian constructivism, Paris Surrealism associated itself politically with the socialist and communist left. But other avant-garde movements and modernists moved to the fascist right. In 1919 Marinetti and other Italian futurists participated in the foundation of the Fascist Party. After spending 21 days in prison with Mussolini at the end of that year, Marinetti became fervently anti-communist. In *Futurism and Fascism* (1924) he proclaimed his avant-garde movement to be the forerunner of Mussolini's "New Italy" and his support remained unabated in his openly fascist journal *Futurismo* of the 1930s. In France, too, some modernists were drawn to fascism. French writer Pierre Drieu la Rochelle was, like many of his surrealist contemporaries, part of the Generation of 1914. But unlike his leftist colleagues, Drieu had been exhilarated by the experience of war and felt deflated afterward. In works of fiction, most notably in *Gilles* (1939), as well as in his life, Drieu flirted with fascist fantasies of power. The American poet Ezra Pound was enticed by fascism as well. Expatriated to London in 1908, Pound was the leading Anglo-American figure in the modernist literary movements of imagism and vorticism. In 1925 he moved to Italy and became an open admirer of Mussolini, even to the point of making pro-fascist radio broadcasts during World War II (arrested as a traitor after the war, Pound was later confined to a mental asylum for the remainder of his life). Revolutionary fantasies within modernism did not inherently drift toward any political direction in particular.

Toward the end of the 1920s the revolutionary fervor of the radical avant-garde from the immediate postwar era began to moderate toward what cultural critic John Willet has called "the new sobriety." Increasingly, modernist ideas were taking form as practical applications, not only by the constructivists in the Soviet Union, but also in public works projects sponsored within the parliamentary nations of France, Germany, and Britain. Domestic collaborations between industry, government programs, and the modernist elite were perhaps most evident in the field of architecture.

In many countries the principles of formalism and functionalism in modernist architectural design were incorporated into public housing and other government-sponsored projects. Le Corbusier (pseudonym of Charles Édouard Jeannert-Gris), a Swiss architect who completed his most famous work after moving to France, became a leading figure in formalist architectural design. Although few of his grand architectural plans for France and its colonies were ever realized, through *Towards a New Architecture* (1922) and his articles in the modernist journal *L'Esprit nouveau*, Le Corbusier's ideas about the fusion of architectural form with function received international attention and were applied worldwide (particularly housing projects in the United States and the urban planning of Brasilia). In Weimar Germany, the Bauhaus school in architecture spearheaded by Walter Gropius was contracted to complete both exterior and interior designs for the Törten housing estates of the industrial city of Dessau, and similar modernist housing projects were realized in Berlin, Frankfurt, Cologne, Dresden, Stuttgart, and several other cities. In Britain, perhaps the most impressive modernist architectural achievement of the interwar era involved the renovation of the London Underground subway system. Everything about the system – from the design of the stations to public art on display within them – became an exercise in educating the public about modernist aesthetics. Modernist architectural design, promoting the new aesthetic of form and function over traditional forms of architecture, was no longer the sole purview of an avant-garde, but was being incorporated into the bureaucratic procedures of urban planning.

In many ways, the years leading up to World War II represented the nadir of modernism in Europe. During the 1930s several radical avant-garde movements experienced substantial setbacks, particularly in the Soviet Union and Nazi Germany. After the death of Lenin, Stalin brought an end to the NEP and embarked upon a project of industrial modernization and agricultural collectivization through a series of state-centralized five-year plans. On the cultural level, this meant an end to the influence of the constructivist avant-garde and the rise of socialist realism as the official cultural policy of the Soviet Union. Some modernists, such as filmmaker Sergei Eisenstein, managed to ride the transition. Others could not bridge the distance between revolutionary creativity and the cultural constrictions imposed by socialist realism, like the poet Mayakovsky, who committed suicide in April 1930. Still other artists and writers would fall victim to Stalin's purges in the late 1930s.

In Germany, the Nazi seizure of power in 1933 not only marked the end of the Weimar republic, but also an end to modernist experimentation. The Nazi Party purged over 20,000 works of modernist art from museums, and then put hundreds of the pillaged pieces on display in the *Entartete Kunst* (Degenerate Art) exhibition in Munich in 1937. Works by Kandinsky, Klee, Picasso, and other renowned modernist artists, as well as a reconstruction of the Berlin Dada Fair, were presented as examples of "Jewish" and "Bolshevistic" art. Simultaneously, the *Großen Deutschen Kunstausstellung* (Great German Art Exhibition) opened in Munich to showcase "heroic" and *Volkisch* "Aryan" works produced by over 1,600 approved German artists. While officially sanctioned Nazi art is generally regarded as kitsch, nonetheless the regime continued to recognize the propaganda value of innovative, if not modernist, design through its patronage of such accomplished individuals as architect Albert Speer and filmmaker Leni Riefenstahl. A similar trend toward heroic art occurred in fascist Italy during the 1930s, although the reaction against modernism was never as pronounced as it was in Nazi Germany. Modernist design in architecture, for example, continued to be used in certain housing projects, and futurist Marinetti remained a staunch supporter of Mussolini's regime.

In response to developments in Nazi Germany and fascist Italy, parliamentary nations of western Europe formed a Popular Front against fascism. At the cultural level, the International Writers Congress for the Defense of Culture held in Paris in June 1935 marked a hiatus in modernism. The meeting, directed by André Malraux and André Gide, featured eminent leftist literary figures such as Ilya Ehrenberg, Boris Pasternak, Henri Barbusse, and Louis Aragon (who had left the surrealist fold and joined the Communist Party). Members of the radical avant-garde, such as André Breton and other surrealists, were simply barred from participation. Experimental modernism barely registered as a cultural challenge, let alone a political one. During the Spanish Civil War, Picasso's *Guernica* (1937) graphically depicted the pain and tragedy of the fascist bombing of that village, yet the painting's cubist aesthetic was no longer perceived as radical. Even surrealism, for that matter, had lost much of its provocative edge. In French newspapers, the International Surrealist Exhibition of 1938 was judged "mysterious but inoffensive."[11] Modernism no longer interrupted the normalcy of modernity, but had become one of its accepted features.

The radical challenge posed by modernism for European aesthetics at the dawn of the twentieth century did not appear as radical four decades later. Not that modernism had lost the impulse towards experimentation and innovation; the "shock of the new" would continue to be an operative principle of modernist art well into the latter half of the twentieth century. After World War II, in the 1950s, the geographic center of modernism would shift from Europe to New York City, and new avant-garde figures and movements would emerge. But the dream of the early twentieth-century modernist avant-garde to transform the consciousness of Europeans, and even to change western civilization itself, had lost something of its radical edge. From our "postmodern" perspective a century later, the aesthetic innovations of the early avant-garde appear nearly commonplace. Modernist art and literature no longer challenge establishment traditions; rather, they have become institutionalized in art museums and canonized in the literature departments of major universities. Techniques of abstraction and montage, as well as the creative impulses to innovate and shock, are no longer the domains of an artistic elite, but have become the stock-in-trade of commercial advertising, feature films, television, and computer-generated graphics. There is little doubt that modernism has revolutionized culture, not only in Europe but also across the globe. Yet the social and political aspirations of the modernist avant-garde of the early twentieth century remain an unfinished project.

NOTES

1   Eugene Lunn, *Marxism and Modernism: An Historical Study of Lukács, Brecht, Benjamin, and Adorno* (Berkeley: University of California Press, 1984), pp. 34–7.
2   James McFarlane, "The Mind of Modernism," in *Modernism: A Guide to European Literature 1890–1930*, Malcolm Bradbury and James McFarlane, eds (New York: Penguin, revd edn, 1991), p. 92. Reference to Yeats's *The Second Coming* (1921) and italics are in the original.

3 Astradur Eysteinsson, *The Concept of Modernism* (Ithaca NY: Cornell University Press, 1990), p. 6.
4 Quoted in Christopher Butler, *Early Modernism: Literature, Music and Painting in Europe 1900–1916* (Oxford: Oxford University Press, 1994), p. 35.
5 Quoted in Butler, *Early Modernism*, p. 67.
6 F. T. Marinetti, "Manifesto of Futurism (20 February 1909)," in *University of Chicago Readings in Western Civilization*, vol. 9: *Twentieth-Century Europe*, John W. Boyer and Jan Goldstein, eds (Chicago: University of Chicago Press, 1987), p. 10.
7 Quoted in Robert Motherwell, ed., *The Dada Painters and Poets: An Anthology*, 2nd edn, Ralph Manheim, trans. (Cambridge, MA: Harvard University Press, 1988), pp. 77, 82.
8 Malcolm Green, preface to *The Dada Almanach*, Richard Huelsenbeck, ed., Malcolm Green et al., trans. (London: Atlas Press, 1993), p. viii.
9 Quoted in John E. Bowlt, "Constructivism and Early Soviet Fashion Design," in *Bolshevik Culture: Experiment and Order in the Russian Revolution*, Abbot Gleason, Peter Kenez, and Richard Stites, eds (Bloomington: Indiana University Press, 1985), p. 204.
10 André Breton, "Manifesto of Surrealism (1924)," in *Manifestoes of Surrealism*, Richard Seaver and Helen R. Lane, trans. (Ann Arbor: University of Michigan Press, 1969), p. 27.
11 Elyette Benassaya, "Le Surréalisme face à la presse," *Mélusine* 1 (1979): 144–5.

GUIDE TO FURTHER READING

Malcolm Bradbury and James McFarlane, eds, *Modernism: A Guide to European Literature 1890–1930*, revd edn (London: Penguin, 1991). A comprehensive survey of modernist literary movements, poetry, novels, and drama across Europe.
Peter Bürger, *Theory of the Avant-Garde*, Michael Shaw trans. (Minneapolis: University of Minnesota Press, 1984). A critical evaluation of the failure of the modernist avant-garde of the interwar era to create an autonomous artistic and intellectual sphere independent of either mass culture or the institutionalized art museum.
Christopher Butler, *Early Modernism: Literature, Music and Painting in Europe 1900–1916* (Oxford: Oxford University Press, 1994). A detailed treatment of the early development of modernist aesthetics, identity, urban poetics, movements, and the avant-garde in France, Italy, Germany, and Britain.
Matei Calinescu, *Five Faces of Modernity: Modernism, Avant-Garde, Decadence, Kitsch, Postmodernism*, 2nd edn (Durham NC: Duke University Press, 1987). A history of ideas that sets modernity, the avant-garde, decadence, kitsch, and postmodernism within a broader concept of the modern extending from the Renaissance to the twentieth century.
Peter Childs, *Modernism* (London: Routledge, 2000). Thematic overview covering major nineteenth-century intellectuals who prefigured modernism, genres of modernist art and literature, and interpretations of key modernist works.
Robert Hughes, *The Shock of the New*, revd edn (New York: Knopf, 1991). Companion book to the BBC/Time-Life series of the same title that provides a comprehensive overview of modernist art internationally across the twentieth century.
Alice Yeager Kaplan, *Reproductions of Banality: Fascism, Literature, and French Intellectual Life* (Minneapolis: University of Minnesota Press, 1986). A provocative treatment of fascist tendencies in the work and thought of French writers and intellectuals.
Stephen Kern, *The Culture of Time and Space 1880–1918* (Cambridge MA: Harvard University Press, 1983). An intellectual history of the multiple technological, cultural, and intellectual innovations that reconceived time and space in such terms as synchronicity, speed, and simultaneity.

Michael Levenson, ed., *The Cambridge Companion to Modernism* (Cambridge: Cambridge University Press, 1999). A collection that critically reevaluates primarily Anglo-American modernism both by theme (philosophy, cultural economy and politics, gender) and by discipline (poetry, drama, novel, visual arts, film).

Donald M. Lowe, *History of Bourgeois Perception* (Chicago: University of Chicago Press, 1982). An intellectual history that argues the epistemic shift from linearity to multiperspectivity occurred in Europe during the decade 1905–15.

Maurice Nadeau, *The History of Surrealism*, revd edn, Richard Howard, trans. (Cambridge MA: Harvard University Press, 1989). The foundational treatment of the origins and developments of dada and surrealism.

Peter Nichols, *Modernisms: A Literary Guide* (Berkeley: University of California Press, 1995). A comprehensive survey of modernist literary movements throughout Europe, from Baudelaire and the symbolists in the late nineteenth century through futurism, dada, and surrealism in the early twentieth century.

Renato Poggioli, *The Theory of the Avant-Garde*, Gerald Fitzgerald, trans. (New York: Icon Editions/Harper and Row, 1971). A classic work that charts the development of the idea of an artistic and intellectual avant-garde in Europe across the nineteenth and twentieth centuries.

Michael T. Saler, *The Avant-Garde in Interwar England: Medieval Modernism and the London Underground* (Oxford: Oxford University Press, 1999). A cultural history that explores the union of modernist aesthetics and industrial craft among British modernists, best illustrated in the renovation of the London Underground during the 1930s.

Ronald Schleifer, *Modernism and Time: The Logic of Abundance in Literature, Science, and Culture, 1880–1930* (Cambridge: Cambridge University Press, 2000). An intellectual history that views modernism as a response to the success of the Enlightenment to produce a new civilization of material, cultural, and demographic abundance.

John Willitt, *Art and Politics in the Weimar Period: The New Sobriety 1917–1933* (New York: Pantheon Books, 1978). A landmark study of the relationships between modernist movements, social transformations, and political change in interwar Europe.

CHAPTER FIVE

The Cult of Youth

ELIZABETH HARVEY

Celebrating youth and youthfulness, and attributing to the years between puberty and young adulthood a whole range of attractive characteristics – beauty, health, purity, energy, idealism, creativity, boldness, vision – had plenty of precedents in Europe before 1900. But there are good reasons for seeing a "cult of youth" as having a particular significance in this epoch. It was a time of burgeoning discourses about youth, youthfulness, and the notion of a "young generation." These were typically produced by cultural critics, politicians, artists, scientists, and educationalists who identified themselves with or claimed expertise about "youth." But the discourses about youth were also shaped by young people in their teens and early twenties, particularly those involved in youth movements of one sort or another, celebrating themselves and promoting their own versions of the "youth myth."

The notion of a "cult of youth" evokes two contradictory meanings. On the one hand, it implies the lavishing of attention on the actual young, based on a view of the life-cycle in which youth is valued all the more because of its transience and its "otherness." From this perspective, youth is expected to express itself, to be rebellious, romantic or escapist, tender or tough, graceful or virile, but at any rate to "be different" and to "be itself." On the other hand, the cult of youth suggests the celebration of the "vital" qualities of youthfulness and the quest for individual and collective "rejuvenation" – making youthfulness not an attribute of the life-cycle but a quality to which society as a whole could aspire. To be eternally "youthful" was to escape, in the imagination, from adult responsibilities and the passage of time and to remain in a constant state of "openness," characterized by uncertainty and vulnerability, but also by energy, mobility, and dynamism. It was an ideal trope upon which to project the idea of the modern individual.

As a slogan of cultural criticism and political campaigning, "Youth!" was as vacuous as they came. It suggested simply a radical rejection of establishments and the old order – "our civilization is senile and rotten" – and a bold message for the future: "make way for the young!" The cult of youth could thus serve as a substitute for political analysis and strategies for political change. As Frank Trommler has pointed out, "myths of youth are easier to produce than revolutions."[1]

At the same time, the cult of youth did carry a distinct political charge in two senses. Firstly, it consistently coded youth as masculine: the creativity associated with youthfulness was typically equated with virility and potency. In an era of feminist challenges to patriarchal thinking, the cult of youth usually functioned as a rearguard defense of masculinity-in-peril. Young women's inclusion within the positively charged discourse of youthfulness, their access to the social power bestowed upon the young, would entail them being constructed as more boyish or androgynous, more "comradely."[2]

Secondly, the cult of youth suggested that the fundamental cleavages in society were generational ones. Generational identities and generational conflict could be presented as a key to contemporary history: accentuated by the watershed of World War I, the impression of a rapid succession of age cohorts, each identified as a "generation" in relation to a distinct historical moment, served to underline the sense of discontinuity and rupture in the modern world.[3] Those who sought to base a political program on the idea of generations tended to reject class struggle and parliamentary government in favor of "organic" notions of solidarity and vaguely conceived "renewal." It was a type of politics that dovetailed easily with hostility to Marxism and classic liberalism as well as feminism.

This essay will consider five aspects of the "cult of youth." Firstly, it will ask how it reflected responses on the part of educated elites before World War I to modernity. Secondly, it will look at how it translated into contrasting formations of youth culture before 1914. Thirdly, it will consider how World War I added new meanings to the cult of youth and fueled the idea of "generations" in political life. Fourthly, it will examine the cult of youth in the interwar period in its guise as a cult of the youthful body. Fifthly, it will explore how fascist movements in the interwar period deployed ideas of youth and the "young generation" as a legitimating claim for their particular brand of reactionary "revolution."

Against Degeneration

One explanation for the virulence of the cult of youth in Europe in the period from the 1890s up to World War I can be found in the "biological thinking" that characterized contemporary comment on issues of the day. Whatever was at stake – the fate of the "white race" versus other races in the global contest, the future of particular nation-states in the struggle for supremacy in Europe, the disorders of societies undergoing modernization or the deficiencies of modern political or intellectual life – diagnoses were offered that drew on evolutionary theory about the survival and adaptation of species and ideas about cycles of human development in which cultures, nations, races, and civilizations naturally grew, flourished, and decayed, to be supplanted by other, more vigorous organisms. Born out of this thinking, the specter of biological degeneration loomed over Europe at the turn of the twentieth century, conjured up by cultural critics, imperialists, military planners, criminologists, and medical experts.[4]

The logic of the biologistic discourse of degeneration suggested to intellectuals that a culture gripped by forces of decay could be rescued only by an infusion of virile youth. In 1874 Friedrich Nietzsche had evoked a race of youthful "warriors and serpent-slayers" that would redeem culture from the dominance of "old men";

at the turn of the century Maurice Barrès condemned the degeneracy and "rootless-ness" of French culture and offered salvation in the shape of vigorous young men, while Moeller van den Bruck declared that Germany needed a blood transfusion: sons had to rise up against their fathers, age had to be replaced by youth.

Alongside the fears of degeneration in *fin-de-siècle* Europe, uncertainties about the future of nations and the survival of bourgeois culture sharpened anxieties about the socialization of the young. Bourgeois reformers constructed working-class and middle-class youth as different types of problem requiring different solutions, but both requiring attention to youth's special needs. Working-class youth was perceived as a phenomenon of degeneration: social observers and criminologists saw them as a vulnerable, but dangerous, social group. Juvenile delinquency and prostitution loomed large in the arguments of social workers in favor of intervening to protect and discipline urban youngsters: against images of delinquency emerged the redeem-ing vision of slum children turned into healthy citizens.

Middle-class youth too was constructed as a site for intensified pedagogical intervention. The late nineteenth century discovered "adolescence," defining it as a period in the life-cycle of bourgeois sons marked by prolonged dependency beyond the age of puberty. A new knowledge about adolescence was created as medics, psychologists, and sociologists proffered opinions on the physiology and psychology of "normal" adolescence as a period of hormonally determined "storm and stress," requiring special care in order to ensure successful maturation into bourgeois adulthood.[5]

How bourgeois daughters fitted into this new thinking was less clear. Girls might feel alienated from their parental homes as well, but what was their place in the model of "storm and stress" as a prelude to mature independence? Like the dreams of cultural rejuvenation through youth developed by radical intellectuals, the theory of adolescence was deeply gendered. The notion of independent adulthood as the goal of maturation remained a problematic aspect of theories of adolescence applied to bourgeois girls in this period, for whom norms of conventional femininity required as a goal for adulthood not so much independence as a new form of dependence – in marriage. Nevertheless, debates about the education of girls formed a part – however marginal – of the discourses on youth.

The spotlight on youth constructed the adolescent, normatively cast as male, as difficult but different, biologically destined to be productively at odds with the world of adults. Coupled with the gloomy tidings of a society in decline, the young could easily be seen – and come to see themselves – as a creative resource from which renewal and rebellion would come. From this belief could be drawn radically different consequences, which found expression in contrasting formations of youth culture in the decade before World War I.

Realm of Youth or Rebellion of Youth?

The early twentieth-century cult of youth constructed an antithesis between male youth and an over-civilized world. From this antithesis some concluded that the young should secede from a society that corrupted them; secession might then give way to a constructive engagement in which the insights gained in the "realm of youthful autonomy" would feed back into society. For others, rebellion rather than secession was in the foreground: youth was seen as the agent of cultural destruction.

A "secession" reaction can be seen in both the prewar *Wandervogel* and in the Scouting movement. The *Wandervogel*, a network of hiking groups that flourished among German and Austrian grammar school pupils from the turn of the twentieth century, stood out from other organizations of the era with its claim to be an autonomous movement *of*, rather than *for*, youth. Its group hikes aimed to give sheltered urban youngsters a new sense of bodily freedom through robust exercise, the chance to explore the countryside and the experience of comradeship within the peer group under a scarcely older chosen leader.[6] The Scouting movement, by contrast, was an organization founded by adults for youngsters; nevertheless, one of the keys to its success was its incorporation of more "adventurous" elements into its activities and a greater delegation of leadership tasks to the young than were typical for other adult-led organizations of the era. Set up in 1908 by the imperialist war hero Robert Baden-Powell, the organization offered a mix of woodcraft, badges for particular skills, and camping. Rather than growing up prematurely, boys were to mature at a natural pace through outdoor activities and challenges during which their self-reliance, hardiness, and alertness could develop. Members sported a "frontier" style of uniform complete with Stetson hat, scarf, and shorts that echoed Baden-Powell's earlier creation, the South African Constabulary, and acquired a repertoire of pseudo-tribal rituals adapted from Zulu and other "native" sources. Baden-Powell's vision was of creating a realm – embodied in the Scout camp – within which the adult world and "civilization" would be held at bay.[7]

In different ways, both the *Wandervogel* and the Scouts offered a form of escape from social conventions into nature and the comradeship of the peer group. In both movements, young males' pursuit of their "own values" was envisaged as entailing them bonding with others in a world imagined as liberation from the bourgeois family – and which specifically excluded girls and women. For the advocates of a new masculinity to be achieved through male bonding, girls who wanted to join the organizations posed a problem. *Wandervogel* groups split over the issue, with girls joining some groups but excluded from others. In the case of the Scouts, girls were quick to grasp at what Scouting offered them, and Baden-Powell was not averse to girls being more active and enjoying the outdoors life, but they were not allowed to join the boys' organization; instead, in 1912 the Girl Guides were set up as a sister organization with a rather tamer program. Baden-Powell's primary interest remained the idea of boyhood and the prolongation of male adolescence – a process that involved denying adolescent sexuality as far as possible in the name of "clean living." For Baden-Powell, whose ideal was the more manly boy and the more boyish man, boyhood was associated with imagination, daring, and a taste for adventure – qualities which he believed might be cultivated even in suburban Britain through the campfires and frontiersman rituals of the Scouting movement.

By 1913 the *Wandervogel* was established and already faction-ridden: if the novelty of its hiking, singing, and sleeping on straw still fascinated new members, others sought to push the German youth movement in a new direction. In the process, they generated new slogans around the theme of youth and its mission to society. As a new network for older members of the youth movement, the *Freideutsche Jugend* was launched at the famous mountainside meeting on the Hoher Meissner in October

1913 as a counter-festival to the jingoistic official celebration of the centenary of the battle of Leipzig. The author of the summons to the meeting, the educational reformer Gustav Wyneken, declared that if youth had been "discovered" by the *Wandervogel*, it was now poised to start upon its mission of spiritually rejuvenating the nation as a whole. The Meissner declaration, in which Wyneken's influence was also evident, declared that the *Freideutsche Jugend* was committed to "shaping its own life according to its own calling, on its own responsibility and with inward authenticity." Endlessly repeated, the formula became the charter of the German youth movement.

In Italy, youthful confrontation with the ills of bourgeois society took more rebellious and scandalous forms. In his appeals to the youth of Italy, Marinetti (born 1876), author, founder of the Futurist movement, and master of the publicity stunt, had no clearly formulated political program but a definite political purpose. Marinetti's myth of youth was coupled with a cult of technology and calls to destroy the past: "We will glorify war – the world's only hygiene – militarism, patriotism, the destructive gesture of freedom-bringers, beautiful ideas worth dying for, and scorn for women." An election manifesto of 1909 declared: "We Futurists appeal to all young geniuses of Italy to fight to the last breath against the candidates who align themselves with the old and the priests."[8] In 1909, still claiming to be under 30, Marinetti stated in the "Founding Manifesto of Futurism" that he was the leader of a movement of youth that would before long – by its own logic – rightly be swept away by a still younger generation: "The oldest among us are not thirty: this means that we have at least ten years to carry out our task. When we are forty, let those younger and more valiant than us kindly throw us into the wastebasket like useless manuscripts."[9] In a speech in 1910, he declared that "to youth we grant all rights and all authority" and evoked a "Government of Youth" that – according to him – could hardly make a worse job of ruling Italy than the present government.[10] Through his lectures, writings, exhibitions, and theatrical stunts Marinetti forged contacts with anarchist circles and gained something of a following among students and young workers.

By 1914, Marinetti had amplified a cult of youth already pervading Italian avant-garde circles and extending more widely in prewar Europe. Marinetti's version of the "youth myth" was crudely anarchistic and aggressive set beside the bluff "boys' adventure" world of Baden-Powell and the convoluted intellectualism of the German youth movement. But some traces of a common pattern can be found in the words of an Italian student explaining his support for futurism at the end of 1913. All the elements of the prewar cult of youth are there, recapitulated once again in a new variation: "The young generation wants to live, LIVE, *LIVE* their *own* life, a life that is intense and strong, without fear of tomorrow, without being afraid of what lies beyond the tombs. LIIIVVVEEE!!! [Fighting + Enjoying] a life of true freedom, of courage, strength, paroxysm, sport, desire, lust, pride, recklessness, of madness if necessary!"[11]

The "Youthful Face of War"

"Sacred youth," declared the Italian poet and agitator Gabriele D'Annunzio in 1915, was called upon by the "priest of Mars" to create a new world through war.[12] D'Annunzio had in his prewar nationalist poems exalted youth and youthfulness;

now, as one of the most prominent spokesmen of the interventionist movement, he urged Italians on to embrace war. The cult of youth that had emerged within literary, artistic, and student circles since the late nineteenth century provided a ready framework for interpreting World War I. Images of young men would come to pervade literary and artistic representations of the war experience, and they left a deep imprint in turn on the popular imagination and memory of the war.

One common theme of early reactions in intellectual circles within the European nations entering the war was the notion of war rejuvenating nations and individual participants alike. The plunge into war conjured up for the supporters of war the prospect of new beginnings, the breaking of political molds, the strengthening of patriotism, perhaps even – in newly unified nations – the forging of a popular national identity for the first time. Imagining the renewal of the national community through war found its counterpart at the individual level in the notion that – regardless of age – those who participated in the fighting would be invigorated by being plucked out of bourgeois life and its mundane concerns and plunged into an existence more intense and more adventurous.

At the same time, the war was associated specifically with the young. The young were depicted as enthusiasts for war; for instance, in the case of Italy, nationalist students were an important element in the interventionist movement that pressured the government in late 1914 and early 1915 to enter the war on the Entente side. The young were also imagined as bearing the brunt of the fighting and the sacrifices of war, even if those who fought included many men in their thirties and forties. The young urban middle-class volunteers who flocked to join up in the early phase of the war straight out of schools and universities became a familiar and potent symbol of the identification of youth and war. Qualities crucial to prewar images of "youth" – daring, idealism, exuberance – made the young seem predestined for heroics on the battlefield. In Germany, the reckless courage and patriotic zeal of young volunteers was encapsulated in the catastrophe of Langemarck, in which a regiment formed from members of the *Wandervogel* suffered overwhelming losses in an assault upon an enemy position. The military record of this episode depicted the troops advancing while singing "Deutschland, Deutschland über alles": this was quickly reported throughout the German press in November 1914 and the young soldiers singing their way to their deaths acquired a mythical status. Meanwhile, the image of the *Wandervogel* in uniform as the embodiment of ideal youth and courage was given lyrical treatment in Walter Flex's posthumously published memorial to his friend Ernst Wurche, *Wanderer zwischen beiden Welten* (Wanderer between Two Worlds). A bestseller, with over a quarter of a million copies sold in the two years following its publication in 1916, it would become a cult book for the German youth movement after the war.

For educated young men primed by the mood of the prewar period to question social conventions and to long for "authenticity," male comradeship, and a simpler life, becoming a soldier could appear to fulfill these aspirations. Enlisting could initially seem to bring – as the playwright Carl Zuckmayer recalled – "liberation from bourgeois narrowness and pettiness, from compulsory education and cramming, from the doubts of choosing a profession, and above all from that which we – consciously or unconsciously – felt as the saturation, the stuffy air, the petrifaction of our world."[13] Rupert Brooke wrote to a friend in January 1915 of his (already tarnished) hopes of war transforming society ("I had hopes that England'd get on her legs again, achieve youth and merriment, and slough the things I loathe – capitalism and feminism and hermaphroditism and the rest") with a bravado that he would not care if he were there to see it or not ("Come and die. It'll be great fun. And there's great health in the preparation").[14]

The experience of war inevitably deepened further the identification of youth with young masculinity, and the association of war with youthful male bonding. Evocations of the experience of the trenches underlined the physical intimacy enforced by cramped living, the importance of male comradeship to survival, and the trauma of witnessing at close quarters the shattered bodies of close friends and comrades. All this contributed to the emergence of a concern with, and celebration of, soldierly masculinity in wartime and postwar accounts of frontline experience. When considering the impact of the war on gender relations, one can see the cult of youth as a factor militating against the visibility of women's part in the conflict – notwithstanding the degree to which women's contribution to the war effort was publicly acknowledged. For young women who volunteered for nursing or other duties at the front, it seemed that their war experience was destined to be submerged by the narrative of their male contemporaries. It was the men who were wounded and died, and any hardships or dangers experienced by the nurses were seen as subordinate to the main story of male heroism and suffering.[15] All the same, contemporary discourses of "youth" could offer young women of the war generation a lever to assert their inclusion in a bourgeois youth profoundly marked by the conflict. In publishing *Testament of Youth*, and in attempting to get her wartime diaries published in the early 1920s and again in the late 1930s, Vera Brittain appropriated the categories of "youth" in which to frame her own experiences. Jotting notes on conclusions to be drawn from her wartime diaries, she wrote, with a note of self-irony, "unfitness of youth of 1913 for its future – contrast between ignorance of that youth & knowledge of present youth, yet universality of certain qualities which belong to youth in all ages – lovely idealism, glorious faith, pathetic verbosity."[16]

The central significance accorded to youth in depictions of war and its victims, coupled with the sense of the war's destructive impact, gave a new inflection to the cult of youth in those countries involved in the war. The idea that "the best were gone" was widespread: the precious qualities of "those who will never grow old" were all the more vivid in the contemplation of their loss. The war also gave a new legitimation to the idea of the mission of youth. The sense that nothing could ever be the same again after such bloodshed gave rise to an intensified thinking in terms of a generation who had shared the experience from a similar age-specific perspective. If before the war the imagined agency of social renewal and transformation had been simply "youth," the talk now was of generations with a mission, specifically the generation of those – young and less young – who were bound by the "comradeship of the trenches." Those who articulated this new consciousness depicted the soldiers who fought and survived the war as a remnant of a generation, homogenized by the experience of fighting, steeled and transformed by their experiences, a generation conceived both in opposition to the "old men" who had been responsible for the war and more generally in relation to the "old order." The downfall of the old world seemed destined to privilege those would be identified with the new – whatever that turned out to be.

Youth in Movement: The Cult of the Body

The cult of youth in the interwar period was not least a celebration of the beautiful body, young, healthy, and whole. Multiple associations and meanings attached to the youthful body in different contexts. In debates on eugenics, the body in its youthful prime represented the repository of the racial stock for future generations, to be managed for the sake of national efficiency. In the world of sport, the record-breaking hero or heroine could be cast as the body-as-machine, tuned to peak performance. In the illustrated press, the pared-down and fashionably attired young woman's body signaled the emancipation of the *garçonne*, the flapper, or the *Neue Frau*. Body culture was also fundamental to the subculture of organized youth in the interwar period. Within interwar youth movements, hardy and suntanned male and female bodies evoked the movements' celebration of the freedom to roam and a life in harmony with nature. But the bodies of boys and young men could also appear – in serried ranks and clad in uniform – as the marching columns of fascism. Images of youthful bodies in motion thus embodied competing visions of interwar modernity.

The growing attempts in this period to harness the principles of "rationalization" to society included a quest to mold the bodies and minds of the young into healthful habits and to promote universal and lasting youthfulness as a key to social efficiency in a fast-moving world. Demographic developments pointed towards an increase in life expectancy and at the same time conjured up the specter of an ageing and debilitated population. The response by biologists and psychologists to this prospect was to maximize the vigor of life across the life span, optimizing human potential and human behavior. From this perspective, "keeping young and beautiful" (in the words of the 1930s song) was not just about retaining one's sex appeal and having a good time. Instead, enterprising scientists, medics, and health reformers promoted the message to keep fit, stay youthful, and maintain an active sex life as an expression of a rationalized lifestyle.[17] "Rejuvenation" techniques included controversial hormone treatments and anti-ageing surgeries as well as regimes of diet and exercise. Magazines depicting implausibly lean and muscular figures wrestling nude in woodland, or performing spectacular leaps on the seashore, provided images of ideal body culture presumably designed to inspire rather than depress readers who might be feeling their age.

The cult of the youthful body was boosted in different ways by the rise of sport. At one level, competitive sport created a space for the display of outstanding physiques. The Olympic Games, revived in 1896 by the Frenchman Baron Pierre de Coubertin, provided in the interwar period a spectacular setting in different European cities – Antwerp, Paris, Amsterdam, Berlin – for record-breaking individual and team performances, with events gradually added to open Olympic competition to women. The *Manchester Evening News* in 1930 celebrated the record-breaking exploits of modern British girls: "One of them won the King's Cup . . . Another flew to Australia. Another won the King's prize at Bisley. More of them have broken motoring, exploring and mountaineering records, and they hardly bother to swim the Channel now. Before long we shall probably see a girl bowler dealing with Bradman."[18] The appreciation of sporting performance was accompanied by a general increase in popular participation in sports. The rise of the seaside holiday and the building of sports grounds and swimming pools by progressive municipalities gave young people of both sexes, but girls and young women in particular, new opportunities for experiencing increased bodily freedom – as well as attracting the scandalized gaze of conservatives outraged by the advent of body-hugging swimwear for women.

For the popular press, it was not just the modern girl as sportswoman that made her such an object of fascination. Across Europe, debates over urban modernity were played out with reference to how the young women of today fashioned themselves: how they looked and behaved in public seemed to sum up the transformations in women's aspirations and to set trends for society more broadly. The look of the young became increasingly the fashion for all. To be in tune with the times, the modern woman presented herself as youthful and, for at least the decade after World War I, androgynous: these were the years of fashions that assumed a boyish figure and haircut, to be offset by make-up.[19] Women were exhorted to diet and exercise, have their hair cut short, and, if tempted by a 1935 tip from the British organization League of Health and Beauty, go skinny-dipping in the middle of the night. The goal was a "healthy, fresh-air body" unencumbered by the trappings of yesterday's femininity.[20]

Youth movements were an important channel for spreading the cult of the body. The interwar period was the era of mass-organized youth, and, where democracy survived, competing organizations reflected the mobilization of the young on the basis of diverse political, religious, and ethnic identities.[21] While intense rivalries and ideological divides separated youth organizations, they shared an emphasis on fresh air and fitness, hiking and camping. Scouting and Guiding grew further in Britain and spread on the Continent, while the hiking excursions of the prewar *Wandervogel* were taken up by a whole range of youth movements. If middle-class youngsters before the war had dominated youth movements, now young Catholic workers in France and young socialist workers in Austria swelled the ranks of those heading for the hills with bare knees, stout shoes, and a knapsack. Czech apprentices and young workers in the 1930s escaped from the cities to "tramp" colonies in the countryside that were given names drawn from the American West.[22] Hiking groups, youth camps, and rallies became a characteristic sight of the era, with uniforms, insignia, and flags heightening their visual impact. Such forays into nature were presented as representing a lifestyle that was rational, moral, and "natural" – in tune with the needs of the young but at the same time setting an example for the rest of society. Leslie Paul, founder of the Woodcraft Folk, a movement that provided a left-wing alternative in Britain to Scouting, typified this in his 1926 statement of the movement's ethos: "We find new life among the green growing things, and new health from the sun and four winds. And this health, together with our understanding, enables us to fight tenaciously for the social betterment."[23]

Youth organizations of the interwar period were so successful because they could build on the trend of the times towards celebrating and liberating the body – making that freedom available to girls as well as to boys. It involved the enjoyable pursuit of fitness, and escape from work, home, and the city streets. It entailed mobility, often under one's own steam, on foot or bicycle, or further afield or even abroad, with companions of one's choice. Coupled with this freedom and mobility was the satisfaction of belonging, a feeling expressed in the paraphernalia that demonstrated one's identity as a group. The physical proximity involved in camping and the comradely intimacy round the campfire intensified the sense of sharing basic experiences. As a template for group activities and group bonding, the strength of this formula of tramping-and-camping lay in its openness. Young socialists or pacifists, Catholics or Zionists, could all form groups within which to combine excursions, and opportunities for leadership and taking responsibility for others, with a consolidation of cultural, political, or religious beliefs. Scouting jamborees – vast encampments with ceremonies, competitions, and games lasting for days on end – could be seen as a way of conjuring up an unsubversive "world of youth" spanning international boundaries.[24] But the uniforming of youth and the ostentatious display of massed bodies could also turn into an aggressive challenge to the existing order, as in the case of Nazi youth in the Depression in Germany and Austria and Falangist youth in republican Spain.

The spectacle of youthful bodies on the move, signaling collective identity through "gear" and insignia, staking out terrain and setting up camp, might convey a range of possible meanings. It could suggest the expanding possibilities for modern travel and adventure, the search for new experiences, and the chance of escape into new worlds. It could suggest a process of democratization and pluralist political mobilization, in which participants demonstrated their rival beliefs through their outward show of strength, advertising their socialist, pacifist, Christian, or nationalist convictions within the public domain. Alternatively, it could suggest a marching column exerting mastery and power over the land it traversed. In an era when popular politics was typically played out on the streets and in public spaces, the deployment of a mobile mass of young fit bodies could be a key political resource – even an offensive weapon. In that process, the rhetoric of generations with a political mission could prove a vital ingredient.

Youth and Fascism: "The Mission of the Young Generation?"

"Modern European politics from Versailles to Munich can be largely explained in terms of a conflict of generations," declared a German political scientist in 1939.[25] Sigmund Neumann, director of an adult education college in Berlin before being forced into exile in the United States, argued that while generational conflict as a social and political phenomenon was nothing new in itself, it was fueled in the contemporary era by specific factors. He identified these as being, firstly, youth's new consciousness of itself and its value ("We are living in the age of self-confident youth"); secondly, the accelerated pace of change in the contemporary western world, with the consequence that "today not only fathers and sons, but older and younger brothers live in a different world, speak a different language, adhere to different values"; and, thirdly, the historical rupture in the continuity of generations brought about by the war, which "not only clearly separated the prewar and postwar period, but also meant the weakening, if not the elimination, of a whole generation."

Neumann's speech went on to analyze the political impact of this generational conflict in contemporary Europe. Prominent in his analysis was the link between a younger generation formed by their war experiences and the rise of European fascism. Fascism in Italy was "the *revolution of the war generation* par excellence"; the Nazi seizure of power was "accomplished almost exclusively by a younger war generation who, different from their elder co-warriors, not only had a romantic concept of war but also lacked experience balanced by a prewar career . . . The Third Reich is led by a capricious generation of young soldiers who, although they returned home, were broken by the war experience." Neumann also diagnosed a "problem of generations" as a cause of weakness in the apparently stable democracies of France and Britain: the missing war generation, he argued, left a gap at the heart of politics, and the Munich agreement was the product of a 68-year-old politician failing to grasp the mentality of the 48-year-old Hitler and the world he represented.

Neumann's analysis is noteworthy as an example of the "generationalism" that featured in political analysis and social commentary of the time. Leftists might reject the talk of the "young generation," seeing it as an obfuscation of the issues of class and poverty. But occasional attempts to deflate the notion of generations were not sufficient to discourage those – even on the left – for whom the idea of generational identities and generational missions had a seductive and even common-sense appeal. Political parties everywhere had, after all, created youth sections in their quest to reach out to new constituencies and shore up their legitimacy. Conservative and nationalist parties saw youth as an agency of cross-class national solidarity; on the left, the rhetoric of youth was combined with the language of class to present youth as a vanguard of socialist revolution and, increasingly in the 1930s, of anti-fascism.[26]

Across the political spectrum, parties and movements claimed to represent "youth" and with it "the future." However, it was fascism and Nazism that appeared to contemporaries as the arch-practitioners of the cult of youth. To comprehend interwar fascism, as Neumann was trying to, required a grasp of the power and appeal of the idea of "youth" and "young generation." That said, historians have revised some common assumptions about fascism and Nazism on the one hand and youth, the cult of youth, and the "mission of a young generation," on the other.

Italian fascism, it is true, seems to fit the characterization of a "revolt of youth." Fascism was born out of a motley assortment of young veterans, futurists, and university students who saw themselves as the shock troops of the nation, determined to smash the left and overthrow the Liberal elite that seemed to have bungled the peace. Its growth and success as a movement from 1920 onwards was largely brought about by the violent actions of young men organized in *squadre*, typically sponsored by landowners who admired their zeal for intimidating, beating up, and killing socialist – and Catholic – activists who had been building the labor movement in the countryside. This onslaught created a bandwagon effect: fascism was clearly where the action was, and every funeral held for a fascist "martyr" was staged for maximum propaganda impact.

The importance of youthful activists to the building of the movement was paralleled by the rhetoric of national rejuvenation in fascist ideology. Its hymn, *Giovinezza*, evoked youth, beauty, and springtime. Fascist ideology was based on the notion of the alleged senescence of Liberal Italy, against which the fascist movement was mobilized to rejuvenate the nation. While the age of the *squadre* members and of the emerging fascist leadership, including Mussolini, gave this claim some legitimacy, Mussolini's backstairs dealing in 1922 with ageing Liberal politicians to secure the premiership rather undercut it – making it all the more essential to stage the "March on Rome" and make the fascist "seizure of power" appear as a supremely energetic and virile act. However, the notion of a permanent revolution of youth – say on the lines of Marinetti's prewar invitation to the rising generation to come and tear up the work of those who had reached forty – was the last thing Mussolini sought. The youth organizations set up by the fascist regime set out to inculcate fascist values into schoolchildren and university students and to create a show of regimented young male and even female bodies to enhance the image of the regime, which by the 1930s had developed a full-blown strategy to project and aestheticize the power of the *Duce* and state through visual display.[27]

In claiming to represent the "will of youth" determined to smash an enfeebled political system, Nazism seemed to repeat the pattern set by Italian fascism. The cult of youth figured prominently in Nazi propaganda before and after the "seizure of power." The Italian fascist cry *Largo ai giovani!* ("Make Way for the Young!") was echoed by Gregor Strasser in 1932 with his *Macht Platz, ihr Alten!* ("Make Way, You Old Men!"). In his recollection of the Nazi takeover published in 1934, Hitler's press chief Otto Dietrich proclaimed the "oneness" of Nazism with youth: "Youth and National Socialism are related to one another in essence, are ultimately two expressions of one and the same concept. Youth is a grappling for a continuously new form of life. National Socialism is the organized will of youth. German youth and National Socialist movement are inwardly one, as spring is one with nature awaking to new life."[28] Such a declaration could suggest not only strong youthful support for the Nazi movement, but also link Nazism with commitment to the radical and the new, and imply a role for youth in shaping Nazism's future. It was true that the Nazi movement had strong support among university students before 1933, and that the SA was an organization largely of younger men. On the other hand the Hitler Youth, while it had grown rapidly from shaky beginnings, was at the end of 1932, together with the smaller *Bund Deutscher Mädel*, still easily eclipsed by other mass-membership youth organizations, particularly those of Protestant and Catholic youth. The simple equation "Nazism = youth = the new" obscured much complexity. If 1934 was a time for emphasizing claims about Nazism's youth and radicalism, this reflected the propaganda challenge of disguising to the movement the compromises with conservatism that Hitler was at that moment set upon – not least at the expense of his "revolutionary" SA. Like Mussolini, Hitler after the "seizure of power" sought to institutionalize repression and to contain the more erratic elements of the movement whose original function – to foment the crisis that his takeover of power promised to solve – now appeared to be over. Meanwhile, it was becoming increasingly clear that the role of youth within the regime was not to be assertive or creative, but, as Hitler put it in 1933, to be "loyal and brave."

Nazism, like fascism, claimed to represent the "front generation" in politics. However, whereas in fascism the "front generation" could be identified with "youth," the passage of time posed difficulties for the Nazi movement even before it was in power. Nazism could present itself as representing the "front generation," whose experiences of comradeship in the trenches had inspired them with the vision of a class-free national community – a myth that disguised the fact that the millions of Germans who had been soldiers during World War I had not only experienced the war in different ways but had also drawn radically different conclusions from it. It might alternatively pose as the "organized will of youth," borrowing the rhetoric of "youth led by youth" and the practices of the "excursion" (*Fahrt*) and the camp from the German youth movement as the basis of its mass formations for boys and girls, and associating itself with its sources of support from those who grew up during and after the war. Connections might be made between "youth" and the "front generation" – for instance, through the evocation of soldierly and disciplined youth. However, they became tenuous now that the veterans were middle-aged and the youthfulness of the front generation was preserved only in the memory of the dead. Pitfalls therefore opened up when Nazi propaganda used generational rhetoric. As Schmidt-Sasse has demonstrated in his analysis of Nazi speeches to youth, such references could have the effect of opening up a generation gap between the regime and the young. When, for instance, the Hitler Youth leader Baldur von Schirach exhorted the "youth of today" to look back in awe at the "youth of Langemarck," it positioned them above all as respectful spectators of a dead young generation that had gone before them.[29]

Conclusion

The "cult of youth" in its early twentieth-century form, together with the "generational politics" with which it was associated, may look to us today like a cul-de-sac. However, at the time it was taken seriously and embraced widely. In the late nineteenth century the belief that society needed infusing with the qualities of youthfulness – vitality, courage, *élan*, etc. – developed alongside discussions about adolescence and the debates on "problem" youngsters. Intellectuals dreamed of liberating the energies of the young to create an alternative culture that would be a catalyst for the transformation of national life. Social reformers and educationalists used versions of the "youth myth" to develop pedagogical models that would combat the ills of "over-civilization" and the distorting and stifling effects of bourgeois conventions upon male adolescents.

The qualities celebrated in mythologized "youth" depended upon constructions of gender. The association of youth with masculinity was evident both in the youth cultures emerging in the pre-World War I period and all the more during World War I, in which a "lost generation of youth" came to stand for all the potential destroyed by the conflict and to legitimate a host of manifestos for postwar political renewal. Girls and young women might contest the exclusively male-bonded nature of generational constructs, but the "mission of the young generation" remained predominantly a vision of virile young men redeeming a society in crisis.

The cult of youth could be associated with escape and subversion as well as with manipulation and the exercise of power. If the liberating potential of myths of youth could most easily be harnessed by boys and male-bonded groupings – to the exclusion and at the expense of girls – there were nevertheless girls and young women who were also fascinated by the notions of breakout from bourgeois convention. But inherent in the new freedoms were also new forms of discipline. By the interwar period, body culture offered a route through which young women could include themselves alongside young men within the category of modern youth on the move. Such inclusion required a degree of conformity with a particular ethos of health, exertion and self-control, and the adoption of a comradely rather than sexualized style of femininity.

Later on in the century, the cult of youth would if anything tighten its grip as the quest for the ageless face and body – both a commodity in itself, to be achieved through particular forms of consumption, and a marketing device for any and every product. In this guise, the cult of youth seems to be a permanent fixture of modern consumer culture, stretching out beyond the present into the future of a globalized capitalism.

Meanwhile, the glorified youth of fascism litters its past. The manipulative and repressive uses to which the cult of youth could be put were nowhere more evident than in the ranks of the "shirted" young men – and women – of the 1930s and 1940s, figuring as a visual display of fascism's rejuvenation of the nation, but at the same time representing the human resources of regimes mobilized for war, "service," and death.

NOTES

1   Frank Trommler, "Mission ohne Ziel. Über den Kult der Jugend im modernen Deutschland," in *"Mit uns zieht die neue Zeit": Mythos Jugend*, Thomas Koebner, Rolf-Peter Janz, and F. Trommler, eds (Frankfurt am Main: Suhrkamp, 1985), p. 14.

2   See Dagmar Reese, "Emancipation or Social Incorporation: Girls in the Bund Deutscher Mädel," in *Education and Fascism: Political Identity and Social Education in Nazi Germany*, Heinz Sünker and Hans-Uwe Otto, eds (London: Falmer Press, 1997), pp. 106–7.

3   See Robert Wohl, *The Generation of 1914* (Cambridge MA: Harvard University Press, 1979), esp. pp. 203–17.

4   See Daniel Pick, *Faces of Degeneration: A European Disorder, c. 1848–c. 1918* (Cambridge: Cambridge University Press, 1989); Robert A. Nye, *Crime, Madness and Degeneration in Modern France* (Princeton NJ: Princeton University Press, 1984).

5   See John R. Gillis, *Youth and History: Tradition and Change in European Age Relations, 1770–Present* (New York: Academic Press, 1981), pp. 95–113; John Springhall, *Coming of Age: Adolescence in Britain 1860–1960* (Dublin: Gill and Macmillan, 1986) pp. 28–37.

6   See Walter Laqueur, *Young Germany: A History of the German Youth Movement* (London: Routledge and Kegan Paul, 1962).

7   See Tim Jeal, *Baden-Powell* (New Haven CT: Yale University Press, 1989), pp. 390–423.

8   Günter Berghaus, *Futurism and Politics: Between Anarchist Rebellion and Fascist Reaction, 1909–1944* (Oxford: Berg, 1996), p. 48.

9   Wohl, *Generation of 1914*, p. 164.

10 Berghaus, *Futurism and Politics*, pp. 57–8.

11 "Spartaco," quoted in Berghaus, *Futurism and Politics*, p. 72.

12 Quoted in Sabina Loriga, "The Military Experience," in *A History of Young People*, vol. 2: *Stormy Evolution to Modern Times*, Giovanni Levi and Jean-Claude Schmitt, eds (Cambridge MA: Belknap Press, 1997), p. 11.

13 Quoted in Dan S. White, *Lost Comrades: Socialists of the Front Generation 1918–1945* (Cambridge MA: Harvard University Press, 1992), p. 3.

14 Quoted in Wohl, *Generation of 1914*, p. 90.

15 See Margaret H. Darrow, "French Volunteer Nursing and the Myth of War Experience in World War I," *American Historical Review* 101/1 (1996): 80–106.

16 Notes for "Introduction to War Diaries" (ca. 1939), in Vera Brittain, *Chronicle of Youth: War Diary 1913–1917*, Alan Bishop and Terry Smart, eds (London: Gollancz, 1981), pp. 14–15.

17 See Anita Grossmann, *Reforming Sex: The German Movement for Birth Control and Abortion Reform, 1920–1950* (New York: Oxford University Press, 1995).

18 Quoted in Claire Langhamer, *Women's Leisure in England 1920–1960* (Manchester: Manchester University Press, 2000), p. 55. Donald Bradman was an Australian cricketer.

19 See Mary L. Roberts, *Civilization Without Sexes: Reconstructing Gender in Postwar France, 1917–1927* (Chicago: University of Chicago Press, 1994), pp. 63–87; Valerie Steele, *Paris Fashion: A Cultural History* (Oxford: Berg, 1999), pp. 247–53.

20 See Catherine Horwood, "'Girls Who Arouse Dangerous Passions': Women and Bathing, 1900–1939," *Women's History Review* 9/4 (2000): 653–73, here p. 665.

21 On interwar organized youth, see the special issue on "Generations in Conflict" in *Journal of Contemporary History* 5/1 (1970).

22 Jiri Koralka, "Spontaneity and Organization in Czech Youth Movements," in *La Jeunesse et ses mouvements* (Paris: Editions du Centre National de la Recherche Scientifique, 1992), p. 225.

23 Leslie Paul, "The Woodcraft Folk: Our Aims and Ideals" (1926). On the Woodcraft Folk, see J. Springhall, "'Young England, Rise Up, and Listen!' The Political Dimensions of Youth Protest and Generation Conflict in Britain, 1919–1939," in *Jugendprotest und Generationenkonflikt in Europa im 20. Jahrhundert: Deutschland, England, Frankreich und Italien im Vergleich*, Dieter Dowe, ed. (Bonn: Verlag Neue Gesellschaft, 1986), pp. 155–7.

24 On the world jamboree held in Liverpool in 1929 and attended by 30,000 Scouts, see Tammy M. Proctor, "Scouts, Guides, and the Fashioning of Empire, 1919–1939," in *Fashioning the Body Politic*, Wendy Parkins, ed. (Oxford: Berg, 2002).

25 Sigmund Neumann, "The Conflict of Generations in Contemporary Europe: From Versailles to Munich," *Vital Speeches of the Day* 5/20 (1938/9): 623–8.

26 On left-wing youth's involvement in combating fascism, see Eve Rosenhaft, *Beating the Fascists: The German Communists and Political Violence 1929–1933* (Cambridge: Cambridge University Press, 1983), esp. pp. 193–6; Sandra Souto Kustrin, "Taking the Street: Workers, Youth Organizations and Political Conflict in the Spanish Second Republic," *European History Quarterly* 34/2 (2004): 131–56.

27 See Sven Reichardt, *Faschistische Kampfbünde. Gewalt und Gemeinschaft im italienischen Squadrismus und in der deutschen SA* (Cologne: Böhlau, 2002); Jens Petersen, "Jugend und Jugendprotest im faschistischen Italien," in Dowe, *Jugendprotest*; Tracy Koon, *Believe, Obey, Fight: Political Socialization of Youth in Fascist Italy* (Chapel Hill: University of North Carolina Press, 1985).

28 Quoted in Radkau, "Die singende und die tote Jugend," in Koebner, Janz, and Trommler, *Mythos Jugend*.

29 Ibid, pp. 135–6.

GUIDE TO FURTHER READING

Christina Benninghaus and Kerstin Kohtz, eds, "*Sag mir, wo die Mädchen sind . . .": Beiträge zur Geschlechtergeschichte der Jugend* (Cologne: Böhlau, 1999). Innovative collection exploring the social history of girlhood and developing gendered perspectives on the history of youth in Europe in the nineteenth and twentieth centuries.

Günter Berghaus, *Futurism and Politics: Between Anarchist Rebellion and Fascist Reaction, 1909–1944* (Oxford: Berg, 1996). Sheds light on futurist ideas and practices and on the cooperation between futurism and early fascism.

Commission Internationale d'Histoire des Mouvements Sociaux et des Structures Sociales, ed., *La Jeunesse et ses mouvements. Influence sur l'évolution des sociétés aux XIX et XX siècles* (Paris: Editions du Centre National de la Recherche Scientifique, 1992). Essays in French or English on a wide range of western and eastern European countries.

Dieter Dowe, ed., *Jugendprotest und Generationenkonflikt in Europa im 20. Jahrhundert: Deutschland, England, Frankreich und Italien im Vergleich* (Bonn: Verlag Neue Gesellschaft, 1986). Excellent contributions in English, German, French, and Italian on demographic, economic, political, and cultural dimensions of youth protest, youth subcultures, and generational conflict in Europe from the late nineteenth century until the 1980s.

John Gillis, *Youth and History: Tradition and Change in European Age Relations, 1770–Present* (New York: Academic Press, 1981). Good introduction concerned mainly with traditions of masculine youth.

Journal of Contemporary History 5/1 (1970), special issue on "Generations in Conflict." Focuses on youth movements and student politics; articles on interwar France, Britain, and Germany.

Thomas Koebner, Rolf-Peter Janz, and Frank Trommler, eds, "*Mit uns zieht die neue Zeit*": *Der Mythos Jugend* (Frankfurt am Main: Suhrkamp, 1985). Explorations of the cult of youth, mostly in German-speaking countries but also in Italy and France.

Tracy Koon, *Believe, Obey, Fight: Political Socialization of Youth in Fascist Italy* (Chapel Hill: University of North Carolina Press, 1985). Illuminating account of fascist efforts to organize young people.

Walter Laqueur, *Young Germany: A History of the German Youth Movement* (London: Routledge and Kegan Paul, 1962). Classic study of German youth movements from *Wandervogel* origins until 1933.

Giovanni Levi and Jean-Claude Schmitt, eds, *A History of Young People in the West*, vol. 2: *Stormy Evolution to Modern Times* (Cambridge MA: Belknap Press, 1997). Broad thematic essays on working-class youth, secondary schooling, military experiences, and involvement in revolutionary movements as well as contributions on fascist Italy and Nazi Germany.

Wendy Parkins, ed., *Fashioning the Body Politic: Dress, Gender, Citizenship* (Oxford: Berg, 2002). Includes three essays – on the Scouts and Guides, on Italian fascism, and the Spanish Falange – concerned with "uniforming" in relation to politics, gender, citizenship, and nationhood in interwar Europe.

Mark Roseman, ed., *Generations in Conflict: Youth Revolt and Generation Formation in Germany 1770–1968* (Cambridge: Cambridge University Press, 1995). Includes essays analyzing pre-1914 youth movements, generation and gender in Weimar society and politics, and the impact and legacy of the Hitler Youth and *Bund Deutscher Mädel* in the Nazi era and beyond.

Heiko Stoff, *Ewige Jugend. Konzepte der Verjüngung vom späten 19. Jahrhundert bis ins Dritte Reich* (Cologne: Böhlau, 2004). Explores the quest for "youthfulness" and techniques of "rejuvenation," ranging from medical interventions to body culture.

Robert Wohl, *The Generation of 1914* (Cambridge, MA: Harvard University Press, 1979). Major study of the "generational thinking" found in the work of European intellectuals after 1900.

Chapter Six

Sexuality and the Psyche

Lesley A. Hall

During the first half of the twentieth century there were radical developments in Europe concerning ideas about sexuality and the psyche, as well as far-reaching changes in sexual attitudes and behavior. New concepts arose concerning the nature of the individual, as well as an increasing belief that issues concerning sex and sexuality were important both in individual life and within society for reasons extending well beyond the "natural" purpose of reproduction. While the extent of the dissemination of new mentalities during this period should not be exaggerated, by the mid-century substantial and significant differences can be perceived. In many parts of Europe, alongside decline in traditional family and community controls over sexual life, there was growing interest in interventions that were not just about regulation or punishment of the illicit, but promoting and improving "good" sex within licit relationships, through measures such as the provision of birth control, scientifically sound and healthy sex education, and marriage guidance.

The historian's understanding of these processes and phenomena is still very partial. Only within the last thirty years or so has sexuality come to be perceived as a legitimate topic for historical investigation, although there were some earlier studies (and early sexologists drew heavily on history as well as anthropology and the life sciences). Besides this issue of the general scholarly acceptability of the subject, there are significant problems of sources and methodology. It can often be difficult to uncover evidence for many aspects of sexual beliefs and activities, while the exact relationship between, for example, codes of law or prescriptive texts dealing with sexual behavior, and what people might actually have been doing, is far harder to establish than merely recording or analyzing what these codes or texts said. Compared to earlier periods the twentieth century has been relatively less studied, and there is little in the way of synthetic studies (there are a number of overviews of what might be described as the modernization of western sexuality, but these usually include North America). Initial research was strongly driven by the concerns of the women's and gay liberation movements of the 1970s, and this had a significant impact on the topics so far addressed.

Certain countries or regions have had much more work done on them (the general availability of the scholarship that exists to an Anglophone audience also presents a problem). There are already significant and sophisticated debates on changing sexual mores in the UK and Germany, and on Russia both before and after the establishment of the USSR, but there are entire countries and important regions for which our knowledge remains extremely scanty for substantial periods of historical time.

What is apparent is that generalization is very difficult and even relatively similar nations may present quite distinct patterns. For example, although the Nordic countries are often regarded as a homogenous entity, recent work demonstrates that there were in fact considerable variations between them. The invocation by the historian Peter Baldwin of a particular "Scandinavian" approach to the control of sexually transmitted and other contagious diseases is increasingly being demonstrated to be about specifically Swedish solutions.[1] Even within discrete political entities there were local and regional differences of attitude and approach: Roger Davidson's work on Scotland reveals rather different traditions and practices of medico-moral policing from those of England.[2]

Attitudes and practices were inflected by numerous other factors. The rural–urban divide was one of these: well into the twentieth century commentators remarked on the persistence in rural communities of the acceptance of premarital sex resulting in marriage when pregnancy occurred. There were also differences between the kinds of sexual opportunities offered by large metropolises with a long historical tradition of license, such as Berlin, Paris, Budapest, and even London, and smaller, less cosmopolitan cities and towns. There were also significantly different perspectives on local moral climates between those who visited and those who lived there: northern Europeans tended to depict the countries around the Mediterranean, especially Italy, as laid-back paradises of (in particular homoerotic) hedonism, which was not the perception of the natives.[3]

While a division of Europe into regions of similar traditions and practices is possible (the Mediterranean, central and eastern Europe, the northwest, the Balkans, etc.), any society within these groupings shows internal variations of considerable significance, such as the north–south divide in Italy. These areas bear some relationship to specific religious affiliations – the Catholic Mediterranean, the Protestant northwest, the Orthodox nations of eastern Europe, the influence of Islam in the Balkans – but these are far from co-terminus, with coexisting groups, or substantial minorities, of different faiths, within most parts of Europe. There were perceptible differences of sexual culture in the various societies falling within one or other of these broad religious divisions. Among Catholic nations, Ireland, for example, was more similar in many respects to mainland Protestant Britain than to the Mediterranean countries,[4] while the differences between the various forms of Protestantism could be almost as great as that between Catholicism and Protestantism. Religion remained a significant factor in most societies throughout the period in question, even if its impact was not usually manifested quite so formally as in the "pillarization" system in the Netherlands. State support was provided for education, social welfare, etc., on the basis of specific confessional affiliation, following a coalition, representing both parties, overturning liberal secularist control of the Dutch government in the late nineteenth century. In spite of their theological differences both churches took a fairly similar (repressive) attitude to sexual matters.[5]

Old traditions of honor and shame continued to influence attitudes and behavior in many societies, independently of religious culture and belief.[6] Different ethnic groups within particular states retained their own traditions. Economic factors also played their part: Simon Szreter has suggested that the difference between the demographic patterns of Portugal and the rest of the "Mediterranean" countries was because its maritime economy affected the status of women obliged to act as heads of households.[7] The increasing entry of women into the workplace and their resultant economic power (even if this only lasted for the few years prior to marriage) was widely perceived by commentators throughout Europe to be having a deleterious effect on conventional moral standards. Marriage patterns altered as improvements in earning opportunities enabled men to get married at younger ages to women of their own generation, instead of marriage being delayed for both sexes, or older men marrying women many years their junior once they were securely established in their professions or ownership of property – changes that had a significant impact on power dynamics within the marital relationship.

While the persistence of all manner of differences must be emphasized, changing ideas and mores were nonetheless an international phenomenon demonstrating numerous commonalities, if following a syncopated time scale in different countries and regions. Certain writers enjoyed wide international influence, transcending the culture in which their works were initially written: the Italian criminologist Cesare Lombroso; the Swedish maternal feminist Ellen Key; the German and Austrian psychiatrists and sexologists Richard von Krafft-Ebing, Magnus Hirschfeld, Otto Weininger, and Sigmund Freud; the English sexologist Havelock Ellis and writer of marriage advice Marie Stopes; the Swiss sexologist Auguste Forel; the Spanish endocrinologist Maranon; the Dutch gynecologist Theodoor van de Velde. Several studies of the development of a twentieth-century modern sexuality have looked at the "west" as an entirety when considering these developments,[8] and in many ways Europe formed part of an "Atlantic" system of the exchange of ideas and technology in which North America was also a leading player (and received numerous émigré European sex researchers and reformers after 1930).[9] While this process of exchange might be represented by guardians of traditional morality as contamination from immoral outside sources, in many cases these ideas were welcomed by individuals and groups already thinking along similar lines. The rise of mass media of popular culture, particularly the cinema, also made a significant impact.

Historians and the popular imagination have often envisaged World War I as a "Deluge" irrevocably changing the world in numerous ways, including sexual morality and the idea of the individual subject. However, the roots of many postwar changes lay in the first decade of the century, or even earlier: certain important strands can be traced back at least to the Enlightenment. The nineteenth century saw the rise of neo-Malthusian arguments for the control of population through contraception (and technical innovations making this more widely available), a social purity movement strongly contesting the assumption that prostitution was an inevitable social phenomenon demanded by the "natural" needs of men, and the rise of attempts to apply science and reason to the analysis and understanding of human sexual life.

In this chapter I provide brief synoptic overviews of four specific aspects bringing about "modern" sexuality in Europe during the years 1900–45: the creation of a sexual science, and the associated or at least overlapping projects for the reform of laws and attitudes; the new solutions arising to the age-old problem of sexually transmitted diseases; issues of birth control and breeding; and changing social attitudes and practices.

Making the Modern Sexual Subject

Much of the work on the rise of sexological science and the associated movement for sexual reforms in law, medicine, and social attitudes has focused on homosexuality (even before the appearance of French philosopher Michel Foucault's *The History of Sexuality* in 1978, which was highly influential in establishing new terms of debate). This was, of course, an important element in provoking the consideration of sexual desires and activities which could not be subsumed to a model of the "normal" concerned primarily with the reproduction of the species. However, the connection between sex and reproduction had been queried at a theoretical level by neo-Malthusians from the early nineteenth century (while restriction of births was practiced much earlier in some societies, notably France). Furthermore, the expansion of European empires led to encounters with other cultures with very different concepts and practices.

An additional impetus to the destabilization of assumptions about sexual drives (particularly those of the male) as normal and natural and demanding social concessions such as the institutionalized "Double Standard" of sexual morality (sexual laxity in the female being severely penalized, whereas the male could sin with impunity), was the rise of a "social purity" movement in the later nineteenth century. This argued that far from prostitution being an inevitable social fact, and preferably regulated by the state for reasons of good social order and public health, it was a manifestation of a culture fostering immoral behavior which could be changed through a variety of strategies. Born in the feminist campaign in Britain, led by the charismatic Josephine Butler, against the Contagious Diseases Acts legalizing the medical examination and incarceration of infected prostitutes in port and garrison towns, this movement struck sympathetic chords elsewhere in Europe. If social purity at one level led to campaigns of censorship and repression, at another it was problematizing topics previously taken as natural and "the ways things had always been," and alongside the vigorous suppression of "obscenity," it advocated disseminating healthy sound scientific knowledge about the mechanics of sex and reproduction. Thus it was creating new discourses about sexuality that were not only not restricted to doctors, lawyers, and agents of government policing, but in many countries were particularly elaborated by women working with voluntary, extra-governmental agencies.[10]

There has been vigorous debate over Foucault's claim for a decisive rupture between acts and identity around 1870, with historians presenting evidence that well before then men with same-sex desires were conceiving of themselves as individuals of a particular kind and part of a like-minded group, and also pointing to the role played by the testimony of "inverts," "urnings," "intermediates," and "members of the third sex" in generating the definitions taken up by medicine and science. The extent to which Foucault dismissed the importance of legal regulation in driving the conceptualization of homosexuality as an unwilled identity, rather than a voluntary sin, applied to a much greater extent to France, where private acts were considered outside the domain of the law under the Code Napoleon (however, there are

indications that laws against public indecency, corruption of minors, etc., were disproportionately applied to homosexual offenders). In countries such as the UK and
Germany, where there were harsh legal penalties – the Criminal Law Amendment
Act of 1885 and Paragraph 175 of the Prussian Penal Code, which applied to the
whole of Germany following unification – there was a significant stimulus to make
the case for same-sex desire and activities neither a sin nor a crime. It also provided
the circumstances for high-profile and extensively reported trials, such as those of
Oscar Wilde in London in 1895, and Philip von Eulenberg, a close friend and advisor
of the Kaiser, and other members of his highly placed social circle, in Germany in
1907/8, bringing the entire issue before a far wider audience. It is therefore perhaps
not remarkable that pioneering studies and polemics emerged within these two
societies.

Attempts to explain "contrary sexual instincts" by physiology or psychiatry emerged
in the German-speaking world during the 1860s. During the following decades both
German and French doctors were gathering cases and essaying definitions over the
whole range of "perversions": "fetishism" as a category was established by the French
psychologist Alfred Binet in 1887. In 1886 Richard von Krafft-Ebing published the
first edition of his compendium *Psychopathia Sexualis*, which went through numerous
expanded editions and was translated into many different languages before his death
in 1902. It remained an influential text, widely read by the public, though intended
as a medical textbook. The Dutch historian of sexuality Harry Oosterhuis has recently
made a persuasive case that its reputation as a mere catalog of stigmatization is
ill-deserved. In *Stepchildren of Nature* he argues that Krafft-Ebing's detailed case
histories provided a voice for (in particular) the "male inverts" who consulted him,
and that their accounts had a substantial impact on his ideas – for example, he was
involved in the campaign to repeal Paragraph 175.[11] Meanwhile, in Britain, John
Addington Symonds published *A Problem in Greek Ethics* and *A Problem in Modern
Ethics* for private circulation, and collaborated with the medically qualified Havelock
Ellis to produce a substantial volume on *Sexual Inversion* (Symonds' name was
withdrawn by his executors following his early death, and the volume as published
was prosecuted for obscenity in 1898, leading Ellis to publish further volumes of his
magnum opus, *Studies in the Psychology of Sex*, outside the UK). Ellis's friend and
colleague Edward Carpenter also addressed the issue of "Homogenic Love," from
the point of view of radical utopian socialism, and published a book-length study,
The Intermediate Sex, in 1909, as well as other influential works.

In 1897 Magnus Hirschfeld founded in Berlin the first organization to campaign
for the rights of the homosexual. Hirschfeld remained a significant and influential
figure on the entire European sex research and reform scene, combining research
and theorizing about sex with activism, until his death in 1935. In 1919 he established a major research institute in Berlin, which attracted international renown. It
was closed, its important collections broken up and destroyed, and Hirschfeld burnt
in effigy by the Nazis in 1933. Hirschfeld's theories were based on a concept of
inborn "intermediacy," in which masculine and feminine characteristics were combined. Though this was a popular way of conceptualizing homosexuality, a number
of other activists at this date, such as Adolf Brand and his group around the journal
Der Eigen, constructed a model of the homosexual as hyper-masculine rather than
effeminate.[12] Otto Weininger, in his influential work *Sex and Character* (1903,

English translation 1906), posited the theory that all individuals, male or female, were in fact made up of differing proportions of male or female characteristics, which he elaborated to advocate marriages between individuals whose balances would add up to one man and one woman.[13]

There were some discussions of same-sex relations between women in sexological works, but usually on the basis of far more scanty materials and case histories. In most European countries there was no legislation against sexual acts between women (which might not even count as adultery for the purposes of divorce), and most cases which came to the attention of the courts related to the specific subgroup of "passing women" living as men and married to women. "Romantic friendships" and "Boston marriages" between women were often regarded with approval, or at least without explicit condemnation, partly, no doubt, because of the pervasive belief that sex in the absence of a penis was not a possibility. Historians have, however, uncovered numerous instances of women who did experience erotic emotions towards other women (though the extent to which these were in any sense consummated remains a matter of speculation). Whereas there were developed homosexual male subcultures in many European urban centers, and networks of male prostitution, female homosexuality was much more associated with private spaces, such as the notorious salon of Natalie Barney in interwar Paris, although there were increasingly some bars and clubs in major cities catering to this clientele. Texts such as Radclyffe Hall's novel *The Well of Loneliness* (1928) therefore constituted important moments for the dissemination of ideas of lesbian identity and the existence of female homosexuality.

Much analysis of homosexuality during this period was trying to explain why those with same-sex desires did not conform to the "natural" direction of sexual desire. Sigmund Freud, however, while seeing libido as the basic driving force of the human personality, was perhaps the first person to consider that "the exclusive sexual interest felt by men for women is also a problem that needs elucidating" rather than "a self-evident fact based upon an attraction that is ultimately of a chemical nature." He claimed that "the sexual instinct and the sexual object are merely soldered together."[14] His arguments for the underlying sexual basis for human emotions and activities, and his theories generally, attracted a wide and international group of disciples, though dissenters also appeared from an early stage of the evolution of psychoanalysis, from C. G. Jung who contested the overarching importance of sexual instincts, to left-wing radicals such as Wilhelm Stekel and Wilhelm Reich, who combined their belief in unconscious drives with political activism, and saw economic and social factors as significant in the formation of the psyche. The rise, development, and internal politics of psychoanalysis, as well as Freud himself, have been the subject of a vast literature. Less attention has been so far given to the various other theorists and movements gathered under the contemporary heading of the "New Psychology."

An entirely different approach to the problems of human sexuality looked to the chemicals secreted by the glands rather than the recesses of the human psyche for an understanding of, and solutions to, problems of sexual desire and functioning. Beginning with the "rejuvenation" experiments undertaken by the eminent Franco-American physiologist Charles Edouard Brown-Sequard in France during the 1890s, and given contemporary discoveries on the role of the adrenals and the thyroid gland on bodily functioning, the potential for a biochemical solution to all sex difficulties attracted a number of researchers. For several decades investigations proceeded on the assumption that there were "male" and "female" hormones peculiar to each gender, and that increasing or decreasing these in the individual would rejuvenate sexual desires, change inverted orientation, and provide a simple fix for these complex problems. A number of treatments supposed to restore youthful vigor, especially in the sexual realm, were being practiced during the interwar period. Russian physiologist Serge Voronoff's "monkey-gland" operations (transplanting the testicles of monkeys and other animals into humans) in Algiers, and Viennese physiologist Eugen Steinach's rejuvenation operations through ligation of the *vas deferens*, attracted a worldwide clientele. On a more sober level an international cadre of researchers pursued research into the secretions of the gonads, finally reaching the startling and counterintuitive conclusion that both men and women had testosterone and estrogen circulating in their systems, though in different proportions. This seemed to hold out (what turned out to be chimerical) possibilities for the readjustment of homosexual desires. This research on the sexual hormones did however eventually lead to the discovery of hormonal contraceptives several decades later.[15]

These projects of research and investigation were largely undertaken by individuals who were also committed to the reform of existing laws and attitudes. Besides locally based organizations such as Hirschfeld's *Wissenschaftlich-humanitären Komitees* (founded in 1897) and the British Society for the Study of Sexual Psychology (founded in 1913), there were numerous international initiatives. Besides those specifically dedicated to particular aspects of the struggle, such as the prevention of venereal diseases or the promotion of birth control, a broadly based World League for Sexual Reform was officially inaugurated at a 1928 congress in Copenhagen, but dated its existence from the 1921 Berlin First International Conference for Sexual Reform on the Basis of Sexual Science. Subsequent congresses were held in London in 1929, Vienna in 1930, and Brno in 1932; a projected Moscow congress was deferred, and then never occurred. There were several vigorous national sections. Because of the spottiness of surviving resources (the central records were destroyed during the Nazi attack on Hirschfeld's Berlin Institute) relatively little is known about the League, its activities, connections, and influence, though it is suggested that political differences caused its break-up after Hirschfeld's death. There was also Albert Moll's *Internationale Gesellschaft für Sexualforschung* (INGESE), which held two conferences, in Berlin in 1926 and in London in 1930, and claimed (somewhat inaccurately) to be "purely scientific" in its ethos. Sex reform was, however, but one of the victims of the political upheavals in Europe during the 1930s and the subsequent outbreak of war, and sex research was also seriously affected.[16]

New Solutions to Ancient Afflictions

While sexologists were evolving new ways of thinking about sex, doctors and governments were struggling with an age-old threat to public health. Throughout the latter decades of the nineteenth century the sexually transmitted diseases had come to seem an ever greater menace to the wellbeing of individuals and society. The long-term results of syphilitic infection in physical and mental debility were becoming more apparent, as were its congenital effects. As the result of the rise of bacteriology and the identification of the *gonococcus* as the causative organism in gonorrhea, this no longer seemed like a mild affliction largely affecting young men (in some European cultures the first dose of "clap" was considered a male rite of passage well into the twentieth century), but was implicated in a large number of cases of hitherto inexplicable infertility, and also responsible for neonatal blindness. Existing treatments might eradicate symptoms, but did not "cure" either disease: gonorrhea tends to be a self-limiting condition, and the early stages of syphilis usually remit with or without treatment. The use of mercury, the standard specific for syphilis, produced its own short and long-term effects on health. The outlook became even more pessimistic in the first decade of the twentieth century, with the identification of the *spirochete* as the microbiological cause of syphilis, and the development of the diagnostic Wasserman test in 1905, which revealed the extent of unsuspected infection within the population and the syphilitic origin of many of the later manifestations.

By the final decades of the nineteenth century the traditional solution to venereal disease control by the medical policing of prostitutes was being increasingly criticized. While many of these attacks were driven by moral and religious objections to making vice "safe" for sinners, there was also a recognition that the system was not working. Even if inspections could have reliably identified infected women, these only took place at intervals, providing significant windows of opportunity for the women to become infected and to infect clients. However, accounts of inspection in practice suggest that any symptom not flagrantly apparent to the naked eye would have eluded the fast and seldom efficient examinations (often undertaken with scant attention to the possibilities of cross-infection), while women with non-venereal discharges might find themselves incarcerated for treatment. Prostitutes and brothel-keepers also had traditional methods of concealing signs of infection. In addition, there was also growing awareness that there were even more "clandestine" and part-time prostitutes operating outside brothels and licensed houses, not subject to even minimal medical inspection.

What to do about this pressing problem was not, however, immediately clear, although there were two major international medical conferences on VD in Brussels in 1899 and 1902. The moral reform of society through the censorship of obscenity, better sex education, and similar methods was at best a long-term approach to an urgent problem. Some authorities advocated premarital health certificates to ensure that men who had been careless in their bachelor days did not carry disease to their wives and offspring: this raised anxieties about what happened if the groom could not obtain a clean bill of health. The importance of greater awareness of the dangers of infection was emphasized, but actually making European populations aware of this threat tended to fall foul of existing obscenity legislation. Propaganda works such as Brieux's play *Les Avariés* (Damaged Goods) were extensively translated but did not always gain exposure to wide, rather than select and already converted, audiences.

There was a huge leap forward in 1909 when German pharmacological researcher Paul Ehrlich unveiled in Berlin his "magic bullet," the arsphenamine compound salvarsan 606. However, while this held out promises of a new therapeutic dawn, there were significant issues over best practice of administration. The drug was periodically injected until a negative Wasserman was obtained (this normally took about two years), but some specialists suggested variations, differences of dosage, intermitting other drugs, and there was no standard opinion. The drug was highly toxic and produced undesirable side-effects. Bringing the remedy to the patient also presented difficulties.

Many countries retained systems of regulation long after any plausible argument could be made for the public health benefits involved. France did not shut down its brothels until after World War II, and regulated prostitution was not abolished in Italy until 1959. Systems introduced for ensuring that the infected availed themselves of treatment also differed. The Lex Veneris passed in Sweden in 1918 was stringent, involving compulsion in certain cases, indeed might be considered as regulation applied to the entire population, whereas the "British system," established in 1917, relied on providing accessible clinics for free, confidential, expert treatment (an ideal somewhat compromised in practice). In the Netherlands the brothels were abolished in 1911, while alongside VD clinics advice centers provided ethical-religious, rather than medical or sanitary, instruction. In Germany, although medical pressure groups were active from the 1900s, new regulations based on a public health rather than medico-moral policing model were not fully implemented until 1927.

The outbreak of World War I caused substantial attention to be paid to the problem of venereal infections among serving troops. Some combatant nations stuck to the traditional expedient of military brothels with regularly inspected prostitutes. Others struggled to find other solutions, from lectures of moral exhortation to the troops, to the provision of early treatment facilities, to the issue of prophylactic packs (these might contain condoms, but at this period often consisted of chemical disinfectants). One by-product of the prewar developments in the understanding of syphilis meant that serving soldiers and sailors were more likely to be diagnosed and reliably treated than in any other era of history, and while a major explosion in infection might have been expected after the end of the war, this was far less than anticipated. In most European countries venereal disease rates declined during the interwar period.

This did not mean that VD disappeared as a subject of concern. Clinics and advice centers were established. Medical and social purity and hygiene organizations mounted extensive campaigns of public education and information, through exhibitions, lectures, campaigns for sex education of children, posters, and the deployment of new media such as film and radio. The level of acceptance and openness differed widely. The Soviet regime in Russia inaugurated a poster campaign aimed at presenting the subject in vivid and simple terms to the populace. The National Council for Combatting Venereal Disease of the UK, however, found its film shows often fell foul of local councils' restrictive policies on cinematic displays. The Spanish government's Antivenereal Executive Committee produced a fictionalized documentary, *La Terrible Lección*, in 1928, aimed at enlightening the public and encouraging them to seek treatment, but there is little evidence about the context within which this was shown or responses to it. In spite of medical support for a public health approach from the 1920s onwards, regulation was not abolished by the Second Republic until 1935. Some countries, including Spain and Italy, issued prophylaxis – which might consist of condoms, otherwise anathema in these Catholic societies – to their armed forces. There was appearing (though far from universally) a concept of the responsible citizen who, if he did indulge in promiscuous sex, took precautions to avoid infection. A medical breakthrough in the treatment of gonorrhea came in 1935 with the introduction of the first antibiotics, the sulphonamides, effective against an ailment previously treated by time- and labor-intensive local applications.

Rates of venereal infection soared once more with the outbreak of World War II, a phenomenon also affecting neutral countries. On the whole, the approach was increasingly about exhorting and enabling members of the fighting forces to use prophylactics or avail themselves of opportunities for early treatment: this might involve the direction of limited supplies of rubber to condom manufacturers. A significant medical advance was the Allied development of mass production of penicillin, which could cure syphilis within weeks rather than the long months required by salvarsan: however, at first, syphilis came very low on the list of priorities for its allocation.

By 1945, though the rate of venereal disease infection remained high, there was an optimism that in the light of these new therapeutic developments, syphilis and gonorrhea were "dying diseases."[17]

Birth and Breeding

During this period the population of Europe was declining overall. The pattern was not uniform and there were significant differences both between and within the various nations. The extent to which the drop in family size was because of the use of contraceptives is a matter of considerable debate, but the most recent research indicates that practices varied widely, between couples using relatively effective methods of birth control (either withdrawal or appliances) at one end of the spectrum and those practicing complete or partial abstention from sexual relations at the other. Contraceptive appliances available at the beginning of the twentieth century consisted of condoms (although the vulcanization of rubber in the 1840s had made these cheaper to produce and more accessible, until the advent of the latex process in the 1930s they remained thick and awkward), spermicidal pessaries and ointments, and female occlusive pessaries such as the "Dutch cap," invented by the German physician Wilhelm Mensinga, but widely publicized by the Dutch birth control campaigner Dr Aletta Jacobs, and many variants on the basic principle of excluding sperm from the uterus by blocking off the cervix. Early versions of the intra-uterine device were expensive and required initial fitting (and often ongoing checks) by a doctor and thus, although the most reliable form of contraception available at the time, were available only to a very limited section of the public. There was a pervasive belief in a "safe period," but until the relationship between menstruation and ovulation was established by the independent researches of Kyusake Ogino in Japan and Hermann Knaus in Austria in 1929, the calculations were made on the basis of wildly misleading assumptions. Abortion was widely practiced among women in probably all European countries, but actual statistics for this secret and private undertaking are hard to ascertain.

The neo-Malthusian case for family limitation on economic grounds had been around since the early nineteenth century, and there were Malthusian organizations in a number of countries, though these were seldom large. By the early twentieth century there was also a case being made for the benefits of spacing pregnancies to maternal and infant welfare. However, artificial contraception was not always regarded with approval: those such as the German feminist and socialist Helene Stöcker and her *Bund für Mutterschutz*, who advocated not only restriction of births but the lifting of penalties on the unmarried mother, were in a small radical minority.

Movements for birth control had a complex relationship with pronatalist attitudes. Many states, or influential groups within them, were profoundly concerned about the perceptible decline in population. In some nations these anxieties were quantitative, whereas in others there was also a concern over the quality of the population and fears that the "fit" members of society were not breeding enough, while the "unfit" were over-breeding. These distinctions tend to map to a considerable extent to Catholic and Protestant nations respectively, though it would be useful to have further studies of regional attitudes in Germany or Switzerland. Eugenics, the idea that it was possible to improve the standard of the population by attempting control over the quality of offspring through selective breeding, is often supposed to have reached its logical culmination in the excesses of the German Third Reich. However, the idea appealed across the political spectrum, being embraced by Spanish anarchists and Russian Bolsheviks as well as German and Italian fascists, British liberals, and Scandinavian social democrats. Its attractions owed much to its association with modernity and the promises of applied science. What "eugenics" meant in any particular context and at any given moment varied enormously. Particularly in the earlier years of the century, there was a blurring between strictly hereditary (genetic) and congenital disorders (first among which was syphilis). In certain cultures there was an explicit or implicit Lamarckian spin (i.e., a persistence of the idea that acquired characteristics could be transmitted across generations) to eugenic beliefs, leading to programs based on the possibility of improving the stock of the nation through environmental and educational strategies. There was also often a simplistic belief in the hereditability of specific qualities, as opposed to physical or mental conditions, both good and bad, and in the mechanism by which genetic factors were transmitted, even after the rediscovery of Gregor Mendel's studies had revealed the complexity of the process. In several European countries programs of sterilization of the "unfit" were put in motion (and persisted well beyond 1945).

Governmental attitudes towards the practice of contraception differed, though none regarded it with enthusiasm. Several nations (e.g., France and Italy during the 1920s) outlawed the dissemination of devices and propaganda completely (French neo-Malthusians were imprisoned), and it was seriously restricted under the Dutch laws of 1911. Sale of birth control devices was not illegal in the UK, but advertising could fall foul of the obscenity laws, which were vague enough that no one knew precisely where the boundary between the obscene and non-obscene lay. During the interwar period movements for the advocacy of contraception and provision of facilities developed in several countries, though the rise of advice centers and clinics in Weimar Germany was brought to an abrupt halt by the Nazis. There were also discussions about legalizing abortion, and in some countries this took place, though usually hedged about with restrictions. The Soviet Republic introduced relatively accessible abortions in the 1920s, but this measure (like other sexual reforms of the early revolutionary period) was severely restricted during the 1930s. Legislation against contraception perhaps suggests that, at least in the perception of governments, it was being widely employed. In 1930 the pope issued the encyclical *Casti Connubii*, hardening Catholic teachings on the matter by explicit condemnations of birth control and abortion, and also artificial insemination.

Although medical and other authorities spoke out about the dangers to health of *coitus interruptus* (withdrawal), it is probable that this, and the condom (the most widely available device, since it was also sold as a prophylactic against VD), remained the most significant forms of contraception. The growing birth control organizations in the UK and 1920s Germany advocated female pessaries, as more reliable and less obtrusive, but for full effectiveness these needed to be fitted by a medical specialist, and presented other problems, both practical and emotional. In theory Ogino and Knaus's discoveries made the calculation of a safe period more accurate, but the rhythm method was still unreliable enough to be known as "Vatican roulette" (it was the only method acceptable for Catholics).

Changing Lives

The extent to which patterns of social behavior around sex changed during this period should not be exaggerated. Manifestations running counter to traditional and conventional expectations were much more likely to be noticed and discussed, while for most life went on much as it always had. Two world wars had significant repercussions on sexual life, but it is debatable whether phenomena occurring during times of wide-reaching upheaval were enduring. After the wars were over, many just wanted to turn back to the status quo, not that this was always possible.

One particular concern aroused by the war periods was the entry of women into the workforce, particularly in occupations previously undertaken by men. While this was perceived as particularly disruptive of gender norms, in most European societies throughout this period women were entering the employment market in greater or lesser numbers (except when specific regimes tried to return women to the home), but certainly to a previously unknown degree. These women were often regarded as a dangerous and disruptive force, violating the previously clear (or assumed to be clear) boundaries between the good woman and the prostitute. This is not perhaps surprising when many occupations previously available to women had been associated with clandestine prostitution, or the necessity to resort to seasonal prostitution. Social purity organizations noted that working women were frequently vulnerable to sexual harassment by the men with whom they worked. Being an earner, if only for a short period before marriage, did have an impact on women and existing sexual mores. Having money of their own might give them some independence from their families (though the vast majority continued to live at home until marriage), and at least some experience of the world outside domestic confines.

Particularly after World War I, commentators wrote of New Women and flappers who were both "unfeminine" (with their fashionably short hair and the new styles) and also sexually transgressive. The extent to which young women were actually experimenting with premarital sex is very hard to ascertain. There was a decline in the institutionalized chaperonage of young unmarried women in many societies, though some groups still continued relatively strict surveillance over marriageable daughters. However, responsibility for maintaining control over her chastity fell increasingly on the woman herself and led to the evolution of new codes of manners to govern interactions between the sexes. Rates of illegitimacy varied widely in different areas of Europe, and there do not seem to have been significant changes during the first half of the twentieth century, except during the wars and their aftermath. While there was some rhetoric about "Free Motherhood" – women deliberately bearing children outside wedlock – in radical circles, both as a protest against the oppressive institution of marriage, and also, after World War I, to enable them to experience maternity if not marriage, this does not seem to have been a demographically significant element. It was claimed that immoral modern girls knew all about contraceptives, and thus were evading conception, but given the problems of access to birth control, and the unreliability of existing devices (experienced even by married women) this seems unlikely on any large scale. Cornelie Usborne has pointed out that in Germany most illegal abortions were performed on married, rather than single, women.[18] If young women were engaging in sexual activity, in many cases this was probably "petting" rather than full penetrative sex. The extent to which first-born children were conceived prior to their parents' marriages suggests the continuation of old traditions whereby a consummated sexual relationship was associated with serious courtship intended to lead to marriage, rather than a revolutionary practice of sexual liberation.

Perhaps the most noteworthy change of sexual mores during the first few decades of the twentieth century was not about extramarital relationships but about a new vision of marriage, as an institution both more companionate in nature and more highly eroticized. This vision was probably most widely disseminated in the works of the British botanist and sex reformer Marie Stopes, and of the Dutch gynecologist Theodoor van de Velde. In 1918 Stopes published *Married Love*, a short guide to erotic bliss within egalitarian marriage, embedding detailed physiological information within poetic emotional appeals. The importance of birth control to this vision was underlined by her issue of *Wise Parenthood*, a guide to what she considered the best methods of contraception, later the same year. These, and her subsequent works pursuing the theme, were translated into many European languages and enjoyed enormous sales. Van de Velde's *Ideal Marriage* was first published in German in 1926, and an English translation in 1928. Again, it combined detailed instructions on the best means of performing coitus to the satisfaction of both parties, with idealistic rhetoric on the importance of monogamic marriage, with extensive quotations from poets and philosophers. Underlying these works was the idea that a sexually gratifying marriage was not only good for the individuals concerned but of wider social benefit by improving the health of the wife and stopping the husband from straying, acquiring venereal diseases, or breaking up other men's marriages, and also by modeling a sound and solid relationship for their children.

As one can see from the immense international correspondence received by Stopes, this vision was clearly one for which the world was ready and waiting. Anne-Marie Sohn has revealed through her examination of letters received by the French Abbé Viollet of the *Association de Mariage Chrétien* that this ideal was shared by the kind of devout practicing Catholics who were attracted to his writings. It remained problematic for many women to whom the idea that sex might be pleasurable for them was almost literally unthinkable, their highest praise for a husband being: "He bothers me very seldom."[19]

A subject which has been much less studied by historians than behavior and expectations of women is the question of changing attitudes and behavior of the "normal" heterosexual male in Europe. Some attention has been given to the effects of war, and the emasculating effects of injury, physical or mental ("shell-shock"), or the psychic effects of national defeat.[20] However, there is some evidence that men's attitudes and behavior were, at least in some parts of Europe, changing, at least partly in response to the altered position of women and the new power dynamics that generated. There were occasional, somewhat anecdotal, indications that men were eschewing prostitutes for non-commercial relationships including some element of personal emotion. The letters received by such authorities as Stopes and Viollet reveal how many men longed for a fulfilling marital relationship. Much work, however, remains to be done more generally on the "normal straight male."[21]

There was an increasing perception of sexuality as an area in which interventions might be appropriate for the better maintenance of chastity before marriage and good relations between husband and wife afterwards. Various forms of sex education developed in different European cultures. Quite often denominational bodies anxious to preserve marriages were active in this field and in the development of marriage guidance and counseling services. In many cases those involved in these initiatives drew on ideas deriving from sexology and psychoanalysis.

In the years following 1945 many of the advances of the interwar period towards new attitudes to sexuality and less traditional forms of behavior seemed to have been stopped or reversed. However, although the 1950s appeared to manifest a return to old-established conventions, many of the issues ventilated during the first half of the century were still seething under the surface, to reemerge in the ferment of the late 1960s. The emphasis on marriage as an individual rather than a family or community controlled relationship, the decline in family size, and the gradual percolation through society of ideas about tolerance for difference first voiced decades before, all signified major differences from fifty years previously.

NOTES

1 Peter Baldwin, *Contagion and the State in Europe, 1830–1940* (Cambridge: Cambridge University Press, 1999).

2 Roger Davidson, *Dangerous Liaisons: A Social History of Venereal Disease in Twentieth-Century Scotland* (Amsterdam: Rodopi, 2000).

3 See Bruno P. F. Wanrooij, "Italy: Sexuality, Morality and Public Authority," in *Sexual Cultures in Europe: National Histories*, Franz Eder, Lesley Hall, and Gert Hekma, eds (Manchester: Manchester University Press, 1999), pp. 114–37.

4 See Tony Fahey, "Religion and Sexual Culture in Ireland," in Eder, Hall, and Hekma, *Sexual Cultures in Europe*, pp. 53–70.

5 See Harry Oosterhuis, "The Netherlands: Neither Prudish Nor Hedonistic," in Eder, Hall, and Hekma, *Sexual Cultures in Europe*, pp. 71–90.

6 Introduction, Eder, Hall, and Hekma, *Sexual Cultures in Europe*, pp. 1–26.

7 Simon Szreter, "Falling Fertilities and Changing Sexualities," in Eder, Hall, and Hekma, *Sexual Cultures in Europe*, pp. 159–94.

8 For example, Vern L. Bullough, *Science in the Bedroom: A History of Sex Research* (New York: Basic Books, 1994); Carolyn J. Dean, *Sexuality and Modern Western Culture* (New York: Twayne, 1996); Angus McLaren, *Twentieth-Century Sexuality: A History* (Oxford: Blackwell, 1999).

9 See Anita Grossman, *Reforming Sex: The German Movement for Birth Control and Abortion Law Reform, 1920–1950* (Oxford: Oxford University Press, 1995), pp. 166–88.

10 See Lesley A. Hall, "Hauling Down the Double Standard: Feminism, Social Purity and Sexual Science in Late Nineteenth-Century Britain," *Gender and History* 16 (2004): 36;

Natalia Gerodetti, *Modernising Sexualities: Towards a Socio-Historical Understanding of Sexualities in the Swiss Nation* (Bern: Peter Lang, 2005).

11 Harry Oosterhuis, *Stepchildren of Nature: Krafft-Ebing, Psychiatry and the Making of Sexual Identity* (Chicago: University of Chicago Press, 2000).

12 See Gert Hekma, "Same-Sex Relations among Men in Europe, 1700–1990," in Eder, Hall, and Hekma, *Sexual Cultures in Europe*, pp. 79–103.

13 See Chandak Sengoopta, *Otto Weininger: Sex, Science and Self in Imperial Vienna* (Chicago: University of Chicago Press, 2000).

14 Sigmund Freud, *Three Lectures on the Theory of Sexuality* (first published 1905, English translation by James Strachey for the *Standard Edition* 1952) (Pelican Freud Library 7: Harmondsworth: Penguin, 1977), pp. 45, 57n, 59.

15 See Chandak Sengoopta, *Glands of Life: Gonads, Sex, and the Body 1850–1950* (Chicago: University of Chicago Press, forthcoming).

16 See Ralf Dose, "The World League for Sexual Reform: Some Possible Approaches," in Eder, Hall, and Hekma, *Sexual Cultures in Europe*, pp. 242–59.

17 This section is largely based on the introduction and chapters 2–8 of Roger Davidson and Lesley Hall, eds, *Sex, Sin and Suffering: Venereal Disease and European Society since 1870* (London: Routledge, 2001).

18 Cornelie Usborne, "'Pregnancy is the woman's active service': Pronatalism in Germany during the First World War," in *The Upheaval of War: Family, Work and Welfare in Europe 1914–1918*, Richard Wall and Jay Winter, eds (Cambridge: Cambridge University Press, 1988), pp. 389–416.

19 Anne-Marie Sohn, "French Catholics between Abstinence and 'appeasement of lust', 1930–1950," in Eder, Hall, and Hekma, *Sexual Cultures in Europe*, pp. 233–54; Hera Cook, *The Long Sexual Revolution: English Women, Sex, and Contraception 1800–1975* (Oxford: Oxford University Press, 2004); Lesley A. Hall, "Eyes Tightly Shut, Lying Rigidly Still and Thinking of England? British Women and Sex from Marie Stopes to Hite," in *Sexual Pedagogies: Teaching Sex in America, Britain, and Australia, 1879–2000*, Michelle Martin and Claudia Nelson, eds (Basingstoke: Palgrave, 2003), pp. 53–71.

20 See Joanna Bourke, *Dismembering the Male: Men's Bodies, Britain, and the Great War* (London: Reaktion Books, 1996); Klaus Theweleit, *Male Fantasies*, vol. 1: *Women, Floods, Bodies, History* and vol. 2: *Male Bodies: Psychoanalyzing the White Terror* (Oxford: Polity Press, 1987, 1989).

21 See Lesley A. Hall, *Hidden Anxieties: Male Sexuality, 1900–1950* (Oxford: Polity Press, 1991).

GUIDE TO FURTHER READING

Anyone interested in pursuing this subject is directed to "SexBiblio: bibliography of the history of western sexuality," online at: www.univie.ac.at/Wirtschaftsgeschichte/Sexbibl/search. html

Edward M. Brecher, *The Sex Researchers* (London: André Deutsch, 1970). Though written from a very 1970s sexual liberationist perspective, includes useful short essays on a number of significant figures.

Vern L. Bullough, *Science in the Bedroom: A History of Sex Research* (New York: Basic Books, 1994). Somewhat US-ocentric, but a helpful overview.

Roger Davidson and Lesley A. Hall, *Sex, Sin and Suffering: Venereal Disease and European Society since 1870* (London: Routledge, 2001). There is a paucity of current scholarship on several countries of significant importance to this subject, and more needs to be known about international initiatives, but this volume provides an overview of attempts to deal with the issue in a range of European cultures.

Carolyn J. Dean, *Sexuality and Modern Western Culture* (New York: Twayne, 1996). A useful, broad overview. The perspective is North American, but Europe is included.

Franz Eder, Lesley A. Hall, and Gert Hekma, *Sexual Cultures in Europe: National Histories* (Manchester: Manchester University Press, 1999) and *Sexual Cultures in Europe: Themes in Sexuality* (Manchester: Manchester University Press, 1999). These two volumes provide national overviews of (mainly) western Europe, 1800–2000, brief analyses of transnational phenomena such as the evolution of sexology and international sex reform organizations, and thematic essays on dangerous sexualities, stigmatized sexualities, and sex and reproduction.

John R. Gillis, Louise A. Tilly, and David Levine, *The European Experience of Declining Fertility, 1850–1970: The Quiet Revolution* (Cambridge: Cambridge University Press, 1992). Essays by demographic historians on the question of the fertility decline that formed such a feature of Europe in the twentieth century.

Angus McLaren, *Twentieth-Century Sexuality: A History* (Oxford: Blackwell, 1999). This elucidates the trajectory of changing sexual attitudes and mores over a broad front, registering both changes and the (sometimes occluded) continuities, and has a strong awareness of particular national traditions and idiosyncrasies inflecting specific developments.

Harry Oosterhuis, *Stepchildren of Nature: Krafft-Ebing, Psychiatry and the Making of Sexual Identity* (Chicago: University of Chicago Press, 2000). A valuable study on one of the pioneers of sexology and his international influence.

George Robb and Nancy Erber, eds, *Disorder in the Court: Trials and Sexual Conflict at the Turn of the Century* (Basingstoke: Macmillan, 1999). Illuminates the effect of both specific legal systems and differing moral concerns on the trials of sexual crimes in the UK, France, and Germany.

Vernon Rosario, *Science and Homosexualities* (London: Routledge, 1997). Although much of the volume is North American in its orientation, several essays address European aspects of the subject.

Richard Wall and Jay Winter, eds, *The Upheaval of War: Family, Work and Welfare in Europe 1914–1918* (Cambridge: Cambridge University Press, 1988). Essays on the impact of World War I on families and family life.

Cas Wouters, *Sex and Manners: Female Emancipation in the West 1890–2000* (London: Sage, 2004). An overview of the transformations in courtship behavior during this period, comparing handbooks of manners from the Netherlands, Germany, the UK, and North America.

CHAPTER SEVEN

The Economy

PETER WARDLEY

The twentieth century was destined to be the American century and its first fifty years saw a transfer of power and influence across the Atlantic. Although the nations of Europe would experience growth after 1900 as indicated by a number of indices, including population, output, standards of living, military capacity, cultural influence, and even territorial scope, from then on the relative position of Europe would diminish in the twentieth century as leadership of the world on all these counts was achieved by the United States of America.[1] If one event has to stand to mark this shift in power and influence from the "Old Empires" to the "New World," it is perhaps the defeat of Spain by an aggressive and expansionist United States of America in 1898 which resulted in the Stars and Stripes flying victoriously over Havana in Cuba and San Juan in Puerto Rico and Manila in the Philippines. The European powers were rather slow to realize the significance of this transformation and even more halting in their recognition of its causes. On at least the first of these two counts, it could be said in their defense that those who determined American foreign policy were also slow in accepting its implications. Many reasons can be suggested for the Europeans' failure to comprehend the shifting balance of world power but, ironically, the successful economic performance of the European economies during the two decades before 1914 did little to prompt a reassessment which would have challenged established views based on inadequate information, traditional outlooks, outdated analysis, or even "Old World" prejudices. At Versailles in 1919, when Europeans were compelled to engage in a radical reappraisal of their world at the end of World War I, lingering nostalgia for a mythic Golden Age, longstanding national rivalries and bitterness generated by the military conflagration, insufficient foresightedness, strategy and even empathy guaranteed the emergence of severe international difficulties within a generation. However, despite its retreat from the European stage in the interwar years, the American achievement, simultaneously beacon and gauntlet, provided Europeans a persistent, ever growing, manifestation of their future. This future arrived in 1945 when, with American troops camped in most of Europe's capital cities, as either allies or occupiers, the ascendancy of the United States was obvious and undeniable.

One factor, and probably the most significant, which explains both the consolidation of European supremacy in the eighteenth and nineteenth centuries and the emergence of the USA as the world's dominant superpower in the twentieth century, is economic performance. In this context, in providing an evaluation of one of the most significant hinges of world history, a valid assessment of European economic performance in the first half of the twentieth century has to be comparative, adopting a perspective which is international as well as continental in its scope. The approach adopted here introduces some of the concepts proposed by economic historians to account for economic development, reviews evidence indicative of the nature and extent of European economic growth before 1945, and uses business history to appraise some of the sources of productivity enhancement which have been proposed to explain relative corporate success and failure. The contemporaneous histories of the US economy and American businesses are reviewed within this framework to provide a comparative perspective.

European Economic Performance 1900–1945

We can begin as an assessment of economic performance within Europe between 1900 and 1945 with two obvious points which apply throughout the period: first, there was considerable variation in the size of the European economies; and, second, across the continent, there was considerable variability in the per capita incomes and the levels of productivity achieved in different countries. However, even at this most simple level, it is easy to demonstrate the instability of "Old Europe" which added to economic uncertainty and fragmented markets, thereby curtailing economic growth. The disintegration of the empires of central Europe added to variability of size of economies, but although war was the most frequent catalyst here, not all these changes were caused directly by World War I.

Czechoslovakia, Estonia, Finland, Latvia, Lithuania, Poland, and the USSR were carved from the war-torn and truncated remnants of the Russian, German, and Austro-Hungarian empires. At almost the same time as the boundaries of these new states were settled, the Irish Free State, after the Anglo-Irish conflict of 1919–20, achieved dominion status within the British Empire, adding yet another independent European economy.

Although Hitler's expansion of Germany, through the *Anschluss* with Austria, the seizure of the Sudetenland, and the establishment of a protectorate over Bohemia and Moravia, is the most famous example of territorial ambition before World War II, such ambitions were not restricted to the major powers. International borders had been redrawn after the First Balkan War of 1912 when Bulgaria, Greece, Romania, and Serbia defeated the Ottoman Empire and almost pushed it out of Europe, leaving only Constantinople and its hinterland as its only remaining European territory. In 1913 a Second Balkan War was fought when the victors quarreled over the territorial settlement, and the size of Greece – in terms of both population and territory – practically doubled within two years. Borders were more certain in North America, though Germany's attempt to entice Mexico into World War I as its ally with promises of territorial adjustments in its favor are a reminder that even the boundaries of the USA were regarded as adjustable by some Europeans. Although changes in international borders present difficulties for economic historians, who search for consistent series that will allow investigation of long-run change, this has not been a major impediment to the constructors of historical national accounts.

Underlying these vital but short-term vicissitudes there remain the dimensions and trajectories of European "Modern Economic Growth." This concept was proposed by Simon Kuznets and it provides a more broadly based interpretation of economic development than those suggested by explanations which stress an "Industrial Revolution." Kuznets constructed historical national income accounts to reveal population growth, increased levels of consumption, rising savings and investment ratios along with major sector shifts in production, with both the manufacturing and services sectors expanding relative to the agricultural sector.[2] Adoption of this framework permits a quantitative appraisal of the characteristics of European economic growth and a relative assessment of economic performance.

One distinguished economic growth accountant, and arguably the most prominent in the field, is Angus Maddison and, if we seek a consistent view of European performance between 1900 and 1945, it is to Maddison's data that we turn in order to examine national economic performance.[3] His national income estimates, which are calculated in constant prices, allow a number of comparative points to be made.

First, the US economy was much larger than that of any single European nation; this is shown in figure 7.1, which illustrates the growth path of national income in the largest economies of western Europe (the United Kingdom, Germany, and France) and the US between 1890 and 1945. The overall pattern is unsurprising: slow but steady growth was achieved in northwest Europe – although the two world wars interrupted this progress while the Great Depression caused a pause in growth

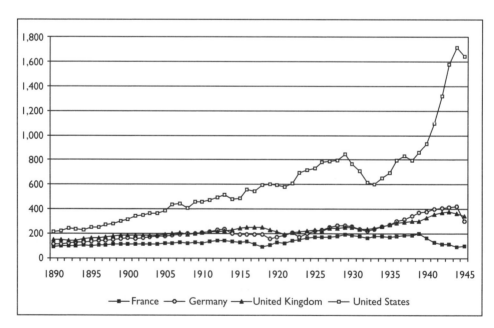

Figure 7.1   Western European and US national income, 1890–1945 (1990 Geary-Khamis international dollars, millions). From Maddison, *The World Economy*.

from which Germany and Britain slowly recovered. During the interwar years French national income barely grew and it diminished significantly in the years of German occupation. In stark contrast stands the American experience of sustained and relatively stable growth until 1929, when a sharp fall marked the Great Depression, after which there was recovery which, after a brief pause in 1938, became rapid expansion as the American economy was mobilized for World War II. Maddison's data also indicates that it was only during World War II that the national income of the United States exceeded aggregate European income.

Second, as figure 7.2 shows, per capita incomes in Europe, estimated as national income, defined as above in constant income terms, divided by total population, varied considerably. Before World War I British per capita income ran in step with that of America, with both economies demonstrating a steady increase. American per capita income level surged ahead in the "Roaring Twenties," while those in Britain sagged in the postwar doldrums, recovering slowly before 1931. Thereafter, freed from the gold standard, British per capita income rose steadily until World War II, matching the American level through the 1930s. Although this was a diminished standard, because per capita income in the USA was reduced by the impact of the Depression, only recovering the 1929 level under the stimulus of World War II, for Britain this represented a significant increase in average income per head over the interwar period. Per capita incomes in France and Germany also ran neck-and-neck, and significantly lower than those achieved in Britain, until the Great War, which depressed incomes. In the 1920s France recovered sooner than did Germany, and appears to have maintained a small lead until the mid-1930s, when stagnation set in.

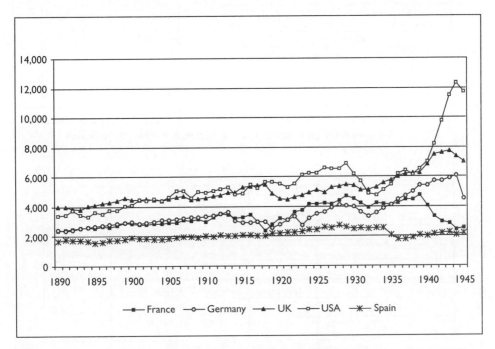

Figure 7.2 European and US per capita income, 1890–1945 (1990 Geary-Khamis international dollars per head of population). From Maddison, *The World Economy.*

The impact of German occupation on France's national income is clearly visible in the fall of per capita income after 1939. Germany, by contrast, after a slow and halting recovery in the 1920s, appears to have experienced rising per capita income until the final stages of World War II. After forty years of slow per capita income growth, civil war in Spain produced a clear fall which was barely restored by 1945, and throughout this period Spanish per capita incomes were significantly lower than those achieved during peacetime in the economies of northwestern Europe.

With Maddison's data we can also compare the per capita income achieved in different economies to examine the disparities between nations within Europe. Figure 7.3 shows income per capita represented as two transverse views of Europe to demonstrate variations from west to east and from north to south in 1912 (American per capita income provides a useful comparator and it is presented as the base index of 100). This figure shows a relatively small gap of about 10 percent between American

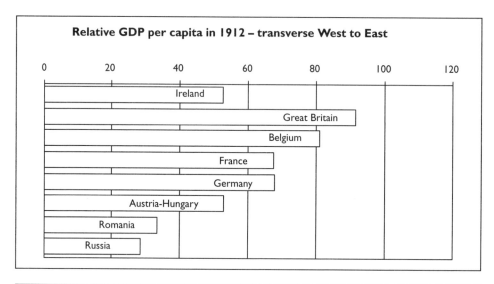

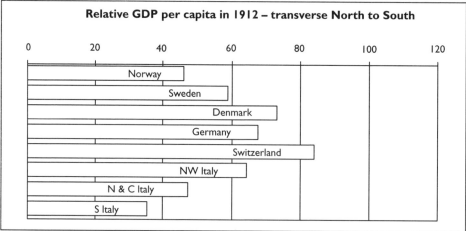

Figure 7.3 European relative per capita income in 1912 (US = 100). From Maddison, *The World Economy*, Zamagni, *Economic History of Italy*.

per capita income and that achieved in Great Britain which, in turn, held a similar lead over Switzerland and Belgium. Germany and France, despite their different economic structures, had per capita incomes which were almost identical. In 1912 Ireland, Norway, Austria-Hungary, and north and central Italy all achieved similar per capita income levels, which were approximately half of that estimated for the United States. By contrast, as shown by the Russian, Romanian, and Italian economies, the eastern and southern margins of Europe experienced lower per capita incomes than northwest Europe, with per capita income equivalent to about 30 percent of that of the United States.

How did the European geographical pattern of per capita income change between 1912 and 1938? Figure 7.4 allows us to adopt the same metric and consider the same geographical traverses across Europe to answer this question. Here the most striking feature is the improved relative performance of both Great Britain and Switzerland,

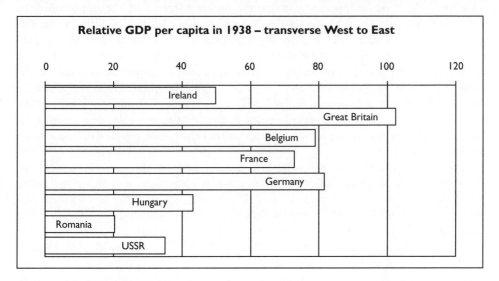

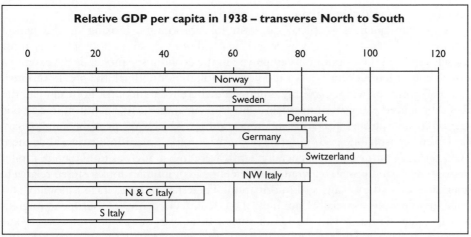

Figure 7.4 European relative per capita income in 1938 (US = 100). From Maddison, *The World Economy*, Zamagni, *Economic History of Italy*.

as both had at least achieved parity with US per capita income. However, with the American economy still recovering from the Great Depression, and controversy over Franklin Delano Roosevelt's New Deal unabated, the diminished status of the American standard has to be recognized. Great Britain still led its closer neighbors, Belgium, France and Germany, and its relative lead had altered by little over the quarter century, during which all had experienced economic growth and higher per capita incomes. In the 1930s the Scandinavian economies, closely associated with Great Britain and members of the sterling area, and benefiting from the recovery of the now protectionist British economy, recovered quickly from relatively mild recession. In Sweden this was assisted by a counter-cyclical fiscal policy introduced by the Social Democrats in response to unemployment that anticipated Keynesian prescriptions. Taken as a group these northwestern European economies resemble a "convergence club" as their growing per capita incomes rose together. This was not the case for Ireland or for Hungary; economic independence and the opportunity to introduce economic policies demanded by nationalists had yielded little in the way of economic benefits to either economy. By this measure of relative economic performance little change is indicated for southern or northern and central Italy as a consequence of policies introduced by Mussolini's fascist regime, though the northwest of Italy saw expansion of the industrial sector and an enhanced level of per capita income. Finally, by this measure, the USSR had made some small progress relative to its tsarist past, though as a broadly based indicator of economic activity, per capita income does not reflect the enormous expansion of industry which had taken place in the 1930s.

Taking a long-run view of European economic growth, the important issues for economists (who are more surprised that history is important than historians) relate to economic growth, convergence, and divergence. Where historians assume that historical differences will be caused by different conditions arising from the past and then explain, at least in part, developments in the ensuing period, economists worry about why these differences exist and persist. In the economist's world, as envisioned in the neoclassical model defined by mobile factors of production, free and full transfers of information, especially technology, and open economies, differences in income should be removed as economic convergence occurs.

As a consequence, a crucial question for economists, looking at the period before World War I, especially as economic conditions in this period of history most closely reflected the assumptions employed in the economists' model, is the extent to which convergence occurred – or did not. Although not optimal, the pre-1914 international economy was remarkably unfettered. There were frictions. For example, the US experienced extensive industrialization while its markets for manufactured goods derived benefits from high tariffs and import duties, which were probably unnecessary and even unjustifiable, even in terms of protection for "infant industries," but these were far from burdensome. Generally, tariffs were low, trade was unhindered, capital moved freely, and postal, telegram, and telephone communications fostered relatively inexpensive rapid exchanges of information. These factors encouraged mobility and millions of people, especially from Italy, the UK, and Germany, left Europe to migrate to the "New Worlds," with the US the major beneficiary of this flow of workers and consumers. This was the world which died in the summer of 1914 – thereby bringing to an end the international economy's first experience of globalization.[4]

By contrast, the interwar period is seen by economists in a most unpromising light. It began with the creation of national states that reflected neither markets, nor established trading patterns, nor areas of product specialization and interrelatedness. To this depleted recipe for economic prosperity was added the collapse of Middle Europe's transport systems as mistrust even prevented trains from crossing new international borders – lest they never return. Although the restoration of peace saw the reestablishment of economic activity, production, investment, trade, and international capital flows looked all too often like pale impressions of those which had been achieved before the war.[5] The protracted establishment of international exchange parities between 1924 and 1928 effectively resulted in competitive devaluations, while long-term monetary stability was also compromised by large stocks of potentially volatile funds and the contentious question of reparation payments.[6] Furthermore, as a result of a shift in the balance of world financial power, effective international economic leadership in a crisis had also become problematic. Britain, previously regarded as the world's undisputed banker, faced potentially serious liquidity problems as a consequence of wartime expenditure and inter-Allied lending, whereas the contender for the role of financial world leader was a reluctant, and perhaps naive, United States, which had emerged from the war as the world's major international creditor.[7]

Further difficulties accumulated as the prices of primary goods, agricultural products, and industrial raw materials fell significantly and, as Kindleberger graphically demonstrates, between 1929 and 1933 world trade collapsed into a black hole.[8] If the economic problems which prompted recession were international and structural, these difficulties were significantly exacerbated by the introduction of deflationary government policies. Although the blame for the depression is often laid at the door of the New York Stock Exchange, which suffered a stock market price fall in 1929, a partial recovery in 1930, but then the long slide to collapse in 1931, it was the sharp downturn in economic activity caused by government induced deflation rather than excessive speculation which generated the unique conditions of the early 1930s. In the United States the introduction of the Hawley-Smoot tariff in 1930 provoked retaliation and further contraction of world trade, and the failure of the US Federal Reserve Board to confront the collapse of the American banking system with an increase in the money supply resulted in external and internal shockwaves that reverberated around the world economy. The international monetary system failed to provide effective cooperation in 1931 as a banking crisis unfolded across central Europe, sweeping away the Austrian Creditanstalt and then the German Danat Bank before threatening London.

The protracted but ultimately futile struggle engaged in by British monetary authorities in the autumn of 1931, as they attempted to keep the pound sterling on the gold standard, was symbolic of the disruption of economic progress which was seen nostalgically by many to have characterized the world before 1914. By contrast, the 1930s saw the United States withdraw from the world economy as it increased tariffs, reduced trade, devalued the dollar, raised interest rates, and reduced international private investment. European governments responded with national economic programs designed to achieve fiscal "retrenchment" that reduced income, introduced "beggar-thy-neighbor" tariffs that distorted trade patterns, and created protectionist trading blocs. As the threat of war grew, autarchic systems were crafted by statesmen that prioritized strategic and military objectives rather than expansion of the international economy.[9] If one extreme case was provided by the Soviet economy, with its centralized planning system directed according to priorities of the Soviet Communist Party, another was Nazi Germany, where the will of the Fuhrer was implemented by state agencies that had been transformed into adjuncts of the National Socialist German Workers Party (NSDAP), but which developed into uncoordinated fiefdoms dominated by high ranking Nazis. Even the British retreated from the international economy to some extent after the British Commonwealth of Nations agreed a system of preferential tariffs at the 1932 Ottawa Imperial Conference. The World Economic Conference held in London the following year failed to provide any impetus towards a reduction in protectionist attitudes. In this environment, international economic prospects were less than propitious. And, when they met at the Bretton Woods Conference in 1944, it was this state of affairs that the policy makers of the United Nations countries were so desperate to avoid as they deliberated upon the establishment of the postwar international economic order.[10]

Between 1900 and 1945 Europe was twice stricken by previously unimagined international conflict. Nevertheless, evidence suggests that significant economic progress was achieved during this period. To some contemporaries it appeared that, with appropriate national and international policies, the possibility of growth and prosperity was not far fetched. A number of material and social indicators suggested that World War II could be followed by better times and the plans made for the return of peace explicitly considered how these might be achieved. This prospect inspired those who were given the task, by their respective governments, of drawing up programs for the new postwar economic order. However, the destructive impact of the two world wars, the bitter experience of the Great Depression, the poisonous legacy which haunted all the many countries which had suffered civil war or invasion, and the ubiquitous dread of unemployment all color our view of the period to the extent that much that was positive is easily lost from view.

Enterprises and Economic Performance

The story so far has looked more closely at one side of economic activity: an investigation of the growth of national income and of per capita income in the European countries between 1914 and 1945 not only explores economic performance at a highly aggregated level – that of the nation-state – but also focuses on income rather than production. While the close relationship between income and production ensures that in most cases the aggregate picture will be very similar, if not identical, the attainment and organization of production is, in itself, important. To present a balanced picture, we must augment an investigation of national income with an examination of the productive enterprise. Here we look to business history.

Business history investigates the activities of firms or enterprises. Enterprises organize the activities which result in the production of goods and services. Enterprises come in all sizes: they range from the independent cobbler or lawyer, who works alone as an owner-manager, to the giant multinational which employs hundreds of managers and overseers (foremen) who, respectively, plan and supervise the daily toil of thousands of workers employed in a number of different countries. It is within the enterprise that production is organized. And it is the effectiveness, or efficiency, with which the owners and managers of enterprises combine the factors of production – land, labor, and capital – that determines productivity and, ultimately, incomes and living standards.

In the context of this essay, this begs two questions: first, how did Europeans organize production at the beginning of the twentieth century? And, secondly, how effective were the people who took the decisions about what to produce and how to produce goods and services? These are very important questions because they allow us to test many of the judgments which have been offered by historians about the nature and effectiveness of national economic performance in this period. Here perhaps the most obvious example is the not uncommon insistence in the literature that the British economy "failed." Within the field of business history the assertion has been made that this was because there was a "failure of British entrepreneurship." However, similar gloomy stories have been told about French businessmen, who are alleged to have been too traditional in their approach to business and innovation, and Russian capitalists, who are charged with timidity and deference because of their failure to challenge the traditional anti-capitalist mentalities of the Russian governing class. And as the German bourgeoisie is often accused of accepting an inferior role in the Kaiserreich, and Italian businessmen are suspected of being adverse to competition, if not incompetent, the emerging pattern would suggest *either* that enterprises across Europe were run, for the most part, by a rather unenterprising bunch *or*, perhaps, that some historians have rushed to offer convenient but overdrawn conclusions. The obvious comparator here is the performance of American enterprise; however, as the standard offered to arrive at this verdict is not uncommonly unspoken, this gauge is not always explicit. Nonetheless, this comparative perspective permits an assessment of European enterprise.

In terms of employment, the majority of enterprises, on both sides of the Atlantic, were small ones, and these provided income for the majority of the occupied labor force. The most frequently occurring enterprise in Europe was the family farm. In this, Europe was not unusual, as this was true of most of the world's richer economies in 1900. In the United States, for example, the "typical" or "representative" enterprise, the most commonly occurring firm, was the family-owned farm which employed permanently few, if any, additional workers; and this remained the case until well into the twentieth century. At the turn of the century only in Britain, Europe's most advanced economy, had the primary sector, consisting of farming, fishing, and forestry, become the smallest of the three major economic sectors, though even here agriculture was to remain a significant employer of labor until after World War II. In 1939 the primary sector was still the predominant one in the Balkans, Iberia, Italy, and eastern Europe and nearly three-quarters of Europe's agrarian workforce were employed in these areas – where labor productivity was relatively low. By contrast, in the high income per capita economies (see figure 7.3) the industrial and services sectors employed three-quarters of the labor force and produced an even larger share of national income.

Europe consisted of a large number of agricultural regions and a great variety of agrarian practices; history collaborated with geography to determine regional and local specializations so that there was considerable variation in the nature of agriculture practices. Reluctance to leave the land was also an almost universal sentiment, which was most often broken by economic necessity, persecution, or ambition. Not infrequently, family possession of land was maintained even when peasants migrated to become workers, as remittance payments supplemented the family's inadequate agricultural income. In many areas of Europe, particularly in the south and east, the owner of a small farm was often the employer of a small number of the landless poor who comprised a large portion of the rural population. However, the existence of very large estates was far from a guarantee that agriculture would be progressive and prosperous.

Spain's territorially extensive and varied agricultural regions demonstrated the characteristics and problems of both the *latifundia*, the large landed estate, and its opposite, the *minifundia*.[11] In both systems traditional crops, age-old agrarian practices, and ossified social relations dominated to replicate low productivity regimes and rural discontent. Demands for agrarian reform revealed political discontent on the part of both those who aspired to land ownership and those whose ownership of the land was threatened; this irreconcilable contest was a major cause of the Spanish Civil War. A different civil war, at the opposite end of Europe, had seen the Bolsheviks triumph with slogans which promised land to the people and a policy that nationalized land ownership but recognized the rights of peasants to use what they had already taken into their own hands. However, by the end of the 1920s a number of factors conspired to provoke Stalin's sudden decision in 1929 to collectivize Soviet agriculture: a scarcity of rural capital; impatience over the growth of agricultural production and reluctance on the part of peasants to amalgamate holdings or voluntarily join state farms; the isolation of "right-wing deviationists," including Bukharin; and the apprehensions of the Communist Party concerning the loyalty of the countryside. Collectivization lurched forward in 1930 and then, after a brief pause, was ruthlessly enforced to transform Soviet agriculture by 1934, without regard for lost production or cost in human lives. Standing in sharp contrast, there were the wealthier regions of northwest Europe, notably Denmark, England, and Holland, where high productivity agriculture was achieved by intensive, mechanized, and highly specialized farming methods combined with well-established distribution networks that linked producers closely to their markets and often adopted cooperative organizations.

It is when we turn to the large-scale enterprise that we find the most obvious contrast between the established literature and recent research. And here we can identify two major themes. First, the large American industrial firm is often assumed to be the source of America's productivity lead at the beginning of the twentieth century and, secondly, the United States is frequently identified as the home of "big business." Both of these assumptions are questionable. On the first count, America's productivity lead over all European countries was the result of a comprehensively superior performance across the full spectrum of economic activities. In every sector, American small-scale firms and medium-size enterprises, as well as large corporations, tended to exhibit greater efficiency than their European counterparts. Consequently, America's relatively high productivity, and therefore the relatively high living standards enjoyed by Americans, owed as much, if not more, to the efficiency of family farms on the prairies as it did to large industrial corporations.

Secondly, large enterprises, however they are measured, be it by output or by inputs of capital or labor, were well established in Europe by 1900. On the eve of World War I Europe provided half of the world's hundred largest enterprises, measured by the size of workforce. The Russian State Railway, the largest enterprise in the world, employed more than half a million workers, as did the second largest, imperial Germany's Prussian-Hessian State Railway. Among the other European enterprises which appear in ranks of the ten largest in the world were Germany's Reichspost, the United Kingdom's General Post Office, the Austrian State Railway, the Italian State Railway, and the Hungarian Royal State Railway Company. Two points stand out: first, the importance of large state enterprise, and, secondly, remembering that telecommunications were provided by the post offices, the very significant contribution of the large firm to the transport and communications systems of the European economies. Only three American enterprises appear in the ranks of the world's ten largest employers in 1912: the US Post Office, the American Telephone & Telegraph Company, and the United States Steel Corporation. The US Post Office, a state-owned communications enterprise, corresponds with its European counterparts. There are only two privately owned companies, both American, but as AT&T operated in a network industry as a provider of telephone services, the US Steel Corporation was the sole manufacturing company. By these criteria in 1912, the world's typical "big business" was European, state owned, and active in the services sector, rather than the American, privately owned manufacturing corporation suggested by conventional wisdom.[12]

It is significant that, at the turn of the century, the large enterprise was a relatively new phenomenon in the United States and this novelty goes some way to explaining why Americans reacted so strongly to its appearance whereas, to contemporary Europeans, this was a less spectacular and far from novel development. The significance of this is all the more striking when one specific element of the conventional story is examined; this is the role which a traditional interpretation awards to Henry Ford.

Ford introduced and developed an industrial system which standardized factory practices, employed machine tools, constructed units from interchangeable components, and honed moving assembly line methods to achieve mass production. In the interwar years, by which time they had been adopted in Europe, these components were to be identified as integral to modern factory organization and, when unified as a system, were often termed "Fordism."

However, far from being typical, Henry Ford was in many ways a revolutionary businessman, a true mold-breaking entrepreneur, who adopted and adapted the assembly line to raise productivity in the automobile industry to unprecedented levels. Furthermore, although Ford established his new enterprise, the Ford Motor Company, in 1903, it was only a decade later at his new Highland Park factory in Detroit that he was able systematically to implement standardization, interchangeability, and assembly line production. Additionally, in the face of absenteeism and a high turnover of labor, Ford introduced a high wage strategy, the $5 day, to compensate workers for the effort and drudgery they experienced on the assembly line. Significant though the Ford Company's output was to become, not only was its contribution too small, relative to the whole US economy, but also its growth occurred much too late to explain America's already significant productivity lead over Europe in the two decades before 1914. Even as late as 1912 the Ford Motor Company employed barely 7,000 workers. Thereafter the company experienced rapid expansion. When the last Model T rolled off the assembly line in 1927 over 15 million had been produced.

While the huge American market provided the primary impetus for this expansion, this was supplemented by the growth of demand in Europe. Almost immediately after the company's creation, Ford's cars and tractors were sold in the European market, with sales offices established in France, Russia, and Scandinavia – although England was the focus of Ford's European activities. In World War I Ford delivered transport equipment urgently required by Allied armies and, with the restoration of peace, it expanded production to meet growing consumer demand. In 1911 Ford started production in Europe at its Trafford Park assembly plant, Manchester and, after World War I, additional factories were built at Barcelona, Bordeaux, Copenhagen, Cologne, Cork, and Paris. In 1928 the company decided that Dagenham, near London, would act as Ford's European Detroit, and a vast complex was constructed to manufacture parts, assemble cars, and supply other subsidiary plants. Managerial difficulties, combined with the difficulties caused by the Great Depression, necessitated a major reorganization of the company and in 1932 the European management at Dagenham coordinated the introduction of the Ford Eight (Model Y), Ford's first car designed specially for the European market, at several of its European assembly plants.

The impact of Ford was even more considerable than the company's impressive contribution to European road transport equipment and farm mechanization. In the 1930s advisors from the Ford Company were influential in both the Soviet Union and Nazi Germany; at the Gorki tractor factory in Russia they assisted in the design of factories and specification of assembly processes and they acted as consultants to the Volkswagen project. Indirectly, the Ford Motor Company also provided a blueprint for European manufacturing companies. At Fiat (*Fabbrica Italiana di Automobili Torino*), for example, Giovanni Agnelli not only adopted its mass production methods at his Il Lingotto factory in 1920 but, by establishing subsidiary companies in France, Germany, and Poland, he also followed Ford's expansionist policy of opening factories in other countries. Henry Ford also exercised personal influence in interwar Europe; greatly admired by Adolf Hitler, Ford was a notorious antisemite and a longstanding supporter of the Nazi Party. Flirting with fascism, however, was not confined to Ford; after World War II several US-owned multinationals, including General Electric, General Motors, IBM, IT&T, and Standard Oil of New Jersey, were to face accusations prompted by their business activities in Nazi Germany.

However, the Ford Motor Company was but one component of the system of big business that impacted upon the economies of North America and Europe between 1900 and 1945. Alfred Chandler, the undisputed pioneering authority of business history, devotes relatively little attention to the Ford Motor Company, as he attributes superior American corporate performance to managerial hierarchy and organizational learning rather than the exercise of personal authority and individualistic flair. Indeed, one consequence of his research was to redirect the attention of historians who previously had concentrated on the less constructive activities of the "Robber Barons."

For Chandler, it was the deployment of the "Visible Hand" of management, achieved by the implementation of departmental structures to exploit unprecedented economies of scale and scope, that enabled the large industrial corporation to supplant the "Invisible Hand" of the market, which economists had identified as the source of economic efficiency ever since the publication of Adam Smith's *Wealth of*

Nations in 1776. The purposeful development of managerial hierarchies by full-time salaried executives provided the crucial ingredient in Chandler's explanation of the success of the large American industrial corporation.

The growth of businesses was often accompanied by an expansion in the range of the economic activities undertaken, so that the scope of a firm often expanded along with its size. Horizontal and vertical integration resulted in the creation of large multi-unit industrial enterprises that could only thrive if order was imposed by senior managers who monitored and co-coordinated the activities performed by middle or lower managers, supervisors, and workers; the implementation of this corporate strategy required a change in organizational structure. Significant economies of scale were achieved by investment in new production processes in the petroleum, chemical, metallurgical, and engineering industries, all of which were relatively more capital intensive than traditional manufacturing industries such as textiles, clothing, furniture, and publishing.

Outstanding examples of America's large integrated industrial corporations at the beginning of the twentieth century include Standard Oil, International Harvester, Du Pont, and the United States Rubber Company. Furthermore, and especially for those that could sell directly to the retailer, there were gains to be obtained by investing in an extensive distribution network; examples here include the American Tobacco Co., Proctor & Gamble, producers of household chemicals, and two meat-packing companies, Armour & Co. and Swift & Co. The most conspicuous was the Singer Manufacturing Company, prominent in North America, the British Empire, and in continental Europe, which created distribution networks across the globe to sell its ubiquitous sewing machine. Singer also illustrates another Chandlerian theme, that of "first mover advantage": although it faced competition, Singer invested in technology and established extensive customer-serving facilities that guaranteed its leading status. By contrast, Chandler suggests that the United States Steel Corporation, the world's largest company at its creation, a bank-sponsored amalgamation which amounted to little more than the sum of its federated parts, failed to invest in management, product research, and distribution and consequently suffered erosion of its first mover advantage.[13]

These influences were not restricted to North America and many of these firms had a presence in, and an impact on, Europe. For example, both Armour and Swift invested in extensive distribution networks, including freezing plants and shipping facilities, which enabled them to sell their processed food products in European markets. In 1901 American Tobacco's expansion into European markets prompted a defensive response in Britain when 17 British firms created the Imperial Tobacco Company. These two industrial giants then cooperated to create a jointly owned company, the British-American Tobacco Company, which was designed to act in markets outside America and Britain. BAT, which became a British company after antitrust action taken by the US Supreme Court saw American Tobacco broken up in 1911, became the dominant tobacco manufacturing company in Germany through its acquisition and expansion of Jasmatzi, previously an American Tobacco subsidiary.

Chandler suggests that America's superior economic performance owes much to the three-pronged investment strategy, which committed resources to production facilities, sales networks, and managerial hierarchies, developed by its industrial corporations. To make a trans-Atlantic comparison, Chandler identifies three national industrial systems: America's "competitive managerial capitalism," Germany's "cooperative managerial capitalism," and Britain's "personal capitalism." Each system is weighed in the balance, to the clear disadvantage of the British. Despite the eagerness of German firms to operate as members of cartels, which uniquely were both legal and amazingly multitudinous, and the active participation of the banks on the boards of industrial companies, reflective of their long-term investments, that Chandler identifies as distinctive features of the German system, he suggests that in their investment strategies, managerial structures, and economic performance, German industrial firms more closely resembled American corporations than did their British counterparts.[14]

Although business organization and practices may explain some aspects of Europe's inferior industrial performance relative to the United States, the adoption of the multidivisional form of corporate organization *per se* can be eliminated as a major explanatory factor before World War II. Far from being a carefully planned organizational innovation, the multidivisional structure pioneered by Pierre Du Pont in 1921 was a response to crisis. As the short-lived boom which followed the end of World War I was succeeded by deep economic depression, like many other US companies Du Pont and General Motors faced financial catastrophe. They were only saved from bankruptcy by radical action in the form of a managerial overhaul which resulted in the imposition of multidivisional structures at both companies. This form of organization spread, both within the USA and abroad, but the rate of diffusion was slow. It is important to remember that until 1921 the departmental structure remained the most advanced form of business organization in the United States, and that it would remain the most prevalent form of organization there until at least World War II.

Chandler's publications have raised a number of salient questions which will prompt comparative research for some time yet. However, it is fair to report that he tends to assume the inferior performance of British firms and that his preferred measure of performance, the relative size of an industrial corporation's assets, is far from optimal. Cassis has shown recently that by this standard and by others, including profitability, size of workforce, and longevity, Britain provided a larger contingent to the ranks of Europe's large industrial companies than did its German and French neighbors throughout the twentieth century.[15]

Furthermore, Chandler has little to say about the services sectors in the twentieth century, though a significant portion of the productivity gains obtained in the half century before 1945 were provided by companies in these sectors. Here he is not alone. Although the national income data at our disposal clearly demonstrate the sizable and significant contribution of services, we are less certain about how this was achieved. Recently published research does not suggest that the large corporations in the services sectors of western Europe lagged behind their American counterparts. British banks, for example, which were much larger than US banks, acted according to the three-pronged investment strategy identified by Chandler.[16] At the end of the 1920s English retail banks consolidated national branch networks, invested in mechanization, and overhauled their management structures while adopting the same enthusiasm to engage in rationalization contemporaneously demonstrated by Chandler's US industrial firms.

In European countries, as in the US, there was a lag between the initial adoption of a new technique or organizational form and the broad diffusion of these innovations across the economy as a whole. Although national circumstances differed – with high per capita income western Europe more closely resembling the United States than poorer regions of southern Europe – big business in interwar Europe was successful, profitable and productive. The shock of World War II, which not only stimulated managerial change within large US corporations but also disrupted and fragmented the corporate systems built by giant European companies, contributed directly to the dominance which American big business would exercise for several decades after 1945.

Conclusion

The European economies experienced discernable economic growth which raised the average income per capita of most Europeans during the four decades after 1900, though the two world wars and the Depression of the early 1930s were detrimental to economic performance. While average incomes increased at a rate which was far from dramatic (the rates of growth were lower than those which were to be achieved during the "Golden Age" of the third quarter of the twentieth century, though higher than those experienced in either the interwar years or during the mid-nineteenth century), the economic gains made in the four decades before 1945 were significant, and for many these resulted in an increase in real living standards.

However, despite the rising average income per capita which was achieved across the continent, poverty remained an obvious feature of every European country, though the incidence, extent, and severity of its impact varied considerably. Marked inequality of income, and even more striking inequality of wealth, is a characteristic of capitalism, which was the dominant form of economic organization in all European countries at the beginning of the twentieth century. While vestigial remnants of previous economic structures survived, remaining to varying degrees in different countries, the market provided the predominant organizing principle of economic activity in Europe. Even if the hegemony of the capitalist class was far from unchallenged, particularly in the less economically advanced countries, where the landed elites resisted threats to their traditional supremacy, capitalism was triumphant.

Nevertheless, economic development was uneven across the continent. Longstanding inequalities in relative incomes were maintained which resulted in large differences in the average level of income experienced in the geographical regions which comprise Europe. Where the inhabitants of countries which fringed the North Sea basin – the Belgians, British, Danes, and the Dutch – enjoyed relatively high levels of per capita income, those who lived in countries bordering the Baltic or Mediterranean or Black Sea experienced significantly lower levels of income. In addition to these disparities in national per capita income, there were significant regional differences within countries.[17] The coal-rich and industrialized areas in northern France and Germany's Ruhr generated higher average per capita incomes than those earned in the more agricultural regions of southern France or eastern Prussia.

However, to view economic growth in Europe largely as a result of a shift from agriculture to industry would not only provide too narrow a perspective but also would exclude recognition of the major structural change in economic activity which would come to dominate all the developed economies of the world. Until relatively recently, however, the significance of the development of the services sectors remained

under-appreciated or even unrecognized. Although this phenomenon had been
noted by some contemporaries, in the aftermath of World War II and for at least
three decades afterwards the implications of this development tended to be under-
appreciated by historians, who continued to stress the primacy of industry; while
often defined more broadly to include all aspects of economic development, the use
of the term "industrialization" often led to an overemphasis on manufacturing.
Similarly, historians have probably placed too much emphasis on the contribution of
the large industrial corporation in the achievement of America's relative productivity
lead. As it is probable that European big business lagged relatively little behind
American practice in the years before 1940, it is more likely that the relative efficiency
of the US economy was a result of superior economic performance across a broad
range of economic activities. In the postwar years the magnitude of America's economic dominance prompted a view that Europe had continued to lose ground relative to the US throughout the first half of the twentieth century. By contrast, it
appears that the US economy faltered significantly in the 1930s, when some European
economies prospered in relative terms, and that it only recovered to achieve its commanding economic lead, in both absolute and relative terms, under the stimulus of
World War II. However, while there were significant differences which characterized
different national experiences, it is important to recognize the similarities which the
European economies had, both with one another and with the United States. One
major commonality was the experience of modern economic growth.

Now, at the beginning of the twenty-first century, it is difficult to fail to recognize
the relative importance and significance of the services sectors, as they provide the bulk
of the jobs and by far the majority share of output in all developed economies. One
hundred years ago this prospect was far from obvious to contemporaries, although our
historical datasets reveal that the more broadly defined process of "modern economic
growth" was already underway. Scholarship undertaken in the last twenty years has
consistently demonstrated the importance of sectoral change, with the services sectors
playing a role which was much more active than had previously been accepted. In the
1930s, contemporaries such as Simon Kuznets and Colin Clark[18] were grappling with
their newly created datasets, trying to recognize the future in their present. Thanks to
the efforts of these pioneering proponents of the concept of modern economic growth
it has been possible to construct a clearer picture which allows us to review the process
of European economic growth in the first half of the twentieth century. However,
there is still much that we do not know.

NOTES

1 See Brian R. Mitchell, *International Historical Statistics: Europe 1750–2000*, 5th edn
   (London: Palgrave Macmillan, 2003); B. R. Mitchell, *International Historical Statistics:
   The Americas 1750–2000*, 5th edn (London: Palgrave Macmillan, 2003).
2 S. Kuznets, *Modern Economic Growth* (New Haven CT: Yale University Press, 1966) and
   S. Kuznets, *Economic Growth of Nations: Total Output and Production Structure*
   (Cambridge MA: Harvard University Press, 1971).
3 Angus Maddison, *The World Economy: A Millennial Perspective* (Paris: Development
   Centre of the Organization for Economic Co-operation and Development, 2001); see
   also A. Maddison, *Phases of Capitalist Development* (Oxford: Oxford University Press,

1982) and A. Maddison, *Monitoring the World Economy* (Paris: Development Centre of the OECD, 1995). Maddison's data for national income, population, and per capita income, which inform the next section, is available as a spreadsheet at his personal website: www.eco.rug.nl/~Maddison/.

4 See A. G. Kenwood and A. L. Lougheed, *The Growth of the International Economy, 1820–1990*, 3rd edn (London: Routledge, 1992), pp. 9–158; J. Foreman-Peck, *A History of the World Economy: International Economic Relations since 1850* (Brighton: Wheatsheaf Books, 1983), pp. 127–82.

5 See Derek H. Aldcroft, *From Versailles to Wall Street* (London: Allen Lane, 1977).

6 See C. H. Feinstein, P. Temin, and G. Toniolo, *The European Economy between the Wars* (Oxford: Oxford University Press, 1997).

7 See C. P. Kindleberger, *The World in Depression 1929–1939*, 2nd edn (London: Penguin, 1987), pp. 70–94.

8 Kindleberger, *World in Depression*, p. 170.

9 See Kenwood and Lougheed, *Growth of the International Economy*, pp. 163–228; Foreman-Peck, *History of the World Economy*, pp. 186–253.

10 See Sidney Pollard, *Wealth and Poverty: An Economic History of the 20th Century* (London: Harrap, 1990), pp. 94–127.

11 See Gabriel Tortella, *The Development of Modern Spain: An Economic History of the Nineteenth and Twentieth Century* (Cambridge MA: Harvard University Press, 2000), pp. 50–72.

12 See Peter Wardley, "Business Size and Performance before 1914: An International Perspective," in Y. Cassis and A. Colli, *Business Performance in the 20th Century* (Cambridge: Cambridge University Press, 2006).

13 A. Chandler, *Scale and Scope: The Dynamics of Industrial Capitalism* (Cambridge MA: Belknap/Harvard University Press, 1990), pp. 131–40.

14 Chandler, *Scale and Scope*, pp. 235–7, 496–502, 591–2, 594–605.

15 Youssef Cassis, *Big Business: The European Experience in the Twentieth Century* (Oxford: Oxford University Press, 1997).

16 See P. Wardley, "The Commercial Banking Industry and its Part in the Emergence and Consolidation of the Corporate Economy in Britain before 1940," *Journal of Industrial History* 3 (2000): 71–96.

17 See S. Pollard, *Peaceful Conquest: The Industrialisation of Europe 1760–1970* (Oxford: Oxford University Press, 1981), pp. xiv–xv, 35, 111–23, 220–51.

18 C. Clark, *The Conditions of Economic Progress* (London: Macmillan, 1940).

GUIDE TO FURTHER READING

Alfred Chandler, *Scale and Scope: The Dynamics of Industrial Capitalism* (Cambridge MA: Belknap/Harvard University Press, 1990). Provides the seminal study of the emergence of the modern industrial corporation in the USA, Britain, and Germany; it augments and expands *The Visible Hand: The Managerial Revolution in American Business* (Cambridge MA: Belknap/Harvard University Press, 1977) and *Strategy and Structure: Chapters in the History of the American Industrial Enterprise* (Cambridge MA: MIT Press, 1962).

Charles H. Feinstein, Peter Temin, and Gianni Toniolo, *The European Economy between the Wars* (Oxford: Oxford University Press, 1997). Short, pithy, and extremely valuable.

James Foreman-Peck, *A History of the World Economy: International Economic Relations since 1850*, 2nd edn (Brighton: Wheatsheaf Books, 1994). An economist's history of the international economy.

A. G. Kenwood and A. L. Lougheed, *The Growth of the International Economy, 1820–1990: An Introductory Text*, 4th edn (London: Routledge, 1992). A highly readable and well-presented student text.

Charles P. Kindleberger, *The World in Depression 1929–1939*, 2nd edn (London: Penguin, 1987). A classic study which remains a storehouse of data and ideas.

Angus Maddison, *The World Economy: A Millennial Perspective* (Paris: Development Centre of the Organization for Economic Cooperation and Development, 2001). Summarizes a lifetime's work to provide a quantitative assessment of economic growth in the long run. Brave in its assumptions, it will provide economic historians with an important resource for future research. Maddison's data, for national income, population, and per capita income, are available as a spreadsheet at his personal website: www.eco.rug.nl/~Maddison/.

Brian R. Mitchell, *International Historical Statistics*, 5th edn (London: Palgrave Macmillan, 2003). A three-volume work which provides essential economic data for Europe, the Americas, Australasia and Africa, and Asia and Oceania.

Alec Nove, *An Economic History of the USSR* (London: Allen Lane, 1969). A highly successful text which inspired many scholars to further research.

Sidney Pollard, *Wealth and Poverty: An Economic History of the 20th Century* (London: Harrap, 1990). An attractively illustrated and concise introductory text.

Gabriel Tortella, *The Development of Modern Spain: An Economic History of the Nineteenth and Twentieth Century* (Cambridge MA: Harvard University Press, 2000). A highly readable account which assesses Spanish economic development in a comparative European framework.

Vera Zamagni, *The Economic History of Italy 1860–1990: Recovery after Decline* (Oxford: Oxford University Press, 1982). Provides an excellent survey of modern Italian economic history.

PART II

Before the Deluge

CHAPTER EIGHT

Europe's World: Power, Empire, and Colonialism

WOODRUFF D. SMITH

Historians of European imperialism do not usually regard the years covered in the first chronological section of the present volume as a discrete period for study. Typically, they subsume those years within a larger span stretching between the late 1870s and World War I. Nevertheless, changes did occur in the political engagement of Europeans with the world overseas in the years immediately around the turn of the century – nuances, alterations in public attitudes and official behavior, rather than major reversals of direction – that make the decade and a half before the outbreak of the Great War significant in imperial history. This is especially true if one is concerned with the links between pre-1914 imperialism and what happened in the rest of the twentieth century. Unexpectedly difficult and expensive resistance by targets of great-power expansion, such as the Boer War of 1899–1902, the American war in the Philippines during the same years, and the rebellions against German rule in what are today Namibia and Tanzania between 1904 and 1907, brought home to the citizens and leaders of imperializing countries the costs of what they were doing and the need, if not to disencumber themselves of their empires, then at least to formulate policies to make sure that they would not have to face such resistance again. After about 1895 the leaders of European states that had carved up almost all of Africa found themselves having to address seriously the problem of what to do with their acquisitions, especially once they realized that most of the new colonial territories could not be quickly turned into profitable adjuncts to the home economies in the ways that colonial propagandists had earlier claimed. One result of this was the formulation of colonial economic expansion programs that were the direct forerunners of the elaborate "Third World" development policies of the second half of the twentieth century. Colonial reform movements, or at least reformist tendencies, appeared that profoundly influenced the ways in which European powers envisioned and ruled their overseas dependencies after 1918.

This essay focuses on recent research and issues of interpretation in the historiography of European imperialism between the turn of the century and World War I, with attention also to continuities between that period and succeeding ones. Much of the most innovative research in the field has concerned imperialism in the context of colonized societies. However, because of the scope of the present volume, the emphasis here will fall on Europe, and on four major themes: relationships among imperialism, modernization, and globalization; the politics of imperialism; colonial reform; and the role of imperialism in constructing identities.

Modernization and Globalization

From the 1950s to the late 1970s the imperialism of the late nineteenth and early twentieth centuries was interpreted by most historians within a framework in which the process of modernization played the dominant role and in which industrialization was the key element of modernization. A classic example of this approach is Hans-Ulrich Wehler's explanation of Germany's sudden grasp for a colonial empire as a policy of "social imperialism."[1] According to Wehler, Chancellor Otto von Bismarck seized colonies for Germany in the mid-1880s in order to exploit class antagonisms created by industrialization and to build a solid basis of support for the new Reich, which primarily represented traditional Prussian landed and bureaucratic elites threatened by modernization. The middle classes were to be wooed away from anti-colonial liberalism by the promise that an overseas empire would offer them a field of opportunity that would offset a movement toward organized corporate capitalism at home. The working class would be diverted from revolution and the Social Democrats by the prospect of jobs protected against economic slumps by "reserve markets" in the colonies. The strategy did not work, not because it was based on an inaccurate assessment of the social effects of modernization but because Bismarck and most of his successors were unwilling to pursue an imperial course vigorously enough. Although they varied in specifics, most other prominent interpretations of pre-1914 imperialism from the same period shared a strong tendency to employ the standard narrative of modernization as a framing structure.[2]

Modernization is still a significant organizing concept for contemporary studies of imperialism, although the notion of a uniform or standard modernization process, a norm from which "developing" societies depart at their peril, has largely been discarded. The fact that the continuing modernization of industrial economies was often accompanied by various kinds of "demodernization" elsewhere in the world has been taken to indicate that modernization is at least a more heterogeneous phenomenon than we used to think. Nevertheless, the idea of turn-of-the-century Europe employing the political mechanisms of colonialism as a means of encouraging modernization at home and overseas forms the background for a substantial amount of historical research. Several developments since the early 1980s have, however, displaced the modernization paradigm from center stage. Of these, the most important has been the rapid rise of "globalization" and the "global economy" as interpretive structures within which to situate the history of European imperialism.

It is possible to view globalization and modernization as entirely compatible processes – the former being simply the expansion of the latter beyond the confines of the European world. Most historians of globalization, however, see it as a long-term historical phenomenon within which the central elements of modernization, including European industrialization, are embedded. This is particularly noticeable in the recent renaissance of British imperial history. Not long ago it was customary to describe the "second" (post-American revolution) British empire as a product of the imperatives of industrialization and the power that the industrial revolution gave to its country of origin, and to explain the decline of British imperial hegemony in the twentieth century as a result of Britain's loss of industrial supremacy.[3] Recent historians have tended instead to emphasize Britain's financial and commercial primacy as the core of Britain's world power and to ascribe that primacy in large part to the political and military success of the British Empire. P. J. Cain and A. G. Hopkins have argued in great detail that British imperialism in the nineteenth and early twentieth centuries was a product of "gentlemanly capitalism" – an amalgam of the financial elite of London and the aristocracy broadly defined, manifested in a distinctive political and economic culture and a set of interests that heavily influenced British policy abroad. The success of gentlemanly capitalism was made possible by, among other things, the success of the British state and its military forces in shouldering Britain into a dominant role in the operation of the global economy in the eighteenth and nineteenth centuries. The achievements of British industry are not disparaged, but Cain and Hopkins and a growing group of historians who think along similar lines see the manufacturing sector as having less influence on policy and far less effect on the long-term operations of the global economy than the banking and commercial sectors, in close alliance with the state and the political elites to which the state – even after the electoral reforms of the nineteenth century – primarily responded.[4] This approach probably exaggerates the autonomous power of elites and underestimates the importance of the public context of politics and the extent to which policy makers in Britain and elsewhere adjusted their external actions to that context. Nevertheless, by emphasizing the importance of the financial sector for defining British imperialism it has performed the major service of placing imperialism in the framework of a global economy in which international finance was the central feature.

Differences have emerged among historians who think along these lines. Niall Ferguson sees the British Empire as the political and military underpinning of nineteenth-century British financial hegemony, which permitted the global economy to develop for the benefit (to greater or lesser degrees) of most countries in Europe and much of the rest of the world. To Ferguson, the sudden appearance of significant imperial rivals to Britain at the end of the nineteenth century, together with a general movement toward protectionism and other forms of government involvement in the economies of the major states, led to a partial breakdown of the global economy as a functioning unit before and during World War I – a breakdown that, despite attempts at reconstruction in the 1920s, became more complete with the Depression of the 1930s. Only after 1945, under an American hegemony that was similar to the earlier imperialism of Britain, could the process of economic globalization be truly resumed.[5] This suggests that a successful global economy requires some form of imperial hegemony by a single state that accepts its role and performs it conscientiously. Others, such as Jürgen Osterhammel, see the explosion of imperial rivalries in the late nineteenth and early twentieth centuries not as a breakdown of globalization, but rather as a sign of its growing complexity, of a necessary movement toward a polycentric global economy and an attempt by governments to develop an appropriate role for their nations in such an economy.[6] Unfortunately, neither the international political system based on nation-states nor the existing body of political and economic theory was able to accommodate such a state of affairs prior to, and for many years after, World War I. Nevertheless, it may be possible to construct a successful global economy on a foundation of cooperation among states and recognition of the transnational character of global enterprise rather than the imperial hegemony of one power suggested by Ferguson.

The first couple of decades of the twentieth century saw serious attempts to articulate economic development programs for most of the European colonial empires. These programs arose in large part from a political need to justify previous – or sometimes ongoing – colonial conquests that were not readily defensible on the basis of current economic realities, but they were framed in terms of broad visions of the economic changes that had occurred during the nineteenth century and that could be anticipated in the twentieth. The most important models for the details of such programs were British India and the Netherlands East Indies, but what is most interesting about them is the general conceptions that lay behind them – conceptions that constituted important sources for later constructions of the idea of modernization itself.

The schemes articulated by British officials for Nigeria and the Gold Coast, by French officials for the interior of West Africa, by German theorists for colonies such as Togo and German East Africa, focused on shaping the economies of those regions as coherent adjuncts to a metropolitan economy that was envisioned as comprising mainly a modern manufacturing and a consumption sector.[7] Colonial subjects were to figure in development schemes mainly as producers of raw materials used by home industry, which would create consumer goods to be sold in Europe and overseas – including the colonies that supplied the raw materials. The basis of economic security for employers and workers in European countries and for the material advancement of colonial subjects was presented in terms of grand modernization projects integrated, under state direction, with the industrial enterprises of the metropolitan economies.

In the early years of the twentieth century, raw cotton was a major focus of most development plans in African colonies. This circumstance reflected an already outdated belief that the textile industry was the foundation of an industrial economy and that the European textile industries were particularly vulnerable to interference with the supplies or prices of their principal raw materials. The British pushed a major cotton scheme in Nigeria, which was followed after World War I by an even larger project in the Sudan. The French had their own cotton project in the Niger basin, while the Germans attempted briefly to create large-scale cotton production in Togo and East Africa. In one way or another, all the cotton schemes failed, in large part because of inconsistencies between the assumptions of the planners and the realities of the global cotton market. Interestingly, what succeeded in many colonies were primary agricultural industries that came about, not as a result of the grand economic strategies of the leaders of empire, but because of small investments by non-European farmers taking advantage of opportunities provided by access to global markets. This was what happened in the cases of the cocoa and coffee industries of Nigeria and the Gold Coast (Ghana). After initially ignoring these sectors of the economy, the colonial authorities moved in the 1920s to control and tax them, in part so as to pay for larger schemes of planned "modernization" that had failed or were in the process of doing so.[8]

Interpreting early twentieth-century imperialism in terms of modernization is therefore a complicated business, in part because one is actually dealing with the

history of the interpretive concept itself. That the formulators of the colonial development schemes were conscious modernizers, that they saw the economic core of
the process they were encouraging as the construction of coherent systems of
economic exchange around industrial production at home, and that they expected
and planned for a wide range of apparently desirable sociocultural changes in the
colonies as a result of economic change, all this is very clear. Modernization as an
explanatory framework thus provides a useful guide to the intentions of the policy
makers, and in terms of those intentions, the ultimate results of the policies can be
seen as "failed" (or occasionally successful) modernization in the latter part of the
twentieth century. On the other hand, it is also possible to place the early development schemes and their successors in other interpretive contexts, especially that of
globalization. It can be argued, for example, that the most important consequence
of British imperial development activities in the first half of the twentieth century was
the creation of the "sterling area" – a secondary aspect of policy, but one that provided a considerable degree of financial stability for colonial economies and a relative
lowering of the transaction costs associated with investment and trade within the
British Empire and Commonwealth.[9] The sterling area had obvious defects. Its
boundaries were defined not by the dynamics of a changing global economy but by
the political structure of Britain's empire. It could not be maintained by a British
economy weakened during World War II. But until a broader dollar-based system
was erected in the late 1940s, it permitted a substantial expansion of commerce
among Britain, its colonies, and self-governing dominions and an increasing level of
articulation between colonial economies and a significant part of the global economy.
Looking back from the twenty-first century, these developments often seem more
important than well-publicized programs of large-scale development and socioeconomic modernization.

The period just preceding World War I also saw the beginning of what was perhaps
the most spectacular connection between imperialism and globalization: the discovery
of oil in southern Persia (present-day Iran) by a British company in 1908, followed
by similar finds elsewhere in the Middle East during the next few years. This brought
significant new strategic considerations to bear on the political futures of Persia and
the Ottoman Empire. It also created an international politics of oil, as extremely
powerful financial consortia, formed to exploit the petroleum resources of the region,
placed great pressure on the governments of the major powers to establish imperial
control. The fact that the Ottoman Empire joined the Central Powers during World
War I and was therefore available for deconstruction at its end led to a massive grab
for colonies (some of them disguised as protectorates and others as League of Nations
mandates) by Britain and France and to a chaos of imperialist initiative, nationalist
response, and eventual Cold War competition in a vital node of the global economy,
with consequences that continue into the present.[10]

Imperialism and Politics

In recent years there has been a growing tendency for historians to portray modern
imperialism as primarily a political phenomenon rather than an economic or social
one. This tendency is by no means universal, but it is quite widespread. It goes against
basic assumptions about the engines of change in modern history that are built into

standard Marxist and modernization-based approaches. So strong were those assumptions as late as the early 1980s that Paul Kennedy, in his excellent study of the origins of the antagonism between Britain and Germany before World War I, after having made what many readers believed to be a good case for understanding that antagonism in largely political and ideological terms, concluded by ascribing it on much weaker grounds to economic competition.[11] Since then, historians have been more willing to challenge both the notion that the orgy of competitive imperial expansion in which the European powers indulged at the turn of the century was a direct product of economic change and the idea that it was caused mainly by class conflict at home (the concept of "social imperialism" mentioned above.)

"Political" can mean many things, of course. It can include the kind of structural–diplomatic interpretation that ascribes pre-1914 imperialism to the collapse of the system created at the Congress of Vienna and to the decline of British global hegemony in the late nineteenth century – both in large part due to the sudden rise of the unified German Reich as a great power.[12] In recent years, historians of imperialism who emphasize diplomacy have tended to focus less on such structural factors and more on the mindsets of those who discussed and made policy in the major imperialist states. In some cases, this takes the form of analyzing the ways politicians and bureaucrats understood (and misunderstood) what they were doing.[13] In others, the focus of attention is broader, encompassing the array of conceptions present in the public discourse in the major European countries regarding trends in the wider world.

A particularly useful way to look at the aggressive imperialism of the turn of the century from a political angle is to connect it to the changes in the political structure, behavior, and culture of European states that are collectively called "democratization" – changes that occurred even in places like imperial Germany that were not, in an institutional sense, democracies. The term refers not just to a broadening of the franchise but also to a vast expansion of participation in the public sphere, a proliferation of interest groups vying to influence public opinion, the appearance of mass political parties, and a host of other alterations in the political scene. The relationship between democratization and imperialism was actually a subject of considerable discussion at the time among politicians and commentators. It was never wholly ignored by historians after 1918. Only fairly recently, however, has it become a central focus of attention among scholars interested in the ways participants in modern political systems seek to establish broad bases of support by creating ideological, discursive, and iconic linkages between their particular agendas and broad social and cultural patterns. In the late nineteenth and early twentieth centuries, imperialism served as a device with which politicians, state officials, leaders of interest groups, journalists – indeed, people of all sorts who took an active part in politics – attempted to operate within democratizing political systems that seemed newly complex and bewildering. Very often, the economic reasoning that plays so large a role in standard interpretations of imperialism reflected not so much the realities faced by businesses functioning in global markets, or even policy problems handled by governments, as it did the expectations of the various audiences that made up the public spheres of the imperialist countries. This helps to explain why so many of the new colonies acquired by European states around the turn of the century had so little economic relevance to their occupiers and why the occupiers turned to development schemes that were intended to create such relevance within the cognitive frameworks that prevailed in imperialist thinking.

It was primarily the success with which nationalism had been used during the course of the nineteenth century as a means of aggregating support – by governments and their opponents, by liberals and eventually radicals and conservatives, by political parties and leaders trying to free themselves from control by parties, and ultimately by the founders of new nation-states such as Germany – that suggested that a nationalism expanded on a global scale could be used for the same purpose under the increasingly complicated circumstances of politics at the century's end. Imperialism appeared to have even more potential than "standard" nationalism for appealing across lines of class, organized economic interest, region, and ideology. It displaced the arena of proposed political action to the world overseas – to a world, in other words, that was more easily fictionalized than the domestic scene. There were plenty of occasions for invoking imperialist thinking. Events arising from the commercial activities of Europeans overseas and from their demands for intervention by governments on their behalf could be interpreted as having vital significance for the nation as a whole. Politicians could attract public attention by connecting such events to an ideology that portrayed the nation's future as bound up with its success in staking its claim to a share of global resources. Business enterprises with overseas interests were often willing to employ such ideologies to obtain enhanced state support for their enterprises. On the basis of perceptions of such possibilities, a new politics of imperialism was constructed.

Attempts by political organizations – often including governments in office – to use overseas expansion (or vigorous defense of overseas possessions already acquired) as a means of appealing for public support occurred between the 1880s and 1914 in Germany, France, Britain, Italy, Spain, Portugal, and Russia, as well as Japan and the United States. In Germany, Bismarck's effort in the 1880s to parlay limited colonial occupation into political support was followed after 1890 by a succession of similar moves by Emperor Wilhelm II and several of the chancellors who served under him. In Germany there also developed a nationalist opposition movement, centered on organizations such as the Pan-German League, which criticized the government for not being imperialist enough. In Italy, the acquisition of an overseas empire was represented by politicians in several parties as a matter of vital importance to the country's economic future as well as an essential sign of great power status. The ill-fated attempt of the Crispi government in 1895–6 to occupy Ethiopia resulted mainly from domestic political aims, while the more successful effort of a liberal government in 1911–12 to seize Libya from Turkey was largely a response to pressure from a newly active nationalist right. In Britain, imperialist wings of both the Liberal and the Conservative-Unionist parties competed with each other for the support of a public that was thought to respond to the need to defend Britain's empire and (weakening) global hegemony as a chief national priority. Colonialism as a factor in French politics went through cycles. In the 1880s, expansion in southeast Asia and in Africa was a major part of the foreign policy and the popular appeal of a number of governments, especially those in which Jules Ferry was a leading figure. Contrary to expectations, however, it proved incapable of serving as a consistent rallying point for any party or coalition. Well-publicized instances of international conflict over colonies, such as the Fashoda incident of 1898 which pitted a French attempt to establish an empire that stretched across northern Africa from west to east against a British effort to do the same thing from north to south, could generate widespread interest, but the interest did not translate into stable popular support for parties supporting colonialism. The same thing was true of the furor that surrounded the Moroccan crises of 1905–6 and 1911. In Russia, the government made a concerted effort in the 1890s and up to 1905 to use colonial thrusts into Manchuria and Korea as (among other things) ways of building public support, primarily among the expanding middle classes. As was so often the case with imperialist politics, the project backfired when Russia's aims were decisively thwarted by Japan in the Russo-Japanese War of 1904–5. Variations on these themes occurred in the other countries noted above.[14]

The politics of imperialism was seldom successful for very long. In a few cases, such as that of Italy, whose attempts to colonize Ethiopia met with disastrous defeat on the battlefield of Adowa in 1896, imperialism backfired and drove the government that employed it out of office. In other cases, such as Britain at the turn of the century, setbacks such as the Boer War lowered the effectiveness of imperialism as a political tool. In Germany, the growth of the nationalist-imperialist opposition put the government into an increasingly difficult position, in which its leaders believed that they could not safely deemphasize imperialism because of public opinion, but at the same time also could not meet the demands of the radical nationalists without taking unconscionable risks in foreign affairs. This was one of the factors leading Germany to become increasingly intransigent in its foreign policy between 1900 and 1914 and encouraging a belief among senior state officials that major war was inevitable. It also led, in Germany as in most other countries possessing newly acquired colonies, to the demands for systematic colonial economic development that were discussed previously. Because much of the territory colonized by European states in the late nineteenth and early twentieth centuries did not immediately yield a significant economic return, it became necessary to create the prospect of such a return in order to validate the process by which colonies had been acquired in the first place. Ideally, validation should have taken the form of substantially enhanced figures for colonial trade and production, but most proponents of development realized that these would take some time to manifest themselves. Instead, the development schemes were constructed so as to validate themselves in terms of the logic of imperialist ideology – that is, to offer the possibility of contributing to a secure economic future for the home economy in an increasingly industrialized world.[15]

Colonial Reform

Imperial politics helped to instigate a phenomenon found in almost all countries with colonial empires during the two decades or so before World War I: movements toward colonial reform. Germany provides many examples. Some of the impetus to making reform of colonial administrations and their policies a matter of public discourse arose from the same sources as schemes for colonial economic development. This was true, for example, of the reforms associated with the tenure in office of Bernhard Dernburg as head of the German colonial administration (1906–10), which were largely directed toward revising labor policies and regulating resource development in such a way that the colonies would become significant participants in the expansion of the domestic economy. Many reformers had other political agendas, although usually they were to some degree compatible with plans for economic modernization. Socialist and left-liberal politicians in the Reichstag regularly directed attention to abuses of indigenous colonial subjects by officials as a way of criticizing authoritarianism in Germany itself, calling for closer oversight of the bureaucracy and an extension of the public sphere as correctives. Still others focused on "native policies," typically with the intention of trying to prevent the proletarianization of colonial inhabitants as a means of emphasizing the need to limit the social consequences of advanced capitalism both abroad and at home. Some colonial reformers, particularly women's groups trying to establish a respectable place for themselves in the national political establishment, also called for racial segregation and the prohibition of miscegenation in the colonies.[16]

In Great Britain, reformist colonial thinking between the turn of the century and World War I tended to be directed toward India and, as in other countries, reflected ideological divisions within the home country. Much attention has been paid by historians to the formation of a fashion for "reform imperialism" that was closely connected to a cult of "national efficiency" among intellectuals and members of the leadership of all major political tendencies. A common factor that cut across party and ideological lines, from members of the Tory Party on the right to many of the Fabians on the left, was a desire to increase the role of intellectual elites in governing both Britain and its empire. However, when it came to the actual formulation of policy, fault lines appeared. The comprehensive attempt of Lord Curzon as Viceroy of India (1899–1905) to reorganize the Indian government as an administrative entity without including increasing native Indian representation reflected the views of conservative imperialists. The Morley-Minto reforms that followed pursued a more liberal line of imperial cooperation, with gradual movement toward increasing the native Indian contingent in the Indian Civil Service and toward representative institutions.[17] Reform could mean quite different things to different people, which was true also of the movements for reform that were a characteristic feature of domestic politics in practically all western European countries (and the United States) in the early twentieth century.[18]

The most heavily publicized movements toward colonial reform in the period before World War I were those that arose from colonial scandals, and of these, none had greater resonance than the uncovering of the horrors of labor exploitation in the Congo Free State in 1903. The Free State, under the personal sovereignty of King Leopold II of Belgium, had been assigned control of most of the Congo basin and its tributaries in order to achieve humanitarian purposes such as eliminating the slave trade, and also to foster the economic exploitation of the region without bringing the great powers into conflict with one another. In fact, the Free State had established a much more closed economy than allowed by the original agreements under which it had been created. Its downfall, however, came about because the system of forced labor it employed to expand its rubber industry in the upper Congo constituted a practical return to a very brutal form of slavery. A number of observers, mostly British, reported what was going on, and an international outcry resulted. Leopold attempted to counter with a series of inquiries and reforms, but this proved to be insufficient to satisfy a Congo reform movement that was mostly located outside of Belgium. In the end, the Belgian state was forced to take over the administration of the Congo rather than see it divided up among the powers.[19]

In most European countries with colonial empires, the period leading up to World War I also saw significant attempts to regularize policy and administration in the colonies themselves. This was generally accomplished by creating colonial services staffed with trained bureaucrats on the models of the domestic civil services and the Indian Civil Service, by establishing standard administrative and financial procedures throughout the colonies, and by adopting a standard ideology of colonialism that could simultaneously frame colonial bureaucrats' conceptions of their missions and legitimate colonial rule to various political audiences at home. The symbolic central figure in this process in the British Empire was Lord Lugard, conqueror of Uganda and Northern Nigeria and, from 1912 to 1919, first governor of a united Nigeria. Lugard was a major exponent of large-scale economic development projects, but he was most famous for expressing what came to be the central features of the ideology of the twentieth-century British colonial civil service: the ideas of the "dual mandate" and "indirect rule." The dual mandate meant that colonial administrators should regard themselves as trustees both for the interests of their home country (interests that were primarily economic and envisioned in terms of the needs of the industrial and consumer sectors) and for protecting and advancing the wellbeing of colonial subjects. Indirect rule was Lugard's generalization from Britain's experience with the princely states in India. Wherever possible, British administrations should operate through traditional native intermediaries and should attempt to maintain the integrity of existing political and religious institutions, as long as these were compatible with British hegemony and orderly modernization.

The classic model of indirect rule was the system Lugard set up in Northern Nigeria, where the Hausa states, with their Fulani ruling families, that Lugard had defeated in conquering the area were kept in power under British oversight. Islam was recognized as the official religion, Islamic law was kept in place, and Christian missionaries were prevented from establishing themselves. Lugard's articulation of enlightened colonialism played very well at home and was extremely popular among the colonial authorities of other countries (France especially) between the world wars. It became the core of the official view of the historical mission of Britain as colonizer that remained in place up to – and after – the time the British Empire was disassembled starting in 1947. It was also part of the ideological framework of the League of Nations mandates system that was set up to justify the distribution of the colonies seized from the Central Powers among the winners in World War I. Lugard, who, like most conscientious colonial officials between the wars, took the dual mandate and indirect rule very seriously, was himself an active member of the League's mandates commission.[20]

In the French overseas empire a similar process of regularization of colonial administration occurred, although the governing ideologies were more varied and tended to be formulated somewhat differently from that of the British colonies. In places like Morocco, which was technically an independent state under French "protection," an approach very similar to that of Lugard was developed by the best-publicized French proconsul, Marshal Lyautey, for use in outlying areas. In other territories official policy veered between attempts at "assimilation" (the full absorbing of at least indigenous elites into French culture, to be followed by close political union between the colony and France) and "association" (the maintenance of formal political differences between a colony and France, matched by a recognition that complete cultural assimilation was impractical.)[21]

Imperialism and Identity

If the experiment with imperialism did not often meet the political needs of its proponents and had so many deleterious side-effects, why was the whole thing not abandoned? This question is similar to one commonly asked about the origins of World War I: why, if so many of Europe's leaders realized the dangers and the potentially awful consequences of what they were doing between 1900 and 1914, did they persist in doing it anyway? It appears that at least part of the answer to both questions lies in the ways in which imperialism (and the kind of foreign policy that took the need to expand and protect empires as one of its central elements) was accepted into the public cultures of the major European states as a device by which individuals and groups defined their identities in relation to the nations to which they belonged. Regardless of the success or failure of specific overseas initiatives, the tropes of imperialist discourse, the icons of imperialist imagery, and the logic of imperialist reasoning came to be widely, and often subtly, adopted by Europeans of differing class and political outlook as means of identity formation. Groups with particular interests, such as the oil companies that wanted European governments to establish control over petroleum producing areas after World War I, or the white settler populations of Kenya and Southern Rhodesia who wanted assurance of their privileged positions, were able to take advantage of the extent to which imperialism informed identities within public culture to make strong arguments for the maintenance of empire even when empire seemed a dubious proposition on other grounds. What would it mean to be British without the British Empire? Governments believed that abandoning even unproductive or marginal colonies would at the very least undermine their credibility with voters. Moreover, many political leaders (Winston Churchill, for instance) strongly and sincerely believed that their nations were defined by an imperial mission. In Germany, after the loss of the colonies in World War I, the return of the overseas empire became a significant theme across the entire political spectrum except on the far left – at least as important a theme as colonialism had been between the 1890s and 1914. The importance of empire was articulated in terms of a number of fictions, including the supposed capacity of the former colonies to support the nation's economic independence and the role of colonies in providing a setting in which the "new German" could develop as a cultural type and in which German cultural superiority could be demonstrated through the "civilizing" of indigenous peoples. These fictions spoke to a constructed identity for Germans as citizens of an autonomous great power and members of a uniquely gifted people with a world-historical mission to advance humankind. The identity was particularly in need of reinforcement in the 1920s when public opinion in many other countries vehemently disparaged it and when Germany lacked the conventional instruments of power.[22]

In recent years the process of constructing identities around aspects of empire has become a major subject of imperial studies. The shaping of national identities has received perhaps the greatest amount of attention. Linda Colley has argued that identification with the empire supplied the finishing touch in the creation of British nationality in the first half of the nineteenth century, permitting Britons to see themselves as members of component nationalities (English, Scottish, Welsh, Irish) while sharing a common Britishness with regard to the empire. British nationality could be extended to encompass the populations of the white colonies and dominions – or at least the segments of those populations that spoke English. Moreover, the empire supplied a variety of attractive meanings to the fact of being British. The conquest of overseas colonies provided comforting images of power and authority which individual Britons could see themselves as sharing. Stories of heroism in defense of the empire, which throughout the nineteenth century were built around cultural stereotypes of British character, contributed to constructing the self-images of Britons of all social classes. Some of the policies associated with the empire – especially the abolition of slavery and the various overseas humanitarian projects associated with it – contributed to defining British nationality as a moral benefit to the entire world. All these forms of national identity-building through imperialism were fully articulated by the middle of the nineteenth century and were available for use in assembling support for a wide variety of political initiatives that could be attached to imperialism.[23]

John Mackenzie has shown that, significant as imperialism was in shaping popular culture and national identity in Britain earlier in the nineteenth century, it had its greatest effect from the 1890s through World War I and into the interwar years. This was in part because the rivalry of other imperial states and the difficulties Britain faced in running its own swollen empire elicited a defensive response, a jingoistic insistence on imperial identity. But mostly it resulted from a vast growth of institutions that deliberately set about propagating British imperial identity as a means of manipulating popular culture and political opinion. The goals of such manipulation were frequently conceived in terms of the greater good of the nation. The Boy Scouts, for instance, and a number of rival youth organizations that ultimately withered in the Boy Scouts' shadow, were an outgrowth of imperialist themes, featuring the skills and character traits supposedly needed to dominate new territories. Their institutional mission was not, however, formulated in overtly imperialist terms. Rather, its aim was to develop discipline, self-control, physical health, and decency among young men, to generalize the ideals of the vigorous part of the British elite across class lines so as to create a people worthy of an imperial democracy and thus avoid some of the dangers of class conflict, proletarianization, and modernization. If the natural leaders of all classes in British society could be persuaded to identify with the nation and its empire through a framework of Boy Scout virtues and attitudes, it might be possible to reach peaceful understanding with the equivalent groups in other countries through the international Scout movement. Like the Rhodes Scholarships, the Boy Scouts were presented as an instrument not just for establishing national identity, but also for building a common identity among the useful citizens of the various empires into which it looked like the world was being divided.[24]

Empire was a means of building national identity in other countries as well. In France, colonial expansion and the French "civilizing mission" were regularly connected in public discourse from about 1880 to 1914 to a renewal of French nationhood in the context of democracy and the recovery of national self-respect after defeat by Prussia. In Germany the idea of overseas settlement was employed even before actual colonies were acquired in order to define an identity for Germans as a people with the global mission of raising the cultural levels of others. Recent studies of colonialism in Germany have also shown how groups representing particular segments of the population, including but not limited to ones that were politically marginalized in the Kaiserreich, attempted to identify themselves and their constituents with imperial patriotism as a means of enhancing their positions. Lora Wildenthal has explored the ways in which women's groups attempted to develop a distinctive women's role in Germany's colonial enterprise as a way of establishing a collective political presence in the country in general. In so acting, the colonial women's movement was partly responsible for the particular emphasis within German colonial reform on the prevention of miscegenation. Other authors have investigated similar uses of colonialism by eugenicists, anthropologists, and southwest African white settlers. In all countries with colonial empires, the early twentieth century also saw a substantial tightening of the connection in public and scientific discourse between imperialism and biological racism. Attempts to reorder and render coherent the systems of control that had been created in the colonies encouraged the assignment of rulers and ruled to fundamentally different human categories, while translating the dominance of Europeans over non-Europeans in the colonial world into racial terms could be turned to advantage at home – for example, by politicians wanting to justify global expansion on terms that transcended considerations of mere profit and loss by claiming that the survival of no less than the white (or Teutonic or Slavic) "race" was at stake in the confrontations of empires with their subjects or with each other.[25]

Overseas empire was a vital part of the public life of many European nations in the first years of the twentieth century, deeply embedded in the dynamics of political culture as well as in the functioning of modernizing economies in a changing global economy. In many respects, the shape of European imperialism between the world wars was laid out in the two decades that preceded 1914, which is an important reason that these decades have recently attracted considerable attention from historians approaching colonialism in new ways.

NOTES

1 Hans-Ulrich Wehler, *Bismarck und der Imperialismus* (Cologne: Knieppenheuer und Witsch, 1969).
2 See, for example, Wolfgang Mommsen, *Das Zeitalter des Imperialismus* (Frankfurt am Main: Fischer, 1969).
3 For example, E. J. Hobsbawm, *Industry and Empire: An Economic History of Britain since 1750* (London: Weidenfeld and Nicolson, 1968).
4 P. J. Cain and A. G. Hopkins, *British Imperialism: Innovation and Expansion, 1688–1914* (London: Longman, 1993); P. J. Cain and A. G. Hopkins, *British Imperialism: Crisis and Deconstruction, 1914–1990* (London: Longman, 1993).
5 Niall Ferguson, *Empire: The Rise and Demise of the British World Order and the Lessons for Global Power* (New York: Basic Books, 2003).
6 See Sebastian Conrad and Jürgen Osterhammel, eds, *Das Kaiserreich transnational. Deutschland in der Welt 1871–1914* (Göttingen: Vandenhoeck and Ruprecht, 2004).
7 See Michael Havinden and David Meredith, *Colonialism and Development: Britain and its Tropical Colonies, 1850–1960* (London: Routledge, 1993); A. G. Hopkins, *An Economic History of West Africa* (New York: Columbia University Press, 1973), pp. 124–236;

Woodrow Smith, *The Ideological Origins of Nazi Imperialism* (New York: Oxford University Press, 1986), pp. 76–8.

8 See Polly Hill, *The Migrant Cocoa-Farmers of Southern Ghana*, 2nd edn (Oxford: James Curry, 1997); Sara S. Berry, *Cocoa, Custom, and Socio-Economic Change in Rural Western Nigeria* (Oxford: Oxford University Press, 1975).

9 See D. K. Fieldhouse, "The Metropolitan Economics of Empire," in Judith Brown and W. Roger Louis, eds, *The Oxford History of the British Empire: The Twentieth Century* (Oxford: Oxford University Press, 1999), pp. 88–113, esp. pp. 93–5.

10 See Glen Balfour-Paul, "Britain's Informal Empire in the Middle East," in Brown and Louis, *Oxford History*, pp. 490–514.

11 Paul Kennedy, *The Rise of the Anglo-German Antagonism* (London: Allen and Unwin, 1980).

12 The classic statement of this approach is W. L. Langer, *The Diplomacy of Imperialism 1890–1902*, 2nd edn (New York: Knopf, 1965).

13 The many vital contributions of W. Roger Louis to our understanding of twentieth-century imperialism can be categorized in this way. See, among other works, *Imperialism at Bay: The United States and the Decolonization of the British Empire, 1941–1945* (New York: Oxford University Press, 1978) and *The British Empire in the Middle East, 1945–1951: Arab Nationalism, the United States, and Post-war Imperialism* (Oxford: Oxford University Press, 1984).

14 See Smith, *Ideological Origins*, pp. 41–140; Richard A. Webster, *Industrial Imperialism in Italy, 1908–1915* (Berkeley: University of California Press, 1975); Claudio G. Segré, *Fourth Shore: The Italian Colonization of Libya* (Chicago: University of Chicago Press, 1974); Ronald Hyam, "The British Empire in the Edwardian Era," in Brown and Louis, *Oxford History*, pp. 47–63; Raymond Betts, *Tricolour* (London: Gordon and Cremonesi, 1978); David M. McDonald, *United Government and Foreign Policy in Russia, 1900–1914* (Cambridge MA: Harvard University Press, 1992).

15 See Havinden and Meredith, *Colonial Development*; Smith, *Ideological Origins*, pp. 112–40.

16 See Lora Wildenthal, *German Women for Empire, 1884–1945* (Durham NC: Duke University Press, 2001); Smith, *Ideological Origins*, pp. 112–65.

17 See Hyam, "British Empire," in Brown and Louis, *Oxford History*, pp. 47–63; G. R. Searle, *The Quest for National Efficiency: A Study of British Politics and Political Thought, 1895–1914* (Oxford: Blackwell, 1971).

18 Janet R. Horne, "In Pursuit of Greater France: Visions of Empire among Musée Social Reformers, 1894–1931," in *Domesticating the Empire: Race, Gender, and Family Life in French and Dutch Colonialism*, Julia Clancy-Smith and Francis Gouda, eds (Charlottesville: University Press of Virginia, 1998), pp. 21–42.

19 A. Hochschild, *King Leopold's Ghost: A Story of Greed, Terror, and Heroism in Colonial Africa* (Boston MA: Houghton-Mifflin, 1999).

20 See I. F. Nicolson, *The Administration of Nigeria: Men, Methods and Myths* (Oxford: Clarendon Press, 1969), which classifies much of the Lugard story as "myth." See also John Cell, "Colonial Rule," in Brown and Louis, *Oxford History*, pp. 232–54.

21 See Raymond Betts, *Assimilation and Association in French Colonial Theory, 1890–1914* (New York: Columbia University Press, 1961).

22 See Smith, *Ideological Origins*, pp. 196–230; Wildenthal, *German Women for Empire*, pp. 172–200.

23 Linda Colley, *Britons: Forging the Nation, 1707–1837* (New Haven CT: Yale University Press, 1992); Kathryn Tidrick, *Empire and the English Character* (London: Tauris, 1990); Andrew Porter, "Trusteeship, Anti-Slavery, and Humanitarianism," in A. Porter, ed., *The Oxford History of the British Empire: The Nineteenth Century* (Oxford: Oxford University

Press, 1999), pp. 198–221; John MacKenzie, "Empire and Metropolitan Cultures," in Porter, *Oxford History*, pp. 270–93.

24 John M. MacKenzie, *Propaganda and Empire: The Manipulation of British Public Opinion, 1880–1960* (Manchester: Manchester University Press, 1984); Kathryn Castle, *Britannia's Children: Reading Colonialism through Children's Books and Magazines* (Manchester: Manchester University Press, 1996).

25 See Horne, "In Pursuit of Greater France"; Susanne Zantop, *Colonial Fantasies: Conquest, Family and Nation in Pre-colonial Germany, 1770–1870* (Durham NC: Duke University Press, 1997); Wildenthal, *German Women for Empire*; Pascal Grosse, *Kolonialismus, Eugenik und bürgerliche Gesellschaft in Deutschland 1850–1918* (Frankfurt: Campus Verlag, 2000); Daniel J. Walther, *Creating Germans Abroad: Cultural Policies and National Identity in Namibia* (Athens: Ohio University Press, 2002); Alice L. Conklin, "Redefining 'Frenchness': Citizenship, Race Regeneration, and Imperial Motherhood in France and West Africa, 1914–40," in Clancy-Smith and Gouda, *Domesticating the Empire*, pp. 65–83; Frederick Cooper and Anna Laura Stoler, eds, *Tensions of Empire: Colonial Cultures in a Bourgeois World* (Berkeley: University of California Press, 1997).

GUIDE TO FURTHER READING

Max Beloff, *Imperial Sunset*, vol. 1: *Britain's Liberal Empire, 1897–1921*, 2nd edn (Basingstoke: Macmillan, 1987). The standard study of British imperialism in the early twentieth century.

Raymond F. Betts, *Tricolour* (London: Gordon and Cremonesi, 1978). French nationalism and imperialism. And *Uncertain Dimensions: Western Overseas Empires in the Twentieth Century* (Minneapolis: University of Minnesota Press, 1985). A comprehensive survey in a major series on imperialism.

Judith Brown and W. Roger Louis, eds, *The Oxford History of the British Empire: The Twentieth Century* (Oxford: Oxford University Press, 1999). A collection of articles (several of them extremely good) covering a wide range of topics on the twentieth-century British Empire.

P. J. Cain and A. G. Hopkins, *British Imperialism: Crisis and Deconstruction, 1914–1990* (London: Longman, 1993). And *British Imperialism: Innovation and Expansion, 1688–1914* (London: Longman, 1993). These two volumes present a thoroughly supported thesis about the nature of British imperialism as a function of "gentlemanly capitalism."

Julia Clancy-Smith and Frances Gouda, eds, *Domesticating the Empire: Race, Gender and Family Life in French and Dutch Colonialism* (Charlottesville: University Press of Virginia, 1998). Gender and family studies, including excellent contributions on identity formation.

Frederick Cooper and Ann Laura Stoler, eds, *Tensions of Empire: Colonial Cultures in a Bourgeois World* (Berkeley: University of California Press, 1997). An extremely influential collection sampling postmodern approaches to colonialism, with a very useful introduction.

Michael Havinden and David Meredith, *Colonialism and Development: Britain and its Tropical Colonies, 1850–1960* (London: Routledge, 1993). A good one-volume survey of development and development policy in the British Empire.

John M. MacKenzie, *Propaganda and Empire: The Manipulation of British Public Opinion, 1880–1960* (Manchester: Manchester University Press, 1984). A major study of the construction of imperialist culture.

Jürgen Osterhammel, *Colonialism: A Theoretical Overview* (Princeton NJ: M. Wiener, 1997). A useful contemporary examination of colonialism from the standpoint of theory.

Andrew Porter, ed., *The Oxford History of the British Empire: The Nineteenth Century* (Oxford: Oxford University Press, 1999). Contains articles on the late nineteenth century.

Woodruff D. Smith, *The Ideological Origins of Nazi Imperialism* (New York: Oxford University Press, 1986). Examines relationships between German colonialism and domestic politics, with a focus on ideology.

CHAPTER NINE

Social Reform or Social Revolution?

GARY P. STEENSON

Was there a serious possibility of social revolution in Europe in the roughly twenty-five years preceding World War I, or is the legacy of this period in European history primarily that of social reform? That this question is even posed reveals a certain bias about the nature of European society during these years. After all, the last major European social upheaval worthy of the name "revolution" came in France in 1870–1 with the rise and bloody suppression of the Paris Commune. Given the relative social tranquility that prevailed from then until 1914, why should there be much question about the matter?

Numerous possibilities come to mind. First of all, powerful movements among the workers emerged during the years before 1914 that, in their propaganda at least, proclaimed the coming of a great revolution in western society. Perhaps most prominent among these were the working-class socialist parties that appeared everywhere in Europe beginning in the 1860s; by 1889, several of these parties had joined together in an informal alliance popularly called the Second International which, while never publicly declaring itself an instrument of the coming revolution, certainly let the impression stand that it was at least potentially a revolutionary body. The vehemence of the governmental assault on these several parties and the repeated denunciation of them in the bourgeois and official press as dangerous threats to the stability and tranquility of society further promoted the notion that they were, in fact, what their intellectuals often claimed them to be, namely, the vanguard forces of an inevitable revolution. Second, perhaps the most powerful source of the notion of revolution was the influence of Marxist thought in the late nineteenth and early twentieth centuries. Marxists everywhere saw revolution to overthrow capitalism as an inevitable result of the development of capitalism itself; the sophistication of Marxist theoreticians at the time, and long after, made this a very seductive theory. Third, in addition to the organized socialist, working-class parties there were other, even more radical groups of anarchists, syndicalists, anarcho-syndicalists, etc., all of whom frightened the dominant society even more than did the socialists. Many of these latter groups engaged in violent activities, including assassination, on a sufficiently frequent basis to rouse the forces of law and order. Fourth, in the aftermath of the war a long period of widespread social disruption and even several revolutions – Russia first of course, then Germany, Hungary, and elsewhere – occurred. Furthermore, given what came later in Europe in the form of the rise of various fascist regimes in Italy, Germany, Spain, Portugal, and elsewhere, is it not reasonable to seek the roots of these upheavals in the years before 1914 as well as in the impact of the war itself?

The "Admirable Century" and Origins of the War

This last question lies at the root of a significant historiographical problem that persists to this day. Namely, if the nineteenth century was such a marvelous time, whence the disaster of the twentieth? John Keegan, author of the best single-volume military history of the war, left no doubt about his view when he called his opening chapter "A European Tragedy" and referred to the war as having "destroyed the benevolent and optimistic culture of the European continent."[1] Frederic Morton specifically identified this problem by concluding his review of Peter Gay's book on pre-1914 Viennese culture with these words: "[Gay's] coda acclaims the Victorian age as 'an admirable century' whereas 'one thinks back on the twentieth century with horror.' So swiftly, so smoothly, then, was the horrible sired by the admirable? There is some novel demonology here. There is also much competent hagiography. Only the historiography is wanting."[2] This apparent disconnect between what came before the Great War and what came after is a problem that has plagued historians for nearly a century.

Older histories discuss almost exclusively the diplomatic activities of these years and their relationship to the war with little or no reference to social, economic, and intellectual matters that might shed some light on the question of continuities in European history across the great gap of 1914–18.[3] Later studies, especially the pertinent volumes of the *Rise of Modern Europe* series, did indeed emphasize the social and economic changes that took place during the years immediately prior to the war.[4] But despite the promise of Oron Hale's title and much of his text, especially his concluding chapter which deals with the origins of the war, the author once again fell back on diplomatic relations to explain the origins of the war. This approach suggests that the causes of the war resided not in broad social-economic developments of prewar society but in the failure of leadership to cope with diplomatic tensions. After reviewing the qualities of major European diplomats at the time, Hale leaves the reader with little doubt about his position when he observes: "No wonder Europe slid easily into war in 1914."[5]

More recently, two British authors, Norman Stone and Eric Hobsbawm, while much subtler and more meticulous in their treatment of economic, social, cultural, and even diplomatic developments, still are largely at a loss when it comes to explaining how such dreadful developments came out of a period of such real advancement and even more promising hope. Stone's book is an unusual piece of work. In an effort, apparently, to capture the spirit of the times rather than to offer critical analysis, the author runs into some problems when it turns out that sources at the time made some serious misjudgments. For example, Stone apparently reports the contention of the German general staff that by 1917, only Russia would be in a position to challenge Germany on equal military grounds. But because we now know the relative military strengths of Germany and Russia in 1917, this statement now seems more than a little absurd.[6] Another problem Stone presents, but does not sort out, is the apparent contradiction between the oft-repeated anti-war position of the organized socialist and trade-union movements in Europe and the eagerness with which worker populations everywhere seemed to greet the outbreak of the war.[7] Investigating the extent to which the movement was the workers and the workers the movement is one of the fields of research that needs to be developed considerably. Stone's work is an interesting and sometimes dramatic extended essay, but it includes little critical judgment of the events it covers.

Hobsbawm's work is rather different. For example, he asserts somewhat circuitously (but plainly enough) that "the idea that somehow or other, but for the unforeseen and avoidable intervention of the catastrophe of 1914, stability, prosperity and liberal progress would have continued, has not even the most superficial plausibility."[8] He further denies that imperialist conflicts of the era were directly responsible for the war, but does contend that destabilization of "the periphery of the single, interdependent world system which [western bourgeois society] had created" inevitably involved this society in "the global revolutionary upheavals" which, he holds, began even before the war itself, namely in Mexico, Persia, Turkey, Russia (1905), and China.[9] In fact, when it comes to explaining the specific origins of the war, Hobsbawm, while again much subtler than most of his predecessors, ultimately refers to the failure of diplomacy, albeit a diplomacy forced to cope with the much more complicated and open-ended situation that was the product of the emergence of a world capitalist economy. While this is a considerably more nuanced version of the crude Marxian view that capitalist economics led to war, it still does not offer much help in understanding how the promise of pre-1914 European society gave way to the disaster of the interwar years. Hobsbawm does toward the very end of his account make passing reference to the increasing inability of governments to control the activities of "subjects in the process of turning into democratic citizens," but without much elaboration, and finally, he quite specifically rejects the idea "that in 1914 governments rushed into war to defuse their internal social crises."[10] Still, the Marxian case for the economic origins of World War I has never been more persuasively made.

More recent works, including revised and updated versions of earlier studies, often include some discussion of the impact of economic and social developments on the origins of the war, and, more specifically, passing mention is often made of the role of the urban masses as a factor shaping the Europe that gave rise to the war. For example, Malcolm Anderson, despite making a seemingly obligatory reference to "the wonderful century which ended in 1914," argues that the end of "the old Europe" was at least in part a result of "the only half-understood destructive powers with which its own achievements had endowed it."[11] Without much elaboration, Anderson specifically refers to three examples of these powers: the apparently serious contemplation by the crown prince of Germany of a Junker-led *coup d'état* in 1913 in response to the continued growth of the *Sozialdemokratische Partei Deutschland* (SPD), the socialist working-class party that had grown so rapidly since the 1880s; the disruptive power of popular nationalism in the Habsburg Empire; and "the growth of the streak of violence and intolerance" in Italy represented by Mussolini's success at the 1912 Reggio congress of the Italian socialist party.[12] These references come early in Anderson's book, and many passages that come later seem to downplay the impact of the organized workers' movement.[13]

Similarly, Robert Gildea argues somewhat ambiguously that one of the four "crucial" factors in the run-up to the war was "the pressure of both nationalist and socialist anti-militarist opinion."[14] However, he then concludes that by virtue of the German *Burgfrieden*, the French *Union sacrée*, and British party unity in August 1914, "the spectre of socialism had been exorcized . . . The moment to begin a revolution, it turned out, was not at the beginning of a war."[15] Because Gildea's account ends at this point, this still leaves open the possibility that the moment for revolution might well be in the midst of a war, as it was for Russia, or at the end of same, as for Germany. Finally, Ken Post, a self-professed unrepentant Marxist, has recently offered an explanation for why Marx and most of his late nineteenth-century followers were wrong in their prediction of an imminent revolution that would bring an end to capitalism. Post argues that development of European capitalism in the nineteenth century on a national, rather than an international, basis "broke up any broad potential social revolutionary movement," and when this was coupled with the globalization of capitalism in the form of imperialism, domestic resources in Europe could be devoted "to socializing workers in [capitalism's] own values and encapsulating [workers'] movements." He calls this process "the emergence of 'social capital.'"[16] Perhaps more plainly than with any of the other authors cited here, Post's argument at least suggests a high degree of continuity between pre- and postwar Europe.

This approach is given further validity when attention is focused on developments in Europe after World War II. The societies that have emerged almost everywhere in western Europe seem now to be much more the products of trends which developed in the 25 years before 1914 than the results of the war and its aftermath. The communism and fascism that arose in the interwar years now seem anomalies of the time, short-lived products of World War I even. Contemporary European society, with its commitment to universal healthcare and retirement programs, decent housing for all, universal education, care for the disadvantaged and elderly, and all the other aspects of regard for human welfare, seems much more clearly to reflect the growing trends of the earlier period than it does the aggressive, hostile, confrontational qualities of the interwar years. Above all, these later developments clearly give the lie to the smug confidence of the rapidly disappearing classical European liberals that theirs was the best of all possible worlds. Perhaps then we are justified in looking back on the years before the Great War to find whence the Europe of today came. If historians are to fulfill their task of understanding the present by explaining the past, then the apparent paradox of the pre-1914 years, an age of promise, leading to the disaster of communism and fascism, only to yield, eventually, the united, prosperous, and generally contented Europe of the twenty-first century, must be dealt with directly.

Marxism and the Workers' Movements

Somewhat paradoxically, at least one obstacle to finding a smoother transition from pre-1914 Europe to what followed has been the prevalence of Marxist interpretations of history, or more particularly, Marxist understanding of the classes of modern industrial societies – their definitions, their relationships, and their role in politics.

The paradox is that while Marxism may well have brought many scholars to focus on the industrial working class as a major force in modern society, the weaknesses of the Marxist view of class tended to direct their attention away from fruitful lines of investigation that might have made it easier to find the continuity that seems to be missing. Certainly, this tendency was greatly strengthened by the claim to Marxian orthodoxy made by the victorious Bolsheviks in Russia and their European defenders and the eventual expansion of communism to much of the rest of the world. The ability of communism to outlast fascism – and spread far and wide – reinforced Leninist claims to orthodoxy and accuracy, which, in turn, perpetuated the notion that Marxist lines of analysis, if not Marxism itself, could yield useful insights into the nature of modern society.

This problem has many facets, not the least important of which is an understanding of the nature of the relationship between political consciousness and the experiences of humans in the day-to-day world. If being determines consciousness, as most Marxists argue, and the most important element of being is one's place in the process of production, again something most Marxists hold, then it follows, for Marxists, that the overthrow of an economic and political system which exploits industrial workers and the rise of those same workers to power is an inevitable result of the further growth of capitalism. Acceptance of this general view, even by those who cannot properly be deemed Marxists, has led to much confusion and misunderstanding, especially about the nature of the working-class movement in pre-1914 Europe. It has, for example, brought a great many people (who should have known better) to accept the notion that the theoreticians of socialism accurately reflected the consciousness of the workers. This was an especially egregious problem with the left-wing faction of the world socialist movement in the prewar years. This self-delusional position strongly suggests that such people believed their own propaganda and never seriously looked into the matter for themselves. Barrington Moore's caution many years ago to "remember that the history of the Social Democratic Party of Germany (SPD) is not the history of the German industrial workers" has increasingly been heeded by some scholars at least.[17] But the myopia suggested by Moore led too many observers to be surprised that while the pre-1914 socialist parties officially called for peace, their followers in a great many cases greeted the war with enthusiasm. For far too long, the facile acceptance of the idea that the consciousness of the working classes corresponds to the claims of the socialist leadership, especially the theorists within it, has resulted in confusion and misunderstanding.

One possible reason for the persistence of this problem was the persistence of the Soviet Union. As long as it survived, the Marxist position, however misunderstood or misinterpreted by the communists, carried considerable weight. Thus, the fall of the Soviet Union in 1991 had a potential liberating influence on scholarship concerned with the working classes in Europe prior to 1914. In fact, the end of the Soviet Union seems to have brought a virtual end to serious study of Marx's influence on the workers' movement of western Europe. Moreover, in the new millennium, there has been a severe drop in the number of studies of any aspect of Marx, his life, and his influence. Works about Marx and his influence used to be published by the hundreds every year; now they appear much less frequently. While this precipitous decline in Marx scholarship does not necessarily signal an end to interest in radical social and political developments in the west during the years Marxism was such an important force, it certainly does suggest that one of the former central concerns of scholars working in this field, namely the role of Marxists and their ideology, no longer attracts much attention.

Sources of Worker Consciousness

Of course, not everyone accepted the Marxian view that the workers would be socialists as a result of their place in the dominant economic system. In sharp contrast to the apparent decline of interest in Marx and his influence on radical social-political movements in the late nineteenth and early twentieth centuries, scholars and activists have recently devoted considerably more time and attention to several major rivals to Marxism as the ideology of worker radicalism. Both anarchism and its variant form, anarcho-syndicalism, have been the subjects of several recent works. Much of the work in this area has been produced by those more or less committed to the ideology, and a great many of the studies concentrate on contemporary political movements, especially those opposing so-called globalization. An excellent example of the first sort is Peter Marshall's *Demanding the Impossible: A History of Anarchism.*[18] Marshall's survey is quite comprehensive and accurate, which makes it a useful and handy study. But it is also clearly marked by the author's own ideological inclination, which at times leads him to be overly generous and forgiving with regard to anarchists and less than generous with regard to their opponents. Curiously enough, given the traditional hostility of anarchists to the theories of Marx, they share with Marxists a predilection to explain workers' political consciousness in ideological terms rather than as a product of self-interest.

Furthermore, not everyone outside anarchist circles waited for the fall of the Soviet Union to begin a reevaluation of the working class in pre-1914 Europe. Contrasting markedly with the decline of interest in Marx and his impact on the working classes of Europe is the vast expansion in the past thirty years of studies that have focused more directly on the experiences, consciousness, politics, and daily lives of workers themselves. In fact, such studies have almost certainly contributed to the decline of interest in Marx as the philosopher of the working class by explicitly challenging several fundamental Marxian concepts, including, especially, the notion that consciousness, and therefore political behavior, is primarily determined by the position occupied by groups in the process of production. By the 1980s, more and more scholars were arguing that factors like language, ethnicity, religion, gender, and race were fundamentally important to shaping consciousness among workers. Among the most influential works in laying the basis for this new view are those by William H. Sewell, Jr, Gareth Steadman-Jones, William Reddy, and Patrick Joyce.[19] Interestingly, many of these writers have been motivated, at least in part, by a desire not only to understand history, but to change the course of society as well. Steadman-Jones concluded his study cited above with a chapter on the failings of the contemporary British Labour Party. In this, scholars bent on rejecting Marx's interpretation of class are also echoing one of his most poignant remarks about the purpose of philosophy, the eleventh thesis on Feuerbach: "The philosophers have only *interpreted* the world, in various ways; the point, however, is to *change* it."

Perhaps the most fruitful line of investigation in this apparent turn away from understanding class exclusively in terms of socioeconomic causality is the work being done by feminist and gender scholars. Although the implications of such work are much broader than just labor and working-class history, much recent work has focused especially on the narrower realm. Above all, the work of Joan Scott deserves special recognition. In works like "Gender: A Useful Category of Historical Analysis"[20] and "On Language, Gender, and Working-Class History,"[21] Scott has presented persuasive evidence and arguments that gender history is a potentially rich source (and in her hands the potential is realized) for better understanding labor and working-class history in the years before 1914. Anyone who has so fundamentally assaulted Marx's positivistic view of the nature of class and can also observe that by following this new approach "the historian can interpret the world while trying to change it," deserves not only our attention, but also our admiration.[22]

Following the lead of Scott and others, several scholars, including Kathleen Canning, have expanded the groundbreaking work into new areas.[23] German historians have been less eager to incorporate the gender-based approach into their work than have American, British, and French researchers, but given the importance of Germany as the birthplace of the first mass workers' party and, even more importantly, as the home of Nazism, a great deal more work needs to be done along these lines in order better to understand this crucial factor in the development of working-class consciousness.

In fact, what is needed now is not only studies of the impact of gender on the formal institutions of workers (Canning, for example, focuses her attention on the *Deutscher Textilarbeiterverband* and its female members), but also much broader efforts to understand the importance of gender issues within the family, neighborhoods, and social-political activities of worker populations. A great many important questions might usefully be rethought from a gender point of view, including why it was that the SPD was the only major group in pre-1914 Germany to espouse the female franchise. It is easy enough to answer this question in terms of the party's putative ideology, socialism, since socialists throughout Europe held similar positions, but if we want to understand the extent to which worker consciousness derived from worker experiences beyond and outside of the work place, the commitment of individual workers to this political position must be investigated in terms of their home and neighborhood situations. Similarly, if, as Canning points out, the male-dominated trade unions in Germany often tended to see female workers as displacing male workers for lower wages, while at the same time, as Canning also contends, females more often than not entered the workforce out of necessity (a fact their husbands, brothers, and fathers were surely aware of), what role did gender issues have in the creation and perpetuation of these apparently contradictory positions? Furthermore, did the majority of individual workers, as opposed to their institutional representatives, hold these contradictory positions or even consider them contradictory?

Moving even further away from the earlier focus on the institutions of the working classes and delving into the collective consciousness of the individuals that comprise this group will require imaginative use of available sources. The fact is that workers were often not literate, and even more often simply did not have the time and leisure to devote to the writing of letters, journals, diaries, or even fiction – sources that might provide valuable insights into what workers themselves were thinking. This may well be one of the most important reasons why researchers in this field have so often turned to the intellectuals of the movements when seeking to understand their character – at least the intellectuals expressed themselves in writing. Some sources that derive from actual workers' experiences do exist, but they are often colored by the fact that their authors had already committed to socialist activities before they launched into an explanation and description of their early lives. Works that draw from the workers' own writings about their lives can provide valuable insights into certain aspects of the development of worker consciousness, but the inherent limitations of autobiographical sources (especially the fact that they constitute a very small, statistically insignificant sample of all workers, and the imbalance in numbers between those written by males and those written by females) limit their value in the search for the origins of worker consciousness.[24]

Autobiographies and memoirs can be combined with other sources to expand our reach a bit. Nicola Verdon added detailed archival research in public and estate records to her reading of autobiographical accounts to give a fuller picture of an admittedly limited but still important element of the working class.[25] However, no matter how sophisticated such work is, the problem of inferring consciousness from impersonal or otherwise suspect sources remains. Oral histories based on personal interviews might at one time have offered real promise, but the people who went through the experience of being workers in the latter half of the nineteenth century and early years of the twentieth are no longer available to scholars, so this source is probably not going to yield much more of interest. The potential was tantalizingly revealed in studies like that of J. Robert Wegs; however, now we must look elsewhere.[26]

Many recent scholars have approached European working-class history with greater sophistication than did older studies.[27] Nonetheless, considerable work remains to be done. New studies that are informed by a greater sensitivity to gender, religious, ethnicity, and racial issues will deepen our understanding of the origins of consciousness. Such undertakings in German working-class history will almost certainly provide very useful insights into another issue – namely, to what extent was the German movement characterized by a collective commitment to Marxism, in however a distorted form, something obvious on the highest levels, and to what extent was the movement cemented together by concerns of workers and voters with the daily, grassroots issues of home, work place, and neighborhood? Anyone familiar with the scorn for theory expressed frequently and loudly by the leaders of the German so-called "free trade unions" will agree that this question is one well worth pursuing. The history of the Austrian workers' movement also provides rich possibilities for similar study, especially with regard to its concern with housing issues, something that was not nearly so prominent in other European workers' movements. Potentially interesting and fruitful studies also might be done concerning the role of women – not just prominent female leaders in the party and trade unions, but also mothers, wives, sisters, daughters, girlfriends, etc. – in shaping the positions of Austrian socialists on the matter of housing. Those more familiar with the other national movements surely can cite similarly promising lines of investigation in France, Italy, Spain, Scandinavia, and other areas.

Besides questions of gender, at least three other areas demand more detailed study to give us a fuller understanding of the nature of the worker-socialist movements in

Europe prior to 1914. One is the relationship between the development of worker consciousness and religion. This is a particularly important question in Germany, where the SPD was far more successful in winning followers among the largely Protestant workers of Prussia's large cities than it was among the predominantly Catholic populations of the south. Furthermore, a Catholic confessional party, the Center Party, frequently challenged the SPD in predominantly Catholic worker districts right up to 1914 and beyond, although the socialists won Reichstag seats in Catholic Alsace-Lorraine as early as 1893 and held a seat in an overwhelmingly Catholic district (2 Oberbayern – Munich II – which was almost 90 percent Catholic) from 1890 on.

The question which naturally arises then is what exactly was going on in workers' minds when they chose to back the Center rather than the SPD or vice versa. Wilfred Spohn discusses the secular tradition in the German movement, confessional dualism, and the ambiguous results of Catholic consciousness versus socialist consciousness.[28] He does not, however, draw from personal sources or memoirs in this brief study. Even if letters, memoirs, and autobiographies are not readily available, it should be possible to look at parish records for some place like 2 Oberbayern to see what baptismal and confirmation entries reveal about the religious consciousness of the worker population. Perhaps such investigations – which can just as well be conducted in the Catholic countries of Austria, Italy, France, and Spain – will disclose a gap between the experiences of the workers and the official atheism and anti-religion stances of the party hierarchy. It might even be possible to use studies of this sort to get at gender issues as well. One widely held assumption is that if worker children were baptized and confirmed, wives and mothers probably pushed for this more than did industrial-worker husbands and fathers. Maybe listening to the intellectuals and leaders has caused us to get this wrong also.

A second area that seems to require further study is the matter of the non-industrial worker following of the various European socialist parties in the years before 1914. Southern French farmers (at least at times of economic crisis), landless Italian agrarian field workers (the *braccianti*), the emerging white collar and lower professional classes (including various kinds of state employees, but especially school teachers), shop owners and workers in working-class districts, and other groups often formed a strong pool of socialist voters and even party activists at various times. None of these was considered prime socialist material by the theoreticians influenced by Marx and his analysis of modern industrial society. What does this say about the relationship between a group's role in the process of production and its political consciousness? Temporary economic crisis was sometimes involved in the turn to socialism of groups that it might not otherwise have attracted; this seems to be true of southern French wine growers during the *phylloxera* disaster of the 1890s. At other times, as in the case of the growing appeal of socialism to the lower ranks of white collar workers, longer-term issues, including, above all, the increasing proportion of the workforce employed by various branches of government, seem to have been more important. The *braccianti* of Italy are a particularly important group, especially given the traditional hostility of Marxism-influenced socialist parties of Europe to rural populations and the role of peasants in the later Leninist interpretation of the master's work. Often the success of socialism among the agrarian workers of the Po valley has been explained as a result of the absentee, capitalistic nature of agriculture pursued there.

But this explanation is flawed in two ways. First, it accepts as a given the now increasingly doubtful assertion that consciousness is determined primarily by place in the process of production; and second, it fails to look into the motives of the people involved. Comparative studies of several of these groups might be another way to discover the variegated sources of worker consciousness.

Finally, there is the vexing question of nationality. Everybody knows that in 1914 the workers of the world did not unite; rather, a great many of them went to war against one another with a rather startling enthusiasm, at least in the beginning. Moreover, anyone familiar with the experiences of the Austrian working-class movement in the years before the Great War knows that transnationalist unity had been abandoned long before 1914. Similar difficulties had also appeared in the German movement (with regard to the Polish population of the east), in the Italian movement (with the German-speaking workers of the north), and even in the Belgian movement (between the Flemish and Walloon populations), to say nothing of the problems between the English and the Irish. Perhaps no issue in the history of the pre-1914 European working class so clearly reflects the conflict between the blinkered ideological view imposed on the movement by its intellectuals and prominent leaders and the reality of the working-class consciousness of the period. Only those who in 1914 ignored reality in hopes of avoiding what was to prove such a disastrous war and those, including later historians and other critics, with much less excuse, who swallowed the myth of the international working class, could so overlook the obvious. As has happened so often, Hobsbawm came closest to the truth: "The masses followed the flags of their respective states, and abandoned the leaders who opposed the war. There were, indeed, few enough of these, at least in public."[29] Determining whether the workers actually "abandoned" their leaders or were never really with them on this issue in the first place will require that someone undertake a sweeping and searching new look at European workers and their relationship to nationalism during these years.

Taken together, studies such as those proposed above should provide a much clearer and more accurate understanding of the nature of the working classes and their organized movements in the years before 1914. If further work strengthens the growing consensus that consciousness is not solely, perhaps not even primarily, determined by economics, but rather by a subtle and complex interaction of a multitude of factors, including, but not limited to, race, ethnicity, gender, religion, family, neighborhood, etc., then the tendency to view the world through Marxist spectacles will be further eroded. This shift will, in turn, allow us to move away from the old notions that the 1914–18 war marks a failure on the part of the workers' movements (which were, on the public level at least, opposed to war) and that somehow this failure contributed to the horror of the interwar years when fascism and communism ran roughshod over the workers as well as much of the rest of humanity. If the Marxist view that the position of a group in the process of production largely determines consciousness is no longer generally accepted, then the notion of the workers failing to act as they should have (according to the erroneous Marxist view) no longer holds much water either. In fact, it may well prove that the dichotomy of social reform versus social revolution is itself mostly a figment of the Marxist imagination and that rejecting it will nudge open a bit wider the door to understanding and enlightenment.

Whence Post-1945 Europe?

Rejecting the reform vs. revolution dichotomy will help in another way also. How can it be that the pre-1914 workers' movement was a failure, while the world that Europe became after 1945 so clearly reflects a great many of the goals and aspirations of that same movement? How can the supposed failure to achieve a revolution be reconciled with the power to have so profoundly shaped society? In fact, leaving aside for the moment the notion of revolution as embodied in the Marxian tradition, especially in its Leninist incarnation (i.e., a relatively short, violent upheaval that shifts power from the bourgeoisie and its allies to the working classes), it seems obvious that the workers' movement did have a revolutionary impact on Europe.

Several writers have provided hints, and even more, about where this view might take us. Eric Hobsbawm's observation cited above about "subjects in the process of turning into democratic citizens," a tantalizing suggestion, was left without elaboration. Fortunately, one of the most active participants in the process of rethinking class, Geoff Eley, in his recent work, has expanded considerably on Hobsbawm's suggestion. Although he somewhat cryptically refers to Hobsbawm as "a career-long mentor, though we've only met a handful of times,"[30] Eley nonetheless admirably picks up on the theme suggested by the older scholar. The scope of Eley's work obviously far outreaches the chronological confines of the present essay, but those portions of *Forging Democracy* that deal with the years before 1914 are based on many of the same assumptions outlined here. Eley asserts "democracy is not 'given' or 'granted.' It requires *conflict* . . . It developed because masses of people organized collectively to demand it."[31] Furthermore, he argues that "for most of the period covered by this book, in fact, the banner of democracy was held up most consistently by the socialist tradition."[32] In this way, not only is the significance of the socialist movements of the pre-1914 years considerably expanded, but Eley also very specifically ties the democratic success of the leftist movements to both the twentieth century's world wars when he writes: "Only the large-scale socioeconomic mobilizations of world war, it seems, created the societal context for the advancement of democratic politics."[33] With this argument, Eley converts the tragic events of 1914–18 from a disruption, even a destruction, of the promise of the prewar years into an essential element of the process of democratizing European society. Thus the puzzlement raised by Gay's assertion turns into an explanation of how history works. Perhaps the Great War may once again be seen as assuming massive, if rather different, significance.

The prevalent notion that the European war of 1914–18 constituted an overwhelmingly important historical turning point cannot, of course, be overturned by the arguments presented here. First of all, from the fall of the Paris Commune in 1871 until the outbreak of the Russian revolution in February–March 1917, the only episode that can be considered a revolution was the rather abortive and remote events in Russia in 1905. Especially when viewed against the backdrop of the tumultuous first three-quarters of the nineteenth century, the years from 1871 to 1914 constitute a very long period of relative domestic peace. Similarly, after the end of the wars that resulted in German unification, again in 1871, Europe was not subjected to extensive fighting on its own territory until 1914. The wars that occurred in the interim, especially the extraordinarily brutal fighting in the Boer War and the Russo-Japanese war of 1904–5, caused hardly a whisper of disruption in most of Europe, which made for a very long period of relative international tranquility also. Such an extended period of order and peace seemed anomalous at the time and, given the character of the 27 years after World War I, would continue to seem abnormal throughout the remainder of the first half of the twentieth century.

But this is viewing human events on the overly generalized level. The years 1871–1914 do encompass events that speak to less tranquility and more internal disruption than the larger view admits. For example, anarchists and other groups and individuals attempted a great many assassinations during this period, and they were successful often enough to disturb the police and military forces of many European nations. The two most important such incidents are the murder of the Russian tsar, Alexander II, in 1881, and, of course, the event which launched the Great War itself, the assassination of Archduke Franz Ferdinand in Sarajevo in June of 1914. The knowledge that this latter event was one of several attacks against the lives of Habsburg officeholders in the four years before 1914 brings the archduke's death into clearer perspective as less an aberrant occurrence and more typical of the times than might be argued by those who view the years before the war as a relatively peaceful time. Furthermore, assassinations of several other prominent figures during this period, including the president of the French Republic in 1894, the empress of Austria in 1898, the king of Italy in 1900, and even an American president in 1901, makes our own time seem rather less unusual that one might think. That terrorists in those days did not kill dozens, hundreds, even thousands by driving explosive-laden cars and trucks, or airplanes, into buildings is almost certainly the result of technical, rather than moral, restrictions. But, of course, we cannot judge reactions to what happened then against the more brutal standards of what is happening now. People in the pre-1914 years did not know that things would get so much worse later.

One further assassination is worthy of special note here. Jean Jaurès was, perhaps, the most able, accomplished, and moderate leader of a factionalized French socialist movement in the prewar years, but he was unequivocally anti-war, not just as a matter of official party position, but also out of personal conviction. In August of 1914, a nationalist extremist assassinated Jaurès, presumably because the assassin thought that Jaurès's position against war would weaken French resolve to become involved in the slaughter that was to come. It must be granted that police and military officials in all the warring states did not respond with particular vehemence to the anti-war elements of their respective societies at the outset of the war. But the assassination of Jaurès does reveal that outside of official circles, sentiments ran high on the matter of socialists' opposition to war. This, then, is a clue to what was to come later. Perhaps the fear among those backing the war was not that the workers' movement could deliver what the Marxists thought it should, namely, stopping the war, but that the increasingly powerful working-class socialist movement posed an irresistible challenge to the old order, an order which did not have to consult with or even consider the will of the mass of the population before taking action that would have a devastating impact on the whole of western society. In this sense, Jaurès's death signaled not the defeat of socialism, but the fear on the part of many who were beholden or otherwise committed to the old order that the end was nigh.

Not the extreme, inward-looking nationalism of the right, but the moderate, though no less deeply held, nationalist and democratic commitment of the left would, after long and terrible struggle, emerge from the disastrous beginnings of the twentieth century to yield the Europe we know today. We know this for certain now – the thousand-year Reich of the Nazi madmen lasted only twelve years, and even the much more enduring regime of Soviet communism is now gone forever. But the society and values urged by the socialist workers' movement of the years before World War I seem set to endure for a long time. Even the incipient internationalism of the pre-1914 years has now taken the form of the European Union, the euro, and the greatly expanded and expanding influence of NATO. The legacy of the socialist workers' movement of these years was not its failing to stop World War I, but rather its laying the groundwork for the European society of the future.

NOTES

1 John Keegan, *The First World War* (London: Hutchinson, 1998), p. 3.
2 Frederic Morton, review of Peter Gay's *Schnitzler's Century: The Making of Middle-Class Culture 1815–1914* (New York: Allen Lane, 2001), *Los Angeles Times Book Review* (August 18, 2002), p. 6.
3 For example, see G. P. Gooch, *History of Modern Europe, 1873–1919* (New York: Holt, 1923).
4 See Carlton J. H. Hayes, *A Generation of Materialism 1871–1900* (New York: Harper, 1941) and Oron J. Hale, *The Great Illusion, 1900–1914* (New York: Harper and Row, 1971).
5 Hale, *The Great Illusion*, p. 287.
6 Norman Stone, *Europe Transformed, 1878–1919* (Cambridge MA: Harvard University Press, 1984), p. 335.
7 Ibid, pp. 330–3.
8 E. J. Hobsbawm, *The Age of Empire, 1875–1914* (London: Pantheon, 1987), p. 277.
9 Ibid, pp. 315–16 and ch. 12, passim.
10 Ibid, pp. 322, 325.
11 Malcolm Anderson, *The Ascendancy of Europe, 1815–1914* (London: Longman, 1972), pp. 60, 306.
12 Ibid, p. 59.
13 Ibid, esp. pp. 151–5.
14 Robert Gildea, *Barricades and Borders: Europe, 1800–1914*, 2nd edn (Oxford: Oxford University Press, 2003), p. 429.
15 Ibid, p. 435.
16 Ken Post, *Revolution and the European Experience, 1789–1914* (London: Macmillan, 1999), p. 3.
17 Barrington Moore, *Injustice: The Social Basis of Obedience and Revolt* (White Plains NY: Sharpe, 1978), p. 174.
18 Peter Marshall, *Demanding the Impossible: A History of Anarchism* (London: Harper Collins, 1992).
19 William H. Sewell, Jr, *Work and Revolution in France: The Language of Labor from the Old Regime to 1848* (Cambridge: Cambridge University Press, 1980); Gareth Steadman-Jones, *Languages of Class: Studies in English Working Class History, 1832–1982* (Cambridge: Cambridge University Press, 1983); William Reddy, *Money and Liberty in Modern Europe: A Critique of Historical Understanding* (Cambridge: Cambridge University Press, 1987); and Patrick Joyce, *Visions of the People: Industrial England and the Question of Class, 1848–1914* (Cambridge: Cambridge University Press, 1991).

20 Originally delivered as a paper at the American Historical Society annual meeting in December 1985, then published in the *American Historical Review* in December 1986, and finally appearing in a sterling collection, Joan Scott, ed., *Gender and the Politics of History* (New York: Columbia University Press, 1988).

21 In *International Labor and Working Class History* 31 (1987): 1–13, and in revised form in Scott, *Gender and the Politics*, pp. 53–67.

22 Scott, *Gender and the Politics*, p. 6.

23 See especially, Kathleen Canning, "Gender and the Politics of Class Formation: Rethinking German Labor History," in *Society, Culture, and the State in Germany, 1870–1930*, Geoff Eley, ed. (Ann Arbor: University of Michigan Press, 1996), pp. 105–41.

24 See, for example, Mary Jo Maynes, *Taking the Hard Road: Life Course in French and German Workers' Autobiographies in the Era of Industrialization* (Raleigh: University of North Carolina Press, 1995).

25 Nicola Verdon, *Rural Women Workers in Nineteenth Century England: Gender, Work and Wages* (Woodbridge: Boydell Press, 2002).

26 J. Robert Wegs, *Growing Up Working Class: Continuity and Change Among Viennese Youth, 1890–1938* (University Park: Pennsylvania State University Press, 1989).

27 For Germany, see Vernon Lidtke, *The Alternative Culture: Socialist Labor in Imperial Germany* (Oxford: Oxford University Press, 1985); Richard Evans, ed., *Proletarians and Politics: Socialism, Protest and the Working Class in Germany Before the First World War* (London: Harvester Wheatsheaf, 1990); and Stefan Berger, *Social Democracy and the Working Class in Nineteenth and Twentieth Century Germany* (London: Longman, 2000). For France, see Robert C. Stuart, *Marxism at Work: Ideology, Class and French Socialism, 1882–1905* (Cambridge: Cambridge University Press, 1992); and Christopher Ansell, *Schism and Solidarity in Social Movements: The Politics of Labor in the French Third Republic* (Cambridge: Cambridge University Press, 2001).

28 Wilfred Spohn, "Religion and Working-Class Formation in Imperial Germany, 1871–1914," in Eley, *Society, Culture, and the State in Germany*, pp. 163–87 (originally published in *Politics and Society* 119 (1991): 109–32.

29 Hobsbawm, *Age of Empire*, p. 326.

30 Geoff Eley, *Forging Democracy: The History of the Left in Europe, 1850–2000* (New York: Oxford University Press, 2002), p. xiv.

31 Ibid, p. 4.

32 Ibid, p. 5.

33 Ibid, p. 3.

GUIDE TO FURTHER READING

Geoff Eley, *Forging Democracy: The History of the Left in Europe, 1850–2000* (New York: Oxford University Press, 2002). Convincingly integrates pre- and post-1914 history with regard to the working class.

Geoff Eley, ed., *Society, Culture, and the State in Germany, 1870–1930* (Ann Arbor: University of Michigan Press, 1996). Essays which look at worker consciousness from many angles.

E. J. Hobsbawm, *The Age of Empire, 1875–1914* (Cambridge MA: Harvard University Press, 1987). Ably presents without exaggeration the influence of workers' parties in pre-1914 Europe.

Leszek Kolakowski, *Main Currents of Marxism*, 3 vols (Oxford: Oxford University Press, 1981). An exhaustive account of the origins and nature of Marx's thought and of many who were influenced by Marx.

George Lichtheim, *Marxism: An Historical and Critical Study* (New York: Columbia University Press, 1982). Focuses on how Marxism changed as it moved eastward from Europe to Russia.

Barrington Moore, *Injustice: The Social Basis of Obedience and Revolt* (White Plains NY: Sharpe, 1978). Insightful view of the relationship between workers and their organized movements.

Ken Post, *Revolution and the European Experience, 1800–1914* (London: Macmillan, 1999). A Marxist's effort to explain why the inevitable revolution never came.

Joan W. Scott, *Gender and the Politics of History* (New York: Columbia University Press, 1988). Fine collection of essays including several pertinent to worker consciousness.

Gary P. Steenson, *After Marx, Before Lenin: Marxism and Socialist Working-Class Parties in Europe, 1884–1914* (Pittsburgh: University of Pittsburgh Press, 1991). Discusses the relationship between Marx's theory and workers' parties before 1914.

CHAPTER TEN

Modernity: Approaching the Twentieth Century

ANGELA K. SMITH

. . . in or about December, 1910, human character changed.

    I am not saying that one went out, as one might into a garden, and there saw that a rose had flowered, or that a hen had laid an egg. The change was not sudden and definite like that. But a change there was, nevertheless; and, since one must be arbitrary, let us date it about the year 1910. (Virginia Woolf, "Mr Bennett and Mrs Brown," 1924)[1]

The relationship between modernity and culture, explored in this chapter, is complex and far-reaching. The beginning of the twentieth century, historically a site of so much dramatic change, saw a blossoming of new ideas throughout the arts, reflecting and cataloging the shifting world around them. Writers and artists built upon the innovations of the last years of the nineteenth century as the pace of change accelerated. A new awareness of the human psyche, ushered in by the growing body of work by Sigmund Freud, began to change the perspectives through which the world, and its occupants, could be viewed. When Virginia Woolf stated, "in or about December, 1910, human character changed," she was well aware of the multiple factors that brought about this notion of change.

For the world was changing in a range of new ways. Politically, the nineteenth century saw a rise in the labor movement with the fight for manhood suffrage and workers' rights accelerating across Europe. Important new leaders such as Keir Hardie emerged, driving socialism on as a political force inspired by the ideas of writers such as Karl Marx. In Britain, the Education Acts of the 1870s ensured that the turn of the century saw the first fully literate adult population, a population receptive to the written word and all its implications. Simultaneously, the women's movement, which had been smoldering for fifty years, took on a new life with the formation of much more militant organizations. In Britain, in 1903, Emmeline Pankhurst, together with her daughters, founded the Women's Social and Political Union, heralding the start of a new phase in the struggle for women's suffrage, that of militancy. Although many established suffrage societies did not support the Pankhursts' methods, they did add another string to the suffrage bow and contributed to the general instability faced by successive governments in the early years of the century. At the same time the internationalism of the movement grew in strength, as women across Europe and America worked together to achieve equality.

Change was also taking place on other fronts. Scientific and technological developments were rapidly altering the physical shape of the world. A shrinking globe was created by inventions such as the telegraph and the telephone, which introduced an immediacy to language and ideas that could never have been achieved through the antiquated postal service. The typewriter transformed the life of the office; the world of leisure was revolutionized by the gramophone and the moving picture. With so much change, new means of expression had to be found to delineate experience in a shifting, transient world.

The subject of the impact of modernity upon culture is a huge one, difficult to do justice to in a small space and time. Inevitably, this chapter can only deal with a sample survey of examples. But it presents an interesting challenge, as space and time were such important concepts to the makers of modern art. The introduction of Greenwich Mean Time in the late nineteenth century was intended to regulate and control time, placing Britain at the center of a universal day. But the explosion of the machine age had a profound effect on notions of space and time. Technological innovation introduced new speeds with the steam train, the omnibus, the tram, and the motorcar, enabling people to travel much more quickly, effectively appearing to shrink space and time. At the same time, courtesy of Freud and other psychoanalytic thinkers, there was a new emphasis on the exploration of inner space, the workings of the mind, which had the effect of dismantling time completely. From within the human mind it was possible to develop new subjective interpretations of time and space and this too is reflected in the artistic production of the period.

Literature presented an ideal forum for such experimentation and it is useful to take one archetypal "modernist" novel to illustrate the complexity of this change. On the surface, Ford Madox Ford's 1915 novel, *The Good Soldier*, deals with the intricate relationships between two couples, the very British Ashburnhams and the equally American Dowells, spanning the first decade and a half of the twentieth century. The confused narrator, John Dowell, tells and retells the story, trying to make sense of events that destroy the old world order and the lives of a number of the central protagonists. He focuses on Edward Ashburnham, the eponymous good soldier, whose clandestine taste for womanizing leads him into a spiral of destruction that destroys hundreds of years of his heredity. Dowell's adulterous wife, Florence, a New Englander set on returning to old England, is a wayside casualty. Dowell himself, the apparent onlooker, ends up owning the ancient Ashburnham estate, while Edward's Catholic wife, later widow, Leonora, reproduces gleefully with a forward-thinking country squire, highlighting her late husband's sterility. The novel engages with a range of topical issues: class, nationality, religion, sex, sentiment, and psychology. But it also does much more than this.

Ford's narrative works on many levels. Dowell invites the reader to take on the role of listener, psychologist, and perhaps psychoanalyst; we delve into his psyche, exploring his unconscious as well as his conscious responses to his fellow characters and thus can identify him as a major player in the drama after all. Time is confused, as Dowell's narrative jumps from one incident to another covering a period of years or days. It is imprisoned within the internal space of his mind as he remembers and misremembers events. But the text also offers a metanarrative, with the unhappy quartet symbolically representing a society and culture, doomed by modernity, destined for extinction on the western front. All the significant events of the novel take place on August 4, ensuring that the guns of World War I resonate throughout the text. Edward Ashburnham, representative of the officer class, the upholder of empire, cannot survive. John Dowell, herald of the new world superpower and later-day imperialist, cannot do otherwise.

The Good Soldier is an almost perfect example of the modernist novel. It rejects the chronological structures of the nineteenth century, draws heavily on the artistic school of impressionism within which Ford grew up (his grandfather was the impressionist painter Ford Madox Brown), and it draws upon contemporary ideas and innovations such as Freudian psychoanalysis, that were changing man's understanding of himself. It explores the condition of late nineteenth-century society and finds it terminally flawed, and it anticipates the cataclysmic event that will transform it. Culturally, *The Good Soldier* illustrates the processes of modernity at play in the first years of the twentieth century, processes located not just in literature, but also in the visual arts, in performance, and in the world of ideas.

Literature

Ideas about the form, structure, and purpose of literature have always been fluid. By the end of the nineteenth century the novel had become established as a major literary force. Writers such as Charles Dickens, George Eliot, Leo Tolstoy, and Gustave Flaubert had given it authority and dignity as well as transforming it into an important political weapon. Culturally, it still ranked below poetry, the highest literary form, but that too was changing. The short story, emerging from the magazines and periodicals of the nineteenth century, was becoming important as an alternative literary form. The writers of the *fin de siècle* were once again searching for difference, for ways of adapting their craft to reflect a changing world.

Within literature, this change took a number of forms, many of which can be linked with shifting ideas about the use of language; whether or not language reflected the world and the ways in which it might be used more effectively to represent the world. A number of writers used these changing ideas about the status of language to explore and develop the genre of the novel. Henry James had already led the way in the late nineteenth century, criticizing the objective prose that had come, for him, to epitomize the Victorian novel. These older books were often "triple deckers"; that is, in three distinguishable parts, extremely long, with a moral or social message to guide the reader's thinking. James argued that the novel should be regarded as an art form, just like any other, and strove in his writing to use language aesthetically as a painter might use paint, to convey the subject rather than the object, to develop the interior life of his characters. A similar effect can be seen in the undulating prose of Thomas Hardy, the tightly constructed words of Joseph Conrad, or the naturalism of Emile Zola. James was also the first writer to identify and construct the notion of a theoretical framework for the novel, analyzing linguistic and structural processes, criticizing it as any work of art may be criticized. He set a trend which was followed in the first decades of the twentieth century by a number of important and influential writers, among them Virginia Woolf, D. H. Lawrence, and Wyndham

Lewis. This exploration of the relationship between reality and art through literature is perhaps most fully realized in Marcel Proust's great work, *A la Recherche du temps perdu*, a series of volumes that search for artistic ways to recapture a lost past.

In the early twentieth century, fiction, on the whole, got shorter.[2] The writing of the "modernists", as they would later be termed, was self-aware, often politically so, and often built around a number of shared characteristics: disruptions to narrative form, concern with issues of temporality, aesthetic self-consciousness, fragmentation and montage, paradox, ambiguity, uncertainty, and juxtaposition. For many, there was a shift in focus from external, objective reality to the internal working of the human mind. Ford Madox Ford's novel *The Good Soldier* embodies many of these characteristics. John Dowell is an unreliable narrator. His narrative moves backwards and forwards in time denying temporal cohesion and thus disrupting the expected narrative form. It is fragmented: pieces of information about the various characters are pieced together almost randomly. Everything is ambiguous, nothing is certain, we have only one person's point of view; all the others are trapped within his. And it is political: when read as allegory, it comments on the state and condition of the world in 1914; the state and condition of modernity.

In 1915, the same year as he published *The Good Soldier*, Ford also published a critical study, *Henry James*. Clearly influenced by James, Ford had spent years considering "how words should be handled and novels constructed."[3] He was also influenced by Joseph Conrad's efforts to develop new literary techniques. Moving on from the experiments of James and Conrad, Ford developed his own brand of "literary Impressionism," a technique that foregrounded language as an artistic tool to create an effective representation of life. It concentrated on the representation of the transitory mental impressions of an observer, in this case John Dowell, rather than giving more conventional descriptions of events. It places an emphasis on interior space, on the complex workings of the mind, indicating the growing importance of Freud's ideas of psychoanalysis in the early years of the century.

John Dowell's narrative explores these ideas. It is almost as though the reader is being asked to psychoanalyze him. He inhabits an internal world that we have to decipher, within which the external world, the events of the novel, are contained or imprisoned. He tells us, "the whole world for me is like spots of color in an immense canvas,"[4] and indeed it is so. The spots of color are provided by Edward Ashburnham, by Leonora, by Florence, by Nancy, flitting in and out according to the light against the background of Dowell's gray uncertainty. Trapped as they are within his gaze, the reader can never be sure of them; we are left instead with an impression that enables us to construct our own narrative upon Dowell's canvas. Nothing in the text is explicit. Each word is carefully chosen and suggestive, leaving it open to the interpretation of the reader: "And then I had my first taste of English life. It was amazing. It was overwhelming. I never shall forget the polished cob that Edward, beside me, drove; the animal's action, its high-stepping, its skin that was like satin. And the peace! And the red cheeks! And the beautiful, beautiful old house."[5]

This is an interesting passage in a number of ways. In terms of its construction, Ford uses short clipped sentences and distinct images to present Dowell's first impression of England: the movement of the horse, the satin skin, the red cheeks. But at the same time, for all its precision, it tells the reader almost nothing. There is nothing about the horse to suggest either Englishness or to appear overwhelming. It is unclear whose cheeks are red; Edward's? the horse's? Dowell's? The impression of the "beautiful, beautiful house" is vague and unhelpful. Dowell's response is almost childlike. There is little in these first impressions to remind the reader that Dowell has been recently widowed, or to warn the reader that he has been called to a household in dire emotional trouble despite the fact the Dowell himself is well aware of this. We are given the spots of color. It is up to us to arrange them and create our own impression without much help from the guide, just as one might be expected to do in life. Dowell's telling and retelling of the Ashburnham story builds up the layers on the canvas, allowing for multiple readings to be made. For example, Dowell's late wife, Florence Hurlbird, is "poor Florence," she is an angel, she is beautiful, later she is a whore, and finally a victim. Most significantly, the reader is left in no doubt from the outset that she is dead and unable to speak for herself. We are reliant on Dowell's changing impressions of her, and all the other characters, and he is the ultimate modernist: an unreliable narrator, confused and yet manipulative in his confusion.

Such narrative and linguistic exploration was not confined to the English language. Across Europe writers were developing new writing techniques to convey their alternate changing worlds. The Viennese doctor, Arthur Schnitzler, experimented with the German language, writing about the middle and upper classes surrounding him, actively portraying Freud's Vienna. Perhaps his most important work, *Leutnant Gustl*, published in 1901, was constructed around an interior monologue that was unique in German literature of the period. A complex tale that was both social criticism and psychoanalytic exploration, it was a precursor to many later European modernist works. Another German writer, Franz Kafka, may perhaps be considered as Schnitzler's heir. Although all of Kafka's work was published posthumously, much of it was written in the period before 1914. Kafka had an innate distrust of established institutions, including that of literary tradition, leading him to search for new ways of literary representation. He analyzes language, seeing it as a source of purity, focusing on the plight of the individual in a world of growing confusion. This is perhaps exemplified in his novel *The Trial*, written in 1914 and published in 1925, with its pessimistic representation of the oppression of bureaucracy. Kafka's work blends comedy, irony, and tragedy, identifying the troubled modern psyche of the world around him.

But similar experiments were taking place in other genres with equally dramatic results. In poetic circles there was a movement away from the wordiness of the Victorians with a focus on the intricacies of language, ideas not dissimilar to those in the arena of prose writing. These notions reached their pinnacle in imagism. Imagism was the brainchild of Ezra Pound and F. S. Flint and was the practice of paring poetry back to present an idea through an image. Also involved in the development of the movement were poets T. E. Hulme, Richard Aldington, and H. D. (Hilda Doolittle). They worked according to a small set of rules:

- Direct treatment of the "thing" whether subjective or objective.
- To use absolutely no word that did not contribute to presentation.
- As regarding rhythm: to compose in sequence of the musical phrase, not in sequence of a metronome.[6]

Pound argued that "An 'image' is that which presents an intellectual and emotional complex in an instant of time."[7] The image at the heart of each poem contained its essence. The image explored the subject of the poem with the painter's eye, bringing out the aesthetics within. The imagists published four anthologies of poetry in the years 1914–17. Pound himself felt that H. D.'s poetry provided the most perfect examples of the working of imagism. The following example illustrates the paradoxical simplicity and complexity of the movement, as well as the brevity of much of the work:

> Whirl up, sea –
> Whirl your pointed pines,
> Splash your great pines
> On our rocks,
> Hurl your green over us,
> Cover us with your pools of fir.[8]

This poem, taken from the 1915 collection *Some Imagist Poets 1915*, was sighted by Pound in his definition of vorticism as the most perfect imagist poem. It appears to reject the existing conventions of poetry, built around a paradoxically abstract, yet crystal-clear image. The image is everything. There is no subject. There are none of the expected structures of poetry, there is no meter or rhyme, only what Peter Jones terms "a rhythm organic to the image itself."[9] Yet it provokes an emotional response from the reader through the sensory and sensual nature of the image itself.

Imagism was one of many cultural and artistic movements of the early twentieth century, the "isms" which have subsequently found space beneath the umbrella term of modernism. They include futurism, cubism, and later surrealism, to name but a few. Vorticism, the manifesto for which was printed in the short-lived publication *Blast*, argued for an attack on old values and an assertion of new ones. In many ways it embodies the nature of these rebellious groups. The ideas of these various "isms," imagism included, were promoted in a range of "Little Magazines" that articulated the voice of new cultures to an unsuspecting population. Publications such as *Poetry Review*, *The Egoist*, and the *Little Review* became mouthpieces for the radical arts and philosophical debates of the time. Such magazines had existed for years, but the nature of their development in the first decades of the century gives an indication of the way in which changing cultural ideas were being disseminated.

The Egoist provides a good example of this development. It began life in 1911 as *The Freewomen*, a radical feminist publication set up by a disillusioned suffragette, Dora Marsden, and her friend and colleague, Mary Gawthorpe. Perceived primarily as a suffrage magazine, *The Freewomen* highlighted the poor conditions of many women, but equally attacked militant suffrage organizations, especially that of the Pankhursts, as misguided in their interpretation of the fight. The paper became more and more anarchic in its subject matter, leading to the withdrawal of its distributor in 1912 – after which it quickly folded. When it reappeared as *The New Freewoman* it had Harriet Shaw Weaver sharing the editorial work with Marsden and the input and support of a number of significant literary women – Rebecca West, May Sinclair, and H. D. among them. Through West, Ezra Pound became involved with the publication and it began to publish experimental literature in addition to the focus on feminist and political issues. In December 1913 the name of the paper was changed again, to *The Egoist*, indicating a new ideology – egoism – that could incorporate artistic and literary experimentation as well as revolutionary politics and philosophical exploration. Although multi-dimensional, *The Egoist* is best remembered for its advance publication of some of the most exciting works of modernism, including James Joyce's *A Portrait of the Artist as a Young Man*, Wyndham Lewis's *Tarr*, and a wide selection of imagist poetry. Indeed, the edition of May 1915 was entirely dedicated to the work and ideas of the imagists. However, it never lost the connection with philosophy and to some degree politics, enabling it to reflect many aspects of cultural modernity.

The Visual Arts

In the visual arts, too, the changes of the early twentieth century manifested themselves through experiments with spatial concepts, both internal and external. Developing schools across Europe found new and alternative ways of representing the world, sharing many of the influences of contemporary writers. When Virginia Woolf made her famous statement, quoted above, that "in or about December, 1910, human character changed," she had in mind the first of two exhibitions of "Post-Impressionism" organized by her friend Roger Fry at the Grafton Galleries, definitively linking literature and the visual arts. The show was seen as shocking by the general public and press alike, and contained works by established artists such as Van Gogh, Gauguin, and Cezanne. Surprisingly, considering the public response, it did not contain examples of any of the more radical experimentation in the arts, most especially cubism, which had been developing in the previous years.

Fry's Post-Impressionism explored aesthetic ideas of pure form, prioritizing the formal characteristics of a work over and above its subject. It is easy to connect these theoretical ideas with the development of modern literature, particularly through the writing of, for example, Virginia Woolf. Woolf examined the formal characteristics of writing in theoretical essays such as "Modern Fiction" (1919) and "Mr Bennett and Mrs Brown" (1924), exploring ways in which writing could develop aesthetically. These ideas are played out in her fiction of the 1920s. Her modernist novels – for example, *Jacob's Room* (1922), *Mrs Dalloway* (1925), and *To the Lighthouse* (1927) – use language in innovative ways to create an aesthetic whole.

In Europe things had developed rather differently. The Post-Impressionism of Fry's exhibition provided the building bricks for artists such as Picasso, Matisse, and Braque to develop alternative routes into abstract art. Matisse elected the route of color, experimenting further along the lines first explored by Cezanne. Indeed, it was Cezanne who inspired the term "cubism" for the art of his contemporaries, describing their developing work as "little cubes."[10] The group of painters involved in the movement regularly met together with writers and critics to develop ideas that related cubism to other areas of the arts. They accepted the term "CUBIST" as a collective description when it was first used in print in 1911 by the poet Guillaume Apollinaire, a supporter of and commentator on the group.

The bridge between the impressionists and the cubists was also Cezanne. Glen Macleod suggests that through broken brushstrokes and the use of pure color,

Cezanne added weight and volume by emphasizing the underlying geometric structure of objects."[11] It was this emphasis on these geometric shapes that would become the trademark of cubism.

Cubism, which developed between 1907 and 1914 in three stages, is perhaps the most influential development in the visual arts of the twentieth century. The two artists generally credited with its development are Picasso and Braque, but a much larger group would meet in Picasso's studio, the *Bateau Lavoir*, in Montmartre from about 1905 onwards. The first stage, still clearly influenced by Cezanne, begins with Picasso's *Les Demoiselles d'Avignon* (1907). It breaks down the subject into geometrical shapes, and while it remains recognizable, it is distorted, breaking with convention. After about 1910, Picasso and Braque moved cubism on to its second stage, which has become known as analytical cubism. In this period, the artists further fragmented and distorted their subjects, removing all color, thus analyzing the form. After 1912 the artists began to move away from the monochrome nature of this second stage, evolving synthetic cubism, which involved the reintroduction of color, along with dialogue and texture. Even physical objects were sometimes incorporated into the works. Macleod states: "This technique, known as *collage*, is a revolutionary invention because it breaks down the boundaries between art and life, causing the viewer to ponder various kinds and degrees of artifice."[12] This phase of cubism explored the three dimensional nature of art and representation which would prove very influential in the years that followed.

The influence of this movement resonates throughout the twentieth century. Picasso in particular was a prolific artist and his works can be viewed in many European cities. An early example of this influence can be found in vorticism, a movement set up by a range of artists including Wyndham Lewis, Henri Gaudier-Brzeska, and the poet Ezra Pound. This, like the Italian-based movement, futurism, claimed to incorporate literature and music as well as art, but was cut short by the outbreak of World War I. It is interesting to further note the impact of cubism on some of the most significant artists of the war, Wyndham Lewis among them, who used modern experimental techniques to represent the unthinkable experience of the battlefield in an authentic way. Just as modernist writers used their new techniques to convey the unspeakable, so artists found alternative ways of illustrating a different and profoundly tragic development in warfare.

In literature, too, the impact of cubism was felt. A number of writers were directly involved with the group of artists, among them Apollinaire, André Salmon and, perhaps most interestingly, the American writer, Gertrude Stein. Apollinaire and Salmon wrote commentaries of the development and processes of cubism, such as Salmon's "Anecdotal History of Cubism" (1912) and Apollinaire's "The Beginnings of Cubism" (1912).[13] For example:

> There lived in Montmartre an adolescent with restless eyes and a face that was reminiscent of those of both Raphael and Forain. Pablo Picasso . . . had abruptly rejected his former style and devoted himself to creating mysterious paintings dominated by a deep blue . . . He dressed in the blue smock worn by electricians; his words were often very bitter . . . His studio, crowded with canvases representing mystical harlequins and with drawings over which we walked and which anyone could carry off, was the meeting place of all the young artists and all the young poets.[14]

This evocative extract is rather like a piece of art in itself. Apollinaire immediately places Picasso within an artistic tradition as both subject and object with his reference to Raphael and Forain. He uses the color blue, rather as Picasso does, to build a picture of the artist and the studio. The studio itself is structured around the pictures, those same geometric shapes. Picasso has the appearance of an artisan and the language of a rebel. He is represented as the center of the movement, perhaps rather romanticized and certainly original.

Gertrude Stein, on the other hand, used cubism in a different way in her writing. Instead of writing about it, allowing it to infiltrate the words, she wrote cubism itself, creating a whole new language based on the same principles. Stein was a patron and friend of Picasso and had lived in Paris for some years. Stein used a portrait by Cezanne to shape her 1909 book, *Three Lives*. She also wrote in response to a number of cubist paintings in her own collection. Stein used language to create geometric shapes in much the same way as the artists, developing patterns within her writing intended to give it dimension. Lacking conventional structure and punctuation, Stein's work is clearly modernist, making a direct link between these two artistic fields.

Performing Arts

> Upon my word, yes, our intimacy was like a minuet . . . You can't kill a minuet de la cour. You may shut up the music-book, close the harpsichord . . . but surely the minuet – the minuet itself is dancing itself away into the furthest stars, even as our minuet of the Hessian bathing places must be stepping itself still.[15]

The central protagonists of *The Good Soldier* perform their roles within the text like the best modern actors. Edward Ashburnham acts out the role of the perfect English gentleman; his wife endorses this with her affected devotion. Florence pretends to be an invalid, to have a "heart" in order to get closer to her precious England. Dowell acts as though he knows nothing. But the old music, the music to which they have all danced, will no longer do. The psychology of *The Good Soldier* is also evident in the modern theater. The European theater, although dependent on public support and critical attention, tied to the commerciality of performance, had begun to change at the end of the nineteenth century, with radical dramatists such as Ibsen, Strindberg, and Shaw starting to use the stage as a forum for political and social ideas as well as for entertainment. But, as Christopher Innes has argued, it is difficult to fit the developments in theater into the same general framework of modernism that can be applied to literature and other art forms:

> On the stage, art could neither assert itself as an autonomous activity, independent of external experience, nor aspire to pure form. In sharp contrast to the modernist drive in poetry or painting, imitation was always present . . . Simply presenting a sequence of actions in a temporal and spatial frame evoked the "narrative method" that Eliot rejected, along with Kandinsky, whose declaration that "the literary element, 'storytelling' or 'anecdote' must be abandoned" was picked up by Pound and the Vorticists.[16]

But modernity did continue to impact on the theater in the first decades of the twentieth century in a number of different ways, ways perhaps more associated with other performing arts such as music and the fledgling art form, the cinema. One example is in the work of George Bernard Shaw. Although at times politically challenging (he was an active member of the Fabian Society) his plays give the impression of being traditional in structure and form. Yet the intellectualism of his work moves it beyond tradition, and he experimented with structures built around those in music to give his drama an alternative feel. Shaw conceived his plays as "musical performances" in which the "long rhetorical speeches" were consciously written "like operatic solos."[17] These allow the audience to glimpse the interior working of the characters' minds; that inner space explored once more. Within this, much of Shaw's drama satirizes the established social order, offering allegorical examples of how this order is heading for disaster. In this way his work parallels *The Good Soldier* despite using a notably different technique.

More experimentally perhaps, Wyndham Lewis turned to drama as a way to articulate his ideas in *Blast*. An early drama, *The Enemy of the Stars*, was published as an artistic manifesto, never intended for performance. "*The Enemy of the Stars* is a composite of fragmented cubist 'visions from within' ":[18] thus it is all that could be expected of modern art. It was significantly influenced by the work of Max Stirner, especially *The Ego and Its Own* which was, coincidentally, a driving force behind much of Dora Marsden's writing for *The Egoist*. Stirner, whose philosophical work focused on the primacy of the individual or the "ego," was an influence on the later nineteenth century philosopher Friedrich Nietzsche, whose writings fed much of the creative development of the early twentieth century, as will be discussed later. Violent and subliminal, this drama of the mind might stand as the epitome of modernism, with human figures expanded to puppet-like monsters in a technologically conceived universe where the stars are "machines of prey" and the imagination determines reality. Needless to say, it has never been produced.[19]

However, plays that are not produced have limited theatrical value. Elsewhere, dramatists were responding to modernity in more productive ways. W. B. Yeats, the successful poet, whose interests in symbolism and primitivism had established him as innovative, worked with the Abbey theater company to produce Irish political drama. Yeats's symbolist past gave him more in common, linguistically, with the imagist poets, but his interests in mythology and Irishness gave his work a different dimension.

The primitivism that can find roots in some of Yeats's work, later to be located in the angry words of Wyndham Lewis and the politics of Eugene O'Neil, perhaps reached its climax in the musical world with the first performance of Stravinsky's *Rite of Spring*. This was a ballet performed by Serge Diaghilev's *Ballets Russes* on May 29, 1913. Its subject was "scenes from pagan Russia," and it was choreographed by Nijinsky. It is structured in two parts, "Dance of the Earth" and "Sacrificial Dance," each beginning slowly and building to a loud, pulsating finale. The performance caused a riot, in part because of the content, subject matter and choreography, but also because of the radical nature of the music.

At the beginning of the twentieth century, musical composition was still built around traditions that had been established with the Renaissance. Harmonic consistency, thematic development, and metrical flow remained fundamental. In the first years of the century, composers, like so many other artists, began to question the uniformity of this tradition and search for more individual expression in their composition. A principle player in this musical experimentation was Arnold Schoenberg. Austrian-born Schoenberg believed in originality as the only means to create an authentic expression of space and vision. His eventual abandonment of tonality in his compositions allowed him to create an expressionist music that he understood to correspond with similar experiments within the visual arts. Schoenberg adopted

> an "atonal" musical universe within which all pitches, at least in principle, were equally related, proclaiming what he called "the emancipation of dissonance": the right of all notes to exist on their own terms, without reference to some higher tonal authority. In so doing he negated a compositional principle that had governed Western music since its beginnings.[20]

Like Schoenberg, Igor Stravinsky broke with tradition to create a new music. He alternated major and minor and disrupted traditional harmony. At the same time he changed rhythm, moving away from beat towards pulse to build irregular bars and irregular phrases. He introduced new musical modes, such as folk or church music, and the combination of all this resulted in a change to the form and structure of the music. As with other modern art forms, there is no clear resolution and the compositions often sound fragmented. These two composers pushed the boundaries of musical composition, influenced by the same factors of change as other artists and the same need to articulate that change. Robert P. Morgan suggests: "Indeed music . . . had been transformed almost as much between 1907 and 1913 – that is, between the appearance of Schoenberg's first post-tonal works and the premiere of Stravinsky's *Rite* – as it had been in the entire preceding 300 years."[21]

There were other impulses of change in music, often directly linked with other radical movements within the arts. For example, the futurist composer Luigi Russolo invented mechanical "noise-makers" in order to create new sound sources. These sources reflected the futurist celebration of the machine age and included things like motorcars, trams, and other engine sounds – a kind of precursor to the makers of electronic music who would become prominent later in the century.

Away from the traditional performance medium of the stage, a new kind of performance art was developing rapidly in the first years of the twentieth century, on the screen. Magic lantern shows had fascinated and frightened Victorian audiences for decades, but the turn of the century saw the birth of a new art form that would become one of the most prominent. The desire to make still photographs move had been growing for some time. Although the name of the American Thomas Edison is commonly associated with the birth of cinema, its real origins were in France. The Lumière brothers, Louis and Auguste, produced the first moving picture on celluloid film in 1895, *Sortie d'usine* (*Employees Leaving the Lumière Factory*). This film was shot with a fixed camera, hidden from the workers so that they would not be distracted by it. The Lumières followed this with other famous tableaux such as *Repas de bébé* (*Baby's Dinner*) and *Arrivée d'un train à La Ciotat* (*Arrival of a Train at La Ciotat*), which frightened viewers with its unexpected realism. Similar films appeared in Britain showing real life experiences, such as the 1901 film *Fire*, one of several depicting the work of the fire brigade. Things began to change in 1903 when an American engineer, Edwin S. Porter, produced the first major film to tell a story,

The Great Train Robbery, and the industry never looked back. Another early film, the French production of *Queen Elizabeth,* committed the famous Victorian actress Sarah Bernhardt to celluloid, allowing her to be seen by more people than ever before.

Early cinema remained much like theater in the way that it was produced and presented. Pioneers in Italy worked to change the format of the moving picture with large-scale films such as *Cabiria* (1914), but World War I had a crippling effect on the industry in Europe. The moving picture was then also used for political purposes, most famously in the propaganda film *The Battle of the Somme* (1916), which shocked audiences despite being manufactured to avoid showing the worst horrors of the trenches.

The cinema stands out from the other forms of art considered here in that, unlike most other disciplines, it was not reacting against a previous tradition. It was new, and an entity in itself. But it was still a product of the same developments in society, the rapid pace of change that forced culture to evolve, the same impulse of modernity, and underlying all these artistic responses, feeding the impulse through the intellect, were the same set of radical ideas.

Ideas

When I set myself the task of bringing to light what human beings keep hidden within them . . . by what they say and what they show, I thought the task was a harder one than it really is. He that has eyes to see and ears to hear may convince himself that no mortal can keep a secret.[22]

The above quotation is from Sigmund Freud in 1905, but the words could equally apply to any readers of Ford Madox Ford's *The Good Soldier,* listening to the monologue of John Dowell as he searches within himself for the story of the Ashburnhams. He recounts his own symptoms and gradually, as the stories unfold, finds his own cure: "So I shall just imagine myself for a fortnight or so at one side of the fireplace of a country cottage, with a sympathetic soul opposite me."[23] Sympathetic soul, reader, psychoanalyst – in such company, Dowell, in the end, can keep no secrets.

In 1900 Freud published *The Interpretation of Dreams.* Much of his most influential work had been published by 1914. Alan Bullock argues: "No single man, probably, has exercised a greater influence on the ideas, literature and art of the twentieth century than Freud."[24] Freud's work was, of course, multi-dimensional, but some of his key ideas relate well to cultural development of the period, particularly in the arts. Freud's principal arguments, set out in *The Interpretation of Dreams* and other important writings, concerning the structure of the psyche (the ego, the super-ego, and the id), place an emphasis on interior life, both conscious and unconscious, that corresponds with and directly influences many literary and artistic experiments. The notion of displacement, the shifting of an emotional reaction from one part of life to another; the idea of the dream as the location for wish-fulfillment, that is the disguised fulfillment of a suppressed wish; the use of interpretation as a key tool for deciphering these – all are concepts that lend themselves well to art and literature. The reader psychoanalyzes Dowell in *The Good Soldier;* Henry James searches for the inside of his characters; later writers such as James Joyce, Virginia Woolf, and Dorothy Richardson find a language for this interior space through "stream of consciousness" narratives. The imagist poets locate the essence of an emotion in an image. Picasso and Braque look inside their subjects for meaning. There are many links and these continue to develop during the course of the century.

Freud himself saw psychoanalysis as a way of interpreting the arts, writing on literature and art, applying his ideas to a range of genres. His understanding of the way that his writings would impact upon the arts is clear. Much later in the century, of course, psychoanalytic literary criticism was to become a major tool of the literary scholar and it is hard now to imagine a world without Freudian ideas.

Similarly influential at the time, although perhaps not quite so integrated into late twentieth-century culture, were the writings of Friedrich Nietzsche. Nietzsche's writing days were over by 1889 when he was committed to an asylum where he spent the rest of his life, but prior to that he had developed ideas that significantly influenced early twentieth-century artistic and cultural development. His 1873 essay, "On Truth and Falsehood in the Extra-Moral Sense," was particularly important. In this very early essay, Nietzsche argued that language itself was inadequate to convey the objective truth about external reality. In 1873 this idea may have been hard to comprehend, but by the early 1900s, when the pace of change in the external world was so great, finding a means to convey it was a real issue in the arts. As we have seen, new languages – literary, visual, musical – had to be devised to keep pace with a shifting world. Such linguistic invention was, perhaps, accelerated by the cultural impact of World War I; how do you articulate the unspeakable events of the western and other fronts. Indeed, during the war years, Dora Marsden wrote a series of philosophical editorials for *The Egoist* that were heavily indebted to Nietzsche's ideas on the inadequacy of language. The high modernism of the 1920s can be read in direct relation to this, searching for an answer to a problem identified by Nietzsche fifty years earlier.

Nietzsche's famous declaration "God is dead," in his 1882 book, *The Joyful Wisdom*, also had a profound impact, picking up as it did on the decreasing popularity of organized religion across Europe, particularly in the wake of Darwin's ideas on evolution. Nietzsche's madman, who declares the death of God, is disbelieved; he has come too early. But the cults of mysticism and spiritualism that grew in popularity at the end of the nineteenth century indicate that he may not be as early as he thinks. Many of Nietzsche's ideas are expressed through different dramatic personae or masks, giving his writings a fictive as well as philosophical dimension. Such techniques can be seen to influence the work of, for example, W. B. Yeats, whose poetry over the following decades reflected his interest in both the use of masks and in spiritualism. For Nietzsche, every word was a mask, hiding something, perhaps another philosophy, within. Words conceal, rather than reveal, both the interior and the exterior worlds, and in a godless world, humanity needed to find a new moral code to live and work by. The world needed to change, and so it did.

"In or about December, 1910, human character changed." Of course, it didn't really. Virginia Woolf's statement can only be metaphorical. Or can it? The old world, the one into which she had been born, was changing rapidly, and would become unrecognizable within the next ten years. The world itself got smaller as mechanized transport literally took off and enabled people to travel as never before. The concept of globalization, so familiar at the beginning of the twenty-first century, was beginning to develop. At the same time, advancements in technology, in medical science, and in the understanding of the human condition led to a greater comprehension of how that world functioned. The people of 1910 had a very different impression of themselves from their grandparents, or even their parents. The writers, artists, and musicians who most embodied this change within their work were still in a minority, but theirs is the work that is remembered a hundred years later and the work that went on to shape twentieth-century culture. They created the new languages of modernity to convey the world around them and to differentiate it from the world of the past.

"This is the saddest story I have ever heard," John Dowell tells us at the beginning of *The Good Soldier*.[25] It is sad because it represents so many endings; accumulatively, the ending of an era. Edward Ashburnham, the good soldier, embodies that era. From the outset we know that he is dead, but it is not until the final paragraphs that Dowell actually tells us the details of his passing. He is the English gentleman, the feudal landlord, the philanderer, the soldier imperialist, "a sentimentalist, whose mind was compounded of indifferent poems and novels."[26] He cuts his throat with a pen-knife. It is a strange postscript, but we, the readers, are somehow not sad despite Dowell's assertion. The world that Ashburnham embodied has been shown to be corrupt, outmoded, and obsolete. The violence of his death parallels World War I, which was literally killing the old world as Ford was writing. The fact of his suicide implies the element of self-destruction that had led the powers of Europe into a conflict that would change the balance of the world forever. Human character changed, and with it the ways in which humanity presented itself. And Ford Madox Ford's perfectly modernist novel, with its own language of modernity, conveys this to great effect.

NOTES

1   Virginia Woolf, "Mr Bennett and Mrs Brown," 1924, reproduced in *A Modernist Reader*, P. Faulkner, ed. (London: B. T. Batsford, 1986), p. 113.
2   There are clear exceptions to this; for example, James Joyce's *Ulysses* and Marcel Proust's *A la Recherche du temps perdu*.
3   Ford Madox Ford, dedicatory letter to *The Good Soldier*, quoted in Randall Stevenson, *Modernist Fiction* (London: Harvester Wheatsheaf, 1992), p. 25.
4   Ford Madox Ford, *The Good Soldier* (London: Penguin, 1946), p. 20.
5   Ibid, p. 25.
6   Ezra Pound, "A Few Don'ts for Imagistes," reproduced in Faulkner, *Modernist Reader*, p. 59.
7   Ibid, p. 60.
8   H. D., "Oread," in *Imagist Poetry*, Peter Jones, ed. (London: Penguin, 1972), p. 62.
9   Jones, *Imagist Poetry*, p. 31.
10 Glen Macleod, "The Visual Arts," in *The Cambridge Companion to Modernism*, Michael Levenson, ed. (Cambridge: Cambridge University Press, 1999), p. 200. I would refer the reader to this chapter for a much more detailed discussion of artistic developments in this period.
11 Ibid, p. 195.

12 Ibid, p. 200.
13 Extracts from these texts can be found in Herschel B. Chipp, ed., with Peter Selz and Joshua C. Taylor, *Theories of Modern Art* (Berkeley: University of California Press, 1968), part 4.
14 Guillaume Apollinaire, "The Beginnings of Cubism" (1912), in Chipp, *Theories,* p. 218.
15 Ford, *The Good Soldier*, pp. 13–14.
16 Christopher Innes, "Modernism in Drama," in Levenson, *Cambridge Companion,* pp. 131–2.
17 Ibid, p. 147.
18 Ibid, p. 133.
19 Ibid.
20 Robert P. Morgan, ed., *Modern Times* (Basingstoke: Macmillan, 1993), p. 6.
21 Ibid, p. 7.
22 Sigmund Freud (1905) "Fragment of an Analysis of a Case of Hysteria (Dora)," in *Sigmund Freud*, Pamela Thurschwell, ed. (London: Routledge), p. 27.
23 Ford, *The Good Soldier*, p. 19.
24 Alan Bullock, "The Double Image," in *Modernism: A Guide to European Literature 1890–1930*, Malcolm Bradbury and James McFarlane, eds (London: Penguin), p. 67.
25 Ford, *The Good Soldier*, p. 11.
26 Ibid, p. 229.

GUIDE TO FURTHER READING

Malcolm Bradbury and James McFarlane, eds, *Modernism* (London: Penguin, 1991). A general guide to European literature, 1880–1930.
Noel Burch, *Life to Those Shadows* (London: British Film Institute, 1990). A detailed study of critical approaches to early film history.
Herschel B. Chipp, ed., *Theories of Modern Art* (Berkeley: University of California Press, 1968). A source book of artists and critics.
Peter Faulkner, ed., *A Modernist Reader* (London: B. T. Batsford, 1986). A collection of original modernist writings and ideas.
Sigmund Freud, *The Interpretation of Dreams* (London: Penguin, 1991). Some of Freud's key ideas.
Paul Griffiths, *Modern Music: A Concise History* (London: Thames and Hudson, 1994). A historical survey of modern music.
Stephen Kern, *The Culture of Time and Space 1880–1918* (Cambridge MA: Harvard University Press, 2000). An examination of culture, modernity, and philosophy.
Michael Levenson, ed., *The Cambridge Companion to Modernism* (Cambridge: Cambridge University Press, 1999). A generic guide to modernisms.
Jesse Matz, *Literary Impressionism and Modernist Aesthetics* (Cambridge: Cambridge University Press, 2001). A study of impressionism in writing.
Mark S. Morrison, *The Public Face of Modernism* (Madison: University of Wisconsin Press, 2001). A study of the audiences and reception of Little Magazines 1905–20.
Randall Stevenson, *Modernist Fiction: An Introduction* (London: Harvester Wheatsheaf, 1992). A comprehensive guide to modernist fiction.
Pamela Thurschwell, *Sigmund Freud* (London: Routledge, 2000). An accessible guide to Freud's principal ideas.

CHAPTER ELEVEN

Politics: The Past and the Future

PETER WALDRON

In the years after 1900, Europeans recognized that they were standing on the brink of fundamental change. The arrival of the new century prompted widespread reflection on the future of the continent. The old political order clung to the remnants of its power, especially in eastern and central Europe, while the forces of democratic politics were pushing their way to the fore in the west of the continent. At the turn of the century, Europe's political structures ranged from the unreformed autocracy of the Russian empire to the near-constitutional monarchy of Britain and to the third French republic. The European old order was clearly on the defensive across the continent and, even in states where traditional political structures endured, it was under severe attack. Radical politics was gaining adherents across Europe and politicians on the left were growing in confidence as they gained increased popular support and saw governments begin to implement programs of social reform in an attempt to appease radical opinion.

It was social change that lay at the heart of this shift in political fortunes. The twin buttresses of church and landed nobility had acted as the main supports for monarchies since the emergence of cohesive European states in the early medieval period. Kings had depended on the nobility and the church to act as their agents, reinforcing royal power across societies that were overwhelmingly rural. The thinly spread agrarian populations of medieval and early modern Europe could be controlled by the local nobility, and the message of obedience to authority that was preached by the clergy served to discourage rebellion. Populations that were overwhelmingly illiterate had little access to other sources of information and, even after the invention of printing, printed material was expensive and hard to come by. Poor communications in pre-industrial Europe also served to help sustain traditional political structures, since they restricted mobility and made it easier for national political and social elites to continue to exercise absolute authority. The changes to Europe's societies and economies that began in the fifteenth and sixteenth centuries had a profound impact on the politics of the continent. The growth of new commercial classes posed a significant threat to the traditional authority of nobility and church, and the political revolution that occurred in Britain in the seventeenth century was the first instance of a monarch being deposed by the burgeoning middle class. The British monarchy that was restored later in the century had its powers significantly restricted by parliament.

As the shoots of industrial revolution began to appear across agrarian Europe, the pace of political change accelerated. Not only were the new industrial and business classes flexing their muscles and demanding a part in the political life of Europe but, increasingly, the people who worked in mines, mills, and factories sought a political voice. The French revolution of 1789 marked the beginning of a process of political change throughout Europe that was reaching its climax at the beginning of the twentieth century. The model that the French experience offered to the downtrodden of Europe was a powerful and magnetic one; it offered an example of the power that ordinary people could wield and of the ideals of liberty towards which they could strive. Even though the French revolution had failed fully to achieve its objectives and the century after 1789 had witnessed reversals as the French monarchy was restored, the ideals of 1789 became the model for revolutions and political upheaval across Europe during the nineteenth century.[1] The revolutionary tradition was well established in Europe by 1900, as rebellions had swept across almost the whole of the continent in the century since the Bastille had been stormed. Only Russia and Britain had been largely immune from the virus of revolution.

Russia: Autocracy and Democracy

As the twentieth century dawned, the political elites of Europe faced unparalleled challenges. In the east of the continent, the Russian state was feared as the most repressive and autocratic regime in Europe. Tsar Nicholas II had come to the throne in 1894 on the death of his deeply conservative father, Alexander III, and believed that it was his duty to pass the empire on unchanged to his own heirs. Nicholas and his ministers argued that Russia needed uniquely strong government to keep its rebellious peoples in check and that any hint of democracy would endanger the entire state. "Senseless dreams" was how Nicholas described liberal aspirations for a national assembly shortly after his accession.[2] The Russian government utilized draconian methods to keep its people in check: much of the empire was governed under emergency legislation after the assassination of Tsar Alexander II in 1881 and this gave very wide powers of arrest and punishment to local officials. The Russian state maintained its traditional paternalist attitudes towards its people, and turned a blind eye to instances of oppression by its own officials. The Jewish population of the empire suffered particularly from antisemitic pogroms, carried out with the collusion of the authorities, most shockingly in Kishinev in 1903 when 47 people were killed. Russia's last tsar harked back to the era of his seventeenth-century Romanov ancestors, ignoring the pressures for change that were developing among the people of the empire, and attempting to project the image of a benign autocrat, keeping a firm grip on his state for the benefit of the people. This policy came under severe challenge after 1900. Even though political parties were illegal, liberal activists were vocal in their calls for the people of the empire to have some say in the government of Russia.

These pressures came to a head in 1905, when Russia was comprehensively defeated in war with Japan and working people took to the streets in St Petersburg to voice their own discontent about their working and living conditions. The regime's troops opened fire on these demonstrators on what became known as "Bloody Sunday" and this massacre sparked off rebellion right across the empire. Both the nascent working class in the great Russian cities and the peasants in the countryside rose up in revolt. Tensions also ran high in areas of the empire dominated by non-Russians. The Poles were overwhelmingly opposed to Russian rule and attempted to take advantage of the apparent weakness of the imperial regime by staging a rebellion, and in Finland attempts were made to extend Finnish autonomy from Russian rule. The tsarist regime was in danger of losing control of the situation, and it was forced to resort to concessions in an attempt to restore tranquility. In October 1905, Nicholas II announced the creation of Russia's first parliament – the Duma – to be elected on a wide franchise. This move was greeted with widespread acclaim, and many Russians believed that it marked the beginning of a process of reform that would set Russia firmly on the path towards becoming a constitutional monarchy. This view was not, however, shared by the tsar and his advisors. Nicholas II deeply resented the existence of the new parliament and attempted to curb its powers and, once the revolts of 1905 had been quelled, wanted to return to a traditional autocratic style of government. Some Russian statesmen recognized that this was not a sustainable course of action. Stolypin, prime minister from 1906 until his assassination in 1911, attempted to drive through a wide-ranging program of economic and social reform, predicated upon establishing a class of small peasant landowners in Russia who would have no interest in supporting rebellion and would instead identify their interests with the tsarist state. Stolypin's land reform had made only limited progress by the time war broke out in 1914 and his vision remained unfulfilled.[3]

The constitutional reforms that were introduced in 1905 included a commitment to significant extensions in civil rights. The Russian people were able to voice their opinions more freely, and they took full advantage of this opportunity. The number of newspapers and magazines in circulation grew as censorship was relaxed. The tsarist regime was faced with a dilemma: Nicholas II fervently believed that he was ordained by God to rule as an autocrat and he wanted to return to governing as he had before 1905. But this was not a realistic option. Once the genie of constitutionalism had been released, it was impossible to reverse the process. The tsarist regime was able to make changes to the franchise in 1907 to restrict the voting rights of the peasantry, even though such a move was illegal, but it dared not go further and entirely neuter the new Duma. Government and Duma maintained an uneasy truce, essentially antagonistic to each other, with the Duma unable to fulfill the lofty aspirations that had accompanied its introduction and the government compelled to accept the existence of the new parliament. The new constitutional system in Russia failed to represent the interests of the people as a whole. The tsarist state was able to restore order in the immediate aftermath of its announcement of concessions, but it became clear by 1908 that the fundamental causes of the discontent that had raged across the empire during 1905 were not being addressed by the new Duma.

Popular unrest began to grow again and calls for the overthrow of the monarchy were heard more loudly. Russia had industrialized very rapidly during the 1890s and St Petersburg and Moscow had developed into huge urban centers. The new migrant working class was a fertile ground for revolutionary ideas. The Russian Social Democratic Party had been founded in 1894 and argued for violent revolution to destroy the monarchy. It was successful in carrying out a series of assassinations of members of the governing elite and in gaining support among working people. Radical parties found their support growing as disillusionment grew with the Duma. This was intensified by widespread labor unrest; in April 1912 a demonstration by workers in the Lena goldfields was fired upon by government troops, resulting in several hundred deaths. Strikes broke out in many Russian cities after 1912, as working people protested about their working conditions and, increasingly, about political issues. In St Petersburg alone, more than 300,000 workers came out on strike in 1912 for political reasons, and this number grew to half a million in the following year, and to more than 650,000 in the first six months of 1914.[4] Political opposition became more vocal and angry in other parts of the political spectrum, too. Liberal political parties became further alienated from the regime: the Kadet (Constitutional Democratic) Party had protested against the government's rapid dissolution of the First Duma in 1906 and, as a result, had been largely excluded from formal political life. They argued that the post-1905 constitutional structures had failed and that Russia needed further fundamental constitutional reform if it was to make progress. Even the most loyal supporters of the new system, the Octobrist Party (named after the October 1905 manifesto that had brought the Duma into being), were disillusioned. Guchkov, one of the most prominent Octobrists, spoke in 1913 of the "inevitable and grave catastrophe" that was facing Russia. His presentiment of disaster was stark: "Never were the Russian public and the Russian people so profoundly revolutionized by the actions of the government, for day by day faith in the government is steadily waning, and with it is waning faith in the possibility of a peaceful issue from the crisis."[5] Russia's history of revolutionary terrorism gave it a particular sense of instability, and a series of government officials had been assassinated after 1900, including Pleve, the minister of internal affairs, in 1904 and prime minister Stolypin in 1911. The threat of violent revolution was never far away and this made the intensification of popular unrest after 1900 especially dangerous for the tsarist government.

Britain: Liberalism and Discontent

Russia's prewar crisis was mirrored elsewhere in Europe. At the western edge of the continent, British politics experienced great turbulence after 1900. As the greatest industrial power in the world, Britain had a large working class and a well-developed tradition of dissent. In contrast to Russia, however, Britain had no real history of terrorism directed at the overthrow of the state. However, Britain had not been immune from political discontent and the seventeenth century had seen a civil war that culminated in the execution of the king and the temporary abolition of the monarchy. By 1900 the British monarchy was a very different creature from the Russian autocracy. In the 1860s the constitutional theorist Walter Bagehot had commented that the rights of the British monarch were reduced to "the right to be consulted, the right to encourage [and] the right to warn."[6] It was the British parliament, and its governing party, that held sway in the political arena. A landslide general election victory brought a Liberal government into power in 1906 with more than 400 MPs, after more than a decade of Conservative rule. The extent of the country's rejection of the Conservatives was hammered home by the election of 29 Labour members of the House of Commons. These results were all the more emphatic since

Britain still did not have universal male suffrage. More than 40 percent of adult men in towns and cities and more than 30 percent of men in the countryside were still deprived of the vote.[7] The new Liberal government was initially cautious, but after the replacement of Campbell-Bannerman as prime minister by Asquith in 1908, and the appointment of Lloyd George as chancellor of the exchequer, the mood changed. Lloyd George set out to make his first budget controversial in an attempt to revitalize the Liberal Party's supporters. The government proposed to introduce an almost universal system of old-age pensions, and it needed to find long-term sources of revenue that would support this major social reform. At the same time, Britain was engaged in building up its naval strength. Germany had begun to expand its navy in the late 1890s, and Britain felt compelled to respond, even though it was clearly impracticable to retain the "two-power standard" by which the British navy was to be greater in size than the next two navies combined. In 1906, *HMS Dreadnought* was launched, the first in a line of new heavy battleships. This program of naval expansion was very costly, and Britain's naval expenditure rose by almost 40 percent between 1900 and 1910. Lloyd George therefore needed to raise significant additional revenue to finance the government's plans and his 1909 budget contained plans to increase income taxes and to impose new taxation on land. These taxation measures were aimed especially at the more prosperous and provoked huge opposition from the Conservatives, who denounced Lloyd George's budget as "socialism." While the Conservatives were hopelessly outnumbered in the Commons, they held an impregnable majority in the House of Lords and the Lords duly rejected Lloyd George's budget in November 1909.[8]

This caused a constitutional crisis and forced a general election early in 1910. The Liberals lost their overall majority in the Commons, but were able to remain in power with support from the Labour Party and from Irish Nationalists. The political crisis was not resolved when the Lords agreed to pass the budget, since the Liberal government was now determined to curb the powers of the Lords once and for all, by legislating to ensure the supremacy of the Commons. This process provoked a second general election during 1910, since the Conservative-dominated Lords vigorously resisted Liberal attempts to subordinate them to the Commons. It was not until August 1911 that the Parliament Act was passed, preventing the Lords from flouting the will of the elected Commons and instead giving them the power to delay legislation for a period of no more than two years.

Political tensions between Liberals and Conservatives were exacerbated by the situation in Ireland. The Irish Question had caused severe problems for successive British governments, as Irish nationalists – both within and outside parliament – pressed for autonomy from the London government. Irish nationalism had provoked great passions and Gladstone, the great Liberal prime minister, had unsuccessfully tried to implement Home Rule for Ireland in the 1880s. The Conservative Lords had proved to be the chief stumbling block to Home Rule, and they had argued that it would lead to the destruction of the united British state. The passage of the Parliament Act meant that the Lords could no longer deal a fatal blow to Irish Home Rule legislation and in 1912 Asquith introduced the measure. The Lords, as was now their constitutional right, delayed the bill for two years and it was in the process of becoming law in 1914. But opposition to Irish Home Rule among Conservatives spread outside the parliamentary arena. The northeastern corner of Ireland was dominated by a Protestant population that did not wish to be ruled by the Catholic majority of the Irish population and was prepared to take extreme measures to resist. Conservative Ulster Protestants wanted to remain an integral part of Britain and, under the leadership of Edward Carson, a former Conservative government minister, they prepared for direct action. "Ulster will fight, and Ulster will be right" was their rallying call and Ulster Protestants began to prepare for armed resistance to Home Rule. Some 250,000 men signed the Covenant, promising to use whatever means they could to defeat the government's proposals, and a private army, the Ulster Volunteers, was formed to show that this was no mere paper threat.[9] There were doubts over the loyalty of British military units stationed in Ireland in the event of them being ordered to put down rebellion in Ulster,[10] and the cause of the Ulster Protestants was taken up by the Conservative Party in parliament. The crisis over Ireland that gripped the British political establishment between 1912 and 1914 showed the deep fissures inside the British state and its society. It brought together the potent forces of nationalism and religion, and these were intermixed with the existing bitter political struggle between Liberals and Conservatives.

British politics and society were also divided over the issue of votes for women. The movement for women's suffrage had developed during the Victorian era, but it gained much greater prominence after 1900 and the emergence of the Women's Social and Political Union.[11] Led by the Pankhursts, the suffragette movement turned to direct action to make its case. Political meetings were disrupted, public buildings were attacked, and government ministers assaulted. Suffragette activists were arrested and imprisoned, responding by going on hunger strike. The government at first attempted to force-feed hunger strikers, but public opinion was shocked by the brutality of the process and the government was forced to release hunger-striking suffragettes, only to rearrest them when they had recovered from their ordeal. In 1913 the suffragette Emily Davison was killed as a result of injuries she received when she threw herself under the king's horse during the running of the Derby. The majority of the suffragette activists were middle-class women and their actions caused significant disquiet among their peers – both male and female. Images of respectable women being dragged out of meetings by policemen, and of women chaining themselves to railings in the centers of large cities, sat awkwardly with the predominant view of women as subordinate to men. The Liberal government attempted to offer concessions in 1912, but was frustrated by parliamentary procedure. The government's failure to address the issue directly and to make female suffrage a significant element of its legislative program provoked the suspicion that leading members of the government were, at best, lukewarm about the idea and, at worst, bitterly opposed to the concept.

Britain was also gripped by labor militancy in the years after 1900. The number of days of work lost because of strikes more than doubled between 1902 and 1910, and trade union membership also showed significant increases. The first-ever national railway strike took place in 1911, and there were also strikes that year by merchant seamen and dockers. The year 1912 was the most significant year for industrial unrest, however, when more than 40 million days were lost due to strikes, especially in the coalmining industry. Dockers in London also struck that year and it appeared at times as if Britain was close to anarchy. The apparent tranquility of British politics and society in the last period of Victoria's reign had been superficial. The persistence of the old order was profound and it required little for the conservative forces in British political life to flex their muscles. Even though the monarch had lost all his formal power, the traditional elites in British society that were represented by the Conservative Party could still wield huge influence. The 1906 Liberal government was successful in reducing the formal power of the House of Lords, but still faced the entrenched influence of its sympathizers in other areas. Coupled with labor unrest and with the militant suffragette movement, Britain was far from political stability in the years before 1914, but the prospect of actual violent revolution seemed remote. The long-established British state appeared able to weather the storms of discontent that were assailing it, even though the cost to its social fabric was severe.

Germany: Kaiser and People

The united German Empire that had been created in 1871 had immediately become one of the great powers of Europe. Bismarck's ideas and personality had formed the political landscape of the new Reich and had ensured significant stability for almost twenty years, until his dismissal in 1890. But this had been achieved largely through the efforts of Bismarck alone, and the new German Empire was still far from being a cohesive social entity. While Germany was expanding industrially at great speed, it did not have the long-established political coherence of Britain, but on the other hand, neither did it have a tradition of revolutionary activity. The accession of Wilhelm II to the throne in 1888 marked the beginning of significant turbulence in German politics, as the Kaiser's impulsive temperament coincided with growing importance for the imperial parliament, the Reichstag, and with increasing social pressures. Wilhelm was not prepared to allow his chancellors the same degree of authority and latitude that Bismarck had enjoyed, instead wanting to establish a "personal regime" in which the Kaiser himself would wield great authority. The ulti-mate sanction that the Kaiser possessed was to dismiss his chancellor and, since he had been prepared to dispense with the services of Bismarck, the architect of the new empire, it was clear that he would not hesitate to use this power. Wilhelm did not, however, possess the degree of application necessary to establish personal rule, and his impact on the German political process was haphazard and unpredictable.[12] He was able to exert particular influence over military and naval policy, and was enthu-siastic about the plans being laid by the navy minister, Tirpitz, to strengthen the German navy to a point where it could challenge British dominance of the seas. The Kaiser was in full agreement with Max Weber who, in his inaugural lecture at Freiburg University in 1895, had argued that "the unification of Germany . . . should be . . . the starting point for a German *Weltmachtpolitik*"[13] and in 1901 the Kaiser himself declared "we have conquered for ourselves a place in the sun. It will now be my task to see to it that this place in the sun shall remain our undisputed possession."[14]

Germany's *Weltpolitik* – its policy designed to place the new empire firmly at the center of world politics – was controversial in both the international and domestic political arenas. Bismarck's German Reich had come into being with universal manhood suffrage for the imperial Reichstag. The wily Bismarck had sought to neu-tralize parliament and to ensure that all significant decisions were removed from the parliamentary arena, but his successors were less skilled and also faced a resurgent

Reichstag. German men voted in large numbers at elections, with turnout in both 1907 and 1912 reaching more than 84 percent, so that parliament could fairly claim to represent the views of the people. The main beneficiary of elections was the Social Democratic Party, the SPD, which saw its share of the vote rise from 20 percent in 1897 to 32 percent in 1903 and 35 percent in 1912, making it the largest single party in parliament after 1912. German socialism contained two central strands: it continued to espouse the cause of revolution that Marx had propounded, but the party's Erfurt program of 1891 showed the influence of revisionism, as Eduard Bernstein advocated the path of reformism. Bernstein stressed that the SPD could achieve its ends by engaging in the parliamentary process and by promoting radical social reform, rather than waiting for revolution to come and for the barricades to be built in German cities, and his message was important in winning voters over to the SPD's side. By 1914 the party had more than a million members and was the focus for a huge variety of cultural and sporting organizations, originally established in response to the left's exclusion from German social life, but which were instrumental in the creation of a "socialist subculture" that could challenge traditional politics. German socialism continued to contain a powerful revolutionary element, however, and Karl Liebknecht and Rosa Luxemburg advocated direct action, such as mass strikes, to press home the socialist case.

   The SPD consistently voted against naval expansion when it was debated in the Reichstag, but the government was able to count on support from the conservative and center majority. German foreign policy after 1900 was designed as much for domestic consumption as for the international stage. Tirpitz's huge naval expansion program was intended to mobilize political support for the Wilhelmine regime, both inside the Reichstag and in the country as a whole, by stimulating German national sentiment. The aggressive foreign policy that Germany pursued in the years after 1900 was conducted with at least half an eye on domestic political opinion, with chancellor Bülow calculating that the threat of impending war would serve to unite opinion behind the government. He argued that "a courageous and generous policy which succeeds in maintaining a positive attitude towards our national life in its present shape and form would offer the best medicine against the Social Democrats."[15] This policy did succeed in denying the SPD a majority in the Reichstag, since the socialists could be outvoted by a combination of right and center parties, but it did not bring about national political consensus. Germany experienced very substantial labor unrest as its economy strengthened after the short recession of 1907 and 1908. Huge strikes broke out across a wide range of industries in 1909 and 1910. Coalminers, building workers, and shipbuilders all came out on strike and parts of Berlin saw violent clashes between strikers and the police. This served to isolate the German left from broader political opinion and made it even less likely that an alliance could be formed between the SPD and center parties to oppose government policy. German politics were in a state of impasse by 1914: the socialists had insufficient power on their own to challenge the government, while the right had proved unable to develop policies that would siphon off socialist support. In the 1880s, Bismarck had tried to win over working people to the regime by instituting schemes of social insurance, but this process did not advance much further after 1900, as his successors did not want to alienate conservative parties by appearing to make concessions to the left. The SPD condemned any move to support the imperial government and withdrew its support from the Baden regional party when it voted in favor of the annual budget in 1910, even though it included a range of welfare provisions.

It was difficult to see how German politics could develop. The Kaiser and his ministers were isolated from public opinion and took no account of the huge popular support enjoyed by the socialists. The imperial regime appeared dislocated from its people, pursuing a policy of imperial and military expansion that ran wholly counter to the internationalist aspirations and rhetoric of the SPD. To the left, the imperial state had no legitimacy and was out of touch with the modern society and economy that Germany possessed after 1900. But the left was condemned to perpetual opposition since it refused to compromise with the regime and could not hope to achieve an absolute majority in the Reichstag. In these circumstances it was unsurprising that the revolutionary element of the SPD retained its strength. Ordinary working people felt themselves alienated from the state and Bernstein's reformism did not appear to have delivered its promised benefits. War in 1914 offered Wilhelm II's government the prospect that it could unite a deeply fractured Germany.

Austria-Hungary: Dualism and the Nationalities

The third great conservative monarchy of Europe – Austria-Hungary – was in scarcely better shape. However, its political problems stemmed from very different pressures from the other European great powers. The Habsburg Empire was comprised of more than a dozen separate national groups and, while the German population was the largest single group, they formed only a quarter of the empire's people. Slav peoples made up almost half of the empire, while the Magyars came close to matching the German population.[16] The 50 million people who populated the Austro-Hungarian empire made it the most nationally incoherent state in Europe. It was a matter of surprise to contemporaries that the empire had actually survived for so long and that it had not been destroyed by national tensions. The continued existence of Austria-Hungary was due in large part to the *Ausgleich* – the Compromise of 1867 between the emperor and the leaders of the Hungarian peoples of the empire. In the wake of Austria's crushing military defeat by Bismarck's Prussia in 1866, the Hungarians saw an opportunity to press their case for greater autonomy from a seriously weakened Vienna. The 1867 Compromise effectively gave the Hungarian part of the empire autonomy in most areas of domestic policy. The imperial government retained control of foreign affairs, war, and finance, but the Hungarians saw themselves as having achieved independence from the empire, with the only real link between Hungary and Austria being provided in the person of the monarch, who was both emperor of Austria and king of Hungary.[17] Franz Joseph, who ruled from 1848 until his death in 1916, was a keystone in ensuring the survival of the imperial state. He recognized that his powers were limited by constitutions in both the Austrian and Hungarian parts of the empire, although he did not relish the restrictions that this posed on his authority. His power had, however, only been limited by constitutional change, not destroyed, so that Franz Joseph enjoyed significantly greater authority than the British monarch. In 1905 and 1906 he played a significant role in discussions to make electoral reform in both parts of the empire, making it plain that his position was to extend the franchise, especially in Hungary. Only 7 percent of the Hungarian people had the right to vote and this ensured that power was retained in the hands of a deeply nationalist Magyar elite, who sought to extend Hungarian influence over the largely Slav peoples of their part of the empire. Franchise reform would have given the vote not just to people from the lower classes but also – much more alarming to the Magyar elite – to people who were from Slav races. While Franz Joseph did not press his support for electoral reform to the limit, his preferences were well known and played a part in the calculations made by politicians.[18]

The system of dualism that developed in the last part of the nineteenth century proved to be successful in conciliating the Hungarians, but it did little for the Slav peoples of the empire. The crisis that erupted over Bosnia in 1908 gives a very clear example of the issues that the substantial Slav population of the empire posed. Austria-Hungary was intimately involved in the Balkans, numbering more than 6 million South Slavs – Croats, Serbs, and Slovenes – among its population. But while the empire included more than 2 million Serbs, the independent Serbian state also claimed their loyalty. National tensions in the Balkans had been accentuated by the way in which the Hungarians had treated the Slav peoples. Both Croats and Serbs were indignant at the way in which the Hungarian language was imposed on them, and the attempts of the Hungarian elite to dominate them both politically and culturally. The Serbs were able to look to independent Serbia in the hope that they could become part of a single Serb state, and Austria always feared that Serbia, with the backing of Slav Russia, might offer support to the empire's Serb people against rule from Budapest and Vienna. With the disintegration of the Turkish empire, the Austrian regime was fearful that a single large Slav state might come into being in the Balkans, thus triggering instability among the South Slav peoples of the empire. The domestic concerns of the Austro-Hungarian regime were thus reflected in its foreign policy and, in 1908, it made the decision to annex the provinces of Bosnia and Herzegovina, in an attempt to prevent them falling under the influence of any other power. A British observer of the scene, Horace Rumbold, commented on what he referred to as the "more decided policy" of the empire in the Balkans, suggesting that it was motivated by a hope to "awaken in both halves of the Monarchy a common sense of solidarity and a feeling of devotion to Imperial interests, irrespective of nationality, which have too long remained dormant in the polyglot empire."[19]

Elsewhere in the empire, national tensions were also becoming more pronounced.[20] The most prosperous parts of the empire were in the Czech lands of Bohemia and Moravia. The Czechs had developed both heavy industrial and consumer goods sectors, and increasingly they were making inroads into the business and professional classes that had been the preserve of the German population. The great controversy that brought national discontent to boiling point was over the use of the German and Czech languages. The German populations of Bohemia and Moravia resented the use of the Czech language in administration and education, while the Czechs believed that, since they were the majority in these areas, it was unreasonable to expect them to learn German. Language disputes raged furiously, bringing both national groups out onto the streets to demonstrate and riot against apparent slights to their own language and, by extension, to their nationality. Segregation became the order of the day, at least in education. Most Czech schools taught no German, and German schools in the Czech lands carried out their education exclusively in German. By 1910, German schools in Moravia were open to legal action if they allowed Czech children to study in them.[21] This segregation was reflected more broadly in social life. Czechs had their own sporting and social clubs and organizations, helping to reinforce their national identity and to demonstrate their separateness from the Germans who ruled from Vienna.

The Austro-Hungarian empire had proved exceptionally adept at coping with its national differences over a long period. But the international tensions that sharpened after 1900 made the empire's domestic situation much more difficult. The strains in the Balkans intensified, while Germany's growing assertiveness had an impact on the German population of the Austrian state. The ageing Franz Joseph was no longer able to govern with the forcefulness of his youth, and he was especially affected by the assassination of his wife, the Empress Elisabeth, in 1898 by an Italian anarchist. The national stresses that Britain was experiencing in Ireland were multiplied many times over in Austria-Hungary. World War I accelerated their development to a stage where the imperial state could no longer cope. Many people had predicted the demise of Austria-Hungary and much of Europe was surprised that it had succeeded in surviving into the twentieth century.

France: Republicanism and Socialism

France, the remaining European great power, was very different from each of the other four in 1900. France was the only republic among the five and its revolutionary heritage was a central part of French political culture. This did not mean that monarchism had been expunged from French political consciousness: republicanism had proved to be a flower that could easily be crushed under the boot of royalist revival. Napoleon Bonaparte had transformed himself from revolutionary general to imperial ruler, subsequently both Bourbon and Orleanist dynasties had worn the restored French crown and, finally, Napoleon III had established the Second Empire in 1851. It was only in 1870, with the trauma of defeat by Bismarck's Prussia, that monarchist rule disappeared once and for all from France. The Third Republic that came into existence in the turmoil of the national humiliation of defeat and the German seizure of Alsace-Lorraine was a political system that, while it had deep intellectual roots in the French revolutionary tradition, proved to be unstable. French governments changed frequently: between 1870 and 1914, France experienced 108 separate administrations, lasting for an average of eight months each.[22] This was symptomatic of structural problems in the French political system: the French lower house of parliament, the Chamber of Deputies, lacked any proper party system until 1910 and it was really only the French Socialist Party that had any real coherence.

There were significant fissures in French society that were reflected in its political life. The Dreyfus affairs still reverberated through the country.[23] There was growing labor militancy after 1900. The number of strikes in the decade after 1900 was more than ten times the quantity of strikes in the 1880s and, by 1901, the average strike lasted for three weeks. Strikes took place in all sorts of industries, including the railways, silk manufacture, and winegrowing, and there was an unsuccessful attempt at organizing a general strike in 1909. The radical prime minister, Clemenceau, formed a new government in 1906 and attempted to drive through a wide-ranging program of social reform that included a statutory eight-hour working day, the introduction of retirement pensions, government control of labor contracts, provisions for workers to receive compensation in the event of industrial accidents, and proper regulation of trade unions. These reform proposals bore significant similarities to the program of the 1906 British Liberal government, but while the British government was able to push through its program – albeit in the face of fierce resistance from the Conservative-dominated Lords – Clemenceau's government had no success in implementing its reforms. While French industry had developed significantly and great urban centers were coming into existence, France remained overwhelmingly a peasant country, where small farmers dominated the rural economy. The divisions between town and country had been very obvious throughout the nineteenth century, and Paris in particular had shown itself to be a center for revolutionary and radical opinion. French socialism was espoused by many of the urban population and, while most of the countryside remained resolutely conservative, socialism did make some inroads in rural France.

Divisions between left and right in politics do not, however, fully explain the contentious nature of French politics. At least as significant were arguments over the place of religion.[24] In rural France, priest and teacher clashed furiously as the teachers sought to inculcate republican values in their charges, while the Catholic clergy continued to assert conservative values and respect for authority. By 1814 there were 120,000 lay teachers spread across France and many of them took on additional roles, such as town clerk or even mayor, in their communities. Social life in many French villages was divided into Catholic groups and republican groups, and these divisions were being formalized at a national level. In 1905, legislation was passed to formalize the division of church and state. The state would no longer be responsible for paying priests' salaries or for maintaining religious buildings and the church no longer needed state approval for its appointments. This process caused riots in some areas as Catholics protested against what they perceived as an attack on the church. But, overall, it was the secular state that emerged victorious, pushing traditional religion into the background.

Politics in the years before 1914 was dominated by three national issues. The process of rearmament that was gripping Europe did not leave France unscathed. To keep pace with the increase in the size of the German army, France had to move from two to three years of military service. This was controversial in itself, but it also had important financial implications. The French taxation system was complex and rested on revenue from land and from tariffs. Successive governments tried to introduce an income tax, but the upper house of the French parliament, the Senate, rejected the measure in both 1907 and 1910. This experience was reminiscent of the passage of Lloyd George's 1909 budget in Britain, and in France too the government was eventually successful in getting its financial legislation through. In 1913 the French parliament finally approved the introduction of an income tax. The third issue that exercised French politicians was electoral reform. The introduction of proportional representation was also mooted by the government, but it proved to be too complex a matter for easy resolution. Like each of the other European great powers, France faced significant political divisions. The French revolutionary tradition made France's position more dangerous. The great revolution of 1789 had been followed by revolution in 1848 and by the Paris Commune in 1871, and each of these events had demonstrated the volatility of French society. But, as in each of the other great powers, the outbreak of war in 1914 was greeted with widespread displays of popular unity. National parliaments right across Europe forgot their party differences and voted in favor of the financial measures needed to wage war.

Conclusion

The success of European governments in rallying their people to the cause of war was surprising, given the apparent strength of European socialism. In 1889 socialist parties across Europe had banded together in the Second International, intending to bring together the working peoples of the great powers and, by emphasizing the common interests that held them together, to prevent war breaking out in Europe. The International was designed to unite the working class and to lead it in a struggle against bourgeois society across the continent, but the very different political situations in each of the great powers made such unity almost impossible. In 1904 the International met in Amsterdam to discuss the issue of the participation of socialist parties in governments led by bourgeois parties.[25] This question of "ministerialism" divided the European left. The German SPD was staunch in its refusal to contemplate such a course of action, and was instrumental in defeating the French socialist Jean Jaurès, who had agreed to the participation of his colleague Millerand in a coalition government in France at the height of the Dreyfus affair. Although the French retorted that the Germans were only able to take such a principled stand because they would never be invited to participate in a government and were thus never going to be faced with this issue, it demonstrated that European socialism was far from united. The Russian socialist movement was even more extreme in its views, arguing that the left should offer no support even to programs of social reform, which Lenin and his Bolshevik Party believed were implemented by conservative governments to dupe working people into abandoning their class interests. This was not entirely far-fetched: the British Conservative prime minister between 1902 and 1905, Arthur Balfour, declared that "social legislation is not merely to be distinguished from socialist legislation, but is its most direct opposite and its most effective antidote."[26] The European left was deeply divided about the tactics that it should utilize in order to win power. The British Labour Party that was founded in 1906 espoused the reformist cause, believing that it could bring about change by winning seats in parliament and promoting socialism by peaceful means. This was anathema to the Russian Social Democrats, who had no prospect of gaining any influence in Russia through the ballot box, even after the introduction of the Duma in 1905. As war was breaking out in the summer of 1914, the leaders of European socialism gathered in Brussels to discuss what action they could take to mobilize opinion against the war. Even though "they spoke for millions, they had little confidence in their ability to prevent the threatened war by direct mass action."[27]

The politics of Europe in the years that led up to 1914 were a microcosm of conflicts that had developed since 1789. Monarchs and traditional landed elites clung tenaciously to their remaining power as they came under severe attack from elected parliaments and from groups who had no representation in elected assemblies, whether they were industrial workers or disenfranchised women. National minorities in multinational states pressed for greater autonomy or for outright independence. Governments across Europe recognized that they were presiding over fractured societies and looked for ways in which they could restore social stability. For the Russian tsar, this meant a return to firm government, after the hiccup of the 1905 revolution. In Britain it included a program of social reform, but in Germany produced only stalemate between government and opposition. The coming of war in 1914 and the mass displays of national unity that it provoked across the continent suggested that the appeal of patriotism was sufficient to seal up the political cracks in each of the great powers. But such unity proved to be short-lived. The failure of European political regimes to meet the aspirations of their peoples before the war, and the catastrophe of World War I itself, meant that the seeds of postwar politics had already been sown by 1914. Disillusion with the venerable old order that had dominated Europe for centuries meant that people turned to political movements at the extremes. Revolutionary socialism proved to be the victor on the left, while the soft-edged conservatism of the pre-1914 world was supplanted by the harshness of fascism on the right. Political failure before 1914 was to give Europe a bleak future after the end of World War I.

NOTES

1   See E. J. Hobsbawm, *Echoes of the Marseillaise: Two Centuries Look Back on the French Revolution* (New Brunswick NJ: Rutgers University Press, 1990), esp. chs 2 and 3.

2   Dominic Lieven, *Nicholas II: Emperor of all the Russias* (London: John Murray, 1993), p. 71.

3   See Peter Waldron, *Between Two Revolutions: Stolypin and the Politics of Renewal in Russia* (London: UCL Press, 1998), pp. 175–7.

4   Robert B. McKean, *St Petersburg Between the Revolutions: Workers and Revolutionaries June 1907–February 1917* (New Haven CT: Yale University Press, 1990), pp. 495–6.

5   "The General Political Situation and the Octobrist Party," *Russian Review* 3/1 (1914): 152.

6   Walter Bagehot, *The English Constitution* (London: Kegan Paul, 1892), p. 75.

7   See Neal Blewett, "The Franchise in the United Kingdom, 1885–1918," *Past and Present* 32 (1965): 31.

8   See Roy Jenkins, *Mr Balfour's Poodle: An Account of the Struggle between the House of Lords and the Government of Mr Asquith* (London: Heinemann, 1954), p. 67.

9   See A. T. Q. Stewart, *The Ulster Crisis* (London: Faber and Faber, 1967), pp. 62–7.

10 See I. F. W. Beckett, ed., *The Army and the Curragh Incident 1914* (London: Bodley Head, 1986), p. 14.

11 See June Purvis, *Emmeline Pankhurst: A Biography* (London: Routledge, 2002), p. 67.

12 See J. C. G. Röhl, "The Emperor's New Clothes: A Character Sketch of Kaiser Wilhelm II," in *Kaiser Wilhelm II: New Interpretations*, J. C. G. Röhl and N. Sombart, eds (Cambridge: Cambridge University Press, 1982), pp. 23–61

13 Immanuel Geiss, "Origins of the First World War," in *The Origins of the First World War*, Hans W. Koch, ed. (London: Macmillan, 1972), p. 40.

14 C. Gauss, *The German Kaiser as Shown in His Public Utterances* (New York: Charles Scribner's Sons, 1915), p. 181.

15 Volker R. Berghahn, *Germany and the Approach of War in 1914* (Basingstoke: Macmillan, 1993), p. 43.

16 See Alan Sked, *The Decline and Fall of the Habsburg Empire 1815–1918* (London: Longman, 1989), p. 278.

17 See Lázló Péter, "Montesquieu's Paradox on Freedom and Hungary's Constitutions 1790–1990," *History of Political Thought* 16 (1995): 86–7.

18 See Steven Beller, *Francis Joseph* (London: Longman, 1996), pp. 168–9.
19 Horace Rumbold, *The Austrian Court in the Nineteenth Century* (London: Methuen, 1909), p. 330.
20 See Gerald Stourzh, "The Multinational Empire Revisited: Reflections on Late Imperial Austria," *Austrian History Yearbook* 23 (1992): 1–22.
21 See S. Konirsch, "Constitutional Struggles between Czechs and Germans in the Habsburg Monarchy," *Journal of Modern History*, 27 (1955): 231–61.
22 See Theodore Zeldin, *France 1848–1945: Politics and Anger* (Oxford: Oxford University Press), 1979, p. 223.
23 See Martin P. Johnson, *The Dreyfus Affair* (Basingstoke: Macmillan, 1999), pp. 150–5.
24 See Maurice Larkin, *Church and State after the Dreyfus Affair: The Separation Issue in France* (London: Macmillan, 1974).
25 See James Joll, *The Second International 1889–1914* (London: Routledge and Kegan Paul, 1974), pp. 102–8.
26 A. J. Balfour, *Essays Speculative and Political* (London: Hodder and Stoughton, 1930), p. 153.
27 Julius Braunthal, *History of the International*, vol. 1 (London: Thomas Nelson, 1966), p. 351.

GUIDE TO FURTHER READING

Abraham Ascher, *The Revolution of 1905*, 2 vols (Stanford CA: Stanford University Press, 1988 and 1992). This ranges much more widely than its title suggests and gives a broad picture of Russian politics in the first years of the twentieth century.

Steven Beller, *Francis Joseph* (London: Longman, 1996). A very good introduction to the Habsburg monarchy.

Chris M. Clark, *Kaiser Wilhelm II* (London: Longman, 2000). A good modern biography of the Kaiser.

George Dangerfield, *The Strange Death of Liberal England 1910–1914* (London: Constable, 1936 and many later editions). A classic view of British politics before World War I.

H. V. Emy, *Liberals, Radicals and Social Politics, 1892–1914* (Cambridge: Cambridge University Press, 1973). A discussion of key issues in British political life.

Robert Gildea, *France 1870–1914* (London: Longman, 1994). A short introduction to the Third Republic.

Dominic Lieven, *Nicholas II: Emperor of all the Russias* (London: John Murray, 1993). The best biography of the last tsar, placing him in a comparative context.

Wolfgang J. Mommsen, *Imperial Germany 1867–1918: Politics, Culture and Society in an Authoritarian State* (London: Arnold, 1995). A wide-ranging introduction to Germany under Bismarck and Wilhelm II.

Alan Sked, *The Decline and Fall of the Habsburg Empire 1815–1918* (London: Longman, 1989). A controversial view of the end of Austria-Hungary.

Theodore Zeldin, *France 1848–1945: Politics and Anger* (Oxford: Oxford University Press, 1979). The outstanding work on French political culture, showing it in all its complexity.

CHAPTER TWELVE

The Coming of War, 1914

ANNIKA MOMBAUER

The Allied and Associated Governments affirm and Germany accepts the responsibility of Germany and her allies for causing all the loss and damage to which the Allied and Associated Governments and their nationals have been subjected as a consequence of the war imposed upon them by the aggression of Germany and her allies. (Treaty of Versailles, Article 231)

Few historiographical debates have been as heated and as long-lived as the controversy over the origins of World War I. The literature on the events that led to war in 1914 is now so vast that it is almost impossible to grapple with. The following account will provide a brief introduction to the subject through an overview of the events prior to 1914 and a summary of the controversy that followed. In three parts, it will first of all look at the long-term and short-term causes of the war, summarizing the development of the alliance system, imperial rivalries and the arms race, and focusing on some of the major prewar crises from which a major war could easily have resulted. To what extent can such international developments really be seen to have caused war? Why, it will be asked, was war averted on so many occasions but not in July 1914?

This "July crisis" will be the subject of the second part of this chapter, in which the events following the assassination of the Austrian archduke, Franz Ferdinand, will be examined. Did this act of terrorism necessarily lead to the outbreak of war in the Balkans? What were the chances of such a war being "localized" (as contemporaries put it) and what were the motivations behind the decisions made in Europe's capitals during these final days of peace?

Finally, the concluding part will briefly summarize the long debate on the origins of the war. So many years after its outbreak, is there any agreement on its causes among historians? Has the once-heated debate on the question of war guilt finally been resolved?

Long-Term and Short-Term Causes of World War I

In order to set the scene and explain the diplomatic background to World War I, most investigations into the origins of the war begin with the wars of German unification (1864, 1866, and 1870–1).[1] Following the defeat of France in 1871 and the annexation of the French provinces of Alsace and Lorraine, the German Empire was founded, with a new emperor, Kaiser Wilhelm I, at the helm. The powerful country at the heart of Europe which had been united through a series of successful wars seemed a threat to the other great powers, although initially the chancellor, Otto von Bismarck, aimed to avoid further conflict and consolidate the gains the country had made.[2] His complicated alliance system served to ensure that what he considered a "nightmare of coalitions" against Germany could not threaten the new status quo. He declared that Germany was "satiated" following its recent unification and that it sought no further conflict with its neighbors. During his time in office, the alliance system that he created preserved peace and prevented Germany's neighbors from uniting against it. Germany was allied to Austria-Hungary in the Dual Alliance of 1879, which became *de facto* a Triple Alliance when Italy joined in 1882. A few years later, in 1887, Germany also concluded the secret "Reinsurance Treaty" with Russia, guaranteeing neutrality in the event of a future war (in contradiction with the alliance agreement with Austria-Hungary). Britain and France remained diplomatically isolated during this time (the former largely by choice, pursuing a policy of "splendid isolation" and reaping the benefits of being the world's largest imperial power), and there seemed little chance of either of them settling their imperial differences with each other. With the accession to the throne of Kaiser Wilhelm II in Germany in 1888, however, and particularly following Bismarck's dismissal in 1890, this carefully constructed system of alliances began to be dismantled. Bismarck's successors were less concerned to preserve the status quo in Europe and envisaged a much more powerful role for the new German Empire, both on the continent and worldwide. As a result, German foreign policy under Wilhelm II became more erratic and began to threaten the European balance of power that had kept Europe relatively peaceful since 1871.[3]

In this age of imperialism, Britain – with its enormous global empire on which the sun never set – was the main imperial power, although new international players were emerging, such as the USA and Japan. France, too, was a great power with considerable imperial clout, while Russia's drive to expand to the east ensured its share of the imperial stakes. It is not surprising that Germany, now a large and economically successful country at the heart of Europe, was eager to make its presence felt. More populous than either France or Britain, it had even begun to overtake Britain as the foremost economic power in Europe.

Under Wilhelm II's erratic leadership and in pursuit of the goal of becoming a *Weltmacht* (world power) and gaining a "place in the sun," the powerful new Germany soon began to challenge its neighbors, who were quick to react to its posturing by forming defensive alliances. Republican France (which still begrudged Germany the annexation of Alsace-Lorraine in 1871) and autocratic Russia overcame their substantial differences in negotiations between 1892 and 1894 which led to the conclusion of a military alliance against Germany and Austria-Hungary which, in turn, gave rise to a feeling of "encirclement" in Germany. Given its geographic situation, Germany, though allied to Austria-Hungary and Italy, now faced potential enemies both in the west and the east, and felt encircled by envious and potentially dangerous neighbors who were forming alliances against it.

At the same time, Germany had stirred Britain into a position of antagonism by deliberately and openly challenging its supremacy at sea with Admiral von Tirpitz's program to build a great navy which would, in time, be able to hold its own against the British. Germany began to construct a high-seas fleet to rival that of Britain in 1897–8. Britain took up the challenge and responded in 1906 with the construction of the first *Dreadnought*. The introduction of this new "all gun ship" leveled the playing field and ruined Tirpitz's grand design. The main result of this Anglo-German naval race was enmity and suspicion in the government and people of both countries, made worse by some ill-advised meddling in South African affairs by the Kaiser, for example during the Jameson Raid in 1895.[4] In Britain, Germany's expanding navy was regarded as one of the ways in which Germany was attempting to improve its international position and challenge its rivals, while in Germany it was felt that the country deserved to play a greater international role and to occupy a more prominent place in the sun, for which a powerful navy was portrayed as an essential prerequisite.

The worsening of Anglo-German relations has often been stressed as playing a major part in leading to a general deterioration of the relations between the great powers, and thus contributing to an increasingly warlike mood before 1914. Although there were some attempts to come to amicable agreements between Berlin and London (for example, the 1912 "Haldane mission"), none came to fruition.[5] Among the reasons for this failure were German insistence on a formal alliance with Britain (which had become impossible once Britain had allied itself to France) and Germany's unwillingness to cease building a strong navy, as well as the threat that German foreign policy seemed to pose to the European status quo, and to Britain's own foreign policy ambitions. In Britain the government faced crucial decisions: who would be the more useful future ally and who the more worrying future enemy among the continental great powers? To British statesmen, the price Germany seemed to be demanding for an understanding with Britain was British neutrality in case of a continental war between Germany and either France or Russia – a price that they believed to be too high to pay, particularly in view of their concerns for the safety of the British Empire.

It has been argued that in addition to the existing Anglo-German antagonism and to Britain's aim of upholding the European balance of power, British policy in the prewar years and its decision to join the war in August 1914 may have been motivated by fears of an overly powerful Russia, and the threat that a victorious Russia would pose for the British Empire, particularly in India. In the British foreign office, some believed that an unfriendly France and particularly Russia would potentially be a much greater threat to the empire than a hostile Germany.[6] While such a view remains contested, it is clear that there were many Francophone voices in the British foreign office, and that an anti-German mood pertained which made more cordial relations between the two countries more difficult. As Sir Edward Grey's private secretary William Tyrrell noted in 1911: "It is depressing to find that after six years' experience of Germany the inclination here is still to believe that she can be placated by small concessions . . . what she wants is the hegemony of Europe."[7]

Anglo-German enmity was such that Britain preferred to settle its colonial disputes with its former rival France to escape its previous relative diplomatic isolation. The conclusion of the *Entente Cordiale* between France and Britain in 1904 was initially a loose arrangement of the two powers that was strengthened as a result of the first Moroccan crisis in 1905–6, during which Germany reacted to French colonial aspirations in the region by attempting to break up the new allies Britain and France. Britain had actually given up its position of "splendid isolation" in 1902 when it had become allied to Japan, but it was the conclusion of the Entente with France that indicated to Germans that Britain would be found on the side of Germany's enemies in any future European conflict. In effect, this Entente also led to a détente between Britain and Russia via their shared partner France. This friendship was given a more solid basis with the conclusion of the Anglo-Russian Convention in 1907. From then on the so-called "Triple Entente" stood in opposition to the Triple Alliance of the Central Powers and two European alliance blocs faced each other in a number of international crises. In both alliance systems, the partners promised to support each other in case one of them faced aggression from a third power. As a result, a conflict between any state in the Entente with one in the Triple Alliance would threaten to escalate and potentially embroil all the major European powers.

The crisis which resulted in the outbreak of war in 1914 was no isolated incident. In the years preceding the outbreak of war, a number of international crises and localized wars had threatened to escalate into a European war. The Russo-Japanese War of 1904–5 involved land battles of almost unprecedented scale, and provided a taste of things to come. Much to everyone's surprise, a European "white" country was defeated by a "non-white" race. The most important result was a significant change in the balance of power in Europe. Following Russia's defeat and the revolution of 1905, Japan emerged as a force to be reckoned with, leading to the renewal and extension of the Anglo-Japanese alliance. Russia, on the other hand, was for the time being so weakened that it could almost be discounted as a great power. The lost war spelt the end of Russia's imperialist aspirations in the far east for the foreseeable future. Any future ambitions would have to focus on Europe. A conflict between Russia and Britain had, however, been avoided and France had been spared the dilemma of having to take sides.

Nonetheless, France was adversely affected by Russia's lost war in the far east, for in the aftermath of its crushing defeat, Russia could be of no support to its French ally in the Moroccan crisis of 1905. Indeed, it was Russia's weakened state which encouraged Germany to challenge France over its Moroccan policy, based on the assumption that Russia would be unable to come to France's aid, thus heightening Germany's chances at achieving a diplomatic victory. At the same time, Germany's military planners developed a new and daring deployment plan (later named the Schlieffen Plan),[8] based on the assumption that the recently defeated Russia would not pose a real threat to Germany in the east in the near future. In fact, Germany's chief of the general staff, Count Alfred von Schlieffen, advocated a preventive war against France at that time because Russia's weakened position meant it would not be able to support its ally, France. However, the military's demand for war found no favor with the German Kaiser or with the chancellor, Bernhard von Bülow, at that time. By 1914, following mounting international tensions, Bülow's successor,

Theobald von Bethmann Hollweg, would be less inclined to resist the demands for war by Germany's military leaders.

While Russia and Japan were fighting in Asia, Germany provoked an international crisis over the Anglo-French agreement regarding the territory of Morocco. Aside from the concerns for some German companies established in the region, Germany felt slighted by not having been consulted by France and Britain, who were increasing their influence over north Africa, and wanted to demonstrate that a great power such as Germany could not simply be passed over when important colonial decisions were made. Friedrich von Holstein, a senior figure in the German foreign office at the time, feared that if Germany allowed its "toes to be trodden on silently" in Morocco, this would amount to allowing a "repetition elsewhere."[9] German policy also aimed at demonstrating that France could not rely on its new Entente partner, Britain, and that Russia was too weak to support it in an international crisis. At the heart of the Moroccan crisis was Germany's desire to expose the newly formed *Entente Cordiale* between Britain and France as useless, to split the Entente partners before they had a chance to consolidate their bond, and to intimidate the French. However, these bullying tactics did not succeed. On the contrary, the newly formed Entente between Britain and France emerged strengthened from the crisis, with both countries realizing the benefits to be had from such a coalition. The international conference at Algeciras, which had been convened following German demands to settle the dispute at the conference table, amounted to a diplomatic defeat for Germany, which found itself isolated, with support only from its ally, Austria-Hungary.

As far as Berlin was concerned, the crisis provided further evidence of German encirclement, while for the country's neighbors it seemed as if Germany was an aggressive bully. This trend was set to continue in the coming years, in which several crises in the Balkans threatened to escalate into a European war on several occasions. It was with the disintegration of the Ottoman Empire that the status quo in the Balkans changed fundamentally. The smaller Balkan states were keen to expand their area of influence into former Turkish territory, and were beginning to pose a direct threat to Austria-Hungary, whose population was made up of numerous national minorities, some of which had ambitions for independence. Austria-Hungary had as much interest in preventing the area from being taken over by Serbs as Russia had in supporting Serbian ambitions in the region. Serbia, Austria-Hungary's main Balkan rival, received moral support from Russia, who considered itself the guardian of the pan-Slav movement. There were disputes over access to the sea, over control of the Straits of Constantinople (providing vital access to the Black Sea), and simply over territorial possessions. For Austria-Hungary, the matter was made worse by the fact that the Dual Monarchy united 11 disparate nationalities in one empire, some of which wanted to establish their independence, notably among them many disgruntled Serbs.

The Bosnian annexation crisis was one such serious dispute which threatened to bring war to Europe as early as 1908. Following the Austro-Russian negotiations of 1897, when the two powers had come to an agreement over the Balkans, relations between the countries had been amicable. The Balkans only reappeared as a potential source of friction after Russia's disastrous experience in the far east, when its interest in the Balkans was reawakened. Revolution in Turkey by the Young Turks[10] in 1908 led to a change of government and policy, and the previously assumed disintegration of the Ottoman Empire seemed to be halted – a threatening development for those European countries that had an interest in Turkey's decline and had welcomed |it. The multinational empire of Austria-Hungary faced numerous internal threats from the nationalist aspirations of its many national minorities, and the policy of Austria-Hungary's foreign minister, Count Alois Aehrenthal, aimed at diverting domestic discontent with the help of an aggressive foreign policy. On the back of the Young Turk revolution, Aehrenthal decided to annex the provinces of Bosnia and Herzegovina, which Austria had nominally occupied following the Treaty of Berlin in 1878, but which had formally remained under Turkish suzerainty.[11]

Russia, too, hoped to gain from the instability in the Balkans, and the Russian foreign minister, Alexei Izvolsky, and his Austrian counterpart, Aehrenthal, came to a secret agreement in 1908. Austria would be allowed to go ahead with the annexation, and in return was expected to support Russian interests in the Bosphorus and Dardanelles. However, Aehrenthal proceeded with the annexation on October 5, 1908 before Izvolsky had time to secure diplomatic support from other European capitals (or indeed from members of his own government). Izvolsky felt betrayed by Aehrenthal, and denounced the secret agreement. Serbia was ready to go to war over the annexation, believing the Bosnian Serbs to belong to its own sphere of influence, but in the event was not supported by Russia, which was still too weak following the war against Japan. Given the fact that Germany gave unconditional support to Austria-Hungary over this Balkan matter and put significant pressure on Russia, it was primarily Russia's mediating influence on Serbia that prevented a war on this occasion. However, the previous accord between Russia and Austria-Hungary in the Balkans had been destroyed, while the German government's open and unconditional support of its ally had significantly changed what had so far been a purely defensive alliance agreement between Germany and Austria-Hungary. From now on, Austria's leaders believed they would be able to count on Germany even if an international crisis resulted from their own actions. The Bosnian annexation crisis marked an important juncture in this respect. In the future, Serbia, humiliated in 1909, would be keen to redress its status in the Balkans, while Russia was now suspicious of German interests in that region and more determined than ever to regain its military power. The European armaments race which followed was started by Russia's desire to increase its military potential, and soon led to army increases by all major European powers.[12] Russia and Serbia had been forced to back down on this occasion, but they were unlikely to do so again.

In 1911 the great powers of Europe again faced each other in a serious diplomatic crisis that brought the continent to the verge of war. When the French sent troops to Morocco to suppress a revolt (and thus, by implication, to extend their influence over that country), Germany considered this to be a move contrary to the international agreements which had been concluded following the first Moroccan crisis. Germany tried again to assert its claim as a great power that could not simply be ignored in colonial affairs. After failing to find a diplomatic solution, Germany's political leaders decided to dispatch the gunboat *Panther* to the port of Agadir to intimidate the French. Germany demanded the French Congo as compensation for the extension of French influence in Morocco. However, as during the first Moroccan crisis, France received support from Britain, and the links between the two Entente partners were only further strengthened as a consequence of German intervention.

Britain let Germany know – in no uncertain terms – that it intended to stand by France, and David Lloyd George's famous Mansion House Speech of July 21, 1911, threatening to fight on France's side against Germany if the need arose, caused great indignation in Germany. Although the crisis was resolved peacefully, and Germany was indeed given a small part of the French Congo as compensation, the affair was in fact another diplomatic defeat for Germany, whose leaders were becoming increasingly worried that their foreign policy adventures were not leading to the break-up of hostile alliances or to proper recognition of the country's great power status. Moreover, Austria-Hungary's lukewarm support suggested that the ally could only be counted on definitely if an international crisis directly affected the Dual Monarchy's own interests. Germany's decision makers arrived at the crucial realization that only a crisis in the Balkans would guarantee the all-important Austro-Hungarian support.

Soon after the Agadir crisis, the Balkans once again demanded the attention of Europe's statesmen. Following the humiliation of 1909, Russia had encouraged the creation of a coalition of Balkan states, and in 1912 Bulgaria, Greece, Montenegro, and Serbia formed the Balkan League. In October 1912 the League declared war on Turkey, and the First Balkan War threatened to embroil Europe's major powers in an armed conflict, too. Against this background, Germany's Kaiser convened an infamous "war council" in which he and his chief of staff demanded war. In the event, that decision was postponed, but the meeting provides evidence for the way international crises such as the Balkan war impacted upon decisions made in Europe's capitals and could easily have led to a European war.[13]

In the First Balkan War, Turkey was quickly defeated and driven out of most of the Balkans, but in the aftermath of the war, the victors fell out over the spoils, and ended up fighting each other in the Second Balkan War of 1913. As a result of the wars, Serbia doubled its territory, and now posed an even greater threat to Austria-Hungary, both externally, and by encouraging the sizable Serbian minority within the Dual Monarchy to demand its independence. This is essential background for understanding Austria's reaction to the Serbian-supported assassination of the heir to the Austro-Hungarian throne on June 28, 1914. Given the longstanding Balkan instability, and Serbia's many provocations, this was a threat to the Empire's international reputation that Vienna's statesmen felt they could not ignore. With the moral right seemingly on their side, the assassination seemed to provide an opportunity to dispose of the Serbian threat once and for all.

The July Crisis and the Outbreak of War

In view of these tensions and underlying hostilities of the prewar years, and given that few contemporaries thought of war as a catastrophe that they should strive to prevent at all cost, it is perhaps not surprising that war resulted from such international rivalries. However, that is not to say that such a turn of events was inevitable, given, for example, the existence of an increasingly vociferous peace movement in Europe, and the prewar attempts at curbing the armaments race, for example during the Hague peace conferences. However, as there had been a general expectation that war would come at some point in the not-too-distant future (and given that war was, after all, still a legitimate way of conducting foreign policy when diplomacy had failed), it is not surprising that all that was needed was the proverbial spark that would set light to the powder keg of Europe.

That spark was provided by the murder of the Austrian heir to the throne, Archduke Franz Ferdinand, and his wife in the Bosnian capital of Sarajevo on June 28, 1914. That act of terrorism committed by Bosnian Serbs against the Austro-Hungarian state would lead to the war between Austria-Hungary and Serbia that quickly escalated into a European war, and ultimately became World War I. With hindsight, it appears almost as if that war could not have been avoided. However, even in July 1914 a European war was not inevitable. Right until the last moment, some decision makers were desperately trying to avoid the outbreak of war and to resolve the crisis at the conference table, while others did everything in their power to ensure an armed conflict would result from the assassination. That war finally broke out was less the product of fate or bad fortune than the result of intention. In order to understand why the crisis escalated into full-scale war, we must look particularly at Vienna and Berlin; for it was here that war (at least a war between Austria-Hungary and Serbia) was consciously risked and planned. France, Russia, and Britain entered the stage much later in July 1914, when the most fateful decisions had already been taken.[14]

In Vienna, the reaction to the assassination was officially one of outrage, although behind the scenes many were secretly pleased because Franz Ferdinand had not been universally popular. It is ironic that the archduke's assassination should have provided the reason for a declaration of war on Serbia, given that Franz Ferdinand had been opposed to war during his lifetime, and had been a powerful opponent to the belli-cose demands of the chief of the Austrian general staff, Franz Conrad von Hötzendorf, for a war against Serbia. Conrad welcomed an excuse for a war with Serbia. He still regretted what he (as well as his German counterpart Helmuth von Moltke) had considered the "missed opportunity" for a "reckoning with Serbia" in 1909.[15] In Berlin, the possibility of a Balkan crisis was greeted favorably, for such a crisis would ensure that Austria would definitely be committed to fighting if a war resulted. Most historians would also agree that Berlin encouraged Vienna to demand retribution from Serbia, and was happy to take the risk that an Austro-Serbian conflict might escalate into a European war. When the Austrian envoy Count Hoyos traveled to Berlin in order to ascertain the powerful ally's position in case Austria demanded recompense from Serbia, he was assured that Germany would support Austria all the way, even if it chose to go to war over the assassination, and even if such a war were to turn into a European war. This was Wilhelm II's so-called "blank check" to Vienna. In a strictly confidential telegram of July 5 to the Austro-Hungarian foreign minister, Count Berchtold, the Austrian ambassador to Berlin, Count Szögyény, reported the following account of his meeting with the German Kaiser:

> The Kaiser authorized me to inform our Gracious Majesty that we might in this case, as in all others, rely upon Germany's full support . . . He did not doubt in the least that Herr von Bethmann Hollweg [the German chancellor] would agree with him. Especially as far as our action against Serbia was concerned. But it was his [Kaiser Wilhelm's] opinion that this action must not be delayed. Russia's attitude will no doubt be hostile, but for this he had for years prepared, and should a war between Austria-Hungary and Russia be unavoidable, we might be convinced that Germany, our old

faithful ally, would stand on our side. Russia at the present time was in no way prepared
for war, and would think twice before it appealed to arms . . . If we had really recognized the necessity of warlike action against Serbia, he [Kaiser Wilhelm] would regret if
we did not make use of the present moment, which is all in our favour.[16]

The Kaiser spoke without having consulted the chancellor, Theobald von Bethmann
Hollweg, whose approval he simply took for granted. Wilhelm II not only actively
encouraged Austria to take action against Serbia, but even insisted that such action
must not be delayed, and that it would be regrettable if the opportunity were not
seized. He clearly expected Russia to adopt a hostile attitude, but felt that the latter
was currently still ill-prepared for war and might therefore perhaps not take up arms.
The Kaiser urged Austria to "make use of the present moment," which he considered
to be very favorable.

While most political and military decision makers in Berlin and Vienna did not
actually want a *European* war, they were certainly willing to risk it. Wilhelm II and
Bethmann Hollweg had been encouraged to do so by Germany's leading military
advisors, who had advocated war "the sooner the better" on many occasions and had
assured the politicians that Germany stood a good chance of defeating its enemies.
Germany's military leaders had been conjuring up the image of a Russia that could
be defeated by Germany at this time, but one which would, in the future, be too
strong to defeat.[17]

Armed with such reassurances from Germany, the Austro-Hungarian ministerial
council decided on July 7 to issue an ultimatum to Serbia. This was to be deliberately
unacceptable, so that Serbian non-compliance would lead to the outbreak of war with
the "moral high ground" on Austria's side. However, much time would pass before
the ultimatum was finally delivered to Belgrade: first the harvest had to be completed,
for which most soldiers of the Dual Monarchy were away on harvest leave. Moreover,
it was decided to wait until the state visit of Raymond Poincaré, the French president,
to Russia was over, so that the two allies would not have a chance to coordinate their
response to Austria's ultimatum. While all this was being plotted behind the scenes,
both Vienna and Berlin gave the impression of calm to the outside world, even
sending their main decision makers on holiday to keep up this illusion. Because of
this deception the other major powers did not play a significant role in the crisis until
July 23, the day when the harsh Austro-Hungarian ultimatum was finally delivered
to Belgrade.

The Serbian response to the "unacceptable" ultimatum astonished everyone. In
all but one point they agreed to accept it, making Austria's predetermined decision
to turn down Belgrade's response look suspicious in the eyes of those European
powers who wanted to try to preserve the peace. Even Kaiser Wilhelm II now decided
that there was no longer any reason to go to war, much to the dismay of his military
advisors. From Britain came the suggestion that the issue could be resolved at the
conference table, but such mediation proposals and attempts to preserve the peace
were not taken up by Vienna or Berlin. Some historians argue that Britain could have
played a more decisive role by declaring its intentions to support France earlier, rather
than trying to be non-committal until the last possible moment. They allege that if
Germany's decision makers had known earlier and with certainty that Britain would
be involved in a war on the side of the Entente, they would have accepted mediation

proposals and would have counseled peace in Vienna.[18] It is certainly worth speculating that Bethmann Hollweg may have urged mediation in Vienna sooner and more forcefully than in the event he did, if he had known earlier of Sir Edward Grey's resolve to come to France's aid in a European war, although in reality London's stance did not really come as a surprise to Berlin. However, some members of the British cabinet objected to a British involvement in a European war, and no definite decision to support France could be made by the responsible decision makers until Germany's violation of neutral Belgium gave Sir Edward Grey the reason for intervention that he had needed. The move against Belgium, necessitated by Germany's deployment plan which envisaged that, whatever the *casus belli*, German troops would initially have to defeat the country's enemies in the west, also ensured that Germany appeared to all the world as an aggressor, and that tales of real and invented atrocities against Belgian and French civilians would haunt Germans for decades to come.[19] In the crucial last days of July, Britain's decision makers were divided on how to deal with the threat of war on the continent. Nonetheless, the ambivalence of Sir Edward Grey's policy can hardly be seen as a cause of the war. After all, this hesitant attitude was motivated by the desire to *avoid* an escalation of the crisis (Grey feared that a definite promise of support might lead France or Russia to accept the risk of war more willingly), while German and Austro-Hungarian decisions were based on the explicit desire to *provoke* a conflict. As the former German ambassador to London, Prince Lichnowsky, summed up in January 1915:

> On our side nothing, absolutely nothing, was done to preserve peace, and when we at last decided to do what I had advocated from the first [he had favored mediation and had wanted to avoid a war], it was too late. By then Russia, as a result of our harsh attitude and that of Count Berchtold [the Austrian prime minister], had lost all confidence and mobilized. The war party gained the upper hand . . . Such a policy is comprehensible only if war was our aim, not otherwise.[20]

Only at the very last minute, when it was clear that Britain, too, would become involved if war broke out, did the German chancellor try to restrain the Austrians – but his mediation proposals arrived far too late and were in any case not forceful enough to be able to halt events. Austria's declaration of war on Serbia on July 28, and its bombardment of Belgrade which ensured that there could not be any last-minute reconciliation, would set in motion a domino effect of mobilization orders and declarations of war by Europe's major powers. Russia, committed to supporting Serbia in case of war, and allied to France, needed to implement its mobilization in order to ensure that it would be able to relieve France from the anticipated early German onslaught in the west. Russia and Germany mobilized in quick succession (the latter waiting until the last moment so that Russia would appear to have initiated mobilization), and Germany declared war on Russia and France, before invading neutral Luxemburg and Belgium. By the time Britain had declared war on Germany on August 4 the Alliance powers (without Italy, which had decided to stay neutral) faced the Entente powers in the "great fight" that had been anticipated for such a long time.

As soon as hostilities began, so too did the battle for the moral high ground over the question of war guilt. For all European governments it was essential that the odium of having started the war was seen to rest firmly with the enemy. Although it is generally now understood that most citizens and subjects of Europe were less enthusiastic in their welcoming of the outbreak of war than has usually been assumed, most believed their leaders that what followed was a defensive war.[21]

However, the war, which was also commonly held to be "over by Christmas," did not go to plan. The longer it lasted, the more victims it took, and the worse it went for the Central Powers, the more important did it become to construct an apologetic version of the events that had led to the war's outbreak, while for those countries who felt they had been victims of the aggression of the Central Powers, attributing blame and – eventually – demanding retribution became a prime concern. Not surprisingly, even before the fighting had ended, the debate on the war's origins had already begun. In the years since the outbreak of World War I, historians have been unable to agree fully on the reasons for the coming of war in 1914. The question of guilt or responsibility for the war is still disputed, and no account of the origins of the war is complete without consideration of its accompanying historiographical controversy.

Conclusion: The Debate on the Origins of World War I

Despite both crude and subtle propaganda efforts on the part of the Central Powers during and after the war, in 1919 the victorious allies were largely in agreement that Germany and its allies were to blame for the outbreak of war, as they stipulated in Article 231 of the Treaty of Versailles. However, their initial harsh war guilt allegations were soon softened by a more conciliatory interpretation in the light of new potential threats to the interwar order, and an apologetic interpretation which allocated responsibility for the outbreak of war to international rivalries became firmly established in the 1920s and 1930s.[22] In Germany, the country that had initially shouldered the blame for having caused the war, and for whom the slowly emerging apologetic consensus had been so welcome, the reopening of the debate following the war guilt allegations of the German historian Fritz Fischer during the so-called Fischer controversy of the 1960s and 1970s caused consternation among historians and the general public that is today difficult to fathom. In the decades immediately following World War II, German history seemed tainted enough without adding guilt for World War I to the country's already shameful past. However, at the beginning of the twenty-first century, this passionately fought debate no longer continues to divide historians along quite such clearly demarcated lines, and it is probably fair to say that today few, if any, scholars would deny Germany and Austria-Hungary's larger share of responsibility for the outbreak of war. Currently, historians are less concerned with attributing war guilt and more with explaining how war had come about; a crucial difference if we are to move away from the passionately fought debate of the interwar years and the 1960s.

Recent trends in the historiography of the outbreak of the war have emphasized the possibility of détente and the "avoidability" or even improbability of war in and before 1914. The relative success of détente in resolving crises had, in the interpretation of some historians, led to a view among contemporaries that war could be avoided, and eventually even led to incredulity that governments really would unleash a war. The long peace and the previous success of diplomacy in resolving the many prewar crises were thus to some extent counterproductive.[23] At the same time, new weight has been placed on understanding long-term factors and why international relations were dominated by an almost phobic fear of the Other, by "mutual suspicion" which "created mutual paranoia." According to such views, once war had broken out, all sides fought it not for reasons of imperialist aggression, but for "national self-defense."[24]

Such views are far removed from the indignant war guilt allegation arrived at by the Allies at Versailles. Ultimately, however, something or someone must have acted to lead the European alliances into war, for whatever the potential for a peaceful resolution of the crisis of July 1914, clearly that chance for peace was squandered. One attempt at explaining this focuses on the importance of human agency. As such, the decisions taken by Conrad von Hötzendorf and Helmuth von Moltke in particular are crucial for explaining why war broke out. Such attempts at explaining the outbreak of war dismiss the "big causes" usually given to explain the outbreak of war, such as the alliance system, nationalism, social Darwinism, imperialism, the influence of the press, domestic pressures, or the accident theory, in favor of the "strategic argument": "the decision makers of the five major powers sought to save, maintain, or enhance the power and prestige of the nation."[25]

In conclusion, while there have been attempts to arrive at a more conciliatory, even apologetic, interpretation in the recent literature on the origins of the war, Germany and Austria-Hungary are still most often named as the main culprits. Yet this does not mean that the Entente powers entirely escape the strictures of historians. Some shift part of the blame for the prewar tensions onto the Entente, for not allowing Germany to reach its full potential: "France, Russia and particularly England" were not willing to give Germany its "place in the sun," it is argued. "Desperately fixated on their own advantage and security they did not grant Berlin the necessary room to expand," and from their unwillingness to do so resulted what they surely had not wanted: that the Dual Alliance dragged "the world into a terrible war."[26] Those who remain convinced of Germany's responsibility for the war might ask why it would have been necessary for Germany to expand (was it not doing very well anyway and set to become the continent's leading industrial power without expanding?). They might also ask where this expansion would have ended, if the other powers had allowed it to go ahead. How much scope should the other countries have given Germany? How much leeway could Austria-Hungary give Serbia?

Throughout the long debate on the origins of World War I, historians' views have been shaped by the political context and climate in which they formulated their arguments, and at the beginning of the twenty-first century this still holds true.[27] Where previously historians were perhaps quick to judge Austria-Hungary's reaction to the assassination as exaggerated and belligerent, they are today more willing to concede that a sovereign nation that found itself exposed to terrorist attacks may have felt obligated to defend itself against the threat that emanated from Serbian terrorists who sought to undermine the Dual Monarchy. As a result, future investigations by historians will have to focus particularly on decisions made in Serbia, about which we still know surprisingly little. We also need to know more about the decisions made in St Petersburg and Paris to accept the challenge that emanated from the Central Powers, although it is arguable what choice they really had in the matter, given Vienna and Berlin's resolve to risk an European conflict.

However, if any agreement has been reached after more than ninety years of debate, it is that World War I, which has rightly been regarded as the seminal catastrophe of the twentieth century, was not an act of fate, need not have happened, and could – even in July 1914 – have been avoided if all the decision makers in the European capitals had wanted to do so. But, tragically, some thought they had more to lose from not fighting a war than from fighting it. Despite the fact that the Treaty of Versailles has been derided by some as a victors' peace, it seems that the victorious Allies were right in their assessment of the war guilt question. War had been no accident, and it had not resulted from the alliance system, the arms race, imperialism, or international rivalries, or at least it had not resulted from them alone. Rather, it was the consequence of decisions taken foremost in Berlin and Vienna, and the result of attitudes which regarded war not as the ultimate catastrophe, but as a necessary, even a desirable, evil and as a way of continuing foreign policy by other means.

NOTES

1   For further details on the political history of the prewar years, see Gordon Martel, *The Origins of the First World War*, 3rd edn (London: Longman/Pearson, 2003) and additional references in the Guide to Further Reading.

2   For a recent biography of Bismarck, see Katharine Lerman, *Bismarck: Profiles in Power* (London: Longman/Pearson, 2004). On the Franco-Prussian war, see Dennis Showalter, *The Wars of German Unification* (London: Arnold, 2004).

3   For details, see Matthew S. Seligmann and Roderick R. McLean, *Germany from Reich to Republic 1871–1918* (Basingstoke: Macmillan, 2000).

4   For more details on the Tirpitz Plan in English, see Paul M. Kennedy, "The Development of German Naval Operations Plans against England, 1896–1914," in *The War Plans of the Great Powers, 1880–1914*, Paul M. Kennedy, ed. (Boston MA: Allen and Unwin, 1979); Volker Berghahn, *Imperial Germany 1871–1914: Economy, Society, Culture and Politics* (Providence, RI: Berghahn, 1994).

5   For details, see R. T. B. Langhorne, "Great Britain and Germany, 1911–1914," in *British Foreign Policy under Sir Edward Grey*, F. H. Hinsley, ed. (Cambridge: Cambridge University Press, 1997), pp. 288–314; Paul M. Kennedy, *The Rise of Anglo-German Antagonism* (London: Allen and Unwin, 1982).

6   See, for example, Keith M. Wilson, *The Policy of the Entente: Essays on the Determinants of British Foreign Policy 1904–1914* (Cambridge: Cambridge University Press, 1985).

7   Cited in Zara S. Steiner and Keith Neilson, *Britain and the Origins of the First World War*, 2nd edn (London: Palgrave/Macmillan, 2003), p. 44.

8   The nature of the Schlieffen Plan has recently been called into question by Terence Zuber, "The Schlieffen Plan Reconsidered," *War in History* 6/3 (1999): 262–305, and his arguments have been advanced in more detail in Zuber, *Inventing the Schlieffen Plan* (Oxford: Oxford University Press, 2003). See also the lengthy debate in *War in History*, with contributions by Terence Zuber, Terence Holmes, and Robert T. Foley. For recent views on this debate, see also Annika Mombauer, "Of War Plans and War Guilt: The Debate on the Nature of the Schlieffen Plan," *Journal of Strategic Studies*, 2006.

9   Cited in Gregor Schöllgen, "Germany's Foreign Policy in the Age of Imperialism: A Vicious Circle?" In *Escape into War? The Foreign Policy of Imperial Germany*, Gregor Schöllgen, ed. (Oxford: Berg, 1990), p. 125.

10   "Young Turks" was the name given to a liberal reform movement in the Ottoman Empire.

11   For more information, see Samuel R. Williamson, Jr, *Austria-Hungary and the Origins of the First World War* (London: Macmillan, 1991).

12   On the armaments race, see David Stevenson, *Armaments and the Coming of War: Europe 1904–1914* (Oxford: Clarendon Press, 1996).

13   On the war council, see John C. G. Röhl, *The Kaiser and his Court* (Cambridge: Cambridge University Press, 1995), pp. 162ff.

14   For details on the diplomatic events of the July Crisis, see in particular Imanuel Geiss, ed., *July 1914: The Outbreak of the First World War: Selected Documents* (London: B. T. Batsford, 1967); Luigi Albertini, *The Origins of the War of 1914*, 3 vols, I. M. Massey, trans. (Oxford: Oxford University Press, 1952–7); James Joll, *Origins of the First World War*, 2nd edn (London, 1992). Further details and references can also be found in Annika Mombauer, *Helmuth von Moltke and the Origins of the First World War* (Cambridge: Cambridge University Press, 2001), ch. 4.

15   See Franz Conrad von Hötzendorf, *Aus meiner Dienstzeit 1906–1918*, 5 vols (Vienna, 1921–25), vol. 1, p. 165.

16   Geiss, *July 1914*, p. 77.

17   See Mombauer, *Helmuth von Moltke*, pp. 121ff.

18   For a summary and critique of such arguments, see Steiner and Neilson, *Britain and the Origins*, pp. 258ff.

19   See John Horne and Alan Kramer, *German Atrocities 1914: A History of Denial* (New Haven CT: Yale University Press, 2001).

20   Lichnowsky's memorandum cited in John C. G. Röhl, ed., *1914: Delusion or Design? The Testimony of Two German Diplomats* (London: Elek, 1973), pp. 79ff.

21   Recent research has questioned that widespread popular enthusiasm for war existed in August 1914. See, for example, Jeffrey Verhey, *The Spirit of 1914: Militarism, Myth, and Mobilization in Germany* (Cambridge: Cambridge University Press, 2000); Jean-Jacques Becker, *1914: Comment les Français sont entrés dans la guerre: Contribution à l'étude de l'opinion publique, printemps-été 1914* (Paris: Presses de la Fondation, 1977); Joshua Sanborn, "The Mobilization of 1914 and the Question of the Russian Nation: A Reexamination," *Slavic Review* 59 (2000): 267–89; L. L. Farrar, "Nationalism in Wartime: Critiquing the Conventional Wisdom," in *Authority, Identity and the Social History of the Great War*, Frans Coetzee and Marilyn Shevin-Coetzee, eds (Oxford: Berghahn, 1995), pp. 133–52.

22   For more details on the historiographical debate, see John W. Langdon, *July 1914: The Long Debate 1918–1990* (New York: Berg, 1991) and Annika Mombauer, *The Origins of the First World War: Controversies and Consensus* (London: Longman, 2002).

23   For a summary of these views in English, see Holger Afflerbach, ed., *The First World War – An Improbable War?*, 2006.

24   See Hew Strachan, "Wer war schuld? Wie es zum ersten Weltkrieg kam," in Stephan Burgdorff and Klaus Wiegrefe, eds, *Der 1. Weltkrieg. Die Ur-Katastrophe des 20. Jahrhunderts* (Munich: DVA, 2004), pp. 240–55.

25   Richard F. Hamilton and Holger H. Herwig, eds, *The Origins of World War I* (Cambridge: Cambridge University Press, 2003), p. 41.

26   Sönke Neitzel, *Kriegsausbruch. Deutschlands Weg in die Katastrophe* (Munich: Pendo, 2002), pp. 194–5.

27   For details on this, see Mombauer, *Origins*, passim.

GUIDE TO FURTHER READING

Luigi Albertini, *The Origins of the War of 1914*, 3 vols, I. M. Massey, trans. (Oxford: Oxford University Press, 1952–7). Still one of the most detailed accounts based on a thorough study of the available source material and an excellent starting point for studying the origins of the war.

Volker R. Berghahn, *Germany and the Approach of War in 1914*, 2nd edn (London: Macmillan, 1993). Part of a series examining the role of the major powers in the coming of war, it provides a useful introduction to the topic.

Fritz Fischer, *Germany's Aims in the First World War* (London: Chatto and Windus, 1967). The English translation of Fischer's first book on the subject, which marked the beginning of the so-called Fischer controversy.

Fritz Fischer, *War of Illusions: German Policies from 1911–1914* (London: Chatto and Windus, 1975). Fischer's second book detailing his arguments on German war guilt.

Richard F. Hamilton and Holger H. Herwig, eds, *The Origins of World War I* (Cambridge: Cambridge University Press, 2003). A collection of essays which focus on the importance of decision makers in the coming of the war.

James Joll, *The Origins of the First World War*, 2nd edn (London: Longman, 1992). An essential introduction to the subject.

John F. V. Keiger, *France and the Origins of the First World War* (London: Macmillan, 1983). Part of a series examining the role of the major powers in the coming of war.

John W. Langdon, *July 1914: The Long Debate 1918–1990* (New York: Berg, 1991). Provides an excellent overview of the historiographical controversy.

D. C. B. Lieven, *Russia and the Origins of the First World War* (London: Macmillan, 1983). Part of a series examining the role of the major powers in the coming of war.

Gordon Martel, *The Origins of the First World War*, 3rd edn (London: Longman/Pearson, 2003). A summary of the debate and the events leading to war, plus useful documents.

Annika Mombauer, *The Origins of the First World War: Controversies and Consensus* (London: Longman/Pearson, 2002). An analysis of the debate on the origins of the war which places the controversy within a historical context.

Zara S. Steiner and Keith Neilson, *Britain and the Origins of the First World War* (London: Palgrave/Macmillan, 2003). An up-to-date revised edition of the original contribution on Britain to the Macmillan series.

David Stevenson, *Armaments and the Coming of War: Europe 1904–1914* (Oxford: Clarendon Press, 1996). An excellent analysis of the importance of the arms race.

Samuel R. Williamson, Jr, *Austria-Hungary and the Origins of the First World War* (London: Macmillan, 1991). An authoritative account of Austria-Hungary's role in the events that led to the outbreak of war. Part of the Macmillan series.

Keith Wilson, ed., *Decisions for War, 1914* (London: UCL Press, 1995). An excellent collection of essays dealing with the decisions of the major combatants to go to war.

PART III

World War I

CHAPTER THIRTEEN

August 1914: Public Opinion and the Crisis

DAVID WELCH

War seemed to creep up unexpectedly on the people of Europe in July 1914. Following the assassination of Archduke Ferdinand on June 28 a few telltale signs of a looming crisis can be discerned. Financial and commercial interests, for example, took fright and the stock exchanges of Berlin, Vienna, Paris, and St Petersburg were severely depressed. Nevertheless, life in Europe had gone on much as usual. Kaiser Wilhelm departed for a Norwegian cruise, Helmuth von Moltke, the German chief of staff, holidayed in Karlsbad, Grand Admiral von Tirpitz in a Swiss spa, and both the German and Austrian ministers of war were also away on holiday. In central Europe, thousands of families gravitated to the seaside and mountains, while millions of peasants toiled the fields under a blazing July sun, among them young men released from military duties under special harvest furlough. In Britain, happy holidaymakers returned from a Bank Holiday at the seaside to discover that the country was at war. Scenes of everyday life would change dramatically for ordinary citizens throughout Europe. *The Times* on its front page declared: "The die is cast. The great European struggle which nations have so long struggled to avert has begun."[1]

Perceptions of War

For the vast majority of ordinary citizens catapulted into war in 1914, the years leading up to that fateful August brought few certainties. Nevertheless, for victors and vanquished alike a myth developed in the postwar world that the Great War had brought to an end an era of tranquility and contentment. Intellectuals looked back longingly after 1918 to a Golden Age that had been disrupted by the savagery and duration of total war. However, the experiences of ordinary people were far more complex – and in many ways more mundane. Fears, hopes, frustrations, and ignorance had been as much a part of Edwardian Europe as of many previous periods. Rather than a Golden Age of innocence, it had been a period of deep divisions and challenges to the status quo.

In the context of perceptions of war, one of the questions often raised is did belligerent states intentionally provoke a war in order to conceal internal problems by means of foreign policy successes. The belief that the "men of 1914" had deliberately contrived a war to resolve internal tensions is too simplistic, although it has proved attractive to historians.[2] Some have argued that the long Victorian century created an implicit belief in progress and that war was viewed as an inevitable part of this process. The "unspoken assumptions" – to use James Joll's phrase – did unquestionably carry influence in military and intellectual circles and the incipient militarism of prewar Europe was fueled, as a consequence, by nationalism and imperialism and was redolent with assumptions of social Darwinism.[3] Furthermore, the alliance system that had unraveled since the turn of the century conditioned expectations about the likely military configuration in the event of war, and the importance of entering war at the most propitious moment. Such considerations no doubt shaped perceptions and the calculations of whether or not to go to war in July/August 1914. Many undoubtedly shared the assumptions not only that war was inevitable but also that it would be short and that victory was assured.[4] The view that the European alliance system had caused the war became popular after 1918 when the principles advocated by President Wilson for a new international order anticipated the establishment of the League of Nations and open diplomacy. However, while the alliance system may have contributed to war, it did not make war inevitable – and certainly not in 1914.

What were the attitudes towards war in the different countries of Europe in 1914? Russia had been severely shaken by defeat in the Russo-Japanese War (1904–5) and in 1914 was the first power to mobilize. Were they aware of what this meant? Whereas in previous crises Russia had not committed itself to mobilization, once Austria had declared war on Serbia, Russia felt compelled to take military action. The decision to mobilize was made, however, not by a disorganized military still smarting from humiliation, nor by an isolated Nicholas II, but unanimously by the full council of ministers. The Italian government took some preliminary measures in August 1914, but deferred mobilization until April 1915 when, after elaborate bargaining, Italy entered the war not on the side of their former allies but in opposition with the Triple Alliance. The punitive peace terms imposed at Versailles were predicated on the guilt of Germany and its allies. There is considerable evidence to suggest that Austria-Hungary seized on the assassination of Archduke Franz Ferdinand as a welcome opportunity to set in motion a belief in the need to settle longstanding scores with Serbia.[5] Most historians would stress intentionality behind German policy in 1914. By giving Austria a free hand and urging her to make war against Serbia as soon as possible, the German government widened the crisis of July 1914.

Did Germany deliberately provoke a war? Certainly, the German military viewed the war as inevitable, and wanted it sooner, rather than later. The need for a preventive war to avoid Germany's having to fight France and Russia simultaneously was an act of faith that shaped the Schlieffen Plan and the German general staff's military strategy. While it is important not to view the German leadership as monolithic in its intentions, such views were also shared by an influential elite within the political leadership. Germany's motivation in July 1914 was based largely on fear of Russia's future military developments and capabilities. If Germany was to successfully implement the Schlieffen Plan and achieve its goal of *Weltherrschaft* (world domination), then at the most propitious moment it was crucial that Britain be persuaded to stay out of the war, at least during the time it would take Germany to defeat France by means of a lightning strike through Belgium. According to John Röhl the motives of the "men of 1914" in Berlin were either to "split the Triple Entente wide open in order to effect a massive diplomatic revolution, which would have given Germany control of the European continent and much of the world beyond, *or* – a better method in the eyes of many to achieve the same goal – to provoke a continental war against France and Russia in what appeared to be exceptionally favorable circumstances."[6] Few historians would disagree with Röhl, although his critics stress the defensive character of the political decisions made in Germany at the time, arguing that the growing tendency in government circles to consider a preventive war does not necessarily prove that Germany was deliberately preparing and planning a major war. In such a context it is difficult to distinguish between a preventive war and a war of aggression. Moreover, as Niall Ferguson has reminded us, a preventive strike "is by no means incompatible with the idea that the outcome of such a strike, if successful, would be German hegemony in Europe."[7]

Set against these military considerations was the fact that Germany in 1914 was arguably the most successful country in Europe, with a dynamic population and a burgeoning economy; a country whose scientific and artistic achievements were the envy of the world. Even if the decision to provoke a war was taken by relatively few, the "men of 1914" took an extraordinarily reckless gamble to risk all this. Such a calculation was predicated on the belief that the German people could be persuaded that the Fatherland was being threatened by a barbarous Russia and that this was a defensive war of national survival and also in the hope that Britain would stay out of the conflict.

And what of perceptions in Great Britain? By 1914, almost 100 years had passed since Britain had fought a war on the European continent. During that time Britain had built a large empire protected by its navy and had largely sought compromise with its European neighbors. British governments were not inspired to intervene in European conflicts, preferring instead to maintain a diplomatic distance from events. Protecting the empire was of paramount concern, and there was a reluctance to become too entangled in European affairs – unless they had imperial consequences. The importance of the empire obscured British military weaknesses and accounted for a self-satisfied indifference to European events. The empire had largely allowed the British to ignore world affairs and concentrate on their day-to-day lives content in the belief that they were superior to any other nation. As a result Britain was militarily weak in 1914 and its army little more than an imperial police force.

Of course, German naval rearmament from the late nineteenth century did not go unnoticed and was perceived by many to represent a real challenge to Britain's naval supremacy. Moreover, the popular press and a spate of "invasion literature" and comics (notably the *Boy's Friend*) encouraged an insular fear of a rampant Germany bent on aggression. The British government was also preoccupied with a number of domestic crises, notably attempts by suffragettes to extend the franchise, militant trade unionism, and Irish republicanism. But the claim that the war represented a welcome diversion from dangerous revolutionary tendencies should be balanced, as Gerard De Groot has outlined, by a whole range of mitigating factors that included a sense of international solidarity between socialist movements in Europe, a growing international cooperation in a number of fields, new developments in international affairs brought about by the Hague Conventions, and the respect for pacifist groups (largely socialist) and the popularity of Norman Angell's pacifist book *The Great Illusion*, published in 1910. Moreover, by 1912, Anglo-German naval rivalry had virtually ceased and British industrialists and intellectuals increasingly held Germany in awe.[8]

And what of France? In many ways the internal circumstances in France are the most complex of all the belligerents – and yet French diplomacy is arguably the most passive and transparent. The elections in 1914 resulted in a shift in power from right to left and the year before there had been considerable domestic controversy over legislation to increase the term of military service to three years. France had little experience of the reality of modern warfare and while the *élan* of large-scale assaults with fixed bayonets was common to all European armies, the French military, under the leadership of Joseph Joffre, Ferdinand Foch, and Colonel Louis de Grandmaison, continued to cling tenaciously to older style "colonial" offensive strategy that exemplified traditional military ideals of honor and glory. However, the possibility of a European war as a result of events unfolding in the Balkans took secondary importance to domestic affairs. For much of July 1914, as the European crisis deepened, French newspapers devoted most of their attention to the trial of Madame Caillaux, the wife of the former finance minister who, incensed by the campaign which *Le Figaro* had orchestrated against her husband, had shot dead the paper's editor. Equally extraordinary, on July 16, a presidential party that had been organized six months previously and included Raymond Poincaré, president of the Republic, and René Viviani, then premier and foreign minister, set off for a state visit to Russia and Scandinavia, leaving France devoid of its senior political and foreign policy decision makers. The obsession with the Caillaux affair combined with the decision to embark on a sea voyage timed to last until July 31 indicates the extent to which the French appeared unconcerned about the deepening crisis in the Balkans. Thus, on the eve of World War I, French leaders were, as John Keiger has reminded us, literally and metaphorically at sea.[9] By the time they cut short their voyage on July 29 (and bearing in mind that radio communication with ships at sea was at best unreliable), events had taken on a momentum of their own. France had been absent from the hub of these events. By now France's overriding objectives in managing the crisis were to ensure that in the event of war the nation would enter the conflict united and with British support for the Franco-Russia alliance.

Complexities and juxtapositions rather than a neat, straight line mark the road to war. While a handful of policy makers weighed up the pros and cons during the weeks of July, most Europeans seemed oblivious to the deepening diplomatic crisis and, as L. L. Farrar has noted, "probably apathetic regarding the question of war."[10] This would change once the ultimatums expired and mobilization orders were issued. Civilians, like soldiers, would be required to "fall-in" and support the war effort and for a brief period they appeared to respond enthusiastically.

War Aims

World War I made greater demands on the material and human resources of the nations involved than any previous conflict. It was no longer sufficient simply to organize industry or to mobilize manpower in order to carry a modern state through a long war. It would prove to be a war of intense industrial competition and scientific innovation; the manufacture of arms and munitions became critically important. But equally important was the need to engage the will and support of whole nations. For the first time, belligerent governments were required to mobilize entire civilian populations into "fighting communities." Consequently, all governments were faced with the urgent task of justifying their entry into the war to their own people. War aims became imperative to the successful prosecution of "total war."

The first to formulate its war aims was Germany. Due to the nature of the Schlieffen Plan and the need for swift military action in the anticipation of a quick military victory, Germany's war aims were formulated in what has become known as the September Program.[11] This document, although of considerable interest to historians, was not, however, the basis on which the people went to war. In the years leading to 1914, Kaiser Wilhelm's claim that Germany had become a world power on the basis of an imperial fleet that could challenge the Royal Navy was enthusiastically received. However, his successes in foreign policy were limited, and the price paid was the self-inflicted isolation of Germany and the forming of an alliance by its rivals: Britain, France, and Russia. When Britain declared war on Germany and the political parties agreed to a *Burgfrieden* (literally, "fortress truce," but in practice, a political truce), the nation appeared united behind a banner of a fully justified war of self-defense. If the Schlieffen Plan were to be successfully implemented then speed was of the essence. The political implications of invading neutral states were secondary to the belief that a swift victory would limit the effects of conflict. In other words, invasion was not only essential to military strategy, but also a political price worth paying for victory.

In Russia, Germany, and France the threat of socialist opposition to the war had been taken seriously. German Social Democrats were committed by congress resolutions to opposing the war. On the other hand a war against tsarist Russia was something that the SPD from the time of Marx had been prepared to envisage. Those sectors of the ruling class who felt most threatened by the socialist challenge undoubtedly looked upon the outbreak of World War I as a possible answer, in the Bismarckian tradition, to Germany's internal problems. For this reason it was important to give the impression that the war was the result of Russian aggression and to play down the fact that Germany was violating Belgian neutrality in order to attack France. As German society rallied behind the war effort and a *Burgfrieden* was proclaimed, the war appeared to demonstrate the soundness of this belief. Provided the Kaiser could deliver the promised swift victory, political quiescence seemed assured. For many socialists, however, the possibility of a European war had been inconceivable, believing as they did that governments would not risk undermining the status quo by subjecting the system to revolutionary strains. Yet the declaration of war against Russia on August 1 aroused – initially, at least – widespread support, with only a minority warning of the dangers. By ending domestic political strife with the *Burgfrieden* the nation was apparently united behind the banner of a fully justified war of self-defense. Even the Social Democrats voted in favor of war credits. In August 1914, therefore, it seemed that the war had created a new sense of solidarity in which class antagonisms were transcended by an entirely fictitious "national community" (*Volksgemeinschaft*).

The belief in such a community spirit was cemented on August 4, shortly after Britain declared war on Germany. A ceremonial session of the Reichstag was held in the White Hall of the Imperial Palace where the Kaiser, wearing an army uniform, outlined Germany's war aims in a speech from the throne. Reaffirming Germany's obligation to defend her ally, he stressed that the war was not one of conquest, but to maintain the nation's economic and political position. After reading his speech, he handed the manuscript to the chancellor and continued freely in a raised voice: "From this day on, I recognize no parties, but only Germans. If the party leaders agree with me on this matter, I invite them to step forward and confirm this with a handshake." To wild applause the leaders of the competing parties stepped forward and extended their hands: the *Burgfrieden*, or "spirit of 1914," had entered into war mythology. Later that day the Social Democrats voted for war credits. During the session the chancellor, Bethmann-Hollweg, took the opportunity to justify Germany's violation of Belgian territory ("we will atone for this injustice") and to accuse Russia and France of aggression: "We are drawing the sword only in defense of a righteous cause," he claimed. "Russia has set the torch to the house . . . France has already violated the peace . . . We are therefore acting in self-defense . . . Germany's great hour of trial has come. Our army is in the field. Our navy is ready for battle. Behind them stands a united people." (Wild applause.) Next, Hugo Haase, the SPD leader, read a brief declaration to the effect that the party would vote for war credits. Explaining this decision, he said that although the SPD had always opposed imperialism, "Russian despotism was threatening the freedom of the German people" and "in this hour of danger we will not leave the Fatherland in the lurch." The announcement was received with endless applause. The chancellor then stood up and concluded: "Whatever we have in store, we may well believe that August 4, 1914, will, for all time, remain one of Germany's greatest days!"[12]

Russia, in fact, had compelling reasons for not committing to war in 1914. The Russo-Japanese war had demonstrated the causal link between war and revolution and ought to have convinced the decision makers to avoid war at all cost. The urban workers' movement had shifted to the left and to Bolshevism and discontent had resulted in more strikes in the first half of 1914 than at any time since 1905. Moreover, Russia's finances were in a perilous state and the army and the navy had only just begun a program of modernization. Nor had the ground been prepared diplomatically. Crucially, however, Russia was aware that its firm stand against Austria had the full support of France.

In France, the trade union movement, the *Confédération Générale du Travail*, had often reiterated its intention of calling a general strike in the event of war, and this policy had been accepted by Jean Jaurès, at the Socialist Party Congress early in July. As events began to unfold in the Balkans, Jaurès and his party made it clear that they did not hold the French government responsible for the worsening diplomatic situation and supported its general position. (This did not save him from being assassinated by a young nationalist fanatic who claimed that he had sold out to the Germans.) Though France had been reacting to events rather than creating them, it did have a strategy; namely, that any French decision for war should be seen as defensive. The assassination of Jaurès on July 31 represented a serious challenge to the strategy of a united domestic front. To diffuse the situation the prime minister spoke at Jaurès' funeral and President Poincaré sent warm condolences to his widow (conveniently published in *L'Humanité*). The syndicalists meanwhile had obeyed their mobilization orders without protest and the government felt confident enough to revoke the orders to arrest militants of the notorious *Carnet B* list likely to sabotage preparations for war. The labor movement was rapidly abandoning its opposition to the war and on August 1 the headline in *La Guerre sociale* summarized the situation: "National Defense above all! They have assassinated Jaurès! We will not assassinate France!" Following President Poincaré's declaration on August 4 of the *Union sacrée* (the sacred union of Frenchmen for the duration of the war) Socialist deputies supported the war budget and on August 26 two of them, including the Marxist leader Jules Guesde, joined the government. It was in this mood of national reconciliation that war began.

Bearing in mind the social and political cleavages that erupted in France during the 1914 election, why did no group of any political relevance oppose the *Union sacrée* in August? One should never underestimate the catalyzing impact of an external threat. Writing in 1928, Georges Bourgin offered an explanation that remains persuasive to this day: that the effect of the war on France was to create the *Union sacrée*, in which all the parties agreed to renounce their differences and unite in a common defense in the face of an aggressive external threat (*la patrie en danger*).[13] To this end a remarkable unity of sentiment was achieved.

Despite what has been termed the "Edwardian crisis" within British society, it remained stable. As Zara Steiner has written, it was "not a society on the eve of dissolution."[14] Nevertheless, as we have seen, Britain in the years leading to 1914 was beset by internal tensions. While Sir Edward Grey was acting out the role of honest broker in Europe, in England the Irish crisis dominated political news. Outside of informed circles few were getting excited about such a familiar problem as trouble in the Balkans. To the man-in-the-street the murder of an archduke whose name he could scarcely pronounce and in a place he had never heard of signified merely another internal Balkan crisis. Ironically, only a few months before his assassination, Archduke Ferdinand had been the guest of King George and Queen Mary at Buckingham Palace.

In Great Britain's case foreign policy was not determined by considerations of domestic politics but rather by the perceived dangers both to its empire and the balance of power in Europe. The implementation of the Schlieffen Plan involved Germany moving its troops through neutral Belgium. On August 2 Grey demanded that Germany promise to uphold Belgian neutrality – and when this was refused, Britain declared war on Germany on August 4. At this stage, according to Gerard De Groot, the war was about empire, capitalism, trade, and food, not democracy, honor, and civilization. But when Germany attacked Belgium, "a war of markets became a war of morality."[15] Belgium, in short, answered all doubts and differences and its invasion was the pretext for an anti-German propaganda campaign that mobilized support behind Britain's war aims. The Belgian issue was a potent factor in uniting public support behind Asquith and Grey. "The menace of Germany – The Neutrality of Belgium," declared the headline in *The Times*. For the opponents of war – the doubters, the waverers, and the pacifists – German aggression had suddenly blunted their voice. This was now a war of honor – noble, just – and forced on Britain. The Catholic journal *Tablet* succinctly encapsulated British war aims: "For the sake of this little people, fighting for its freedom against desperate odds, England will go out by land and sea . . . So she will vindicate the honor of her sacred word and there is no nobler cause for which any man may die."[16]

In France, the news of Britain's declaration of war after all the uncertainty was greeted with profound relief and joy. "C'est fait," declared *Le Figaro*. "L'Angleterre s'est prononcée."

Responses

An overriding impression provided in popular history and television documentaries of the beginning of the war is of nations and populations united, and of men going cheerfully and confidently to war throughout Europe. This, of course, is the impression that leaders wished to encourage. After all, the Kaiser and his advisors could not guarantee that the socialists would agree to a political truce; the French thought after the assassination of Jaurès that as many as 13 percent of French males would not heed the call to arms, and the British government did not feel confident to introduce conscription until 1916. Russia, on the other hand, wished to convey the impression of military preparedness so as not to expose its lack of funds, technology, and general modernization necessary for total war. The need to justify war aims meant that politicians were eager to proclaim a new kind of national unity and solidarity. Hence the declarations from the Kaiser that "I recognize no parties, but only Germans" and from the President of the French Chamber of Deputies: "There are no more adversaries here, only Frenchmen."

Contemporary accounts of the first month of the war are redolent with phrases such as the "August experience" or the "spirit of 1914." While it is understandable that internal tensions should be forgotten in times of crisis, do these terms accurately describe the feelings and emotions of the German, French, or British people in 1914? Curiously, only recently have historians begun to question many of the assumptions that there was a prevailing "spirit of war" and that the people were "enthusiastic."

The illusions with which World War I began stemmed from the widely held belief that the war would be short. When war did erupt in August 1914, it was for a long time conventionally depicted by images of excited and enthusiastic reservists clamoring to participate in the conflict in the belief that they were defending their country. The declaration of war was undeniably welcomed by some who glorified in the patriotic *élan* which it evoked. The drama and expectations of war lent an almost mystical status to the "spirit of 1914." Intellectuals were quick to record the exhilaration that accompanied these events and the sense of mission. The German historian Friedrich Meinecke described the scenes as "One of the greatest moments of my life, which suddenly filled my soul with the deepest confidence in our people, and the profoundest joy." The poet Rupert Brooke celebrated the apparent mood of euphoria as follows:

> Blow, bugles, blow! They brought us, for our dearth
> Holiness, lacked so long, and Love, and Pain.
> Honour has come back, as a king, to earth
> And paid his subjects with royal wage;
> And nobleness walks in our ways again;
> And we are come into our heritage.

The key to an understanding of the optimism and enthusiasm with which the war was initially greeted in the summer of 1914 was the widespread conviction that the war would be an adventure and of short duration. Sporting analogies abounded, particularly in Britain: it would be a "good match," but "over by Christmas" – and Great Britain would win![17] When German reservists chalked "Excursion to Paris. See you on the Boulevard" on the railway wagons taking them to the front, they assumed that this would be a short but exciting campaign. No doubt many imagined it would be another 1870-type war, a brief adventure that offered escape and excitement from a humdrum existence. For many youth, war offered a rite of passage, a true test of masculinity.

The illusion that the war would be a short one was not uniquely German, but it partly explains the attitude and behavior of different social and political groups to the announcement of hostilities. The initial enthusiasm aroused by the war (not the same as *for* the war), the emergence of the *Volksstaat*, and the apparent *volte face* of the Social Democrats can all be traced to this belief that the war would be quickly and gloriously concluded. The events leading up to and including the fateful month of August reveal a curious mixture of rising nationalism, superficial harmony, and hatred of tsarist Russia, but also a nervousness and uncertainty as the shock of war began to sink in.

The failure of diplomacy to resolve the Balkan crisis ushered in mounting tension and jingoism in all the major European cities. In Germany, events were reaching a climax. On July 25, 1914, Austria-Hungary severed diplomatic relations with Serbia, which it alleged had been responsible for the assassination of Archduke Ferdinand and his consort. That evening in Berlin crowds gathered outside the Reichstag and the Austro-Hungarian embassy and began burning Serbian flags. Describing these events, the Socialist newspaper *Vorwärts* reported that the crowds consisted mainly of young people. Meanwhile, the Kaiser, apparently unaware of the growing serious-ness of the situation, was still enjoying a cruise in the Norwegian fjords. His hasty return to Potsdam on July 27 was greeted by the usual enthusiastic crowds, only this time patriotically singing "Deutschland, Deutschland, über alles." Equally revealing was the response of ordinary bank depositors who reacted to the worsening diplo-matic situation by withdrawing savings and gold and silver. Food prices were also rising as anxious citizens, fearful of shortages, began hoarding provisions. Within a few days, as stock exchange values plunged, some municipal banks actually suspended dealings and in the provinces paper money was invariably refused altogether. All these factors highlight the pervading uncertainty.

In Austria the initial excitement soon faded and subdued crowds on the streets rapidly ebbed away. Despite an intense propaganda campaign whipped up by the press there was little immediate sign of a *démarche*. Most striking was the pugnacity of the Hungarian opposition that only began to fall into line towards the end of July when war seemed inevitable and the Austrian censor threatened. In Russia there was little discernible indication of "popular" support for the war. Public opinion was restricted largely to educated elites that articulated its views through the Duma, the press, and the public organizations. The peasantry remained a largely silent majority. The meeting of the council of ministers on July 24 believed that it had limited options. The belief that Russia had conceded too much in the past and now required a robust stand had been aired in the press for some time. Foreign minister Sazonov argued that concession made now would mean that Russia would have to face similar challenges by Germany in the future. It was the civilian-dominated council, consumed by Russia's international and diplomatic failures in the past, that made the fateful decisions in July 1914.

By July 31 Germany was gripped by war fever and hysteria with rumors abounding. A *Kriegsgefahrzustand*, or "condition of state of war," was proclaimed and Germany demanded that Russia should cease mobilizing within 12 hours. The afternoon special newspaper editions announced that the Kaiser had decreed a state of siege throughout Germany. Later that day he and his family appeared before a huge crowd on the balcony of the Imperial Palace in Berlin. In what was virtually an announcement of war he regretted, apparently more in sorrow than anger, that "The sword is being forced into my hand . . . This war will demand of us enormous sacrifices in life and money, but we shall show our foes what it is to provoke Germany." Even at this late hour *Vorwärts* prepared a sober edition pleading for sanity and a just compromise. Its editorial entitled "Europe's Hour of Destiny" courageously drew a distinction between the true wishes of the ordinary people and the machinations of governments and concluded: "If, nevertheless, the hideous specter should become reality, if the bloody torrent of a war of nations should sweep over Europe – one thing is sure; Social Democracy bears no responsibility for the coming events." During the night of the 31st and the following day, people waited anxiously for the ensuing moves. On August 1 the anticipated order for mobilization was given, signed by the Kaiser and Bethmann-Hollweg, and to take effect the next day. At 7.10 p.m. Germany declared war on Russia, Wilhelm II proclaiming the news from his balcony to a large crowd in Berlin.

In the period of mobilization immediately after the declaration of war against Russia the mood of the people fluctuated dramatically, reflecting the pervading uncertainty. James Gerard, the American ambassador, noted the excitement of large crowds in Berlin "pervading the streets and singing 'Deutschland über alles' and demanding war." Similar demonstrations supporting the war took place in Leipzig. The departure of soldiers for the front at first undoubtedly created enthusiasm and provided a much needed emotional release from the mounting tensions of previous weeks. Princess Blücher, an Englishwoman married to a German nobleman, noted that the whole life of Germany was moving to the tune of *Die Wacht am Rhein*, just as the soldiers marched to the rhythm of its refrain. The attitude of the ruling class was summed up by Kurt Riezler, advisor to the chancellor, who wrote in his diary: "War, war. The people have risen – it is as though they were not there at all before and now all at once, they are immense and touching." Peter Hanssen, on the other hand, a Reichstag deputy from Schleswig Holstein, recorded vividly the mobilization scenes on his way south to Berlin and the oppressed atmosphere in the capital: "People were standing close together on the sidewalks of Unter den Linden to catch a glimpse of the Kaiser . . . But there was no rejoicing, no enthusiasm; over all hung that same heavy, sad, and depressed atmosphere."[18] A pastor in a working-class suburb of Stuttgart noted "the declaration of war left people stunned – it was horrible." Jeffrey Verhey, who has subjected the "August experience" to a systematic study, identified three areas in Germany that were decidedly not "enthusiastic"; the countryside, the urban working class, and the areas near the border. Indeed, the war was "extraordinarily unpopular" with workers; rather, they accepted it as a "heavy, unavoidable duty."[19] As the effervescence of the demonstrations quickly subsided, patriotic duty towards the Fatherland, and not glory, was increasingly emphasized.

The French government rallied its people to the cause of national defense by proclaiming a *Union sacrée* and, as with Germany, French politicians made extravagant claims that this union transcended political, class, and religious differences. Similarly in France, as in Germany, there was no unified "August experience." In their ground-breaking works on French public opinion in World War I, Jean-Jacques Becker and P. J. Flood utilized a rich variety of unpublished contemporary governmental reports, often written by local school teachers.[20] Their findings reveal that French public mood fluctuated between extremes of wild euphoria and pessimistic foreboding. Highlighting the former, the distinguished French historian Ernest Lavisse expressed his joy that "he was not dead before having seen this war." Newspapers reported high French morale and heavy German losses. The headline in *Le Matin* claimed: "Following terrible shortages, Berlin seems to be on the eve of revolution." All this led to wild speculation about the state of affairs in Germany and the imminent defeat of its imperial army. "As far as I am concerned," wrote Francis Laur in *Journal*, "the German army has been knocked out." Like all the belligerents, the French naively thought only in terms of a victoriously short campaign. Becker's work has shown that to suggest that the public were wildly enthusiastic about the war is an exaggeration. Moreover, when discussing the "spirit of 1914," it is important to distinguish between responses to the announcement of war and to the actual mobilization of the troops. That is not to say that enthusiasm was contrived or whipped up by propaganda. Photographic evidence, for example, records excited and enthusiastic French reservists clamoring to participate in the conflict in the belief that they were defending their country. But it is equally important to remember that most of the departures captured in photographs or in newsreels took place in train stations and had been carefully constructed for the occasion. The trains had been decked with flowers and patriotic posters and slogans ("à Berlin") and departing husbands and sons were surrounded by their families seeing them off. Such conditions combined to swell patriotic pride that could easily manifest itself in the appearance of enthusiasm. But appearances can be deceptive – a point noted by a teacher from Mansle, who wrote: "The cars of the trains are decorated with flowers. Vulgar drawings and inscriptions, usually poorly written, indicate hatred of the Hun . . . The soldiers sing, joke, call back and forth and attempt most of all to work themselves into a daze. The affectedness of this clamorous gaiety is easy to grasp." French public opinion at the time of mobilization was diverse, contradictory, and far from unanimous.

In the case of Britain, the public had little time in which to react to events. As we have seen, the Irish crisis continued to dominate press coverage – certainly until July 31. The gravity of the situation in Europe only began to unfold over the Bank Holiday weekend. "The rush to the seaside during the next few days," observed the *Daily Mirror* on August 1, "is likely to be the biggest in living memory." Both talk of war and newspaper sales were on the increase. However, everyday life continued much as usual – in striking contrast to the situation in many European cities, which by now were gripped by the ferment of warlike excitement. The invasion of Belgium changed the demeanor of the British and gave this war a purpose. On August 6 the prime minister Herbert Asquith informed the House: "I do not believe any nation ever entered into a great controversy . . . with a clearer conscience and a stronger conviction that it is fighting, not aggression, not for the maintenance even of its own selfish interest, but . . . in defense of principles the maintenance of which is vital to the civilization of the world." The violation of Belgian neutrality represented a moral issue of the kind to which British liberalism would habitually respond. The war now became a crusade to be fought by crusaders.[21] Only the *Manchester Guardian* remained implacably opposed to the war. For the rest of the press it was now a matter of honor and if the response to the initial recruitment drive is anything to go by then it would appear that British public opinion was resolutely behind its government's war aims.

The armies of continental Europe were made up of conscripts and they really had little choice about going to war. The British army in contrast was made up of volunteers and professionals. If the eagerness to go to war was manifested by volunteering alone then the figures are revealing. August 3, 1914 was a Bank Holiday and as such the recruiting offices were closed. But for the rest of that first week of war there was an average of 16,000 volunteers a day. Between August 4 and September 12, 478,893 men enlisted.[22] The spontaneous response would suggest that the fears, hopes, anxieties, and illusions that had buffeted Britain during the July crisis were swept away in support for a noble and just war. Or were they?

Mobilization began on August 4 and almost immediately the British Expeditionary Force (BEF) became an auxiliary of the French army and marched proudly and confidently to the music-hall song "It's a Long Way to Tipperary" – although few would have known or cared where Tipperary was. The silent film and photographic evidence of volunteers and families waving cheerfully at the cameras tells only part of the story. Marc Ferro has made the telling point that: "They marched off to war, their faces a picture of delight. Film is of course deceptive and a more searching examination would show other images – the anguish of the father, a fiancé, or a husband."[23] Furthermore, as the testimonies that have been cataloged in the Imperial War Museum reveal, the motives for going to war in 1914 were many and complex and cannot be explained simply in terms of exhilaration and jingoism – although that is not to deny that these were not present at the time. There were a variety of reasons for volunteering: patriotism, the desire for adventure – particularly the belief that they would share this adventure together with friends – peer pressure, and the ever-present pressure from newspapers, the pulpit, and the accusing finger of Kitchener that stabbed at young men (and women) on every bill posting. (Remember, also, that in France less than 2 percent of men called to the colors in 1914 failed to respond to the call.)

Conclusion

There can be little doubt that there existed a general euphoria in these early weeks of war, no doubt partly due to the release of tension now that war had finally arrived after all the declarations, ultimatums, and preparations. However, the notion that belligerent states entered the war in euphoric unanimity requires qualification. Jean-Jacques Becker's work on (mainly) rural France can be applied to most of the belligerent states: the traditional view of popular opinion when mobilization orders were received was distorted by the failure to account for the consternation felt by substantial sections of the population. There is considerable evidence to suggest that negative responses, ranging from helpless grief to sober resignation, permeated sections of the population. In fact – with the exception of Austria-Hungary – when mobilization orders were first received, enthusiastic responses were rare, although not entirely absent. For Britain, the catalyst was clearly the German invasion of neutral Belgium. However, by the time the soldiers departed for the fronts those who had previously held misgivings about mobilization swung behind the war and supported the menfolk and war aims. That is not the same as the claim made by some historians that the peoples of Europe were swept up by a wave of enthusiasm for the war – a sort of "war fever" – as the troops mobilized.

Such shifting responses are not unique to August 1914: one only need think of the widespread anti-war feelings and demonstrations that were generated in Britain in the run-up to Gulf War II in 2003 – however, once the soldiers began leaving for Iraq, opinion swung – not in favor of the war – but in support of the soldiers sent to fight the war. In 1914 most of the soldiers who marched to war put on a brave face for the newsreel cameras and crowds who had formed to send them off. Yet while many left willingly, convinced that they had a duty to perform, and some undoubtedly felt enthusiastic about the war, they were not typical. Flag waving and bravado are more commonly associated with the need for solidarity and unity in the face of a common enemy, than wholehearted approval of war. It is too simplistic to make sweeping generalizations about the "spirit of war." While the scenes in London, Paris, Berlin, Vienna, and St Petersburg that accompanied the announcement of war appeared to be indistinguishable, there were many different August experiences, and anxiety was as widespread as jubilation.[24]

What conclusions then can be drawn about popular attitudes to war during the crisis of 1914? All governments had a stated purpose for going to war and these war aims were largely supported by those required to make the sacrifices. Every nation framed support for the war in terms of a righteous cause and the need to defend its own against external aggression. Most civilians and soldiers went to war in the belief that they were fighting for a just cause. However, popular attitudes did not in themselves make war inevitable. Propaganda came of age during the conflict and has been associated unfairly with pejorative associations ever since. Public opinion is an amorphous thing at the best of times. In a crisis it tends to coalesce around traditional, unifying themes and symbols. The acceptance of war aims did not necessarily mean that the people of Europe were enthusiastic or indeed that there existed a "war fever." What united them was the belief that this war would be clinical, controllable and victorious, and be over by Christmas. This, more than anything, explains the bitterness of postwar recriminations. Having been led to believe that the war would be of short duration, it is remarkable that combatants and civilians continued to endure stoically such unspeakable deprivation and suffering. It is surely not surprising that in the postwar years so many writers and poets should take refuge and comfort in a world that was allegedly more innocent, secure, and self-confident.[25] The idealization of 1914 has become part of European mythology – in more ways than one.

NOTES

1 Geoffrey Marcus, *Before the Lamps Went Out* (London: Allen and Unwin, 1965), p. 284

2 The clearest pressure for war to "solve" internal difficulties was to be found in Austria-Hungary. Arno Mayer's pioneering comparative study of this period suggested that during the early years of the century, the "erosion" of the Center exacerbated the "symbiotic growth of domestic and international tensions" leading to a "diversionary war." See A. J. Mayer, "Causes and Purposes of War in Europe, 1870–1956: A Research Assignment," *Journal of Modern History* 41 (1969): 291–303.

3 For a further discussion, see Caroline E. Playne, *The Pre-War Mind in Britain* (London, 1928).

4 See Ian Beckett's magisterial synopsis of these issues, *The Great War 1914–1918* (London: Pearson, 2001), pp. 18–34

5 See Derek W. Spring, "Russia and the Coming of War," in *The Coming of the First World War*, R. J. W. Evans and H. Pogge von Strandmann, eds (Oxford: Oxford University Press, 1988), pp. 57–86. For Austria-Hungary, see Samuel R. Williamson, *Austria-Hungary and the Origins of the First World War* (New York, 1991) and Fritz Fellner's brief but perceptive "Austria-Hungary" in *Decisions for War*, Keith Wilson, ed. (London: UCL Press, 1995), pp. 9–25.

6 J. C. G. Röhl, "Germany," in Wilson, *Decisions for War*, p. 35.

7 Niall Ferguson, "Germany and the Origins of the First World War: New Perspectives," *Historical Journal* 35 (1992): 734–42. Ferguson has claimed that Germany's leaders acted out of a "sense of weakness" in 1914: Germany believed it had lost, or was losing, the arms race, "which persuaded its leaders to gamble on war before they fell behind." See Ferguson, *The Pity of War* (London: Penguin, 1998).

8 Gerard J. De Groot, *Blighty: British Society in the Era of the Great War* (London: Longman, 1996), p. 2. See also Michael Gordon, "Domestic Conflict and the Origins of the First World War: The British and German Cases," *Journal of Modern History* 46 (1974): 191–226.

9 John Keiger, "France," in Wilson, *Decisions for War*, p. 122.

10 Lancelot L. Farrar, Jr, "Reluctant Warriors: Public Opinion on War during the July Crisis, 1914," *Eastern European Quarterly* 16 (1983): 436.

11 For a discussion of the September Program, including the actual wording of the program, see David Welch, *Modern European History 1871–2000: A Documentary Reader* (London: Routledge, 2000), pp. 76–9.

12 For a more detailed analysis of these events in Germany, see David Welch, *Germany, Propaganda and Total War 1914–1918: The Sins of Omission* (London: Athlone, 2000), pp. 1–10.

13 G. Bourgin, J. Carrère, and A. Guérin, *Manuel des partis politiques en France*, 2nd edn (Paris, 1928), p. 13. Cf. Gerd Krumeich, *Armaments and Politics in France on the Eve of the First World War* (Leamington Spa: Berg, 1984), p. 8.

14 Zara Steiner, *Britain and the Origins of the First World War* (London: Macmillan, 1977), p. 153; Beckett, *Great War*, p. 27. The term was first coined by David French, "The Edwardian Crisis and the Origins of the First World War," *International History Review* 4 (1982): 207–21. The first historian to emphasize the restlessness and disharmony in Britain from the late nineteenth century was George Dangerfield. Writing in 1936, Dangerfield challenged the romanticism that had characterized the period leading to 1914 as one of contentment and stability: *The Strange Death of Liberal England* (London: Constable, 1936). Trevor Wilson subsequently went even further and claimed that the British government was saved from a potentially ruinous position in 1914 by the outbreak of war: *The Downfall of the Liberal Party* (London: Collins, 1966).

15 De Groot, *Blighty*, p. 7.

16 Quoted in Marcus, *Before the Lamps Go Out*, p. 307.

17 See Colin Veitch, "'Play up! Play up! And Win the War!' Football, the Nation and the First World War 1914–15," *Journal of Contemporary History* 20 (1985): 363–78.

18 All quotations taken from Welch, *Germany, Propaganda and Total*, pp. 14–19.

19 Jeffrey Verhey, *The Spirit of 1914: Militarism, Myth, and Mobilization in Germany* (Cambridge: Cambridge University Press, 2000), p. 94.

20 Jean-Jacques Becker, *1914: Comment les Francais sont entrés dans la guerre* (Paris: Robert Laffont, 1977, 1983); see also Becker, *The Great War and the French People* (Oxford: Berg, 1993); P. J. Flood, *France 1914–18: Public Opinion and the War Effort* (London: Macmillan, 1990).

21 Sadly, I cannot claim this as an original phrase. I have taken it from De Groot, *Blighty*, p. 9.

22 See Clive Emsley's excellent summary of these issues in *Total War and Social Change 1914–1955* (Milton Keynes: Open University Press, 2000), pp. 45–53.

23 Marc Ferro, *The Great War 1914–1918* (London: Routledge, 1973), p. xi.

24 For examples of different layers of experience during the August crisis outside the capital cities of Europe, see Michael Stöcker, *Augusterlebnis 1914 in Darmstadt: Legende und Wirklichkeit* (Darmstadt: E. Roether, 1994).

25 A theme expanded by Mark Connelly, "'Never Such Innocence Again': Grossbritannien und das Jahr 1914," *Aus Politik und Zeitgeschichte* 29/30 (2004): 13–20.

GUIDE TO FURTHER READING

Jean-Jacques Becker, *The Great War and the French People* (Oxford: Berg, 1993). A wealth of information on popular attitudes in wartime France.

Ian F. W. Beckett, *The Great War 1914–1918* (London: Pearson, 2001). An impressively wide-ranging comparative analysis.

John M. Bourne, *Britain and the Great War* (London: Arnold, 1989). Particularly strong on the military and political aspects.

Hugh Cecil and Peter Liddle, eds, *Facing Armageddon: The First World Experienced* (London: Leo Cooper, 1996). A wide-ranging collection of essays.

Roger Chickering, *Imperial Germany and the Great War, 1914–1918* (Cambridge: Cambridge University Press, 1998). A thoughtfully written study of the military, political, and social effects of the war.

Geoffrey J. De Groot, *Blighty: British Society in the Era of the Great War* (London: Longman, 1996). Intensely thought-provoking analysis based on considerable scholarship.

Niall Ferguson, *The Pity of War* (London: Penguin, 1998). Provocative generalizations, particularly strong on economics.

P. J. Flood, *France 1914–18: Public Opinion and the War Effort* (London: Macmillan, 1990). Well-researched treatment of the French experience.

Patrick Fridenson, ed., *The French Home Front 1914–1918* (Oxford: Berg, 1992). Ten perceptive and wide-ranging essays.

Holger H. Herwig, *The First World War: Germany and Austria-Hungary 1914–1918* (London: Arnold, 1997). A comprehensive treatment that has the benefit of including analysis of Austria-Hungary.

David Stevenson, *1914–1918: The History of the First World War* (London: Allen Lane, 2004). An impressively written and researched global history of the conflict.

Hew Strachan, ed., *The Oxford Illustrated History of the First World War* (Oxford: Oxford University Press, 1998). A good general introduction, heavily illustrated and analytical.

Jeffrey Verhey, *The Spirit of 1914: Militarism, Myth, and Mobilization in Germany* (Cambridge: Cambridge University Press, 2000). A systematic analysis of German public opinion and the myth of the "spirit of 1914."

David Welch, *Germany, Propaganda and Total War 1914–1918: The Sins of Omission* (London: Athlone, 2000). An examination of the interaction between politics, propaganda, public opinion, and total war, drawn from a wide range of archival sources.

Keith Wilson, ed., *Decisions for War* (London: UCL Press, 1995). An authoritative and comprehensive collection of nine essays that examine the weeks of crisis management that led to the outbreak of war.

CHAPTER FOURTEEN

The War in the Trenches

TIM TRAVERS

Land warfare in World War I included many variations, but the most intense and significant campaign occurred on the western front, and within the western front the warfare that most soldiers experienced was trench warfare, so that topic will be the focus of this chapter. Trench warfare comprised daily life in the trenches, interspersed with trench raids against opposing trenches, also rest periods and training behind the front lines, and the constant fatigues – such as carrying up supplies or bringing forward artillery shells, or digging fresh trenches, or repairing destroyed wire and trenches. Soldiers could expect to spend about one third of their time in the front line trenches, otherwise they could be in reserve trenches, at rest, training, or very occasionally, on leave. Most stressful was participation in major offensives, which could last for weeks and months. Soldiers living in the trenches could also expect to be bombarded by enemy mortars and artillery, raked by machine gun fire, gassed by gas shells or drifting gas waves, and shot by sharpshooters if any part of the body was exposed above the trench.

When the soldier was ordered to take part in an offensive, there would first be training to familiarize the participants in the tactics to be used, and the aims and conditions of the attack. Toward the end of the war, artillery preparation for the attack could last just a few hours, but in the first years of the war, a week or more before the date of the offensive a continuous preparatory artillery bombardment would start, in order to cut enemy wire, destroy enemy trenches opposite, and disable as many enemy machine guns and artillery pieces as possible before the offensive began. Some half an hour before the actual time of the attack, the artillery bombardment would intensify into a drumbeat of shells, and then as the troops went over the top, the offensive artillery barrage would start, leading the attacking troops forward, either moving ahead in "lifts" in the early stages of the war, or "creeping" ahead in later stages of the war. The attacking waves of troops learnt to "lean" on the barrage by keeping close to the moving rain of their own shells, since the barrage would protect the attackers across the dangerous open ground before reaching the enemy trenches. It was always safer to sustain a few casualties from one's own barrage than to "loose" the barrage ahead of the troops, as this would expose the soldiers to the enemy's defensive artillery barrage, machine guns, and rifles. If all went well, the troops would reach their objectives, dig in, and get ready for the likely enemy counter-attack. The wounded and dead would be dealt with, and the troops would try to hold onto their territorial gains before the next attack or "push" would commence, sometimes within hours, or perhaps days later. If the attack did not go well, casualties would be heavy and the troops would likely find themselves back in the trenches they had started from.

Trench warfare actually began in France and Belgium around mid-September 1914, after the battle of the Marne. The opposing trenches crept across the country-side until they covered the whole front line between Switzerland and the sea, extending some 350 miles long. Soon entire armies and millions of men were concealed in the earth in a strange subterranean existence. Veterans particularly disliked the daily conditions of mud and rain, lice and rats, lack of sleep and poor food, frost in the winter, hosts of flies in the summer, and the diseases that went along with trench life, such as trench foot. It would be possible to write an entire book about trench life, but in this chapter the focus will be on certain aspects of trench warfare: firstly, the dangerous moments when enemy soldiers might be captured or killed; then the emergence and treatment of shell shock; the controversial problem of executions during the war; the attempt to escape trench warfare through self-inflicted wounds; the question of fraternization with the enemy; and the officially encouraged trench raid.

Capturing Prisoners of War

One of the largely unwritten stories of trench warfare concerns the treatment of prisoners of war at the point of capture.[1] In this situation, while an attack or large-scale offensive was under way, the offensive spirit of the troops was at its height, and unfortunate incidents sometimes took place. The well-known writer and junior German officer in World War I, Ernst Junger, described one such incident during the German offensive of March 1918: "No quarter was given. The English hastened with upstretched arms through the first wave of [German] storm troops to the rear, where the fury of the battle had not reached boiling point. An orderly . . . shot a good dozen or more of them with his 32 repeater. I cannot blame our men for their bloodthirsty conduct," wrote Junger, and explained that

> the defending force, after driving their bullets into the [German] attacking one at five paces' distance, must take the consequences. A man cannot change his feelings again during the last rush with a veil of blood before his eyes. He does not want to take prisoners but to kill. He has no scruples left; only the spell of primeval instinct remains. It is not till blood has flowed that the mist gives way in his soul.[2]

Here Junger sees the problem as one of warlike instinct. The same warlike instinct was alleged against the Turks in the Gallipoli campaign of 1915, who were thought not to take prisoners as a matter of course. Hence, the Turks responded with a leaflet in June 1915:

> We hear from the prisoners we made lately, that your officers try to make you believe that we Turks kill and massacre our prisoners. Not just the international law, but also

our religion as well tell us to treat prisoners and wounded kindly. Be sure, English soldiers, that we will receive every single man of you who come to us friendly, that he will return safely home to wife and children.[3]

It seems likely that the Allied troops were not persuaded.

In other contexts there was sometimes a more deliberate intention. Hence, in September 1916 on the western front, one Canadian soldier claimed that he and his comrades were given

> strict instructions to take *no* prisoners until our objectives had been gained. The reason for this was that so often in British advances, when the Germans had thrown down their arms in surrender and our men had moved through them, at the same time indicating to them to go to our rear where they could be collected as prisoners, the Germans had picked up their rifles again and shot our men in the back.[4]

In fact, rightly or wrongly, British troops were always on the alert for German "tricks" throughout the war. Hence, in August 1918, orders for the major Allied offensive of August 8, 1918 listed common German ruses: the white flag; men shamming death; machine guns concealed on stretchers; and Germans shouting "Retire!" in English. In regard to this last trick, it was ordered that any officer or man giving this order would be shot at once.

The fear of German treachery was a common attitude. But revenge was another frequent motive for killing prisoners of war. In this context, a Canadian soldier went on to tell a poignant story which occurred during operations in September 1916:

> One young German, scruffy, bareheaded, cropped hair, and wearing steel-rimmed glasses, ran, screaming with fear, dodging in and out among us to avoid being shot, crying out "Nein! Nein!" He pulled out from his breast pocket a handful of photographs and tried to show them to us (I suppose they were of his wife and children) in an effort to gain our sympathy. It was all to no avail. As the bullets smacked into him he fell to the ground motionless, the pathetic little photographs fluttering down to the earth around him.[5]

Other soldiers in this same attack bayoneted Germans trying to surrender, and in this case, it seems that the motive was revenge for German mines fired under the Canadian trenches, or for Canadian losses sustained earlier at St Eloi and Mont-Sorrel. As a result the senior general in charge of this particular division wrote later: "The men were not looking for prisoners, and considered a dead German the best." Even at the very end of the war, on November 2, 1918, revenge among some soldiers was a reason for killing German prisoners of war, in this case because the men had spoken to French civilians and had heard stories of German abuses.[6]

In fact, fear of enemy treachery, or actual enemy treachery, seems to have been the most common rationale for killing potential prisoners of war. Yet other reasons existed also. Sometimes, relief at escaping death provided a reason for killing soldiers who wanted to surrender. One such case occurred during Passchendaele in 1917, when a junior British officer was trapped in no man's land between British and German trenches, with his own attack failed, and death imminent. Suddenly, British

reinforcements arrived, and then fortunes reversed as the German troops began trying
to surrender:

> I saw straight to the front and a hundred yards away a crowd of men running towards
> us in grey uniforms. Picking up another rifle, I joined . . . in pouring rapid fire into this
> counter-attack. We saw at least one drop . . . then we noticed that they were running
> with their hands up. Laughing, we emptied our magazines at them in spite of that.[7]

On other occasions, there were more "legitimate" reasons for killing potential
prisoners of war, as Ernst Junger relates of two British soldiers killed at Guillemont on
the Somme: "Two members of an English ration party who had lost their way appeared
at dusk on No. 1 platoon front. Both were shot down at point blank range." Junger
explained that "None of the men would take prisoners, for how could we get them
through the barrage? It was bad enough on our own without prisoners to see to."[8]

In summary, it appears that the killing of potential or actual prisoners of war took
place among all armies through reasons of fear of enemy treachery or actual treachery,
because of feelings of revenge, through official or unofficial orders, from relief at
one's own survival, because of the inability to control prisoners during enemy attacks,
or simply because of hate of the enemy. Yet although the killing of prisoners did
happen, it was certainly more common for soldiers to be able to surrender. Usually,
the upraised arms, the taking off of military gear, and throwing down one's weapon,
were sufficient to be taken prisoner safely. If the situation seemed particularly threatening, the extra supplication of going down on one's knees, and the production of
a crucifix or bible, or showing photographs of family, or the circumstance of being
wounded, all meant greater likelihood of immediate survival.

Shell Shock: Post Traumatic Stress Disorder

Not surprisingly, given these experiences, and the stress of trench life, there developed
in the soldiers of all armies what has more recently been called post traumatic stress
disorder, or as it was initially known in World War I: shell shock. There was considerable difficulty in understanding and treating mental breakdown, so different terms
were used to describe the problem. The British army used shell shock because it was
thought to be associated with the nearby explosion and concussion of a shell. Later
on, a more open term was used: "Not Yet Diagnosed (Nervous)." In the French
army, similar confusion as to the causes of mental stress led to the use of a number
of terms, such as "commotion cerebrale," "accidents nerveux," "obusite" (shell-it
is), and finally, simply "commotion." The German army used a number of terms also,
usually around the word "neurose" (neurosis), such as "kriegsneurose," meaning
battle neurosis.

In all armies, symptoms of shell shock manifested themselves in a number of ways.
In about 70 percent of all cases, there was anxiety or fear, revealed by shaking and
trembling limbs, tremors and tics, crying, headaches, dizziness, confusion, stumbling
gaits, and often temporary unconsciousness. In about 20 percent of cases, there was
mutism (lack of speech), and various forms of paralysis. One such case of paralysis
was reported when a certain Private C. M., aged 32, was near a shell-burst a few days
after going up the line. He was blown up, and when he got up, he was fixed in the

attitude called camptocormia, meaning a bent over state. Early suggestion produced some improvement, but then there were rapid relapses. As late as 1920, Private C. M. was still bent over, and was quite sure that his back was dislocated. The final 10 percent of cases related to various situations such as intense mental confusion, amnesia, dissociation, and neuroses.

The German army tried to ignore shell shock, but eventually treatment stressed immediate attention at the front, because it was thought necessary to remove symptoms before they became "fixed." As in the British army, there was an attempt by the German army to keep the patient as close to the front as possible, to give the patient the sense that he was still at war, and so prevent him from giving up the will to fight. But as elsewhere, this was found to be only partially successful, and patients would in the end have to be evacuated from the front. Meanwhile, French ideas about treatment were complicated by a refusal to accept the legitimacy of non-organic war injuries, and by a fairly strict military attitude to mental stress, which also included treatment close to the front. French treatment generally seems to have varied between a rather harsh approach which favored isolation, and the use of the electric battery to cure mutism, paralysis, and the more severe cases, and a relatively mild approach, using warm baths and extended rest.

Perhaps the best-known literature on mental stress during World War I comes from the British army. Here there were two basic schools of thought, although they were not mutually exclusive. One was the discipline approach, and the other, the analytic therapy approach. The first, the discipline treatment, might include scolding, a regimented existence, a milk diet, bromides, the use of ether or chloroform followed by massage and manipulation of limbs, electrical faradizations, and even the infliction of pain in cases of longstanding neglect or suspected malingering. On the other hand, the analytic therapy approach tended toward psychoanalysis, and the "talking cure," such as free association conversations. Hypnosis might also be used to reach the patient's buried fears and repressed memories, which could be gently brought to the surface.

An example of the analytic therapy approach would be Charles Myers, a medical specialist in nerve shock who served in France in 1915, and then created four special centers for the nerve shocked in 1916. Myers argued that when shell shock occurred, the normal personality was replaced by an emotional personality, representing the emotional experiences of the shell shock episode. After a period of time an apparently normal personality returns, but this is the normal personality without memory of the shell shock episode. This apparently normal personality was frequently disturbed by the dissociated emotional personality, working subconsciously beneath the apparently normal personality. The treatment, according to Myers, was to restore the emotional personality, deprived of its pathological character, to the apparently normal personality, which had been ignorant of the emotional personality until the treatment. With this integration of the purified emotional personality with the apparently normal personality, the completely normal personality then returns. Myers' normal method to achieve this rather complicated "cure" was to use suggestion, aided if necessary by hypnosis. If this did not work, then in extreme or obstinate cases, it might be necessary to apply electrical faradization or an anesthetic.[9]

Myers' recommended treatments seemed to have wavered between a more progressive analytic therapy approach, and a more aggressive physical approach. Thus, in obstinate cases of functional deafness, lip reading should be taught, or in obstinate cases of blindness, the patient should plunge his head, with eyes wide open, into a basin of cold water several times daily, while in cases of severe headaches, lumbar punctures could be tried. In general, a spirit of optimism should greet every patient on arrival.

Turning to the more sympathetic wing of the analytic therapy approach, the best-known practitioner of this method was the psychoanalytically inclined doctor, W. H. R. Rivers, who treated the poet and writer Siegfried Sassoon at Craiglockhart hospital in Scotland. Rivers was an early convert to Freudian ideas, and tried a different tack in regard to alleviating underlying emotional problems. This was the idea that terrible war experiences should not be repressed by the patient. Instead, Rivers advised patients to face the unpleasant memories of the war experience, and actually deal with them. Rivers cited a case in which his patient had gone out of the trench to seek a fellow officer, and found his body with head and limbs lying separated from the trunk. From that time forward

> he had been haunted at night by the vision of his dead and mutilated friend. When he slept he had nightmares in which his friend appeared, sometimes in the still more terrify-ing aspect of one whose limbs and features had been eaten away by leprosy. The muti-lated or leprous officer of the dream would come nearer and nearer until the patient suddenly awoke poring with sweat and in a state of the utmost terror. He dreaded to go to sleep, and spent each day looking forward in painful anticipation of the night. He had been advised to keep all thoughts of war from his mind, but the experience which recurred so often at night was so insistent that he could not keep it wholly from his thoughts, much as he tried to do so. Nevertheless, there is no question but that he was striving by day to dispel memories only to bring them upon him with redoubled force and horror when he slept.[10]

Rivers believed that the way to deal with this and similar cases was to stop the patients, and in this case, the officer, from continually trying to repress their horrible experiences, and instead to face the reality of their experiences, and to find some aspect of their situation that was positive. Hence, in this particular case, Rivers drew the attention of the officer to the fact that

> the mangled state of the body of his friend was conclusive evidence that he had been killed outright and had been spared the long and lingering illness and suffering which is too often the fate of those who sustain mortal wounds. He brightened at once and said that this aspect of the case had never occurred to him . . . He said he would no longer attempt to banish thoughts and memories of his friend from his mind, but would think of the pain and suffering he had been spared. For several nights he had no dreams at all, and then came a night in which he dreamt that he went out into no man's land to seek his friend and saw his mangled body just as in other dreams; but without the horror which had always previously been present. He knelt beside his friend to save for the relatives any objects of value . . . a pious duty he had fulfilled in the actual scene, and as he was taking off the Sam Browne belt he woke with none of the horror and terror of the past, but weeping gently, feeling only grief for the loss of a friend.[11]

The officer was on the road to recovery, according to Rivers, suffering later only one other unpleasant dream with a different content. Rivers theorized that the recovery of this officer and several others came about because of the effect of catharsis. Rivers believed that catharsis occurred when a repressed or dissociated body of experience was brought to the surface so that it could become reintegrated with the ordinary personality. In conjunction with the cathartic process Rivers also applied the concept of reeducation, which Rivers saw as helping the patient to a new view of himself and his experience.

Unfortunately for Rivers and all those seeking to "cure" shell shock, whether employing the analytic or discipline approaches, with the object of returning the patient to the battlefield, shell shock, or post traumatic stress disorder, often remained resistant to cures, and was often remarkably long lasting for the patient. This is demonstrated by the statistic that in Britain, two years after the armistice, 65,000 exservicemen were drawing disability pensions for neurasthenia, while 9,000 were still undergoing hospital treatment. A typically poignant story, concerning a dairyman who had served in World War I and had broken down under the strain, reinforces the idea of long-lasting shell shock:

> He nods and smiles every time one looks at him, frantic to please. He will sit in a chair for hours, raising and lowering his eyebrows and fitting imaginary gloves to his fingers. An inspecting general, pausing at his bed this morning, said, "A dairyman are you? Afraid of horses are you? Then what do you do about cows?" He was pleased with his own joke and the dairyman smiled too, his eyebrows shooting up and down like swallow's wings. Such jokes meant nothing to him. He is where no jokes but his own will ever please him any more.[12]

Execution of Serving Officers and Soldiers

Even more unfortunate was the perception that some shell shocked men might have been executed during the war for cowardice. After the war, the 1922 British inquiry into shell shock considered that of the 346 men executed during the war in the British Expeditionary Force (including 25 Canadians and 5 New Zealanders), some 18 were executed for cowardice. This was an offense that might well derive from shell shock, and undoubtedly some men were executed, especially early in the war, who were in fact suffering from shell shock. For example, Private Harry Farr, in the BEF, was executed in 1917 despite having suffered from traumatic neurosis during the Somme campaign of 1916. Farr had refused to enter the line, saying he could no longer cope with the sound of gunfire. In another case, 2nd Lieutenant Eric Poole, also in the BEF, was executed in 1917 for desertion, despite witnesses testifying that he suffered from mental confusion. In addition, courts martial in the British army were often rather short and casual affairs, with little in the way of defensive arguments. Other examples come from the Gallipoli campaign of 1915.

One such case concerned Private Davis of the Royal Munster Fusiliers, who faced a court martial in late June 1915. Davis had previously been sentenced to be shot in May 1915, which was commuted to 10 years in prison, but he reoffended by being absent from duty and was awarded 28 days Field Punishment number 1 (being strapped to a wheel, fence or wall, or other suitable structure for a number of hours per day). Then on June 20, 1915, Davis was posted as a sentry at headquarters at 1 a.m. until 3 a.m., but was discovered to be absent from his duty at 2.30 a.m. by the sergeant in charge of sentries. Davis said that he had stomach cramps at 2.15 a.m., and went to the latrines for the remaining 45 minutes of his duty. Davis did not cross-examine any of the witnesses or offer any plea for mitigation. Meanwhile, the two witnesses were only asked whether Davis had been on duty or not, and not whether he had been seen in the latrine area. The court martial proceedings were very brief, there was essentially no defense, and Davis was sentenced to be shot, which was carried out at 5 a.m. on July 2, 1915. In this case, Davis could certainly have been suffering from dysentery, which was rampant in Gallipoli at the time, and he may well have been suffering from mental instability, but he was probably executed rather than being sentenced to a prison term because of his previous convictions.[13]

One other example from Gallipoli is also of interest because it involved a sergeant from the Wiltshire Regiment, by name, Robins. This was a high non-commissioned officer rank, and the prosecution in Robins' court martial had a difficult time explaining why the regiment thought highly enough of Robins to promote him to this rank, and at the same time suggest that he was a poor soldier. Robins' crime was that he refused to go on patrol on December 3, 1915, saying he was not feeling well. The regimental medical doctor examined Robins but could not find any medical problem, although he did give Robins some (unspecified) medicine. Robins claimed he had contracted fever and ague from long service in India, and this was his problem on December 3, 1915. Before sentencing, the acting regimental adjutant admitted he could not produce Robins' service record because it had been lost in the recent flood on Gallipoli. Robins did not deny his actions, and he was sentenced to death and executed on January 1, 1916. It is not clear why Robins was given the death sentence, especially because the recent floods and freezing temperatures of November 1915 on Gallipoli had created very bad conditions, and many other soldiers had abandoned their posts because of these conditions. Robins may well have suffered a reoccurrence of his India symptoms because of the weather, but his execution probably occurred because as a sergeant he held significant rank, and thus his crime could not have been overlooked.[14]

These two specific examples at the micro level show that various factors could go into receiving the death sentence and subsequent execution. However, at the macro level, the executions of serving men by their own justice systems reveal a strange contrast among different countries involved in the trench warfare of World War I. The facts are not entirely well established, and exact numbers are disputed. However, it is considered during the war that the following numbers of men were executed: 18 Belgians; 346 British and Dominion officers and men; 700 French (a disputed number since only 49 men were executed for participating in the large-scale French mutinies of 1917); 35 US soldiers (only 10 of whom committed offenses in France); 48 Germans (allegedly); and the surprising number of 750 Italians. Numbers for Russia, the Ottoman army, and the Austro-Hungarians are not available. It seems that the Italian forces suffered the largest total number of executions, with 141 alone being shot in November 1917, in order to halt the collapse of the Italian army after the disaster of the battle of Caporetto, in late 1917. General Luigi Cadorna, the Italian commander in chief, apparently resorted to floggings and summary executions to stem the tide of indiscipline in the Italian army after Caporetto.

Of course, discipline had to be maintained, and there were then considered to be legitimate reasons for maintaining morale through use of the death penalty. But the

Australian government refused to allow Australian soldiers to be executed in World War I, and yet it is clear that Australian forces in World War I maintained their high morale without the ultimate penalty. In regard to the differences between the executions of officers and men, while some officers were shot in all armies, it was generally easier for officers to avoid punishment by simply getting themselves sent home to some less dangerous job. On the other hand, the average soldier found it much more difficult to avoid punishment. Yet even for the average soldier, the unit commander would do much to avoid a court martial, and would try to deal with the soldier within the unit. It should also be emphasized that a court martial death sentence did not automatically result in execution, since most death penalties were commuted. For example, in the BEF, there were 346 executions out of 3,080 convictions, for a death rate of 11.23 percent of convictions. If the figures are roughly correct, the French execution rate per conviction was very much higher, at 35 percent, while the Italian rate was 18.62 percent, and the Belgian rate was relatively low at 8.18 percent.[15]

There is no easy way to summarize these statistics, but a British memoir of the war voiced what was probably the general sentiment among front line troops:

> A man was shot for cowardice. The volley failed to kill. The officer in charge lost his nerve, turned to the assistant provost marshal [APM] and said, "Do your own bloody work, I cannot." We understood that the sequel was that he was arrested. Officially this butchery has to be applauded but I have changed my ideas. There are no two ways. A man either can or cannot stand up to his environment. With some, the limit for breaking is reached sooner. The human frame can only stand so much. Surely, when a man becomes afflicted, it is more a case for the medicals than the APM. How easy for the generals living in luxury well back in their chateaux to enforce the death penalty.[16]

Self-Inflicted Wounds

If men could not stand the war in the trenches, and did not break down mentally, and wanted to avoid the death penalty, there was always the hope that they might get a "Blighty," meaning a non-critical wound that might mean a period of time in base hospital, convalescence in Britain, and hopefully, honorable discharge from the war entirely. Some soldiers encouraged this possibility by raising hands or even feet above the trench line, hoping for a disabling wound. And some went even further by inflicting on themselves what were called self-inflicted wounds (SIWs). As one extreme example, in the Canadian Corps, a soldier planted his foot and a grenade in the ground, and blew his foot off. In all there were 582 detected cases of SIWs among the Canadian Corps, but rarely as dramatic as the grenade and foot method.[17]

Joseph Murray, who wrote a fine memoir of his service on Gallipoli in 1915, described an SIW in which he was unwillingly involved. Murray's section was much reduced by fighting, and his friend, nicknamed Tubby, was unable to stand the strain any longer. Just before an attack, Tubby put his thumb over the mouth of his rifle and pulled the trigger. Unfortunately, the thumb was not completely severed, and Tubby danced around with blood squirting out. A bandage did not help, so Murray decided to use his pocket knife to saw off the thumb. Despite much sawing this did not work, and Tubby howled in pain: "By now Tubby had lost a lot of blood. Something had to be done quickly and the alternative was to try chopping it off. I placed the thumb on the butt of his rifle, inserted the blade and, with a sharp tap with my fist, the operation was complete." With tears streaming down his face, Tubby begged Murray not to report him. But now came the difficult part – how to explain the powder marks on the remains of the thumb? A story was concocted that in the excitement just before the attack, a fellow soldier had fired his rifle as Tubby was climbing out of the trench. Somehow the officer believed the story, or what was far more likely, the officer realized that Tubby would not be any future use in the trenches anyway, and so Tubby was discharged back to Britain.[18]

Fraternization with the Enemy

SIWs are often mentioned in memoirs, but the statistical side is difficult to analyze due to the often disguised nature of the problem. Nevertheless, the existence of SIWs can be balanced by more positive experiences, in this case, fraternization with the enemy. It was to be expected that with opposing trench lines so close to each other on the western front for three or four years, that there would be communication between the two sides, and that this might develop into something more. There were essentially five aspects to fraternization: truces during special times of year, such as Christmas or Easter; medical truces to deal with dead and wounded in no man's land; a general system of "live and let live" in quieter sections of the line; communication between trench lines that were close together; and finally, truces created by extreme weather conditions.

The most famous truce occurred over the Christmas holiday of 1914. On Christmas eve Allied soldiers in some sectors were surprised to see Christmas trees appear in the German trenches and on their parapets, followed by singing of Christmas carols, especially "Stille Nacht, heilige Nacht" (Silent Night). Then on Christmas Day men called across no man's land to each other, and finally, small groups came out of the trenches to shake hands and exchange gifts such as cigars, cigarettes, tobacco, and newspapers. In some areas a Christmas dinner was shared, and it was rumored that a soccer match took place between a Saxon regiment and a British regiment, with the score 3–2 in the British favor. However, as senior officers began to hear of the fraternization, orders went round the trenches on the evening of Christmas Day forbidding such activity, and the next day, the war resumed, although at a low level. In fact, in some places, the truce continued to New Year's Day, while January 1915 remained remarkably quiet in the trenches. Yet in other areas there was no Christmas truce, as Ernst Junger relates:

> We spent Christmas Eve in the line. The men stood in the mud and sang Christmas carols that were drowned by the enemy machine guns. On Christmas Day we lost a man in No. 3 platoon by a flanking shot through the head. Immediately after, the English attempted a friendly overture and put up a Christmas tree on their parapet. But our fellows were so embittered that they fired and knocked it over. And this in turn was answered with rifle grenades. In this miserable fashion we celebrated Christmas Day.[19]

Medical truces were quite common, either to bring in the wounded or to bury the dead between trench lines. A typical truce of this sort occurred on May 24, 1915, in Gallipoli, after severe fighting. Bodies had begun to decompose in the heat, to smell, and to attract swarms of flies, which posed a medical threat to both sides. It may have been the Australian troops which first proposed the truce, after some Turkish stretcher bearers had come out of the trenches the previous day, had been captured, and then released. A truce was arranged for May 24, with both sides wearing white arm bands to distinguish the burial parties. The burial parties took identification from the bodies, and then buried the dead in mass graves. At a specified time in the late afternoon, both sides retreated to their trenches, and the war resumed. However, there had been opportunity for an exchange of cigarettes, and some halting attempts at conversation. According to a New Zealand soldier: "Many of the Turks expressed a wish to surrender to us but of course the conditions of armistice do not permit of deserters being accepted during its existence."[20]

Similar medical truces took place throughout the war, but particularly in places like Gallipoli where heat and disease were prevalent. More frequent perhaps was the truce system known as "Live and Let Live." In this system, sections of the line mutually "agreed' to live in relative peace with each other, especially in the quiet areas of the western front. These truces meant that firing would be restricted to certain times of the day and night, sniping might be outlawed at meal times, and patrols might "agree" not to be violent with each other. Charles Sorley, a British officer, wrote later: "Without at all 'fraternizing' we refrain from interfering with Brother Bosch seventy yards away, as long as he is kind to us." Again:

All patrols – English and German – are much averse to the death and glory principle; so, on running up against one another . . . both pretend that they are Levites and the other is a good Samaritan – and pass by on the other side, no word spoken. For either side to bomb the other would be a useless violation of the unwritten laws that govern the relations of combatants permanently within a hundred yards of distance of each other, who have found out that to provide discomfort for the other is but a roundabout way of providing it for themselves.

Even without an understanding like this, conflict would sometimes be avoided, as in the case of a German patrol in June 1916, with rifles slung over their shoulders, which unexpectedly ran into a French outpost in the fog. A German non-commissioned officer simply said in French: "Triste guerre, messieurs! Triste guerre!" and the French simply allowed the patrol to fade away in the fog.[21]

It was generally considered on the western front that Saxon regiments were the German regiments most inclined to be passive. At St Eloi in 1915 it was understood that when Saxons were in the line, there would be little shooting, and when patrols went out, there would be a low warning whistle, and then both sides would exchange food at night in the mine craters of no man's land. According to one memoir of the St Eloi sector, also in 1915: "The enemy shouted out 'Good morning' to me. When I was in front of the largest crater, I watched six Germans coming out into the open and getting into one of their advanced posts. Six more got out with their rifles slung and with braziers in their hands yelling 'Goodbye' to me and went back to their main trench."[22]

This Live and Let Live system did operate on quieter sections of the front, and elsewhere from time to time, depending on the units in the line. But generally, the overall attitude of the troops was to kill the enemy, and the war was normally prosecuted with some intensity. Nevertheless, trenches were often close to each other, and communication did take place, although this did not amount to a Live and Let Live system. Robert Graves, the poet and author, recalled that when he arrived at the Cuinchy brickworks area on the western front, he found the Germans opposite wanted to be friendly. They sent over messages in empty rifle grenades, evidently intended for an Irish regiment that had just left, inviting the English over for a dinner, and informing them that their pet dog had run over to the German trenches, and was being looked after. Graves' regiment did not respond. Edmund Blunden, a junior officer, remembered an incident when a German officer and perhaps twenty men emerged from their trench and called out "Good morning, Tommy, have you any biscuits?" There was an exchange of shouted remarks and both sides then returned to their trenches. Meanwhile, the junior British officers had told their men not to fire and, for this lack of aggression, were placed under arrest. It is possible that the German intention had simply been to find out how strongly the opposing trench was held.[23]

The closeness of the trenches and the similarity of their situations also led to some reluctance to fire on the enemy. The French liaison officer Paul Maze wrote that he once visited a British forward observation post and noticed a bald headed German clearly visible opposite, but he was not fired upon. It seems that the German was involved in the universal problem of delousing himself, and this was sufficient to prevent him from being shot. Similar situations took place when rescuers went out to find wounded men, or in the unusual case of Canon Frederick Scott, who on July 2, 1916 was allowed to walk around in no man's land without interference, searching for his dead son.[24]

A more unusual form of communication occurred in Gallipoli, according to the memoir of Joseph Murray. A bayonet fight had taken place in no man's land between some men of the Dublin Fusiliers and a Turkish unit. After the fighting died down, a single combat continued between an Irish soldier and a Turkish soldier, both using bayonets. The combat carried on until both men sank down, exhausted. Then some men of the Dublin Fusiliers and of the Turkish unit got out of their trenches and moved forward to collect their respective combatants. Murray wrote:

> We were within arm's length of each other, but no one spoke. We, and they, hauled our men to their feet, both still holding their rifles at the ready. Both parties turned and walked slowly away to their respective trenches. Not a shot was fired from either line though there were at least a dozen men ambling about at point-blank range.[25]

Finally, extreme weather could also force the two sides out into the open, whatever their attitudes to each other. Ernst Junger, the German officer, reported an incident in December 1915 after days of heavy rain:

> One morning, when, thoroughly wet through, I went up out of the dugout into the trench, I could scarcely believe my eyes. The field of battle that hitherto had been marked by desolation of death itself had taken on the appearance of a fair. The occupants of the trenches on both sides had been driven to take to the top, and now there was a lively traffic and exchange going on in schnapps, cigarettes, uniform buttons, etc., in front of the wire. The crowds of khaki-colored figures that streamed from the hitherto so

deserted English trenches had a most bewildering effect. Suddenly there was a shot that dropped one of our fellows dead in the mud . . . Whereupon both sides disappeared like moles into their trenches.[26]

Trench Raids

However, a much more frequent element of life in the trenches was not fraternization, but trench raids and patrols. Trench raids were called patrols if they were small and essentially unplanned. Supposedly invented by the Canadians in 1915, trench raids were almost always undertaken at night, and were conducted primarily to obtain information about the enemy forces opposite. In the BEF, trench raids were also used to theoretically maintain the morale and fighting offensive spirit of the troops, who might lose that spirit by simply staying in their trenches. Trench raids and patrols were also used to maintain dominance over the enemy in no man's land. Finally, as the war progressed, much larger trench raids took place, with considerable and precise planning, artillery support, and lengthy orders. They were, in effect, minor offensives. Whether trench raids maintained morale and offensive spirit is questionable, but among BEF armies a number of trench raids were required to be launched every month by each division, to show that that division was active in fighting the enemy opposite.

A typical trench raid involved Ernst Junger, who on June 20, 1916 was asked to go out into no man's land to discover whether the enemy was mining or not. Junger took three soldiers with him and crawled through the long grass toward the British trenches: "Once there were loud crackling sounds behind us. Two shadows passed along swiftly between the trenches. Just as we made ready to jump on them they vanished. Immediately after, the thunder of two bombs in the English trench told us it was two of our men who had crossed our path." Junger paused, and then crawled on. Suddenly, rustling in the grass indicated that the British had detected the patrol. Junger's breath came in gasps and he could hardly suppress the noise. The click of Junger's safety catch going back went through his nerves, as did his teeth grating on the fuse pin of his grenade: "The fray will be short and murderous. You are aquiver with two violent sensations – the tense excitement of the hunter and the terror of the hunted." However, the British soldiers had come out to repair wire and the raid was undetected. Slowly, Junger and his men crawled back safely to their trench. But the next night, Junger's raid to capture a prisoner was discovered, and lights lit up the dark ground. Rifle and machine gun fire swept across no man's land, and it was safer to stand up and run. By good luck, all returned safely.[27]

Conclusion

Trench raids and patrols were a constant feature of trench life on the western front, and were probably successful about half the time. It was always more dangerous to attack than defend, but every day life in the trenches, despite the comradeship of the men, was also full of tension, with the occasional moments of relief, as can be seen from the previous discussion of the moment of capture, shell shock, executions, SIWs, fraternization, and trench raids. Moreover, death and wounds could occur at any time in trench warfare, so it is no surprise that the casualty figures for World War I are very large. Including wounded, prisoners, missing, and those who died from disease, the statistics are: France 3,844,300; Britain 2,556,014; British Empire 646,850; Germany 6,861,950. Outside the Western Front, the numbers are equally large: Italy 2,055,000; Russia 6,761,000; Austria-Hungary 6,920,000.[28] The tragedy is that so much death and destruction in the trenches did not prevent another world war twenty years later.

NOTES

1   An exception is Niall Ferguson, *The Pity of War* (New York: Basic Books, 1999), pp. 373–86.
2   Ernst Junger, *The Storm of Steel, From the Diary of a German Storm-troop Officer on the Western Front* (New York: Howard Fertig, 1996), pp. 262–3.
3   Cited in Tim Travers, *Gallipoli 1915* (Stroud: Tempus Publishing, 2001), p. 192.
4   Lance Cattermole, "Attack on the Somme," 92/26/1, p. 2, Imperial War Museum.
5   Ibid.
6   John Terraine, *To Win a War: 1918, The Year of Victory* (London: Sidgwick and Jackson, 1978), p. 238.
7   Charles Edmonds, *A Subaltern's War* (London: Peter Davies, 1929), pp. 134–5.
8   Junger, *Storm of Steel*, p. 102.
9   Charles Myers, *Shell-Shock in France* (Cambridge: Cambridge University Press, 1940).
10 Captain W. H. R. Rivers, "The Repression of War Experience," *The Lancet* 1 (1918): 174.
11 Ibid.
12 The World War I nurse, and author of children's books, Enid Bagnold, cited in Denis Winter, *Death's Men: Soldiers of the Great War* (Harmondsworth: Penguin, 1979), p. 135.
13 Davis Court Martial record, War Office 71/431, Public Record Office, London.
14 Robins Court Martial record, War Office 71/442, Public Record Office, London.
15 Statistics taken from David Englander, "Mutinies and Military Morale," in *The Oxford Illustrated History of the First World War*, Hew Strachan, ed. (Oxford: Oxford University Press, 1998), p. 192.
16 M. Evans, *Going Across* (London: Constable, 1952), cited in Denis Winter, *Death's Men*, p. 140.
17 Desmond Morton, *When Your Number's Up* (Toronto: Random House, 1993), p. 249.
18 Joseph Murray, *Gallipoli 1915* (London: NEL, 1977), p. 106.
19 Junger, *Storm of Steel*, pp. 53–4.
20 Travers, *Gallipoli 1915*, pp. 86–9, 196.
21 Charles Sorley, *The Letters of Charles Sorley* (Cambridge: Cambridge University Press, 1919), cited in Modris Eksteins, *Rites of Spring: The Great War and the Modern Age* (Toronto: Lester and Orpen Dennys, 1989), p. 105; Leonard Smith et al., *France and the Great War, 1914–1918* (Cambridge: Cambridge University Press, 2003), p. 110.
22 F. Hitchcock, *Stand-To* (London: Hurst and Blackett, 1937), cited in Denis Winter, *Death's Men*, pp. 218–19.
23 Robert Graves, *Goodbye to All That* (London: Penguin, 2000), p. 116; Edmund Blunden, *Undertones of War* (Harmondsworth: Penguin, 1982), p. 81.
24 Paul Maze, *A Frenchman in Khaki* (London: Heinemann, 1934), cited in Denis Winter, *Death's Men*, pp. 217–18.
25 Joseph Murray, *Gallipoli 1915*, p. 206.

26   Junger, *Storm of Steel*, p. 51.
27   Ibid, pp. 71–3.
28   Figures taken from Ferguson, *The Pity of War*, p. 295.

GUIDE TO FURTHER READING

Edmund Blunden, *Undertones of War* (London: Penguin, 1982). A classic of trench warfare by a young officer.

George Coppard, *With a Machine Gun to Cambrai* (London: HMSO, 1969). Evocative first-hand account of trench war and daily life in the trenches.

Niall Ferguson, *The Pity of War* (London: Allen Lane, 1998). Some innovative chapters on aspects of the war.

Robert Graves, *Goodbye to All That* (London: Penguin, 2000). Striking vignettes of the war by a junior officer and distinguished writer and poet.

Richard Holmes, *Tommy: The British Soldier on the Western Front, 1914–1918* (London: Harper Collins, 2004). The most recent account of the life of the British soldier, with a more positive view of the trench experience.

Ernst Junger, *The Storm of Steel* (New York: Howard Fertig, 1996). First-hand story of the trenches from a German point of view.

Peter Leese, *Shell-Shock: Traumatic Neurosis and the British Soldiers of the First World War* (Basingstoke: Palgrave/Macmillan, 2002). In-depth study of the medical approaches to shell shock.

Desmond Morton, *When Your Number's Up* (Toronto: Random House, 1993). The Canadian experience of trench warfare.

Joseph Murray, *Gallipoli 1915* (London: New English Library, 1977). A poignant account by a soldier who served throughout the campaign.

Julian Putkowski, *Shot at Dawn: Executions in World War One by Authority of the British Army Act* (Barnsley: Leo Cooper, 1996). Accusatory examination of British army executions.

Leonard Smith et al., *France and the Great War, 1914–1918* (Cambridge: Cambridge University Press, 2003). One of the very few books to look at the French side of the war.

Hew Strachan, ed., *The Oxford Illustrated History of the First World War* (Oxford: Oxford University Press, 1998). Useful general studies of the war.

Tim Travers, *The Killing Ground: The British Army, the Western Front, and the Emergence of Modern Warfare, 1900–1918* (London: Allen and Unwin, 1987). An overview of the prewar and World War I experience of the British army.

Tim Travers, *Gallipoli 1915* (Stroud: Tempus Publishing, 2001). An analysis of the campaign, using new Ottoman and German material.

Denis Winter, *Death's Men: Soldiers of the Great War* (London: Allen Lane, 1978). The life of the British soldier in World War I, emphasizing trench warfare and a critical view of the conduct of the war.

CHAPTER FIFTEEN

The War from Above: Aims, Strategy, and Diplomacy

MATTHEW STIBBE

Prior to 1914 wars were still fought for limited aims and usually ended in a negotiated settlement and the immediate restoration of trade. The growing liberalization of world markets and commerce reinforced this trend, as did the emergence of new international conventions governing the rules of military and naval engagement. During World War I, however, the mass mobilization of industrial resources and the apparent steadfastness of the two rival coalitions (the Allies or Entente and the Central Powers) went hand in hand with a ruthless disregard for the rights of combatants, civilians, and occupied populations, and a determination to fight on to the bitter end. For the generals and politicians on both sides, the stakes were simply too high to contemplate anything other than total victory, even as total victory seemed increasingly unobtainable. The continued German occupation of 95 percent of Belgium, including the strategically significant ports of Antwerp and Zeebrugge, proved to be one of the major sticking points. Whereas Britain and France insisted on the full and unconditional restoration of Belgian independence as a precondition for any peace settlement, Germany was determined not to abandon its demands for appropriate "guarantees" and "securities," lest Belgium should join the anti-German camp in the future. In addition, after 1915 Germany and Austria-Hungary developed rival plans to expand their sphere of influence over Russian Poland, while in 1918 Britain, France, and the United States championed the right of self-determination for the Poles and other subject nationalities of east-central Europe, a move with far-reaching consequences for Russia as well as for the two Central Powers.

The deadlock over Belgium and Poland, combined with Allied plans to weaken the German economy and deny Germany equal trading rights after the war, in turn doomed all attempts to achieve a peace settlement via neutral mediation. To round the circle, the history of war aims and of failed attempts to negotiate a compromise peace provides the background to understanding changes in military strategy, especially after the first winter of the war. With stalemate in the west, both sides looked for alternative fronts or for "miracle weapons" which could deliver victory in one knockout blow. Compromise was not an option for either side; total war required total commitment. Only when the German high command finally conceded defeat at the end of September 1918 was the way open for an armistice and the end of the conflict. Until then, the outcome of the war was still uncertain, in spite of America's intervention on the side of the Allies.

In what follows we shall look at each of these three issues in turn, beginning with war aims, moving on to strategy, and ending with diplomacy.

War Aims

Over the past forty years or so the volume of literature on the war aims of the great powers has continued to grow, thanks largely to the discovery of fresh archival evidence. A major turning point was the publication in 1961 of Fritz Fischer's book *Germany's Aims in the First World War*, which has shaped international debate ever since. Fischer's conclusions were at first extremely controversial, not least because he argued that Germany's leaders had deliberately unleashed war in Europe in July 1914 as part of a "grasp at world power" which in many ways paralleled Hitler's ambitions in the 1940s. In fact, though, a closer reading of Fischer reveals that his argument was considerably more subtle than some of his detractors claimed. Throughout the years 1914–18 different government departments put forward ambitious war aims programs, and argued over how much Germany could or should demand from the enemy at peace negotiations. The most famous statement of war aims was the secret memorandum drawn up on behalf of the chancellor, Theobald von Bethmann Hollweg, in September 1914, which called for substantial annexations on the European continent at the expense of France, Belgium, and Luxembourg, as well as a new German colonial empire in central Africa. In the east, Russia would have its borders pushed back "as far as possible" and its "domination over the non-Russian vassal peoples" would be "broken." In western and central Europe, Germany would establish a customs union as a means of obtaining indirect control over the economies of several independent states, including the Netherlands, France, Belgium, and Denmark. If necessary, Britain could be excluded from the continent by this means, thus ensuring its defeat in a "Second Punic War."[1]

Bethmann's program represented the aims of the moderate imperialists in Berlin. On the extreme right, however, there were organizations like the Pan-German League and the Independent Committee for a German Peace which wanted to go even further in subjugating Europe to Germany's will. The Independent Committee, for example, demanded the wholesale annexation of the Polish frontier districts, Lithuania, and the Baltic states, regardless of the wishes of their inhabitants. The annexed territories would be used not only to create a security zone against Russia (as Bethmann had suggested), but also for purposes of colonization (i.e., they would be resettled with German farmers who would exploit the east's abundance of natural resources and thereby reduce Germany's dependence on international trade).[2] Other annexationist groups were more interested in the expansion of the German colonial empire and trading posts overseas, an enthusiasm shared by several government departments, including the colonial office, the naval office, and the admiralty. In November and December 1916, for instance, the chief of the admiralty staff, Admiral Henning von Holtzendorff, outlined an ambitious program for the acquisition of new naval bases along the coasts of Belgium and Courland, west and east Africa, the west and east Indian Ocean, the Azores and Dakar, and the Mediterranean. The key objective, as he wrote to the Kaiser on May 18, 1917, was to "retain control over the colonial empire in a future war and to fight a trade war and protect our trading interests." This, combined with extra spending on naval armaments, would eventually allow Germany to challenge Britain's domination of the seas.[3]

While Germany arguably had the most aggressive war aims between 1914 and 1918, imperialism was a global phenomenon and was certainly not confined to one side. Among the Central Powers, Turkey and Bulgaria were more or less willing to follow Germany's lead as far as military operations were concerned, although Turkey in particular remained suspicious of Berlin's attempts to interfere in its domestic affairs.[4] Germany's most important ally, Austria-Hungary, on the other hand, was keen to assert from the beginning that it had ambitions of its own. These included some minor frontier changes on the borders with Italy and Romania, as well as a major drive towards expansion in the Balkans at the expense of Serbia and Montenegro and the establishment of a protectorate over Albania. More controversially, the Habsburg Empire also claimed a say in the future of Russian Poland, insisting first of all on the unification of the Austrian province of Galicia and Russian Poland under Habsburg tutelage (the so-called Austro-Polish solution), and later, after Bethmann and his advisors rejected this plan, demanding equal rights with the German Reich in the newly proclaimed "independent" Kingdom of Poland in November 1916. Austrian ambitions in Poland were of course regarded with great suspicion in Berlin, not least because an increase in the Polish population of the Habsburg Empire would also weaken the influence of the German-speaking element, which was not in Germany's long-term interests. The Hungarian Prime Minister Count István Tisza was also wary of any arrangement which might upset the delicate balance between the two halves of the Habsburg Empire, and argued that Hungary should be compensated with Bosnia-Herzegovina and Dalmatia if Austria acquired parts of Russian Poland.[5]

Turning now to the Allies, Japan and Russia were the first to draw up a comprehensive set of war aims in August 1914. Japan demanded support for its claims to Kiaochow (the Chinese port leased to Germany) as a condition of its entry into the war on August 23, 1914; later, it sought to expand its markets and influence in southern Manchuria and China's Shantung province, while weakening the influence of other powers in these regions. Russia likewise revealed a series of aggressive war aims in the opening stages of the war. The 13 point program drawn up by the foreign minister Sergei Sazonov in September 1914 and presented to the British and French ambassadors in St Petersburg/Petrograd provided details of the planned seizure of German territory in Posen and Silesia, and of Austrian territory in Galicia. Most of this land would be handed to a new "Kingdom of Poland" under Russian sovereignty, but some of it would be directly annexed by the tsar. In the west, France would acquire Alsace-Lorraine and parts of the Rhineland, while the remainder of the German empire would be further weakened through the confiscation of its overseas colonies, the return of Schleswig-Holstein to Denmark, and the restoration of the Kingdom of Hanover. As for east-central Europe, Sazonov's program envisaged the division of the Habsburg Empire into three independent kingdoms: Austria, Hungary, and Bohemia. Serbia, Russia's principal ally in the Balkans, would be handed Bosnia-Herzegovina, the Dalmatian coastline, and the northern part of Albania. Through its alliance with Greater Serbia, Russia would be in a position to exert a significant influence on the future shape of Balkan politics, effectively canceling out any German or Habsburg presence there.[6]

Unlike Japan and Russia, Britain and France at first resisted the temptation to put forward specific territorial demands of their own, fearing that this would be divisive and a potential threat to national as well as Allied unity. Instead, they stuck to much vaguer formulations about the need to "liberate" Europe from the dangers of "Prussian militarism." A formidable propaganda campaign was set in motion in order to convince the world that Germany had committed a monstrous act by violating the neutrality of Belgium and terrorizing its civilian inhabitants; German counter-claims were far less successful. Indeed, the one aim to which Britain and France remained committed from the beginning was the restoration of Belgian independence. In Britain in particular it was the Belgian issue that had persuaded nominally pacifist members of parliament on the Liberal and Labour benches to swing round in support of the war.[7]

France, admittedly, had another agenda after 1914: the return of the provinces of Alsace and Lorraine, lost to Germany in 1871 and since then a bone of contention for nationalist opinion on the left and the right. French politicians were also keen to secure financial compensation from the Germans for the devastation caused in occupied northern France and Belgium, and some on the extreme right even wished to see the Reich destroyed and split up into several different states. Secretly, the French government and general staff were also moving in a similar direction, although French ministers stopped short of calling for an end to German unity. During 1915 and 1916 the government of Aristide Briand considered various schemes for the annexation of the industrialized Saar region and for the separation of the Rhineland from the rest of Germany. This formed the basis of a confidential agreement with Tsar Nicholas II in February–March 1917 whereby Russia pledged to recognize French claims to hegemony on the left bank of the Rhine in return for "complete liberty" to redraw its own borders with Germany and Austria-Hungary in the east. Although the French cabinet had not collectively approved this agreement before it was signed, Briand's successor Alexandre Ribot remained committed to it, at least until the changing situation in Russia forced a serious reconsideration.[8]

British leaders, on the other hand, were very wary about taking substantial amounts of territory from Germany after the war, fearing that this would upset the balance of power on the continent. Alsace-Lorraine was considered an acceptable French war aim, but the Rhineland was not. David Lloyd George, prime minister from December 1916, was also personally committed to the establishment of a completely independent Polish state after the war, and, as a former radical, had few sympathies for the claims of hereditary rulers, whether German, Austrian, or Russian. Self-determination for subject peoples indeed became a key British goal inside Europe in 1918. This involved the restoration of prewar Belgium, Romania, Montenegro, and Serbia, and a more vague declaration of sympathy for the national aspirations of the Czechs, Romanians, and south Slavs living under Habsburg rule.[9] Beyond this, the British cabinet and the British press wanted to punish the Kaiser and his senior generals for having caused the war, both for reasons of "justice" and also to set an example. In Lloyd George's estimation, Germany's military rulers were a "dangerous anachronism in the twentieth century," while no peace was possible without "reparation for injuries done in violation of international law."[10]

This appeal for "justice" and "freedom" does not mean that Britain had no imperialist goals outside Europe, however. Indeed, as David Stevenson argues, "British
[war aims] policy combined uncertainty and even altruism within Europe with
Realpolitik outside."[11] In particular, British leaders demanded that the German navy
should be eliminated in its entirety and that German naval bases in Africa and elsewhere should be permanently occupied or at least rendered harmless to British
interests. In March–April 1917 the Curzon Committee on war aims called for
Germany to be dispossessed of all its overseas colonies, regardless of their strategic
worth, but Lloyd George refused to be bound by this. Instead, he kept open the
option of returning some of Germany's colonies in return for concessions on other
matters. Nonetheless, it was clear that Britain intended to annex substantial parts of
German east Africa, including Tanganyika. Australia, New Zealand, and South Africa
also expected to hold on to German possessions they had captured in Africa and the
south Pacific soon after the beginning of the war.[12]

In addition to looking after its own imperial interests, Britain sponsored imperialism in a wider sense in that it supported the territorial ambitions of its allies, usually
at the expense of freedom for oppressed colonial peoples. Thus in August 1914 and
February 1916 agreements were reached with France over the future of Togoland
and the Cameroons. Likewise, Italy and Romania were brought into the war in 1915
and 1916 respectively through secret offers of territorial gains at the expense of
Austria, Hungary, and the future Yugoslavia. Italy was also offered a sphere of influence in Asia Minor, even though this broke with a longstanding British commitment
to uphold the integrity of the Ottoman Empire. And in February 1917 the Lloyd
George government came to a new arrangement with Japan over the division of
Germany's colonies in the Pacific region. Like other wartime deals between the Allies,
this agreement was made behind closed doors and was not subject to public discussion or approval.

The most controversial aspect of British war aims policy, however, was the ambitious program for the expansion of western interests and capital in the middle east
at the expense of both the Ottoman Turks and the Arabs. Here, a breathtaking concession to tsarist Russia over Constantinople in March 1915 was followed by the
infamous Sykes-Picot agreement of January 1916 outlining British and French areas
of "direct or indirect" control over Syria, Lebanon, Palestine, the Transjordan, and
Mesopotamia in the event of a collapse of Turkish power there. This agreement
contradicted the spirit, if not the exact text, of a letter sent by Sir Henry McMahon,
the British high commissioner in Cairo, to Hussain ibn Ali, the Sharif of Mecca, in
October 1915, in which McMahon promised British recognition of the Arab claim
to independence in return for Hussain's willingness to side with the Allies and accept
British advisors. Meanwhile, in November 1917, the British government added to
its other undertakings by publicly committing itself to the "establishment in Palestine
of a national home for the Jewish people," a key aim of the World Zionist Federation.[13]
How this project could be realized without leading to a rise in intercommunal hatreds
and without infringing on the rights of the native Arab and non-Arab populations
remained unclear, however, leaving Britain vulnerable to accusations that it had seriously underestimated the complexities of the Palestinian question.

At first sight it seems that the United States government, which came into the
war on the Allied side in April 1917, was determined to do things very differently

and above all to avoid involvement in the kind of secret deals and covenants that had characterized the war aims policies of the European powers. Indeed, in his message to Congress on April 2, 1917 and in his Fourteen Points of January 1918, President Woodrow Wilson outlined his vision for a new world order based on open diplomacy, the limitation of armaments, and the establishment of a League of Nations. Some of the Fourteen Points, if taken at face value, were directed more against Britain and France than against Germany, in particular the demand for a "free, open-minded and absolutely impartial adjustment of all colonial claims" and for "absolute freedom of navigation upon the seas." In general, Wilson made it clear to his coalition partners and to the American people at home that the USA was not an allied but an "associated" power, bound by no treaties and free to act independently at all times. The USA would not and could not fight a war for British, French, Japanese, or Italian imperial interests. Nonetheless, after April 1917 Wilson ruled out any peace settlement with Germany that involved leaving the existing regime in power, and even rejected an offer of mediation by Pope Benedict XV in August 1917 on the grounds that "no man [and] no nation could depend on" the word of Germany's military rulers.[14]

In many ways, indeed, America after 1917 was even more concerned to stand up to German militarism and aggression than the older democracies in Europe. The desire to hold Germany to account for alleged war crimes, for instance, was as much a part of Wilson's agenda as it was of Lloyd George's. At the same time, America wished to expand its world trade interests, and Germany's desire for economic and political hegemony in Europe stood in the way of this. In a speech in Philadelphia on May 10, 1915 Wilson declared that the American nation was "too proud to fight," but behind the scenes most members of the Wilson administration were pro-Ally and became more so as time went by. One person who had to be more circumspect in public than others was the senior American diplomat Joseph C. Grew, first secretary at the US embassy in Berlin between 1912 and 1917, who was often accused of having pro-German tendencies by his friends and family back home in Massachusetts. In a fascinating letter written to his father-in-law on December 6, 1914 he revealed his innermost feelings, and those of his wife:

> Whatever may be our sympathy for individual Germans . . . we are, at heart, entirely pro-Ally. We are opposed to the German cause, and all it stands for, the origin of the war, the method of conducting it, the dropping of bombs on defenseless cities, killing innocent people, the shooting of non-combatants, the violation of the Red Cross, the maiming of the wounded – all these things have horrified and disgusted us as much as they have you – so far as they are true, though we are convinced – with our many sources of information – that of every ten such reports published and told in the US, nine are exaggerated or false. We believe that a German victory would be a step backward in civilization and a misfortune to mankind, and we realize that if militarism is not now killed once and for ever, the progress of the world will be retarded for many generations to come.[15]

Once America had entered the war on April 6, 1917, the country's "extraordinary capacity for industrial production and human organization took possession of the nation's energies," as John Keegan puts it.[16] Economic self-interest and genuine idealism combined to make the USA's "moral imperialism" as much a force for violence as the imperialism of the older European powers. Washington nonetheless continued to present itself as an "impartial" mediator in international affairs, and many radicals and socialists in Germany as well as in Britain and France looked to Wilson to prevent an imperialist "peace of victors."

Strategy

In August 1914 the Germans were faced, as they were briefly in September 1939 and again in June 1941, with the specter of war on two fronts. Their strategy – based broadly on the so-called Schlieffen Plan of 1905 – was to knock out France quickly in the west, capture Paris, and then move with equal rapidity against Russia in the east, before the tsar could bring the full weight of his armies into the field. Accordingly the Germans advanced into Belgium and northern France in the opening days of the fighting, but were halted about 40 miles short of Paris on the River Marne just six weeks into the war. Meanwhile, the Russians mobilized more quickly than the German general staff had predicted, and invaded East Prussia at the end of August 1914. Paul von Hindenburg, the new German commander-in-chief in the east, counter-attacked and the Russians were badly beaten at Tannenberg with 90,000 taken prisoner. The Russians arguably never recovered from this first defeat, while Hindenburg rapidly advanced to fame in Germany as a national hero and possibly even as an *Ersatzkaiser*, once Wilhelm II had turned out to be an uninspiring war leader. The Habsburg army too had been exposed as weak and ill-prepared, a liability rather than an asset to Germany, although it is notable that there were no major revolts among the empire's subject nationalities until 1918.

Meanwhile, the building of defensive trenches from Flanders to the Swiss border and the failure by Germany to capture Paris or the French Channel ports ended the war of movement in the west and with it the expectation of rapid victory. In spite of this, neither the Central Powers nor the Allies tried to limit the war or to sue for a general peace. In the coming months, as the stalemate on the western front solidified, both sides looked for new allies and new strategies. The Central Powers scored the first notable successes when they brought Turkey into the war on their side in October 1914, followed by Bulgaria in October 1915. The alliance with Turkey in particular was crucial, as it enabled the closing of the Dardanelles Straits, disrupting the Allies' main supply route to Russia and tying down British troops in Egypt and elsewhere. On December 18, 1914 the Russian commander-in-chief, Grand Duke Nikolai Nikolaevich, admitted to his French and British counterparts that shortages of ammunition were hampering the Russian war effort on all fronts; efforts to increase domestic production had failed and the rerouting of supplies through Arctic ports like Archangel could not plug the gap left by the closing of the Straits.[17] In addition, the Turkish sultan had now declared a *jihad* or holy war against the Allied forces in the middle east, enabling Germany to put into motion plans to stir up discontent among the Muslim subjects of the British and Russian empires. This undoubtedly put further pressure on Russia in the Caucasus region.[18]

Throughout 1915 German military advisors led Turkish forces in shoring up the Ottoman Empire's defenses on the Dardanelles, which, in the end, managed to repel an attempted Anglo-French invasion at Gallipoli, southwest of Constantinople. Up to 300,000 Turks and 265,000 Allied servicemen were killed or wounded in this campaign before it was finally abandoned in January 1916, with particularly severe losses among the Anzacs, volunteers from Australia and New Zealand.[19] Combined German, Austro-Hungarian, and Bulgarian forces also succeeded in overrunning Serbia at the end of 1915 and Romania at the end of 1916, allowing the Central Powers to create a continuous strip of territory from Berlin through to Constantinople and beyond. There was more good news for the Central Powers when a British expeditionary force sent into Mesopotamia (Iraq) was surrounded and captured at Kut al-Amara in April 1916. On the western front, the German army managed to repel several major British and French offensives in 1916–17, while inflicting maximum damage at Verdun and on the Somme. The biggest blow for the Allies came in December 1917, when the new Bolshevik government in Russia sued for peace on terms highly favorable to Germany and Austria-Hungary. This seemed to be a vindication of the decision taken by the German high command to allow the Bolshevik leader Lenin safe passage through Germany on his way home from Zurich to Petrograd (later renamed Leningrad) in April 1917.

In other respects, however, the Central Powers fared less well. The plan to create a pro-independence Irish army from captured Irish prisoners of war under the rebel leader Sir Roger Casement, first hatched in Berlin in November 1914, came to nothing, as Casement could not find the necessary recruits. In the end the Easter Rising in Dublin in 1916 went ahead without German support, only to collapse within days of its outbreak. Likewise, an attempted German–Turkish invasion of the Suez Canal ended in complete failure, as did plans to encourage Islamic revolts against British rule in Egypt and India. In fact, it was the Turkish sultan who turned out to be more vulnerable to nationalist unrest in the Middle East, especially after the announcement of the British-backed Arab revolt in June 1916. Above all, however, Austria-Hungary proved to be a weak and unreliable ally for Germany, and was always having to be bailed out, most notably in the summer of 1916 when the Russians launched a surprise offensive on the eastern front under General Brusilov. Only after the intervention of German troops was the Brusilov offensive pushed back, leading to a momentary crisis of confidence in Berlin. As the chief of the general staff, Erich von Falkenhayn, put it on August 21, 1916: "Every redeployment in one direction leads inevitably to a dangerous weakening in other places which – if even the slightest error is made with regard to our assessment of the enemy's next moves – could lead to our destruction."[20]

How to break the stalemate on the western front remained the crucial strategic question for both sides. As well as mass bombardments followed by orders to go over the top, poisonous gas, flamethrowers, and other deadly weapons were used, causing huge numbers of casualties for no immediate gain. The brutalizing effects of trench warfare were also evident in occasional, but very real, instances of prisoner killing on both sides in contravention of international law. This had important strategic as well as humanitarian implications, for, as Niall Ferguson has argued, in the end it was numbers captured rather than numbers wounded or killed that determined the outcome of the war. Thus high levels of desertion and surrender heralded the collapse of the Russian army on the eastern front in late 1917, and of the Italian army after the battle of Caporetto (October 1917). A similar pattern, albeit on a slightly lesser scale, was seen with the German army on the western front in the late summer of 1918. Crucial here, according to Ferguson, was a shift in Allied propaganda towards bombarding frontline German soldiers with offers of food and humane treatment if they surrendered; this, he argues, was a more effective means of undermining enemy morale and discipline than the order to "take no prisoners."[21]

The war at sea was very different in this respect. Here the main target was civilians (via economic blockade and submarine warfare) and they were encouraged to surrender not through promises of food and comforts but through disruption to living standards and slow starvation. In this sense, Britain possessed a decisive strategic advantage over Germany. Its geographic position allowed it to mount a distant blockade of the German coastline using surface ships, effectively cutting off the Central Powers from trade with the outside world and with America in particular. German propagandists reacted angrily, accusing Britain of gross violations of the rules of war and the rights of neutrals. However, in reality the Central Powers could strike back against British supply lines only by unleashing the submarine, a dangerous weapon when used indiscriminately, as the international outcry caused by the sinking of the *Lusitania* off the coast of Ireland in May 1915 showed. The alternative option of breaking the blockade by drawing the Royal Navy into an all-out showdown for control of the North Sea was considered too risky, particularly as Britain still had a numerical advantage in terms of battleships. Indeed, only once did the British and German fleets face each other for a serious fight: at the battle of Jutland on May 31, 1916. The result was inconclusive, although Admiral von Scheer, the commander of the German High Seas Fleet, subsequently advised the Kaiser against further naval engagements as "there can be no doubt that even the best possible outcome . . . would not force England to make peace in this war."[22]

Instead, Scheer joined the growing number of naval strategists in Germany calling for the resumption of unrestricted submarine warfare as the only possible means of compelling Britain to surrender. During the first half of 1916 the Kaiser and Bethmann Hollweg still resolutely refused to countenance such a move, on the grounds that it would bring America and other neutrals into the war without securing any significant strategic advantages for the Central Powers. However, a major turning point came at the end of August 1916 when the chief of the general staff, Falkenhayn, was replaced by Hindenburg, with Erich Ludendorff as first quartermaster general. The latter were determined to force through an ambitious program of total mobilization of all the nation's resources for victory: unrestricted submarine warfare was a necessary part of this plan. At a Crown Council meeting at Pleß on January 9, 1917 Bethmann's objections were overruled and the decision was reached to unleash the submarines from February 1. According to the calculations of a host of civilian experts, backed by German admirals and the naval high command, Britain would now be defeated within six months or less, rendering any American assistance irrelevant.

At first it seemed as if they might be right. In the spring of 1917, the German U-boats managed to sink even more than the predicted 600,000 tons of food per month.[23] However, the British agreed to adopt the so-called convoy system, which made the transatlantic run far less hazardous for ships in the second half of 1917, and helped, in the end, to defeat the German blockade of the western powers. At the same time, the German submarine campaign did more than anything else to bring the United States into the war. Wilson broke off diplomatic relations with Germany on February 2, 1917, and declared war on April 6. In the short term, America's intervention had little noticeable effect, but in the long run it tipped the military and economic balance decisively in favor of the Allies. By December 1917 there were already 176,000 American troops in France, and by March 1918 the total had reached 318,000. These were the forerunners of a much larger force of 1.3 million Americans and several million British, French, Canadian, and Belgian troops deployed in the Allied counter-offensive on the western front in August 1918, which finally forced the German high command to sue for peace.[24]

Diplomacy

War aims and the search for alternative strategies to win the war both involved an avoidance of the question of peace. Restoration of the *status quo ante bellum* was unacceptable to both sides. Indeed, those who talked of peace were marginalized and persecuted in all countries. In Germany the socialists Rosa Luxemburg, Clara Zetkin, and Karl Liebknecht were imprisoned, and bourgeois pacifists were subject to close police surveillance. In June 1917 Britain, France, Italy, and America joined together to thwart a proposed conference of neutral and belligerent socialist parties in Stockholm, and without their support the project – part of a joint Russian–Dutch–Scandinavian initiative – eventually collapsed. When the British cabinet minister and former Unionist foreign secretary Lord Lansdowne wrote a letter to the editor of the *Daily Telegraph* in November 1917 calling for a negotiated settlement on pragmatic and humanitarian grounds, he was disowned by his own party and widely vilified in the British press.

Even so, behind the scenes the Germans and the Russians were already discussing possible peace terms by the end of 1914, and all the belligerents were involved at one time or another in secret negotiations with the enemy. Throughout the war Germany hoped to detach one of the Allies from the rest, and at first it seemed that Russia was the best bet. Subsequently, channels of communication between the Kaiser and the tsar were developed through various intermediaries, including the king of Denmark, Christian X, and one of his aides, the shipping magnate Hans Niels Andersen. Contacts were also made with the former Russian prime minister Count Sergei Witte, who was known to have pro-German sympathies.[25] For the time being, however, the Russians stuck to the Pact of London (September 1914) by which the Allies were bound not to make a separate peace with the Central Powers. After Italy joined the war in May 1915, it too signed up to the terms of the Pact of London in return for a promise of Allied support for its territorial demands against Austria and the Ottoman Empire.

In 1915 and 1916 fresh opportunities for a general peace settlement came through the offices of Colonel Edward M. House, Woodrow Wilson's special envoy to Europe. House traveled across the Atlantic three times in a failed bid to persuade the warring powers to specify their minimum terms. At the end of January 1916 his efforts collapsed when Bethmann Hollweg refused to relinquish his demands for "safeguards" in Belgium and Poland, and also asked for territorial compensations in northern France, terms which were completely unacceptable to London and Paris. Subsequently, House proposed to the British foreign secretary Sir Edward Grey that a conference be held to end the war, and that minimum peace terms would include "the restoration of Belgium, the transfer of Alsace and Lorraine to France, and the acquisition by Russia of an outlet to the sea." Germany would be offered territorial concessions outside Europe; but if it refused to attend the conference, then the United States would "probably" enter the war on the side of the Allies (the House–Grey memorandum, February 22, 1916). Wilson knew of and approved House's statement to Grey, but later tried to distance himself from direct involvement in the affairs of Europe when it became clear that this might jeopardize his chances of being reelected as president in November 1916. The French and British governments were also reluctant to commit themselves to specific peace terms before they knew the views of their other alliance partners (i.e., Italy, Russia, and Japan).

Wilson's election victory in November enabled him to return to his quest for peace in Europe and the reordering of international relations. A key turning point came on December 5 when the Central Powers offered a general peace without specific terms, thereby preempting Wilson's own offer of mediation which was issued two weeks later. Wilson's offer enabled Britain and France to put forward their own peace proposals, while highlighting the fact that Berlin was simply looking for an excuse to resume unrestricted submarine warfare. Allied unity remained unshaken, in spite of the Central Powers' victory over Romania and a worsening supply crisis in Russia.

In the early part of 1917 German diplomacy made its most serious blunder yet, when, in anticipation of a final break with the United States over unrestricted submarine warfare, the foreign secretary Arthur Zimmermann sent a secret telegram to the German ambassador in Mexico instructing him to offer the Mexican government financial support and the chance to reconquer the lost territories of New Mexico, Texas, and Arizona in return for a joint declaration of war against America. This so-called "Zimmermann Telegram" was intercepted by British intelligence and published in the United States on March 1, 1917, thus playing straight into the hands of Wilson and the advocates of war. The offense caused by Zimmermann was made even worse by his apparent offer of a similar deal to Japan to join in an attack on the USA. It was only a matter of time before Wilson made a formal declaration on this issue, and he now had most of the nation behind him, including the previously isolationist states in the southwest.[26]

Meanwhile, the overthrow of Tsar Nicholas II in Russia in March 1917 opened up new opportunities for a settlement in the shape of the Petrograd Soviet's call for a peace without annexations or indemnities. Strikers in Germany in April 1917 raised the same demand, but it was ignored by both the German and Russian governments, and by the western Allies, who preferred to engage in secret talks with the new rulers in Petrograd, as well as with contacts in Vienna. A French plan to negotiate a separate peace with Austria-Hungary via Prince Sixtus de Bourbon, the brother-in-law of the new Emperor Karl, foundered because of Italian opposition in April 1917, while the provisional government in Russia publicly confirmed its claim to Constantinople and the Straits in May 1917. In Germany, the new Chancellor Georg Michaelis paid lip-service to the Reichstag peace resolution of July 19, 1917, which rejected "territorial acquisitions imposed by force" and called for a "peace of understanding" in order to banish "hostility between nations." In reality, though, the high command under Hindenburg and Ludendorff now controlled German war aims policy behind the scenes and were able to block any moves towards what they saw as a policy of surrender.

The nearest the powers came to a negotiated settlement was in the late summer of 1917, when the Papal Peace Note of August 1, coupled with reports of the imminent collapse of Russia's war effort on the eastern front, encouraged the opening of tentative channels of communication between Germany and Britain. In September 1917 Lloyd George came close to accepting the idea of a separate peace at the expense of Russia, but his cabinet colleagues were unwilling to jeopardize the unity of the Entente and insisted that Britain's partners would have to be approached first. In Berlin, however, the new foreign secretary, Richard von Kühlmann, was unwilling to negotiate with the Allies as a whole, believing that this was not to the Central Powers' advantage. Fierce opposition from the admiralty, backed by the high command, also prevented him from offering Britain the one concession that might have ended the war: unconditional restoration of Belgium, including the Flanders coast.[27] Meanwhile, another channel of communication, this time between Germany and France, was closed after the French foreign minister, Alexandre Ribot, vetoed a proposed meeting between French and German officials in Switzerland. In the end, as David Stevenson argues, the rulers in Berlin were unwilling to sacrifice any meaningful part of their war aims program in the west in exchange for peace. What was offered was too vague to persuade either France or Britain to abandon Russia, which was still at this time ruled by a provisional government under the moderate socialist Alexander Kerensky and remained – at least in theory – committed to the war.[28] Events in Petrograd and on the eastern front were nonetheless to prove critical in the following weeks.

The Turning Point: November 1917–November 1918

While the summer of 1917 had seen a flurry of diplomatic initiatives in favor of a negotiated peace, in the last few months of that year both sides suddenly became more optimistic that victory could be achieved by military means. In Germany, for instance, Hindenburg and Ludendorff believed that they could knock Russia out of the war before the end of the winter, allowing them to plan a new offensive in France for the following spring. The Bolshevik seizure of power in November 1917 led to the complete collapse of the Russian army on the eastern front, and an armistice was signed in December. Foreign Secretary Kühlmann's pleas for a moderate peace settlement with Russia were brushed aside by Ludendorff, and the eventual Treaty of Brest-Litovsk gave Germany direct or indirect control over vast swathes of non-Russian (but formerly tsarist-ruled) territory in eastern Europe. Austria-Hungary, the junior partner in the negotiations, was now on its last legs, with Germany taking ruthless advantage of the weakness of its ally to demand a dominant position in Poland, Courland, Lithuania, the Baltic provinces, Finland, and the Ukraine.

Britain and France were also more optimistic about the possibility of victory by the end of 1917. The German submarine blockade had been largely overcome through the adoption of the convoy system, and American credits had restored Allied finances to a reasonable state of health. The news from the east was grim, and up to 300,000 Italians had been captured at Caporetto in October 1917, but this was at least partly offset by the growing number of US soldiers arriving in France. Furthermore, there were signs that the home fronts in Germany and Austria-Hungary were beginning to crack, with big strikes in Vienna, Leipzig, Berlin, and other major industrial cities in January 1918. Above all, Wilson's Fourteen Points seemed to add moral force to the Allied cause, and although the president had clearly not endorsed all of the Allies' war aims, he at least seemed to support the demand for the full restoration of Belgium, Serbia, Romania, and Montenegro, the return of Alsace-Lorraine to France, the creation of an independent Poland, the granting of "autonomous development" to the subject nations of Austria-Hungary, and the "readjustment of the frontiers" between Austria and Italy "along clearly recognizable lines of nationality." There was thus everything still to fight for.

Nonetheless, when the German spring offensive began in March 1918, the Allies were caught on the defensive and Ludendorff's armies again got perilously close to reaching their target, Paris. Only after the military turn-around in July and August, when German units were forced into full-scale retreat on the western front, followed by the total collapse of Bulgaria, Turkey, and Austria-Hungary a few weeks later, did Hindenburg and Ludendorff call for the opening of secret talks with the enemy. Constitutional reforms were also announced, in order to make Germany appear more democratic. In the course of negotiations, however, the issue of the monarchy arose, with Wilson again calling for the Kaiser to abdicate as a precondition for an armistice. In late October the extreme right-wing Fatherland Party, a successor to the Independent Committee for a German Peace, briefly considered the idea of launching a popular uprising in defense of the monarchy and in favor of continuation of war, but this project never got off the ground. By the beginning of November 1918, with naval mutinies spreading from Wilhelmshaven and Kiel to other German ports, and workers' and soldiers' councils taking control of many key cities, rumors circulated that the government had fallen and the socialists had seized power. Other rumors suggested that the Kaiser might be gathering together an army from loyal remnants in Belgium which would march back into Germany to restore law and order. Civil war was indeed in the air and it was now clear that the war was lost.

In the end, the German revolution, when it came, was considerably less violent than at first feared. The Kaiser was advised to go quietly on November 9, fleeing from Supreme Headquarters in Spa, Belgium to the safety of the Netherlands, where he formally abdicated on November 28. Meanwhile, moderate socialists led by Friedrich Ebert and Philipp Scheidemann prevented a fully-fledged communist takeover by negotiating a secret deal with the new first quartermaster general of the army, General Groener, to crush any "Bolshevik" disturbances. The new German republic was to be a western-style parliamentary democracy, and not a Leninist "dictatorship of the proletariat." Nonetheless, the total surrender of November 11 came as a shock to the German people, who had been led by the press to believe in victory almost up until the last week of the war. Some could never accept defeat: instead, they took flight in myths about the invincibility of the German army and the alleged treachery of the home front.[29] Most soldiers were glad to go home, however, and it is interesting to note that in September 1939 enthusiasm for war was far less evident in Germany – and elsewhere in Europe – than it had been in August 1914.

NOTES

1 Fritz Fischer, *Germany's Aims in the First World War* (London: Chatto and Windus, 1967), esp. pp. 103–6.
2 On the Independent Committee see K.-H. Schädlich, "Der 'Unabhängige Ausschuß für einen deutschen Frieden' als Zentrum der Annexionspropaganda im Ersten Weltkrieg,"

in *Politik im Krieg. Studien zur Politik der deutschen herrschenden Klassen im Ersten Weltkrieg*, Fritz Klein et al, eds (Berlin: Akademie Verlag, 1964), pp. 50–65.

3 Helmut Stoecker, ed., *German Imperialism in Africa* (London: Hurst, 1986), p. 290. See also Holger H. Herwig, "Admirals *versus* Generals: The War Aims of the Imperial German Navy, 1914–1918," *Central European History* 5 (1972): 208–33.

4 See Ulrich Trumpener, *Germany and the Ottoman Empire, 1914–1918* (Princeton NJ: Princeton University Press, 1968), p. 370.

5 Holger H. Herwig, *The First World War: Germany and Austria-Hungary, 1914–1918* (London: Arnold, 1997), p. 160.

6 See Horst G. Linke, *Das zarische Rußland und der Erste Weltkrieg. Diplomatie und Kriegsziele, 1914–1917* (Munich: W. Fink, 1982), p. 39.

7 On the Belgian question, see John Horne and Alan Kramer, *German Atrocities 1914: A History of Denial* (New Haven, CT: Yale University Press, 2001).

8 See David Stevenson, *French War Aims against Germany, 1914–1919* (Oxford: Clarendon Press, 1982), pp. 53–6.

9 On British war aims the key book is Victor H. Rothwell, *British War Aims and Peace Diplomacy, 1914–1918* (Oxford: Clarendon Press, 1971). See also Kenneth J. Calder, *Britain and the Origins of the New Europe, 1914–1918* (Cambridge: Cambridge University Press, 1976).

10 David Lloyd George, *British War Aims: Statement by the Prime Minister on January 5th 1918* (London: HMSO, 1918), pp. 6, 14.

11 David Stevenson, *The First World War and International Politics* (Oxford: Clarendon Press, 1988), p. 107.

12 Ibid, p. 112.

13 David Lloyd George, *War Memoirs*, vol. 2, new edn (London: Odhams Press, 1938), p. 1092.

14 Wilson's reply to Pope Benedict XV, as reproduced in Lloyd George, *War Memoirs*, pp. 1220–2.

15 Joseph Grew to his father-in-law, Tom Perry, 6 December 1914, in Houghton Library, Cambridge, MA, Grew Papers, MS Am 1687 (5). Cited by permission of the Houghton Library, Harvard University.

16 John Keegan, *The First World War* (London: Hutchinson, 1998), p. 402.

17 See A. J. P. Taylor, *The Struggle for Mastery in Europe, 1848–1918* (Oxford: Clarendon Press, 1954), p. 535.

18 See Fischer, *Germany's Aims*, pp. 120ff.

19 See Keegan, *The First World War*, p. 268.

20 Matthew Stibbe, *German Anglophobia and the Great War, 1914–1918* (Cambridge: Cambridge University Press, 2001), p. 135.

21 Niall Ferguson, "Prisoner Taking and Prisoner Killing in the Age of Total War: Towards a Political Economy of Military Defeat," *War in History* 11 (2004): 148–92. Cf. Ferguson, *The Pity of War* (London: Allen Lane, 1998), pp. 339–88.

22 Stibbe, *German Anglophobia*, p. 135.

23 See Herwig, *First World War*, p. 318.

24 See Keegan, *First World War*, p. 401.

25 See Lancelot L. Farrar, Jr, *Divide and Conquer: German Efforts to Conclude a Separate Peace, 1914–1918* (London: East European Quarterly, 1978), esp. pp. 13–34.

26 See Barbara Tuchman, *The Zimmermann Telegram* (London: Constable, 1959).

27 See Herwig, "Admirals *versus* Generals," p. 220.

28 David Stevenson, "War Aims and Peace Negotiations," in *World War I: A History*, Hew Strachan, ed. (Oxford: Oxford University Press, 1998), pp. 210–11.

29 See, for example, Annelise Thimme, *Flucht in den Mythos. Die Deutschnationale Volkspartei
    und die Niederlage von 1918* (Göttingen: Vandenhoeck and Ruprecht, 1969); Ulrich
    Heinemann, *Die verdrängte Niederlage. Politische Öffentlichkeit und Kriegsschuldfrage in
    der Weimarer Republik* (Göttingen: Vandenhoeck and Ruprecht, 1983).

GUIDE TO FURTHER READING

Lancelot L. Farrar Jr, *Divide and Conquer: German Efforts to Conclude a Separate Peace,
1914–1918* (London: East European Quarterly, 1978). An important monograph on an
important subject.

Niall Ferguson, *The Pity of War* (London: Allen Lane, 1998). Offers fresh perspectives on a
whole range of issues, including a useful chapter on prisoners of war.

Fritz Fischer, *Germany's Aims in the First World War* (London: Chatto and Windus, 1967).
The English translation of the 1961 classic that launched the so-called "Fischer
controversy."

Holger H. Herwig, *The First World War: Germany and Austria-Hungary, 1914–1918* (London:
Arnold, 1997). Provides an extended analysis of the German and Austrian war efforts.

Gerhard Hirschfeld, Gerd Krumeich, and Irina Renz, eds, *Enzyklopädie Erster Weltkrieg*
(Paderborn,: Ferdinand Schöningh, 2003). A substantial reference book, with hundreds of
entries by leading scholars in the field.

John Keegan, *The First World War* (London: Hutchinson, 1998). A detailed military history
written by an expert in this genre.

Hort G. Linke, *Das zarische Rußland und der Erste Weltkrieg. Diplomatie und Kriegsziele,
1914–1917* (Munich: W. Fink, 1982). A thorough investigation of Russian war aims.

Ernest R. May, *The World War and American Isolation, 1914–1917* (Cambridge MA: Harvard
University Press, 1959). Good on the submarine controversy from an international
perspective.

Wolfgang Michalka, ed., *Der Erste Weltkrieg. Wirkung, Wahrnehmung, Analyse* (Munich: Piper,
1994). Forty-two essays, including many on the question of strategy and war aims.

Victor H. Rothwell, *British War Aims and Peace Diplomacy, 1914–1918* (Oxford: Clarendon
Press, 1971). The best and most detailed book on British war aims.

David Stevenson, *French War Aims Against Germany, 1914–1919* (Oxford: Clarendon Press,
1982). The best and most detailed book on French war aims.

David Stevenson, *The First World War and International Politics* (Oxford: Clarendon Press,
1988). Provides a clear and concise synthesis.

Matthew Stibbe, *German Anglophobia and the Great War, 1914–1918* (Cambridge: Cambridge
University Press, 2001). Focuses on the domestic background to the submarine controversy
in Germany.

Ulrich Trumpener, *Germany and the Ottoman Empire, 1914–1918* (Princeton NJ: Princeton
University Press, 1968). An intelligent and well-written monograph on German–Turkish
relations.

Barbara Tuchman, *The Zimmermann Telegram* (London: Constable, 1959). Still the standard
account after nearly fifty years.

The World War I Document Archive at www.lib.byu.edu/~rdh/wwi/. A useful website containing the full texts of the key treaties, declarations, speeches, and memoranda discussed
in the above essay.

CHAPTER SIXTEEN

The War and Revolution

MARK BAKER

One of the most widespread and consequential results of the Great War was revolution. While most non-specialists think only of the Russian revolution in this regard, in fact the war sparked several upheavals of various kinds and varying magnitudes across the European continent. In 1917–18 the three dynastic empires that ruled over much of the land area of Europe (Romanov, Habsburg, and Hohenzollern), worn down by the intense, protracted economic and social strains of fighting industrial warfare, collapsed into chaos and revolution. Although nineteenth-century Europe is often portrayed by contrast as a sort of paradise lost, there were in fact serious class and national tensions in many countries in the period leading up to the war. Along with an increasing life expectancy, material improvement, and technological advances, industrialization brought a large and growing urban working poor, living in vast, dirty, disease-ridden and alienating cities. These working people were increasingly drawn to and inspired by the ideas of social democracy, creating a formidable working-class movement before 1914 (particularly in Germany). At the same time, industrialization (especially by requiring literacy) and democratization (inspired by the American and French revolutions) promoted and encouraged the nationalisms of the various subject peoples of these empires, especially in Austria-Hungary. And because the ruling elites of these empires repeatedly rejected or ignored the have-nots' demands, many of the latter increasingly looked to a general war as a possible path to improving their lives. While this prewar situation certainly played an important role in the outbreak of revolution, this essay will focus on the ways in which the Great War contributed to the collapse of these empires, to show how the war exacerbated existing tensions and turned discontent into revolution. These empires encountered similar problems as the war progressed, but reacted in different ways depending on their particular circumstances.

Revolutions in the Russian Empire

Certainly, a revolutionary movement among some sections of the educated classes emerged in the Russian Empire long before World War I, at the latest by

1861, when Alexander II finally emancipated Russia's huge serf population (the last major European state to do so) and instituted a number of other reforms in response to defeat in the Crimean War, 1853–6. The members of this "intelligentsia," as it came to call itself, demanded a radical transformation of the empire and frequently the end of autocracy. They gradually formed into political parties, the most important of which were the Socialist Revolutionaries (SRs) and the Social Democrats (SDs); the latter in about 1903 split into the Mensheviks and Bolsheviks. In 1905 this revolutionary movement, along with Russia's defeat in the Russo-Japanese war, Bloody Sunday, January 9, 1905 (when government troops were ordered to fire on peaceful workers petitioning the tsar), workers' strikes, and peasant land seizures, combined to provoke the first Russian revolution. In the face of mounting chaos, Tsar Nicholas II begrudgingly issued a Manifesto (not a constitution), granting "his subjects" inviolability of person, freedom of speech, assembly, and association; and a kind of parliament, called a Duma, elected by estates. These changes appeared to be and were celebrated as fundamental and promising: Russia was finally moving toward democracy. In fact, they were illusory: neither Nicholas nor the educated public was committed to playing by the new rules of the game. The government soon took steps to change the rules; in June 1907 newly appointed prime minister Petr Stolypin had Nicholas dissolve the quite radical and oppositionist Second Duma. Stolypin then used a special emergency law to pass legislation sharply curtailing the Duma's electoral franchise, favoring the propertied classes (about 1 percent of the empire's population now elected a majority of deputies). Over the next seven years other rights were curtailed and frequently violated. After a brief respite, a renewed strike wave began in 1912, sparked by the massacre of workers at the Lena goldfields, and culminating in massive strikes on the eve of the war.

Almost since the outbreak of the February revolution, historians have debated the war's role in the Russian Empire's sudden collapse. While historians in the west stressed the war's decisiveness, Soviet historians increasingly proclaimed the revolution's inevitability: the war was the tsarist regime's last ditch effort to stop the great revolutionary upsurge engulfing the country; it only *delayed* the revolution. The "scientifically determined progress" towards the Great October Socialist Revolution was inevitable. These positions held until about 1964, when Leopold Haimson published the first serious attempt to analyze social change in the Russian Empire on the eve of the war. Based on his analysis of the available published documents, Haimson argued that in the period leading up to World War I dual polarizations were splitting the empire: a growing political and social rift between industrial workers and the better-off members of urban society; and another divergence between all urbanites (workers and non-workers alike) and the ruling elite supporting Nicholas and autocracy. Charting these widening cleavages, Haimson concluded: "What the war years would do was not to conceive, but to accelerate substantially, the two broad processes of polarization that had already been at work in Russian national life during the immediate prewar period."[1] Haimson's work sparked a flurry of debate on the inevitability of the revolution and a great deal of research into the role of the masses in the upheavals of 1917.[2] Although the question of the revolution's inevitability has not been settled, there is no doubt that Russia's participation in the war greatly contributed to the revolutions of 1917.

The proclamation of war provoked some fleeting enthusiasm and expressions of unity, but these were quickly dashed. Although educated society earnestly embraced the initial call to arms and thought that the masses would follow their lead, in fact most soldiers (the majority of whom were peasants) trudged off to war with sullen resignation. At the front, after some initial successes, especially against the weaker and poorly mobilized Austro-Hungarian army in Eastern Galicia, the army's repeated defeats and retreats greatly depressed and defused early enthusiasm. Horrific battle-field experiences – death, destruction, and incompetent command – turned resignation into resentment. By late 1916, 3.6 million were dead, seriously sick, or wounded.[3] Not surprisingly, frontline soldiers numbered prominently among the most radical revolutionaries in 1917.

As in all belligerent countries, more civilian involvement was provoked in Russia than in all previous wars. Although the government was resistant to such public participation, by 1915, facing a catastrophic shortage of munitions, it agreed to the organization of War Industries Committees, set up by leading industrialists to coordinate and expand military supplies. The state was characteristically suspicious of these very patriotic committees; not only was it resistant to the creation of worker representatives on the committees, but it also denied even the leading industrialists essential access to state institutions and information. In essence the bureaucracy saw the committees (and the public in general) not as partners, but as rivals.[4] Other similarly composed organizations were established to deal with various aspects of the war, especially food supply, with similar results. In consequence, the war mobilized not only soldiers, but also much of educated society, whose efforts the state largely frustrated. And as defeat followed defeat, greater public involvement led to greater public criticism.

Russian liberals and even some conservatives became increasingly disparaging of the government; their main criticism was not its continuing unwillingness to share political power with them as much as its horrid prosecution of the war. In November 1916 a leading liberal, Pavel Miliukov, concluded a poignant speech to the Duma on the government's conduct of the military campaign by asking the deputies: "What is it, stupidity or treason?" The deputies overwhelmingly (and more confidently than Miliukov) supported the latter interpretation.[5] The war, into which the tsar had stumbled in an effort to prop up Russia's waning great power status, delegitimized his authority more than any other event in 300 years of Romanov rule.

Another very consequential result of the war was a rapid increase in the price and decrease in the availability of basic foodstuffs, which the urban working population especially resented. Recent research has shown that this was not a result of lower harvests but rather the empire's insufficient transportation system and the demands of the front. In early 1917 railway cars full of spoiling food sat on rails in the south, while most of the locomotives were being used to move men, weapons, and food to the front. Territorial squabbles among provincial officials added to the problem. Hence, food, especially bread, became increasingly rare and expensive, contributing greatly to the urban working population's anger, unrest, strikes, and other disturbances, especially in the capitals, Moscow and Petrograd.

By early 1917 the war had created an explosive concoction in Russia: educated society considered the government inept and the tsar no longer in control; economic conditions were terrible; workers, despite the danger of being sent to the front, increasingly went on strike; peasants at home believed that a radical reordering of rural land relations was in the offing; radicalized soldiers at the front were on the verge of revolt. All were extremely war-weary and there was a creeping feeling that something had to give.

A new strike wave began on January 9, 1917, when about 140,000 Petrograd workers downed their tools and took to the streets, commemorating the anniversary of Bloody Sunday. On February 23, 1917, International Women's Day, a large demonstration of working women, protesting the scarcity and price of bread, turned into a massive revolt against the authorities; locked-out, striking workers from the Putilov works joined in. The demonstrators grew in boldness and demands; the authorities responded with violence, ordering police and troops to fire on demonstrators. From the start the troops appeared reluctant to fire. Over the next week more and more of the Petrograd garrison's soldiers refused to fire on the demonstrators. On February 27 the Volynsky Guard Regiment rebelled, shooting their commanding officer. By that evening workers and soldiers were in control of the capital of the largest empire on earth. They created a Soviet (Russian for council) of Workers' and Soldiers' Deputies to represent their interests and agreed to the creation of a Provisional Government composed of leading Duma deputies. Nicholas did not even manage to return from the front to Petrograd before he was persuaded by his generals, hoping to save the war effort, to abdicate in favor of his brother Mikhail. On March 3 Mikhail met with the Provisional Government and, learning that they could not guarantee his safety, declined the throne. Thus ended the 300-year old Romanov dynasty. As Hasegawa has argued, the February revolution resulted from the coincidence of the revolt of the masses against the regime, its handling of the war and food supplies, the soldiers' revolt, and middle-class opposition to the entire institution of tsarism.[6] In this revolution Russia's educated elite, whether liberals or socialists, did not lead; they followed the masses.

The February revolution was not a conclusive event. It took a long time for the revolution to spread across the vast empire; in some cities there was a violent struggle; in others the authorities quickly ran away. It took longer still to spread to the empire's many villages, where one could still find tsarist police in place as late as May 1917. And this was only the beginning; for "Glorious February" spawned a number of other revolutions.

The empire's many nationalities (who composed more than half its population) took the birth of "Free Russia" as an opportunity to explore their own national development. The year 1917 was for them also a year of national revolution, often beginning with troops of the former tsarist army organizing themselves into national units. National committees (composed mostly of educated elites) were set up to express the interests of each nation. The most successful movements combined national and economic interests; for example, Ukrainians were also (even primarily) peasants with a strong interest in land reform. Sometimes these movements sought only the right to develop their national culture or territory within a federated Russia; but most educated Russians, including the leading socialist parties and the Provisional Government, proved surprisingly resistant to such modest demands. Later, especially after the Bolsheviks seized power and revealed their great willingness to violate their own official policy of national self-determination, some nationalities sought outright independence from the former empire. Their armies then played independent roles in the emerging civil war.

Peasants also carried out their own revolution. Beginning in late spring 1917, once they began to realize just how free they had become, they embarked on an agrarian revolution, seizing land, forests, and property from all non-peasants by violent and non-violent means. This peasant revolution was massive in scale but local in scope. Indeed, the localness of these struggles suggests that there was not one peasant revolution but many, many village revolutions. Moreover, soon after they had acquired some land and forest, many peasant villages began to squabble among themselves over the appropriate redistribution; these squabbles sometimes turned into small battles between villages.[7]

Finally, there occurred one more revolution in 1917, sometimes called the "October Revolution," sometimes the "Bolshevik revolution." This one has provoked the most intense study and controversy. The Provisional Government, discredited by its continuing prosecution of the war, inability to solve the food supply problem, delay in holding the constituent assembly elections, and unwillingness to give peasants the land, came under increasing attacks from the Petrograd Soviet, especially from its Bolshevik members. On October 25, 1917, the soviet's Military Revolutionary Committee (which Leon Trotsky created to fight the counter-revolution and was Bolshevik-controlled) resolved to depose the government and declare "All Power to the Soviets!" that is, all power should belong to the councils set up and elected by workers, peasants, and soldiers across the empire. A Soviet of People's Commissars (Sovnarkom), led by Vladimir Lenin and composed of Bolsheviks, was then declared the new government, promising that it would hold the elections to the constituent assembly as soon as possible and give the people "Bread, Peace, and Land!" Very few objected to the overthrow of the Provisional Government. Many workers and soldiers, especially in Petrograd, supported the Bolsheviks' actions. Most non-Bolshevik socialists and their supporters, however, objected to the Bolsheviks' unwillingness to share power. Across the empire most people approved of the idea of "All Power to the Soviets!" but interpreted this to mean local power, not Bolshevik one-party, centralized rule from Moscow. It took a while for most to realize that Lenin had the latter interpretation in mind. Only when pro-Bolshevik "Red Guards" dispersed the constituent assembly (the Bolsheviks won only about 25 percent of the seats; the SRs 51 percent) the morning after its first day of meeting, January 5, 1918, did most come to understand what the Bolsheviks envisioned. The result was a massive civil war (1918–21), in which the combatants employed the brutal practices and weaponry of the world war against each other. The total number of deaths is unknown; 5 million is a conservative estimate.[8] Total war evolved into total, extremely violent revolution.

Revolutions in the Habsburg Empire

Compared to the Russian revolution, there has been less politically driven debate about the causes and legitimacy of the revolutions that broke up the Habsburg Empire in the fall of 1918. Most historians have argued that the empire was in decline, its political life characterized by "absolutism and anarchy,"[9] long before 1914. Born centuries before the appearance of modern nationalism, the Habsburg monarchy, to the twentieth-century observer, appeared to be an outdated, ramshackle conglomeration of many peoples and lands, whose only common feature was the long-ruling emperor, Franz Joseph (1848–1916). Over the course of the nineteenth century many of his subjects came to identify primarily with one or another national group, from Poles, Czechs, and Magyars, to Ukrainians, Romanians, and Croats. Rising national movements then clashed with the empire's very structure. Having agreed to the creation of a dual Austro-Hungarian state in 1867, Franz Joseph, along with most Germans and Hungarians, refused to make any serious concessions to the other nationalities. The late nineteenth-century advent of mass politics hamstrung the government with endless obstructionism from various political parties (at least nine different ethnic groups were represented in the parliament, divided into as many as 35 parties).[10] The arbitrariness of the hulking, inefficient bureaucracy, often ruling by default, greatly exacerbated these problems, making the empire increasingly precarious before 1914.[11] The war only accelerated the empire's final fall.

More recent research into the relations between state and society has challenged this roundly negative interpretation, revealing that there was far more going on than decline in late imperial Austria-Hungary. The arrival of mass politics certainly led to considerable party bickering, but this period also saw the appearance of various useful public services, such as education, sanitation, agricultural assistance, public health, and welfare. And the state had to use civic organizations to make these services work. A lively civil society emerged across the empire, including numerous mass parties and broadly based interest groups. These largely grassroots organizations initiated and pursued a variety of political and social activities, penetrating into state institutions, especially at the local, district, and provincial levels. Even imperial ministers at times felt compelled to accommodate them. These studies have revealed that the late Habsburg Empire was more flexible, democratic, and responsive than had earlier been thought.[12] Indeed, Alan Sked has argued that the empire did not fall because of its unwillingness to reform or provide sufficient concessions to its many nationalities. "It fell because it lost a major war."[13]

The more recent historiography, presenting a more positive view of the late empire, in fact makes the war's role in its destruction more decisive. Whether collapse was inevitable or not before 1914, it is certainly true that the ruling elite provoked the war at least in part because it feared collapse. The chief of the Austro-Hungarian general staff, Franz Conrad von Hötzendorf, the most insistent advocate of a war against Serbia, confessed to his lover immediately after Archduke Franz Ferdinand's assassination that "it will be a hopeless fight; nevertheless it must be waged, since an old monarchy and a glorious army must not perish without glory."[14] Robert Kann poignantly called this committing "suicide from fear of death."[15]

The outbreak of the war was met by most of the empire's national groups with an initial expression of unity, which dissipated quickly following news of the loss of Galicia to Russia's massive, rumbling, peasant army. Conrad's long-desired campaign went from bad to worse. After a confused and bungled mobilization, the army managed to lose almost half of its regular soldiers by the end of 1914. Most humiliating to the formerly great Imperial Army, little Serbia successfully repulsed the first three attacks. By the end of 1915 Conrad estimated that more than 2 million of his troops had been killed or irreparably disabled. Because these losses fell disproportionately on certain nationalities (Germans, Magyars, Slovenes, and Croats), which the commanders had deemed "reliable" enough to lead engagements, they greatly exacerbated national antagonisms. In April 1915 Italy entered the war on the Entente's side and opened up a third front against Austria, whose army now became virtually dependent on Germany.

On the home front matters went from bad, to better, to worse. After the initial shock, the empire's economy recovered somewhat in 1915, but by 1916 the strains of the war – the Entente's blockade, decreasing food production (because many peasants were mobilized), and poor distribution – were producing great shortages of food and clothing. By January 1915 the empire already had an overall grain shortage of 26 million quintals (2.6 billion kilograms). The per capita potato ration, 493 grams before 1914, dropped to 118 in 1916. In 1917 the average meat ration was decreased from 82 to 17 grams per day (to 35 in Hungary). In January 1918 the government further reduced the flour ration from 220 to 165, and to 82 in June. While rations to the troops were larger, they decreased at a similar pace.[16]

Adding to the almost deadly atmosphere of people, especially children, going hungry, in October 1916 left-wing socialist Friedrich Adler assassinated the ultra-conservative Austrian Prime Minister Stürgkh. More important, in November 1916, the old emperor Franz Joseph finally, quietly, passed away. He was replaced by his 29-year-old grandnephew, Karl, a devout Catholic full of good intentions, who proclaimed that he would recall the Reichsrat (Austrian parliament), strive to secure an early peace, and to create a constitutional regime despite the opposition of Austro-German, Magyar, and military elites. Karl's promise of peace and the recalled Reichsrat did much to force a relaxation of wartime censorship. In the Reichsrat, South Slav and Czech deputies, while expressing loyalty to the monarchy, called for autonomy and federalism. Meeting determined resistance from Austro-German deputies and the government, they made increasingly radical demands, moving rapidly away from compromise; their speeches were quite freely published uncensored. Rather than carrying out a vigorous pro-monarchy propaganda campaign, the authorities responded with uneven and arbitrary repression, heavily censoring some newspapers, while allowing others to print; they presented no viable or appealing alternative to the nationalists' calls for independence. While Karl expressed concern about his subjects' lack of patriotism, he scorned to take part in the propaganda war, asserting that thoughts and ideas "could not be recommended like laxatives, tooth-paste and foodstuffs."[17] Hence, the empire lost the war of ideas largely by default.

At the same time the Entente leaders encouraged discord within the monarchy by supporting (to varying degrees) the autonomy or independence of its nationalities. President Wilson's "Fourteen Points" speech in January 1918 suggested autonomy for the empire's diverse peoples within some sort of federal Habsburg structure, but also called for an independent Poland, cutting away the Polish-populated part of Galicia, and the turnover of Italian-populated lands to Italy. In April the Entente approved the resolutions of the Congress of Oppressed Peoples in Rome, calling for the creation of a south Slav state. Over the summer of 1918, impressed by the efforts of the Czech legion (composed of Czech POWs) to fight pro-Bolshevik forces in Russia, the Entente recognized the Czech National Council in Paris as the "basis" of a new government of Czechoslovakia, implying that Bohemia, Moravia, and Slovakia would also no longer be part of a future Austria. On October 2, finally realizing that defeat was inevitable, Austria-Hungary sent President Wilson a plea for armistice on the basis of his Fourteen Points, that is, a federation of autonomous national states. This was too little too late. Wilson replied that he had already recognized Czechoslovakia as a co-belligerent and had agreed to the south Slavs' national unification.

Emboldened by these declarations, the non-dominant peoples of the empire took more decisive steps. The Czech National Committee in Prague plainly proclaimed its approval of an Allied victory and Czech deputies soon walked out of the Reichsrat. After lengthy negotiation, the Croats, Serbs, and Slovenes formed a National Council in Zagreb in early October. Rapidly losing both his authority and the war, Karl, on October 16, issued a manifesto for the federalization of the empire. In response, Hungarian Premier Wekerle, insisting that Hungary could not make any serious concessions to its many Slavic peoples, proclaimed that the kingdom no longer felt bound by the constitutional compromise of 1867. No other national group even bothered to reply.[18]

While it was the non-German nationalities of the empire that most undermined its continued existence, the German-Austrians themselves hammered the final nail in the coffin. On October 21, the German members of the Reichsrat proclaimed themselves the "Provisional National Assembly of independent German-Austria," electing an executive committee that assumed governmental authority. The assembly soon issued a proclamation claiming for their state "territorial power within the entire area settled by Germans, especially the Sudeten lands," warning all other nations (especially the Czechs) against annexing these territories. On October 29 the National Committee in Prague proclaimed the founding of a new Czechoslovak republic, confirmed the following day by the Slovak National Council. The next day the working people of Vienna carried out mass demonstrations calling for the declaration of a republic; that evening large crowds, including many soldiers, tore the imperial eagles from government buildings and the black and yellow imperial colors from their uniforms, and those of their officers. The National Assembly then created a State Council as the state's new executive (assuming the emperor's rights without consulting him). Noting that "the authorities of the former Austrian state do not render any resistance to the taking over of the administration by the new people's government," the council called for peace and quiet.[19]

The Czechs and Germans were not the only ones headed for confrontation. In Galicia, Ukrainian deputies and party and church leaders gathered to form the Ukrainian National Council (Rada), proclaiming its intention to unite all of the empire's Ukrainian-populated lands in a Ukrainian state. On October 24 Galician Poles established the so-called Liquidation Commission in Lviv to sever relations between "Austrian Poland" and the monarchy. A surprise to the Poles, on the night of October 31 a squadron of young, impulsive Ukrainian officers disarmed imperial troops and took control of the provincial capital, Lviv. The next morning yellow-and-blue Ukrainian flags flew over city hall, government offices were in Ukrainian hands, and everywhere posters proclaimed the creation of a Ukrainian state. Shocked at these bold actions, Galician Poles soon resisted. After some negotiations, both sides resorted to violence, leading to the Polish–Ukrainian war, a particularly bloody conflict between erstwhile neighbors lasting until July 1919.

Strangely, despite all the demands and actions of his subjects, emperor Karl refused to abdicate. By November 4, when the armistice was signed at Padua, only some sections of the army still recognized his authority. Finally, on November 11, two days after Wilhelm II abdicated, Karl renounced participation in the public affairs of Austria; on November 13, in those of Hungary. He never abdicated, but Austria and Hungary immediately declared themselves to be republics.

Clearly, the break-up of Austria-Hungary was provoked mostly by national revolutions among the empire's subject peoples, though its defeat in the war was also crucial. In contrast to these national revolutions, the goal of which was basically accomplished with independence, in the new republics of the previously dominant peoples – Hungary and Austria – class struggle soon became the issue. Military defeat, economic collapse, and the dismemberment of a former great power brought great disillusionment to the citizens of the new German-Austrian republic. Almost from the start the republic's Social Democratic leaders, Karl Renner, Otto Bauer, and Friedrich Adler, realized that matters stood quite differently in Austria than in Russia, especially concerning the peasants. Radical socialist revolution was impossible. They rejected both Bolshevism and a return to the old order. Because they had the support of the working class, these leaders were able to implement this decision, while avoiding both violent social revolution and reaction. Austrian workers and soldiers did establish councils on the Soviet model in some cities, but the Social Democrats managed to keep them under control. They organized a People's Guard, composed mostly of workers, which two times stopped communists' attempts to stage a coup. In the February 1919 elections to the constituent assembly, the Social Democrats won 69 seats, the Christian Socialists 63, and the German Nationalists 26; as a result, the socialists formed a coalition government and made large concessions to the republic's regions. The Social Democrats gradually lost support outside of Vienna, but turned the latter, which ended up containing about one third of the republic's population, into a sort of socialist experiment of working-class housing, healthcare, and adult education, soon dubbed "Red Vienna."

While independence from the Habsburgs was popular in Hungary, the social repercussions of falling on the losing side of the war were catastrophic. The victorious Allies had great sympathy for the Slovaks, Serbs, Croats, Slovenes, and Romanians, all of whom made territorial claims on the former kingdom, and no sympathy for the latter. This indifference turned to hostility, when, on the evening of March 21, 1919, the Workers' and Soldiers' Councils of Budapest proclaimed a dictatorship of the proletariat. The new Revolutionary Governing Council, led by the communist Béla Kun, promised Hungary the Red Army's support against the invading armies of Romania and Czechoslovakia, but the Red Army never made it across the Carpathian mountains. Kun proceeded to nationalize the entire economy with one crucial exception: land redistribution, thereby losing the peasants' support. He hoped that the Hungarian revolution would spark a greater central European communist revolution, one that never really materialized, which was a grave disappointment not only to him, but also to Lenin and the Bolsheviks in Moscow. The majority of socialists across the region preferred national consolidation to world revolution. But the main factor in the fall of Kun's government was its defeat by the Romanian army. On August 1 the communists stepped down in favor of a more moderate trade unionist government. A few days later the Romanians entered Budapest, helped to remove the socialists, and installed a more conservative regime. In November Admiral Miklós Horthy, with the Allies' approval, led an army into Budapest and soon installed a right-wing regency. The revolution was over.

Revolution in the German Empire

In contrast to the historiographies on the collapse of the Romanov and Habsburg empires, there is not a great deal of debate about war's role in the collapse of the Hohenzollern empire: the war, especially Germany's quite sudden and unexpected defeat, was the crucial and decisive cause. Certainly, prewar German society was not without class conflict. As Sean Dobson has recently shown, workers were for the most part *not* integrated into the social order and were greatly displeased with their lot in life, resenting especially the authoritarian political system and the owner–worker wage relationship. In this environment the Social Democratic Party of Germany (SPD), which strongly encouraged the working class to act for democratic change, flourished. While in 1890 only 35 members of the SPD were elected to the Reichstag (German parliament), in 1912, 110 SPD candidates won seats, making it the Reichstag's largest single party (about 35 percent of all seats). By 1913 SPD-dominated trade unions had about 2.5 million members. Indeed, many pre-World War I Marxists believed (at least until February 1917) that *the* revolution was most likely to break out in Germany. And yet even Dobson admits that this thriving working-class movement was not at all a sufficient cause for revolution, that the elite's "political dominance was insecure but not in crisis," and that only the Great War removed the main obstacles to revolutionary action.[20] Hence, it is not surprising that the central debate of the German revolution has not focused on its causes, but rather on whether it failed or succeeded.

In many ways the war's effects on Germany were similar to those on Russia and Austria, though at the time the disruption was less obvious. Indeed, it was the appearance of success until the spring of 1918 that made the shock of defeat so devastating to both soldiers and civilians. The supreme army command (Oberste Heeresleitung, OHL), headed by Erich von Ludendorff and Paul von Hindenburg, strove vigorously to the bitter end to put a positive spin on all military successes and failures; it is only in hindsight that we can see that the army and empire were beginning to fall apart long before the actual defeat.

The home front was harshly affected by the prolonged war effort. The crucial question for most civilians was again food supply. Almost from the beginning of the war most internal political controversies revolved around the production and distribution of food. Not all layers of German society were hit equally hard. Much of the German middle and upper classes could still afford sufficient food. Buoyed up in the fall of 1917 by the Bolsheviks' call for an immediate peace, they continued to support the war effort and believed that Germany could obtain a "victorious peace." German workers, on the other hand, became increasingly radical and politically mobilized by the war's exactions. While some workers, especially in the armament industry, received wage increases, even these did not keep up with food prices. By 1918 the official food ration per individual provided only about 60 percent of that needed for light work, less for those who did heavier labor. Consequently, workers increasingly went on strike. While in 1915 there were only 137 strikes, in 1917 there were 561. Workers became more frustrated because the organizations that claimed to represent them, the trade unions and the Social Democratic Party (SPD), refused to encourage and sometimes even opposed strike actions, stubbornly sticking to their wartime pro-unity position.[21] In January 1918 a massive strike wave broke across much of Germany, alarming the police and military authorities. In Berlin, Hamburg, Bremen, and else-where, hundreds of thousands of workers quit their work in a protest against the terrible food situation. Workers began forming their own councils (called *räte* in German). To some extent following their Russian counterparts, German workers and some of their more radical leaders in the councils and the Independent Social Democratic Party (USPD, which broke with the SPD in April 1917) demanded an end to the war, calling for an immediate peace without annexations or indemnities.

In the army, shirking of military duty became widespread already in the fall of 1917 as the OHL moved many troops from other fronts to the west in preparation for the last great offensive beginning in March 1918. The soldiers who did fight in this last desperate effort were motivated by the desire to end their suffering sooner and by the great opportunity for plunder, a more than reasonable response to their meager rations.[22] Ludendorff's last great offensive made some important advances, but was accompanied by massive losses of men, contributing greatly to "the slow but steady deterioration of discipline," as a May 1918 order to the Sixth Army noted.[23] According to one contemporary military analyst, Erich-Otto Volkmann, there were between 750,000 and 1 million "shirkers' on the western front in the last few months of the war. Deist has argued that the spring 1918 offensive's failure provoked a massive, though covert, refusal of soldiers to follow orders. Ludendorff was shocked to overhear on August 8 that an attack division heading for the front was greeted by retreating guard troops with shouts of "strike-breakers" and "war-prolongers." The soldiers' refusals, a "covert strike," contributed much to Ludendorff's decision to admit defeat.[24]

On September 29, Ludendorff suddenly declared that the war was lost and the government now had to negotiate an immediate armistice. The German government believed that President Wilson (based on their reading of his Fourteen Points) was amenable to creating a just and equitable peace, but to deal with Wilson, they soon realized, they would have to make serious constitutional changes. A new government was formed under the leadership of the liberal Prince Max von Baden, supported by a parliamentary majority of Catholics, Progressives, and the Majority Social Democrats. After a lengthy period of indecision, the Kaiser issued a proclamation making the government responsible to the Reichstag, placing foreign and military policy under its control, and democratizing the franchise. The hope was that a truly constitutional monarchy, with responsible government, would suffice. It did not. Wilson's note of October 23 recognized the constitutional changes made thus far, but made it clear that the Allies were not interested in negotiating with the Hohenzollern dynasty.[25] At the same time, the German peace offering and change of government greatly transformed the public mood and further radicalized the masses, especially those who had been fighting for Kaiser and Vaterland for more than four long years.

On October 29, the very day on which Kaiser Wilhelm signed the new constitu-tional laws, sailors at Wilhelmshaven revolted in response to rumors that the Supreme Navy Command was about to order a suicidal attack – a death sortie or "Admirals' Rebellion" – on the British Grand Fleet.[26] The navy's commanding officers (without informing the Kaiser or government) were attempting, or so they thought, to save the navy's future and to die with honor – motivations that did not interest rank-and-file sailors in the least. As ship after ship mutinied, the commanders began to panic. On November 1, the commander of the high seas fleet, Admiral Franz Hipper, ordered the squadrons, then assembled at Wilhelmshaven, to disperse to other ports, thereby unwittingly spreading the revolt. On November 3, a full-blown rebellion broke out at Kiel, sparked by the most mutinous Third Squadron, and transferring rapidly to the city's workers. Sailors,' soldiers,' and workers' councils were spontaneously created and began to claim authority. On November 7, the King of Bavaria was forced to abdicate in favor of a soldiers' and workers' council. The next day many key German cities fell to the revolutionary masses. Almost to the very last moment the Kaiser refused to abdicate, threatening to gather those troops loyal to him and march on Berlin. On November 9, von Baden decided on his own to issue a declaration that Kaiser Wilhelm had abdicated and then, stepping down, asked MSPD leader Friedrich Ebert to form a new government. A few hours later, to Ebert's annoyance, another MSPD leader, Philipp Scheidemann, fearing the further radicalization of the revolution, proclaimed Germany a republic from a balcony of the Reichstag. He had no authority to do so, but that proved to be the end of the Hohenzollern dynasty. Wilhelm fled to Holland early the following morning, cursing von Baden for his "treachery" and retaining hopes of returning some day.[27] He never did.

On November 10, a new government was created, the Council of People's Representatives, composed of three members each of the MSPD and USPD and led by Ebert and Hugo Haase (of the USPD). The same day delegates from Berlin's workers' and soldiers' councils gathered at the Circus Busch and confirmed the new government; the delegates also expressed admiration for and sent their "fraternal greetings" to the Russian workers and soldiers, "who took the lead on the path of revolution"; they even called for "the speedy and thorough socialization of the capitalist means of production."[28] The new leaders, however, strove to ignore such enthusiasms. Indeed, Ebert, Scheidemann, and the other MSPD leaders fell into a sort of fetish of moderation in the face of mounting chaos. Viewing themselves as the realists, "they made a virtue of hardheaded realism, of taking the tough decisions left-wing dreamers refused to face."[29] Ebert's government soon issued its program, which demanded a maximum eight-hour day, unemployment legislation, improved social insurance, better housing, democratic elections, sexual equality, the removal of wartime restrictions on civil liberties, and the calling of a constitutional assembly. This was a strong democratic program, sympathetic to the working class, but it disappointed those demanding the socialization of production and other radical economic changes.

The German revolution then turned into a struggle between the MSPD leaders' consistent efforts to preserve the achievements of the revolution, as they viewed their actions, and the attempts of the more radical left (the USPD,[30] Spartacists, and Communists) to advance the revolution (from their perspective). The council movement was caught in the middle, not always agreeing with the radical left, but demanding more than the moderate republican government was willing to give. Ebert's government won out, basically by gaining the support of the political center, the army's officer corps, and new military organizations, called *Freikorps*. Always a reluctant revolutionary, Ebert agreed to utilize the *Freikorps* in order to suppress the council movement, whose radical demands he feared. In January 1919 the *Freikorps* put down an attempted communist coup against the government in Berlin, killing about 100 insurgents and the leaders of the newly founded Communist Party – Rosa Luxemburg and Karl Liebknecht. At the elections to the national (constituent) assembly, held on January 19, the MSPD took almost 38 percent of the vote, compared to 7.6 percent for the USPD; the MSPD allied with the Democrats and Catholic Center to obtain a parliamentary, republican majority.[31] Although a number of localized disturbances followed, this was basically the end of the German revolution.

Debate on this revolution has focused more on whether it succeeded than on its causes. With the exception of a few early writers such as Arthur Rosenberg, interwar German historians generally defined the revolution as a choice between the imposition of "Russian Bolshevism," represented by the councils and communists, and some moderate form of republicanism, an alliance of the MSPD with conservative elements in the bureaucracy and army. In effect, these historians argued that Ebert had no choice but to side with the forces of order, no matter how conservative, or face the horrors of Bolshevik Russia. After World War II, and especially in the 1960s, historians of the revolution came to support the idea, first proposed by Rosenberg, that there was in fact a third choice open to Ebert: the councils.[32] These historians uncovered considerable potential in the council movement for compromise with the governing MSPD. The councils were not at all the communists' tools, but rather democratic, grassroots organizations that sprang up spontaneously as the imperial authorities disappeared. Ebert's government missed a rare opportunity to cooperate with the councils to democratize German society thoroughly and create a much stronger Weimar republic, one more resistant to the radical right. More recently, however, some historians such as Mommsen and Bernbach have questioned the viability of the councils as a democratic alternative. The councils were not really that interested in democratizing society, but rather only in defending workers' and soldiers' interests; they rarely attempted to claim political leadership.[33] Because this debate is linked to the weakness of the Weimar republic and therefore the rise of National Socialism, it is unlikely that it will be resolved any time soon.

Conclusion

Clearly, World War I played a crucial role in the collapse of the empires of eastern Europe and the outbreak of both national and class-based revolutions. In the Russian empire participation, not defeat, led to the February upheaval, which spawned numerous other revolutions, including that of October, a crucial issue of which was getting out of the war. In the Habsburg and Hohenzollern empires, defeat after four long years of struggle was the catalyst to collapse and insurrection; these revolutions were, overall, more moderate in tone, less violent, and less radical, partly in reaction against the Russian example. While historians attribute to the war varying degrees of responsibility for these revolutions, its great contribution to their outbreak is unquestionable.

NOTES

1   Leopold Haimson, "The Problem of Social Stability in Urban Russia, 1905–1917," *Slavic Review* (part 1) 23/4 (1964): 618–42; and (part 2) 24/1 (1965): 1–22; quotation is from part 2, p. 17.

2   This literature is massive; for useful surveys see Ronald G. Suny, "Revision and Retreat in the Historiography of 1917: Social History and Its Critics," *Russian Review* 53 (1994): 165–82; and "Toward a Social History of the October Revolution," *American Historical Review* 88 (1983): 31–52.

3   See Allan K. Wildman, *The End of the Russian Imperial Army: The Old Army and the Soldiers' Revolt (March–April 1917)* (Princeton NJ: Princeton University Press, 1980), p. 95.

4   See Lewis H. Siegelbaum, *The Politics of Industrial Mobilization in Russia, 1914–17: A Study of the War-Industries Committees* (London: Macmillan, 1983).

5   P. N. Miliukov, *Vospominaniia, Tom vtoroi (1859–1917)* (Moscow: Sovremennik, 1990), p. 237.

6   Tsuyoshi Hasegawa, *The February Revolution: Petrograd 1917* (Seattle: University of Washington Press, 1981).

7   See Orlando Figes, *A People's Tragedy: The Russian Revolution: 1891–1924* (London: Jonathan Cape, 1996), p. 364.

8   Ibid, pp. 773–5. Another 5 million starved to death in the famine crises of 1921–2, which resulted in part from the ruthless food requisitioning of the civil war's various occupying armies. For comparison, about 1.7 million soldiers of the Russian Imperial Army died in the world war.

9   Lothar Höbelt, "Parliamentary Politics in a Multinational Setting: Late Imperial Austria," Working Paper 92–6, Center for Austrian Studies, University of Minnesota, 1992, p. 8.

10 Only 50 deputies were needed to force a roll-call, which would last several hours; only 20 were needed to force an emergency debate; all of which greatly facilitated minority parties' obstructing the passing of bills. See Höbelt, "Parliamentary Politics," p. 6.

11 The best of the classic works are C. A. Macartney, *The Habsburg Empire, 1790–1918* (New York: Macmillan, 1969); and Robert A. Kann, *A History of the Habsburg Empire, 1526–1918* (Berkeley: University of California Press, 1974).

12 For a thorough and insightful discussion of the older and more recent historiography, see Gary B. Cohen, "Neither Absolutism nor Anarchy: New Narratives on Society and Government in Late Imperial Austria," *Austrian History Yearbook* 29 (1998): 37–61.

13 Alan Sked, *The Decline and Fall of the Habsburg Empire 1815–1918*, 2nd edn (London: Longman, 2001), p. 269.

14 Samuel R. Williamson Jr. and Russel Van Wyk, *July 1914: Soldiers, Statesmen, and the Coming of the Great War: A Brief Documentary History* (Boston MA: Bedford/St Martin's Press, 2003), p. 57.

15 Kann, *History of the Habsburg Empire*, p. 519.

16 See Horst Haselsteiner, "The Habsburg Empire in World War I: Mobilization of Food Supplies," in *East Central European Society in World War I*, Béla K. Király and Nándor F. Dreisziger, eds (Boulder CO: East European Monographs, 1985), pp. 89–90.

17 Mark Cornwall, "News, Rumour and the Control of Information in Austria-Hungary, 1914–1918," *History* 77/249 (1992): 50–64; quotation from p. 64.

18 See John C. Swanson, *The Remnants of the Habsburg Monarchy: The Shaping of Modern Austria and Hungary, 1918–1922* (Boulder CO: East European Monographs, 2001), pp. 8–9.

19 Francis L. Carsten, *Revolution in Central Europe, 1918–1919* (Berkeley: University of California Press, 1972), pp. 21–3.

20 Sean Dobson, *Authority and Upheaval in Leipzig, 1910–1920: The Story of a Relationship* (New York: Columbia University Press, 2001), p. 290.

21 See Jürgen Kocka, *Facing Total War: German Society 1914–1918*, Barbara Weinberger, trans. (Cambridge MA: Harvard University Press, 1984), pp. 61–7; statistics from pp. 25, 61.

22 See Wilhelm Deist, "The Military Collapse of the German Empire: The Reality Behind the Stab-in-the-Back Myth," E. J. Feuchtwanger, trans., *War in History* 3/2 (1996): 199–201.

23 Ralph. H. Lutz, ed., *Fall of the German Empire, 1914–1918*, vol. 1 (Palo Alto CA: Stanford University Press, 1932), doc. 215, p. 652.

24 Deist, "The Military Collapse," pp. 202–5.

25 See Klaus Schwabe, *Woodrow Wilson, Revolutionary Germany, and Peacemaking, 1918–1919: Missionary Diplomacy and the Realities of Power*, Rita and Robert Kimber, trans. (Chapel Hill: University of North Carolina Press, 1985), p. 59.

26 See Daniel Horn, *The German Naval Mutinies of World War I* (New Brunswick NJ: Rutgers University Press, 1969), p. 212; and see pp. 198–233.

27 Giles MacDonogh, *The Last Kaiser: The Life of Wilhelm II* (New York: St. Martin's Press, 2000), pp. 412–15.

28 F. L. Carsten, *War Against War: British and German Radical Movements in the First World War* (London: Batsford Academic and Educational, 1982), p. 227.

29 Geoff Eley, *Forging Democracy: The History of the Left in Europe, 1850–2000* (Oxford: Oxford University Press, 2002), p. 166.

30 The USPD leaders left the government on December 31, 1918, after the MSPD leaders ordered (without consulting the USPD) *Freikorps* to crush the revolt of some mutinous sailors in Berlin, killing about a dozen sailors.

31 Eley, *Forging Democracy*, p. 168.

32 Arthur Rosenberg, *A History of the German Republic*, Ian F. D. Morrow and L. Marie Sieveking, trans. (London: Methuen, 1936), pp. 23–4.

33 See Wolfgang J. Mommsen, "The German Revolution 1918–1920: Political Revolution and Social Protest Movement," J. Williams, trans., in *Social Change and Political Development in Weimar Germany*, R. Bessel and E. J. Feuchtwanger, eds (London: Croom Helm, 1981), p. 31.

GUIDE TO FURTHER READING

Francis L. Carsten, *Revolution in Central Europe, 1918–1919* (Berkeley: University of California Press, 1972). The only serious attempt (in English) to study the revolutions in both Austria-Hungary and Germany.

Gary B. Cohen, "Neither Absolutism nor Anarchy: New Narratives on Society and Government in Late Imperial Austria," *Austrian History Yearbook* 29 (1998): 37–61. A comprehensive discussion of the historiography on the late Habsburg period.

Mark Cornwall, ed., *The Last Years of Austria-Hungary: A Multi-National Experiment in Early Twentieth-Century Europe*, revd edn (Exeter: University of Exeter Press, 2002). A stimulating set of essays on the main nationalities.

Wilhelm Deist, "The Military Collapse of the German Empire: The Reality Behind the Stab-in-the-Back Myth," trans. E. J. Feuchtwanger, *War in History* 3/2 (1996): 186–207. A wonderful study of the collapse of the army and the covert German soldiers' strike of 1918.

Sean Dobson, *Authority and Upheaval in Leipzig, 1910–1920: The Story of a Relationship* (New York: Columbia University Press, 2001). A refreshing local study that takes a longer period and argues that the seeds of revolution were present before World War I.

Orlando Figes, *A People's Tragedy: The Russian Revolution: 1891–1924* (London: Jonathan Cape, 1996). A compelling, inclusive history of the entire revolutionary period.

Leopold Haimson, "The Problem of Social Stability in Urban Russia, 1905–1917," *Slavic Review*, (part 1) 23/4 (1964): 618–642; and (part 2) 24/1 (1965): 1–22. The landmark studies that initiated research into the social history of the Russian revolution.

Peter Holquist, *Making War, Forging Revolution: Russia's Continuum of Crisis, 1914–1921* (Cambridge MA: Harvard University Press, 2002). Conceives of the revolution as part of a longer period of industrialized violence and modern political practices.

Jürgen Kocka, *Facing Total War: German Society 1914–1918*, Barbara Weinberger, trans. (Cambridge MA: Harvard University Press, 1984). A path-breaking investigation of the war's social impact.

Stephen C. MacDonald, *A German Revolution: Local Change and Continuity in Prussia, 1918–1920* (New York: Garland, 1991). A very useful local study of the revolution.

Wolfgang J. Mommsen, "The German Revolution 1918–1920: Political Revolution and Social Protest Movement," Jane Williams, trans., in *Social Change and Political Development in Weimar Germany*, R. Bessel and E. J. Feuchtwanger, eds (London: Croom Helm, 1981), pp. 21–54. An excellent summary of the historiography.

Robin Okey, *The Habsburg Monarchy: From Enlightenment to Eclipse* (New York: St Martin's Press, 2001). The most thoughtful and well-researched book in English on the Habsburgs' last 150 years.

Klaus Schwabe, *Woodrow Wilson, Revolutionary Germany, and Peacemaking, 1918–1919: Missionary Diplomacy and the Realities of Power*, Rita and Robert Kimber, trans. (Chapel Hill: University of North Carolina Press, 1985). A comprehensive study of Wilson and his impact on the German revolution.

Alan Sked, *The Decline and Fall of the Habsburg Empire 1815–1918*, 2nd edn (London: Longman, 2001). A controversial but stimulating set of interpretive essays on the Habsburgs' final years.

Ronald G. Suny, "Revision and Retreat in the Historiography of 1917: Social History and Its Critics," *Russian Review* 53 (1994): 165–82; idem, "Toward a Social History of the October Revolution," *American Historical Review* 88 (1983): 31–52. Two thorough discussions of the social, revisionist work on the Russian revolution.

Rex A. Wade, *The Russian Revolution, 1917* (Cambridge: Cambridge University Press, 2000). The best concise synthesis of western historians' work on the revolution.

Allan K. Wildman, *The End of the Russian Imperial Army: The Old Army and the Soldiers' Revolt (March–April 1917)* (Princeton NJ: Princeton University Press, 1980). A magisterial study of the army's collapse and its role in the revolution.

PART IV

The Aftermath of War

CHAPTER SEVENTEEN

Peacemaking after World War I

ALAN SHARP

The 1919 Paris Peace Conference at the end of World War I acknowledged the end of four great multinational empires and the emergence of nine new states, based theoretically on national self-determination. Its mission was to encourage liberal and democratic values where previously autocracy had prevailed. It set itself the goal of applying higher moral standards than any previous peace conference in its decision making. Once billed as the first of the twentieth-century summit meetings,[1] the Paris conference seems now to be rather the last of a kind – more the rearguard of the tradition of Vienna and Berlin than the vanguard of twentieth-century peacemaking. Neither World War II nor the Cold War was followed by such a far-reaching attempt, in a structured meeting in one location, to reorder the affairs of a globe emerging from conflict.

Indeed, it could be argued that, despite the greater magnitude, scope, and reach of World War II, the task facing the peacemakers in 1919 was more formidable than that in 1945. Then the victorious Anglo-American, French, and Soviet forces occupied and administered the defeated states. In 1919 there had been an unprecedented collapse of long-established rule across most of central and eastern Europe and into the near east. At no time before or since have four major empires more or less simultaneously experienced revolution, the disintegration of governmental systems, and the destruction of their hold over both their metropolitan and imperial domains. While Germany did not experience revolution on the scale of Russia, nor imperial implosion on the scale of Austria-Hungary, and the ending of the Ottoman Empire seemed less immediately pressing than events nearer the heart of Europe, the sweeping away of authorities that had controlled territories for centuries did set the peacemakers in 1919 a daunting challenge, requiring executive action on a wide scale. Given these responsibilities, and the personnel involved, Margaret MacMillan's assessment is that "In 1919 Paris was the capital of the world . . . the world's government," yet as Sir Henry Wilson, the British chief of the imperial general staff told his prime minister, David Lloyd George, "The root of evil is that the *Paris writ does not run*."[2] The conference might make decisions but often had no means of enforcing them in areas where the allies had neither troops nor reliable local agents.

This unenviable position of having responsibility without power meant that the peacemakers have often been blamed for both contemporary and subsequent events over which they had, in reality, little control.

Attitudes to the Settlement

The conference and its results were not well received by commentators in the first fifty years after it met. Since the 1970s there has been some softening of attitudes among scholars using the newly available archival material to reveal more of the complexities of policies and attitudes of peacemakers facing a task of bewildering proportions. As President Woodrow Wilson predicted, crossing the Atlantic en route to the conference in December 1918, many, buoyed by a belief in his "program for the peace of the world," had unrealizable expectations of a peace that would satisfy all. These hopes were shared as much by those within governments as by less informed observers outside them. Their disappointment, eloquently expressed by conference participants like Stephen Bonsal, James Headlam-Morley, John Maynard Keynes, and Harold Nicolson, followed by the outbreak of a new major European conflict which many blamed on the inadequacies of the peace settlement, left the peacemakers with few friends. Only more recently – and still not yet widely disseminated in textbooks or classrooms, perhaps because it has mainly appeared in specialized monographs or learned journals – has there emerged an assessment that tries to balance the shortcomings of some of the solutions advanced by the statesmen in Paris against the immensity and intractability of the problems they faced.[3]

This more generous interpretation – that they did the best they could in the circumstances – has made little impression on the more negative popular assessment that the peacemakers not only failed to solve the problems with which they were faced but also sowed the seeds of future European and world disaster. Most recent scholarly approaches to the Paris conference stress its position in a wider process of shifting European and world power balances before, during, and after World War I, arguing it is neither fair nor sensible to take the situation in 1919 as a completely fresh start without past baggage or encumbrances. In addition, there is the role of the decision makers who replaced the peacemakers in the 1920s and 1930s and whose implementation, neglect, or abandonment of the settlement must play a crucial part in any explanation of 1939. Nonetheless it is clear that MacMillan's claim that the Versailles settlement was not exclusively, or even mainly, to blame for the outbreak of a second major European conflict struck some reviewers as a new, even revolutionary, interpretation. This is perhaps unsurprising when respected historians like Jay Winter continue to suggest, in a book aimed at the wider interested public, that

> The Peace Conference which ended the Great War was more about punishment than about peace. Perhaps inevitably, anger and retribution followed four years of bloodshed, ensuring the instability and ultimate collapse of the accords signed in the Hall of Mirrors at Versailles on 28 June 1919. The road to World War II started here.[4]

Winter's claim has plausibility, not least because the hopes of those who believed that the horrors of World War I were suffered in order to end war were cruelly dashed in 1939 (if not before). Nonetheless it is wrong, even if parts of it are true. There can be no doubt that the peoples of the victorious states were angry and expected Germany to pay, both literally and metaphorically, for the war. The peacemakers were aware of these expectations and knew that, as democratic leaders, they must attempt to satisfy their electoral masters. The election in Britain in December 1918 provided solid evidence of desire for revenge. Georges Clemenceau, the French premier, knew that he would have to satisfy the unforgiving constituency in France championed by the formidable Raymond Poincaré, the president of the French Republic, and his major ally, Ferdinand Foch, the commander-in-chief of the Allied armies, both of whom were fretting at their lack of influence and power in the peace discussions. Throughout the conference Clemenceau and Lloyd George reminded Woodrow Wilson that their positions depended upon the democratic support of their parliaments and peoples and that there were certain limits beyond which they dare not go. This was not the only reason for their attitudes, and the Calvinistic beliefs of Lloyd George and Wilson should not be underestimated. While both might wish to be fair and just to Germany, justice might require retribution. "It was not vengeance, but justice," Lloyd George suggested to his cabinet in October 1918, ". . . whether we ought not to consider lashing her [Germany] as she had lashed France."[5] The delegates in Paris wanted to make a lasting peace but knew they could not create a perfect world. The conference was a staging post on the road to the outbreak of another major European war in 1939, but it was not the point at which that road began.

The Longer View

The conference gathered in 1919 because a major war had begun in 1914. Some of the leaders of the great powers believed that their problems required the breaking of the existing international system and its remaking in a form more satisfactory to them. They resorted to the highly risky and unpredictable stratagem of war. That war "solved" only a handful of the issues at dispute. If it was a colonial contest between Britain and France on the one hand and Germany on the other, then there was a clear outcome. Germany's colonies, unprotected by its expensive battle fleet, were (with the notable exception of German east Africa) rapidly overrun by British, Dominion, or allied forces. The short-lived German overseas empire was gone. Similarly, Anglo-German naval rivalry seemed settled when the Royal Navy and other allied ships escorted the German High Seas fleet into internment in Scapa Flow. Despite the prewar race to build them, it had not been these massive battleships that had constituted the near-fatal threat to Britain's control of the seas, but Germany's submarines.

Little else had been resolved. Now, in addition to the problems of a changing European power balance and a wider world international structure that had provided the background to the outbreak of the war, there were complicated interwoven questions that the war itself had either created or exacerbated. States that had failed the test of war had been overthrown, had collapsed, or had been severely weakened. What should be put in their place? The experience of 1914 suggested that an international system, which had helped to prevent a general war involving all the major European powers at once since 1815, might require radical alteration. How might this be accomplished? The war had been expensive, both in terms of men and money. Some 8–10 million young men had been killed in the armed forces of the belligerents, millions more people died as collateral damage, victims of the war itself and the ensuing smaller interstate and intrastate wars that persisted elsewhere after the armistice in western Europe. Some were simply not conceived because of wartime separations; others died of famine and disease. A virulent influenza epidemic took an estimated further 20–30 million lives of victims frequently exhausted by the strain of war. The British treasury estimated that it had cost the allies £24 billion (in 1914 gold values) to win the war. The damage caused by industrialized warfare on a massive scale required repair – on the western front alone a hasty postwar survey suggested this might cost between £3–5 billion in contemporary values. The lost lives could not be retrieved but who should meet these massive bills and who would ease the plight of crippled soldiers, widows, and dependants?

Organizing Peace?

What struck almost all contemporary observers of the conference was a lack of organization verging on the chaotic. This was partly because the end of the war arrived much sooner than the victors expected and their thoughts were only beginning to turn to peace planning. They did agree on Paris as the location and that English and French would enjoy equal status in the negotiations – these decisions foreshadowed many other compromises that would not be palatable to all the parties concerned. There was, however, no agreed agenda, no shared set of priorities, and no clear plan of action. No one quite knew how peace was to be made – would it begin with an inter-Allied meeting to establish Allied demands and priorities? Would there then be, as there had been at the end of the Revolutionary and Napoleonic Wars, a preliminary treaty between the major belligerents that would establish the boundaries of the defeated powers, the military, territorial, and political consequences of defeat, and the contribution payable to the victors? Would a more general gathering follow involving prominent neutral states, again as in 1814–15, which would deal with the wider consequences of a long war and the reordering of the international system? Contemporary diplomatic shorthand distinguished between the two, terming the first a peace conference and the second a peace congress.

These issues had not been resolved when Poincaré opened the official proceedings, rather strangely, on a Saturday – January 18, 1919. This was not an accident; it was the 48th anniversary of Bismarck's humiliating proclamation of the German Empire in the Hall of Mirrors in Louis XIV's palace of Versailles in 1871, after French defeat in the Franco-Prussian war. The French saved Versailles for later, opening the conference in the Salle de l'Horloge in their foreign ministry, the Quai d'Orsay, but they did not miss the symbolic date. Nor did Clemenceau neglect to make his own statement – the British diplomat Esmé Howard noted in his diary – "I hear that when the Delegates were putting on their hats to leave, Wilson, who saw Clemenceau putting on an old soft felt, said, 'I was told I must wear a tall hat for this occasion.' 'So was I,' retorted C., cramming his soft hat over his eyes."[6]

Harold Nicolson, another British diplomat participating at the conference, explained in *Peacemaking 1919* – his half-diary, half-historical reflection – that the uncertainties about what would happen to their conclusions had a profound effect on the demands presented by the various commissions established by the leading powers to advise them on boundaries and other technical matters.

Many paragraphs of the Treaty, and especially in the economic sections, were in fact inserted as "maximum statements" such as would provide some area of concession to Germany at the eventual Congress. This Congress never materialized . . . Had it been known from the outset that no negotiations would ever take place with the enemy, it is certain that many of the less reasonable clauses of the Treaty would never have been inserted.[7]

The French proposed an agenda for the conference in November 1918, but Wilson rejected it. Its priorities and perspectives smacked too much of the "old diplomacy" and it paid scant respect to Wilson's ideas, suggesting that they lacked sufficient precision to form the basis of a settlement. This not necessarily incorrect judgment was both tactless and tardy because Lloyd George and Clemenceau had already grumpily accepted, after Germany approached Wilson to arrange an armistice in October, that the president's 1918 speeches would form the basis of the eventual peace settlement. The note by Robert Lansing, the American secretary of state, sent on November 5, 1918, was a pre-armistice contract with Germany. Wilson's uplifting and inspiring but often ill-defined and contradictory statements were accepted as the guiding principles and practical foundations for the forthcoming settlement. A broad spectrum of opinion and peoples now expected Wilson to deliver both the tone and substance of his program.

Peace Conference Structures

Wilson had promised "open covenants of peace, openly arrived at." His speeches implied that great and small powers should have a role to play in these transparent negotiations. The conference met instead behind closed doors and, although 32 states attended, it was dominated by the great powers, among which some were clearly greater than others. Initially, the main decision-making forum of the Paris gathering was the Council of Ten consisting of the prime ministers of France, Great Britain, and Italy, the American president, their respective ministers of foreign affairs, and two Japanese delegates. The smaller powers were allowed only glimpses of the process when they appeared as petitioners to the various commissions set up to advise the Ten, or, like the press, attended the infrequent (eight in all) plenary sessions of the conference. Even then their voices were rarely heard: "Are there any objections?" asked Clemenceau, the peremptory president of the conference. "No. Adopted!"[8]

The Council of Ten proved to be unwieldy, there were too many people milling about, and the Japanese had only a very limited interest in European affairs, while the Italians had their own focused agenda. It had taken very few decisions by the time it broke into two unequal parts in mid-March 1919 – Germany's colonies were forfeit and the first draft of the Covenant of the League of Nations was agreed. Yet it had enormous responsibilities that stretched beyond the already formidable task of making peace with Germany, not to mention the other defeated powers. In addition to dealing with the technicalities of armistice renewal and the establishment of commissions on territorial and military matters, it was an emergency European government, grappling with famine relief and the dangers of the spread of revolution. It met 72 times between January and March, and created 58 subcommittees, so it did not lack diligence, but it found itself caught in a log-jam of interlocking and unresolved problems. These included: the German frontiers in the east and west; financial compensation from Germany – its extent and basis; Polish claims to Danzig and a corridor to the sea; Italian demands for Fiume; growing Anglo-French tensions in the middle east; and an increasingly resentful Japan, smarting at the insult of the refusal of Wilson's League commission to agree to a clause embodying racial equality.

The delegates knew they had to reach decisions quickly. The premiers could ill-afford to be absent from their national capitals as their states struggled to dismantle the mechanisms created to fight a total war. The conference also feared Bolshevism would fill the vacuum of power in eastern and central Europe unless it made rapid decisions. Communist regimes in Munich and Hungary increased this concern. As Lansing noted on April 4, "It is time to stop fiddling while the world is on fire, while violence and bestiality consume society. Everyone is clamoring for peace, for an immediate peace."[9] The Ten could not make progress; a new, more incisive body was needed.

The Council of Four – Lloyd George, Clemenceau, Wilson, and Vittorio Orlando, the Italian premier – evolved during March as the crucial decision-making body of the German settlement. It began with meetings in early March between Lloyd George, Clemenceau, and Colonel Edward House, Wilson's most trusted advisor. After his mid-conference trip to the United States, Wilson replaced House. Orlando joined them on March 24. Professor Paul Mantoux acted as interpreter and, from early April, Sir Maurice Hankey, the secretary to the British cabinet, provided much-needed administrative support, recording their proceedings and decisions. Their foreign ministers, plus the Japanese delegate, became the second-string Council of Five, which made most of the less controversial territorial decisions. But it was the Four who had to resolve the crisis of the conference.

They did so, still working without a firm agenda, though it had by then become clear that there would be no real negotiations with the Germans. Mindful of the difficulties they had in reaching even tentative and grudging agreements between themselves on a number of questions, and aware of the havoc in the victorious alliance wrought by Talleyrand, the French delegate in Vienna in 1815, the current winners tacitly agreed to dictate a peace to Germany. An offer of dubious sincerity by Lloyd George and Wilson to guarantee the full support of Britain and the United States if Germany again attacked France encouraged Clemenceau to be more flexible on the fate of the Rhineland. Gradually the log-jam was released, with agreements on the fate of the Saar, Danzig, the Polish Corridor, and a decision to postpone a decision on the extent of Germany's liability to pay compensation for the damage caused by the war. They decided the mandatories for the former German colonies and they made some progress about the future of former Ottoman territory in the near and middle east. The Four became Three when Orlando stormed from the conference on April 21, unable to persuade Wilson that the Adriatic port of Fiume should become part of Italy. This tactic was singularly unsuccessful and, when a frustrated Orlando returned "fiuming" to the conference on May 7, he discovered that Italy (probably very fortunately) had also missed out in the near east, where the Greeks had been authorized to land troops at Smyrna (Izmir). The main beneficiaries of the Italian walk-out were the Japanese because Wilson dare not risk a second major ally quitting the conference, and thus conceded their claims to the former German concessions in China, despite deploring them.

On May 7 the allies handed the Germans their draft terms. To many, particularly in the British delegation, the effect of the proposed treaty was greater than the sum of its parts. It incorporated undiminished all the demands that the commissions had expected to be the subject of bargaining. The Germans were now permitted to make written representations about the terms, but such few alterations that were made before the final signature were the result of British rather than German intervention. The unease in the British camp encouraged Lloyd George to seek a mandate for treaty revision from his cabinet, brought to Paris for the meeting. Their major concerns were reparations, the Rhineland occupation, Germany's exclusion from the League, and the need for a plebiscite in Upper Silesia rather than its automatic transfer from Germany to Poland. The Silesian plebiscite was Lloyd George's only success (one he may have come to regret). The German government prevaricated, then resigned, but the new government had no choice – sign the treaty or face invasion. It capitulated, and the signing ceremony in Louis XIV's palace at Versailles on June 28 completed the symbolic revenge for 1871.

By this time Orlando had left office, but even when present he was often the peripheral figure of the Four. It was Wilson, Lloyd George, and Clemenceau that became the principal targets of *The Economic Consequences of the Peace*. This magnificent polemic was penned by John Maynard Keynes, then a British treasury advisor at the conference. His vitriolic attack on the conference and all its works has had a huge impact on public and scholarly perceptions of the peacemakers since its publication in late 1919.[10] Part of its appeal was that it offered a manageable explanation of the enormous complexities of the postwar world by reducing them to the decisions of three men, caricatured as the wily Welsh wizard, the cynical defender of France, and the failed American philosopher-king. Any treatment of the conference faces such an organizational dilemma because, if the different areas of peacemaking – the territorial settlements, the League, reparations and so on – are treated as discrete entities, with a chronological and analytical explanation of how the final decision evolved in each case, one loses sight of the interconnected, persistent, and debilitating effect of their totality. An alternative approach might show the peacemakers moving from issue to issue, hour by hour, day by day, but would risk overwhelming the reader with the same confusion and exhaustion that they experienced.

An Overview

The remainder of this chapter will offer a brief overview and then consider three key aspects of the settlement: national self-determination, the League, and reparations. Chronologically, the period of peacemaking might be divided into four: from October 1918 to January 1919; January to March 1919; March to June 1919; and July 1919 to July 1923. The first period was dominated by wartime bodies and had to cope with the end of the war, the armistice, and preliminary peace planning. The first half of 1919 was mainly concerned with drawing up the peace treaty with Germany. The first quarter was the era of the Council of Ten, the second that of the Council of Four. The final four years cover the period between the signatures of the treaties of Versailles and Lausanne. Versailles on June 28, 1919, was followed by Saint Germain with Austria on August 20 and Neuilly with Bulgaria on November 27. The Paris conference wound down to be replaced by a rather confused period of conflicting conferences in early 1920. The Treaty of Trianon was signed with Hungary on June 4 and the Ottomans signed Sèvres on August 10, 1920, apparently concluding the process. The Turks, who had accepted the most abject of the armistice conditions of all the defeated enemies in 1919, and who had been last in the peacemaking queue, now revolted against the Ottoman system and the peace settlement. The new secular state of Turkey, led by Mustafa Kemal, became the only one of the former Central Powers to negotiate a peace settlement. The final act of World War I ended in Lausanne on July 24, 1923; peacemaking had lasted longer than the fighting.

National self-determination

The peacemakers had to decide what had caused the war, and then propose their prescriptions for cure and the prevention of future conflict. Wilson's ideas, inevitably, dominated. His world vision was that of a Gladstonian liberal with a belief in the basic goodness of his fellow humans. For Wilson, Europe's problems in 1914 lay in multinational empires that denied their subjects proper expression of their cultural and political rights and an international system that did not allow the good sense of informed and rational public opinion to curtail the aggressive behavior of autocratic states. "This war," he said on February 11, 1918, "had its roots in the disregard of the rights of small nations and of nationalities which lacked the union and the force to make good their claim to determine their own allegiances and their own forms of political life."[11] Wilson believed that people should choose their states and their governments and would be able to guide those governments away from dangerous adventures in foreign policy.

Both sets of warring multinational empires indulged in the potentially suicidal practice of encouraging revolts by the discontented national minorities of their opponents, though often in a rather half-hearted and ambiguous manner. The Central Powers targeted the Irish, Indians, and Poles; the Entente also targeted the Poles as well as Arabs and Czechs (whom they were assured were Czechoslovaks). Wilson's advocacy, and the circumstance that swept away the old order in Europe, transformed this ambivalent tactic of war into "an imperative principle of action," leaving national self-determination as the one credible basis for the new states system. Wilson's concept of nationality was, however, civic rather than ethnic, thus placing him firmly in a western liberal philosophical camp. For him, the accident of birth had no bearing on someone's allegiance to a state, hence people had the right (with certain caveats) to self-determine their nationality (by which Wilson really meant citizenship). East Europeans saw things very differently and believed that nationality was ethnically determined by birth, race, and religion. The two concepts did not readily mix.

National self-determination was, wrote Lansing, "a phrase simply loaded with dynamite."[12] In eastern and central Europe Wilson's principle encountered a complicated intermingling of ethnic and religious groups that defied the creation of homogenous states. Competing nationalities (of which there were many more than he had imagined) accepted no compromise to their ambitious plans for statehood. The practical considerations of defense, economic viability, and communication needs vied with linguistic and historical allegiances and considerations of administrative convenience, all suggesting differing lines of demarcation. In addition there were the ambitions and fears of the great powers, some of which regretted Wilson's demand "that peoples and provinces are not to be bartered about from sovereignty to sovereignty as if they were mere chattels and pawns in a game."[13]

The need to match the wishes of inhabitants with wider geopolitical considerations created a number of crisis points: the Rhineland, the Saar, Upper Silesia, the Banat of Temesvar, and the South Tyrol. The problem is best encapsulated in the attempt to deliver Wilson's thirteenth point, which proposed an "independent Polish state" including territories "inhabited by indisputably Polish populations" assured of "a free and secure access to the sea." Russia's collapse removed one embarrassment – Wilson was suggesting independence to the subjects of a wartime partner. The subsequent collapse of the Central Powers meant Poland existed before the peacemakers met. Here, as elsewhere, it was not the conference that created the new states; its role was to recognize their existence and adjudicate their disputed boundaries. But how were "indisputably Polish populations" to be defined? How could his requirement that the new state should have access to the Baltic be squared with the problem that the land linking the Polish heartland to the sea was not "indisputably Polish" and that the obvious port, Danzig, was indisputably German? Polish ambitions for the restored state backed by French plans to deprive Germany of as many resources as possible threatened Anglo-American hopes of a solution acceptable to Germany. The conference decided to make Danzig a free city, under the League, but linked economically to Poland. A corridor of land, whittled away by Lloyd George's insistence that the location of railway lines should not consign unwilling inhabitants into another state, linked Poland to Danzig and separated East and West Prussia. Plebiscites in Allenstein and Marienwerder went in favor of Germany and the Germans left on the wrong side of the new Polish frontier were guaranteed minority rights, illustrating two methods used by the conference in attempts to soften its decisions and their outcomes.

In 1914 there were some 60 million Europeans living in states in which they were minority nationalities. After 1919 that was reduced to 30 millions, though the problem was not necessarily halved because every person left on the wrong side of a new frontier was living proof that the principle had not been applied. On average 25 percent of the populations of the new states were still minorities; it would take the Holocaust and ruthless "ethnic cleansing" after 1945 to reduce that to 7 percent by 1970. Hitler's use of the Sudetenland Germans' discontent to destabilize Czechoslovakia in 1938 realized one of the peacemakers' nightmares.

The League of Nations

Wilson insisted that the first priority be the drafting of the Covenant of the League of Nations. He chaired all but one of the drafting commission's ten meetings in eleven days from February 3–14 and was, with one of the British delegates, Lord Robert Cecil, the main force driving the League's creation. Wilson's fourteenth point demanded that "A general association of nations must be formed under specific covenants for the purpose of affording mutual guarantees of political independence and territorial integrity to great and small states alike."

The idea was partly a development of growing internationalism in the prewar period, partly an enhancement of the existing European concert, and partly driven by what were perceived as the flaws in the existing structures that had permitted the precipitate collapse of peace in July 1914. It had gained support on both sides of the lines and both sides of the Atlantic as the consequences of that collapse became more and more tragic. It was at once simple and yet full of complications. War must not break out quickly; there must be attempts to settle any dispute. During that delay the weight of informed public opinion would change the minds of those intent on conflict. If a member state went to war with another member, without exhausting all the League's dispute-resolving mechanisms, then the rest of the League was bound to assist the victim of that aggression. In Wilson's original draft that obligation had been expressed as an automatic requirement to be at war with the aggressor. This posed, in its starkest form, the dilemma of creating a collective security system in a world of sovereign states. The guarantee on which any state could base its security must be automatic and unambiguous. That required that the members surrender their sovereignty over their most sensitive and important decision: whether or not to go to war. As Lansing pointed out, the American Constitution did not allow this, only Congress could declare war. The final version thus stated that the aggressor would be "deemed to have committed an act of war against all other members." This enabled each individual member's government to decide what its response to that act of war would be. This safeguarded national sovereignty but did little for the credibility of the League's guarantee, which would now be, at best, a delayed response of uncertain composition.

Cecil claimed: "For the most part there is no attempt to rely on anything like a superstate: no attempt to rely on force to carry out a decision of the Council or the Assembly of the League. What we rely on is public opinion . . . and if we are wrong about it, then the whole thing is wrong."

One of the French delegates whispered, in an audible aside, "Am I at a Peace Conference or in a madhouse?" The French wanted something more secure than public sentiment, preferring the League to have armed forces and a general staff to provide its members with assistance. It was, however, mainly an Anglo-American document that emerged, relying on delay and the force of world opinion to deter preemptive aggressive attacks. It did contain an impressive promise in Article 10 of the Covenant to "respect and preserve as against external aggression the territorial integrity and political independence of all members of the League" but, as Cecil remarked, "Yes, but do any of us mean it?"[14] This uncertainty was reinforced by possible contradictions between preserving the territorial status quo as promised here, and the possibility of peaceful change set out in Article 19, which gave members the right to refer to the League "treaties which have become inapplicable and . . . international conditions whose continuance might endanger the peace of the world." Wilson set great store in the ability of the League to put right the inevitable mistakes and injustices that the peacemakers would, under such severe pressure, commit. If, however, one state's territorial integrity was perceived to be a condition endangering world peace, which Article would prevail?

The League expressed the hopes of many that World War I should not be repeated and it was impossible for any democratic government to ignore the force of that sentiment in any public expression of its policies. Yet most policy makers remained unconvinced about collective security and happier in a balance-of-power world where states looked after their own security and made suitable alliances with limited numbers of other states. So they said one thing and did another and this was revealed dramatically in the Abyssinian crisis of 1935, when the need to maintain good relations with Italy for the sake of the balance of power clashed with collective security obligations to Abyssinia, a League member against whom Italy had committed aggression. The British government tried to juggle both policies but, predictably, failed. The League collapsed and Italy became the ally of Nazi Germany, the state against which Britain and France were seeking Italian support. The League did undertake good work in minority protection, disease control, and in hindering trades in drugs and women for prostitution. It oversaw the government of the Saar and Danzig and had responsibilities for former colonial territories. It did make a difference in disputes involving small powers but, in its main mission, to transform the way in which international relations were conducted and to prevent another major war, it failed. Nonetheless, a quarter of a century later, the peacemakers of 1945 believed that the experiment should be repeated and created a new version of the League of Nations, this time calling it the United Nations.

Reparations

If the League represented the noblest of the peace conference's aspirations, the bitter disputes about the amount and type of compensation Germany would have to pay for the damage caused by the war showed a very different side to the negotiations. The American banker Thomas Lamont, who was engaged in those discussions, declared: "The subject of reparations caused more trouble, contention, hard feeling and delay at the Paris Peace Conference than any other point of the Treaty."[15] The questions were deceptively simple: how much damage had been done; what part of that damage should Germany repair; should Germany's liability be determined by adding up all the legitimate bills against it; or should the allies try to establish what Germany could afford and then agree a figure, certainly less than any calculation of its total debt, which the allies would nonetheless accept as discharging all Germany's responsibilities (a fixed sum)? There were, of course, complicating factors. How were these calculations to be made? What would be a reasonable estimate of Germany's capacity to pay after it recovered from its present weakened condition? How would Germany actually pay? For how long? And who would get what in terms of receipts? As with the broader negotiations each of these variables intertwined and affected thinking about the others.

Underlying all these questions, however, was an even deeper issue, well expressed by Sally Marks:

> At heart, reparations were about two fundamental and closely related questions: who won the war and who would pay for it, or at least the cost of undoing the damage . . . If the Allies, and especially France, had to assume reconstruction costs on top of domestic and foreign war debts, whereas Germany was left with only domestic debts, they would be the losers, and German economic dominance would be tantamount to victory. Reparations would both deny Germany that victory and spread the pain of undoing the damage done.[16]

The term "reparations" reminds us that one of the main issues in Paris was whether Germany should pay simply for damage to civilian property (reparations) or should pay for the whole cost of the war (an indemnity). Historically, the rule was that the loser paid, but, as part of his higher moral package of peacemaking, Wilson rejected this in his "Four Principles" speech of February 11, 1918: "There shall be no annexations, no contributions, no punitive damages." He had, however, mentioned on several occasions in the Fourteen Points, that invaded territories should be "evacuated and restored." Lloyd George and Clemenceau included in Lansing's note of November 5 the pious hope that "the Allied Governments feel no doubt ought to be allowed to exist as to what this provision implies."

> By it they understand that compensation will be made by Germany for all the damage done to the civilian population of the Allies and their property by the aggression of Germany by land, by sea and from the air.

This seemed to be conclusive, but when the Paris conference opened Britain and France both made claims for full war costs, driven in part by domestic expectations fired by politicians' promises that it would be Germany, not allied taxpayers, who would foot the bill. Wilson was adamant, there would be no indemnity, Lloyd George and Clemenceau were equally determined and the conference was threatened. Two American delegates, the young John Foster Dulles and Norman Davis, produced a compromise: Germany should, morally, pay for all war costs, but, because it could not possibly afford this, would be asked only to pay for civilian damages. This formed the basis of Articles 231 and 232. Article 231 stated:

> Germany accepts the responsibility of Germany and her allies for causing all the damage to which the Allied and Associated Governments and their nationals have been subjected as a consequence of the war imposed upon them by the aggression of Germany and her allies.

Article 232 then recognized

> that the resources of Germany are not adequate . . . to make complete reparation for all the loss and damage. The Allied and Associated Governments, however, require . . . that she will make compensation for all damage done to the civilian population . . . and to their property.

This is one of the classic examples of something done for what seemed to be compelling reasons at the time but which proved to be rich in unintended consequences. Germany seized on what it claimed was an accusation of sole German responsibility for the outbreak of the war. The "war guilt" clause proved a useful lever for Germans trying to undermine the credibility of the settlement, but of more practical importance at the time was what would be defined as "damage to the civilian population."

This was significant both to Germany because it would be a major factor in setting its eventual bill, and to the Allies because it would help to determine their individual shares of the receipts. If civilian damage was interpreted strictly then France and Belgium, where most of the fighting in the west had occurred, would get the lion's share. Britain would get relatively minor sums to cover its merchant shipping losses and bomb and gun damage caused by German air and sea raids. Australia and the other British Dominions, which had spent more men and money than Belgium, would get nothing. For domestic and imperial reasons, therefore, Lloyd George needed a wider definition. His South African colleague, Jan Smuts, a lawyer by trade, provided Wilson with an excuse to offer what he saw as a fairer division of German payments between the Allies. Smuts argued that civilian conscripts were not, properly speaking, military personnel, but civilians in uniform and hence pensions paid to injured soldiers and their dependants could be categorized as "civilian damage." Wilson's heart, if not his head, was persuaded. "Logic? I don't give a damn for logic, if you will excuse my French. I am going to include pensions."[17]

Wilson almost certainly believed that the conference would name a fixed sum and hence that his decision would not increase German liability, merely the distribution of the receipts. Various figures of varying credibility were mentioned, with British claims often the most extravagant.[18] Lloyd George later claimed that his policy had been more moderate but that he was trapped by the implacability of his advisors, Lords Cunliffe and Sumner, "the Heavenly Twins."[19] Here, as elsewhere, Lloyd George's truthfulness has been questioned. A fixed sum proved politically inexpedient in 1919, so the conference agreed to postpone the quantification of Germany's debt, perhaps to allow realistic expectations to evolve. Germany thus signed a "blank check" on which no numbers would appear for two years. When in May 1921 the reparations commission set the bill at £6.6 billion, roughly half represented pensions and other allowances. Given the terms of the bonds Germany was required to deliver, payment much beyond £3 billion was never anticipated, the rest was "phoney money" for the benefit of public expectations. Germany's capacity to earn and to transfer such sums has been much debated, though Gerald Feldman has suggested that "apparently the only people who really believed that the Germans could fulfill their reparations obligations . . . are some historians."[20] Nonetheless the cost of the war and its aftermath did represent genuine burdens. A more generous attitude from America about the debts incurred by the Allies in order to fight the war might have helped, but Wilson and his successors would admit no linkage between reparations and inter-Allied debts. As President Calvin Coolidge apparently remarked: "They hired the money, didn't they?"[21] Reparations bedeviled international relations and international finance throughout the 1920s, providing a useful tool for discontented revisionists.

Conclusion

The Versailles settlement recognized the creation of nine new states. It deprived Germany of over 6.5 million people and 27,000 square miles of land (10 percent and 13 percent, respectively, of its prewar resources). Germany's losses included Alsace-Lorraine, Eupen and Malmédy, northern Schleswig, Danzig and the Polish corridor (which split East and West Prussia), Posen, Memel, and half of Upper Silesia. The Saar coalmines went to France, the territory was ceded for 15 years to the League, after which a plebiscite would decide its fate. The Rhineland was demilitarized permanently and occupied by the Allies for 15 years. Germany also lost over 1 million square miles of colonial possessions, with 14 million inhabitants, surrendered technically to the League, though the mandates system was little more than a camouflage for an imperial division of the spoils. It was forbidden an air force, heavy artillery, tanks, poison gas, and a general staff, with its army restricted to 100,000 long-service volunteers and its tiny navy to 15,000 men. It was obligated to deliver as yet unnamed "war criminals" (the Dutch were pressed to surrender Kaiser Wilhelm II but refused) and it had agreed to pay as yet unspecified reparations to the victors. It was forbidden union with the rump state of Austria. The Sudetenland, with 3 million German speakers, remained part of Czechoslovakia. Germany did not accept the verdict or the results of the settlement and attacks on the *diktat* (which it was) and "slave treaty" (which it was not) became standard fare for disgruntled right-wing nationalists throughout the 1920s. It should be noted, however, that Nazi electoral success had infinitely more to do with 1929 than 1919.

Elsewhere, the Balkan states, with the exception of Bulgaria (which experienced minor losses of territory and population), made important gains – with Yugoslavia (technically until 1929 the Kingdom of the Serbs, Croats, and Slovenes) the biggest winner. Serbia in 1914 had 33,900 square miles and 4,600,000 people; Yugoslavia by 1921 had 101,250 square miles and a population of 13,635,000. Greece and Romania also made significant gains, while Austria, Hungary, and Turkey were the losers. The Balkans seemed much less fragmented than in 1914, though eastern and central Europe went in the opposite direction. Finland, Estonia, Latvia, Lithuania, Poland, and Czechoslovakia (in addition to Yugoslavia and the rump states of Austria and Hungary) filled the vacuum left by the collapsed empires, creating thousands of miles of new frontiers. In the middle east the settlement created new states and contributed towards tensions that still occupy newspapers and television screens today – Mesopotamia (now Iraq), Transjordania (Jordan), the Hijaz (Saudi Arabia), Syria, and Lebanon, together with the enduring problem of the twice, or thrice, promised land, Palestine (Israel). In the near east Turkey made Lausanne an important part of its founding myth.

The peace treaties at the end of World War I were truly a global settlement, reflecting the scope of the conflict and the struggle to come to terms with an unfamiliar world. Some powers had lost their previous status: for Germany and Russia, reborn as the Soviet Union, this was temporary, for Austria-Hungary and the Ottoman Empire, permanent. Others, namely the United States and Japan, emerged as major international players, while the European victors, France and the United Kingdom (and the ambivalent Italy), seemed to have greater influence and control than they could actually sustain. Facing an enormous task, after an exhausting war and aware of their daunting responsibilities, the peacemakers strove to recreate order from the shipwreck of the old world. Nicolson's 1933 judgment (before Hitler's ambitions were clear and before contemporaries knew they were living in the interwar period) was harsh on himself and his colleagues: "We came to Paris convinced that the new order was about to be established; we left it convinced that the old order had merely fouled the new."[22] A more realistic judgment might be that the settlements were not perfect and contained many potential seeds of future conflict, but yet also the potential for a more hopeful world. The outcome depended on the decisions of later leaders, but was also heavily influenced by tensions that had existed before the Paris Conference met and that would continue after the Four had vanished into political oblivion. Our contemporary record of dealing with virulent ethnic nationalism, ideological extremism, and the collapse of only one major empire, should at least give pause to those who would condemn too readily the efforts of those trying to make the world anew in 1919.

NOTES

1 Keith Eubank, *The Summit Conferences 1919–1969* (Oklahoma: Oklahoma University Press, 1966).
2 Margaret MacMillan, *Peacemakers: The Paris Conference of 1919 and Its Attempt to End War* (London: John Murray, 2001), p. 1 and, quoting Wilson, p. 7.
3 See Manfred Boemeke, Gerald Feldman, and Elisabeth Glaser, eds, "Introduction," in *The Treaty of Versailles: A Reassessment after 75 Years* (Cambridge: Cambridge University Press, 1998), pp. 11–20; Zara Steiner, "The Treaty of Versailles Revisited," in Michael Dockrill and John Fisher, eds, *The Paris Peace Conference 1919: Peace without Victory?* (Basingstoke: Palgrave, 2001), pp. 13–33; Mark Mazower, "Two Cheers for Versailles," *History Today* 49/7 (1999): 8–14.
4 Jay Winter and Blaine Baggett, *1914–1918: The Great War and the Shaping of the Twentieth Century* (London: BBC Books, 1996), p. 338.
5 CAB 491B, 26.10.18, in CAB 23/14, National Archives, Kew.
6 Esmé Howard Diary 18.1.19 D/HW1/5 in the Cumbrian Record Office, Carlisle.
7 Harold Nicolson, *Peacemaking 1919* (London: Constable, 1933), p. 100.
8 Ibid, p. 242 (author's translation).
9 Quoted by David Perman, *The Shaping of the Czechoslovak State* (Leiden: Brill, 1962), p. 169.
10 John Maynard Keynes, *The Economic Consequences of the Peace* (London: Macmillan, 1919).
11 Harold Temperley, ed., *A History of the Peace Conference of Paris*, 6 vols (Oxford: Oxford University Press, 1920 onwards), vol. 1, p. 438.
12 Robert Lansing, *The Peace Negotiations: A Personal Narrative* (New York: Houghton Mifflin, 1921), p. 97.
13 Temperley, *Peace Conference*, vol. 1, p. 437.
14 All quoted by A. Sharp, *The Versailles Settlement: Peacemaking in Paris, 1919* (Basingstoke: Macmillan, 1991), pp. 62, 57.
15 Quoted by MacMillan, *Peacemakers*, p. 191.
16 Sally Marks, "Smoke and Mirrors: In Smoke-Filled Rooms and the Galerie des Glaces," in *Versailles After 75 Years*, Boemeke et al., eds, pp. 337–8.
17 Arthur Walworth, *Wilson and His Peacemakers: American Diplomacy at the Paris Peace Conference, 1919* (New York: Norton, 1986), p. 281. Antony Lentin in "Maynard Keynes and the 'Bamboozlement' of Woodrow Wilson: What Really Happened at Paris? (Wilson, Lloyd George, Pensions and Pre-Armistice Agreement)," *Diplomacy and Statecraft* 15/4 (2004): 725–63, argues that Smuts' claim, while not accepted by Wilson's American advisors, was not dismissed as readily as a legal concept as some historians (including the present writer) have done.
18 The figures of £3–5 billion occurred in several contexts, but British claims began at £24 billion and rarely fell below £8 billion. See Sharp, *Versailles*, pp. 89–96.
19 They were called this because they were always together and demanded astronomical sums. A. Lentin, *Lloyd George and the Lost Peace: From Versailles to Hitler, 1919–1940* (Basingstoke: Palgrave, 2001), pp. 23–46.
20 G. Feldman, in *Versailles after 75 Years*, Boemeke et al., eds, p. 445.

21 See Arthur Turner, *The Cost of War: British Policy on French War Debts 1918–1932* (Brighton: Sussex Academic Press, 1998).

22 Nicolson, *Peacemaking*, p. 187.

GUIDE TO FURTHER READING

Anthony Adamthwaite, *Grandeur and Misery: France's Bid for Power in Europe 1914–1940* (London: Arnold, 1995). A good survey of French foreign policy.

Lloyd Ambrosius, *Woodrow Wilson and the American Diplomatic Tradition* (Cambridge: Cambridge University Press, 1987) and Klaus Schwabe, *Woodrow Wilson, Revolutionary Germany, and Peacemaking 1918–1919* (Chapel Hill: North Carolina University Press, 1985). Excellent studies from differing angles.

Manfred Boemeke, Gerald Feldman, and Elisabeth Glaser, eds, *The Treaty of Versailles: A Reassessment after 75 Years* (Cambridge: Cambridge University Press, 1998) and Michael Dockrill and John Fisher, eds, *The Paris Peace Conference 1919: Peace without Victory?* (Basingstoke: Palgrave, 2001). The proceedings of two international conferences involving most of the leading specialists.

Michael Dockrill and J. Douglas Goold, *Peace Without Promise: Britain and the Peace Conferences 1919–1923* (London: Batsford, 1981) and Erik Goldstein, *Winning the Peace: British Diplomatic Strategy, Peace Planning and the Paris Peace Conference 1916–1920* (Oxford: Clarendon Press, 1991). Reliable overviews of British policies.

Seamus Dunn and T. G. Fraser, eds, *Europe and Ethnicity: World War I and Contemporary Ethnic Conflict* (London: Routledge, 1996) and Derek Heater, *National Self-Determination: Woodrow Wilson and His Legacy* (Basingstoke: Macmillan, 1994). Helpful studies of the ethnic conflict legacies of the war.

Bruce Kent, *The Spoils of War: The Politics, Economics and Diplomacy of Reparations, 1918–1932*, revd edn (Oxford: Clarendon Paperbacks, 1991) and Marc Trachtenberg, *Reparation in World Politics: France and European Economic Diplomacy 1916–1923* (New York: Columbia University Press, 1980). Good analyses of a controversial subject.

Antony Lentin, *Guilt at Versailles: Lloyd George and the Pre-History of Appeasement* (London: Methuen, 1985). Witty, acerbic, and informative.

F. S. Northedge, *The League of Nations: Its Life and Times 1920–1946* (Leicester: Leicester University Press, 1986). An accessible history of the League.

Margaret MacMillan, *Paris 1919: Six Months that Changed the World* (New York: Random House, 2001); also published as *Peacemakers: The Paris Conference of 1919 and Its Attempt to End War* (London: John Murray, 2001). Elegantly written and wide ranging.

Sally Marks, *The Illusion of Peace: International Relations in Europe, 1918–1933*, 2nd edn (Basingstoke: Palgrave, 2003). Splendid analysis of the aftermath.

Alan Sharp, *The Versailles Settlement: Peacemaking in Paris, 1919* (Basingstoke: Macmillan, 1991). A succinct overview.

CHAPTER EIGHTEEN

Demobilization and Discontent

JAMES M. DIEHL

In 1929 the perceptive French historian Elie Halévy noted: "Certainly no responsible statesman would have said, at the beginning of 1914, that he felt safe against the perils of some kind of revolutionary outburst."[1] As the international crisis deepened in the summer of 1914, all of the future European belligerent powers were experiencing severe domestic crises. In each country the Forces of Order, composed of the traditional elites and their conservative allies, were being challenged by the Forces of Movement, represented primarily by rapidly growing socialist parties.

The long-held view that the outbreak of war was greeted with general enthusiasm has proven to be exaggerated.[2] Some among the Forces of Order welcomed the war, seeing it as an opportunity to rally support to the existing state and repress opposition. Some intellectuals greeted the war with enthusiasm, believing it would regenerate complacent and stifling bourgeois societies. The oft-pictured crowds shown celebrating the war's outbreak in cities and capitols were largely middle class. In working-class districts there were demonstrations against war, followed by sullen acceptance, as labor leaders rallied to their governments. In the countryside, the war's outbreak was met by resigned acceptance. In all countries the war's outbreak produced a series of social truces and, at least initially, national unity was achieved. Domestic issues were buried in the face of the common external threat. Regardless of what else they thought about it, Europeans were convinced that the war would be short.

The War

Instead of quick victory, the war produced a prolonged, bloody stalemate. Instead of the expected "great adventure," the war became a nightmare of muddy trenches, rats, lice, and death. Terrifying bombardments, unprecedented and unimaginable mayhem, and, above all, unending slaughter with no discernable progress became the hallmarks of what was to become known as the Great War. The stark contrast between expectations and reality came as a great shock, especially for middle-class soldiers, who had been raised on romantic images of war. For working-class soldiers, the contrast was less dramatic, since the routine of backbreaking, boring, mundane work in the trenches, punctuated by danger, was not that different from ordinary work routines.[3]

Stalemate presented new challenges to the belligerent governments. Mobilization of military forces was no longer enough to ensure victory. It was necessary to mobilize the entire nation, above all the economy. In short, governments had to create a home front that could sustain the fighting front. The resources of the nation, both material and human, had to be fully mobilized and harnessed to the war effort. Non-essential sectors of the economy were allowed to languish or were shut down. All available sources of labor were tapped. The unexpected complexity of directing the first industrial war led to an unprecedented increase in the state's power, an experience that was to provide a model for diverse political persuasions after the war.

After two years of total war, war weariness gripped the belligerent nations. Both the home and fighting fronts were affected. On the military front, discipline began to break down. Soldiers despaired and increasingly felt that they were victims, not heroes. The endless slaughter that they experienced seemed to be for no purpose, as the battle lines remained fixed. While the troops experienced a disconnect and isolation from the home front, which was increasingly alien, furloughs and letters provided a connection to families, and soldiers' anger with their governments grew as a result of reports from loved ones of inadequate separation allowances and insufficient food. In Russia, the most autocratic regime failed the test of total war. Both the home front and the army collapsed. Soldiers deserted in droves and the country was engulfed in revolution.[4] On the western front, the French army mutinied in the spring of 1917. Here the troops' actions were not directed against the regime *per se*, but against the military leadership and the way in which the war was being fought. French troops were willing to fight for their country and its liberation from foreign occupiers, but they wanted an end to the continuation of tactics that produced nothing but senseless slaughter. The French mutinies were more like an industrial strike against unbearable working conditions than a prelude to revolution, a fitting response to the first industrial war.[5]

On the home front, social truces began to break down. The massive slaughter at the front touched nearly every family by death. The home front combatants chafed at increasing regimentation and deprivation. The legitimacy of governmental policies was questioned. Domestic politics began to reassert themselves under the guise of the debate over war aims.[6] Governments were increasingly pressed to explicate what they were fighting for. Demands for a negotiated peace began to be raised. Governments were forced to remobilize their exhausted populations on both the home and fighting fronts.[7] The terms for further support of the war had to be negotiated (or renegotiated), a process that involved concessions in the present and promises of reform in the future. The democratic governments, Britain and France, succeeded in this process, largely because they had more credibility and their citizens felt they had a stake in their government's success. Italy and the authoritarian monarchies failed to succeed in remobilizing their people because it was clear that their governments were not seriously committed to correcting the glaring inequities that the war had so clearly revealed. War, even if it ended in victory, would not bring reform, and support declined accordingly.

Once the war ended, demobilization, longed for by the combatants of both the fighting and home fronts, brought not the promised and expected better world, but disappointment, disillusionment, and discontent. While many in the Forces of Order camp had welcomed the war and the ensuing social truces as a way of blocking reform, they now discovered that the strains of prolonged war and continued resistance to change weakened morale and delegitimized the state, creating an environment in which defeat meant revolution. Following their defeats, the eastern monarchies were swept away. In Russia the tsarist regime was replaced by a revolutionary Soviet regime, which called for a world revolution. In Austria-Hungary, the Habsburg Empire disintegrated into its component ethnic parts. In Germany, Wilhelm II was forced to abdicate and the conservative Bismarckian Reich was replaced by a liberal parliamentary government, the Weimar republic. Although Italy was nominally a victor and the monarchy remained intact, the nation emerged from the war bitterly divided.

Postwar Problems

In the years immediately following the war, it appeared that the Allies' claim that the war was "to make the world safe for democracy" had been vindicated. The democracies had been victorious and the new regimes that emerged from the wreckage of the defeated authoritarian states were democratic. But the apparent triumph of democracy was short lived. By the early 1920s Russia and Italy were dictatorships. By the end of the decade the successor states were almost without exception authoritarian, and Germany entered a crisis that ended with the Nazi takeover. Even the established democracies foundered. The war had created a new political landscape peopled with democratic institutions, but the socioeconomic, political, and psychological strains and dislocations of the war created powerful obstacles to their successful operation.

If in international terms the interwar years represented an era of cold war between defenders and opponents of the order created at the Paris Peace Conference, in domestic terms it was an era of civil war, open and latent, between the (primarily Marxist) left and the (primarily bourgeois) right. In terms of domestic politics, the interwar years opened not with the end of World War I in 1918 but with the Russian revolution of 1917 and closed not with the beginning of World War II but with its end.[8] If before 1914 war was the continuation of politics by other means, after 1917 politics became a continuation of war by other means.

Postwar societies were deeply divided and badly fractured. Prewar problems had not been solved by the war, but were exacerbated, while new ones had been created. All of the belligerent states, including the victors, faced enormous problems. The main and most debilitating of these was class conflict. The war had dramatically changed the prewar socioeconomic and political balance of power. Because labor formed the backbone of industrial warfare, its position was strengthened. To ensure uninterrupted production, governments had to make concessions and socialist parties and trade unions emerged from the war stronger. This was in sharp contrast to the middle-class experience. Key areas of middle-class economic activity such as consumer goods and service industries had languished or shut down during the war, since they were non-essential. While all sectors of society were hurt by war-induced inflation and postwar hyperinflation, the middle classes were hit hardest.[9] War bonds, bought with patriotic enthusiasm, declined in value and in some cases became worthless.

Savings disappeared. Salaried employment, an asset before the war, became a liability in an inflationary environment. Long-term economic planning, a staple of the bourgeois lifestyle, became impossible. As a result of these factors, the socioeconomic position of the middle classes eroded, while that of labor, at least in relative terms, improved. The war also deepened mistrust between urban and rural populations. The result was sharpened class conflict, which became the keystone of postwar politics.

The war also deepened another prewar social division. The division of the belligerent countries into home and fighting fronts was more than a functional one. It was also gendered, with a masculinized fighting front and feminized home front. Women were pulled into the labor force to replace men who had been drafted and killed. This was not the result, as it is often portrayed, of a massive influx of previously unemployed women, but primarily a transfer of working women from sectors of the prewar economy that had been dominated by women into areas that had been monopolized by men.[10] After the war some women welcomed the increased independence provided by working outside the home and wanted to remain in the labor force. Many, widows and younger women with reduced prospects of marriage, had no choice. In any case women were quickly pushed out of industry and returned to traditional sectors. The threat, feared by many males, that they would be replaced by unskilled women never became reality, except in the clerical and retail sectors. Although the emancipating effects of war are often exaggerated, women after the war were more visible and assertive and this fed misogynist anger among many males and cultural conservatives. Some soldiers resented the way expected wartime roles did not play out the way they were expected to, but were reversed: the mobilization of women freed them geographically and socially, while the mobilization of men immobilized them in the trenches and made them dependent and passive.[11] Moreover, at the same time that wartime service appeared to masculinize women, the growing number of shell shock cases, "male hysteria," raised fears that war, rather than enhancing male soldiers' virility, was feminizing them. Postwar anxiety over gender roles was compounded by demographic concerns.[12] One of the several shared goals of cultural conservatives and fascists in the interwar years was the restoration of women to their traditional roles as wives and mothers.

The deepened gender gap was also accompanied by a deepened generation gap. Soldiers were angered by the policies of politicians and senior staff that consigned them to the hellish world of the trenches. Wartime memoir literature is replete with soldiers' outrage with the older generation, which, safe in its armchairs, sent the war generation to its death and repeatedly bungled the war effort. On the home front parental authority was weakened as a result of the drafting of fathers and the wartime employment of mothers. Children were unsupervised and through wartime employment gained a certain economic independence. They no longer were willing to accept control by traditional sources of authority, parents, teachers, clergymen. As with women, the changed role of youth was the source of a chorus of Cassandra calls by cultural conservatives, who, like the fascists, believed the way to tame wild youth was through military service and the inculcation of military values. While the older generation deplored the changes caused by the war, the war and postwar generations resented the fact that there had not been enough change and that the old, prewar leaders were still in charge.

Interwar politics were dominated by economic issues. Ultimately, the question was who was going to pay for the war and, then, the Depression, itself a product of the war. In the broken postwar world, classic economic solutions no longer worked and often exacerbated the problems they sought to solve. Would inflation be combated through reduced government spending or higher taxes? Would the Depression be solved through deflationary or inflationary measures? Economists notwithstanding, the solutions were not value-free. They had consequences that favored some social groups and hurt others. In an age of mass politics it was no longer possible, as it had been in the nineteenth century, to disregard the interests of the weaker elements of society. Because they represented discrete socioeconomic constituencies that were directly and oppositely affected by the different solutions to economic problems being considered, it was difficult for working-class and middle-class liberal parties to work together. While cooperation was often possible on political and foreign policy issues, when it came to economic and fiscal issues cooperation broke down. As a result, parliamentary government foundered.

The postwar empowerment of previously disenfranchised groups made mass politics a reality. In the abstract, it might be expected that wartime socioeconomic leveling and postwar political reform would help ease the way for postwar democracy, but the opposite occurred. The aspirations of those who had, at least in relative terms, benefited, were raised, while the fears of those whose positions had been weakened grew. Wartime sacrifice combined with postwar economic difficulties created widespread disillusionment. Everyone felt that they had been victimized and that their socioeconomic and political rivals had unjustly gained at their expense. As postwar social and political tension mounted, the wartime practice of dividing the world into friends and foes and demonizing enemies was carried over into peacetime and furthered by the increasingly ideological nature of politics. Postwar politics became a no-holds-barred, zero-sum game in which more people were fighting for a smaller pie. Compromise was ruled out.

A concrete manifestation of postwar polarization was a new phenomenon that became a hallmark of the interwar years: street violence produced by clashes between the "political soldiers" of opposing social and political "fronts." Demobilized soldiers formed the core of these paramilitary organizations in the immediate postwar years, but by the end of the 1920s their ranks were increasingly being filled by young men who had missed the war but now sought their own war experience in the streets, rather than in the trenches.

Moderate centrist parties declined as the ferocity of political conflict increased. Postwar politics increasingly become polarized around the opposing poles of communism and fascism. The war convinced many on the left that liberal democracy and social democracy were bankrupt and that the more radical communist program was the correct roadmap of the future. Similarly, the war and postwar developments convinced many of the middle and upper classes that the liberal parliamentary state, as well as traditional conservatism, was bankrupt and incapable of defending their interests against a strengthened left. The fact that each ideology became embodied in a state, the Soviet Union and Mussolini's fascist regime, worked to frighten opponents and embolden proponents. Above all, the formation of national communist parties fed fears of the propertied classes, and many, especially in the revolution-wracked defeated states, turned to fascism to defeat both their "internal" and "external" enemies. The success of fascism depended on a number of factors: the extent of the threat from the left; the confidence of the bourgeoisie in the state's ability to counter leftist threats; the loyalty of civil and military institutions – the bureaucracy, police, and army. In Italy and Germany these institutions were dominated by traditional elites who distrusted democratic government and consequently forged alliances with the fascists to destroy it. In England the weakness of the communist threat combined with the almost uninterrupted rule of the Conservative Party reassured the propertied classes and checked the growth of fascism. In France the political pendulum swung back and forth. When the Republic's institutions seemed able to protect the interests of the bourgeoisie, as in 1919–24 and 1928–32, fascism waned. When, however, institutions appeared to be captured by the left, after the victories of the *cartel des gauches* in 1924 and 1932, then fascism waxed. Following the victory of the Popular Front in 1936, France was in a state of virtual civil war, a *guerre franco-française*.[13]

Veterans

The war produced a new social group, veterans, which played an important and often disruptive role in the fractured postwar societies. Veterans, the human war surplus of the Great War, had already emerged as a political force before postwar demobilization. The first to take collective action were those who had been wounded and disabled, those demobilized by disability. By 1916 two years of unremitting slaughter had exposed the inadequacies of existing systems of disability treatment, rehabilitation, and pensions. The vast numbers of wounded and maimed overwhelmed systems that were designed to care for professional soldiers and only limited numbers of conscript casualties. Prewar care for disabled veterans was piecemeal and heavily dependent on voluntary charitable organizations. World War I sounded the death knell of voluntarism. By the end of 1916 war-disabled organizations were being formed in all the belligerent nations. The new organizations demanded an acknowledgment of the modern wartime social contract: since the state had compelled them to defend it, and while doing so they had been injured, the state was obligated to provide compensation. As they repeatedly asserted, the war disabled wanted justice, not charity: comprehensive, state-supported programs for the treatment of disabled veterans. They also demanded rehabilitation and reintegration, rather than the warehousing that had characterized prewar treatment of disabled veterans. This demand found favor with many state officials, who wanted to reclaim the labor potential of the disabled.

The original impetus for the foundation of organizations for the war-disabled came from the left, and welfare demands were increasingly coupled with political demands. After the Russian revolution governments could ill afford to ignore the political potential of veterans. Efforts were made to establish organizations that would mobilize veterans in support of the existing political and social order. Piecemeal reforms were implemented and promises were made, but nothing substantive was done until after the war. The resulting war-disability systems were complicated and costly, prompting discontent among both the disabled and taxpayers.

Like those demobilized by disability, the able-bodied veterans demobilized by victory or defeat were a volatile force. For millions of men the war remained the decisive formative experience of their lives and they were unable to free themselves from its spell. Their experience in the liminal, troglodyte world of the trenches scarred and embittered them and made their reintegration into civilian society difficult.[14] As a result, every belligerent nation was host to a substantial postwar army of men unable or unwilling to demobilize psychologically.

While veterans were a universal product of the war and shared much in common, their postwar experience was filtered through the particular national matrix to which they returned. In Russia, soldiers, who had demobilized themselves by "voting for peace with their feet," were soon remobilized into a brutal civil war and a new war against foreign invaders. Although veterans of the Red Army received recognition by the Soviet state, those of World War I did not.[15] Elsewhere, veterans fared better, but their treatment and postwar roles varied considerably.

British veterans, like others, began to organize in 1916. Because of its tradition of a small, voluntary army, Britain, even more than the other belligerent countries, was unprepared to cope with the staggering number of casualties. With the introduction of conscription in 1916, the issue became even more pressing, since one could no longer say one joined the army at one's own risk. Scattered groups of disabled soldiers were formed in 1916. In January 1917 the first major organization, the National Federation of Discharged and Demobilized Sailors and Soldiers, was founded. In November Conservatives, headed by Lord Derby, created an organization, the Comrades of the Great War, which was designed to mobilize veterans in support of the status quo. Other groups were also established and by war's end there were four separate veterans' organizations in Britain.[16]

Following the armistice, the discontent of veterans became a major problem and a source of concern for the British government, which, mindful of the role of veterans in the Russian revolution, maintained close surveillance of their actions. The slow pace of demobilization combined with high levels of unemployment fueled discontent, producing riots and "soldiers'strikes." Veteran unrest and disruptive activity reached its peak in the summer and fall of 1919. Thereafter, discontent subsided as the labor market improved and the government acted to fulfill demands for pensions. In 1921 the remaining veterans' organizations merged to form the British Legion, which largely limited its activity to lobbying for improved benefits and avoided the pursuit of "external" (i.e., political) goals.[17]

The story in France was similar, though there ideological and political differences, reflecting French society, were more diverse and deeper.[18] The initial impulse to organize veterans came from the author Henri Barbusse, who used the royalties from his bestselling anti-war novel, *Under Fire*, to found the Republican Association of War Veterans (ARAC), which was dedicated to bringing peace and establishing pensions for the war-disabled. ARAC claimed to be apolitical, but it soon, like its founder, became affiliated with the communists. By 1923 it was little more than the veterans' auxiliary of the French Communist Party, which doomed it to insignificance.

In France, as elsewhere, there were two cohorts of veterans: those demobilized by disability and those demobilized by the ending of the war. In November 1917 a national congress was held of local disabled veterans' organizations that had been spontaneously formed throughout France during the previous year, and the Federated Union of Veterans (UF) was founded the following February. The UF's political composition was centrist; it concentrated its efforts on expanding the pension system and avoided partisan politics. In November 1918 the National Union of Veterans (UNC) was founded. It consisted primarily of non-disabled veterans and was politically conservative. Unlike the UF, the UNC was formed from the top down and was an effort by traditional elites to control veterans and steer them away from radical activity. Despite the organizations' different constituencies and political orientations, they were able to cooperate in lobbying for benefits. Although the UNC's leaders periodically flirted with radical right-wing organizations, they were reined in by the rank and file, and extremist efforts to gain control of the UNC failed. As a consequence, the major veterans' organizations in France were on the whole moderate, more regime stabilizing than destabilizing.

The various fascist leagues were a different matter. The first leagues, which emerged in the early 1920s, were inspired by, and modeled on, the Italian *squadristi*. Like the latter, they included many veterans, but they were not, strictly speaking, veterans' organizations. The leagues flourished following the leftist victory in the 1924 elections, but declined after the rightist victory in 1928. The Croix de Feu (Cross of Fire), founded in 1928, initially limited membership to veterans who had fought at the front. In its early years the organization was conservative and nationalist, but largely apolitical. This changed in the early 1930s, when it became fascist, but by then its membership had been broadened to include non-veterans.[19]

Unlike other belligerent nations, where the outbreak of war initially produced consensus and unity, in Italy the war divided the country from the beginning.[20] The war was imposed on an unwilling majority. Italy's entrance was not dictated by defensive needs or treaty obligations, but by the opportunistic calculations of its leaders and extra-parliamentary pressure from nationalist organizations. The country was unprepared for war, and the illusion that it would be short faded quickly. The war greatly distorted Italy's already weak economy and Italians suffered accordingly. The resentment and alienation of the lower classes, exploited and excluded before the war, steadily mounted. Aware of the general discontent, the government reacted harshly, militarizing society and the economy. The measures taken in Italy to mobilize the nation for war were more like those taken by the militaristic authoritarian Central Powers than those of the western democracies to which Italy nominally belonged.

Victory brought to Italy, not peace, but a revolutionary crisis. The postwar demobilization was as clumsy and ill-managed as the mobilization of 1915. There was unrest among workers not only in cities but also in rural areas, where promises of land reform had not been kept. High rates of unemployment and inflation added to the general turmoil. The government, fearful of revolution, kept soldiers scheduled for demobilization in active service to combat potential uprisings, a move which further angered soldiers and their families.

Italians across the political spectrum felt they had been betrayed by the Liberal government and emerged from the war convinced that wartime policies had favored their rivals while hurting them. The left denounced the state's favoring of the propertied interests, while the right denounced the state's concessions to labor and charged that leftist opposition had weakened Italy's war effort and undercut its position at the peace conference, producing a "mutilated victory." Democratic institutions, never strong in Italy, were irreparably weakened and unable to regain legitimacy. At the same time, the enormous power that the state had wielded during the war made clear the desirability of capturing control of it.

With the end of the war, a bitter struggle for power broke out with the pendulum swinging first to the left and then to the right. The relaxation of wartime controls unleashed a strong shift to the left, the *Biennio Rosso* or "two red years." The leftist surge was fueled by a number of factors: solidarity generated by prewar and wartime grievances, organizational consolidation of the Italian Socialist Party (PSI) and its affiliated unions, vacillation by the Liberal government, and disarray on the right. The results were huge gains for the PSI in the national elections of 1919, socialist control of local and regional governments, and favorable wage and labor contracts, both in factories and in rural areas. By 1921 the leftist wave began to ebb, weakened by indecisive leadership and partisan divisions. The right, galvanized by the *Biennio Rosso*, went on the attack, led by Mussolini's reconstituted fascist movement. The rightist offensive was spearheaded by the fascist *squadristi* which violently smashed leftist organizations, beat and murdered their leaders, and forcibly ousted recently installed socialist governments. The murderous assaults of the *squadristi* were not only tolerated but also openly applauded by the traditional elites, the police and military, and the frightened middle classes, who feared a socialist revolution. The fascist victory culminated in the March on Rome and Mussolini's installation as prime minister in the fall of 1922. Veterans were a key ingredient in the violent postwar struggle for power in Italy. Initially they were associated as much, if not more, with the left as with the right, but eventually they became primarily identified with the right as a result of their prominent role in the fascist *squadristi*.[21] Once in power the fascist party brought veterans under state control and appropriated the romantic, heroic version of the front experience for the regime.

In Germany, as elsewhere, disabled veterans began to organize and make their voices heard in late 1916 and early 1917. Their demands for improved treatment and compensation for their sacrifice were quickly linked to demands for political reform in general and, in particular, reform of the inequitable Prussian suffrage system. The argument that wartime sacrifice should be rewarded with political equality was a powerful one and was adroitly exploited by the Social Democrats. Conservatives responded by attempting to organize veterans in support of the status quo, building upon existing veterans' organizations which had been an important prop of the empire. The Forces of Order hoped to postpone welfare reform until after the war, when Germany's defeated enemies would be forced to pay for them, and to blunt demands for political change through military victory.

In November 1918 the German nation was rocked by the dual traumas of defeat and revolution: the German army was defeated and the country was swept by revolution. Germany's "external" and "internal" enemies had triumphed. The nation could no longer resist the former and the propertied classes appeared defenseless against the latter. By coupling the emancipation of the "internal" enemy with national defeat in an inverted cause and effect relationship through the infamous stab-in-the-back (*Dolchstoss*) legend, Germany's displaced elites delegitimized the former and denied the latter. Germany had not been defeated, but betrayed, "stabbed in the back," by the founders of the republic. The previous "state supporting" elements now became the most vitriolic opponents of the new democratic German state. Prominent among these were organized veterans, which were a major source of instability in Weimar Germany. In spite of the republic's efforts to meet the needs of veterans, German veterans' organizations, with the exception of the war-disabled, were violently anti-republican.[22] The claim that the republic was ungrateful to veterans is a myth created by its rightist opponents. In contrast to other belligerent nations, the transition to a peacetime economy was relatively smooth and unemployment among veterans was low. The National Welfare Law (RVG), passed in 1920, provided a progressive system of rehabilitation and benefits for the war-disabled and the next-of-kin of soldiers killed in the war. But, like the war itself, the RVG remained a source of contention, considered inadequate by its beneficiaries and too indulgent by others.[23] Defeat made it impossible to come to some sort of reconciliation with the enormous human damage caused by the war. Disabled veterans could not console themselves with the belief that they were heroes who had successfully defended their nation, and for German society as a whole the war-disabled were human placards advertising the futility of the war effort. Meanwhile, former officers happily pocketed generous pensions while attacking the new democratic order.

The collapse of the imperial army created a power vacuum. Obsessed with restoring order and avoiding "Russian conditions," the new Social Democratic government filled the vacuum with volunteer forces that brutally suppressed the workers' and soldiers' councils that had spearheaded the revolution. The volunteer forces were recruited from the middle classes and through their actions many ordinary and respectable middle-class Germans came to appreciate the use of armed force to achieve political ends. The volunteer forces became the seedbed for a violent paramilitary subculture that was instrumental in undermining the Weimar republic.[24]

In 1920 the Allies ordered the dissolution of German volunteer forces. This did not mean their end, however. They reemerged as Military Associations (*Wehrverbände*), private organizations, composed primarily of veterans of World War I and postwar volunteer associations. They were uniformed, militarily organized, and violent. Despising traditional political activity, the Military Associations hoped to achieve their political aims, the destruction of Germany's "internal" and "external" enemies, by means of military rather than political action.

The explosive events of 1923, culminating in Hitler's abortive "March on Berlin," in which the Military Associations played a prominent role, seemed to clear the air, as the social and political turmoil of 1918–23 gave way to comparative peace and prosperity. Confronted with a "crisis" of stability, the Military Associations transformed themselves into Political Combat Leagues (*politische Kampfbünde*). Putschism was to be replaced by politics. The Combat Leagues sought to expand their influence through the formation of youth groups, women's auxiliaries, and the development of a vigorous press. The newspapers, periodicals, and other publications of the rightist Combat Leagues provided a heady brew of anti-democratic thought cloaked in a "Front Ideology" that romanticized war and the "Front Experience." Meanwhile, political violence not only continued but was also compounded by the formation of leftist Combat Leagues by supporters of the republic and by the communists.[25] Because of the activities of paramilitary formations, political meetings became scenes of angry shouting matches and physical confrontation. The constant demonstrations, counter-demonstrations, and bloody clashes became a surrogate for Germany's unresolved civil war. It was during the 1920s that the cadres were trained for the enormous outburst of violence that crippled the republic in its final years. The activities of the Combat Leagues created not only an intellectual but also a physical environment that paved the way for the Nazis, whose paramilitary violence did not seem all that strange to Germans already accustomed to it.

According to proponents of the Front Ideology, the war had been the crucible of a new era, one in which armed conflict would not disappear, but become central. The massive slaughter of German youth had not been in vain, it was asserted, but was a blood sacrifice, one that was necessary for the regeneration of the nation and the destruction of its internal and external enemies.[26] The Political Combat Leagues, as well as the Nazis, portrayed themselves as agents for the fulfillment of the Front Generation's mission. The "community of the trenches," represented in their militarized ranks, was to be transferred to peacetime society, creating a people's community (*Volksgemeinschaft*) that in turn would become an armed community (*Wehrgemeinschaft*) that would permit Germany to reverse the defeat of 1918.

Conclusions

Fed by the German example, much has been written about the psychological impact of the war on veterans' postwar political views. The stereotype is one of brutalized veterans flocking to fascist movements. The war unquestionably had an enormous psychological impact on veterans, but its political consequences are less clear. Memories of the camaraderie and unity of purpose of the trenches, which most veterans shared, did not provide a coherent political program in the postwar world. Some veterans were brutalized and predisposed to fascism, but this was true for civilians as well. Generally, it seems that the war did not change but reinforced prewar political tendencies, though the war experience and postwar disillusionment often radicalized these predispositions, especially in defeated countries. Many radicalized veterans (as well as non-combatants) sought a brave new world, modeled on the Soviet Union or the fascist regime that emerged in Italy; most just wanted to get back to normal civilian life. Some, mostly older, veterans hoped to go back to a restored prewar world. Veterans who had come of age during their military service expected to see a reformed postwar order which would recognize their sacrifice, provide material benefits, and open doors of opportunity for them. When these hopes were not met there was much anger and disillusionment, but the vast majority of veterans did not want revolution: they wanted to expand democracy, not destroy it.

Outside of Germany and Italy the romantic, redemptive view of war propagated by proponents of the Front Ideology found only a weak echo and the vision of veterans as heralds of a new age, while given lip-service, was ignored. For most Europeans, once the euphoria of peace wore off, the war was seen as an unmitigated catastrophe. Nothing had been solved and much had been made worse. It was unbearable that all the blood and sacrifice had been in vain. Even those in victorious countries began to doubt whether the war had been worth the cost. It had suspended or even inverted the just and predictable laws of causality that had governed the prewar world. The prewar virtues of thrift, prudence, and abstinence no longer brought the promised rewards: those who practiced them were ruined, while those who flouted them flourished. Optimism was replaced with bitter irony, which became a marker of the twentieth century.[27] The seismic changes wrought by the war were irreversible, and attempts to restore the secure "world of yesterday" were futile, quixotic, and politically irresponsible.[28] Those who came of age during the war or after it had no nostalgia for the past. The war had showed the folly of planning ahead and deferring gratification, and the postwar "lost generation" lived for the day, seeking to escape both the war and an uncertain present through hedonistic excess.

But it was impossible to escape the war. Its destructive consequences were revealed daily in the fragmented postwar societies, the stagnant economies, and the broken bodies of the war-disabled on whose bodies the horrors of the war were indelibly inscribed. Above all it was the silent presence of the dead, the truly lost generation, which weighed upon postwar Europe. Their loss and sacrifice were commemorated both officially and privately. Official observations of Armistice Day and/or Memorial Day were introduced. Tombs dedicated to Unknown Soldiers were built. Personal shrines were constructed and bereaved families made pilgrimages to battlefront gravesites. Séances were held by distraught parents, hoping to make contact with lost sons on "the other side."[29]

While official commemorative activity sought to create a uniform memory of the war, its meaning remained contested. This was reflected in postwar literature. After years of digesting their experiences, novels and autobiographies by participants in the war began to appear. Some, such as Ernst Jünger, celebrated the war, but most deplored its folly and waste. Were the soldiers heroes or victims? How were they to be portrayed in graveyard statuary and courthouse monuments? The debate was most intense in those countries which had been defeated. Germany never built a national monument as a result of division over where it should be and what it should represent and there were struggles everywhere, on both the national and local level, over how the war dead were to be honored and depicted.[30]

Memories of World War I obsessed Europeans in the interwar years, but the lessons that were drawn from it diverged sharply. Most wanted to avoid another war at all costs. This desire went far beyond traditional pacifist circles. Even those, primarily conservatives, who had romanticized war in 1914, now realized its cost in an age of mass politics: the warfare state led inevitably to the welfare state and a further erosion of the wealth and power of traditional elites. Democratic regimes, reflecting this broad consensus, pursued peaceful policies, even appeasement. In contrast, fascists and fascist regimes glorified war. The fascist lesson of World War I was not to avoid war, but to prepare to wage it more effectively. This had domestic and international consequences. For fascists, the militarized wartime organization of society during World War I became the model for their political movements and for future society. Militarized fascist movements were mobilized to defeat domestic, "internal" enemies, and the militarized societies of fascist regimes prepared their nations for confrontation with "external" enemies and the overthrow of the postwar international order. Twenty years after the end of the Great War, the "war to end war," the seeds sown during that conflict sprouted with a terrible vengeance, plunging the world into a new, even more bloody and destructive war.

NOTES

1   Elie Halévy, *The Era of Tyrannies* (New York: Doubleday, 1965), p. 222.
2   See Jean-Jacques Becker, *The Great War and the French People* (Providence RI: Berg, 1993); Jeffrey Verhey, *The Spirit of 1914: Militarism, Myth, and Mobilization in Germany* (Cambridge: Cambridge University Press, 2000).

3   See Michael C. C. Adams, *The Great Adventure: Male Desire and the Coming of World War I* (Bloomington: Indiana University Press, 1990); Eric J. Leed, "Class and Disillusionment in World War I," *Journal of Modern History* 50/4 (1978): 680–99.

4   See Allan K. Wildman, *The End of the Russian Imperial Army*, 2 vols (Princeton NJ: Princeton University Press, 1980, 1987).

5   See Leonard V. Smith, *Between Mutiny and Obedience: The Case of the French Fifth Infantry during World War I* (Princeton NJ: Princeton University Press, 1994).

6   See Arno J. Mayer, *Political Origins of the New Diplomacy* (New York: Random House, 1970).

7   See John Horne, "Introduction: Mobilizing for 'Total War,' 1914–1918," in *State, Society and Mobilization in Europe during the First World War*, John Horne, ed. (Cambridge: Cambridge University Press, 2002), pp. 1–17.

8   Although the Spanish Civil War came to an end in March 1939, elsewhere the interwar civil wars continued after September 1939 as wars within a war: in the west, this took the form of collaboration versus resistance; in the east, it was played out between contending factions within resistance movements. Cf. Paul Preston, "The Great Civil War: European Politics, 1914–1945," in *The Oxford Illustrated History of Modern Europe*, T. C. W. Blanning, ed. (Oxford: Oxford University Press, 1998), pp. 148–81.

9   See Gerald D. Feldman, *The Great Disorder: Politics, Economics, and Society in the German Inflation, 1914–1924* (New York: Oxford University Press, 1997); Benjamin F. Martin, *France and the Après Guerre, 1918–1924* (Baton Rouge: Louisiana State University Press, 1999).

10 See Gail Braybon, "Women, War, and Work," in *The Oxford Illustrated History of the First World War*, Hew Strachan, ed. (Oxford: Oxford University Press, 1998), pp. 149–62.

11 See Sandra M. Gilbert, "Soldier's Heart: Literary Men, Literary Women and the Great War," in *Behind the Lines: Gender and the Two World Wars*, Margaret Randolph Higonnet et al., eds (New Haven CT: Yale University Press, 1987), pp. 197–226.

12 See Joanna Bourke, *Dismembering the Male: Men's Bodies, Britain, and the Great War* (Chicago: University of Chicago Press, 1996); Mary Louise Roberts, *Civilization Without Sexes: Reconstructing Gender in Postwar France, 1917–1927* (Chicago: University of Chicago Press, 1994); Susan Kingsley Kent, *Making Peace: The Reconstruction of Gender in Interwar Britain* (Princeton NJ: Princeton University Press, 1993).

13 See Robert Soucy, *French Fascism: The First Wave, 1923–1933* (New Haven CT: Yale University Press, 1986) and *French Fascism: The Second Wave, 1933–1939* (New Haven CT: Yale University Press, 1995); Henry Rousso, *The Vichy Syndrome: History and Memory in France since 1944* (Cambridge MA: Harvard University Press, 1991).

14 See Eric J. Leed, *No Man's Land: Combat and Identity in World War I* (Cambridge: Cambridge University Press, 1979).

15 See Hans-Heinrich Nolte, "Stalinism as Total Social War," in *The Shadows of Total War*, Roger Chickering and Stig Förster, eds (Cambridge: Cambridge University Press, 2003), pp. 295–311; Catherine Merridale, *Night of Stone: Death and Memory in Twentieth Century Russia* (New York: Viking, 2001) and "War, Death, and Remembrance in Soviet Russia," in *War and Remembrance in the Twentieth Century*, Jay Winter and Emmanuel Sivan, eds (Cambridge: Cambridge University Press, 1999), pp. 61–83.

16 See Stephen R. Ward, "Great Britain: Land Fit for Heroes Lost," in *The War Generation: Veterans of the First World War*, Stephen R. Ward, ed. (Port Washington NY: Kennikat, 1975), pp. 10–37.

17 See Andrew Rothstein, *The Soldiers' Strikes of 1919* (London: Macmillan, 1980); Graham Wootton, *The Politics of Influence: British Ex-Servicemen, Cabinet Decisions, and Cultural Change, 1917–57* (London: Routledge and Kegan Paul, 1963).

18 See Robert Soucy, "France: Veterans' Politics between the Wars," in Ward, *The War Generation*, pp. 59–103; Antoine Prost, *In the Wake of War: "Les Anciens Combattants" and French Society, 1914–1939* (Providence RI: Berg, 1992).

19 On the fascist leagues, see the works by Soucy cited in note 13.

20 On Italy, see Jonathan Dunnage, *Twentieth-Century Italy: A Social History* (London: Longman, 2002); Paul Corner and Giovanna Proacacci, "The Italian Experience of 'Total' Mobilization, 1915–1920," in Horne, *State, Society and Mobilization*, pp. 223–40; and Giovanna Procacci, "A 'Latecomer' in War: The Case of Italy," in *Authority, Identity and the Social History of the Great War*, Frans Coetzee and Marilyn Shevin-Coetzee, eds (Providence RI: Berghahn, 1995), pp. 3–27.

21 See Michael A. Ledeen, "Italy: War as a Style of Life," in Ward, *The War Generation*, pp. 104–34.

22 See James M. Diehl, "Germany: Veterans' Politics under Three Flags," in Ward, *The War Generation*, pp. 135–86; Richard Bessel, "The Great War in German Memory: The Soldiers of the First World War, Demobilization, and Weimar Political Culture," *German History* 6/1 (1988): 20–34.

23 See Michael Geyer, "Ein Vorbot des Wohlfahrsstaates. Die Kriegsopferversorgung in Frankreich, Deutschland und Grossbritannien nach dem Ersten Weltkrieges," *Geschichte und Gesllschaaft* 9/2 (1983): 230–77; Robert W. Whalen, *Bitter Wounds: German Victims of the Great War, 1914–1939* (Ithaca NY: Cornell University Press, 1984).

24 See James M. Diehl, *Paramilitary Politics in Weimar Germany* (Bloomington: Indiana University Press, 1978).

25 Ibid, ch. 7; Karl Rohe, *Das Reichsbanner Schwartz Rot Gold: Ein Beitrag zur Geschichte und Struktur der politischen Kampfverbände zur Zeit der Weimarer Republik* (Düsseldorf: Droste, 1966); Kurt G. P. Schuster, *Der Rote Frontkämpferbund 1924–1929: Beiträge zur Geschichte und Organisationsstruktur eines politischen Kampfbundes* (Düsseldorf: Droste, 1975).

26 See George L. Mosse, *Fallen Soldiers: Reshaping the Memory of the World Wars* (New York: Oxford University Press, 1990); Modris Eksteins, *Rites of Spring: The Great War and the Birth of the Modern Age* (New York: Doubleday, 1989).

27 See Paul Fussell, *The Great War and Modern Memory* (New York: Oxford University Press, 1975).

28 See Richard Bessel, *Germany after the First World War* (Oxford: Oxford University Press, 1993). The phrase "World of Yesterday" is Zweig's. See guide to further reading.

29 See Jay Winter, *Sites of Memory, Sites of Mourning: The Great War in European Cultural History* (Cambridge: Cambridge University Press, 1995); Adrian Gregory, *The Silence of Memory: Armistice Day, 1919–1946* (Providence RI: Berg, 1994).

30 See Mosse, *Fallen Soldiers*; Winter, *Sites of Memory*; Sean A. Forner, "War Commemoration and the Republic in Crisis: Weimar Germany and the Neue Wache," *Central European History* 35/4 (2002): 513–49; Daniel J. Sherman, *The Construction of Memory in Interwar France* (Chicago: University of Chicago Press, 1999) and "Bodies and Names: The Emergence of Commemoration in Interwar France," *American Historical Review* 103/2 (April 1998): 443–66.

GUIDE TO FURTHER READING

Derek H. Aldcroft, *From Versailles to Wall Street, 1919–1929* (Berkeley: University of California Press; London: Allen Lane, 1977). A clear account of postwar economic problems.

Volker Berghahn, *Der Stahlhelm, Bund der Frontsoldaten, 1918–1935* (Düsseldorf: Droste, 1966). History of the largest and most dynamic of the anti-Weimar veterans' organizations.

Deborah Cohen, *The War Come Home: Disabled Veterans in Britain and Germany, 1914–1939* (Berkeley: University of California Press, 2001). An interesting, if flawed, attempt to explain why German veterans were hostile to the state, while British veterans remained loyal to it, even though benefits were more generous in Germany than in England.

Victoria DeGrazia, *How Fascism Ruled Women: Italy, 1922–1945* (Berkeley: University of California Press, 1992). Has much to say not only about women in fascist Italy, but in interwar Europe in general.

David, A. Gerber, ed., *Disabled Veterans in History* (Ann Arbor: University of Michigan Press, 2000). Useful survey of a long-neglected problem.

Robert Graves, *Good-bye to All That* (New York: Doubleday, 1957). Graphic descriptions of trench warfare as well as instructive accounts of Graves's life before and after the war.

Charles P. Kindleberger, *The World in Depression, 1929–1939* (Berkeley: University of California Press, 1973). Describes the origins of the Depression and the socioeconomic consequences of the various remedies employed to end it.

Rudy Koshar, ed., *Splintered Classes: Politics and the Lower Middle Classes in Interwar Europe* (New York: Holmes and Meier, 1990). Provides new insights by challenging old stereotypes.

Gregory M. Luebbert, *Liberalism, Fascism, or Social Democracy: Social Classes and the Political Origins of Regimes in Interwar Europe* (New York: Oxford University Press, 1991). A useful and overlooked analysis of why democracy succeeded or failed in the interwar years.

Charles S. Maier, *Recasting Bourgeois Europe: Stabilization in France, Germany, and Italy in the Decade after World War I* (Princeton NJ: Princeton University Press, 1975). A sophisticated analysis of how bourgeois conservative social and political forces contained the postwar leftist surge.

Stanley Payne, *A History of Fascism 1914–1945* (Madison: University of Wisconsin Press. 1995). A comprehensive survey.

Raymond J. Sontag, *A Broken World, 1919–1939* (New York: Harper and Row, 1971). A classic gem that still shines.

David Stevenson, *Cataclysm: The First Word War as Political Tragedy* (New York: Basic Books, 2004). A detailed and up-to-date synthesis of the war and its aftermath.

Jay M. Winter, *The Experience of World War I* (New York: Oxford University Press, 1989). Lavishly illustrated, brief, but thorough, account of the war and its consequences.

Stefan Zweig, *World of Yesterday: An Autobiography* (Lincoln: University of Nebraska Press, 1964). An excellent account by a perceptive contemporary observer of the impact of the war on European society.

CHAPTER NINETEEN

The Socialist Experiment

WILLIAM J. CHASE

When the Russian Communist Party held its Eighth Congress in March 1919, the fate of the party and the new Soviet republic was anything but certain. The party, commonly known as the Bolsheviks, had come to power in October 1917 proclaiming a new type of government, a Soviet government of workers and peasants, devoted to ending Russian participation in World War I and to creating a socialist society. Those goals angered many Russians and many European governments. Within months, civil war and foreign interventions turned Russia once again into a battleground. The treaty of Brest-Litovsk, the civil war, and the government's early policies led to a hemorrhaging of the nation's wealth. The party that met in March 1919 governed (if that is the appropriate verb) a Russia that was but a fraction of its former size and was besieged by foreign and domestic armies.

Yet there was also cause for optimism and optimists abounded within the party. Much to everyone's surprise, the Soviet republic still existed. The end of World War I meant the collapse of old empires and the rise of new nation-states, the political definition of which remained uncertain. The hopes the Bolsheviks had for other socialist revolutions were not unfounded in 1919. Just as the Eighth Congress opened, a Soviet republic was proclaimed in Hungary. Although it lasted only eight months, it exemplified the revolutionary unrest that swept through sections of Europe. Sympathy and support abroad for the new socialist experiment were substantial. That same month, the Communist International (Comintern) was founded in Moscow. Its creation marked a decisive break with moderate socialist parties in Europe and elsewhere, and Russia's intentions to promote revolutions abroad. Communist parties, the members of which had belonged to socialist parties, came into being throughout Europe and elsewhere. Some were large and influential, some not, but all forced their governments to confront issues raised by the Soviet experiment. Between 1918 and 1923, communist-led uprisings in Germany, Austria, and Bulgaria threatened fragile governments. European governments refused to recognize the new Soviet sate. Fascist and nationalist parties in Europe gained support by offering themselves as defenders against "Bolshevik" revolution at home.

After 1917, Europe and the world closely watched the Soviet socialist experiment. Governments treated it as a pariah state because it offered a stark political alternative to liberal democracy and fascism. Some applauded its efforts to build a new world. Others watched carefully and reserved judgment, fascinated by its bold social experiments yet dismayed by restrictions on political freedom. Few Europeans were agnostic about the socialist experiment.

The "Program of the Communist Party of Russia," which the Eighth Congress adopted, conveyed succinctly what attracted or scared people.[1] The program outlined the party's vision of the kind of socialist society it intended to construct and some of the means by which it envisioned doing so. It also provides themes that enable us to appreciate the means, ends, and dynamics of the socialist experiment that unfolded in the USSR during the interwar years.[2] Like all revolutions, the October Revolution sought to destroy the old order and to construct a new one, although the dimensions of the destruction and construction exceeded those of all previous revolutions. Not everyone viewed the processes of destruction and construction in the same ways. Conflicts over differing revolutionary agendas, differing visions of what the revolution promised, and different visions of socialism fragmented the party and society, and extended into Europe.

While scholars tend to focus on the Communist Party because it formulated policy and its members staffed important state offices, the Soviet state was charged with defending the revolution and implementing the party's program. As Marxists, the Bolsheviks believed that all governments represented the ruling class and implemented policies that served its interests. The revolution had not changed that cornerstone of Bolshevik thought. Guided by party policy, the state was the driving force in the destruction of the old order, the process of socialist construction, and the realization of the socialist experiment.

Central to the new regime's identity was its understanding of those it viewed as enemies. There were many enemies, real and perceived: some were foreign, some were domestic; some took up arms against the new state, some used economic or political means to destroy socialism. Whatever their means, these enemies threatened the socialist experiment and made it imperative for party members and their supporters to be vigilant. The civil war and foreign intervention by European, US, and Japanese troops legitimized the view that "capitalist encirclement" threatened the USSR. Their fear of war is understandable. Less obvious, but no less important, is that many party members and Soviet citizens broadly interpreted politics in terms of enemies.

Appreciating the importance of these four overarching themes – destruction and construction; competing revolutionary agendas; the transformative role of the state; and fear of war, enemies, and capitalist encirclement – makes it easier to understand the dynamics that defined the world's first socialist experiment, and its relationship to Europe. Using the party program to structure our exploration enables us to focus and organize our discussion, and to judge the experiment on its own terms. We must also impose a chronological framework so as to give temporal definition to this unfolding experiment. This essay examines three periods: the Civil War years (1918–21); the years of the New Economic Policy (NEP, 1921–8); and the Stalin years (1928–41, although Stalin ruled until his death in 1953).

The Experiment Outlined

When the Bolsheviks came to power in October 1917, they set out to destroy root and branch the Romanov autocracy and its social base, as well as the "bourgeois" Provisional Government that had replaced the tsar in February 1917. They announced their intention to create a new form of government: a revolutionary democracy based on the dictatorship of the proletariat and peasantry. Known variously as Soviet or proletarian democracy, it was based on Marx's belief that hitherto all governments had been dictatorships of that minority class. Proletarian democracy was to be "a higher type of democracy"[3] because workers and peasants, the majority, would rule. Declaring the principles of the new government and bringing them to life were distinct realities. The party's call for "All power to the Soviets" in October 1917 hastened the collapse of central governmental power and fueled the assertion of local power. According to the party's program, this was how it should be because the "Soviet State realizes . . . local self-government, without any sort of authority imposed from above." Yet fighting a war without "any sort of authority imposed from above" proved impossible. The government increasingly asserted central direction of the economy and, in many cases, local officials pleaded for help from the central government. The state's need to mobilize scarce resources for the Red Army and to keep the economy going overwhelmed the dreams of a decentralized political system. Although the ideal remained alive, when the party adopted its program in 1919, the centralization of power was well advanced. Still, the central government had a difficult time of governing at the local level. Holding power and wielding it effectively are different realities.

The contrast between the program's idealistic vision and political reality was not confined to issues of democracy and state power. The Bolsheviks embraced a vision of socialism different from that held by many socialists of the time. Most European socialists believed that a socialist government required electoral legitimacy and that a socialist society could only exist in an economically developed and democratic society. The Bolsheviks, the self-proclaimed vanguard of the proletariat, rejected this view. Their program announced "a pitiless struggle against that bourgeois perversion of socialism which is dominant in the leading social democratic and socialist parties."[4] They rejected the label socialist and embraced the label communist. They broke with moderate socialist parties and urged their supporters to do the same, to form communist parties, and to join the Comintern.

The Bolsheviks enacted policies designed to destroy Russia's social and economic order and the principles on which it was based. They abolished private ownership of land and productive property; they authorized peasants to confiscate and redistribute the lands of the aristocracy and church; they empowered local soviets (locally elected councils) to confiscate and redistribute the housing of the former elite; they nationalized key sectors of the industrial economy; they declared the legal equality of all people regardless of race, gender, or ethnicity (although they denied legal rights to the former "exploiting classes"); and they abolished the existing military and judicial systems. These early proclamations sought to destroy the former elite's bases of power so as to construct a new socialist order ruled by the dictatorship of the proletariat and the peasantry and based on the principles of egalitarianism and decentralized power. The ideals underlying these proclamations infused the party program, which was militantly idealistic. Consider, for example, the call to abolish a market-based system for the distribution of goods and to replace it with a system of "consumers' communes" that would create "an apparatus for mass distribution more perfect than any known to the history of capitalism" and would be administered "in the communist spirit."[5] European governments were horrified.

The Bolsheviks envisioned the use of state power to destroy the old order and to construct a socialist society defined by local power and infused by the "communist spirit." It was a vision of socialism unlike any other and one which, by 1919, did not always conform to reality. It was also a vision that inflamed many Russians who organized anti-soviet armies and many foreign governments who supported them. It was a vision that split the European left and working class. It was a vision that opened a Pandora's box.

The Experiment in the Civil War Years (1918–1921)

Following the October 1917 decree nationalizing land, peasants moved quickly to confiscate the former elite's property. The Bolsheviks initially viewed this destructive urge as a progressive force. Many peasant communities used the processes of land confiscation and redistribution to reinvigorate the village commune, where traditional agricultural practices, such as the three-field system, strip farming, and periodic redistribution of land, were common. The new government's food policy also contributed to the revival of communes. By mid-1918, the country faced a food crisis. Given rampant inflation and dire shortages of consumer goods, peasants withheld their produce. Faced with desperate urban food shortages, the government ordered the requisitioning of peasant produce, angering peasants and driving a wedge between them and the government that ruled in their name. By late 1920, peasant armies ruled vast tracts of land and the food crisis deepened, threatening the government at the moment of its victory in the civil war. Communes, which envisioned local control as central to socialism, often organized this resistance. In early 1921 the party relented. It ended requisitioning and legalized rural trade, quickly calming an angry peasantry.

The party had failed to achieve its goals of organizing "large-scale socialist agriculture," promoting scientific and cooperative agricultural methods, and crushing the resistance of "rich peasants" to state policy – but it had deepened peasant suspicions of centralized state power. The Bolsheviks continued to believe that building socialism on the foundations of medieval agricultural practices was impossible. The struggle between the government's and the peasantry's conflicting revolutionary agendas put both sides on notice that the other threatened to block the realization of their dreams. During the 1920s the government and peasants coexisted, although the issue of how to modernize agriculture went unresolved.

The government's decrees abolishing private property and nationalizing key economic resources hastened economic collapse just when the civil war demanded increased production. Destroying the old order threatened the defense of the embryonic new order. Factories offer a microcosm of the confusion and contradictions that arose from efforts to realize competing revolutionary agendas. Workers and Bolsheviks alike wanted to raise workers' standard of living, shorten their workday, improve working conditions, and give them greater influence over the workplace. The program envisioned the economy being coordinated by a "general government design" and the centralization of production, with the trade unions administering the "whole economic life of the country" so as to assert "effective popular control over the results of production."[6] Like many Europeans of their generation, the Bolsheviks viewed science and rationality as crowning human achievements, and industrialization and rational administration as social panaceas – so long, of course, as they were administered according to the proper class values. Here, too, the destructive and constructive agendas came into conflict.

In 1917 the Bolsheviks made workers' control a central plank of their platform. Following the October Revolution, many workers moved quickly to enact that promise. But there was sharp disagreement over what workers' control meant. Many Bolsheviks and workers believed that workers should control factories and allow factory committees and trade unions to run enterprises. Others argued that control should initially take the form of worker oversight of and participation in factory administration alongside knowledgeable personnel, even if those personnel were "bourgeois specialists." For Lenin, the party's founder and leader until his death in 1924, workers' control committees were schools of communism where workers would learn how to administer properly a socialized enterprise.

The nationalization of enterprises and workers' demands for control led many owners and administrators to abandon the factories, leaving them in the hands of workers who had no administrative experience.[7] Modern industrial enterprises are complex and workers' inexperience and lack of knowledge exacerbated problems created by economic collapse. Workers' ignorance of accounting, sources of credit and raw materials, technical and engineering issues, and wholesale networks resulted in diminishing production and revenue that undermined efforts to raise wages and assert control. To reverse the situation, workers often demanded that the state nationalize their enterprise, but the state had few resources and fewer solutions. The program called for the "universal increase in the productive forces of the country . . . by all available means."[8] But the available means were few. To increase production, party leaders asserted central control over the economy, demanded greater work discipline, and tied wages to output. "Bourgeois" technical specialists returned to factories to direct a sullen workforce. When such efforts failed, the party and its social base found themselves at odds. By late 1920, widespread worker unrest swept the country, and debate raged over what roles trade unions and workers should have in administering the nation's economy. Some cited the party program's call for unions to direct "the work of administration in the whole economic life of the economy." Others argued for militarizing labor and making unions focus on industrial production. In 1921 a compromise was reached. Unions would focus on protecting workers and on increasing their productivity and labor discipline. The state, guided by party policies, would administer the economy.

Equality infused the socialist vision – and the Soviet government was the first state to outlaw ethnic and racial inequality. But how to deal with nationalist aspirations within the former tsarist empire confounded many. As Marxists, Bolsheviks understood the world in class terms. Their program announced that "primary importance is the policy of uniting the proletarians and semi-proletarians of various nationalities in a joint revolutionary struggle for the overthrow of the landlords and the bourgeoisie." Class, not ethnicity, was the essential characteristic. Yet they were often realists. They accepted the declarations of independence by Finns, Estonians, Latvians, and Lithuanians in 1918, although in areas such as Georgia party leaders struggled to keep lands within the new Soviet federation. Establishing a federation of ethnic or national groups seemed to most Bolsheviks to be the appropriate, democratic way to address the legitimate concerns of the Russian Empire's former subjects. Soviet leaders acknowledged that Great Russian chauvinism had alienated many non-Russians. Hence the program deemed it "essential to annul any and every privilege of any national group [read: Russians], to secure complete national equality, and to recognize that colonies and oppressed nationalities have a full right to secede." The new Soviet state was a union of socialist republics defined along national lines. The party called for the "utmost consideration" of the "survival of national sentiment" as the surest way to ensure a "durable and amicable union between the diverse national elements of the international proletariat."[9] Republics, autonomous regions, even districts organized on an ethnic basis, came into being. But finding ways for class values to replace nationalist values proved illusive. The Bolsheviks' innovative approach to ethnicity intrigued or alarmed many in Europe, where issues of class and nationality were also flashpoints.

Education was central to the socialist experiment's long-term success. As Marxists, Bolshevik leaders viewed educational institutions as venues where the ruling class inculcated students with its political, social, and cultural values. The program was quite explicit: schools must contribute to the "complete abolition of the division of society into classes" and to "the communist regeneration of society." Toward this end, it announced its intention to provide free, compulsory, secular education for all children (to age 17), to provide students with free school materials including school clothing and footwear, to create a network of crèches and kindergartens to prepare children for school, to train teachers "permeated with the ideas of communism," to provide "easy access to the universities for all who may desire it," especially workers, and to organize citizens to "participate actively in the spread of enlightenment." Local soviets and party committees organized members to participate in anti-illiteracy campaigns by going to villages and neighborhoods to teach children and adults how to read. Creating an educated population and inculcating socialist values were essential to enabling workers and peasants to achieve positions of power and responsibility. Social promotion was essential if the proletariat was to become the ruling class. Only when educated and trained workers and peasants staffed the offices of government, commerce, industry, and culture would the destruction of the old elite's power be complete.[10] Many did so during the civil war years.

The platform of 1919 envisioned a new political order, "a higher type of democracy" in which "local self-government, without any sort of authority imposed from above," would rule. That did not happen. Defense against the military onslaughts of domestic and foreign enemies justified a centralized state. The new Soviet government had promised to build the foundations for a socialism of abundance, to improve the working and living conditions of workers and peasants. That did not happen. The economic collapse triggered by revolutionary policies, civil war, and foreign interventions brought the economy to a near standstill, and pitted many workers and peasants against the government that ruled in their name. So total was the collapse of 1918–21 that reality made a mockery of everyone's vision of socialism, of each group's revolutionary agenda. It was as if they had to start all over.

The Experiment During the NEP (1921–1928)

And that is what they began to do in 1921. The civil war years had witnessed the destruction of the old order; the years of the New Economic Policy (NEP) heralded the search for the basis of the new order, Soviet socialism. The party's program offered principles and guidelines, but how to achieve the new order in an economy of scarcity with an exhausted population divided the party and society. By 1923, hopes for socialist revolutions in Europe were dashed. The USSR was going to have to go it alone, to establish "socialism in one country," as Stalin put it. That idea shocked many Bolsheviks and European Marxists who believed that socialism had to be an international system, that it could not exist in one country. During the NEP, party leaders clashed over what was the proper road to socialism. They debated means, not ends; they debated the timing and pace of change, not the need for change; they debated the consequences of the NEP and how to ameliorate them, not whether NEP represented the desired socialism; they debated which policies the state should enact, not whether the state was the appropriate vehicle for revolutionary transformation.

The NEP was a collection of policies that evolved over several years rather than a single policy. Lenin called it a "strategic retreat" in the campaign to establish socialism. In this retreat, market mechanisms replaced central governmental direction in many sectors of the economy and fiscal restraint restricted funding for many social services. Reconstruction replaced destruction. The retreat disappointed many Bolsheviks; many Europeans viewed it as a welcome restraint on state power. The NEP began by ending food requisitioning and legalizing private trade by peasants, which soon extended to other commercial activities. To provide incentives for peasants to sell their produce, the state enacted policies to lower the costs of consumer goods. It ended many financial subsidies to nationalized industrial and commercial enterprises, and demanded that they balance their books. To cut costs, enterprises fired workers and increased output norms. Although the industrial labor force grew sharply, unemployment rose more quickly. The shortage of jobs generated conflict between urban workers and peasants who flooded to cities in search of work. In 1927, urban unemployment rates nationwide exceeded 12 percent, but in some places, like Moscow and Leningrad, that figure hovered around 20 percent. Mass unemployment had not been on anyone's revolutionary agendas. By 1927 the economy had reached 1913 levels of production, and discontent with many aspects of the NEP was widespread.

The Soviet state had outlawed inequality based on gender, race, or ethnicity and written these principles into its laws and the 1918 Constitution. Henceforth, women were the legal equals of men. But changing laws is easier than changing customs and cultural values. During the civil war, women dominated the industrial workforce; during the NEP, women were the first to be fired, often to make room for returning Red Army veterans. Female unemployment soared. Some party leaders viewed the destruction of "bourgeois marriage" as central to revolutionary transformation. While not all members held such radical views, most believed that women and children were victims of bourgeois marriages and that liberating them was central to the creation of an egalitarian socialist culture. The state legalized divorce and abortion on demand so as to give women more control of their lives and hasten the destruction of "bour-

geois marriage." Many women availed themselves of both rights. In 1926 the so-
called "postcard divorce" made divorce even easier by enabling one to dissolve a
marriage by simply signing a form. The possibly unwitting spouse received a postcard
announcing the divorce. While many party members lauded the new policy, many
women condemned it for enabling men to walk away from their paternal and financial
obligations. The tensions between the revolutionary agendas of some party members
and women underscore the point that the legal destruction of discrimination proved
easier than the construction of new social values. Europeans had never seen anything
like this. Some praised the granting of abortion, divorce, and equal rights to women,
while others vociferously condemned the policies.

During the NEP, fiscal realities meant that students had to pay to attend higher-
level schools, yet the number of primary schools and courses for adults expanded.
Literacy and training were essential to social promotion and the realization of a new
society. Many citizens took advantage of the available opportunities. One such person
was Masha Scott, one of eight children in a poor peasant family. She and her siblings
availed themselves of whatever educational opportunities they could, attending the
local village school, then the provincial school, and later college in Moscow. She
became a math and science teacher. Her parents learned to read in their fifties. Masha
and her family were not exceptions.[11] Soviet educators also pioneered new ways to
use education, especially vocational education, to reform juvenile delinquents, even
criminals. Such a radical and democratic approach to education intrigued many
in Europe and the Americas, where debates over pedagogical theory became
passionate.

During the 1920s the Soviet government continued to address the nationality
issue. It pursued a policy of *korenizatsiia* (indigenization) in national regions as part
of its efforts to acknowledge and direct national sentiment. In schools, classes were
taught in the dominant native language; newspapers and cultural events also used
the native language. There were constraints. The central government financed most
of these operations, and Bolsheviks dominated key state and party positions. The
state hoped to infuse national practices with proper class content and socialist rhetoric; overt anti-soviet activities were illegal. Terry Martin has aptly described the USSR
as an "affirmative action empire" in which, into the 1930s, national culture, language,
and custom flourished in many regions and Russian influence not only diminished,
but also was legally constrained. No other empire, no other country, had made such
an effort to cultivate and direct national practices and sentiment. In the 1920s such
policies were a source of pride; in the 1930s they became a source of anxiety as the
consequences of nationalism in Europe turned nasty.

By 1927 agriculture and industry had reached 1913 levels of production.
Educational opportunities and the supply of consumer goods had increased, but so
too had unemployment. There were more women in the industrial workforce and
among the ranks of the unemployed. There was social insurance, but not enough to
pay for the promised universal insurance plan. Squalid factory housing had been
closed and the homes of the former elite redistributed, but overcrowding continued
and homelessness was a mounting urban crisis. It was against this backdrop that
debates within the leadership over the proper policies for and pace of socialist construction unfolded. Outside of the party, debate was severely restricted. By 1923 all
political parties other than the Bolsheviks had been outlawed. The party used its

powers of appointment and budgetary control to assert editorial control of the press and media. The Bolsheviks had constructed a one-party state that sought to enact socialism in one country. Whether they lauded or condemned Soviet initiatives, Europeans carefully followed the unfolding socialist experiment.

The Experiment Redefined (1928–1932)

Such was the state of the Soviet experiment in 1927 on the tenth anniversary of the October Revolution. After a decade of turmoil and revolutionary experimentation, few in the country viewed the results as the realization of their revolutionary agenda, few viewed the construction of socialism as finished. Many supporters welcomed the anniversary with the rhetorical question, "Is this what we fought the revolution for?" The celebration took place at a time of anxiety. A war scare had erupted in spring 1927. The war scare passed but its consequences remained, harming tentative Soviet efforts to normalize relations with Europe. In reaction to that threat and unfavorable agricultural prices, many peasants withheld their harvest. Food prices rose and, by early 1928, food shortages prompted rationing in selected cities. Debate raged over which economic policies could best construct a socialist economy. Some leaders, fearing a split between the party and peasantry, advocated adjusting prices and market mechanisms. Others had tired of market solutions and tailoring economic policies to peasant demand. For them, the market symbolized a return to capitalism. They demanded more forceful policies and their arguments carried the day. Stalin, a long-time party leader, became their spokesman. During 1928–32 the party rejected the principles of the NEP and reembraced the goals outlined in the 1919 program. The radical policies enacted during these years – collectivization of agriculture, planned industrialization, and Cultural Revolution – are often referred to as "the Stalin revolution." That revolution consisted of a set of destructive and constructive policies that had short-term and long-term objectives, and were carried out in an atmosphere of revolutionary enthusiasm and social crisis at home, and depression in Europe.

We tend to lump the various policies by which the party transformed agriculture under the rubric of collectivization, but the transformation resulted from several hastily enacted processes rather than a single policy. The pressing need in 1927 was to increase the flow of agricultural produce to cities. As during the civil war, peasants and urbanites found themselves pitted against each other. To increase the shipment of food to cities, the state ordered the requisitioning of produce. Fearing a return to civil war policies, peasants resisted. Some party leaders argued that increasing food supplies did not provide a solution to the longstanding agricultural problems and that a wholesale reorganization of the agricultural system – collectivization – was essential.

Collectivization sought to destroy the traditional peasant commune, traditional agricultural practices, and the market as a means of exchange. In 1929 Stalin called for the elimination of so-called "rich peasants" (kulaks) as a class. Other policies sought to construct a new agricultural order by replacing traditional agricultural practices with large-scale, enclosed collective farms, introducing mechanization and scientific farming, and promoting a new local elite to administer the collective farm system that replaced the traditional commune. But the requisitioning of produce, the assault on the traditional order, and the drive to create a new collective farm system became hopelessly intermingled. Many peasants resisted; agricultural production plummeted. When peasants resisted, and in some cases even before they did, the state applied force. Alleged kulaks were arrested, local communes forcibly dissolved, and new collective farms decreed. In Ukraine and the northern Caucasus, repression and resistance were violent. In areas that collectivized somewhat later, such as Smolensk province, better planning enabled party activists to mobilize support for the policies, thereby reducing the level of violence and increasing the rate of voluntary association.[12]

Between 1928 and 1933 the old agricultural system was destroyed. Many peasants lost their lives or were arrested and sent to forced labor. Some 3 million fled the countryside for the cities; millions slaughtered their livestock rather than let the state tell them how to manage it. The quantity and quality of food shrank markedly. In 1932–3, famine wracked parts of the country. The standard of living suffered until 1935. One vision of socialism, founded on scientific and industrial rationality and social engineering but hastily and violently imposed, came into being in the countryside. It had many opponents in the villages, people willing to sacrifice their lives to oppose it, people who viewed it as a "second serfdom," even the apocalypse. It also had supporters. New groups of peasants came to hold responsible collective farm offices, the gradual mechanization of agriculture expanded employment opportunities for men and women, the spread of state-supported schools, libraries, and cultural activities opened new ways of viewing the world for many. The 1919 program had envisioned the ends, but not the means, by which "socialized agriculture" came into being.

The collectivization of agriculture unfolded within a larger universe of revolutionary change. The 1927 war scare helped to bring the debate over industrial policy to a head. In 1921 many Bolsheviks had accepted Lenin's argument that the NEP represented a strategic retreat in the socialist offensive. Some party members accepted this but nonetheless bristled at its social costs: high unemployment, homelessness, the return of a bourgeois strata, and reliance on market mechanisms. They believed in the inherent superiority of planning and were impatient to fulfill the 1919 promise of the "centralization of production" and coordination of the economy by "general government design." Other party members endorsed the NEP's principles, including the use of limited market mechanisms, as a viable path to socialism. The debates over the direction of industrial and economic policy, over the shape of the socialist experiment, proved deeply divisive. In spring 1929 a majority of the Bolshevik leadership chose to abandon market principles and introduce a centrally planned economy. A new economic order, the era of the five-year plans, began. No society had ever tried such an experiment, but many Bolshevik leaders believed that the achievement of socialism was impossible without a planned economy because only planning could ensure rapid industrial development and economic growth, generate capital for an extensive social welfare system, and raise the standard of living.

The onset of the First Five-Year Plan (1928–32) required the destruction of the private market and private entrepreneurs, and the creation of innumerable offices to plan, direct, and oversee the economy. It was a Herculean task that the Bolsheviks tackled with an enthusiasm and naïveté that leaves observers slack-jawed. The amount of inefficiency, waste, and administrative confusion that accompanied the Five-Year Plan was staggering. In the absence of market mechanisms, offices authorized money to be spent without rigorous accounting. Steep inflation ensued; the standard of living plummeted.

The results were also staggering. During these years, the USSR laid the foundations for a virtually self-contained industrial economy. The Plan stressed the construction of capital industries: electrical power, iron, steel, machine-building, transport, coal and petroleum production. Most of it was built by manual labor. Some workers were enthusiastic, others reluctant. Workers who adopted efficient work techniques and surpassed output norms won material rewards and social praise. Brigades of younger workers competed to break production records, while more experienced workers struggled to keep control of output norms. Unemployment ended during the First Five-Year Plan and industrial output increased by more than 20 percent per annum at a time when the rest of the industrialized world experienced economic depression. The contrast emboldened the Stalinists and added legitimacy to their policies, as did the fact that tens of thousands of workers from abroad moved to the USSR in search of work or to participate in the socialist experiment.

The First Five-Year Plan was more than an experiment in economic planning and rapid industrialization. It also produced materials necessary for national defense. Enhancing the country's military strength so as to protect it from external enemies was an important aspect of the Plan. As Stalin put it in 1931: "We are fifty or a hundred years behind the advanced countries. We must make good this distance in ten years. Either we do or we shall go under."[13] Defending the socialist experiment from its enemies was central to the Stalin revolution.

These years also witnessed the Cultural Revolution that revealed the destructive aspects of some revolutionary and utopian visions. A class war was launched which sought the final destruction of the so-called "bourgeois" elements. Public show trials of "bourgeois" elements received widespread press coverage; some defendants were charged with being foreign agents. Students with the "proper" class credentials denounced "bourgeois" teachers and professors. Personnel with dubious class backgrounds were denounced, demoted, or fired. Class war between the workers and "bourgeois" specialists, workers and kulaks, communists and their perceived enemies was a defining feature of the Stalin revolution.

Although Stalin and other party leaders sounded the tocsin of class war, many people, especially younger people, participated. The motives were many, and included social mobility. In 1928 Stalin called for the creation of a new proletarian technical intelligentsia to replace the "bourgeois" specialists who allegedly obstructed industrial production. To train this new technical intelligentsia, the state invested heavily in expanding the number and types of schools – universities, higher technical institutes and schools, workers' faculties – so as to train a generation of engineers and technical personnel to staff the new industrial enterprises. Workers, poor peasants, and their children received priority in admissions; education was free. People flocked to take advantage of the opportunities for improved education and social mobility, to realize one aspect of their revolutionary agenda. To work an eight-hour day, grab one's ration, and then attend class was not at all unusual. Sheila Fitzpatrick has dubbed the beneficiaries of these policies of open access to education and rapid social mobility the "Brezhnev generation," after its best-known member.[14] The revolutionary agendas of some in this generation, which provided the social base of support for Stalin and Stalinism, were being fulfilled. Europeans, reeling from the effects of the Great Depression, took careful note.

While the state financed expanding educational opportunities, the Cultural Revolution also witnessed battles within professions over how to hasten the construction of socialism. Examples abound within literature, the visual arts, legal theory, theater, and history, but urban planning is particularly illuminating. Like many early twentieth-century thinkers, Bolsheviks and their supporters viewed cities as both symbols of the scourge of capitalism and as symbols of hope. For them, the city should represent the pinnacle of human achievement, planning, collective interdependence, and individual independence. The reality of Soviet urban life was dramatically different. Before 1917, Russian cities had been overcrowded, dangerous, and expensive. Epidemics of cholera and typhus routinely wracked the poorer neighborhoods. Moscow was the most crowded, unhealthful, and expensive city in pre-World War I Europe. Urban conditions deteriorated sharply during the civil war years and insufficient funds during the NEP slowed repairs. Although improved water and sewage systems reduced the incidence of diseases, overcrowded housing, homelessness, inadequate municipal transportation, and other problems meant that daily life was a struggle for most urbanites. During the 1920s many urban planners and municipal officials explored and debated how best to improve urban life and to create genuine socialist cities. During the Stalin revolution some urban planners proposed to reconstruct existing cities and to build new cities. They believed in social engineering, so long as the "proper" political values were applied. For them, cities were Petri dishes in which socialist values and behaviors would germinate.[15]

Urban planners put forth various proposals, but all insisted that essential amenities – water purification and sewer systems; centralized energy generating plants; mass transit; easy access to work, school, and culture; and green space – would remedy the ills that beset cities and lay the basis for the socialist city. Many planners, like advocates of the Garden City movement elsewhere, sought to meld the benefits of urban and rural life. They viewed easy access to green spaces as crucial to the health of residents of a socialist city. Some planners deemed congested cities as beyond redemption and advocated abandoning them. Some advocated linear cities, in which residential complexes, public space, economic enterprises, and transportation lines ran parallel to each other through the open country.

As important as urban design was, the design of living and public spaces was crucial. Many planners condemned the concept of the single-family apartment, asserting that housing design should hasten the destruction of the bourgeois family. Single-room dwellings in buildings that provided communal dining halls, laundries, libraries, movie theaters, and daycare centers would enable people to blossom as individuals while simultaneously inculcating a communal spirit. Communal apartments in which several families shared kitchen and bathing facilities became common. The emancipation of the individual and the fostering of collective values were visions that excited many planners.

Such utopian plans were, however, impractical and sometimes unpopular. By 1932 their advocates had lost influence, although some of their principles endured. The 1931 plan for the reconstruction of Moscow called for a dramatic increase in green space, public transit, public utilities, and housing construction, all of which were to be centrally planned.

The Experiment Institutionalized

By 1932 the destructive goals of the Stalin revolution had been achieved. The "bourgeois" elements, be they specialists, kulaks, or intellectuals, had been vanquished; the private market and the traditional agricultural order had been destroyed. In their place were proletarian technical specialists and collective farmers, a state-controlled distribution system, and a planned economy. In this "revolution from above," the state was the agent of change. Destroying the old order was easier than constructing a new one, as the steep decline in the standard of living, resistance of many peasants, and the chaotic aspects of the Five-Year Plan made clear. These realities help explain why the leadership was anxious about the state's ability to govern and to defend the USSR. Hitler's coming to power and the rise of fascism in Europe heightened the fear of war and need for national security. The once pariah state joined the League of Nations and sought to forge anti-fascist collective security agreements. It began to engage Europe as a citizen.

There was also cause for optimism. At the Seventeenth Party Congress in 1934, the "Congress of Victors," some speakers announced that the foundations of socialism were in place. In 1935 Stalin told an audience that life was "getting better" and "more joyous." In 1936 a national referendum approved the so-called Stalin Constitution that granted equal rights and liberties to all citizens, regardless of class. The era of class war was over. These pronouncements signaled the end of the destructive phase of the socialist experiment. Attention and energies now turned to "consolidating the gains already won," as one slogan of the era put it. The Second Five-Year Plan (1933–8) stressed accountability, efficiency, increasing productivity, and lowering costs. The mid-1930s witnessed the reassertion of more traditional family and social values, and increased opportunities for individual advancement. Divorces and abortions became more difficult to obtain. Motherhood became extolled. Yet more women than ever held full-time jobs and responsible positions. The new Soviet woman was expected to balance the demands of work and family. Educational opportunities expanded, yet traditional curricula returned to the schools, as did entrance exams, uniforms, textbooks, and structured classrooms. This was a different vision of socialism than the utopian vision in the 1919 program, a vision that confounded once again many European observers.

In these ways "Stalinist civilization," to use Stephen Kotkin's term, emerged. Some view this as the abandonment of the socialist experiment; supporters and beneficiaries viewed it as its realization. Members of the Brezhnev generation and Stakhanovites were the bearers of this new civilization. Named after Andrei Stakhanov, an overachieving coal miner, the ideal Stakhanovite embodied the characteristics that defined the new Soviet person. Such people sought to use initiative to find ways to increase production and to apply their knowledge to improve Soviet socialism. They received public praise and material rewards; their wives received public praise for aiding their husbands' efforts by creating a supportive domestic environment. In this way, they served the public good. They exposed shortcomings on the job, criticized practices or people who stymied improvements, and acted as role models for proper socialist behavior. They were models for the new Soviet person. They possessed self-discipline, time discipline, and party discipline, and were rewarded and acknowledged for such. They were conscientious in their work and social service. They lived to serve the cause of socialism. By achieving personal fulfillment through the fulfillment of social needs, they served a positive didactic function. They had the confidence to criticize the shortcomings of others and the humility to be self-critical. And they were tireless in their vigilance.

Given that the Stalinist vision of socialism was victorious, the class struggle had ended, and the class enemies had been routed, against whom or what were such people supposed to be vigilant? There were real and perceived threats, but in the long run the distinction became moot because Soviet citizens were expected to unmask any perceived threat. From 1933, the foreign fascist threat loomed large. During 1936, concerns about alleged internal enemies mounted; in 1937–8, it became the basis and justification for mass violence against many who lived in the USSR. That violence, known variously as the Great Purges, the Great Terror, the Stalinist mass repression, the *Yezhovshchina*,[16] heralded the end of socialist experimentation and the deformation of Soviet society. It accounted for more than 1.5 million arrests and 681,000 executions.[17] It was a horrific period of police repression that had not been on anyone's revolutionary agenda. It shocked sympathizers and they condemned it.

Fear of enemies drove the repression. That fear was not new, but the face of the enemy changed. Prior to 1934, the class enemy posed the greatest danger. During the Cultural Revolution, several show trials alleged that these class enemies acted as spies and foreign agents. As anxiety about foreign intervention grew in the early 1930s, so too did official suspicions about certain groups within the USSR. The first were the advocates of *korenizatsiia* (indigenization) in the various national republics and regions. That policy had proved more successful than Bolshevik leaders could have imagined. They found themselves unable to keep the rise of national sentiment within desirable bounds. They particularly feared that sentiment in the border regions. In the 1920s the Soviet state had hoped to make the border regions, such as Ukraine, showcases to attract Ukrainians who lived across the border in Poland. In the early 1930s Soviet leaders began to fear that the forces of attraction pulled the other way. The influx of hundreds of thousands of émigrés from border states, like Poland, Finland, Korea, and the Baltic countries, deepened that fear. Hitler's coming to power in 1933 extended that fear to German émigrés and native German communities in the USSR. Some leaders feared that ethnic communities harbored "saboteurs" and "enemy agents" who sought to weaken the country at a time of intensifying "capitalist encirclement." In 1937–8 these communities experienced widespread repression.

State agencies conducted the repression, but this was not like the pre-1936 period when the state openly spoke of smashing class enemies. According to the 1936 Constitution, the class struggle had ended. Henceforth the police moved against "enemies of the people." Some alleged enemies had advocated different revolutionary agendas than had the Stalinists; overzealous and vigilant police interrogators interpreted their past behaviors as a potential peril. But Stalinists were also victims. The armed might of the state struck at those suspected of opposing the existing version of the socialist experiment. The defense of the Soviet state on the eve of a war provided the justification to destroy those who might weaken it.

Europe watched this repression with shock and bewilderment. One of the causes of bewilderment was that, while the Soviet government unleashed the police on certain groups at home, it was the only European power to take up the anti-fascist cause during the Spanish Civil War. In 1936 Spain elected a Popular Front government that began to enact its own socialist experiment. Its moves to nationalize property, to secularize and expand education, and to grant wide-ranging civil rights challenged the power of the aristocracy, military, and Catholic church. The Spanish army with the military and economic assistance of Nazi Germany and Italy moved quickly to squash this experiment. The USSR did the same for the Popular Front. The Comintern organized the International Brigades consisting of anti-fascist volunteers from all over the world. The contrast between mass repression at home and its principled stand in Spain confounded Europeans. The repression angered many European communists, who quit the party. In 1939 the socialist experiment in Spain was defeated. In the USSR by 1939, fear had deformed the socialist experiment that the Bolsheviks had envisioned in 1919.

NOTES

1   An English translation of the "Program of the Communist Party of Russia" can be found in N. Bukharin and E. Preobrazhensky, *The ABC of Communism: A Popular Explanation of the Program of the Communist Party of Russia* (Ann Arbor: University of Michigan Press, 1966). *The ABC* was written to provide an accessible explanation of the program to party members and working people.

2   The USSR (Union of Soviet Socialist Republics) was not officially proclaimed until 1924, but for the sake of convenience this essay uses that label.

3   Bukharin and Preobrazhensky, *ABC*, p. 379.

4   Ibid, p. 377.

5   Ibid, p. 396.

6   Ibid, pp. 390–1.

7   See Carmen Siriani, *Workers Control and Socialist Democracy: The Soviet Experience* (London: Verso/NLB, 1982).

8   Bukharin and Preobrazhensky, *ABC*, pp. 389–90.

9   Ibid, p. 383.

10 Ibid, pp. 387–8. See also Sheila Fitzpatrick, *Education and Social Mobility in the Soviet Union, 1921–1934* (Cambridge: Cambridge University Press, 1979).

11 On Masha Scott, see John Scott, *Behind the Urals: An American Worker in Russia's City of Steel* (Bloomington: Indiana University Press, 1989); Pearl S. Buck, *Talk about Russia with Masha Scott* (New York: John Day, 1945).

12 On resistance, see Lynne Viola, *Peasant Rebels under Stalin: Collectivization and the Culture of Peasant Resistance* (New York: Oxford University Press, 1996); Lynne Viola, ed., *Contending with Stalinism: Soviet Power and Popular Resistance in the 1930s* (New York: Oxford University Press, 2002).

13 J. V. Stalin, *Works*, vol. 13 (Moscow: Foreign Language Publishing House, 1955), pp. 40–1.

14 Sheila Fitzpatrick, "Cultural Revolution as Class War," in *Cultural Revolution in Russia, 1928–1931*, Sheila Fitzpatrick, ed. (Bloomington: Indiana University Press, 1978). Leonid Brezhnev was the Communist Party's general secretary from 1964 to 1981.

15 See Anatole Kopp, *Town and Revolution: Soviet Architecture and City Planning, 1917–1935*, Thomas E. Burton, trans. (New York: G. Braziller, 1970).

16 *Yezhovshchina* translates as the "time of Yezhov." Nikolai Yezhov headed the People's
    Commissariat of Internal Affairs (NKVD), the police, from September 1936 to December
    1938, and directed its operations during 1937–8. Historians heatedly debate the causes,
    dynamics, and dimensions of the *Yezhovshchina*. For a sample of views, see Robert
    Conquest, *The Great Terror: A Reassessment* (New York: Oxford University Press, 1990);
    Roy Medvedev, *Let History Judge: The Origins and Consequences of Stalinism* (New York:
    Columbia University Press, 1989); J. Arch Getty, *Origins of the Great Purges: The Soviet
    Communist Party Reconsidered, 1933–1938* (New York: Cambridge University Press,
    1985); William J. Chase, *Enemies Within the Gates? The Comintern and the Stalinist
    Repression, 1934–1939* (New Haven CT: Yale University Press, 2001).

17 There is debate over the number of victims. These figures, from NKVD documents, can
    be found in J. Arch Getty, Gabor T. Rittersporn, and V. N. Zemskov, "Victims of the
    Soviet Penal System in the Pre-war Years: A First Approach on the Basis of Archival
    Evidence," *American Historical Review* 98/4 (1993): 1017–49.

GUIDE TO FURTHER READING

Kendall Bailes, *Technology and Society under Lenin and Stalin: Origins of the Soviet Technical
    Intelligentsia, 1917–1941* (Princeton NJ: Princeton University Press, 1978). The best treat-
    ment of the topic.

William J. Chase, *Workers, Society, and the Soviet State: Labor and Life in Moscow, 1918–1929*
    (Champaign-Urbana: University of Illinois Press, 1987). A crisp study of workers and urban
    life.

Davies, R. W., *The Socialist Offensive: The Collectivization of Soviet Agriculture, 1929–1930*
    (Cambridge MA: Harvard University Press, 1980). A thorough study of the onset of
    collectivization.

Fitzpatrick, Sheila, ed., *Cultural Revolution in Russia, 1928–1932* (Bloomington: Indiana
    University Press, 1978). A fine collection of essays.

Fitzpatrick, Sheila, ed., *The Russian Revolution*, 2nd edn (Oxford: Oxford University Press,
    2001). A lucid survey of the revolutionary process from 1900 to 1938.

J. Arch Getty and Oleg V. Naumov, *The Road to Terror: Stalin and the Self-Destruction of the
    Bolsheviks, 1932–1939* (New Haven CT: Yale University Press, 1999). A blend of translated
    documents and analysis about the mass repression.

Wendy Z. Goldman, *Women, the State, and Revolution: Soviet Family Policy and Social Life,
    1917–1936* (New York: Cambridge University Press, 1993). The title says it all.

James R. Harris, *The Great Urals: Regionalism and the Evolution of the Soviet System* (Ithaca
    NY: Cornell University Press, 1999). A fine case study of politics and economics during the
    1920s and 1930s.

Stephen Kotkin, *Magnetic Mountain: Stalinism as a Civilization* (Berkeley: University of
    California Press, 1995). An insightful study of the building of the city of Magnitogorsk and
    Stalinist civilization.

Hiroaki Kuromiya, *Stalin's Industrial Revolution: Politics and Workers, 1928–1932* (New York:
    Cambridge University Press, 1998). An engaging study of workers and the Five-Year
    Plan.

Terry Martin, *The Affirmative Action Empire: Nations and Nationalism in the Soviet Union,
    1923–1939* (Ithaca NY: Cornell University Press, 2001). The most insightful book on
    nationality policies.

Evan Mawdsley, *The Russian Civil War* (Boston MA: Allen and Unwin, 1987). An accessible
    study of a complicated period.

Alec Nove, *Economic History of the USSR* (New York: Penguin, 1989). The most balanced textbook on the topic.

Matthew Payne, *Stalin's Railroad: Turksib and the Building of Socialism* (Pittsburgh: University of Pittsburgh Press, 2001). A fascinating study of labor and nationality issues during the Five-Year Plan.

CHAPTER TWENTY

The Fascist Challenge

MARTIN BLINKHORN

> If you had asked me why I had joined the militia I should have answered: "To fight against Fascism," and if you had asked me what I was fighting *for*, I should have answered: "Common decency." (George Orwell, *Homage to Catalonia*, 1938)

The English writer George Orwell was just one of thousands of foreigners who volunteered to "fight against Fascism" in the Spain of 1936. In the course of the Spanish Civil War of 1936–9, over 40,000 non-Spaniards made the difficult journey to what for most of them was an unfamiliar country in order to resist a right-wing rebellion backed by Fascist Italy and Nazi Germany. Most enlisted in the legendary International Brigades; a few, like Orwell, joined one of Republican Spain's left-wing party militias; and several thousand served as doctors, nurses, or ambulance drivers.[1] Many never returned. Those who did survive left Spain only to become embroiled within months in the definitive "fight against fascism": World War II. In Spain, the victory of "fascism" gave birth to the 36-year dictatorship of the rebellion's eventual leader, General Francisco Franco.

The epic of the foreign anti-fascist volunteers in the Spanish Civil War was unique in the twentieth century. Other "local" conflicts, from the South African War of 1899–1902, through Vietnam, down to the Balkan struggles of the 1990s, aroused strong feelings among non-combatants of many nationalities, without tempting significant numbers to change and risk their lives by voluntarily taking part. That "Spain" could do this testifies to the conviction, widely held in Europe and beyond by 1936, that the continent was being crushed by an evil, oppressive force to which the term "fascism" was commonly applied. Whatever the appropriateness of the label, the conviction itself had very real substance. By 1936, the liberal-democratic Europe of 1920 was a mere memory. Throughout most of the south, center, and east of the continent, dictatorships and authoritarian regimes now prevailed. Within the previous three years, the final vestiges of Germany's Weimar democracy had succumbed to Adolf Hitler's Nazis, a "clerical-fascist" regime had installed itself in Austria, and authoritarian regimes of one kind or another had been imposed in Bulgaria, Estonia,

Latvia, and (soon after the outbreak of war in Spain) Greece. Even where democracy lived on, in the continent's northwestern quadrant (Britain and Ireland, France, the Benelux countries, and the Nordic countries) and in Czechoslovakia, "fascism" appeared to be on the march. For sincere devotees of democracy and for adherents of socialism – especially the latter – who had witnessed parliamentary democracy, free trade unionism, and the organized left crushed or politically castrated throughout so much of Europe, it was time for ordinary people to do in Spain what democratic governments elsewhere had proved unwilling or impotent to do – confront and defeat a fascist challenge that was coming to seem irresistible.

The "fascism" that its enemies in the 1930s saw as devouring Europe took its name from the political force founded in Italy in 1919 and the Fascist dictatorship finally established there in 1925.[2] Especially following Hitler's achievement of power in 1933, the term's analytical and emotive power was reinforced by widespread recognition of the family resemblance linking Italian Fascism with Nazism. Fascist Italy and the Nazi Third Reich indisputably constituted a new kind of political regime: new in appearance, style, language, and a powerful drive towards totalitarian control. Nevertheless the continent-wide and potentially worldwide threat identified by Orwell and so many others was actually a broader and looser phenomenon than this might suggest. It involved the demolition or undermining of parliamentary democracy, and the disempowering or downright crushing of the left, by an assortment of authoritarian, right-wing forces. Many of these were essentially conservative in outlook and keen to deny that they were fascist at all, a denial readily accepted by self-proclaimed fascists or National Socialists who saw themselves as authentic revolutionaries.

These differing perceptions of "fascism" need to be borne in mind when we consider the "fascist challenge" presented to the Europe of the 1920s and early 1930s – the period with which this chapter is chiefly concerned. Since the end of World War II, historians and political scientists have grappled with the problems of definition and understanding arising from the discrepancy between, on the one hand, fascism and National Socialism as their self-conscious devotees saw them, and, on the other, a wider "objective" fascism as chiefly understood by committed liberals, democrats and, especially, socialists.[3] For Orwell and his contemporaries, such problems barely registered; they knew fascism when they saw it, knew it was inimical to "human decency," and – certainly by 1936 – knew it must be fought. Differences between manifestations of self-proclaimed "fascism" and more conventional forms of authoritarianism were matters of degree and theoretical nuance, not of essence or practical urgency. While demanding more of the intellect, present-day scholarly study of fascism asks little of the character and spirit. Comfortable, early twenty-first-century academics, while legitimately anxious in discussing fascism to exercise analytical rigor and achieve terminological precision, accordingly owe it to their forebears of the 1920s and 1930s never to forget or diminish the less neatly defined realities they faced.

For the purposes of this chapter, "fascism" and "fascist" will refer "generically" to the Italian example and to those ideas, movements, and regimes that consciously took inspiration from it – and later from its German National Socialist variant. Then, as the chapter progresses, it will become necessary to confront the implications of a broader use of the term such as that much employed at the time. First, however, we need to consider what it was that the "fascist challenge" was actually challenging.

The New Europe

Although as we have just seen, and as we shall see again later, it was during the 1930s that Europe truly faced a full-blown threat from fascism, it was certainly in the 1920s that this challenge was born and took shape. Whether we view fascism as a genuinely novel and even revolutionary phenomenon, or as an essentially counter-revolutionary one, it was – at least in what might be called its "first phase" – a product of World War I and the postwar environment. It is true that many of fascism's ideas and attitudes had prewar origins. Nor was there any shortage in pre-1914 Europe of political organizations seeking to mobilize, for instance, ultranationalism, authoritarianism, racism and antisemitism, anti-Marxism, "national" variants of socialism, and various forms of cultural revolt.[4] Movements such as *Action Française*, the Italian Nationalist Association, Portuguese Integralism, and numerous German political leagues are only a few examples of what, in the generation before 1914, was a general phenomenon.[5] Yet while historically significant, these were mostly symptoms of stirring political dissatisfaction rather than serious threats to the privileged liberal and conservative political elites of Europe's nations and empires. The 1914–18 war, the 1917 Bolshevik revolution, the 1919 peace settlement, and the convulsive conditions of the postwar years generated new issues and released new social forces. This transformed setting helped give birth to fascism in its original "Italian" sense, nurtured it and propelled it to power, and then made it relevant and attractive to individuals and interests well beyond Italy. In addition, the postwar climate encouraged the growth and articulation of other, less outwardly "revolutionary" expressions of authoritarianism which, thanks to the attention lavished upon developments in Italy, became associated in many minds with fascism. It is accordingly vital to consider more closely the relationship between the emergence of fascism and the setting from which it emerged.

During its closing stages, the extensive conflict that was unprecedented in its destructiveness had assumed the character of a crusade on behalf of liberal values and political democracy. With the entry into the war of the United States in 1917 and the withdrawal in early 1918 of a recently tsarist and now Bolshevik Russia, the Allies – led by Britain and its Dominions, France, the United States and Italy, but also embracing other European states such as Greece, Portugal, and Romania – were able to proclaim their victory as that of liberal democracy over the alleged authoritarianism of the losers: Germany, the Austro-Hungarian and Ottoman empires, and Bulgaria. However shaky and/or dubious prewar parliamentary liberalism may have been in some places, superficially at least it emerged from the struggle as Europe's dominant system of politics, economics, and general values. Ideological and cultural pluralism, religious and ethnic toleration, national self-determination, free-market economics, representative and responsible government, free trade unionism, and the peaceful settlement of international disputes through a new body, the League of Nations – all of these liberal precepts were embraced, west of the USSR and admittedly (as we shall soon see) with widely varying degrees of enthusiasm and sincerity, by the elites of Europe's old and new nations.

As the last phrase indicates, fundamental to the new Europe was the redrawing of the territorial and political map in the peace settlements of 1919–22.[6] Out of the defeat of the old German, Habsburg, and Ottoman empires arose a number of new or reborn independent states: Finland, Estonia, Latvia, Lithuania, Poland, Austria,

Hungary, Czechoslovakia, Yugoslavia, and Albania. Some of these conformed more or less closely to the principle of national self-determination beloved of President Woodrow Wilson, though most nevertheless contained substantial minority populations. Two, Czechoslovakia and Yugoslavia, were born as problematical multinational states with serious ethnic and cultural tensions. Austria and Hungary, previously dominant and competing partners within the Habsburg Empire, found themselves separated and independent but territorially and demographically truncated. Austria's very viability as a small German-speaking state overshadowed by a new Germany was questionable, while Hungary saw substantial Magyar-speaking regions attached to Yugoslavia, Czechoslovakia and, most importantly, Romania. Romania's new situation, vastly expanded in both area and population and facing difficult problems of assimilation and national identity, indicates that being on the winning side in the war was no guarantee of future stability. If generous territorial gains promised difficulties for Romania, rewards widely considered inadequate provoked a sharp sense of national grievance in Italy, where disappointed patriots and especially war veterans bemoaned a so-called "mutilated victory." Literally central to the settlement and to the continent's future was of course Germany: stripped of German-speaking populations on the Baltic coast and in Bohemia, its sovereignty undermined along the Rhine, and thrust into a problematical relationship with Austria. Thus, across much of the continent, issues of unredeemed national territories and peoples, contested borders, and internal minorities provided fuel for international and ethnic tensions. The opportunity for ultranationalist elements to exploit this situation was enhanced by the presence of numerous demobilized ex-combatants, infected by military values and habits and uncomfortable with a sudden adjustment to civilian life.

Not only were many territorial boundaries shifted by the war and the 1919 settlement, but Europe's overall political complexion changed too. Before the war, while most European countries had acquired constitutional governing systems of some kind, many of these were actually far from being true democracies. With real power held by wealthy conservative and liberal oligarchies, the popular will was obstructed by a variety of constitutional limitations (Germany, Austria-Hungary), narrow suffrage (Italy to 1912), or institutionalized corruption (Italy, Spain, Portugal). It is impossible to know whether, had there been no World War I, most of the European countries that existed in 1914 might have evolved more or less peacefully into viable parliamentary democracies. What we can say is that the demands of war on governments and peoples encouraged two potentially conflicting tendencies relevant to the story of European democracy. The first was a pronounced strengthening of state machinery, notably bureaucracies and the military, which entrenched authoritarian habits and sentiments among their personnel. The second was a pronounced acceleration in a shift, already apparent before 1914, towards truly "mass politics" involving modern political parties, organized interest and pressure groups, and large, powerful labor movements.

This "massification" of politics, especially evident from the mid-point of the war, merged after its conclusion with a heady and illusory "vogue for democracy" fed by the Allied victory and America's newly arrived influence. The result was a continent containing several new states that were also young democracies, many born in settings and circumstances that were far from conducive to their chances of achieving maturity. All of the newly created countries began their lives as constitutional democracies, though some like Hungary and Albania began to show signs of reverting to authoritarianism from an early date.[7] While the establishment of new republics in Germany and Austria raised wider hopes of a decisive stride towards democracy among the German-speaking peoples, in both countries powerful anti-democratic forces still operated. Italy offered a particularly complex picture: although the fundamental constitutional position remained unchanged, postwar Italy became something like a true democracy almost overnight, as the full effects of near-universal male suffrage, introduced in 1912, combined with those of proportional representation, added in fulfillment of a wartime governmental promise to the Italian people. The outcome was the immediate weakening of Italy's previously dominant "liberal" political elites, the emergence of mutually mistrustful socialist and Catholic mass parties, and a state of political paralysis.[8] In all of these countries democracy was either an accompaniment to the challenges of new nationhood or, at the very least, inextricably intertwined with the negative consequences of war and peace. Even in countries less dramatically affected by the peace settlement, such as Portugal, Spain, and Sweden, postwar political adjustment was far from easy.

Had the postwar years been years of economic and social stability, even of reasonably smooth recovery from the disruption caused by war, the prospects for European democracy could have been very different. New democracies and a newly democratized Italian polity might have established themselves more securely, weak not-quite-democracies like those of Spain and Portugal might have had the chance to mature more or less peacefully into genuine ones, and the fascist challenge might never have emerged. In the wake of so massive a conflict, however, such a scenario is sheer counterfactual fantasy. The reality was one of dislocated industry and agriculture, mass demobilization contributing further to large-scale unemployment, and waves of nightmarish inflation affecting middle-class salaries and savings. Economic grievances, status insecurities, and heightened social tensions between 1919 and 1924 meant that new – and even more established – democracies, many forced also to grapple with problems arising from defeat, disappointing victory, ethnic tension, etc., also became the victims of social discontents of one kind or another. It is important to stress here that, because its particular forms were new across so much of Europe, it was often democracy as *system* of politics and values – involving, ironically, acceptance of free discussion and the right to question those in power – that attracted criticism and even contempt for the failures of individual *governments* to solve postwar problems. To some at least of its attackers, democracy could appear *intrinsically* weak, indecisive, shabby, compromising, and inimical to a nation's interests.

A particular concern of democracy's critics as they began to express themselves after 1919 was its relationship with a newly powerful political left, whether the latter was seeking to work within the system for gradual reform, determined to overthrow it by revolutionary means, or hovering uncertainly between these two positions. From the later nineteenth century onward, most European countries had witnessed the emergence of left-wing political and trade union movements wedded to the redistribution of wealth and the transformation of society, either by parliamentary or by outright revolutionary means. The 1914–18 war and the demands it placed on the economies of belligerent and even neutral nations gave an enormous boost to the European left in three main ways. First, it stimulated a massive growth in the labor force and concomitant expansion of trade union membership. Secondly, employer and state pressures on labor, together with the excesses of war profiteering, provoked intensified labor and social conflicts. Thirdly, the effects of war and defeat helped precipitate in Russia a revolution that transformed the hopes, fears, and perceptions of postwar Europeans. In the short term almost all European leftists, longstanding and newly recruited, drew inspiration from the Russian example, even if many were sooner or later alienated by Bolshevism's increasing authoritarianism and repressiveness. Most European socialist parties in the 1920s were theoretically Marxist and inclined to use revolutionary rhetoric. Some, like the French and Spanish parties, were revolutionary in theory only; others, like the main body of the Italian Socialist Party during 1919–20, flirted with revolution sufficiently to spread alarm among its possible victims without ever seriously approaching its achievement. The Austrian Socialist Party sought revolutionary transformation by peaceful means, while the powerful German SPD left belief in revolution to the breakaway German Communist Party, the KPD. The latter, like the new communist parties in Hungary and elsewhere, actively engaged in revolutionary activity which generated a "red scare" mentality in upper- and middle-class circles and played an important part in preparing the ground for fascism.

For many Europeans during the early 1920s, the essence of the postwar European left was revolutionary whatever its militants said or did; socialism in power, whether at the national level as in Weimar Germany or, more briefly, the Austrian republic, or at the local level as happened in many parts of northern Italy after 1919, was believed to mean a "Bolshevik" assault upon property, capital, and middle-class status. Postwar democracy, by tolerating left-wing trade unionism and political socialism, seemed to such terrified bourgeois to represent – like the Kerensky government in post-tsarist, pre-Bolshevik Russia – a mere stage within a descent into "Bolshevism" that must therefore be resisted or forestalled by any available means. In several countries – most notably Finland, Poland, Germany, Austria, Hungary, and Spain – the end of the war and/or the immediate postwar months had witnessed either actual revolutionary attempts or at the very least mass left-wing militancy with revolutionary overtones, and the employment of the army or paramilitary armed bands to suppress them. The legacy was to prove a powerful one.

Italy and the First Fascist Challenge

During the revolutionary and counter-revolutionary conflicts of 1918–20, Europe witnessed numerous foretastes of what would come to be called "fascism." Paramilitary squads such as the German *Freikorps* and Austrian *Heimwehr*, made up of war veterans and, in the latter case, sympathetic peasant farmers and members of the urban middle class, exemplified a direct and violent response, either to real or exaggerated threats of communist revolution or to territorial and ethnic rivals.[9] Frustrated nationalism was also a factor: in Italy the nationalist poet and war hero, Gabriele D'Annunzio, led a private army of war veterans in seizing the Adriatic city of Fiume, disputed between Italy and Yugoslavia, holding it for a year until finally ejected by the Italian authorities. D'Annunzio's theatrical style and his experiments with a new kind of state were not lost on an admirer, Benito Mussolini.

Related, but more unambiguously "institutional" reactions to the "Bolshevik menace," came from conservative military cliques and their well-heeled civilian supporters. Such forces were involved in defeating left-wing movements in Finland and Poland, and in 1920 promoted the unsuccessful Kapp Putsch against Weimar. By this time authoritarian conservatives were already in control of Hungary, where in 1919 they overturned the unpopular Soviet Republic of Béla Kun and destroyed the power of the Hungarian left for a generation. Brushing aside their country's genuine liberals and democrats, the triumphant Hungarian counter-revolutionaries installed, behind a transparent veneer of so-called "liberalism," a reactionary semi-dictatorship under their leader Admiral Miklós Horthy.[10] The Horthy regime, which was to last until 1944, was the first of Europe's many interwar dictatorships. Its rapid emergence, together with stirrings elsewhere, signaled how fragile and conditional, if it existed at all, was the support of many establishment forces for newly created liberal democracies – especially when these appeared vulnerable to the left.

While counter-revolutionary, anti-democratic activity of an essentially conservative character may have been widespread in postwar Europe, and might well have continued regardless of developments in Italy, it was these that ensured the label "fascism" would gain worldwide and lasting currency. Fascism's rise was dramatic. In March 1919 Benito Mussolini, a leading socialist militant until late 1914, led a mixed bag of around a hundred political malcontents in forming a new organization, the *Fascio di Combattimento* (Combat Group). After failing to attract support as a kind of "alternative socialism," Fascism changed course and quickly became a mass movement of a kind unprecedented in Italy or anywhere else, contemptuous of liberal democracy and devoted to the use of violence against socialists, communists, and Catholic peasant leagues. In late October 1922 Fascism's fast-increasing numbers, its power to intimidate, and the political establishment's desperate ineptitude enabled Mussolini to become premier in a Fascist-led government. Finally, in January 1925, Mussolini inaugurated a Fascist dictatorship advertised, and widely accepted, as a wholly new way of organizing the state.

Unlike Hungary, now something of a European backwater, Italy was a leading European country whose public affairs attracted enormous outside interest. This, coupled with Fascism's sheer *differentness*, guaranteed the new regime continent-wide publicity and, in many quarters, sympathy. For many Europeans Italian Fascism, for all its rough edges, radiated youthfulness, energy, excitement, and novelty. First as a movement and then as a regime it appeared to combine a counter-revolutionary, anti-democratic role with a distinctive and completely original revolutionary posture. The former it demonstrated by ruthlessly crushing the Italian left and freeing Italy from what was actually a largely illusory revolutionary threat. The latter's emergence was more piecemeal. Between 1922 and the end of 1924, even without an outright dictatorship and still facing elements of criticism and opposition, Fascism began to project a sense of national renewal and reborn pride. With the establishment of Mussolini's dictatorship in January 1925, what was now an unambiguously Fascist regime managed to persuade sympathetically inclined Europeans that it was utterly transforming Italian politics, society, and culture; perhaps, it was also possible to believe, Fascism was even altering the character of the Italians themselves. Crucial to all this was Fascism's unprecedented presentational skills and carefully constructed image of discipline. Here, historical perspective is vital to our understanding. As yet, in the 1920s, the uniforms and parades, the stiff-armed salutes, the symbols and sloganizing, in fact many of those external features which excited and attracted many observers, had not acquired the associations – chiefly with Nazism and the Holocaust – that were later to discredit them. Fascism in its first decade was above all *new*.

This may help us to understand why by no means all those non-Italians who found themselves attracted to, and even inspired by, Italian Fascism during the 1920s were instinctive reactionaries or even conservatives. Many Europeans, while rejecting the recipes of the orthodox left, nevertheless did dream of radical solutions to postwar problems: solutions perhaps impossible within the framework of pluralistic politics. In Fascism, especially as the new Italian state developed after 1925, sympathizers saw an alternative, patriotic radicalism, apparently capable of cutting through the chatter, delays, and compromises of parliamentary democracy. Fascism appeared to promise the restoration of economic health; the elimination of market uncertainties in favor of planning through a "corporate" state; the replacement of class conflict and the Bolshevik threat by social cohesion and collaboration; and the mobilization of a people's energies and enthusiasm in a collective patriotic mission. Fascism's desire and seeming intention to transform individual and collective mentalities through education, propaganda, and mass participation in its public displays also appealed to intellectual minorities in other countries who found the postwar world drab and "decadent."[11]

The challenge with which Italian Fascism confronted the Europe of the 1920s thus had, or seemed to have, much more to it than the mere replacement of democracy with a defensively minded, *destructive* authoritarianism. Present-day historians, both inside and outside Italy, disagree sharply among themselves regarding the sincerity, consistency, and success of Fascism's social and cultural purpose,[12] but few deny the effectiveness of Fascist propaganda in persuading substantial numbers of non-Italian contemporaries that Fascism had something *constructive* with which to challenge liberal democracy. Even so, many other Europeans were less bewitched by militaristic display, punctual trains, triumphalist rhetoric, and the strutting *machismo* of Mussolini and his henchmen. For its critics and enemies, Fascism, behind the superficial glitter, was first and foremost an oppressive, reactionary force. Unconditional supporters of liberal democracy were appalled by Fascism's increasing authoritarianism, its proclaimed "totalitarian" goals, and what all this meant for individual and collective freedom. For socialists of all kinds, Fascism was the armed guard of capitalism and the enemy of the working class.

However Italian Fascism was viewed, its impact was such that from 1922 onward, "fascism" assumed a salient position within European political discourse. From the very start, though, it was – as it remains – a slippery term, with important implications when it comes to assessing the true character and seriousness of any "fascist challenge" to liberal democracy and its socialist alternatives. Broadly speaking, we can discern three main positions in relation to the term as it emerged in the 1920s. Two have just been touched on. For some in every European country (save the USSR) "fascism" meant a political revolution of nationalist, populist, authoritarian character, forged and developed in Italy but capable and worthy of imitation anywhere in Europe. Critics saw its essential character as demagogic and oppressive, its function that of propping up capitalism and broader conservative forces. The third position grew out of the second, holding that behind its facade Fascism's essential character and role were sufficiently similar to those of other, less experimental authoritarian regimes to justify applying the now fashionable term to all of them. It is now time to explore these matters further.

Between 1922 and the end of the decade many of Europe's parliamentary democracies, together with the socialist, communist, and anarchist left, found themselves confronted by organized challenges from the political right which fell into three broad categories. The most straightforward consisted of newly formed organizations which, appearing in most European countries, took direct inspiration from the supposedly *revolutionary* character of Italian Fascism and proposed something similar for their own national communities. The second comprised new or ongoing organizations which borrowed *something* from Fascism, or in some respects resembled it, without attempting to disguise their own essentially non- or counterrevolutionary character. The third category embraced a range of elite elements such as conservative parties, army and naval officer corps, bureaucratic cliques, organizations of industrialists and landowners, ecclesiastical hierarchies, and royal courts. From beneath the sometimes disturbing revolutionary surface of Fascism, their members drew a generalized inspiration and comfort from its defeat of the left and its essential *authoritarianism* as a system of power. It was precisely this aspect of Fascism, of course, that made it acceptable to so many conservative Italians, whatever their reservations and however little they may have shared its more ambitious social, cultural, and institutional goals. But conservative groups outside Italy often concluded that the "best" of Fascism was achievable without recourse to those of its features they mistrusted.

During the 1920s a definite vogue for "fascism" seduced significant numbers of individuals throughout Europe and stimulated the formation of countless self-consciously fascist organizations. Examples are the French *Faisceau*, the creation of Georges Valois, a former militant of *Action Française*; the British Fascisti (later British Fascists); the Spanish (though predominantly Catalonian) group "La Traza"; the Academic Karelia Society in Finland; and the largely military Iron Wolf movement in Lithuania – but others can be identified in virtually every European country west of the Soviet frontier. While it would be simple to produce an impressive list of such parties and movements, a sense of proportion is called for. The majority of such imitative movements, like those just mentioned, in reality presented little or no threat to their country's political establishment. Some, it is true, did lay down an intellectual or ideological template which they or other movements were able to employ with greater profit during the 1930s. Viewed overall, however, the experience of outright fascist parties in much of Europe in the 1920s did much to confirm Mussolini's early assertion (he was later to change his mind) that Fascism was "not for export." Fascism in Italy was an extraordinary, highly distinctive political phenomenon, the product of a unique combination of circumstances at a specific historical moment. Artificially replicating elsewhere a movement that had formed and developed organically out of Italian conditions, and which achieved power in the midst of a distinctively Italian political crisis, was never likely to be easy.

In only two settings can a species of "fascism," formed in the 1920s, be said eventually to have flourished, and in both cases it flourished because it possessed highly particular roots of its own. Here, the "fascism" of the Romanian Legionary movement and German National Socialism, although similar to the Italian model, did not imitate it.

The "Legion of the Archangel Michael," later the Legionary Movement and better known as the Iron Guard, was formed in 1927 by ultra-patriotic Romanian students led by the charismatic Corneliu Codreanu. Drawing on Romania's powerful tradition of nationalistic, antisemitic populism it borrowed little directly from Italian Fascism save perhaps an unambiguous detestation of liberalism and a vitalistic belief in the ability of a "new man" to transform political reality. From modest beginnings in the 1920s, the Legion was to become a major force in the next decade, challenging both the country's corrupt liberal political class and the authoritarian alternative eventually posed by the monarchy of King Carol II.

The Germany of the early 1920s threw up a kaleidoscope of rightist organizations opposed to Weimar democracy, the German left, and the Treaty of Versailles. The NSDAP (National Socialist German Workers Party), founded as the German Workers Party in 1919 and renamed by its new leader, Adolf Hitler, in 1920, was initially just one of these, and indeed became the country's dominant far-right organization only during the mid-1920s. Even then its popular and electoral success was limited, and up to 1929 there was little sign that it would ever emulate the successes of Italian Fascism, much less surpass them. Only with the 1930 general election can it be said to have achieved the kind of breakthrough that positioned it for a serious attempt on power. As it developed, Nazism clearly assumed ideological and presentational characteristics linking it with Italian Fascism, while remaining quintessentially Germanic in ideology, outlook, and horizons. One preoccupation which distinguished it, and indeed the Romanian Legion, from Italian Fascism was antisemitism, which played little part in Italian affairs before the late 1930s.

If closely plagiarizing Italian Fascism produced relatively meager results, organizations borrowing more selectively from the Italian model sometimes achieved more. Some of the most successful – that is, in drawing attention to themselves, recruiting members, attracting financial backing, and influencing the course of their country's history – emerged, as did Italian Fascism, Nazism, and the Romanian Legion, where there existed what might be termed indigenous *roots*. In particular, they grew where postwar conditions and conflicts had already contributed to a militarization of politics. Thus in Austria, Finland, and Germany, for example, paramilitary organizations, formed in the immediate postwar period to combat the revolutionary left and the national enemy, were already active when the example of Italian Fascism began to make its mark. So, in an admittedly very different context, were the groups in Hungary who came to be known as "Szeged fascists": military and bureaucratic extremists keen to push the Horthy regime towards more open authoritarianism.

From 1922 onward organizations such as these, particularly the *Heimwehr* and the "Szeged fascists," fell at least partly under the Italian spell. The magic nevertheless had its limits. It would be 1930 before the *Heimwehr* openly embraced fascism, despite receiving Italian financial sponsorship, and its underlying ideological conservatism was always present. For their part, the "Szeged fascists," despite the confusing terminology, provide a good example of an Italian-influenced movement which ignored those aspects of Italian Fascism, essentially the more radical ones, that lacked appeal to its socially snobbish militants. Other relatively vigorous movements of the 1920s which, while influenced by Fascism fell well short of fascist maximalism, were the *Jeunesses Patriotes* (Patriot Youth), founded in France in 1924, and the longer-standing Portuguese movement, *Integralismo Lusitano*. The former achieved some success, especially among French war veterans; by the late 1920s it claimed 100,000 adherents. It did this with a mixture of rather half-hearted fascist "style" and conventional authoritarian–nationalist ideas: a combination that was to enjoy greater success in France (and elsewhere) during the 1930s. *Integralismo Lusitano*, a movement strongly influenced by *Action Française*, had been firmly established in Portugal since before the war; now, in the 1920s, this elitist organization of academics, students, and younger army officers drew psychological nourishment from, and owed its growing influence to, Italian Fascism, without ever looking convincingly fascist itself. Even so, for some of its members it was to serve as a way-station en route to fascism.[13]

The Wider Challenge of Right-Wing Authoritarianism

The sense of a remorseless "fascist" wave, threatening and in many countries over-turning parliamentary democracy, derived much of its validity and power not so much from the emergence of self-consciously fascist or fascist-influenced movements, much less their actual achievements, as from the installation by more established right-wing forces of authoritarian regimes which then became linked with "fascism" – chiefly in the perceptions of their victims, critics, and enemies, but also sometimes in those of their adherents. As with fascism in its stricter sense, here too origins can be discerned that went back well before 1914. Authoritarian ideas of essentially conservative character were widely held in, for example, prewar Germany, Italy, Spain, and France: ideas, that is, favoring a strengthening of the state, of the executive, even where relevant of the monarchy, all in the face of mass politics, supposed cultural degeneration, and the threat of leftist revolution.[14] Especially at times of political and social crisis – Italy at the turn of the century, Spain after the humiliation of the Spanish–American War in 1898, Portugal in the early twentieth century, Germany following dramatic SPD advances in 1910 – the introduction of a dictatorship was widely discussed. In a single case, that of Portugal in 1907–8, it even became a reality. Since analyses of fascism not infrequently counterpoise "fascist" regimes to supposedly "traditional" dictatorships, it is worth stressing that the latter, in interwar Europe, were not really traditional at all, since dictatorships of any kind were rare in Europe before 1914. The demands of the war itself, however, strengthened executive power and in several countries, Germany and Italy among them, gave increased influence and authority to army generals. State responses to social and political unrest between 1917 and the early 1920s had a similar effect in countries throughout eastern, central, and southern Europe, from Finland to Portugal.

Generalizing, it is possible to say that the kinds of forces under discussion here – senior army and navy officers, high-ranking bureaucrats, monarchical courts, landed magnates, bankers, and industrialists – tended to nurse hierarchical, authoritarian instincts. Both before and after the war, these elites were comfortable with parliamentary liberalism as long as it stopped short of actual democracy, and grudgingly accepted the latter only as long as it did little to threaten their interests or, worse, allow latitude to the political left. As already suggested, the establishment of Horthy's thinly veiled dictatorship in Hungary provided early evidence that the new democracies of post-1919 Europe might be under serious threat from authoritarian elements of broadly conservative character. While the Italian Fascist achievement of power may have presented a different kind of challenge, Fascism's dependence on establishment support, both in 1922 and during difficult times in 1924, was plain enough; Italy was distinctive, indeed unique, in the reluctance of its conservative elites to act on their own behalf, and in its spawning of a mass fascist movement capable of assuming the task. Elsewhere during the 1920s it was a different story, as military, royal, and presidential *coups d'état* subverted or overthrew parliamentary government in Spain (1923), Greece (1925), Lithuania, Poland, and Portugal (1926), Albania (1928), and Yugoslavia (1929).

Inevitably, even during the 1920s and still more during the following decade, authoritarian regimes became associated with fascism and were even viewed as fascist. This is an immensely complicated area, but at the cost of some over-categorization it is possible to suggest a number of features about the relationship. First, it cannot be denied that the success of Italian Fascism, simply in winning and holding on to power, showed that an authoritarian alternative to both parliamentary democracy and Soviet communism was possible, with or without Fascism's other attributes. Primo de Rivera in Spain (1923–30), Piłsudski in Poland (1926–35), Pangalos in Greece (1925–6), Smetona in Lithuania (1926–40), and the Portuguese junta (1925–ca. 1930) – all in a sense rode to power on Mussolini's coat-tails without being themselves fascists as most convinced fascists would have understood it. Secondly, however, it might be argued that most of these dictatorships played a broadly similar *role* to that of Fascism: ultra-patriotic to the point of chauvinism, hostile to parliamentary democracy and the revolutionary left, and protective towards established interests. Thirdly, the leaders of such regimes found it difficult, if they lasted long enough, to resist the temptation to graft on more openly fascist/Fascist characteristics: the corporate state, the cult of leadership, and elements of the outward display and choreography especially associated with Mussolini's regime. While it cannot be denied that, in its totalitarianism intentions and outward thoroughgoingness, Italian Fascism remained in a class by itself until the birth of the Third Reich in 1933, the conviction of the European left that Fascism represented at most an extreme variant of a much wider trend remains both perfectly understandable and by no means absurd.[15]

At the same time, it must be acknowledged that the picture presented by the more "establishment" regimes imposed in the 1920s is sometimes less tidy than is suggested by the notion of an essentially monolithic "fascist" tide. One aspect of this untidiness is their reversibility. The Greek dictatorship of the decidedly fascist-influenced Pangalos lasted only a year, while that of Primo de Rivera collapsed in January 1930 after little more than six, at least in part precisely *because* its political elite, in attempting a "fascistization" of the regime, bit off more than it could chew. The fates of Pangalos, removed by rival generals, and Primo de Rivera, abandoned by the rest of the general staff, by most of the old political elite, and finally by his king, illustrate the vulnerability to shifts in elite loyalties of dictatorships which lacked the autonomous support of a fascist mass movement. The Greek dictatorial interlude of the mid-1920s gave way to a by-no-means doomed reversion to parliamentary government, while the fall of Primo de Rivera was followed a year later by that of the Spanish monarchy and the advent of the democratic Second Republic. A second and very different complication arose from relations between authoritarian regimes and the far right. Poland under Pilsudski and Yugoslavia under the Royal Dictatorship of King Alexander, like the enduring regime of Horthy, combined an intrinsic authoritarianism with enough political pluralism to permit the activity of more extreme and more openly fascistic organizations. This emerging tension was to prove a significant one, capable during the 1930s of giving rise to outright conflict in, for example, Hungary, Romania, and Portugal.[16]

From a democratic or left-wing perspective such disagreements represented little more than squabbles among the Four Horsemen of the Apocalypse. And for all the foregoing qualifications, when it came to assessing the underlying significance of authoritarian regimes the suspicions of early anti-fascists had at least some justification. The 1920s had shown how throughout much of central, southern, and eastern Europe powerful interests were lukewarm and opportunistic in their support for parliamentary democracy and liable under pressure to embrace authoritarianism of one kind or another, but preferably a "conventional" one. Only in Italy, where this option was not readily available, and where for other distinctive reasons the mass movement of fascism appeared, did the mutual embrace of mass movement and establishment forces produce an unambiguously fascist regime.

The Real Fascist Challenge: The Second Wave of the 1930s

As the 1920s drew towards their close, Europe as a whole can scarcely be said to have been seriously challenged by fascism as it was understood in Italy and by those elsewhere who embraced the Italian example or a homegrown variant of it. It is true that by the end of 1929, following the conclusion of the Lateran agreements between the Italian state and the papacy, the Fascist regime was completely secure and Italy poised to enter the years of what many historians of Fascism consider to have been "consensus."[17] Nevertheless Mussolini's regime presented no significant threat to international peace, while self-consciously fascist movements in most other European countries struggled to make progress. Even in Germany and Romania the threat they posed their country's rulers was as yet hardly a massive one. This is not to say that democracy was in a particularly strong position, for not only in Italy but also in several southern and eastern European countries authoritarian regimes had replaced democracies in what the human casualties of that process now considered fascism, even if most fascists and authoritarian conservatives did not. And, in some places where it survived, democracy's health was in doubt. In Germany, for example, it is arguable that the greater stability achieved by Weimar from the mid-1920s was at the cost of dependence on some intrinsically unreliable conservative forces. Even in Spain, which by late 1929 was already embarked on a course *towards* democracy, anti-democratic elements remained ominously powerful. The overall balance was thus a delicate one.

While the main emphasis of this chapter has been on the decade of the 1920s, it would thus be misleading to leave things as they stood at the end of 1929, passing over completely those events of the years 1930–6 which convinced Orwell and so many others of the need to reverse an advancing fascist tide. What changed the picture as it stood in 1929, and made the second wave of European fascism, that of the 1930s, far more serious than the first, was the onset and impact of the world economic depression unleashed by the Wall Street Crash of October 1929. Even allowing for differences in timing and degree, all European countries, from the industrialized like Germany and Britain to the predominantly agricultural like Greece and Romania, were hit by the Depression. What then encouraged German National Socialism to take off, and a host of other fascist or fascist-influenced movements to attract support elsewhere, was not so much the embracing of fascism by the Depression's principal casualties, the unemployed, as a complicated set of responses to the confusion and failures of parliamentary government. Germany was of course the most dramatic case. There, between 1930 and 1933, the NSDAP swept up support from collapsing middle-class liberal and Protestant parties until by July 1933 it was the country's most popular party. Given the importance of the "Nazi seizure of power," which began with Hitler's appointment as chancellor in January 1933, it must be recognized that here too, as with Italian Fascism a decade earlier, it was the machinations and complaisance of the country's conservative elites which opened the way to power to a force which, while undeniably strong, was by no means irresistible. Even the Italian elites had sometimes found coexistence with Fascism unexpectedly uncomfortable, but for many German conservatives the equivalent experience was to be far more difficult.

The Nazi achievement of power, followed by the decisive and ruthless process of "Coordination" which produced a dictatorship in a fraction of the time it had taken Mussolini, was one of two factors which, against the background of the Depression, gave European fascism a significant new boost. The other was the apparent ability of the Italian Fascist regime to cope with the effects of the Depression more successfully than most of Europe's democracies. Even if, like so much to do with Fascism, this achievement was actually a triumph of presentation over substance, it attracted fresh waves of foreign admirers and helped to inspire a new generation of would-be emulators. Notable examples are the British Union of Fascists (BUF), founded by Sir Oswald Mosley, a former Labour Party minister (1932); the *Parti Populaire Français* (PPF), founded by Jacques Doriot, a lapsed communist (1936); and *Falange Española*, created by José Antonio Primo de Rivera, son of Spain's late dictator (1933). The BUF, while never seriously threatening the British political status quo, was by far the most significant expression of fascism in interwar Britain; the PPF became a genuinely mass movement during the late 1930s; and the Falange in 1937 became the core of Franco's single party. Elsewhere during the first half of the decade openly fascist or national socialist movements, or movements displaying some features of fascism, proliferated. In 1932 a coup by the fascist-style Lapua movement was only averted in Finland by, significantly, a rallying of conservative forces to the country's democratic system. In 1930 the Austrian *Heimwehr* became officially fascist by adopting the so-called Korneuberg Oath. From 1933 the country's right-wing Catholic government adopted an increasingly authoritarian posture, and allied with the *Heimwehr* established an authoritarian regime, militarily crushing the country's socialist movement in the process. New dictatorships were imposed in Estonia and Latvia during 1934, and in Portugal during the early 1930s dictatorial authority was assumed by the country's right-wing financial savior, Salazar. In Spain between 1931 and 1936 the democratic Second Republic was plagued almost from the outset by right-wing forces whose authoritarian tendencies became increasingly tinged with fascism. It was these forces that produced the rising of 1936 which precipitated Spain into civil war. Within a couple of weeks of the outbreak of hostilities in Spain, Greece's parliamentary democracy, thrown into paralysis by the economic and political effects of the Depression, had succumbed to takeover by the Fascist- and Nazi-influenced General Metaxas. Against this background it is not difficult to grasp why, as the Spanish rebel forces advanced on Madrid in the autumn of 1936, Orwell and his fellow volunteers should have felt it was time to act.

Conclusion

Knowing what we do of the 1930s, and more especially of the horrors accompanying World War II, we must be careful not to read back those events into the very different decade of the 1920s. The explosion onto the political scene of Italian Fascism unquestionably did pose a challenge to liberal-democratic institutions and values. To be more accurate it posed a two-sided challenge: a negative, destructive one based on violence, and authoritarianism, and an ostensibly more positive, constructive one based on ideas of a new kind of state, culture, and individual. As far as the 1920s were concerned the latter in fact made less headway than might be supposed from later events, since in no other European country had a movement similar to Italian Fascism come close to equaling its success by the end of 1929. Fascism's more negative side, on the other hand, had done much to stimulate a broader authoritarianism across much of Europe, insinuating itself into many a movement and party, and influencing authoritarian regimes like that of Primo de Rivera. In much of Europe, mainly the north and northwest, liberal institutions and cultures had survived the decade's vicissitudes without too much difficulty, largely thanks to the mid-decade economic recovery.

It was the onset of depression from 1930 onward, and one of its most dramatic consequences, the meteoric rise of Nazism between 1930 and 1933, that truly created the fascist specter against which George Orwell was so determined to fight.

NOTES

1 On British volunteers in the Spanish Civil War, see Richard Baxell, *British Volunteers in the Spanish Civil War: The British Battalion in the International Brigades, 1936–1939* (London: Routledge, 2004). For Orwell's role, see Peter Davison, ed., *Orwell in Spain* (London: Penguin, 2001): a collection containing *Homage to Catalonia* as well as numerous other material.

2 In this chapter, "Fascism/Fascist" refers to the Italian version, "fascism/fascist" to the wider phenomenon.

3 See Martin Blinkhorn, "Afterthoughts. Route Maps and Landscapes: Historians, 'Fascist Studies' and the Study of Fascism," *Totalitarian Movements and Political Religions* 5/3 (2004): 507–26.

4 See Stanley G. Payne, *A History of Fascism, 1914–1945* (Madison: University of Wisconsin Press, 1995), pp. 23–70.

5 See Martin Blinkhorn, *Fascism and the Right in Europe, 1919–1945* (London: Longman/Pearson, 2000), pp. 8–16.

6 See chapter 17.

7 On Hungary, see below.

8 On the rise and early stages of Fascism, see Adrian Lyttelton, *The Seizure of Power: Fascism in Italy, 1919–1929*, 2nd edn (London: Weidenfeld and Nicolson, 1987).

9 See Jill Lewis, "Conservatives and Fascists in Austria, 1918–34," in *Fascists and Conservatives: The Establishment and the Radical Right in Twentieth-Century Europe*, Martin Blinkhorn, ed. (London: Unwin Hyman, 1990), pp. 98–117.

10 Horthy was officially "Regent" pending the unlikely restoration of the Habsburgs.
11 Despite its age, the most satisfactory overview of fascism's attraction for intellectuals remains Alastair Hamilton, *The Appeal of Fascism: A Study of Intellectuals and Fascism, 1919–1945* (London: Anthony Blond, 1971).
12 See R. J. B. Bosworth, *The Italian Dictatorship: Problems and Perspectives in the Interpretation of Mussolini and Fascism* (London: Arnold, 1998), pp. 12–36 and passim.
13 Notably for Rolão Preto, leader of the principal Portuguese version of fascism, National Syndicalism. See Antonio Costa Pinto, *The Blue Shirts: Portuguese Fascism in Interwar Europe* (New York: Columbia University Press, 2000).
14 A wide-ranging treatment of this theme is still awaited, but the issues can be sampled in Alexander De Grand, *The Italian Nationalist Association and the Rise of Fascism* (Lincoln: University of Nebraska Press, 1978).
15 The analyses of fascism produced by the European left are considered in David Beetham, ed., *Marxists in Face of Fascism: Writings by Marxists on Fascism from the Inter-War Period* (Manchester: Manchester University Press, 1983), pp. 1–63.
16 Colorful accounts of these conflicts in Hungary and Romania are given in Nicholas Nagy-Talavera, *The Green Shirts and the Others: A History of Fascism in Hungary and Romania*, 2nd edn (Portland OR: Center for Romanian Studies, 2001). On Portugal, see Costa Pinto, *The Blue Shirts*.
17 Bosworth, *Italian Dictatorship*, pp. 120–7. Bosworth is decidedly skeptical towards the notion of "Fascist consensus" particularly associated with the Italian scholar Renzo De Felice and his followers.

GUIDE TO FURTHER READING

Martin Blinkhorn, ed., *Fascists and Conservatives: The Radical Right and the Establishment in Twentieth-Century Europe* (London: Unwin Hyman, 1990). Edited essay collection with expert contributions exploring the relationship between fascism and conservative forces in several European countries.

Martin Blinkhorn, ed., *Fascism and the Right in Europe, 1919–1945* (London: Longman/ Pearson, 2000). An attempt by the author of this chapter at a brief overview and interpretation of fascism and its place within the wider European right.

R. J. B. Bosworth, *Mussolini* (London: Hodder Arnold, 2002). Currently the best single-volume biography of Mussolini in any language, and a thoroughly enjoyable read.

Richard Evans, *The Coming of the Third Reich* (London: Allen Lane, 2003). Excellent and up-to-date account of Nazism's origins, development, and rise to power.

Roger Griffin, *The Nature of Fascism* (London: Routledge, 1991). Important statement of what is now a widely – though not universally – accepted view of fascism by the most prominent British scholar in the field.

Ian Kershaw, *Hitler 1889–1936: Hubris* (London: Penguin, 1998). The first volume of Kershaw's monumental and surely definitive life of the Nazi dictator.

Martin Kitchen, *Europe between the Wars: A Political History* (London: Longman, 1988). One of the most satisfying and stimulating general treatments of European political history during the years of the "fascist challenge." (A new edition is expected in 2005 or 2006.)

Adrian Lyttelton, *The Seizure of Power: Fascism in Italy, 1919–1929*, 2nd edn (London: Weidenfeld and Nicolson, 1987). This remains the most thorough and illuminating account of Italian Fascism's emergence, rise to power, and establishment of a dictatorship.

Charles S. Maier, *Recasting Bourgeois Europe: Stabilization in France, Germany, and Italy in the Decade after World War I* (Princeton NJ: Princeton University Press, 1975 and 1988).

An extraordinarily ambitious – and successful – exploration of the different ways in which postwar problems were confronted in three European countries.

Mark Mazower, *Dark Continent: Europe's Twentieth Century* (New York: Knopf, 1998). The most thought-provoking recent history of twentieth-century Europe, with interesting things to say on the matters discussed in this chapter.

Stanley G. Payne, *A History of Fascism, 1914–1945* (Madison: University of Wisconsin Press, 1995). The most satisfying attempt at a comprehensive history of fascism in its heyday, by the leading American authority on the subject.

Stanley G. Payne, *Fascism in Spain, 1923–1977* (Madison: University of Wisconsin Press, 1999). Comprehensive study of Spanish fascism in all its forms by the subject's senior scholar.

Robert Soucy, *French Fascism: The First Wave, 1924–1933* (New Haven CT: Yale University Press, 1986) and *French Fascism: The Second Wave, 1933–1939* (New Haven CT: Yale University Press, 1995). Two volumes by a leading American specialist comprising the best available analysis of the French "fascist challenge."

CHAPTER TWENTY-ONE

Revisionism

CAROLE FINK

We looked for peace, but no good came. (Jeremiah 8:15)

Revision of the Versailles *Diktat* was the overriding aim of all Germans.[1]

Treaty revisionism is nothing new. Beginning with the creation of the modern European state system in 1648, vanquished powers such as Spain, France, Austria, and Russia have applied a number of devices, including cunning statesmanship and propaganda as well as acts of force, to reverse their defeats. Indeed, the very nature of the European state system, with its unstable balance of power sustained by ephemeral wartime coalitions, meant that peace treaties were often short-lived conventions. Not only did the losers invariably obstruct their terms, but the winners might also disregard them once the ink was dry. Indeed, for almost three centuries every European power, buffeted internally by religious, national, or social unrest, and vying outside for continental or overseas territory and markets, has recognized that yesterday's enemy might well be tomorrow's collaborator.

Nonetheless, the treaty revisionism that emerged after World War I was distinctive because it was so pervasive. In their efforts to eliminate the causes of future wars, the exhausted and often divided victors devised treaties that touched practically the entire globe. Because of the length, ferocity, and huge costs of World War I and the distinctive circumstances surrounding their negotiations, the peacemakers' prodigious work was also laced with gaps and contradictions, leaving them open to challenges from both sides. Inside the Allied camp there was widespread disappointment with their accomplishments and, among the losers, an almost unanimous opposition to accepting the consequences of defeat. It was this all-encompassing revisionism, ideological, territorial, and military, which not only impeded the creation of a solid international system during the interwar period but also lay the groundwork for another world war.

Revisionism Among the Victors

Among the Allies and Associated Powers, there was an unusually large number of discontented governments. All the new and enlarged states of east central Europe complained about the curtailment of their territorial goals and also their imposed and despised minority treaties, which they were determined to ignore.[2] Italy chafed at the "mutilated victory" that had rewarded its huge wartime suffering with meager territorial and colonial gains and had spawned unfriendly new neighbors in the east. Poland's use of military force in Vilna and Italy's in Fiume set two early bad examples of unilateral territorial change.

Overseas, there was even greater indignation. The British Dominions were irritated by the restrictions tied to the assignment of their new Mandates. Japan, although admitted at least formally as an equal to the victors' councils, resented the denial of the prizes it had sought in China and Siberia. And the greatest victor of all, the United States, which failed to ratify the Versailles treaty and signed a separate agreement with Germany, not only withdrew from any collective enforcement procedures but also assailed the very economic, military, and territorial provisions it had helped to write in Paris and ignored the League of Nations it had worked to create.

Behind the official pronouncements there was also a deeply disillusioned Allied public, buffeted by the shocks of postwar inflation, unemployment, and social unrest. In public utterances and writing little remained of the wartime animosity towards the enemy. Instead, left wing and internationalist publicists blamed the peace treaties for Europe's economic and political misery. Visual artists depicted ruined urban landscapes, and poets lamented the postwar "waste land."

The political and moral epicenter of treaty revisionism on the Allied side was Great Britain. The world's largest empire, Britain considered itself the most vulnerable of the victors to the post-Versailles order, a susceptibility that was intensified after the United States rejected the treaty. Once Britain's leaders had achieved their principal aims at the peace conference, they became obsessed with creating a more just and workable treaty with Germany. Once they left Paris, they were even more outspoken in their pursuit of correcting as many of the aberrant details as possible.

The apogee of this policy was reached at the Genoa Conference of 1922, when Prime Minister David Lloyd George proposed to revive European peace and trade by easing the distinction between victors and vanquished.[3] After raising high expectations and fears, and after six long weeks of dreary technical as well as political negotiations, Genoa resulted in failure. This was due partly to the "Easter Sunday surprise," the separate treaty between Weimar Germany and Soviet Russia that was signed in Rapallo one week after the opening. However, the threat of a revisionist conspiracy by these two, still weak, governments did less to undermine Genoa than the firm resistance by France and its allies, abetted by Lloyd George's political opponents in London. Despite the failure of Lloyd George's great project of opening relations between the west and Russia, his goal of meliorating the German peace settlement remained a constant in British foreign policy.

There were several reasons why Britain's leaders and the majority of its cultural, intellectual, and religious elite were obsessed with revising the Versailles treaty and creating a new European order. London's goals, reinforced by the behavior of its ex-enemies and ex-allies, incorporated very specific practical, moral, and ideological considerations.

Britain's foremost concern was strategic. A small, overpopulated island with an exposed coastline, undersized army, and far-flung empire, Britain had always required a balance of power in Europe. Facing a chaotic continent after World War I, Britain's leaders were convinced of the menace of a dominant France and a feeble Germany to the pacification of Europe and to its own security.[4] To evade French demands for strict treaty enforcement and forestall German–Soviet irredentism, London was prepared to conciliate Berlin in a number of ways, including a nod to territorial changes. To be sure, this stance also reflected the objectives of Britain's Dominions, whose leaders constantly preached the appeasement of Germany and refused to assume military responsibility for the contested regions of eastern Europe.[5]

Britain's second concern was economic. Plagued by dwindling trade, a weakened pound, huge war debts to the United States, industrial unrest, and unemployment that hovered at 1 million throughout the 1920s, Britain linked its recovery to the revival of peace in Europe. Immediately after leaving Paris, John Maynard Keynes, a junior technical advisor to the British delegation, penned his now-famous attack on the Treaty of Versailles. Echoing the German critique, he condemned the territorial and economic clauses and warned that the inflated reparations figures would "degrade the lives of millions" of Germans and "sow the decay of the whole civilized life in Europe." Keynes implored the United States and the Allies to revise the peace treaty at once.[6]

Avidly grasping Keynes's message, British political and financial leaders became convinced that the solution to Britain's domestic problems lay in a new settlement of the German question.[7] Prewar Germany had been London's foremost continental trading partner, and the Weimar republic now offered prospects for potentially lucrative collaborative projects in eastern Europe and Russia. Across the ranks of class, party, and region, many Britons became converts to the principle of scaling down reparations and resisting French efforts to "enslave" this indispensable collaborator in Britain and Europe's economic recovery.

These practical considerations were bolstered by bursts of moral outrage. Keynes's savage pen portraits of the mordant Clemenceau, cunning Lloyd George, and tedious Wilson set off Britain's national preoccupation with deflating the peacemakers and their treaties. The flood of memoirs by other conference participants augmented Britain's emotional and practical disengagement from specific treaty terms. When France invaded the Ruhr in 1923 to punish Germany's obstreperousness over reparations, all the British stereotypes of a vindictive France, helpless Germany, and doomed Europe were confirmed; indeed, some Britons privately hoped that Paris would be punished for its intemperate demands.[8]

Moreover, British statesmen and journalists were notably unsympathetic to France's pugnacious clients, the Poles, Czechs, and Romanians, who, in the name of militant anti-Bolshevism, had aggrandized themselves by force and wile and created "dozens of new Alsace-Lorraines."[9] Whitehall officials regretted the loss of the Habsburg monarchy and the chaotic landscape between a ruined Germany and an isolated Soviet Russia, scoring the new governments who persecuted their minorities, practiced a reckless economic nationalism, and continued to provoke their neighbors. A favorite culprit was the Czechoslovak foreign minister, Eduard Beneš, the "eternal go-between" and small-power spokesman, who ardently championed the treaties, the League, and collective security. Reinforced by the British public's lack of interest in eastern Europe, these private misgivings were manifested in almost every aspect of Britain's foreign policy, from its disapproval of France's alliance system to its tacit encouragement of German territorial revisionism.

As Catherine Cline has written, one of the most powerful ideological weapons of Britain's revisionists was the war guilt issue. Immediately after the signing of the Treaty of Versailles, liberal and left-wing historians in Britain and the United States, appalled by the "tough peace," suddenly reversed their wartime stance, denying Germany's sole guilt and insisting that structural causes – "imperialism" and a rigid alliance system – had caused the hideous conflict.[10] The swell of revisionist history undoubtedly bolstered the revisionist impulses of British foreign policy. Taking their cue from the careless comment of the Great Warlord, David Lloyd George, that all the parties had "stumbled" and "staggered" into war,[11] British leaders and British intellectuals questioned not only the moral basis of the treaties, but also all their punitive clauses.

Although the historians, and their audience, may have believed that they were engaging in objective scholarship, the political results of their exculpation of Imperial Germany were nonetheless momentous. The spokesmen for treaty revision nurtured the image of a noble, wronged Germany. Throughout the tumultuous period of the Weimar republic, they ignored the persistent nationalist rhetoric and right-wing violence as well as the official chicanery and defiance that not only challenged the peace treaty but also undermined German democracy from within.

These Britons also endorsed another political myth, which survives to this day. Avidly fostered by Berlin, many of the British elite insisted that without treaty revision Germany's first republic would fail and chaos ensue. Keynes chimed in, echoing Berlin's alarms over the threat of Bolshevism to central Europe. From Baldwin to MacDonald, British leaders expressed a bad conscience towards Germany that reinforced their essentially revisionist inclinations, claiming that they were fulfilling a "moral responsibility" to right the wrongs of Versailles.[12]

There were very few dissenters to the revisionist consensus. A handful of British journalists, scholars, and government officials continued to insist on Germany's responsibility for World War I, the merits of the treaties, and the necessity of banding together with France and supporting the League of Nations to preserve the peace settlement.[13] But these sober voices were drowned out by the flood of memoirs, novels, and poetry depicting World War I as a cruel and pointless sacrifice of Britain's youth and portraying the peace treaties as an indecent form of victors' retribution. Widely read and admired, the searing testimonies of Wilfred Owen, Siegfried Sassoon, Vera Brittain, and Robert Graves undoubtedly bolstered the resolve of British leaders to prevent a repetition by removing as many of their ex-enemy's grievances as possible.

Revisionism Among the Vanquished

This revisionist camp comprised a diverse group, from tiny and impoverished Austria, Hungary, and Bulgaria, to Turkey and Russia at the periphery, to Germany at the very center. They drew support from other "victims" of the peace treaties, particularly from former wartime neutrals hurt by postwar economic conditions and from 35 million of the losers' kin people who had been involuntarily transferred to new governments. Although there was some coordination, these groups often worked for separate goals, with different methods.

Early on, there were some dramatic feats of revision. By force of arms, and with the diplomatic support of France and Italy, Kemal's Turkey reversed the dictated Treaty of Sèvres and achieved a negotiated agreement at Lausanne that all but eliminated Allied control. Equally spectacular were the feats of Lenin's Russia. After losing vast amounts of former tsarist territory to Finland, the Baltic states, Poland, and Romania, it survived the Allied intervention and a brutal civil war, and, in a major diplomatic coup in 1922, it aligned itself with Germany. However, neither Turkey nor Russia raised further challenges to the European peace settlement. Turkey, faced with its gigantic nation-building project, withdrew into diplomatic isolation; and Soviet Russia, notwithstanding the Comintern's attacks on the postwar order, ceased to threaten its neighbors.[14]

The smaller losers in east central Europe were incapacitated by their economic weakness and diplomatic ineptitude. The new Austrian republic, whose leaders and people overwhelmingly favored *Anschluss* (union) with Germany, was forced to bow to the dictates of the Allies in return for their rescue from bankruptcy. A more pugnacious Bulgaria, which threatened its neighbors with secret irredentist movements and complaints over mishandling their minorities, was stymied by its isolation and meager resources. Hungary, the foremost protester, refused to recognize the frontiers established by the Treaty of Trianon; it deployed a variety of devices, including military force and a harebrained Habsburg restoration scheme as well as petitions to the League over the expropriation of Hungarian landowners and to preserve Hungarian schools and religious life in Romania. However, Budapest's incessant pleas for "justice" were thwarted by a determined "Little Entente" of its immediate neighbors and by a lack of support in London and Paris.[15]

Germany, under the Weimar republic, was the heartland of the revisionism of the vanquished. This weak, factionalized regime, born of military defeat and political collapse, made the destruction of Versailles its primary diplomatic goal: the step-by-step erosion of the peace provisions that had stripped German military, naval, and air power, removed territory and population, stolen its empire, demoted its economic, financial, and commercial influence, and subjected the Reich to hundreds of large and petty humiliations.

The revolution of 1918 had scarcely changed Germany's political culture. Divided as they were over political and economic questions, the Germans presented a far more solid front than any of their neighbors in their attitudes towards the peace treaties. Few accepted the military verdict of 1918 and fewer still strove for reconciliation with their former enemies. Where the Germans differed was over the means of overcoming their defeat: by toughness or conciliation. Still a great power, now surrounded by weak and divided neighboring states and with almost intact industries and infrastructure, the new Germany was determined to secure its place in Europe.

Like Britain's, Germany's revisionist tactics began at the peace conference itself. Displaying their art as Wilsonians, the German delegates castigated the violations of the Fourteen Points in the treaty's territorial, economic, military, and colonial settlements. Combining propaganda and behind-the-scenes maneuvers, they aimed at widening the peacemakers' divisions and gaining sympathy from Allied and neutral populations. Warning constantly of the menace of Bolshevism to central Europe, they also prepared for a future entente with the Soviets. And once the treaty was signed, the Weimar republic used all its resources to discredit the treaty, block Allied control, and regain the Reich's freedom of action.

One of the Reich's first initiatives was its massive propaganda campaign against the treaty. The war guilt section (*Kriegsschuldreferat*) of the foreign ministry worked tirelessly to refute the charges of Germany's aggressive intentions in the summer of 1914 and to spread the blame to others. The new republican government granted generous subsidies for this purpose. It assigned the task of presenting a more balanced interpretation of the prewar period to a small scholarly institute, staffed by eminent scholars, which produced the 40-volume collection, *Die Grosse Politik der Europäische Kabinette, 1871–1914*. In addition, it made payments to individuals and groups at home and abroad whose aim was to mobilize popular support for treaty revision.[16]

Between 1920 and 1924 a great international duel took place over treaty enforcement. Germany won a remarkable victory, but not as the result of its aggressive tactics. Indeed, despite their many differences, Britain and France stood together on several difficult issues, including the Reich's refusal to disarm, its vicious criticisms of Paris and Warsaw, its stubbornness and deviousness over reparations, and its self-imposed hyperinflation that thwarted European recovery.

Instead, it was the sensible revisionism of Gustav Stresemann that rescued Germany from ruin. The French invasion of the Ruhr in 1923 – labeled by some historians the last battle of World War I – deeply alarmed Britain and the United States.[17] Although it could seize German coal assets, France failed to secure peace on its own terms, because Prime Minister Raymond Poincaré lacked a long-term plan as well as a strategy for eliciting cooperation from his friends and his enemies. In the midst of the crisis, Stresemann acted adroitly on the political, economic, and diplomatic levels. The former annexationist, monarchist, and "practical republican" boldly ended passive resistance, which had brought financial ruin and political chaos to the Weimar republic. He then deployed his foreign-policy skills to involve Britain and the United States in the Reich's rescue, scale down reparations, and end France's bid to force compliance with the peace treaties.[18]

With the signing of the Dawes Plan in 1924, Germany's road to revision was open. Like Talleyrand at the Congress of Vienna, Stresemann had decisively altered the victor–vanquished relationship, replacing dictated terms with negotiations among (at least almost) equals. He had presented the face of a firm but reasonable Reich, driven by nationalist goals but willing to apply them patiently and peacefully. To the great bafflement of his more militant countrymen, Gustav Stresemann made a revisionist Germany an indispensable element in the pacification of Europe.

Treaty Revision Begins: Locarno, 1925

Few historical agreements have stimulated as much controversy as the 1925 Locarno treaties, whose authors won the Nobel Peace Prize a year later. If their defenders have applauded these negotiated agreements for bringing peace to Europe, their critics have long detected in their conciliatory language the seeds of Nazi aggression and World War II.[19]

It was Stresemann who initiated the Locarno treaties. Aiming to hasten the evacuation of the Rhineland and stave off a possible Anglo-French agreement, he revived an earlier Reich proposal for a five-power pact guaranteeing Germany's western borders and establishing the permanent demilitarization of the Rhineland.[20] Not surprisingly, Britain responded positively and, with Washington's support, pressured France to agree. Despite the howls of German nationalists over his "surrender of Alsace-Lorraine," Stresemann had undoubtedly accomplished a great deal. The Cologne zone would be evacuated; and Germany entered the League of Nations as a permanent Council member without loosening its ties to Moscow.

According to the terms of Locarno, the Reich was now secure against any further French coercion. In addition, the 1925 agreement diluted the terms governing the demilitarized Rhineland. In the text of Versailles, *any* violation would be regarded as a "hostile act," but under the Locarno arrangements, British and Italian aid for France would be invoked only if a "flagrant violation" occurred.

Of even greater significance, Germany had also evaded an eastern Locarno. On Stresemann's insistence, Germany's borders with Poland and Czechoslovakia had now become second-class frontiers, not guaranteed by the Locarno signatories but subject merely to non-binding arbitration treaties. Later, he boasted how Britain and France, intent on winning an understanding with Germany, had excluded the foreign ministers of Poland and Czechoslovakia from the Locarno negotiations; relegated to an anteroom, these once-pampered clients had to wait to be invited in. Although Stresemann foreswore the use of force, he had signaled the direction of his policy, opening the door to future territorial revision in the east.

During the next four years Germany's rewards multiplied. Foreign loans flooded into Germany and its economy and trade revived. In September 1926 Stresemann made a triumphant entry into Geneva, signaling Germany's restoration to the family of nations. As part of the "Big Three," Stresemann was an active partner in the quarterly hotel room tête-à-têtes during League Council meetings; he was also an admired speaker in the League Assembly and a favorite of foreign journalists. In 1927, international military control was completely removed from Germany. By 1929, Stresemann succeeded in reducing Germany's reparations bill further, and he convinced the Allies to evacuate the Rhineland five years ahead of the Versailles schedule. Eighteen hours before his death on October 3, 1929, Stresemann exulted, "We are again masters in our home."[21]

The other great winner, who had celebrated his sixty-second birthday at Locarno, was Britain's foreign secretary, Austen Chamberlain.[22] For British leaders, Locarno represented the *real* peace that had eluded Europe since 1919. Chamberlain was untroubled by Germany's incomplete disarmament, by Stresemann's openly revisionist goals in the east, or by Berlin's insistence on exempting itself from the League's collective defense obligations in the event of a Soviet attack on Poland. What mattered were Britain's strategic and economic interests, which only a peaceful Europe, based on German compliance, US financial aid, and French willingness to relinquish the use of force, could make possible. Britain had not only avoided a pact with France and any obligation towards France's east European allies, but also had assumed the role of arbiter between a fearful, dependent France and a determinedly revisionist Germany, making clear its readiness to remove further abrasive elements in the peace treaties.[23]

Why did the French acquiesce? The French foreign minister, Aristide Briand, based his decision on the reality of France's political and economic weakness. Not only had the franc fallen drastically during and after the Ruhr crisis, but France was now compelled to negotiate a war-debt settlement with the United States. Although Briand recognized the revisionist danger, he could do little against the overwhelming Anglo-German pressure. With the loss of France's Russian ally, France was entirely dependent on Great Britain, and Locarno represented the limit of London's commitment to its security.

When the elation over Locarno evaporated, Paris did what it could to preserve its hard-won victory and bolster its diminishing power. France renewed its treaty bonds with its east European allies, although these military guarantees had to be reformulated within the new, reduced multilateral framework of Locarno. France supported Poland during Berlin's brutal trade war with Warsaw and helped check the Reich's clumsy efforts to negotiate the return of the Corridor. Paris also backed its east European partners against Stresemann's campaign in the League of Nations in 1929 to expand the protection of German minorities.

Briand's other efforts to reassert France's authority were less successful. He failed to achieve an economic entente with Germany, to draw the United States into the affairs of Europe, or to gain support for his proposal to contain a resurgent Reich within a united Europe. Recognizing the inevitable, France, with the construction of the Maginot Line three years after Locarno, acknowledged the primacy of defending its own borders and its inability to stop Germany from eventually moving eastward.

One of Germany's new initiatives after Locarno was both audacious and ominous. Article 8 of the League of Nations Covenant obliged all its signatories to "disarm to a level consonant with their own national security." Once it entered the League, Germany led a noisy political and propaganda campaign calling for general disarmament. Linked to its impossible insistence that France disarm to its level was the demand that Germany achieve *Gleichberechtigung* (equality of treatment).

The other side resisted, at great cost to themselves and the League. During the long, dreary hours of the Preparatory Disarmament Conference, France and its allies, citing the gaps in European security exposed by Germany's rapid recovery and its persistent revisionism, resisted the Reich's demands. Standing on the sidelines, Britain was reluctant to commit its power and prestige to act as a mediator between the two sides, and the Soviet Union and the United States remained aloof.

The unresolved debate between disarmament and security cast a dark shadow over the post-Locarno era, creating public confusion and cynicism. Germany's inexorable pressure for equality contributed as much to the erosion of the League's authority and effectiveness as did the divided and incoherent policies of France and Britain. The world's first international organization, torn between its mandate to preserve the peace and its lack of power to do so, was undoubtedly weakened during the Stresemann era, and ill-prepared to face the even greater dangers ahead.

We can never know the direction German revisionism would have taken had Stresemann lived beyond 1929. Some historians have argued that his diplomacy, more akin to Bismarck and Adenauer's than to Hitler's, was tempered by his commitment to the values of western civilization and aimed only at gradual and peaceful change of Germany's borders in the east. Others, quoting Stresemann's private correspondence, his bombastic speeches to nationalist audiences, his support of secret German rearmament, and his tough bargaining stance with Poland and his western partners, remain unconvinced of his peaceful intentions.[24] The reality, as E. H. Carr long ago pointed out, may have been more commonplace. Stresemann was simply

> A German patriot who valued the Western connexion, the League of Nations and Locarno not for any sentimental or ideological reasons but for the advantages which they brought to his country; for the same reason he valued the eastern connexion, however little he, in common with most German industrialists, appreciated the theory or practice of the Bolsheviks. He exercised a great economy of truth when he repeatedly assured the Allies that Germany was loyally carrying out her obligations under the disarmament clauses of the Versailles treaty . . . Few statesmen fail in an emergency to lie for their country.[25]

It is nonetheless clear that Gustav Stresemann's achievements were spectacular: the exploitation of Germany's weakness, the balancing acts between east and west, and the liberation of German soil. But the negative aspects of his short tenure in power were also damaging. His failure to bolster German democracy, temper German irredentism, and inspire trust among Germany's neighbors left a serious question mark in the volatile center of Europe. It was Stresemann's achievement to erode the Versailles treaty, and his legacy to accustom Germany and Europe to expect more of the same.

German Threats, Allied Appeasement

Between Stresemann's death in October 1929 and the Nazis' stunning electoral victory 11 months later, there was a transformation of German and European politics. Germany's new foreign minister, Julius Curtius, who lacked his predecessor's skill and finesse, became the mouthpiece of the fanatic German nationalism that was ignited in June 1930 when the Allies departed from the Rhineland five years ahead of the schedule set by the Treaty of Versailles. During the electoral campaign that summer, Germany's right-wing parliamentary candidates sent shudders through the capitals of Europe, excoriating France and Poland and demanding the return of the Corridor.

Mirroring the radicalization of German politics after September 1930, the imposition of presidential rule, and the deepening of the Depression, the Reich's new diplomacy demanded a release from the remaining fetters of Versailles. Curtius taunted his eastern neighbors over their "servitude" to the minority treaties and in 1931 launched Germany's most aggressive campaign in the League of Nations on behalf of the Germans in Poland.

The Reich's former Locarno partners, also under new political leadership, offered only weak opposition to Berlin's tougher stance. Burdened by the world economic crisis, their predicament over Manchuria, and US and Soviet isolationism, as well as by their own disagreements, Britain and France wavered between resistance and accommodation. Recognizing Weimar's weakness and the Nazi danger, they nonetheless acted together to block an Austro-German Customs Union and stave off the Reich's demands for military equality; but, with America's help, they also effectively cancelled reparations in 1932. In the waning days of the Weimar republic, the western powers and the League lacked the vision, skill, and strength either to call Berlin's bluff or issue further concessions.

After Hitler came to power in January 1933, Germany's revisionist project was drastically altered. With the establishment of a dictatorship, the brutal persecution of German Jews, and the exit from the League in October 1933, Nazi Germany renounced the role of an aggrieved but reasonable diplomatic partner and set out not only to destroy Versailles but also to establish German hegemony over Europe. Step by step, combining shrewd bilateral diplomacy and startling unilateral moves, the Third Reich moved to dismantle every fetter of the peace treaties and prepare for the next war. Its most remarkable move was the non-aggression pact with Poland in January 1934. By temporarily disarming the longtime object of its antagonism, Germany hastened the disintegration of France's alliance system in eastern Europe and made itself the key player in the region. One by one, the east European governments fell into the Third Reich's economic and political orbit; and Poland, Hungary, and Romania imitated its racist practices as well.

The west offered even feebler resistance to Hitler than to his Weimar predecessors. Weighed down by their colonial troubles and military unpreparedness, the French and British governments reeled from crisis to crisis. When Benito Mussolini embarked on the conquest of Abyssinia, the western powers neither stopped nor appeased him. Their feeble, contradictory moves created panic among the small states and left the League's collective security apparatus in ruins. Berlin profited from its fascist neighbor's unopposed defiance. In 1935 Germany renounced the treaty's disarmament clauses, only to be rewarded with a bilateral naval agreement with Great Britain.

With the unopposed entry of German troops into the Rhineland a year later, Britain and France once and for all lost their role as the enforcers of Versailles. Having failed to construct a firm barrier against the Reich, the western powers now simply caved in to Hitler's demands in order to delay, and perhaps divert the inevitable conflict. To be sure, some British leaders and journalists at both ends of the political spectrum continued to insist on Nazi Germany's legitimate grievances against the peace treaties, thus providing the moral and political justification for the active appeasement of Hitler's demands.

Encouraged by the west's signals of compliance, Germany began its assault on the territorial settlement of 1919; it seized Austria in March 1938 and threatened war with democratic Czechoslovakia over the alleged mistreatment of its German minority. Berlin was preparing for war, but the west was determined to appease Hitler's threats while it began, finally, to rearm.

Britain revived the old revisionist language of righting the wrongs of Versailles. Having readily acquiesced in the *Anschluss* (which it justified as the union of one German state with another), it now strove frantically to remove the threat of a war over another questionable border between Germany and Czechoslovakia. By going to Munich in September 1938, Prime Minister Neville Chamberlain reendorsed the Locarno precedent of a four-power concert to adjust the peace settlement. British objectives were also served by the exclusion of Czechoslovakia and Soviet Russia. And Chamberlain rejoiced in his personal understanding with Hitler and the reestablishment of stability in central Europe.

Britain's appeasement of Nazi Germany at the fateful Munich Conference had both historic roots and new features. As the dynamic element of British revisionism, appeasement, by 1938, had developed into a full-blown ideology combining national goals and practical realities: its fervent anti-communism, global rivalry with the United States, and the new threat from Japan along with an aversion to European commitments, the recognition of Britain's economic frailty, and the acknowledgment of its dependence on the Dominions.

Recently, historians have attempted to resuscitate Chamberlain's stature, from "a weak-kneed, naive Prime Minister who swallowed all of Hitler's lies" to that of a proactive statesman who followed a "double policy" of appeasing the fascist dictators, Mussolini and Hitler, while rearming Great Britain.[26] But none of Chamberlain's partisans has weighed the consequences of Britain's equivocal commitments to France and its small eastern allies, its refusal to negotiate seriously with Soviet Russia, and its conviction that Germany had a good case for revision.

In the absence of Britain's moral and material leadership, the other World War I victors mounted no resistance to an openly expansionist Third Reich. Italy and Japan became allies of Nazi Germany. The Little Entente had ceased to exist. And France, politically divided and militarily weak, hid behind the Maginot Line. The sole resistance was mounted by Soviet Russia, whose offers to block the German threat were, however, tainted by Stalin's own revisionist demands against his small neighbors.

Until the end, Chamberlain and his supporters persisted in their misguided image of Hitler as simply a coarser, more irrational Stresemann who, nevertheless, could be appeased with concessions. British leaders were astoundingly ignorant or insouciant over the prospects of Berlin's uniting with Moscow. And Britain's last major diplomatic signal, the guarantee to Poland, was a stillborn gesture, based on the questionable assumption that London could withhold a real moral and military commitment to the state it had helped to create in 1919 and force accommodation on Warsaw in order to preserve European peace a few months longer.

According to Antony Lentin, the war that began in 1939 and spread to the entire world was not over the terms of the Paris peace treaties, which had disintegrated much earlier.[27] Nor, as some have asserted, did it mark the climax of a 30-year European civil war that began in 1914. Nazi Germany's invasion of Poland, like its audacious moves over the previous six years, represented a bid to dominate Europe and the world. And all those who resisted between 1939 and 1945, repealing two decades of German cleverness and threats and Allied bad conscience and submission, had to take up arms not to defend Versailles but in sheer self-defense.

Conclusion

Were there alternatives to the dreary erosion of the Paris treaties? Would more timely corrections have altered the atmosphere of disrespect and resentment and promoted a more internationalist *esprit* from victors and losers alike? Or were there simply overwhelming obstacles in the mentalities of the interwar period: the victors' mistrust of each other, their fear of another war, and Germany's unremitting demands to cancel its defeat?

Good or bad, the Paris peace treaties were not self-enforcing. They required either strict implementation or orderly, negotiated change. Weakened and divided, Britain and France could do neither of these on their own, without the support of the United States. The former Entente emerged from World War I profoundly shaken, with insufficient preparation, will, and resources to enforce the treaties or revise them. After France failed to compel Germany to accept its defeat, the Allies embarked on a slow, painful process of dismantling the peace settlement, often allowing Stresemann to call the shots. Even before 1933 it was evident that the victors had failed to protect their essential interests and those of their small allies.

The Weimar republic, with its bullying tactics and refusal to accept the new order, contributed substantially to the revisionist climate. Stresemann, for example, referred repeatedly to his eastern neighbors as *Saisonstaaten*, ephemeral entities that would soon disappear, and he protested every document that acknowledged the Treaty of Versailles. With the early evacuation of the Rhineland and the end of reparations, Weimar Germany was no longer a pariah state, dependent on the Allies' acquiescence; and after Hitler launched German rearmament, the Third Reich could take action on the territorial grievances that its predecessor had repeatedly declared and postponed.

Interwar revisionism filled the ideological and political space left by the unachieved internationalism of Wilson and Lenin. It united indecisive victors, resolute losers, and a populace vulnerable to blaming and mythmaking. Easy to kindle and slow to extinguish, revisionism merged *Realpolitik* with high-minded professions of justice and humanitarianism. Favoring arbitrary change over prudent adjustments, the revisionism practiced by both sides placed state interest above long-term European security. By reigniting nationalism in both camps, this revisionism also created a permissive environment for fear and dissimulation, threats and capitulation, the destruction of the peace treaties and, ultimately, a new war.

NOTES

1   Hans W. Gatzke, Introduction to *European Diplomacy Between Two Wars, 1919–1939* (Chicago: Quadrangle Books, 1972), p. 7.

2   See Carole Fink, *Defending the Rights of Others: The Jews, the Great Powers, and International Minority Protection, 1878–1938* (Cambridge: Cambridge University Press, 2004), pp. 232–5 and passim.

3   Details in Carole Fink, *The Genoa Conference: European Diplomacy, 1921–1922*, revd edn (Syracuse NY: Syracuse University Press, 1993).

4   See Sally Marks, *The Illusion of Peace: International Relations in Europe, 1918–1933*, 2nd edn (Basingstoke: Palgrave Macmillan, 2003), p. 38.

5   See John Ferris, *Men, Money, and Diplomacy: The Evolution of British Strategic Policy, 1919–26* (Ithaca NY: Cornell University Press, 1989), pp. 104–5.

6   John Maynard Keynes, *The Economic Consequences of the Peace* (New York: Harcourt Brace and Howe, 1971), pp. 56–225; the quotation is on p. 225. For a useful critique of Keynes's position that evaluates his ties with the Germans, see Niall Ferguson, "Keynes and the German Inflation," *English Historical Review* 110 (1995): 368–91.

7   See Cedric J. Lowe and Michael L. Dockrill, *The Mirage of Power: British Foreign Policy, 1914–22* (London: Routledge and Kegan Paul, 1972), pp. 350–2; Marc Trachtenberg, *Reparation in World Politics: France and European Economic Diplomacy, 1916–1923* (New York: Columbia University Press, 1980), pp. 193–5.

8   On the eve of the Ruhr occupation, Sir John Bradbury of the treasury, who was Britain's representative on the Reparations Commission, argued in a confidential memorandum to Stanley Baldwin that only "a further fall in the franc" would bring the French to their senses. See W. N. Medlicott and Douglas Dakin, eds, *Documents on British Foreign Policy, 1919–1939*, First Series, vol. 20 (London: HMSO, 1976), p. 286.

9   G. H. Bennett, *British Foreign Policy during the Curzon Period, 1919–24* (New York: St. Martin's Press, 1995), p. 43. According to Keynes's grim characterization in *The Economic Consequences of the Peace*, p. 291, "Poland is to be strong, Catholic, militarist, and faithful, the consort, or at least the favorite, of victorious France, prosperous and magnificent between the ashes of Russia and the ruin of Germany. Roumania, if only she could be persuaded to keep up appearances a little more, is a part of the same scatter-brained conception. Yet, unless her great neighbors are prosperous and orderly, Poland is an economic impossibility with no industry but Jew-baiting. And when Poland finds that the seductive policy of France is pure rhodomontade and that there is no money in it whatever, nor glory either, she will fall, as promptly as possible, into the arms of somebody else."

10   Catherine Anne Cline, "British Historians and the Treaty of Versailles," *Albion* 20 (1988): 43–58.

11   Quoted in G. P. Gooch, *Recent Revelations in European Diplomacy* (London: Longmans Green, 1927), p. 3.

12   Ferris, *Men, Money and Diplomacy*, p. 128.

13   See Ephraim Maisel, *The Foreign Office and Foreign Policy, 1919–1926* (Brighton: Sussex Academic Press, 1994), pp. 42–54.

14   Details in Marian Kent, ed., *The Great Powers and the End of Ottoman Empire*, 2nd edn (London: Frank Cass, 1996); Richard Debo, *Survival and Consolidation: The Foreign Policy of Soviet Russia, 1918–1921* (Montreal: McGill-Queen's University Press, 1992).

15   Details of Hungarian revisionism in Bela Király and László Vezprémy, eds, *Trianon and East Central Europe: Antecedents and Repercussions* (Boulder CO: Social Science Monographs; Highland Lakes NJ: Atlantic Research Publications, 1995).

16   Johannes Lepsius, Albrecht Mendelssohn Bartholdy, and Friedrich Thimme, eds, *Die Grosse Politik der Europäische Kabinette, 1871–1914: Sammlung der Diplomatischen Akten des Auswärtigem Amtes*, 40 vols (Berlin: Deutsche Verlagsgesellschaft für Politik und Geschichte, 1922–7). For details of the propaganda campaign, see Herman J. Wittgens, "War Guilt Propaganda Conducted by the German Foreign Ministry During the 1920s," *Canadian Historical Association, Historical Papers/Communications Historiques* (Montreal, 1980), pp. 228–47; Stefan Berger, "William Harbutt Dawson: The Career and Politics of an Historian of Germany," *English Historical Review* 116 (2001): 76–113. On a parallel enterprise, see Gregory T. Weeks, "Forcing the Colonial Issue: German Attempts to Regain African Colonies in the Weimar Republic and Third Reich, 1918–1945" (MA thesis, Purdue University, 1993).

17   See Elspeth Y. O'Riordan, *Britain and the Ruhr Crisis* (Basingstoke: Palgrave, 2001), p. 180.

18   See Stephen A. Schuker, *The End of French Predominance in Europe: The Financial Crisis of 1924 and the Adoption of the Dawes Plan* (Chapel Hill: University of North Carolina Press, 1976).

19   The former position is held by A. J. P. Taylor, *The Origins of the Second World War* (London: Hamish Hamilton, 1964), p. 82; the latter by Ruth Henig, *Versailles and After, 1919–1933*, 2nd edn (London: Routledge, 1995), pp. 71–2, and Marks, *Illusion of Peace*, pp. 78–80.

20   See Jonathan Wright, "Stresemann and Locarno," *Contemporary European History* 4/2 (1995): 109–31. See also Jon Jacobson, *Locarno Diplomacy: Germany and the West, 1925–1929* (Princeton NJ: Princeton University Press, 1972).

21   Cited by Georges Castellan, *L'Allemagne de Weimar, 1918–1933* (Paris: A. Colin, 1969), p. 339.

22   In his speech to the British press on October 23, 1925, Chamberlain called the treaties "the real dividing line between the years of war and the years of peace." Quoted in C. A. Macartney, ed., *Survey of International Affairs, 1925*, vol. 2 (London: Oxford University Press, 1928), p. 56. See also Anne Orde, *Great Britain and International Security, 1920–26* (London: Royal Historical Society, 1978), p. 210; Paul Kennedy, *The Realities behind Diplomacy: Background Influences on British External Policy, 1865–1980* (London: Allen and Unwin, 1981), p. 269.

23   See Frank Magee, "Limited Liability? Britain and the Treaty of Locarno," *Twentieth Century British History* 6/1 (1995): 1–22.

24   The first perspective in supported in Henry Ashby Turner, "Continuity in German Foreign Policy? The Case of Stresemann," *International History Review* 1/4 (1979): 509–21, the second in Marshall Lee and Wolfgang Michalka, *German Foreign Policy, 1917–1933: Continuity or Break?* (Leamington Spa: Berg, 1987), p. 98.

25   E. H. Carr, *German–Soviet Relations between the Two World Wars, 1919–1939* (Westport, CT: Greenwood Press, 1983), pp. 88–9.

26   Peter Neville, *Neville Chamberlain: A Study in Failure?* (London: Hodder and Stoughton, 1992), pp. 93, 68.

27   Antony Lentin, "Decline and Fall of the Versailles Settlement," *Diplomacy and Statecraft* 4/2 (1993): 374.

GUIDE TO FURTHER READING

Edward Hallett Carr, *International Relations Between the Two World Wars, 1919–1939* (London: Macmillan, 1947). Still valuable survey by an insightful witness.

Keith Eubank, *The Origins of World War II*, 3rd edn (Wheeling IL: Harlan Davidson, 2004). Standard, if dry, account of interwar diplomacy.

John Robert Ferris, *Men, Money and Diplomacy: The Evolution of British Strategic Policy, 1919–26* (Ithaca NY: Cornell University Press, 1989). Clear explication of the aims of, and restraints on, British diplomacy.

Hans Gatzke, ed., *European Diplomacy between Two Wars, 1919–1939* (Chicago: Quadrangle Books, 1972). Although based almost entirely on German documentation, an important selection of essays by notable scholars.

Richard S. Grayson, *Austen Chamberlain and the Commitment to Europe: British Foreign Policy, 1924–29* (London: Frank Cass, 1997). Excellent study of a key figure's aims and policies.

John Hiden, *Germany and Europe, 1919–1939*, 2nd edn (London: Longman, 1993). Detailed account of Weimar revisionism.

Julian Jackson, ed., *Europe, 1900–1945* (Oxford: Oxford University Press, 2002). Part of the Short Oxford History of Europe, containing useful essays on imperialism, and foreign and economic relations.

Jon Jacobson, *When the Soviet Union Entered World Politics* (Berkeley: University of California Press, 1994). A balanced analysis of Moscow's reintegration into international diplomacy.

Carolyn Kitching, *Britain and the Problem of International Disarmament, 1919–1934* (London: Routledge, 1999). Clarifies an important element of London's diplomacy.

Marshall M. Lee and Wolfgang Michalka, *German Foreign Policy, 1917–1933: Continuity or Break?* (Leamington Spa: Berg, 1987). Balanced survey of Weimar's leadership and policies.

Antony Lentin, *Lloyd George and the Lost Peace: From Versailles to Hitler, 1919–1940* (Basingstoke: Palgrave, 2001). Sound analysis of one of the leading contributors to interwar revisionism.

Brian J. C. McKercher, ed., *Anglo-American Relations in the 1920s: The Struggle for Supremacy* (Basingstoke: Macmillan, 1991). Covers various aspects of collaboration and rivalry.

Sally Marks, *The Illusion of Peace: International Relations in Europe, 1918–1933*, 2nd edn (Basingstoke: Palgrave Macmillan, 2003). Classic study of the divided victors and an unrepentant Germany.

Maarten L. Pereboom, *Democracies at the Turning Point: Britain, France, and the End of the Postwar Order, 1928–1933* (New York: Peter Lang, 1995). Provocative study of the post-Locarno era.

Stephanie Salzmann, *Great Britain, Germany, and the Soviet Union: Rapallo and After, 1922–1934* (London: Royal Historical Society; Rochester NY: Boydell Press, 2003). Inserts the ideological factor into Britain's revisionist policies.

Part V

The New Age

CHAPTER TWENTY-TWO

The Jazz Age

THOMAS J. SAUNDERS

"So, Vasia, what class do you consider yourself coming from?"
"Frankly speaking – the *dance-class*!"[1]

Cultural history thrives on the discovery of upheavals, collisions, and maelstroms. Its metaphors come frequently from nature and evoke the dramatic arts which constitute one of its objects of study. The "jazz age"; the "roaring twenties"; the "golden twenties"; the "crazy years" – each metaphor frames the era after World War I distinctively, even as together they signify cultural effervescence and revolt. The "jazz age" conjures images of exuberance and transgression – fast cars, wailing saxophones, seminude chorus girls, frenetic dancing, and celebrities from movies and sports. Beyond these individual associations it highlights three broad features of European popular culture after the war: first and foremost its newness, both in form and affront to traditional values; second, its indebtedness to (black) America; and third, its unprecedented shaping by music and dance. All three were refracted in the early Parisian performances of the black American dancer, Josephine Baker. Clothed only in a feather skirt, feather collar, and anklets, slithering off the back of a black man to perform with him a *dance sauvage*; or, naked but for a skirt of bananas, climbing monkey-like down a tree to dance provocatively for a white explorer in the jungle, Josephine became the premier icon of the European jazz age. The power of her appearance and her movements to subvert conventions of art, entertainment, and propriety has been paralleled to the impact of the world war in shattering the assumptions that governed the age of progress and marking the advent of modernity.[2]

If Baker embodied the new and foreign, the jazz age can be represented as an epic clash between everything she stood for and the values and traditions of prewar Europe. This clash exhibits some convenient parallels with the political conflicts of the age. The recognized hub of modern culture was Weimar Germany, a republic in which all forms of censorship were initially abolished and whose capital led Europe's new entertainment industry and became a byword for Americanization and artistic and sexual experimentation. National Socialists joined cultural conservatives in denouncing the fashions and values of the jazz age which they saw rampant in Berlin. Right-wing movements in other countries adopted similar positions. In Stalinist Russia, conservative social values and xenophobia likewise provoked resistance to forms of popular culture associated with America.

There is no denying the importance of the war of values after World War I, but on the field of popular culture battle lines were less neatly drawn. Here the context and the positions adopted proved somewhat confusing. Conservatives decried the frivolous, immoral, and foreign character of contemporary popular culture, but so too did socialists and communists for whom the entertainments of the jazz age stupefied the masses. Nazis denounced Weimar's modern entertainment industry for its alleged domination by Jews, but showed enormous interest in harnessing it for national purposes. Their later purge of non-"Aryans" meant anything but dismantling of the infrastructure and the ethos of the industry.

The initial question to ask about the jazz age is therefore not how it came under siege by reactionary forces or authoritarian regimes. If we take the jazz age to signify a sea-change in cultural sensibilities, the first task of the historian is to pinpoint the most striking breaks with prewar popular culture. Part of that task, given that interwar popular culture borrowed from America as never before, is to clarify the nature and extent of America's expanding presence after 1918. This permits reflections on the wider question of how successfully the elements of popular culture crossed boundaries of class, nation, and politics. These reflections reveal in turn the limitations of the paradigm of cultural war for grasping developments in the 1920s and 1930s. The final, brief task is therefore to suggest a substitute for a binary reading of interwar popular culture.

Elements of Popular Culture

To address these issues in a chapter-length survey requires the exercise of several kinds of historical shorthand. The first of these involves a working definition of popular culture, a term which has been used in different ways. Some historians of the twentieth century prefer the term "mass culture" in order to distinguish new and media-driven entertainments from the traditional culture of the people or the subculture of the proletariat. Mass culture also refers to the rapidly broadening reach of the new media. It highlights the range of entertainment and attraction experienced live by tens of thousands and consumed in mediated form by millions of both sexes and various social backgrounds that is the focus of this chapter. In interwar Europe this included everything from the most popular and burgeoning spectator sports – football, boxing, cycling – to music, dance, and literature, and media such as the gramophone, radio, and cinema.

The term mass culture is a useful marker of changes in audience, scale, and mode of delivery. "Popular culture" has been retained here for two broad reasons. First, the attractions of the interwar years were in some respects derivative rather than original: they perpetuated or borrowed from the creative achievements and genre conventions of the stage, music hall, pulp fiction, and fairground of nineteenth-century popular culture. As they absorbed or displaced earlier forms, they became the new popular culture. In the process they also borrowed personnel. Stage performers had parallel careers in moving pictures; popular singers, such as Maurice

Chevalier in France or Leonid Utesov in Russia, used the music hall as a springboard to fame in early film musicals, effectively bridging two eras.

In addition, although "mass culture" has been criticized for its populist connotations, for masking the capitalist logic of the "culture industry," it can also suggest manipulation of the masses parallel to the political domination by Europe's dictators. It is undeniable that the popular arts have been increasingly dependent upon and identified with media since the early twentieth century, and that these media have been largely profit driven. To disguise this reality would fundamentally distort the history of the crucial years between the wars when the media became widely institutionalized – a prominent theme in what follows. However, the film industry or the recording companies or the radio stations that proliferated in the 1920s did not invent the popular. Nor could they dictate it. Consumers still made choices, so that popular culture was a "negotiated" as much as a "managed" realm.[3]

A second historical shorthand is implicit in the title. Borrowed from America, it refers not only to notable cultural contributions of New World to Old, such as music and dance, but also to a broader ethos. It represents the mood and mores associated with jazz. In the United States, jazz signified revolt against the traditional constraints of fashion, morality, and gender roles, set within the context of prohibition and embryonic consumerism. These were all epitomized by the syncopation, insouciance, and improvisational nature of jazz music and the dances accompanying it. The flapper – bobbed-haired, short-skirted, cigarette-smoking, flirtatious, and independent – symbolized the style and attitude. Self-indulgence and self-assertion were the rage.[4]

It was clear already in the 1920s that this rage was primarily about the lifestyles of self-appointed and wealthy trend-setters. Nonetheless, the challenge to convention was not confined to the columns of fashion magazines and the lives of world-travelers and the literati. Nor was it confined to the United States. Europe too witnessed a break, mourned by some and embraced by many, with traditional values. The wide granting of female suffrage and the presence of women in new areas of employment and public life; the coming of age of the generation whose fathers, brothers, and uncles died or were maimed at the front and whose ties to the prewar world were attenuated; the extremely unsettled economic conditions and the search for meaning after the war to end all wars – these were essential components of change for which America could not be made responsible, even if America offered some of the forms by which that change was expressed. Fashions of dress and conduct changed, with shorter skirts and hair signaling a shift, if not revolution, in sexual behavior and gender relations; leisure and pursuit of pleasure occupied a growing share of human activity as trade unions negotiated shorter work weeks and holidays became widespread; the "culture industry" expanded rapidly to engage public interest, feeding the fads, crazes, and celebrity worship which marked the age.

One could elaborate on this rupture in values and styles in the aftermath of World War I. The "jazz age" refers to this discontinuity, those features of postwar European culture that distinguished it from the prewar era, not least its borrowing from America. It tends, of course, to prejudge the case for newness and threatens to Americanize doubly – once through original indebtedness and a second time through foreshortening of perspective and the screening out of what did not mirror American trends. It treats the war as the principal watershed and ignores the appearance already before the war of styles that won broad acceptance in the 1920s. Yet it underscores

the fact that there was no going back to the *belle époque* and that America was part
of European modernity. American culture did not sweep away a rich heritage of
European popular music, dance, literature, and stage entertainment, or national
forms of the newer entertainments, such as cinema. Nonetheless, it was increasingly
difficult to imagine European culture in America's absence.

The third and somewhat more arbitrary shorthand concerns the focus on popular
culture over the arts as conventionally understood. This emphasis is not motivated
by a judgment that what is somewhat awkwardly labeled "high culture" – architecture, painting, literature, theater, and classical music – is less deserving of attention.
The 1920s are remembered as the apogee of cultural modernism. The cult of newness
and experimentation, associated with names from Jean Cocteau to Wassily Kandinsky
and movements from surrealism to the Bauhaus, has been a central theme of interwar
cultural history. The period also witnessed noteworthy appropriations of popular
culture by prominent artists, writers, and composers. Fascination with specific entertainments, boxing in particular, but also the music hall and motion picture, inspired
poems, paintings, and literary reflections. Celebration of primitive cultures and
peoples, familiar among modernist artists and intellectuals before the war, provided
the foundation for postwar appreciation of jazz music and dance by sections of the
European avant-garde. Igor Stravinsky's *Ragtime* dates from 1918; in 1923 Darius
Milhaud published a jazz ballet; Ernst Krenek's well-known jazz opera, *Jonny spielt
auf*, was first staged in 1927.[5] Yet the writers, artists, and composers who frequented
the cafés and studios of Montparnasse or Berlin borrowed more than they gave back.
Focus here remains fixed on the culture they appropriated.

The fourth shorthand is largely prescribed by the existing historiography. Some
aspects of interwar popular culture have received extensive attention. There is, for
instance, a wide literature on interwar cinema, more than enough to justify a monograph integrating its findings. Recent work on radio and literature has begun to fill
gaps in understanding. Yet we know much less about other important areas, such as
the gramophone and the recording industry or popular dance and sport. To this
unevenness must be added a more fundamental kind of fragmentation. Whereas for
the United States the jazz age provides a conceptual umbrella under which to synthesize the elements of popular culture, historians of Europe face a dual challenge.
Research tends, first, to divide along national lines and, second, to focus on one
aspect of popular culture, such as music or sport or film. Consequently, there is very
little to which one can turn bearing on the topic as a whole.

"Americanization": Music and the Movies

Where then does one begin? A useful jumping-off point is provided by jazz itself. As
a musical idiom, it came to Europe late in the war with black soldiers in the American
Expeditionary Force. When the soldiers, having played a crucial role in ending the
European civil war, went home, their music and dance stayed behind. In their wake
American jazz bands and soloists toured Europe, while recordings gradually widened
the circle of jazz enthusiasts. The performances (and recordings) in Europe of
premier American jazz dancers and musicians, among them Josephine Baker, Sidney
Bechet, Sam Wooding, Louis Armstrong, and Duke Ellington, were at once revela-
tion and provocation, proof of possibilities for intonation, rhythm, movement, and

showmanship that exploded Old World boundaries. The conflicting passions these stirred give some measure of the jolt they administered. Significantly, Afro-American music and dance were denigrated and embraced on remarkably similar grounds. Detractors took its sensual, primitive, and foreign qualities as evidence that it was degenerate and uncivilized; enthusiasts welcomed these same features as liberation from the dead weight of European civilization.[6]

Even as music, however, jazz was an elastic term. Europe primarily encountered the "symphonic" jazz created by white musicians in America and championed most famously by Paul Whiteman and his orchestra. The distinctiveness of so-called "hot jazz" was only belatedly appreciated, and then mainly by specialists. Moreover, jazz was initially identified with gimmickry and showmanship. Novelty percussion instruments and vocal sounds, unusual performing techniques (playing the slide on the trombone with the feet or juggling with the sticks while playing drums), and cacophony were taken as its trademarks. Finally, jazz instrumentation became enormously popular for European bands whether or not they played jazz music.[7]

In Europe as in America the term "jazz" came to be used quite loosely – to the dismay of purists ever since – as a synonym for popular dance music or even popular music in general. Only in these terms can it be said that jazz became widely popular. With the emergence of "swing" in the early 1930s, the domestication of jazz was essentially complete. Yet the association of race, instrumentation, and rhythm that identified jazz as Afro-American remained, even when the music itself adopted smoother rhythms and intonations and lost much of its improvisational nature. It is in this context that one can comprehend the ambivalence toward jazz that characterized the Soviet Union and Nazi Germany. In origins and nature it was perceived as alien and subversive, but as a form of dance music, its smoother variants became such a part of domestic culture that intermittent attempts to ban it foundered.[8]

Jazz was the spearhead of a series of American contributions to interwar European popular culture. The European jazz age was one in which America served as a source of entertainment, creative inspiration, and cultural debate. American popular culture showed little respect for boundaries of nation, politics, or class; it steamrolled its way into virtually all parts of Europe. Apart from jazz music and dance, America's contributions had perhaps less shock value but more pervasive public and commercial impact. Motion pictures stand out. Already during the war Hollywood had supplanted French studios as the major supplier of global film entertainment. British and French cinemas came to rely on American shorts and feature films. After the war Hollywood's reach extended eastward to encompass central Europe and the Soviet Union. By the mid-1920s it attained a position of dominance everywhere but in Germany, where domestic production roughly matched the volume of American imports. The jazz age was, therefore, the era in which Hollywood's enduring presence in European cinemas was established.[9]

Apart from the sheer volume and variety of celluloid produced by the Hollywood assembly line, and the promotional juggernaut that sustained it, the glamor and polish of American movies and their wealth of human types earned them a leading place in cinemas from France to Russia. Douglas Fairbanks in *The Thief of Bagdad*, Rudolph Valentino in *The Sheik*, Lillian Gish in *Broken Blossoms*, and Charlie Chaplin in numerous shorts and *The Gold Rush* were early representatives of a pool of creative talent that appeared almost limitless. Westerns, society dramas, slapstick, and gangster films projected images of America and figured centrally in defining the language of the medium. American movies also disseminated American values and lifestyles. Automobiles, hair-styles, fashions of dress, and behavior were among the lifestyle advertisements imported with American movies.

Hollywood's numerical preponderance and influence generated responses as mixed as those provoked by jazz music. From a purely quantitative perspective European theaters needed American films. In terms of the variety and production values of American movies, theater owners and viewers likewise welcomed them. Some artists and writers found them a source of refreshment and fascination. However, dependence on Hollywood was resented by some members of the film trade and by critics alarmed at the perceived Americanization of European culture, especially where American film companies created European affiliates or invested in existing companies. Some charged Hollywood with undermining domestic film industries by buying up outstanding European film personnel for its own studios. Others went so far as to allege that European audiences were fed up with a steady diet of American film entertainment and were consequently abandoning the cinema in general. The first charge, at least in the active recruiting of leading producers, directors, and performers with lucrative dollar contracts, was undeniable. The second allegation was harder to sustain and remains historically difficult to verify. Some types of American film understandably proved more attractive to European audiences than others. It is also arguable that the postwar boom in movie-making and theater-building resulted in overproduction and relative stagnation in the second half of the 1920s.[10]

Hollywood's omnipresence and recruiting of continental talent certainly did not stifle European filmic activity. Indeed, it can be argued that the competition from America was a necessary, if not sufficient, stimulus to the cultivation of national cinemas, represented most notably in the works of Soviet and German filmmakers of the 1920s and the French *auteur* in the 1930s. Although the "revolutionary" films of Sergei Eisenstein, Aleksandr Dovzhenko, and Vsevolod Pudovkin could not generally rival American imports at the box office, they were internationally acclaimed and plundered for filmic technique. In Germany and France the work of such directors as Ernst Lubitsch, F. W. Murnau, Fritz Lang, Jean Renoir, and René Clair was equally influential in shaping the language of moving pictures. Historians have frequently focused on cinematic milestones, particularly those which could broadly be termed socially realistic, but European studios also manufactured a wide range of light entertainment, even if they could scarcely compete with Hollywood in terms of volume and variety. With the introduction of "talkies" they encountered the challenge faced by Hollywood – how to market their product in other languages – but also enjoyed a breathing space provided by the language barrier, behind which domestic sound production could be nurtured.

Media and the Masses

Discussion of film underscores the second fundamental feature of interwar popular culture, namely, its unprecedented media saturation. Whether new or previously established, the media experienced remarkable growth. For serial publishing, the interwar years represent a historic pinnacle. Leading cities boasted multiple daily papers; in Berlin there were roughly a dozen major and many minor, local papers.

Inexpensive paperback fiction, aimed, like cinema, at a market whose contours and tastes were closely calculated, became big business, led by the phenomenon of the bestseller.[11] The range of periodical literature was unprecedented, as publishers targeted specific audiences, among them women and youth, and as newer media such as film and radio spawned related print material, from critical journals to fan magazines. Sports magazines and dedicated sports sections in newspapers grew rapidly with the sharp rise in popular appeal of the mass spectator sports. There were, of course, variations in the extent of media coverage across the continent, but interwar popular culture was largely media driven.

Several media stand out for their newness or modernity, prominent among them cinema and the gramophone. In the decade before the war the former had begun to find permanent accommodation in urban areas; the latter, from the uneven statistical evidence available, was at home primarily among the growing middle classes. It was after the war that each became accessible on a very wide front. A postwar boom brought motion pictures to widening circles of the urban working class and smaller towns. The movies also climbed the social ladder toward bourgeois respectability and at least in the larger cities acquired palatial surroundings which rivaled or outdid traditional theaters. Movie programs also adopted features of vaudeville, combining live acts and music with short and feature films. The number of cinemas rose rapidly in most parts of Europe. Beyond the towns and cities, especially as one traveled east, coverage remained thin, but movies still qualify as the premier form of public entertainment between the wars.

In addition to rapid expansion, the cinema underwent a revolution from silence to sound. Strictly speaking, film had never been silent, since musical accompaniment was an integral part of film screenings. The motion picture palaces of the 1920s boasted their own house orchestras, while the modest suburban or provincial theaters usually provided a small ensemble or at least piano accompaniment. Cinemas were the leading employer of musicians in the 1920s – in Germany alone it is estimated that 12,000–15,000 musicians found work in them. Strikingly and ironically, "silent film" provided the experience of live *musical* entertainment for more people than had ever frequented concert halls. It offered a wide range of music, including classics and popular and original songs. All this being said, the introduction of sound at the end of the 1920s represented a very significant break. The ability of film to synchronize the visual and the aural made it a central forum for the music, dance, showmanship, and sensation which characterized the age.

The gramophone became increasingly accessible to the lower classes and fueled a dramatic postwar growth in record sales. Although we know much less about their cultural impact than we do about motion pictures, it is clear that by the early 1920s recordings began to supplant sheet music as the primary vehicle for transmission of popular music. For a brief period, before radio and sound movies assumed a fair share of this role, they were the main link between musical artists and the public. On the eve of the Depression, record sales in Germany were almost 30 million annually and perhaps half that number in France, evidence that as many as half of all households owned a gramophone. Even though this boom was less about jazz, strictly speaking, than popular music in general, it was sustained by the dance fads of the decade. It has been estimated that at least three-quarters of all records sold in the second half of the 1920s were either popular songs or dance music.[12]

Among the leading media of interwar Europe one was entirely new. If we set television aside as a novelty of the 1930s whose popular history belongs to the period after the second war, radio was the lone medium to penetrate domestic space between the wars. Its rapid ascent from curiosity to household item is a case study in media dissemination and in the harnessing of that medium for the primary purpose of entertainment. From its inception in the early 1920s, broadcasting became, within a decade (again with considerable national variations as one traveled south and east), a fixture in middle-class homes. Italy was an exception among the industrialized nations of western Europe, lagging well behind, but otherwise by the end of the 1930s radio was also familiar in working-class households in western Europe. Germany and England led the way: in the former case there were already a million radio licenses in 1925, a figure which quadrupled by 1932 and then tripled again by 1939. France showed a slower growth curve, but even there the number of radios rose from about half a million in 1930 to 5.5 million in 1939.

Unlike cinema and the recording industry, broadcasting was largely, though not exclusively, in public hands. Launched with a mandate to educate and cultivate, it initially addressed the middle classes capable of affording the unwieldy and expensive radio sets manufactured in the 1920s. Its mandate therefore ran somewhat at cross-purposes with those of the other popular media. Indeed, a determination that radio should not become just another medium of popular culture pervaded official opinion about it. The commitment to elevation of the audience in the national interest was almost universal. Programming ranged from live concerts to news, lectures, radio plays, and sporting events, with emphasis on music and talk which would edify and enlighten. By the early 1930s, with improvements in the technology of both broadcasting and receiving, radios became increasingly attractive and accessible to the working class. Radio stations responded to growing public demand to provide a variety of light entertainment, including comedy and increased quotas of popular dance music. A socially more diverse listenership, and transmitters capable of reaching beyond towns and cities into rural areas, gave radio the ability to speak nationally, connecting a disparate audience. It brought cultivation to the masses and popular music to the elite.[13]

Spectators and Participants

As the modern media claimed a growing share of discretionary spending, traditional forms of culture were inevitably affected. Media competition represented a relentless challenge to the *café concert*, music hall and, to a lesser extent, cabaret, which were vibrant forms at the turn of the century. By the mid-1920s the music hall faced decline with the surge in popularity of records. At the start of the next decade sound movies and radio delivered an even more telling blow. Yet live entertainment did not of course disappear. In some respects the radio served its interests by the exposure it offered to otherwise little-known performers who toured concert halls and stages. Moreover, the traditions of popular song and the music hall remained alive in other guises, such as the dance hall and in the "silent" movie theaters.

The music hall tradition had already been enriched before the war with the emergence of the revue. For a better-off clientele in large cities the 1920s became its heyday. Borrowing from variety shows a mix of bands, skits, singers, and well-drilled chorus lines, the revue added increasingly extravagant stage presentation, particularly magnificent and exotic backdrops, and various stages of nudity (censored in film). Its subject matter, like that of vaudeville or the music hall, cohered only in the loosest sense, but the purpose was not to convince but to overwhelm the senses and provide diversion. Revues became enormously popular. The leading producers vied with each other in the opulence, exoticism, and sheer variety of their numbers. Until the beginning of the depression and the release of the early musical films they offered an unrivaled combination of titillation, sensation, and spectacle. For the metropolis of the postwar years they acquired an iconic quality, short-lived though their popularity proved to be.[14]

As the example of the revue suggests, rather than draw a hard line between live and media-based entertainment, roughly old and new, we should be attentive to their intersection, indeed reciprocity. Radio and motion pictures were unique modes of communication and entertainment and spawned their own audiences. Yet they also appropriated the traditions of live musical and theatrical entertainment. Moreover, they reproduced for millions, in the pre-television age, the life of their time. It was in this period that sporting events became accessible via radio to remote "spectators." But this accompanied, rather than undermined, the attractions of live attendance. Indeed, radio interest in sporting events catered to the growing fan base and is difficult to imagine without it. Across Europe new stadiums were built, in number and size far exceeding the requirements of the prewar era, to accommodate football fans. Film and broadcasting also captured the outstanding feats of the age, feats which drew massive live audiences, such as Lindbergh's triumphant reception in France after the first transatlantic solo flight in 1927. Similarly, the gramophone brought music to an enormous audience and, like film, crossed boundaries of geography and tradition.

The importance of media should also not be understood to imply that popular culture can be reduced to various forms of passive consumption or spectatorship. In the first place, one should not assume that audiences in cinemas or football stadiums were inert. It is simpler for us to imagine enthusiastic and vocal behavior at sports events than in movie theaters, but there is ample evidence that interwar movie-goers engaged motion pictures much as they would live entertainment, not only with laughter and tears but also with cheers, boos, applause, catcalls, and whistling. Second, some media directly fostered participation. The popular music of the 1920s, available on gramophone and radio, fed a dance craze serviced by thousands of dance halls and clubs. Indeed, it is arguable, as in the case of the emergence of jazz music in America, that the causal sequence should be reversed: new dances and public venues to engage them made the music and recordings popular.

At the burgeoning dance halls the mostly young and single could meet, mix, and learn new steps. Restaurants, clubs, and beer gardens likewise employed live bands to cater to a clientele enthusiastic about dancing. The most famous of the American dances of the 1920s to land in Europe, the Charleston, was a rather short-lived craze at mid-decade, and less widely adopted than often imagined. It nonetheless represents a wider trend that went back to the arrival of the tango before the war. A series of imported dance steps, such as the foxtrot, cakewalk, and shimmy, like the Charleston, transformed the meaning of popular dance. Whether Europeans danced in order to forget the war, to enjoy the relative freedom of relations between the sexes, or because the rhythms of jazz proved as irresistible as the blend of contortion, eroticism, and celebration of the body performed by Josephine Baker, they danced publicly as never before.

A similar observation can be made with regard to sports. Media coverage of the three most popular sports of the age – football, boxing, and cycling (six-day races and the *Tour de France*) – not only extended, rather than replaced, the experience of live spectatorship. It also, in the case of football, reflected the widening popularity of the sport as a pastime for millions of young males. The interwar years witnessed a remarkable expansion of amateur football clubs on the continent. The English game, introduced to the continent in the late nineteenth century among the better classes, became a staple of working-class culture and the national sport of Europe. France, which had about a thousand local football associations in 1920, had four thousand by 1925 and six thousand by the late 1930s. In Germany there were a half million active members in 3,100 associations in 1920; a decade later total member-ship had doubled. Active participants and a wide circle of mostly male spectators constituted the fan base for the sport. Thus spectatorship followed the growth of participation as much as it was fostered by media. With the enormous rise in the number of participants and spectators went the commercialization and professional-ization of football, just as the *Tour de France* had commercialized road cycling. The leading clubs competed financially for the best players, whose names and pictures were used in advertising: football cards helped sell cigarettes. The World Cup was held for the first time in 1930, giving formal dimensions to national rivalries which were already crucial for stimulating public interest in the sport.[15]

Music and the Public Realm

Jazz music and dance, a rich and diverse film culture, the gramophone, sports, and radio: these are the outstanding elements of interwar popular culture. Only the first and last of these were unique to the era, yet enough has been said about the remain-der to suggest how changes in scale and technology meant a significant departure from the norms of prewar Europe. Taken together with Americanization, these ele-ments point to two conspicuous features of interwar popular culture in addition to its dependence on media and its ability to cross lines of class and nation. The first is that in a manner never before experienced, music saturated the public (popular) realm. Live on stage and in the dance hall, in "silent" movie theaters and then sound films, via radio and recordings, someone's song went continuously around the world and was heard by unprecedented numbers of people, a condition that has since become so normal as to be completely unremarkable. The second is the impressive synergy of the various means by which music found its audience, notwithstanding intervals of competition between them. Live performances were broadcast on the airwaves and recorded for sale; studio recordings found outlets in radio; film com-panies crafted motion pictures around singers and hit songs and then distributed the latter as records and sheet music; radio picked up the popular movie tunes as well as initially supporting its own live ensembles. All of these phenomena are now so familiar as to be commonplace. But it was the interwar years that witnessed the convergence of the media which made music as ubiquitous as print or still photography and the moving picture.

What can be said about the nature of this music? First and foremost, it encompassed a range of styles both new and old. In addition to dance and jazz hits, waltzes, folk songs, sentimental ballads, operetta, choral music, and symphonic and operatic music were recorded, broadcast, and featured in films as well as at live performances. The jazz age was not dominated by jazz in any strict sense. One of the popular musical forms of the period was the operetta, and one that generated its own series of hit songs. From the early days of sound movies it became accessible to audiences of millions. Some operettas used modern styles of popular song and dance; others drew on the musical traditions of the nineteenth century. Sometimes these were juxtaposed. As noted earlier, the instrumentation of the jazz band was adopted widely for other musical styles. If we add military music to the list above, especially the patriotic and marching tunes without which Soviet socialism and German Nazism are scarcely imaginable, and which were also heard on screen, radio, and records, some idea of the richness of popular music can be gained. In variety as well as availability this was an age inundated by music.[16]

While there are a number of illuminating studies of popular music in this period, the phenomenon just outlined has not been comprehensively assessed. A convenient and fascinating window on it is offered by early musical films, the entertainment form that married music and moving image, thus uniting the leading attractions of the age. More than photographs, which capture the fashions and settings of the time, or recordings, which preserve many of its sounds, including those of some sporting events and radio programming (including radio plays), musical films archive contemporary tastes, emotions, and illusions. As in other aspects of interwar cinema, Hollywood's leading role brings to mind such pictures as *The Jazz Singer* (1927) or *Broadway Melody* (1929). Yet all the major film-producing nations in Europe made musicals and operettas, many of which were enormously popular. René Clair's *Le Million* (1930), early German works such as *Three from the Filling Station* (1930) or *Congress Dances* (1931) and the films of the Soviet song-writing/directing duo of Isaak Dunaevsky and Grigori Alexandrov, especially *Jolly Fellows* (1934) and *Volga, Volga* (1937), invented worlds in which song and dance overcame all obstacles. Light-hearted, optimistic, irrepressible, these often chose "everyday" settings but transcended socioeconomic circumstances which were anything but hopeful.

It is easy to dismiss these musicals as vapid and inane, the ultimate form of escapism in extremely difficult circumstances. When three snappy and good-looking German males return to their flat to find its contents being repossessed because their bank has collapsed (*Three from the Filling Station*), they break into a plaintive but good-natured and ultimately playful song about their plight – this in 1930, as the Depression in Germany moved from dire to catastrophic. Soviet performers celebrated the power of music to create individual happiness and national strength, anticipating Stalin's famous pronouncement in late 1935 that life had become more joyous – this in the interval between the monstrosities of industrialization and collectivization and the nightmare of the purges to come.[17] In France, René Clair's enchanted spoof, *Le Million*, again set during the Depression, revolved around a winning lottery ticket. It is difficult to deny the opportunism of the culture industry in this sugar-coating of the real world. Yet it is likewise difficult to deny the cleverness with which these films enlisted contemporary song, dance, comedy, and romance, their promotion of existing or creation of new musical talent, their boon to record sales in launching hit songs, and their enlistment of a mix of musical styles. Whether produced in democratic or socialist or fascist societies, they testify to dreams and aspirations that are as recognizable as they were remote from reality for their audiences.

Reading Popular Culture in the Jazz Age

The musical film can be read as a type of popular culture in general, identifiable by its ephemeral and inconsequential content as much by its stylistic features and broad audience. By this account, superficiality and cliché characterize everything from popular songs to movies. This reading renders popular culture a weak source for understanding the world of those who produced and consumed it. However, it can be argued with at least as much force that the motifs of popular culture recur precisely because they engage fundamental human concerns, situated in concrete times and places. Their dependence upon genre conventions such as comedy, romance, or tragedy by no means undermines their significance. Moreover, the relationship between motif and genre treatment is historically conditioned. Popular literature, movies, and music inescapably treat contemporary issues, even if their treatments and resolutions displace and distort. How they distinguish themselves stylistically and engage contemporary issues can be highly revealing.

What then was characteristic of the content or main themes of interwar popular culture? To respond to this question is to gloss the final query raised in the introduction to this chapter about the significance of popular culture for understanding interwar Europe. At first glance the thematic trends yield a straightforward answer: broken hearts and romantic fulfillment; satire and slapstick; heroism and adventure; triumph and tragedy, spectacle and action: these formed the backbone of entertainment on the stage and in film and popular literature. In this respect little appeared to have changed. Yet the answer is not as simple as classifying genres and narrative traditions. Even if we except jazz music and dance as outsiders – though they quickly became insiders – popular culture appropriated new thematic territory after the war by engaging the issues of its time. Shifts in modes of delivery went hand in hand with changes that transcended one national or regional context, notwithstanding the varieties of European experience.

One clue to these broad changes has already been noted: the extent to which American music, dance, and movies found a home across Europe. America was clearly the outstanding source of transnational popular culture, but it was not alone. Although no European movie-making nation could compete seriously even on the continental market, Swedish, German, Russian, and French films still circulated widely. While identified with their respective places of origin, they were ingredients in a truly international film culture. Popular music, whether music hall songs or marches and patriotic melodies, had specifically national provenance, but thanks to radio, recordings, and motion pictures, also circulated more widely. In short, internationalization of popular culture did not only mean Americanization. It can be paralleled to the nationalizing effects of motion pictures, recordings, and broadcasting in their transcendence of regional and class boundaries.

Another clue can be found in examination of the authoritarian states of the period – primarily Stalin's Russia, Hitler's Germany, and Mussolini's Italy – for evidence that official ideologies and state control created distinct popular cultures. Historians have devoted considerable energy to this search, particularly for evidence that popular culture was ideologically contaminated. Sport history, for instance, has been written largely from the perspective of the state, focusing on the role of physical training in national health and militarization and on the politics of international competition.[18] Until recently the same has been true of much research on film, radio, and the press. The aim has been to pinpoint how the aspirations of the seemingly omnipresent state remade national culture.

The results of the search have been equivocal. There is no doubt that the state had ambitions to mold the culture of the people, or that substantial apparatuses were constructed and that they functioned to this end. The range of controls was unprecedented and the visions for cultural renewal were boundless. There is also no doubt that media were instrumentalized for specific propaganda purposes, especially newsreels or radio talks. Nonetheless, what remains in great doubt is that the millions of people who went to the movies and football matches, purchased records and visited dance halls, had a particular interest in the politics of their entertainment. Thematically, perhaps socialist realism in the Soviet Union of the 1930s came closest to attaining a life of its own, though even it has been dubbed a "tortuous compromise."[19]

While each regime acknowledged the importance of sport or film or radio for national life and appropriated popular culture wherever it could, it has yet to be demonstrated that any of them knew how to create a popular culture in its own image. Indeed, despite proclamations of national superiority and quotas to protect it – a notable oxymoron, though one familiar as well in the democracies – they generally permitted circulation of foreign, especially American, films and jazz music. In fact, the dictators often enjoyed Hollywood's top productions, just as their people adopted American-inspired dance music. To the extent that audiences showed preference for domestic over foreign films or music, there is little to suggest that political questions intruded. Notwithstanding significant attempts to draw firm lines between political and non-political entertainment, to tease out hidden ideological content or to credit popular culture for reconciling consumers to an otherwise oppressive social and political system, historians have found that popular culture spoke to concerns that could not be neatly bounded by race, nation, or class.[20]

This is not to whitewash or suppress manifest evidence of manipulation in the interests of an ideology. But in Europe as in America, popular culture generally emphasized individual, private fates, rather than the collective so prized by fascism, socialism, or National Socialism. This was consonant with a central impulse of the modern age. Paradoxically, the authoritarian political movements defined and presented themselves according to the categories and values of genre entertainment at least as much as they reshaped those images and values for ideological purposes. In important regards their key personalities were stage managers and spin-doctors, otherwise known as politicians.

If the case for reading popular culture according to political agendas is problematic, a more convincing and intriguing argument has been made for the gendering of interwar popular culture. A central motif for historians interested in the intersection of culture and society has been the emergence of the "new woman" as archetype and consumer. While partly myth, spawned by male apprehensions in the postwar world, the "new woman" was both enough of a reality and a large enough myth to generate impassioned discussion and to become a favorite figure of popular film and literature. Male anxieties in the face of a cohort of young, single, working women with little prospect of marriage, given the gender imbalance after the war, is one side of the phenomenon. The other is the role of women as consumers of films, magazines, novels, cosmetics, and clothing (i.e., as a majority of the "masses"). Women's choices acquired novel public, cultural, and commercial weight. These choices intersected with changing images of feminine roles, dress, and ideals of beauty. Popular culture therefore played a crucial role in the process of what has been called female "subjectivity formation."[21]

Not the least intriguing aspect of this theme is the coding of popular culture itself as feminine, that is, as a *public* realm that thematized *private* concerns traditionally associated with the female sphere, that projected a novel role for women, and that was open to females as much as to males. Feminization can thus be linked to mass media in general and the inroads of American culture in particular, to the expanding public space for consumption of popular culture and the invasion of the private (female/family) sphere, not least by radio. The "new woman" featured in popular novels, films, and songs became associated with contemporary media and forms of marketing. (Sport alone remained broadly "male" in its ethos and following, although here too the thrall of mass spectatorship suggested feminization parallel to that witnessed in mass adoration of Mussolini and Hitler.) Women were targeted by publishers, broadcasters, and film producers, becoming conspicuous consumers of popular culture at the same moment that their social roles and identities were highlighted there and in broad public debate. American popular culture, foremost in overriding national boundaries and the traditional divide between high and low culture, represented a comparable challenge to gender boundaries, demonstrating that inherited categories were unstable and subject to overthrow.[22]

The gendering of popular culture frames the final question starkly: have we abandoned one binary reading of the subject – the war between tradition and modernity – only to be enmeshed in a second – the gender divide? If so, is the latter the key to popular song, film, and literature after the Great War? The short answer to both questions is a simple negative. The slightly longer answer is that issues not new to the 1920s – from expanding leisure time and disposable income to female suffrage and widening employment, urbanization and its attendant social opportunities and stresses, and a generation of youth in search of meaning – were transformed by the war into matters of central interest and received both overt and coded airing in the popular culture of the postwar decade. Gender roles and images were prominent, but questions of class, morality, or national identity were also prevalent. In addition, America's presence was pervasive and much debated. Moreover, as a model and as competitor in music, dance, film, and marketing, America helped shift the terms of debate not only on a wide range of social issues but also on the nature and significance of popular culture itself.

The tug-of-war, new to this era but still with us, was no longer between tradition and modernity. Thanks largely to the supraregional and supranational reach of new media, the challenge was how to engage ever wider audiences without imitating or surrendering to America. The challenge rested on a simple discovery: resistance to, or outright rejection of, the American political and social model generally proved no bar to adoption of its popular culture. With that culture came the panoply of values that can be broadly termed individualistic and consumerist, rooted in self-realization and self-fulfillment. This is a world we have not yet lost.

NOTES

1 Soviet satire of 1927, cited in Anne E. Gorsuch, *Youth in Revolutionary Russia* (Bloomington: Indiana University Press, 2000), p. 116.

2 See Phyllis Rose, *Jazz Cleopatra: Josephine Baker in Her Time* (London: Chatto and Windus, 1989), pp. 18–28, 97: her performance was of course stage-managed by Europeans to conform to their notions of the primitive.

3 Cf. Richard Stites, *Russian Popular Culture: Entertainment and Society since 1900* (Cambridge: Cambridge University Press, 1992), pp. 1–6; Regina M. Sweeney, *Singing Our Way to Victory: French Cultural Politics and Music during the Great War* (Middletown CT: Wesleyan University Press, 2001), pp. 7–8.

4 See Kathy J. Ogren, *The Jazz Revolution: Twenties America and the Meaning of Jazz* (New York: Oxford University Press, 1989).

5 See Jody Blake, *Le Tumulte noir: Modernist Art and Popular Entertainment in Jazz-Age Paris, 1900–1930* (University Park: Pennsylvania State University Press, 1999); Nancy L. Perloff, *Art and the Everyday: Popular Entertainment and the Circle of Erik Satie* (Oxford: Clarendon Press, 1991).

6 See Chris Goddard, *Jazz Away from Home* (New York: Paddington Press, 1979); Gorsuch, *Youth in Revolutionary Russia*, pp. 116–38.

7 See Ronald Pearsall, *Popular Music of the Twenties* (London: David and Charles, 1976), pp. 55–62.

8 See Michael Kater, *Different Drummers: Jazz in the Culture of Nazi Germany* (New York: Oxford University Press, 1992); S. Frederick Starr, *Red and Hot: The Fate of Jazz in the Soviet Union, 1917–1980* (New York: Oxford University Press, 1983).

9 See Victoria de Grazia, "Mass Culture and Sovereignty: The American Challenge to European Cinemas, 1920–1960," *Journal of Modern History* 61 (1989): 53–87.

10 See Tom Saunders, *Hollywood in Berlin: American Cinema and Weimar Germany* (Berkeley: University of California Press, 1994).

11 See Lynda J. King, *Best-Sellers by Design: Vicki Baum and the House of Ullstein* (Detroit MI: Wayne State University Press, 1988).

12 See Pekka Gronow, "The Record Industry: The Growth of a Mass Medium," *Popular Music* 3 (1983): 62; see also P. Gronow and Ilpo Saunio, *An International History of the Recording Industry*, Christopher Moseley, trans. (London: Cassell, 1998), p. 41.

13 Cf. Karl C. Führer, "A Medium of Modernity? Broadcasting in Weimar Germany, 1923–32," *Journal of Modern History* 69 (1997): 722–53; Cécile Méadel, "Programmes en masse, programmes de masse?" in *Masses et culture de masse dans les années 30*, Régine Robin, ed. (Paris: Editions ouvrières, 1991), pp. 51–68.

14 See Peter Jelavich, *Berlin Cabaret* (Cambridge MA: Harvard University Press, 1993), pp. 165–86.

15 See Geoff Hare, *Football in France: A Cultural History* (Oxford: Berg, 2003), pp. 15–21. On cycling, see Richard Holt, *Sport and Society in Modern France* (London: Macmillan, 1981), pp. 81–102; Christopher Thompson, "The Tour in the Inter-War Years: Political Ideology, Athletic Excess and Industrial Modernity," in *Tour de France, 1903–2003*, Hugh Dauncey and Geoff Hare, eds (London: Cass, 2003), pp. 79–102.

16 See James J. Nott, *Music for the People: Popular Music and Dance in Interwar Britain* (Oxford: Oxford University Press, 2002); David MacFadyen, *Songs for Fat People: Affect,*

Emotion and Celebrity in the Russian Popular Song, 1900–1955 (Montreal: McGill-Queen's University Press, 2002).

17 See James von Geldern and Richard Stites, eds, *Mass Culture in Soviet Russia* (Bloomington: Indiana University Press, 1995), pp. 234–5, from *March of the Happy-Go-Lucky Guys* (1934).

18 See the essays in James Riordan and Pierre Arnaud, eds, *Sport and International Politics* (London: Routledge, 1998).

19 Stites, *Russian Popular Culture*, p. 67.

20 Cf. Robert Edelmann, *Serious Fun: A History of Spectator Sports in the USSR* (New York: Oxford University Press, 1993); Eric Rentschler, *The Ministry of Illusion: Nazi Cinema and its Afterlife* (Cambridge MA: Harvard University Press, 1996).

21 See Mary L. Roberts, *Civilization without Sexes: Reconstructing Gender in Postwar France, 1917–1927* (Chicago: University of Chicago Press, 1994); Richard W. McCormick, *Gender and Sexuality in Weimar Modernity* (New York: Palgrave, 2001); Eugenia Paulicelli, *Fashion under Fascism: Beyond the Black Shirt* (New York: Berg, 2004).

22 See Victoria de Grazia, *How Fascism Ruled Women: Italy 1922–1945* (Berkeley: University of California Press, 1992), pp. 201–33; Billie Melman, *Women and the Popular Imagination in the Twenties: Flappers and Nymphs* (Basingstoke: Macmillan, 1988).

GUIDE TO FURTHER READING

Wolf von Eckardt and Sander Gilman, *Bertolt Brecht's Berlin: A Scrapbook of the Twenties* (Lincoln: University of Nebraska Press, 1993). A photographic record of the culture of the metropolis, both high and low.

Modris Eksteins, *The Rites of Spring: The Great War and the Birth of the Modern Age* (Toronto: Lester and Orpen Dennys, 1989). Provocative and impressive in breadth and in suggesting connections between artistic sensibilities and popular passions.

Chris Goddard, *Jazz Away from Home* (New York: Paddington Press, 1979). Well-informed and rewarding study of European attempts to assimilate jazz, especially in the Parisian context.

Hans Gumbrecht, *In 1926: Living at the Edge of Time* (Cambridge MA: Harvard University Press, 1997). International, idiosyncratic, and intriguing: from boxing and bullfighting to movie palaces and revues, it evokes and decodes the age.

Richard Maltby, ed., *Dreams for Sale: Popular Culture in the 20th Century* (London: Harrap, 1989). Well illustrated overview which situates the jazz age internationally.

Princesse Tam Tam (1934) (New York: Kino on Video, 1989). Josephine Baker in a semi-autobiographical Pygmalion tale of the clash between European civilization and African primitiveness. Features a magnificent revue and Baker in a trademark "native" dance.

Charles Rearick, *The French in Love and War: Popular Culture in the Era of the World Wars* (New Haven CT: Yale University Press, 1997). A national survey of broad scope which inquires into the "Frenchness" of the subject.

Jacqueline Reich and Piero Garofalo, eds, *Re-viewing Fascism: Italian Cinema, 1922–1943* (Blooomington: Indiana University Press, 2002). A dozen essays illustrating the richness of current approaches in film and cultural studies.

Richard Stites, *Russian Popular Culture: Entertainment and Society since 1900* (Cambridge: Cambridge University Press, 1992). Comprehensive in its coverage of the range of popular culture and perceptive in suggesting overarching national themes.

Denise, J. Youngblood, *Movies for the Masses: Popular Cinema and Soviet Society in the 1920s* (Cambridge: Cambridge University Press, 1992). An important study of film as popular culture, attentive to its foreign and domestic elements as well as social context.

CHAPTER TWENTY-THREE

The Nazi New Society

DICK GEARY

It is difficult to derive any single Nazi vision of a new society from the statements of its leaders before 1933. The initial program of the National Socialist German Workers Party (NSDAP) contained a mixture of nationalist, racist, and socially radical demands (nationalization of industrial trusts, communalization of department stores, and confiscation of war profits), but it was far from clear that Hitler ever believed in these last elements of the program. By 1928 the Nazi leader was reassuring rural and middle-class voters that it was "only Jewish capital" which would be expropriated. In the elections which preceded Hitler's appointment as chancellor in late January 1933, the NSDAP made a wide variety of promises about the future under Nazism. The unemployed were promised jobs. Agriculture was promised protection and lower taxation, and was lauded as the healthy backbone of the German nation. Small shop-keepers were promised protection against large department stores and small businesses protection against banks and corporate giants. Yet at the same time the leaders of German industry were promised the restoration of management's right to manage, the destruction of trade-union power, and fewer taxes. Differences and contradictions in the area of economic policy were bridged over by the more general aims of restoring national greatness, reviving traditional family values, and destroying socialism/communism, as well as by the most fundamental of Nazi goals: the creation of a "People's Community" (*Volksgemeinschaft*), in which divisions of region, religious denomination, social class, and political affiliation would be overcome in a single German identity.[1]

Economic Reality: Productivity, Income Distribution, and Property Ownership

Economic change under Nazism was limited in scope. Although several historians have credited the regime with a Keynesian approach to economic problems and noted that Germany pulled out of the Depression with relative speed after 1933, the growth of the German economy in the mid-1930s was not that spectacular: over the whole period from 1913 to 1938 many of Germany's competitors enjoyed greater growth rates and the economic spurt of the 1930s simply saw the Reich catching up with the growth that had been achieved earlier elsewhere. Certainly, Hitler's coming to power set the scene for economic recovery. This was not so much the result of a specific Nazi economic policy, however, but rather because of the resolution of political conflicts, the destruction of trade unions, the prohibition of strikes, wage controls, and the default on international debts. Significantly, the fall in world prices, especially food prices, in the 1930s were not passed on to German consumers. Here the contrast with British and US economic growth is instructive; for this was driven by cheap imports, rising real incomes (of those in jobs) and a subsequent increase in consumer demand for manufactured goods, which led in turn to greater investment in new technology and a reorganization of industry. In Germany, on the other hand, the state-led stimulus to increased consumer demand in the first two years of the Third Reich was quickly replaced by increased demand for capital goods and industrial raw materials in the armaments boom of 1936 to 1938. Moreover, despite full employment in Germany between 1936 and 1939, private consumption and the output of consumer goods responded slowly to the economic upturn. It was only in 1941 that real earnings reached the level of 1929. The product of German economic growth in these years was increasingly redistributed to profits, which rose significantly faster than wages, and to the German state, rather than to German consumers. Moreover, high rates of investment in the mid-1930s did not lead to commensurate increases in the productivity of German industry. Indeed, despite the recent claims that the Nazis were a force for modernization, increases in industrial productivity in Germany in the 1930s only look good in comparison with the disastrous years of the Depression and compare unfavorably with those of many other countries. The "Americanization" of German industry took place after, rather than before, 1945 and the continued production of consumer goods during the armaments boom was largely a consequence of lowering quality rather than technological innovation. Furthermore, the economic boom of 1936–8 was generated by expenditure on armaments or arms-related activities. Mass consumption and a new consumerism, which, according to Rainer Zitelmann and Michael Prinz, were central to the aims of Hitler and the German Labor Front, remained figments of the imagination. It should also be noted that the realization of Nazi economic aims was predicated on the exploitation of non-Aryan labor and plundered resources from beyond the boundaries of the Reich.

Thus Nazi economic policy was in no sense "Keynesian." For Keynes had argued that state expenditure was to serve the role of job creation primarily in order to increase pay packets and thus give rise to a self-sustaining recovery, led by consumer demand. But the reverse of this happened in Nazi Germany. The Nazi government used public spending to gain greater control of the German economy, not to relinquish that role to consumer spending power. It did not encourage private consumption, but, as we have seen, restricted it. It did not lower interest rates *á la* Keynes or reestablish links with the world economy, but embarked upon policies of autarky and investment in producer goods industries. Moreover, it sought to replace dependence on international trade with national self-sufficiency and a series of bilateral trade agreements with countries in eastern Europe. From *Anschluss* with Austria in 1938 the Nazi economy was also increasingly dependent upon plunder from occupied territories and dispossessed foreigners and Jews. It was not only for its raw materials and industrial capacity that Nazi-occupied eastern Europe was exploited after 1939, however, but also and above all for its manpower. This included not only the forced labor of the Jews and other prisoners in the ghettoes, concentration camps, and death camps, but also of up to 8 million foreign workers imported into the Reich, mainly, though not always, forcibly. By 1944, 7–8 million foreign workers were domiciled in the Reich. This system of servile labor was a distinguishing feature of the Nazi economy and casts no little doubt on its supposed "modernity."

The Nazi economic system remained capitalist. Except for non-Aryan or foreign capital, the ownership of private property was not disputed, though the long-term trend of capital concentration, so often denounced by the Nazis in their appeals to small businessmen and shopkeepers, not only continued but accelerated. At the same time the profits of large industrial concerns rose significantly and the share of Germany's national product consumed by profits increased, while that of wages declined. This was no accident: Hitler had promised that he would restore profitability to German industry and management's right to manage. Furthermore, many of the "Nazi radicals" had left the NSDAP by 1933, while the murder of the SA leadership in the "Night of the Long Knives" in 1934 further reduced the prospects of a fundamental challenge to the prevailing economic and social order. Subsequently, the plans of the German Labor Front (DAF) to expand its role, plans likened by Michael Prinz to the welfare program of Beveridge in the UK (a flawed comparison, given the complete absence of racism in the latter and its centrality to the former), never came to fruition. Industrialists benefited from the destruction of socialist and union influence in government and the prohibition of strikes. Moreover, the larger firms, which were most successful in the intense competition for labor and raw materials after 1936, were the major beneficiaries of forced labor. The power of corporate capitalism was reflected in the continuing process of industrial concentration: the number of independent artisans declined from 1.65 million in 1936 to 1.5 million three years later.

The Third Reich did take some steps to protect artisans and small retailers. Special taxes were introduced on large stores, the creation of new department stores was prohibited, some consumer cooperatives were closed, and restrictions were placed on itinerant salesmen. To establish a business, independent craftsmen now had to belong to a guild and possess certificates of qualification. Yet the major beneficiaries of economic growth and government contracts were the large firms: to build the industrial infrastructure of German national greatness, the Nazi regime required efficient, large-scale production.

Similar points can be made about the relationship between the regime and agriculture. Nazi ideology proclaimed the significance of "Blood and Soil" for the Aryan race and portrayed the peasantry as the healthy core of the German *Volk*. However, schemes to re-ruralize German society soon proved illusory. The regime began by addressing some grievances of peasants and farmers: introducing strict import controls on agricultural produce; pegging food prices at levels higher than those of the Depression; subsidizing agriculture; introducing the Farm Inheritance Law to make it illegal for agricultural land to be alienated from its owners. However, until 1935 agricultural subsidies were more likely to be distributed to large or medium size estates than to the smallholdings of peasants. Moreover, the Farm Inheritance Law proved to be a very mixed blessing; for, by preventing the alienation of farmland, it also prevented peasants from using their farms as collateral to raise loans from financial institutions. As a result of these developments and above all of the fact that the gap between rural and urban incomes continued to grow to the detriment of agriculture, Germans continued to leave the countryside for the towns in large numbers. By 1939 more Germans lived in cities than ever before. At the same time the number of agricultural workers declined by half a million and attempts to achieve agricultural self-sufficiency failed. Thus industrial and urban growth was not halted by the Nazis.

So far we have seen that industry in the Third Reich was not subjected to major state interventions in property relations, that large concerns continued to thrive under private ownership, and that the role of agriculture in the total German economy continued to decline. However, this did not mean that big business was free to do whatever it wanted. In return for lucrative armaments contracts, the suppression of strikes and unions, and access to cheap servile labor, business leaders either complied or were forced to comply with the wishes of their political masters. Wage and price levels were now dictated by the regime, as was the distribution of raw materials and manpower, capital flows and foreign exchange. Moreover, private entrepreneurs found themselves in competition with a new and privileged economic player in the shape of Göring's personal industrial empire. Thus capitalists in the Third Reich competed less for markets and more for their share of contracts in the arms economy and for labor and raw materials. State, rather than private, demand became the driving force of economic life; and representatives of industry were largely excluded from the most important decisions. Yet most industrialists were not expropriated; and significantly they were absent from the activities of elite resistance groups in the final years of the Reich. Earlier, in the first six years of the Nazi regime, the profits of German industry rose by over 36 percent. At the same time the share of profits in gross national income rose from 43 percent to just under 48 percent, while that of wages fell proportionally.[2]

If capitalists remained capitalists, what of German labor in this period? Most obviously millions of Germans welcomed the return of full employment and the rise in real wages, although most of that rise can be explained by longer working hours and it was not until 1941 that real wage levels reached those of 1929. Significantly, the distribution of wage increases in Germany after 1933 became increasingly uneven, as collective wage agreements were abandoned for the *Leistungsprinzip*, the "performance principle," which meant an individualization of pay packets. The *Refa-Verfahren* of wage calculation, which was partly modeled on Fordist/Taylorist concepts of scientific management, together with greater supervision of labor, served to fragment the solidarity formerly generated by collective wage agreements and trade-union membership and to some extent cut across older hierarchies of skill and gender. Moreover, medical and welfare support was increasingly delivered by individual factories, which further served to tie the worker to his or her place of employment, while dissent within the "work community" could lead to the withdrawal of benefits and other forms of punishment. Whatever workers may have thought of these changes, they certainly made collective opposition increasingly difficult. However, that some workers drew advantage from increases in the number of jobs available and greater purchasing power is indisputable.

Although the changes described above did significantly reshape the experience of German labor, it is far from clear that a completely new labor force, untouched by older solidarities, was created in these years. In the first place, it is questionable that class identities and solidarities are forged by experiences on the shop floor alone, for there have always been divisions of skill and gender here. Secondly, the extent to which the new systems of payment created hierarchies genuinely different to older shop floor hierarchies needs to be investigated in relationship to different kinds of concerns and not only in the large and newest plants, which have formed the focal point of recent research. Thirdly, there is considerable evidence that processes of rationalization in German industry between 1933 and 1945 were extremely uneven. If anything, modernization in some sectors increased the difference between the new enterprises, for example in the aircraft and automobile industries, with their serial techniques of production, conveyor belts, and new buildings, and older concerns, which were much more difficult to reorganize according to Taylorist precepts.[3]

Together with full employment and rising real wages, the Nazi regime instituted a number of measures to increase worker loyalty to the regime. The "dignity of labor" and "German craftsmanship" were praised, and a national skills competition for younger workers proved very popular. Attempts were made to make factories lighter and less congested by the "Beauty of Work" organization; and May Day was declared a public holiday as the "Day of National Labor." Workers now received a second paid day of leave at Easter, longer vacations, and various benefits from the "Strength through Joy" leisure organization. This provided many German workers with decent leisure facilities and their first experience of holidays away from home. Just how successful these attempts were to seduce workers into the arms of Nazism is far from clear, however, and will be discussed later. What is undeniable is that this worker-friendly strategy was accompanied by a range of coercive measures.[4]

The leverage of the regime over workers, generated by new systems of payment, rationalization, and factory-based welfare, was further enhanced not only by the generally repressive nature of Nazi rule, but also by legislation relating specifically to labor. In June 1938 labor mobility was restricted and infringements of industrial discipline were criminalized. As a result, absenteeism or shirking at work could result in fines or imprisonment. A proliferation of labor camps emerged to discipline the "work-shy" and in 1939 one worker was actually hanged for persistent absenteeism. With the onset of World War II labor was subject to ever more restrictions.[5]

Simultaneously, the German working class was restructured, partly because of the geographical uprooting of millions of Germans and partly because of a new racial division of labor. The development of new centers of industrial production, such as the aircraft industry in Bremen and the *Reichswerke Hermann Göring* in Salzgitter, saw the recruitment of workers from all over Europe, as well as from different parts of the Reich. This brought into existence a new labor force without traditions of solidarity and segmented by new methods of payment. Migration, enforced by the Allied bombing of industrial centers, disrupted established residential and work communities, which had sometimes formed the basis of class solidarity. Moreover, workers could now be intimidated by the threats of employers to call in the Gestapo and were cut off from traditional forms of working-class socialization (labor clubs and unions), which the Nazis had destroyed. In consequence many workers concentrated on maximizing their earnings and thought in terms of individual strategies of advancement, especially as the prospect of both increased wages and upward mobility were increased by shortages of labor and the emergence of a racial underclass of foreign workers. By 1944 there were 7–8 million such *Fremdarbeiter* in the Reich. Italian, French, Dutch, and Scandinavian workers in German concerns were rewarded at rates roughly equivalent to those of German employees, but the bulk of the foreign work force (Russians and Poles) was treated most brutally. This racial restructuring of the labor force created significant opportunities of upward mobility for German workers, who might now find themselves in supervisory positions. Racial difference thus constituted one more factor which cut across class identity in the Third Reich and increased the mobility prospects of significant numbers of German workers.[6]

The issue of labor in the Third Reich was inextricably bound up with that of gender. That the Nazis had "traditional" attitudes towards female employment is well known. When they first came to power, they thought that women belonged in the home and adopted pronatalist policies for "healthy" Aryan women, who were encouraged to leave their places of paid employment, marry, and procreate through the provision of loans and subsidies. However, such policies were not as extensive as they might have been. For example, there were no mass firings of female employees, nor any laws passed against the hiring of women in or after 1933. Moreover, the National Socialist Women's Organization sought to prepare German women for paid employment, as well as for motherhood; and both the total number of women and the number of married women in paid employment in Germany continued to increase from 1933 to 1939, became significantly larger with the onset of war, and grew even larger from 1942–3, with a move towards total mobilization. In 1933 almost 5 million women worked outside the home. Six years later rising real wages and increasing labor shortage drew 7.14 million women into paid employment. This was another example of the partial conquest of ideological imperatives by economic logic. However, the industrial mobilization of women in the Third Reich continued to lag behind that in other industrial nations, even in the early years of the war, and the rise in the number of women in paid employment scarcely outstripped the overall growth of the arms economy. Significantly, the increased industrial employment of females between 1933 and 1939 was almost matched by an increase in the number of women taking up jobs in that most traditional of female economic roles, domestic service. Pressure from the DAF to pay women workers the same rates as their male colleagues and to move to the total mobilization of female labor in the war were repeatedly rebuffed by Hitler, even as late as 1942. Only in 1943 was the Führer forced to change his position. Even thereafter the largest increase in the number of female laborers in the Reich was provided by foreign females. Many German women seem to have tried to avoid conscription into the factories.[7]

Class, Mobility, Gender, and Race

From the above it is clear that the Nazis brought about no fundamental changes in property relations, except where Jews and foreign nationals were concerned. The profits of large corporations continued to grow and inequality was further compounded by both an increased gap between agrarian and industrial incomes and the new system of wage calculation, which increased inequalities of income within the German working class. The economic foundations of capitalist class relations (private ownership of the means of production, production for profit, and the commodification of labor) remained intact in Germany between 1933 and 1945. Workers remained workers and their bosses remained bosses. Moreover, the control of capital over labor was reinforced by the destruction of unions, the prohibition of strikes, and the disappearance of the traditional working-class parties (SPD and KPD), as well as by the changes on the factory floor described above. Yet, if Nazi Germany remained a capitalist society, it was one, nonetheless, in which various important aspects of social relations were transformed. This was the case, for example, as far as patterns of social mobility were concerned. It was true above all, however, in terms of race, which became the defining criterion of life chances in Nazi Germany and in the territories it occupied and plundered after 1939.

The Third Reich made deep inroads into the power and influence of the traditional German social elite. In the realm of politics, membership of the Nazi Party and not aristocratic birthright or worldly riches conferred advancement. The dismissals in the army, the foreign office, and the finance and economics administration in 1937–8 saw members of the German elite lose their positions to Nazis of lower social status. The army also witnessed a significant reduction of aristocratic influence in its ranks, though this process had already begun in the Weimar republic. The massive expansion of the German military and the events of war accelerated this change even further: of 166 infantry generals during the conflict, 140 came from middle-class families. Nazi vengeance after the abortive "Bomb Plot" of July 1944 hammered a further nail into the coffin of Junker power, for many of the 5,000 "conspirators" then executed came from the most famous families of the German aristocracy. The expansion of the German army and the experience of war did far more than rid the military of Junker dominance, however. For vast numbers of Germans from all walks of life, including many former "workers," military service now constituted the crucial life experience, in which traditional social divisions paled into insignificance beside the imperative of survival. World War II became the crucible of change, as the possibilities of plunder in eastern Europe opened up for many "ordinary Germans" apparently endless opportunities for advancement and enrichment. It remained true in Nazi Germany that most academics, university students, diplomats, senior civil servants, and leading businessmen were recruited from a very restricted elite. Only 1 percent of university students in 1939, for example, came from working-class homes. Yet new avenues of social mobility did arise; and not only in the army. The massive proliferation of Nazi Party agencies created a huge number of jobs, access to which was determined by political or racial and not social criteria. As early as 1935 some 25,000 Germans received salaries from the NSDAP. Subsequently the expansion of the DAF, the NSF, the Hitler Youth, and the League of German Maidens provided more employment opportunities, through which politically reliable Germans could escape from their humble origins. Göring's Office of the Four Year Plan gave jobs to over 10,000 people, while Himmler's SS grew to monstrous proportions. By 1944 there were 40,000 concentration camp guards (though many of these were non-Germans), 45,000 officers of the Gestapo, 100,000 police informers, and 2.8 million policemen. Death and destruction, brutality and plunder thus created a space for individual Germans to improve their life chances at the expense of the defeated, the occupied, and the exploited; and it is this that makes various forms of complicity with the regime comprehensible. Traditional social cleavages were also dissolved by the evacuations and bombings of wartime, which threw Germans from different regions and backgrounds together, and by the racial reordering of society. As already indicated, "racially superior" German workers now found themselves in supervisory positions over millions of foreigners. It has also been argued that class identity became less significant in determining the fate of Germans than other factors. These included whether or not one was sent to the front, whether one was on the western or the eastern front, and whether or not one lived in an area subject to Allied bombing. For some commentators, such developments eroded earlier traditions of working-class solidarity.

The opening up of mobility chances and the reduction of the power of the traditional elites has been seen as a fundamental moment in the history of German society. For the sociologist Ralf Dahrendorf, this denoted the modernization of German social relations, though in his view this was an unintended by-product of Nazi rule, a consequence of economic imperatives, labor shortage, and above all World War II, which frustrated the anti-modern (anti-industrial, anti-urban, anti-feminist) sentiments of the leading National Socialists. For Rainer Zitelmann and Michael Prinz, on the other hand, the modernization of Germany was the intended consequence of the modernizing vision of Hitler and the German Labor Front. According to Zitelmann, Hitler was an advocate of "equal opportunity," with a strong desire to exalt the manual worker and increase his social standing at the expense of the materialistic bourgeois. In his view the Führer was a Keynesian modernizer, an advocate of an industrial and consumerist society, and a prototypical social engineer. Hence his enthusiasm for the People's Radio and the People's Car. Prinz paints a similar picture of the DAF, stressing its enthusiasm for modern technology, industrial rationalization, the emergence of functional rather than status elites, and a sweeping program of public welfare. Now it is true that one can find various remarks in the totality of Hitler's writings and speeches that are amenable to Zitelmann's interpretation. However, compared to the centrality of race in those writings and speeches, such remarks are few and far between. In fact Zitelmann confuses ends and means in Hitler's *Weltanschauung*. War and racial hygiene were the goals, which in passing brought about significant social change, rather than the other way round. In any case, even if Hitler did make complimentary remarks about manual labor, he also sent reassuring noises to big business, which reaped far more benefits from Nazi rule than did the German working class. Much as Hitler may have been keen on *Autobahnen*, cars, and airplanes, no "modern consumerist society" came into existence in the Third Reich. Economic policy favored armaments, not consumers. The great majority of German workers remained workers, even if limited mobility chances offered themselves, and even though they were better off than the slave laborers they often supervised. In any case this supposedly "modern society" rested upon the barbarous exploitation and plunder of non-Aryan capital and labor. It was only "open" for "healthy Aryans." The increase in mobility chances was not universal and social position was not determined by function alone. For economic inequality, racial discrimination, and political correctness directly affected the life chances of millions of German citizens. Nazi Party members and sympathizers might do well and experience rising living standards, but social democrats and communists suffered persecution and a reduction in their job prospects, unless they converted to the gospel of Nazism. Jews, Gypsies, "asocials," the incurably ill, alcoholics, mental patients, Freemasons, Jehovah's Witnesses, and gays were also excluded from the benefits of this "modernity." All of which suggests that modernity was not what the Third Reich was about.

Racial and political imperatives subverted the emergence of a society genuinely open to talent. Similar points can be made about the plans of the German Labor Front, which were continuously thwarted by opposition from Hitler, as in the case of pleas for the total mobilization of women.[8]

The extent to which Nazi rule transformed the role of women is hotly contested. The Third Reich did remove women from significant posts in the German government and administration. Where women were active in public life, they were expected to be so in specifically female agencies. Early initiatives of the regime to persuade married women to abandon employment outside the home, as well as the provision of marriage loans to encourage single women to remain at home and procreate, seemed to reinforce the traditional segregation of male and female roles. They certainly fitted ill with images of modernity. The closure of birth control clinics, attempts to restrict access to contraceptives, and the prohibition of abortion pointed in the same direction. However, the "pronatalist" policies of National Socialist Germany did see significant extensions of pre- and postnatal care, as well as other forms of mothers' welfare and family allowances. These have been seen as a more "modern" aspect of gender relations in Nazi Germany. So have the increased employment of women outside the home, the fact that the NSF sought to prepare German women for work as well as motherhood, and the rise in the percentage of university students who were female: from 17 percent of the student body in 1933 to 40 percent in 1940. There was also an increase in the percentage of female German doctors: from 6 percent in 1930 to 8 percent in 1939.

Nevertheless, the Third Reich did not deliberately modernize gender relations. In the first place Hitler resisted the total mobilization of female labor until economic imperatives forced him to recant in 1942–3. He also opposed the equalization of male and female wages. On the shop floor of the factories they entered, women still did not fill skilled, supervisory, or managerial posts. Increases in the numbers of female doctors and students were chiefly a consequence of the drafting of males into the Labor Service and the armed forces. Secondly, the "pronatalist" and welfare policies of the regime were dominated by considerations of racial hygiene. Female Jews, Gypsies, asocials, the incurably ill, and chronic alcoholics were excluded from the welfare system and from entitlement to marriage loans, making it clear that the logic of Nazi welfare was not care but racial selection. Women (and some men) in the categories listed above were subject to a program of compulsory sterilization, which involved some 400,000 victims. According to Gisela Bock, Nazi racial policy actually turned women into the "prime victims" of the Nazi era. If women were "healthy" and Aryan, the Nazi regime deprived them of control over their own bodies by making abortion and contraception illegal. If they were "unhealthy" or "non-Aryan," they were forcibly sterilized or shipped to concentration and extermination camps.

Needless to say, Bock's view that women were invariably "victims" of the Third Reich has not gone uncontested. Aryan women were clearly superior to non-Aryan men in both Nazi ideology and reality. Women denounced their fellow Germans to the Gestapo, just like their male counterparts. Moreover, as Claudia Koonz points out, significant numbers of German women were complicit in the sustenance of the regime's objectives. They did breed for the Fatherland, rear Germany's soldiers, and care for their Nazi menfolk. Nazi women's organizations were hugely popular, though rarely for ideological reasons; and many young German girls even experienced their time in the League of Maidens as a liberation from parental control. It should also be noted that many women participated – as nurses, doctors, welfare professionals, and even concentration camp guards – in the campaigns of sterilization, euthanasia, and extermination. There was no single female fate under Nazism.

To return to the theme of gender and modernization, although a new Marriage Law made divorce easier, it did so primarily for men, who could now dissolve their marriages on the new grounds of race or physical and mental infirmity, rather than for women. Again, therefore, the clear imperative was racial hygiene rather than any identification with "modern" social trends. Furthermore, divorce by mutual agreement was not permitted by Nazi legislation; and most of the grounds for divorce, apart from those relating to racial hygiene, remained the same as before in both law and practice.[9]

Although few aspects of social existence were fundamentally transformed between 1933 and 1945, in one area of social engineering the Nazis did realize radical goals and did so with enormous violence: that of race. It has become increasingly clear that the "racial hygiene" campaign of the Third Reich touched virtually all aspects of life, including the delivery of welfare, the treatment of criminals, and relations at work and in the family. The aim of creating a racially pure "People's Community," purged of "unhealthy" and "alien" elements, intruded into the lives of Germans in a multitude of ways. All those deemed by the Nazis to be "of no biological value," "useless eaters," and "community aliens" were to be removed from the *Volksgemeinschaft*. Political opponents (communists and social democrats) experienced terror at the hands of local Nazis in the spring and early summer of 1933. Many were subsequently moved into concentration camps. Others, whose loyalties were deemed suspect (Freemasons, Jehovah's Witnesses), suffered a similar fate. From 1936–7 onwards, however, other "outsiders," whose problems were held by the Nazis to be genetically determined, were carted off to camps or subject to various forms of medical intervention. These groups included "asocials" (the homeless, tramps, prostitutes, the "work-shy"), "hereditary criminals" (deemed predisposed to a life of crime by their genes), and homosexuals. Until 1939 relatively few of these "community aliens" had been killed, but the onset of war radicalized their treatment, especially after 1941. Now some were shot, given lethal injections, subject to medical experiments, worked to death, and transported to the death camps.

Programs of genetic engineering were also unleashed on those the Nazis held to be "unhealthy." The term "hereditarily ill" was used by the regime to describe a large number of people: "the congenitally feeble-minded," "schizophrenics," "manic depressives," "chronic alcoholics," those with serious physical deformities, and sufferers from Huntington's chorea, hereditary blindness, and deafness. Welfare support was removed from such people, many of whom (some 320,000 Germans) were forcibly sterilized. Dangerous criminals were not infrequently castrated and all prisoners held in the Reich were subject to medical testing. The most infamous example of Nazi inhumanity towards its own sick was the so-called "euthanasia" campaign, in which over 70,000 mentally ill and physically impaired Germans were murdered.

Outside the Reich the Nazi racial program had further consequences. In the areas under German occupation in the east the allocation of land, material resources, and power followed a clear racial hierarchy. Germans plundered whatever they wanted without regard to the needs of the Slavic populations, millions of whom were forced into servile labor both inside and outside the boundaries of the Reich. Furthermore, the regime embarked on a policy of racial resettlement ("ethnic cleansing") in Poland, in which Poles and Jews were transported out of areas to be settled by ethnic Germans. Most notoriously of all, Nazism attempted to exterminate European Jews and Gypsies, a story told elsewhere in this volume.[10]

A German Identity?

There is yet another perspective from which the issue of social change under Nazi rule may be addressed: to what extent did the regime succeed in changing the attitudes and identities of its citizens? Even if inequalities of wealth and income continued, was it still not possible that the Third Reich oversaw the destruction of traditional group identities and created a united German consciousness? We have long known that some aspects of the Nazi regime and its policies were popular: foreign policy successes before 1939, speedy military victories between 1939 and 1941, and the conquest of unemployment, as well as the restoration of "law and order," "traditional family values," and national greatness, and the repression of social democrats and communists. Recent literature has taken this picture of approval even further. On the basis of oral history testimony, which remembers the peacetime years of the Third Reich as quiet and prosperous; of the huge numbers who flocked to join Nazi organizations; of the participation of many "ordinary" Germans in the implementation of Nazi racial policy; and of the fact that a significant number of the Reich's citizens were prepared to denounce their workmates, neighbors, and even family members to the Gestapo, it has been argued that the regime rested on the consent of its citizens, or that at the very least most Germans were prepared to accommodate themselves to that regime.[11] Research on the Saarland has claimed that distinctive Catholic and working-class identities were overridden by this process, while Nazi success in winning the loyalty of industrial workers has been stressed by a number of studies.[12]

While it is certain that the Third Reich had a great deal of support, a generalized concept of consent is problematical on a number of counts. Firstly, the reports of both the Gestapo and the SPD in Exile make it quite clear that the popularity of some aspects of the regime was matched by the unpopularity of others. Hitler enjoyed widespread public support, but the Nazi Party was loathed. Foreign policy successes without war were popular, but German public opinion was not in favor of another war before 1939. Attacks on communists appealed to many, but this did not apply to attacks on the churches.[13] Moreover, the concept of consent needs to be differentiated. Consider, for example, the experience and attitudes of the working class under Nazism. The worker-friendly discourse of the regime and the removal of unemployment may have had a positive impact on some workers, while new systems of payment, the creation of workforces in new industries and places, industrial rationalization, and the racial restructuring of the labor force may have undermined traditional structures of class solidarity. However, some workers, who had been unemployed in the Depression, could still be found complaining that they earned less in 1938 than in 1929. The individualization of pay packets may have been supported by young and energetic workers, but others denounced the new working practices. In any case, it is questionable whether living standards provide a key to class identity and solidarity.

The factory floor and worker solidarity were not as transformed by technological rationalization as some would have us believe. This may have been true of the largest companies, which have been the focus of scholarly attention, but it was far from true across the whole of German industry, where a lack of uniformity was the most striking characteristic. In any case, even if shop-floor hierarchies had been transformed, the impact this would have had on class identity is far from clear. For thirty years labor historians have become increasingly insistent that solidarities are rarely formed on the shop floor – or at least on the shop floor alone – but rather by factors exogenous to the labor process. For in the factory there have always been differential systems of skill and reward that have had the potential to divide rather than unite interests. This takes us into the most important reason for doubting that the identity of the German working class was unequivocally transformed by Nazism: there never was a single, monolithic, German working class. Different groups of workers had different histories and identities – of occupation, skill, religion, race, gender, region, ideology – which cut across or undermined the solidarity of class long before 1933. The experience of mass and long-term unemployment had done a great deal to fracture, demobilize, and demoralize German labor before the Nazi seizure of power: a united working class was and remained a fantasy.

This diversity of working-class experience and identity did not disappear after 1933. Where class loyalties had never been strong, as in the Saarland, or where labor forces were new, as in the aircraft industry of Bremen, or where workers possessed strong nationalist traditions, as at Krupp in Essen, it is not surprising that class identity is difficult to find. That letters from former workers serving on the front tell us little about class identity is also scarcely surprising in the context of a brutal conflict, in which the distinction between Germans and the enemy was bound to dominate. Perhaps most crucially, class identity has never been easy to forge across skill, occupational, gender, and generational divides. Solidarity was never a given; it had to be created by the agencies of the labor movement (parties, unions, social clubs). In this context the complete destruction of the institutions of the German labor movement and the incarceration of its leaders by the Nazis was crucial. It robbed labor of a collective voice and an institutional backbone of solidarity. In the absence of these, many workers retreated into a privatized existence; and in this context such a retreat (or even collusion with the regime) may be better understood as opportunistic survival strategies rather than the result of ideological affinity. We know that many joined the NSDAP to get or keep jobs, for example, and that most denunciations to the Gestapo were inspired by self-interested and non-ideological motives. These actions certainly constituted collusion with the regime. Whether they can be construed as consent, however, is a different matter, for consent can only be measured where historical actors can choose between real alternatives without detriment to themselves. No such choice existed in the Third Reich, not least because of terror and persecution.

Recent literature has played down the Nazi terror, pointing out that there were relatively few Gestapo officers and violence was targeted at specific "outsiders" rather than the German people as a whole. Though true, these observations miss the point; for those "outsiders" included that 30 percent or more of the German electorate, which had voted "left" (for the SPD or KPD) in virtually every German election between 1912 and 1932. Against this group terror was exercised not only by the

Gestapo but by the SA and Nazi Party thugs, as in the spring and early summer of 1933, when large numbers of social democrats and communists were carted off to "wild" concentration camps, where they were beaten, tortured, or murdered. Between 1933 and 1945, 150,000 KPD members were "detained" in prisons or concentration camps and 42,000 communists were murdered. The destruction of the SA leadership in 1934 and the antisemitic pogrom of November 1938 offered further examples of what any opponent of the regime might expect. These – as well as the concentration camps, the absence of civil liberties, and the destruction of independent institutions – set the context in which Germans had to live and work between 1933 and 1945. The context was further radicalized in the later stages of World War II. In the first half of 1943 alone, 982 Germans were convicted of treason, of whom 948 were executed. At the same time almost 9,000 were charged with left-wing activity, 8,727 with "resistance," and just over 11,000 with "opposition." A further 10,773 were arrested for fraternizing with foreign workers and prisoners of war.

The significance of this repressive context for the behavior of Germans was made clear by developments when that context was removed. After 1945 trade union, socialist, and even communist organizations reappeared with remarkable rapidity, indicating the continued existence of older group solidarities. The 1949 national election in West Germany has also been described as the last Weimar election, with both Catholic and socialist camps surviving the Nazi onslaught. Subsequently, the combination of the Cold War and Germany's "economic miracle" created a new politics. This transition, however, may also have been a consequence of generational change, in which Nazism did play a major role. Though an older generation may have returned to pre-Nazi identities after 1945, the younger generation, which grew up under Nazi rule, was cut off from those traditions and subject to a distinct, homogeneous, and pervasive socialization. This new generation produced the individualist and income-maximizing workers of the "economic miracle."[14]

NOTES

1   For the original Nazi Party program and examples of Nazi electoral promises, see Jeremy Noakes and Geoffrey Pridham, eds, *Nazism 1919–1945*, vol. 1 (Exeter: University of Exeter Press, 1983), pp. 14–16, 70–81. On the contradictions of Nazi economic promises, see Henry Ashby Turner, *German Big Business and the Rise of Hitler* (New York: Oxford University Press, 1985), pp. 60–71.

2   On the Nazi economy, see Noakes and Pridham *Nazism*, vol. 2: *State, Economy and Society 1933–1939* (Exeter: University of Exeter Press, 1984); Tim Mason, *Social Policy in the Third Reich* (Providence RI: Berg, 1993); Richard Overy, *The Nazi Economic Recovery*, 2nd edn (Cambridge: Cambridge University Press, 1996); Richard Overy, *War and Economy in the Third Reich* (Oxford: Oxford University Press, 1994); Harold James, *The German Slump* (Oxford: Oxford University Press, 1986); Volker Berghahn, *The Americanisation of the German Economy* (Leamington Spa: Berg, 1986); John Gillingham, *Industry and Politics in the Third Reich* (London: Methuen, 1985); Neil Gregor, *Daimler Benz in the Third Reich* (New Haven CT: Yale University Press, 1998); Arthur Schweitzer, *Big Business in the Third Reich* (London: Eyre and Spottiswoode, 1964); Daniel P. Silverman, *Hitler's Economy* (Cambridge MA: Harvard University Press, 1998). On the

exploitation of foreign labor, see Ulrich Herbert, *Hitler's Foreign Workers* (Cambridge: Cambridge University Press, 1998). On the modernization thesis, see Rainer Zitelmann, *Hitler: Selbstverständnis eines Revolutionärs* (Leamington Spa: Berg, 1987); Michael Prinz, *Vom neuen Mittelstand zum Volksgenossen* (Munich: Oldenbourg, 1986); Michael Prinz and Rainer Zitelmann, eds, *Nationalsozialismus und Modernisierung* (Darmstadt: Wissenschaftliche Buchgesellschaft, 1991); Mark Roseman, "National Socialism and Modernisation," in *Fascist Italy and Nazi Germany*, Richard Bessel, ed. (Cambridge: Cambridge University Press, 1996), pp. 196–229. On agriculture, see Gustavo Corni, *Hitler and the Peasants* (Oxford: Oxford University Press, 1990) and John G. Farquharson, *The Plough and the Swastika* (London: Sage, 1976).

3   For a continuous index of real wages, see Gerhard Bry, *Wages in Germany* (Princeton NJ: Princeton University Press, 1966); Mason, *Social Policy*, p. 132 and the statistical appendix of Tim Mason, *Arbeiterklasse und Volksgemeinschaft* (Opladen: Westdeutscher Verlag, 1975). On living standards, see also Noakes and Pridham, *Nazism*, vol. 2, pp. 349, 370–1; Günther Morsch, *Arbeit und Brot* (Frankfurt am Main: Peter Lang 1993); Overy, *Recovery*, pp. 26–31. On rationalization, see Tilla Siegel, *Leistung und Lohn in der nationalsozialistischen "Ordnung der Arbeit"* (Opladen: Westdeutscher Verlag, 1989); Rüdiger Hachtmann, *Industriearbeit im Dritten Reich* (Göttingen: Vandenhoeck and Ruprecht, 1989); Tilla Siegel and Thomas von Freyberg, *Industrielle Rationalisierung unter dem Nationalsozialismus* (Frankfurt am Main: Campus Verlag 1991); Tilla Siegel, "Rationalizing Industrial Relations," in *Reevaluating the Third Reich*, Thomas Childers and Jane Kaplan, eds (New York: Holmes and Meier, 1993), pp. 139–60; Overy, *War and Economy*, pp. 343–75. On the limits of rationalization, see Alf Lüdtke, "The 'Honour of Labour'," in *Nazism and German Society*, David Crew, ed. (London: Routledge, 1984), pp. 67–109; and Morsch, *Arbeit*, which stresses the diversity of workers' working and living conditions. On the diversities of working-class identities and what shapes them, see Dick Geary, "Working-Class Identities in Europe, 1850s–1930s," *Australian Journal of Politics and History* 45 (1999): 20–34.

4   See Lüdtke, "Honour of Labour"; Noakes and Pridham, *Nazism*, vol. 2, pp. 331–2, 346–53; Stephen Salter, "Structures of Consent and Coercion," in *Nazi Propaganda*, David Welch, ed. (Beckenham: Croom Helm, 1983).

5   See Noakes and Pridham, *Nazism*, vol. 2, pp. 369–73; Matthias Frese, *Betriebspolitik im Dritten Reich* (Paderborn: Schöningh, 1991); Mason, *Social Policy*, p. 141; Carola Sachse et al., eds, *Angst, Belohnung, Zucht und Ordnung* (Opladen: Westdeutscher Verlag, 1982).

6   Herbert, *Foreign Workers;* Noakes and Pridham, *Nazism*, vol. 4: *The German Home Front in World War II* (Exeter: University of Exeter Press, 1998), pp. 247, 359–65.

7   On women under Nazism, see Mary Nolan, "Work, Gender and Everyday Life," in Crew, *German Society*, pp. 311–42; Dagmar Reese et al., eds, *Rationale Beziehungen? Geschlechtsverhältnisse im Rationalisierungsprozess* (Frankfurt am Main: Suhrkamp, 1993); Carole Sachse, *Siemens, Nationalsozialismus und die moderne Familie* (Hamburg: Rasch and Röhring, 1990); Renate Bridenthal, Anita Grossmann, and Marion Kaplan, eds, *When Biology became Destiny* (New York: Monthly Review Press, 1984); Claudia Koonz, *Mothers in the Fatherland* (New York: St Martin's Press, 1987); Adelheid von Saldern, "Victims or Perpetrators," in Crew, *German Society*, pp. 141–65; Anita Grossmann, "Feminist Debates about Women and National Socialism," *Gender and History* 3 (1991): 350–8; Tim Mason, "Women in Germany, 1925–1940," in *Nazism, Fascism and the Working Class* (Cambridge: Cambridge University Press, 1995), pp. 131–211; Gabriele Czarnowski, "The Value of Marriage for the *Volksgemeinschaft*," in Bessel, *Fascist Italy and Nazi Germany*, pp. 94–112; Noakes and Pridham, *Nazism*, vol. 4, p. 247; Shaaron Cosner and Victoria Cosner, *Women under the Third Reich* (Westport CT: Greenwood Press, 1997);

Matthew Stibbe, *Women in the Third Reich* (London: Arnold, 2003); Lisa Pine, *Nazi Family Policy* (Oxford: Berg, 1997); Elizabeth Heinemann, *What Difference Does a Husband Make?* (Berkeley: University of California Press, 2003); Jill Stephenson, *The Nazi Organisation of Women* (London: Croom Helm, 1981); Jill Stephenson, *Women in Nazi Germany* (London: Longman/Pearson, 2001); Karen Hagemann and Stefanie Schüler Springorum, *Home/Front: The Military, War and Gender in Twentieth-Century Germany* (Oxford: Berg, 2002).

8 See Michael Geyer, "Restorative Elites, German Society and the Nazi Pursuit of War," in Bessel, *Fascist Italy and Nazi Germany*, pp. 134–64; Ralf Dahrendorf, *Society and Democracy in Germany* (London: Weidenfeld and Nicolson, 1966). For Zitelmann and Prinz, see note 2. See also Roseman, "National Socialism and Modernisation."

9 See note 7 above.

10 See Jeremy Noakes, "Social Outcasts in the Third Reich," in *Life in the Third Reich*, Richard Bessel, ed. (Oxford: Oxford University Press, 1987), pp. 83–96; Michael Berenbaum, ed., *Mosaic of Victims* (New York: New York University Press, 1990); Michael Burleigh and Wolfgang Wippermann, *The Racial State* (Cambridge: Cambridge University Press, 1993); Michael Burleigh, *Death and Deliverance* (Cambridge: Cambridge University Press, 1994); Robert Gellateley and Nathan Stolzfuss, eds, *Social Outsiders in Nazi Germany* (Princeton NJ: Princeton University Press, 2002).

11 See Robert Gellately, *Backing Hitler: Consent and Coercion in Nazi Germany* (Oxford: Oxford University Press, 2001); Eric Johnson, *The Nazi Terror* (New York: Basic Books, 1999).

12 See Klaus Michael-Mallmann and Gerhard Paul, *Herrschaft und Alltag* (Bonn: J. H. W. Dietz, 1991); Inge Marsollek and René Ott, *Bremen im Dritten Reich* (Bremen: C. Schünemann, 1986); Herbert, *Foreign Workers*; Alf Lüdtke, "The Appeal of Exterminating Others," in *The Third Reich*, Christian Leitz, ed. (Oxford: Blackwell, 1999); Alf Lüdtke, ed., *The History of Everyday Life* (Princeton NJ: Princeton University Press, 1995), esp. "What Happened to the Fiery Red Glow?" pp. 198–251; Lüdtke, "Honour of Labour."

13 For variations in public opinion by policy, time, and place, see Ian Kershaw's seminal *Popular Opinion and Political Dissent in the Third Reich* (Oxford: Clarendon Press, 1983).

14 For a much more extensive account of this argument about the German working class under Nazism, with detailed references, see Dick Geary, "Working-Class Identities in the Third Reich," in *Nazism, War and Genocide: Essays in Honour of Jeremy Noakes*, Neil Gregor, ed. (Exeter: University of Exeter Press, 2005). On labor in the immediate postwar years, see Dick Geary, "Social Protest in the Ruhr, 1945–49," in *A Social History of Central European Politics, 1945–52*, Eleonore Breuning, Jill Lewis, and Gareth Pritchard, eds (Manchester: Manchester University Press, 2005). On the significance of generation, see Roseman, "National Socialism and Modernisation," p. 224.

GUIDE TO FURTHER READING

Richard Bessel, ed., *Fascist Italy and Nazi Germany* (Cambridge: Cambridge University Press, 1996). Contains important articles on class and gender.

Renate Bridenthal et al., eds, *When Biology Became Destiny* (New York: Monthly Review Press, 1984). Contains significant contributions on gender in Weimar and Nazi Germany.

Michael Burleigh, *The Third Reich: A New History* (London: Macmillan, 2000). Often brilliant, sometimes wayward, has relatively little to say on economy and social change.

Michael Burleigh and Wolfgang Wippermann, *The Racial State* (Cambridge: Cambridge University Press, 1993). Seminal in underlining the significance of racial policy for all areas of life.

David Crew, ed., *Nazism and German Society* (London: Routledge, 1994). Contains many significant contributions on class, gender, consent, and coercion in the Third Reich.

Dick Geary, *Hitler and Nazism*, 2nd edn (London: Routledge, 2000). A brief, basic survey.

Robert Gellately, *Backing Hitler* (Oxford: Oxford University Press, 2001). Goes further than other historians in claiming popular support for the regime.

Ulrich Herbert, *Hitler's Foreign Workers* (Cambridge: Cambridge University Press, 1998). An important study of the racial reorganization of the German working class and the latter's treatment of foreign labor.

Eric Johnson, *The Nazi Terror* (New York: Basic Books, 1999). A subtle study of the interaction between coercion and consent.

Ian Kershaw, Hitler, *Popular Opinion and Political Dissent in the Third Reich* (Oxford: Oxford University Press, 1983). A seminal and nuanced account of public opinion under Nazism.

Ian Kershaw, *Hitler*, 2 vols (London: Allen Lane, 1998/2000). The definitive biography that contains a host of insights into all aspects of the Third Reich.

Ian Kershaw, *The Nazi Dictatorship*, 4th edn (London, Allen Lane, 2000). By far the best summary of historical debates about Nazi rule.

Claudia Koonz, *Mothers in the Fatherland* (New York: St Martin's Press, 1987). Sees female collusion with Nazi aims.

Christian Leitz, ed., *The Third Reich* (Oxford: Blackwell, 1999). Another collection of useful essays.

Tim Mason, *Social Policy in the Third Reich* (Providence RI: Berg, 1993). An often brilliant though problematical account of labor in Nazi Germany.

Jeremy Noakes and Geoffrey Pridham, eds, *Nazism 1919–1945: A Documentary Reader*, 4 vols (Exeter: University of Exeter Press, 1998). By far the best English-language collection of sources with incisive commentary.

Richard Overy, *The Nazi Economic Recovery*, 2nd edn (London: Macmillan, 1996). Brief, clear, and convincing.

Detlev Peukert, *Inside Nazi Germany* (New Haven CT: Yale University Press, 1987). Contains interesting material on non-conformity.

David Schoenbaum, *Hitler's Social Revolution* (New York: Doubleday, 1966). An early claim that the Nazis succeeded in changing German society, at least as far as status and subjective consciousness were concerned.

Rainer Zitelmann, *Hitler: The Policies of Seduction* (London: London House, 1998). The classic statement of the view that Hitler was a "modernizer."

CHAPTER TWENTY-FOUR

The Popular Front

MICHAEL RICHARDS

The gradual but very public erosion of democratic principles in Italy after 1922 and the rapid curtailment of all vestiges of the democratic Weimar republic in Germany from 1933 were huge setbacks to the cause of the political left across Europe. The rise of authoritarianism undermined social peace and liberalism as the foundations of progress. For many reasons it proved impossible during the 1920s and early 1930s to secure a unified political program that would be effective in resisting the rise of Nazism. Historians have speculated, with good reason, that left-liberal unity might have prevented Hitler coming to power, thereby avoiding war in 1939. Generally, however, they have concluded that the depth of the political divisions within the left in Germany between 1918 and 1933 is to a significant degree explicable through the seismic fracturing of German society itself. Most obviously, divisions were exacerbated by mass unemployment following the great economic Crash of October 1929. In the end, the political left could have done little to prevent the economic and social crisis that heralded Nazi rule.

Nonetheless, Hitler's seizure of power was the great turning point in the balance of power between fascism and its opponents in Europe. The closest the political left in Europe came to an effective strategy of unified anti-fascist action in the wake of this accession to power was the series of written agreements, joint actions, electoral platforms, and – briefly, in France and Spain – governmental authority, assumed under the broad banner of the Popular Front. At a formal level, the Popular Front constituted an alliance of political parties, including Marxists, socialists, liberals, moderates, and even some conservatives, representing a common defense against and rejection of fascism.[1] The electoral victories of the French and Spanish coalitions of 1936 were its greatest achievements, but the Popular Front was more than a political pact. The propaganda posters produced in its name illustrated both the need to defend the French Third Republic (1870–1940) and the Spanish Second Republic (1931–9), and the modernizing and popular aspects of the Front's struggle against fascism. Such images represented collective desires to bring about social and cultural change, to preserve international peace, and attack the causes and symptoms of economic crisis.

These positive aims have, however, to be set beside the undoubted failings of the Popular Front. The negation of fascism – though it contained within it a positive promotion of peace, democracy, and an end to hunger – would ultimately prove a rather weak basis for unity. The effects of the far-reaching social legislation enacted by Popular Front governments in France and Spain were severely constrained by the advance of the fascist threat, by economic circumstances, and by the internal differences within the Front itself. The menacing pursuit of expansionism in Fascist and Nazi foreign policy posed a grave threat also to *international* peace. Popular Frontism was unable to develop an active and effective alternative to the policy of appeasement of Nazism pursued by the major democracies. The Front proved incapable of becoming a political focus of collective security largely because such a strategy was associated by the democracies with the interests of communist Russia. The domestic, social, and international threats combined, relatively unhindered, therefore, as fundamental causes of World War II.

Mass Politics in 1930s Europe

In his monumental study of British writers during the 1930s, the cultural commentator Valentine Cunningham has argued that never previously, "not even in the Victorian 'age of great cities,' had people been so conscious that modern industrialised, urbanised life was mass life . . . Inescapably, the post-First-World-War sensibility had to grasp that it was in an age of mass-production, mass-demonstrations, mass-meetings, mass sporting occasions, mass-communications, mass-armies, a time when things would be done in, and to, and for crowds."[2] The rise and fall of democracy in Europe during the interwar years can be charted in the attempts by democratic and anti-democratic movements to absorb and channel the economic and political demands of this mass society. These demands were imperfectly met by politicizing growing areas of everyday experience in the 1930s.

While the late nineteenth-century extension of the franchise saw the arrival of mass politics, the sacrifices of the war of 1914–18 had been made possible through mass conscription and made real through mass "industrialized" slaughter. "Total war" provided more than enough justification to the soldiers, workers, and producers for radicalizing their collective idea of what democracy was. At the same time, war seemed to threaten bourgeois morality on the home front. The threat to the "life-blood of nations" represented by the human losses of the war heightened fears of degeneration and decline and hardened middle-class doubts about modernity.

War and revolution led to unprecedented upheaval and a new and precarious political balance in Europe. But in this mass age the forms that politics took depended on other influences in public life that were not directly political. Intellectual, moral, economic, and religious life also reflected and responded to the arrival of the masses. Collective habits, fashions, and means of entertainment and amusement – radio and cinema, the expansion of the mass media – all channeled the great dynamism of Europe in the 1920s. In urban Europe, the private sphere of family merged with the political sphere in struggles, for example, over the public consumption and growth of leisure in the interwar years.

The conditions of daily life for many Europeans in the 1930s were noticeably different even to those pertaining as recently as the 1890s. This fast-changing cultural landscape interacted with the requirements of political mobilization and manipulation. Exhortations were made to the masses to consume both goods and ideas. Politics became *mass* politics – quasi-theatrical and often polarized and violent. It is perhaps because of this new overlap between politics and other forms of mass public behavior – and because of the unprecedented depth and breadth of the effects of the economic crisis – that people seemed so susceptible to political myths during the 1930s.

The Popular Front theoretically linked two significant social forces: bourgeois liberals and the working class. Progressive liberals, guided by the principles of the Enlightenment and the French revolution, were disaffected by the conservative turn of bourgeois politics when confronted with the demands of the masses at the end of the nineteenth century and were horrified by World War I. To all of those who thought about such things, the enormous political potential and incipient threat of massing crowds were obvious. Liberals optimistically believed that demands from below could be directed through enlightened "tutelage" and measures of reform.

This sense of directing the popular will was epitomized by Manuel Azaña, liberal architect of the Spanish Popular Front in 1935–6. The Spanish Second Republic had been proclaimed in 1931, chiefly by the popular classes represented by a coalition of republicans and socialists. By the mid-1930s the Republic was in danger of succumbing to anti-democratic forces, as had already happened in Germany and Austria. Azaña, middle-class intellectual, reluctant political leader, and no advocate of proletarian revolution, set out to return Spain to the original reforming spirit of the democratically elected republican–socialist coalition of 1931. A central part of the rallying of "the republican masses" was his open-air speech at Comillas (Madrid) in October 1935, delivered to what was possibly the largest crowd that any European politician had ever mobilized without recourse to paramilitary methods.[3] Before some half a million supporters Azaña called for a democratic "redemption of the Republic" based on resistance to authoritarianism and fascism. He recognized explicitly the great potential power of the masses as a positive moral force: "I have no fears of the popular torrent, nor that it will overwhelm us; the question is to know how to guide it so that we do not allow this enormous popular force to lose its way or be wasted or ruined."[4]

The sense of channeling the will of the people directly echoed the liberal philosopher José Ortega y Gasset who, in his *Rebelión de las masas* of 1930, argued that since the masses had become the dominant social force, it was imperative that they could not be left to "direct their own personal experience," and still less that they should "preside over society in general."[5] This problematic notion of *direction* was intrinsic to Popular Front unity and its program of reform in Spain on the eve of the civil war in 1936.

While this synergy of liberals and masses was idealistic enough, other European intellectuals were captivated by a more romantic idea of moral self-regeneration through integration with "the masses" by joining the communist movement. The English poet Stephen Spender typified this experience. He later explained that his 1937 book, *Forward from Liberalism*, was aimed at people who cared for progress and peace rather than reaction and imperialist aggression: "I believed that if the implications of this attitude of mind were clearly stated many liberal individualists would find themselves set on a path which would lead them ultimately to the idea

of the classless international society and to an acceptance of the action necessary –
such as the formation of a United Front – to achieve that society."[6]

The masses, often favoring socializing measures that radically altered the balance
of economic power, took the proletarian Russian revolution of 1917 as an example
rather than the bourgeois French revolution of 1789, and were not always willing to
be directed. In an era of modern economic and social crisis, the very basis of cross-
class alliances was to be constantly and severely challenged.

The Origins of the Popular Front

For over a decade prior to Hitler's grasp for power, leftist leaders and analysts – many
of them direct participants in the political struggle – wrestled to determine the causes
of generic fascism. How had Mussolini's regime been able to sustain itself once power
had been seized, and what was the likelihood of its spread to other states? Marxist
analysis, specifically, had a further purpose: to provide an impulse towards proletarian
revolution. Partly because the form and extent of the capitalist system varied greatly
across the continent, however, it was no easy matter to relate anti-fascist strategies
to coherent Marxist critiques of capitalism. Moreover, the relationship between fascism's violent use of the instruments of the state, on the one hand, and its use of
political means for procuring partial consent from society, on the other, proved especially difficult to explain.

The principal institutional channel of these strategies and tactics was the Communist
International, or Comintern, founded in 1919. A legacy of the Russian revolution
had been a Soviet aspiration to dominate national communist parties, and during the
1920s the Comintern degenerated almost completely into an instrument of Soviet
raison d'état. Stalin was indifferent to the internationalist ideals of the Comintern.
It was clear even in the 1920s, from his declaration in 1924 in favor of "Socialism
in One Country," that world revolution took a back seat. The priority of Stalinist
foreign policy was not the promotion of progressive forces in Europe but rather an
insular and all-pervasive preoccupation with Soviet security.

The Comintern's own organizational weaknesses, doctrinal disputes, and rivalries,
and the effects of internal terror within the Stalinist system, also limited its effectiveness: the International's initial president, Zinoviev, was executed in August 1936 after
the first of the fake show trials. Under such pressures, considerable tension existed
between Comintern orthodoxy, expressed in publicly declared strategic "theses,"
national Party leaderships, and the activist rank and file. Attempts were made to
impose broad strategic measures from outside regardless of specific national factors.
In the process, the division of the European labor movement, begun by the secession
of revolutionaries from social democratic parties following the 1917 Russian revolution and the immediate aftermath of war in 1918, became irreconcilable. The fatal
divide opened up in spite of sporadic attempts by rank-and-file activists to achieve a
pragmatic unity of action.

The *Biennio Rosso* ("two Red years") from 1919 to 1921 in Italy witnessed an
irreparable split in the ranks of the Socialist Party (PSI), resulting in the secession of
a "Bolshevik" wing and the founding of the Italian Communist Party (PCI) in
January 1921. This fragmentation of the left preceded the ultimate destruction of
the left's organizations by Mussolini's Fascist movement. By early 1926 the PCI's

leaders would be arrested, imprisoned, or forced into exile and the party's Congress that year would have to be held in Lyons. The right to strike was formally abolished as a prelude to establishing a dictatorial state structure, including a "fascistized" judicial system complete with special courts for political crimes. In 1928, Antonio Gramsci, a founding leader of the PCI and its best-known and most insightful thinker, would be condemned to 20 years' imprisonment by such a court.

Following Germany's defeat in November 1918 there had been a deep, though chaotic, political and social revolution. Politically, the revolution succeeded in ending the discredited and unpopular Wilhelmine empire. While a republic was proclaimed, the working-class movement, until 1917 united within the socialist SPD, split into two, the communist KPD eventually being formed as a breakaway movement. With the new republic, political power shifted to the left, though property relations were not overturned and the consciously socialist aspects of the revolution were restricted through direct intervention by paramilitary forces loyal to the government, now in the hands of the social democrats of the SPD. It was partly for this reason that the Comintern's crude depiction of social democracy as "social fascism" would later ring true to many of the ordinary activists of the KPD. Similar rebellions and risings from below took place and were defeated in Hungary and in Austria, again leaving a legacy of bitterness within the left. In October 1923, during the first great economic crisis of the years of the Weimar republic, further uprisings occurred, supported by elements of the SPD and KPD in parts of Germany that ended in failure, with the regional left-leaning governments deposed by the army at the orders of the republican state.

The various "theses" adopted by the Comintern rarely did much to make unity more likely. At its notorious Sixth Congress, held in 1928, revolution with no compromise was the guiding principle, and the unbending slogan of "class-against-class" was adopted. Although revolution was far from being Stalin's desire, once sanctified by the Congress, this thesis was accorded the status of analysis by the leader's acolytes. Its shaky theoretical foundation was the belief that the rise of fascism signified a world crisis of capitalism that would lead to its inevitable collapse. The weakness of this somewhat arbitrary theory was that it failed to recognize that fascism, and the capitalist system it supported, was still strong and dynamic. Evidence on the ground ought to have suggested that fascism was far from static both in the way it successfully mobilized support and in its use of state power to remake the existing system.

An element of this dynamism was fascism's ability to repress and effectively defeat the organizations of proletarian political power. Under such pressure, the Comintern's mistaken prognosis led to a highly damaging strategy in relation to leftist unity. Social democrats were deemed to be artificially propping up the "doomed" social, economic, and political system because they did not preach immediate workers' revolution in order to take advantage of capitalism's "crisis." As the main obstacles to the workers' revolution, social democrats thus became "social fascists" and were considered leading enemies rather than allies in the fight against fascism.

With the benefit of hindsight, the International's insensitivity to the scale of the setback to democracy represented by fascism is shocking. Even as the delegates to the 1928 Congress rubber-stamped the new strategy, right-wing extremism in Austria, in the shape of the paramilitary "Home Defense Units" (the *Heimwehr*, principal organ of Austro-fascism), was rapidly growing. More important still, the Comintern's analysis presented a justification to activists of the German Communist Party (KPD) and the Socialist Party (SPD) to hurl insults and sabotage each other's initiatives during the Weimar years while Nazi Party support burgeoned.

The signs remained doom-laden in Germany even before the economic Crash of October 1929. The May Day demonstration, held that year in Berlin, was suppressed with such violence by the SPD police chief that 29 participants were killed. The tendency for political violence to surface would become generalized with the economic depression. German economic health was closely linked to the fortunes of the US economy through the financing of postwar recovery programs and it was not long before the conservative German government of Brüning reacted by imposing an austerity budget through emergency decree in July 1930. Millions of workers had come to regard a full-time job as the normal, indispensable basis for their existence. Mass employment thus brought with it the possibility of mass unemployment and by July 1930 there were 3 million Germans without jobs. In September the NSDAP (Nazi Party) gained 107 seats. Two years later, in July 1932, there would be 4.7 million unemployed and in the Reichstag elections the Nazis would win 230 seats. It was in the wake of the Depression – and with 6 million unemployed – that Hitler became chancellor in January 1933, backed by a mass *Volkisch* movement able to project powerful images onto an ailing German society. These images were reinforced by national and racial myths and a highly theatrical choreography of the crowd. The Reichstag fire in February 1933 gave the Nazi state an apparent justification for institutionalizing authoritarian measures – paradoxically by appealing to "the people" through the Decree for the Protection of the *Volk* and the state.

No immediate change in political strategy was initiated in Moscow. As late as December 1933 the Comintern was still able to declare that fascism and "social fascism," though not identical in every respect, were indeed "twins." In the end, the impulse for change came from below in the form of rank-and-file initiatives from the workers' movement in various parts of Europe, including France, Czechoslovakia, and the industrial regions of Spain. Belated calls for a workers' alliance against fascism-Nazism seemed pointless once free trade unions were abolished by the Nazi regime and the SPD outlawed. The one-party state was declared in July 1933 and the first concentration camps for political enemies soon began to function.

In Austria the combination of a campaign of anti-democratic threats and propaganda led to the gradual incorporation into government and state institutions of authoritarian parties. In September 1930 the leader of the *Heimwehr* had joined the governing cabinet. In November the Austro-fascist electoral effort was subsidized financially by Mussolini. In September 1931 the *Heimwehr* attempted a *putsch* against the government and the vote for the Austrian Nazi party increased in the provincial elections. In May 1932 a Christian Social coalition with the *Heimwehr* was formed; in March 1933 parliament was suspended and government by decree introduced as a prelude to the proclamation of a Christian-Social authoritarian regime. The first concerted and armed attempt of the left to face the fascist challenge head-on would be mounted on the streets of Vienna. Indefinite martial law was declared in Austria in January 1934 and an all-out attack on the Social Democratic Party (SDAP) was staged in February by the *Heimwehr*, which to all intents and purposes had become the paramilitary wing of the Christian-Social government. The anti-government, anti-fascist rising by the workers in response to this attack was crushed within weeks and the SDAP and trade unions were made illegal.

The lessons of the collapse of Weimar and the authoritarian drift of Austrian politics gradually combined with the demands of Stalinist *Realpolitik* to produce a climate of change. Fearing Japanese expansion in Manchuria, the Soviet Union began to look for technical assistance from France for its air force during 1933 and 1934. The push by Stalin for a European strategy of collective security was crowned by Soviet entry into the League of Nations in May 1934 and by the Stalin–Laval pact (between the Soviet Union and France), signed a year later.

But the real catalyst for the change of direction can be found within the rank and file of the European left and, specifically, in the events in France in February 1934. On February 6 demonstrations inspired by the far-right Leagues culminated in a show of strength outside the Chamber of Deputies in Paris. Faced with this discontent, which may have been an attempted fascist coup against the Third Republic, and reeling from a financial corruption scandal, the government resigned, giving way to a reactionary "national bloc" regime. As a counter to the action of the right, the organized left staged an impressively supported general strike on February 12. The Comintern's obsolete "class-against-class" strategy was thereby revealed as a sham and communists and socialists marched together to the rallying cry of "Unity!" The process of unity culminated in July 1934 with a socialist–communist pact, at this stage to be known as the United Front. This would become the *Front Populaire* in October, with incorporation of the Radical Party that stood to benefit from identification with defense of republican ideals such as popular sovereignty. Radical support, gained with encouragement from the PCF, was forthcoming on the tacit assumption that class-based economic demands would not go too far.

The widespread enthusiasm for unity was undeniable. The Socialist Party leader, Léon Blum, noted its presence not only in Paris but throughout France: "The same electric current can be experienced in the most diverse places and at the furthest distance from each other."[7] The PCF resolution adopted at its national conference the same month stressed the demands not simply of the working class but of "*all* working people" regardless of their proletarian credentials: "the unemployed, peasants, tradesmen, intellectuals, ex-service men, invalids, young people, women, the lower and junior ranks of the army" which, although they "are often under reactionary influence," could not be neglected as part of the new cross-class strategy. Blum remained skeptical, noting how the PCF had been slow to respond to unitary sentiment. He was only too aware that the communist change of tack had been induced under the watchful eye of Moscow and that the PCF's own agenda was its priority: France held the key to the European security of Soviet Russia. The Socialist Party had to beware of being carried away by PCF overtures. At the same time, Blum was pragmatic enough to recognize the need for unity as the basis of anti-fascism and defense of the Republic.

The unity of the French socialists, communists, and radicals was confirmed by a joint Paris demonstration, both celebration and political protest, by hundreds of thousands of supporters who marched from the Place de la Bastille to the Place de la Nation on July 14, 1935. The sense of collective historical memory was palpable. Blum published an editorial in *Le Populaire* entitled *Vive la Nation et Vive la Révolution!* The red, white, and blue tricolor of the Republic mingled with the traditional red flag of militant labor. As the leaders of the communist and radical parties, Maurice Thorez and Edouard Daladier, marched side by side, the *Marseillaise* was sung with what Blum described as the spirit of 1790, binding the republican nation together afresh. Ten thousand delegates took the oath of the *Rassemblement Populaire*, committed to unity of action, to dissolve the fascist Leagues, and to develop democracy.[8]

The Comintern was sufficiently influenced by events in France to pursue a new strategy of cross-class unity that had been underway since the appointment by Stalin of the Bulgarian communist Georgi Dimitrov as general secretary of the Comintern in the spring of 1934. Dimitrov, who had direct experience of Hitler's rise and had been calling for a common working-class struggle against fascism since 1932, would play a vital role in the International's change of line. By the summer of 1934 other leading communists were arguing for broader alliances to encompass petit bourgeois groups and peasants. The new strategy converged conveniently with Stalin's foreign policy objectives and with French pressure "from below." Thus, the idea of broad anti-fascist alliances would be embraced at the Seventh Congress of the Comintern in July 1935. The formal abandonment of the sectarian tactics of the preceding years made some sense to the rank and file, though there remained an unresolved tension between the new line emanating from Moscow and a failure to admit to the mistakes of the old class-against-class thesis.[9] National communist parties would now place anti-fascism above all other priorities, putting revolutionary initiatives on "hold" in the interests of unity with the middle classes and denying the possibility of class struggle.

The Popular Front in Practice: France and Spain, 1935–1936

The medievalist historian Marc Bloch would reflect in 1940 on how the Popular Front seemed symbolic of French divisions: "Overnight there was a crevice in the stratum of French society, separating social groups into two blocs."[10] In both Spain and France the experience of Popular Front government was curtailed by national and international authoritarianism – in Spain the popular alliance was gradually reduced to ruins during the civil war and the deep conservatism of French society ended the reforming experiment well before the country's fall to the Nazis in 1940. There were also great tensions *within* the Popular Front. The level of commitment to the socioeconomic aspects of its program varied considerably and some parties to the coalition seemed more attracted by the possible electoral gains to be won by coalescing with the left. Moscow's obsession with building an international collective security system implied an anti-revolutionary stance from communist parties in order not to scare the democratic powers. In both France and Spain communists became the most conservative adherents to the pact.

The French election in May 1936 produced a gain of 40 parliamentary seats for the combined parties of the Popular Front, even though their total combined vote only increased from 54 to 57 percent. Following the electoral victory of the *Front Populaire*, Léon Blum, as leader of the coalition party with most seats, became France's first socialist premier on June 5, heading a government that would last only a year. The limited, rationalist objectives of the Popular Front were seen by its leaders, including Blum, who sympathized with the plight of the workers, as being jeopardized by working-class dissent. Like Manuel Azaña in Spain, Blum would successfully mobilize huge crowds in support of the Popular Front while, in fact, standing for non-threatening constitutionalism and non-revolutionary aims. Blum was received with huge acclamation at the annual ceremonies, held at the end of May, to honor the martyrs of the Paris Commune of 1870. Already, pressure from below and from the left was mounting for action in the shape of substantial reform. This pressure, aimed at more radical measures, was the product of years of worker frustration and submissiveness. In socioeconomic terms, both leaders would, however, keep scrupulously to their respective Popular Front electoral programs, published separately in each country in January 1936.

Blum made a clear distinction between the exercise of power within the framework of capitalist society, on the one hand, and the revolutionary conquest of power and transformation of the means of production, on the other. One new remedy for the depression was the nationalization of certain industries. At this time socialism in France was more or less synonymous with pacifism and Blum's government targeted the arms industry for public ownership. He saw state intervention as a measure of republican defense. This responded to French society's post-1918 mood of pacifism and revulsion at private profiteering from warfare. It was an anti-imperialist position that could be cloaked in the anti-fascism of the *Rassemblement Populaire*. The Front's critics, who depicted Stalin as puppet-master of the new government, were able to point to a possible contradiction with the alliance's focus on peace, since the socialists were in a pact with the PCF which, following Comintern directives, preached *active* anti-Nazism. Blum countered with realism: participating in an international front against the expansionism of Hitler and Mussolini necessarily entailed building French military strength. Against his natural inclination towards disarmament, the extension of military service by the Nazis in Germany would therefore force the government to sponsor a rearmament program.

Fissures within the Front made problem resolution difficult. Of the 31 members of Blum's cabinet, 18 were Socialists, 13 Radicals, and four Republican-Socialist Unionists. There were no women ministers, but three women served as departmental undersecretaries. The representation of the conservative Radical Party did not faithfully represent the spirit of the Popular Front among the lower classes. Combined with the Radicals' entrenchment within the Senate (the upper house within the French National Assembly that ratified decisions of the elected Chamber of Deputies) this meant that reforming initiatives were subject to limitation. Meanwhile, the PCF, not wanting to be tarred with the brush of "bourgeois" government, decided not to participate directly. This meant they could apply pressure on the government without having to shoulder any responsibility for decisions.

In mid-May, the greatest strike movement of the Third Republic began when Paris metalworkers called for a wage increase and paid holidays. Towards the end of the month a second wave of sit-down strikes for collective-bargaining rights broke out in metalworking, automobile, and airplane factories, spreading quickly to construction workers. Following the anti-revolutionary thesis of the Comintern, the PCF was firmly on the side of moderation. Although the CGT labor confederation sought to moderate excessive demands, by June 4 – the day Blum was handed the reins of power – the strikes were moving beyond Paris. Almost a million workers were involved. The sit-in protests were not under the control of the trade unions: this was a social explosion. It was not irrationally chaotic, though it frightened the middle classes. At the trial of Blum staged by the Vichy regime in 1942 the socialist premier would recall the state of "panic and terror" that reigned among the employers. He argued that it was the tranquility of the protests, the "calm majesty" with which the workers had installed themselves beside the machines, "watching over them, keeping them in order, without leaving the buildings, without any sign of external violence whatsoever," that contributed most to "the Great Fear" of June 1936, since it seemed to justify the workers' co-ownership of the means of production.[11]

On June 7 the "Matignon agreement" was signed by the government, employers, and unions. Blum's moderate socialist colleagues hoped this would satisfy worker demands and cement working-class support. Most socialist deputies therefore hailed the agreement, recognizing collective bargaining and labor organization and wage increases as a great victory. The agreement did not put an immediate end to the strikes. The argument of the PCF leader, Thorez, that the unity of the Popular Front against fascism was being jeopardized proved decisive in the end, however, with the all-important metalworking sector.

With the help of Thorez, who again was following the party line, a greater conflagration, bloodshed, and even a civil war, were avoided by agreeing to the workers' demands. The 40-hour week, collective bargaining, and paid vacations would be introduced legally. Blum, well versed in modern industrialism, such as mass production (Fordism) and corporativism, argued that although concessions altered the balance between employer and worker, they were strictly rational in productive terms. One of his mantras was "leisure is not laziness"; a shorter week and vacations represented rest after labor and "reconciliation" with family and "natural life." Moreover, the need to maintain production as Nazi Germany rearmed at a hectic pace made concessions inevitable, as employers recognized. Blum had been the savior of industry, but this did not save his government from revenge for the concessions they had made.

Events in Spain were to cause the fault lines in the *Front Populaire* to open up. In the middle of July 1936, only six weeks after Blum's accession to power, there was an attempted *coup d'état* against the democratic Spanish Popular Front government. This was the start of the Spanish Civil War. Following in the slipstream of the Italian invasion of Abyssinia in October 1935 and Nazi Germany's remilitarization of the Rhineland in March 1936, the Spanish *coup* precipitated a crisis for Blum's government. His instinct was to aid the Spanish Republic, particularly since Hitler and Mussolini were soon to be sending substantial military assistance to the Spanish rebels. The Spanish crisis, however, gave the French right an opportunity to point to the contradictions of the Popular Front. The posters and cartoons of conservatives claimed that one had only to look at Spain to see that a Popular Front government led only to "war and bombs": what started with strikes would end with "communism." Indeed, the slogan "Better Hitler than Blum" summed up the attitude of many French conservatives. Such was the level of hatred that Blum feared the Spanish conflict might cause such tensions that civil war in France was a real possibility. Moreover, leading elements in the Radical Party, the French socialists' main *Front Populaire* partners, followed the line of appeasement and were set against sending aid to the Spanish government. Arms supplies to the Spanish Republic were therefore halted. Meanwhile, the aid sent by Germany and Italy to the rebels effectively cemented the Rome–Berlin Axis, an alliance formalized in October 1936.

As in France, the nature of the Spanish Popular Front had been determined by national political conditions. The year 1931 was a watershed: municipal elections in April became, in effect, a referendum on the monarchy which had supported a military dictatorship since 1923. The victory in these elections of a coalition of republicans and socialists heralded the Second Republic – an experiment in democratization similar to that initiated by the Weimar republic in Germany in 1918. At the heart of the Second Republic's program of modernization were reforms of the land structure, political recognition of regional identity, the separation of church and state, the laicization of education, depoliticization of the army, and improvement of the conditions and wages of the rural and urban workforce. The constitution of the Second Republic would formally symbolize full popular sovereignty, consciously representing the interests of *el pueblo republicano*, and enunciating such liberal principles as freedom of conscience, equality before the law, universal suffrage, and parliamentary democracy. It would also veer uncertainly towards satisfying the economic desires of the proletarian masses.

Popular expectations of a shift in power were thus awakened, only to be frustrated by entrenched elites spurred on in their obstructionism by the successes that fascistic regimes had won elsewhere in Europe. In turn, this obstructionism widened the divisions of the left. The Republic had to contend with mass politics at a moment of economic crisis and from 1933 left-liberal efforts were shaped by the need to avoid a reactionary and authoritarian backlash as had already happened in Germany and would shortly happen in Austria. Though failure was not inevitable, the Republic was weakened politically by serious divisions between republicans, socialists, and anarchists, and by the internal factionalism of the Socialist Party (PSOE). As with the unfortunate rigidity of the French communists, many PSOE leaders and activists adhered doggedly to Marxist orthodoxy, viewing the Republic merely as the beginning of a middle-class or "bourgeois" revolution with which they ought to be cooperating only sparingly. This quietism played into the hands of anti-democratic forces just as had happened in Germany. At the same time, the more activist wing of the PSOE preached social revolution while abjectly failing to develop any rational strategy for revolution.

The left's divisions aided the populist and conservative Radical Party and mass Catholic party, the *Confederación Española de Derechas Autónomas* (Spanish Confederation of Autonomous Rightist Groups, CEDA), which sympathized with the authoritarian aims of European fascism and shared some of its methods and rhetoric. A Radical–CEDA coalition was able to win the elections of November 1933 because the left was so divided. Government by the Radical Party and the CEDA until the end of 1935 saw severe attacks on the reforming program of 1931, the closing down of the offices of left-liberal political organizations, and the removal of "unreliable" mayors. This all threatened to destroy the republican–socialist alliance as the political essence of popular republican expectations. It also fueled the left's fear of fascism and appeared to justify giving free rein to the left wing of the PSOE. A number of ineffective essays in direct action followed which were intended to force the political right to relinquish its hold on state power.

In June 1934 the land workers' section of the socialist trade union called a peaceful general strike. Declared illegal and repressed by the authorities, the action became an opportunity for the right to defeat one of the most rapidly growing sections of the labor movement. When in October 1934 CEDA was given control of three key government ministries by the conservative president of the Republic it appeared to the left that the Republic was being handed over to its enemies – a repetition of what had happened in Austria in February, where armed resistance in Vienna had been too weak to halt the assumption of power of authoritarianism. A revolutionary general strike aimed at grasping back power for the Republic and the left was declared, but lacked coordination in Barcelona and Madrid, where it failed miserably. In the coalmines of Asturias the strike was organized through the Workers' Alliance (*Alianza Obrera*), a form of leftist unity, incorporating socialists, anarchists, and communists. For two weeks the local traditions of militant action against the bureaucracy of mine companies and state were crystallized in the form of a revolutionary commune. After a couple of weeks the rebellion was violently suppressed. Among the thousands of leftists across Spain imprisoned for "complicity" was Manuel Azaña. The former prime minister drew an important lesson from the October events. Unity among the parties of the working class was effective but required broadening into a "popular" alliance with liberal republicans and sections of the middle classes.

Unified political mobilization meant resurrecting the essence of the Republic through its natural mass support base. The 1931 republican–socialist coalition would have to be rebuilt as the basis of a political bloc strong enough to survive the challenge of the Republic's enemies. A minority government would not do. This, rather than any signals from the PCE or the Comintern, was the primary origin of the Spanish Popular Front, whose electoral manifesto was published in January 1936.

In France the workers' organizations remained powerful after February 1934. There had certainly been a moment of real crisis, but not of defeat for the trade unions. In Spain, by contrast, the unions were defeated and were in no position to resurrect leftist unity after October. The initiative in reducing the left's crippling fragmentation therefore depended on two political groupings which would have considerable strategic and tactical input, but which possessed hardly any genuine mass following: the Communist Party (PCE) and Azaña's liberal Republican Left (*Izquierda Republicana*). Azaña's task would not be easy. Following the Comintern thesis, the PCE promoted united action through factory, workshop, and neighborhood committees. Cooperation from the PSOE, which was suffering the effects of division and defeat, was limited to aid for the 30,000 political prisoners of October. The middle-class republican parties, meanwhile, were ideologically ill-disposed towards unity with the communists. Azaña's campaign therefore depended on peculiarly Spanish conditions and would come to fruition only in early 1936 once the Radical–CEDA government had collapsed as a result of a financial scandal.

Because it had a mass following, participation of the divided PSOE was a prerequisite of a united electoral platform. But Azaña foresaw the difficulties of linking a reformist republican program to the collectivist aspirations of the socialist left. What form would the electoral discourse and day-to-day tactics assume if the campaign was for a Workers' Front? If a coalition with the socialists based on recuperation of republican popular authority as in 1931 was perfectly "legitimate, normal and desirable," the same did not apply to the communists: "While bringing in no appreciable number of votes electorally, they will scare away voters." In a prophetic summary of the dangers that were to be realized a year or so later in the republican zone during the

Spanish Civil War, Azaña feared that the PCE would "corrupt the nature of the coalition."[12]

In September 1935 the governing Radical Party collapsed and the prime minister resigned. This increased fears that CEDA might assume leadership of the government and intensify the "fascistization" of the Republic. In October, Azaña delivered his speech to the republican masses at Comillas, calling for a return to the ideas and essential values of the Republic.[13] Like the activists of the PSOE, Azaña was acutely aware of the threatening international context: "All of Europe is a battlefield between democracy and its enemies, and Spain is no exception. You have to choose between democracy, with all of its difficulties and faults, with all of its equivocations or errors, or tyranny with all of its horrors. There is no choice. We have made ours." The Republic had to be liberated from those who had seized it and provoked the exasperation of the republican masses that had been forced to "sacrifice their rights and freedoms." A pact had to be constructed of all like-minded organizations, representing republican popular opinion, and including groups which were not specifically republican but which wanted to preserve and promote the assumptions of the Republic. Azaña appealed to both the liberal values of 1931 and to those more closely held by the working class: the privileges of the moneyed classes had to be "absolutely destroyed . . . not with a spirit of retaliation, nor of revenge, nor of social dissolution, but with a creative spirit, with the stabilization of Spanish society."

The left wing of the PSOE insisted on including the hitherto insignificant PCE in the *Frente Popular*. This exacerbated tensions between the PSOE and its more left-leaning union confederation, the UGT, just as the Republic was about to face its greatest challenge. The Popular Front coalition was elected to power in the general parliamentary elections of February 16, 1936. Azaña became head of the new government. But the Spanish Front was a circumstantial electoral coalition rather than a rationalized tool of government. The limited nature of the signatories' commitments, their divisions, and the disparity of their ultimate objectives made a precarious basis for unity. The government failed to reflect the nature of the coalition that had won the election and the socialist UGT declined calls upon it to commit politically to government. In effect, the Popular Front dissolved as a political entity.[14]

Government became partially by-passed, therefore, as the initiative for action passed back to the trade unions and their revolutionary program for the repossession of agricultural land, fueling the street clashes between fascist Falangists and leftists in the few months before the illegal rebellion against the government on July 18. Much of the unrest the government had to deal with came in the form of labor strikes and land seizures. This direct action lacked coherent political direction or leadership, but there was also little coherent basis for a more considered program. Communist activists, preaching conservatism, were jeered off the stage when they tried to introduce more moderate proposals at workers' mass meetings.

The Popular Front would be subsumed by the civil war that began with the attempted *coup d'état* by a section of the Spanish army in July. Popular Front unity would become a central part of the rhetoric of war mobilization from July 18, 1936. The PCE was especially adept at broadening the meaning of what was now known as "the People's Front," stressing unity for the sake of "victory and liberty." But the enormous pressure of wartime mobilization laid bare the contradictions of the Front.[15] Military assistance to the military rebels from Hitler and Mussolini was part of the inexorable march of fascism to which the Popular Front, in Spain and else-where, had been the principal democratic response.

Conclusions: Decline of the Popular Front, 1937–1939

In both France and Spain, therefore, the inherent divergences of the Popular Front, partly because of external circumstances, could not be suppressed. The historian Marc Bloch, who lived through the years of the Front and its tragic aftermath, explained how quickly "it expired in spirit if not in form, a victim of the equivocations of its supporters and of the obstructions and contempt of its enemies."[16] In late September 1936 the reticence of French business forced Blum to devalue the French franc and in December the PCF abstained from a parliamentary vote of confidence on the Blum government. By February 1937 the government was settling merely for consolidation and retrenchment. When in June 1937 the Senate refused to grant Blum decree powers to deal with the financial crisis, France's first Popular Front government resigned. Its Radical successor struggled on until January 1938. Blum's second government, in March 1938, lasted only a month. In the aftermath of the *Anschluss* between Germany and Austria, a conservative government under Edouard Daladier took office. The demise of the Popular Front was thus consummated amid the appeasement of Hitler and Mussolini. In September 1938 the French government, with the British, signed the Munich Agreement to partition Czechoslovakia. By the time of General Franco's victory in the Spanish Civil War in April 1939 the Spanish Popular Front had long ceased to exist, except as a requirement of war mobilization. The Nazi–Soviet pact, signed in August 1939, formally ended the Comintern's search for collective security and paved the way for the dismemberment of Poland.

The Popular Front in Europe represented an uneasy compromise between political necessities in the age of the masses and a mission to preserve parliamentary democ-racy. A central weakness was that the Comintern played a substantial role in pushing the notion of cross-class unity for the sake of Soviet security, while believing neither in bourgeois democracy nor in revolution. Theoretically, the lessons of Germany in the period 1929–33 could be learned, but the experience of power would heighten the contradictions of interclass unity. The various compromises became a huge problem in the exercise of political power in France and Spain when the Popular Front formed the basis of reforming governments that aimed simultaneously to achieve progressive change in the interests of the popular classes and halt the rise of fascism. The ultimate failure of the Front, wrecked by the unbearable pressures it had to resist, symbolized the failure and defeat of European liberalism and the European left. This defeat contributed in a very real sense to the onset of the European war in 1939.

NOTES

1 While "fascism" (lower case "f") refers to the *generic* form of extreme nationalist–racial ideology and action in Europe, "Fascism" (upper case "F") refers specifically to the Party, regime, and state in Italy (or part thereof), 1922–45. The generic notion of *fascism*, as used in this essay, incorporates Nazism.

2   Valentine Cunningham, *British Writers of the Thirties* (Oxford: Oxford University Press, 1989), p. 266.

3   See Santos Juliá, "The Origins of the Spanish Popular Front," in *The French and Spanish Popular Fronts: Comparative Perspectives*, M. Alexander and H. Graham, eds (Cambridge: Cambridge University Press, 1989), p. 29.

4   M. Azaña, *Obras completas*, vol. 3 (Mexico: Ediciones Oasis, 1967), p. 292.

5   J. Ortega y Gasset, *The Revolt of the Masses* (New York: W. W. Norton, 1993).

6   Stephen Spender, "I Join the Communist Party," *Daily Worker*, February 19, 1937, reproduced in Stephen Spender, *The Thirties and After* (Glasgow: Collins, 1978), pp. 80–2.

7   "Les problèmes de l'unité," *Le Populaire*, July 7, 1934, in *L'Oeuvre de Léon Blum*, vol. 4, part 1 (Paris: Éditions Albin Michel, 1964), p. 157.

8   Cited in Joel Colton, *Léon Blum, Humanist in Politics* (Cambridge MA: MIT Press, 1974), pp. 109–10.

9   See Kevin McDermott and Jeremy Agnew, *The Comintern: A History of International Communism from Lenin to Stalin* (London: Macmillan, 1996), pp. 124–5.

10 Marc Bloch, *L'Étrange défaite: Témoignage écrit en 1940*, 2nd edn (Paris: Armand Colin, 1957), cited in Carole Fink, *Marc Bloch: A Life in History* (Cambridge: Cambridge University Press, 1989), p. 188.

11 Hearing before the Supreme Court at Riom, March 11–12, 1942, *L'Oeuvre de Léon Blum*, vol. 4, part 2, pp. 259, 327.

12 Azaña, *Obras completas*, vol. 3, p. 602.

13 See Paul Preston, "The Creation of the Popular Front in Spain," in *The Popular Front in Europe*, H. Graham and P. Preston, eds (London: Macmillan, 1987), p. 99.

14 See Juliá, "Origins," p. 33.

15 See Helen Graham, *The Spanish Republic at War, 1936–1939* (Cambridge: Cambridge University Press, 2002).

16 Fink, *Marc Bloch*, p. 197.

GUIDE TO FURTHER READING

Martin S. Alexander and Helen Graham, eds, *The French and Spanish Popular Fronts: Comparative Perspectives* (Cambridge: Cambridge University Press, 1989). An essential collection of essays by leading scholars comparing the politics and culture of the Popular Fronts.

David Beetham, ed., *Marxists in Face of Fascism* (Manchester: Manchester University Press, 1983). Indispensable collection of writings on fascism by Marxists in the period 1922–38, with a critical introduction.

Edward. H. Carr, *The Twilight of Comintern, 1930–1935* (London: Macmillan, 1982). A detailed study of the Comintern at work in the 1930s.

Joel Colton, *Léon Blum, Humanist in Politics* (Cambridge MA: MIT Press, 1974). First published in 1966, a political biography which focuses on Blum's humane qualities pitted against the great conflicts of 1934 to 1945.

Helen Graham, *The Spanish Republic at War, 1936–1939* (Cambridge: Cambridge University Press, 2002). An extended study of the wartime experience of the Republic, stressing pre-existing political tensions that made the Popular Front problematic as a basis for wartime mobilization.

Helen Graham and Paul Preston, eds, *The Popular Front in Europe* (London: Macmillan, 1987). Including a useful introductory summary, this places the Popular Front within political tensions of the interwar period and looks at each significant country in turn.

Jonathan Haslam, *The Soviet Union and the Struggle for Collective Security in Europe, 1933–1939* (London: Macmillan, 1984). Standard work on the security rationale as the basis of Stalin's support for the Popular Front line.

Julian Jackson, *The Popular Front in France: Defending Democracy, 1934–38* (Cambridge: Cambridge University Press, 1988). Thematic and historiographical study concentrating on the relationship between culture and politics in France in the 1930s.

Santos Juliá, *Orígenes del Frente Popular en España (1934–1936)* (Madrid: Siglo Veintiuno, 1979). Focusing on the specifically *Spanish* origins of the Popular Front in Spain. A useful summary can be found in Alexander and Graham, *The French and Spanish Popular Fronts*, above.

Kevin McDermott and Jeremy Agnew, *The Comintern: A History of International Communism from Lenin to Stalin* (London: Macmillan, 1996). Narrative and interpretive account drawing on research carried out since the opening of Soviet archives.

Paul Preston, *The Coming of the Spanish Civil War: Reform, Reaction and Revolution in the Second Republic* (London: Methuen, 1983). Detailed account of the political origins of the civil war, focusing on the struggle for state power between the PSOE and CEDA.

Sian Reynolds, *France Between the Wars: Gender and Politics* (London: Routledge, 1996). Places gender at the center of analysis of political, cultural, and economic change.

Eve Rosenhaft, *Beating the Fascists? The German Communists and Political Violence, 1929–1933* (Cambridge: Cambridge University Press, 1983). Major study of the German social crisis and left political divisions on the eve of the Nazi seizure of power.

CHAPTER TWENTY-FIVE

The Strategic Revolution

TAMI DAVIS BIDDLE

When Napoleon stunned the heads of Europe with a string of seemingly unstoppable victories at the dawn of the nineteenth century, he had done so by relying on means and methods of warfare that were largely familiar to the military officers of the day. Surely, he had refined them, honed them, and opened up vast new opportunities by presiding over an army that was, initially at least, committed to an ideological cause. But Napoleon fought his battles in a way that would have been quite recognizable to generations of officers before him. A century later, warfare had changed so dramatically that Napoleon himself would not have recognized it. The speed, range, and accuracy of small arms and long-range artillery had undergone radical transformation, producing a battlefield environment that was vastly more lethal than it had ever been before.

The years leading up to 1914 had seen sweeping, dramatic change in the tools of modern warfare. The industrial revolution had placed a great array of new, highly destructive weapons in the hands of the military. This same revolution had allowed for the equipping, clothing, and supporting of the mass armies that would eventually march off to war. Those large armies were the result not only of the increased nationalism and militarism of the late Victorian and Edwardian eras, but also of the basic changes in sanitation and sewage that had reduced disease in Europe and thus made possible a dramatic increase in population. The new weapons arriving on the battlefield – especially the tank and the airplane – changed the look and feel of modern warfare. At sea the submarine had the same effect. All three weapons would make their presence felt even more dramatically between 1939 and 1945, forcing armies and navies to make ongoing, sweeping changes in their conduct of warfare.

During the interwar years Europe witnessed, for a time at least, a social and cultural rejection of the politics and militarism that had paved the way to the "Great War." But the twenty years between the two world wars did not see a halt in the evolution of the tools and technology of warfare. This was true despite a serious attempt to de-claw Germany through the Versailles treaty, and despite several sweeping attempts at disarmament and arms control. This chapter will examine the "strategic revolution" that first manifested itself during the Great War, and continued through the conclusion of World War II in 1945. It will address the ways that armies and navies adapted to dramatic change in the scope, methods, and tools of warfare during the first half of the twentieth century.

Armies and Land Warfare

The central problem facing soldiers at the start of World War I has been summed up succinctly with a few telling statistics: a Napoleonic infantry battalion of 1,000 men with smoothbore muskets could project 1,000 rounds to an effective range of 100 yards twice a minute; a bayonet charge by a comparable formation would thus receive about 2,000 rounds before reaching its target, or about two shots per soldier. By 1916 an infantry battalion with 1,000 magazine rifles and four machine guns could project over 21,000 rounds to distances over 1,000 yards every minute. An assault by a comparable unit would thus absorb over 210,000 rounds in the time needed to close, or more than 200 per targeted soldier – an increase of over two orders of magnitude.[1] How to cope with this new degree of lethality on the battlefield was the main issue faced by all World War I generals.

An extraordinarily daunting and difficult problem to solve, it took years – and millions of lives – before military professionals found their way to an answer. The problem was complicated and intensified by the powerful synergy that developed between small arms and long-range artillery and by the primitive state of battlefield communications. The speed with which these problems could be solved was slowed by the hierarchical nature of military organizations, by class structures, and by inadequate systems of training and education.

Many theories have been advanced to explain the seemingly desultory performance of World War I armies, particularly on the western front. The best of these combine an appreciation of the culture of Edwardian-era armies with an appreciation of the difficulty of the problem they faced. If the World War I generals are still remembered as "donkeys" who led lions (and if this thesis has been embedded in European popular culture through literature and the media), a good deal of recent scholarship has sought to redress it.[2] By the end of 1918, all of the major combatant nations had come to understand the principles of what one scholar has recently termed the "modern system" of warfare. These principles enabled soldiers to employ the components of industrialized, twentieth-century war fighting – to employ modern "combined arms" – in a sophisticated way.

A means of breaking the western front's trench stalemate was first demonstrated by the Germans during the Michael Offensive of March 1918, when they used surprise, suppressive fire, dispersion, cover and concealment, and maneuver to advance dramatically in a short period of time. These foundational elements of contemporary land warfare have remained consistent, even as ever more sophisticated weapons have made their way to battlefields over the past 100 years. And wide-ranging, extensive developments in communications technology have greatly facilitated the command and control of large, complex military forces operating over extended areas. But the principles of modern combined arms warfare require a high degree of professionalism, discipline, and dedicated training; indeed, their demands are so strenuous that only a small number of armies have been able to master them fully.

The thinking and behavior of European armies following the war was influenced by a number of factors, most notably the political, economic, and social contexts in which they operated. Having suffered so grievously from 1914 through late 1918, Europeans were weary of war and anxious to embrace the promise held out by the League of Nations. If Germany was actively prohibited from keeping a large, standing army, other nations were disinclined to invest more than necessary in their land forces. The French, spent by the long, exhausting battle of Verdun in 1916, never fully recovered from it. After the war they adopted a defensive mentality, hoping to keep themselves safe through a doctrine of *couverture* behind the Maginot Line of static defenses.

Anti-war attitudes and limited budgets shaped the context of the British interwar army. Neither its analysis of its wartime experience nor its interwar investment in training and doctrinal rigor was as robust as it might have been. The new states that emerged from the dissolution of the Austro-Hungarian empire were fully engaged in trying to develop political and economic stability; they had little energy or funding left over for their military establishments. Russia, enmeshed in civil war, and, later, in the ongoing turmoil of the early Stalinist era, saw only halting progress towards the development of a sophisticated, professionalized army.

Nonetheless, planning for the next war did take place inside European military organizations. It often proceeded in fits and starts, and was characterized by ongoing and largely unresolved contests between those who sought radical change and those who sought to preserve the traditional and the familiar. Among the radicals were those who became outspoken proponents of armor and battlefield mechanization, including J. F. C. Fuller, Basil Liddell Hart, and Charles de Gaulle.

The tank was a natural enough response to the lethality of the new battlefield: it combined protection and firepower in one machine, thus helping to restore movement, and to expand the opportunities for the reconnaissance and exploitation phases of warfare. But during World War I the tank was primitive, difficult to use, and mechanically unreliable; it never emerged as a decisive weapon prior to 1918. Its proponents saw its possibilities, however, and thus promoted it as a central tool of warfare for the future.

By the start of World War II the British would have the only fully mechanized army. But British planning was affected by an assumption that the defense would continue to predominate on land, and conservatives generally won the day over more radical thinkers. Fuller argued for all-tank formations, and Liddell Hart argued, somewhat less radically, that tanks and aircraft were the means to restore movement on the battlefield. He insisted, as well, that tanks could break up enemy lines and drive deep into the enemy rear to disrupt command and control efforts. But conservatives, who were invested in justifying their wartime tactics, were not generally moved by these non-traditional ideas; they continued to insist on the predominance of more traditional means, especially infantry and cavalry. In 1935, twice as much money was spent on cavalry as on tanks and armored cars.[3]

A defensive mindset also infused French interwar thinking. De Gaulle's arguments for replacing the large, indifferently trained French conscript army with a smaller, fully mechanized, more professional one seemed too radical a step to win wide support in interwar France. By the time World War II commenced, the French had large numbers of capable tanks, but the doctrine for their employment was defensive and limited in imagination. The most innovative tank supporter in the Soviet Union, Tuchachevsky, perished in Stalin's political purges.[4]

Ironically, the Germans would develop and utilize the power of mechanized forces most successfully in the early stages of World War II. The small, tightly knit, professional German army remaining after Versailles engaged in a great deal of analysis and introspection in the interwar years – far more than their counterparts in the victorious nations. Innovators like Hans von Seekt and Heinz Guderian laid the groundwork for a fast-moving, offensive, mechanized style of warfare. Though it would look revolutionary to Germany's opponents, it was simply a natural evolution of the combined arms tactics the Germans had worked out by 1918. What became known as *Blitzkrieg* or "lightning war" was the utilization of infantry, artillery, armor, and aircraft in interoperative, mutually supporting ways. It focused on decentralized authority, flexibility, speed, and exploitation.[5] Employed effectively by a German army that expanded rapidly between 1933 and 1939, the new vanguard of combined arms warfare posed a deadly and difficult problem for Germany's opponents. During World War II, all other combatant armies in Europe would find themselves working to catch up to and surpass the *Wehrmacht* in its employment of mechanized combined arms.

The Germans took advantage of new advances in technology, integrating these into the combined arms methods they had worked out and improved – through attention and close study – through the interwar years. Using advanced small arms, powerful artillery, armor, and aircraft in close support and aerial bombing roles, they quickly overwhelmed their initial opponents in Poland and France. This placed Britain on the defensive – fighting for independence and survival in 1940. Through a tenacious fight during the aerial Battle of Britain they managed to beat off the early advances of the Luftwaffe, but initially they had no offensive weapon, save for strategic bombers, to throw against the Germans. The Soviets would find themselves similarly on the defensive in the summer of 1941, well before Stalin had expected that Hitler would violate the non-aggression pact he had made with the Soviets in 1939. And these two unlikely Allies – Britain and Russia – against the Axis powers would be joined by the United States following the attack on Pearl Harbor, Hawaii in December 1941. For much of the war the Soviets carried the burden of the fighting.

World War II revealed that the tank is utilized best in a combined arms role; armored forces can take the initiative and can move quickly to exploit breakthroughs; indeed, the psychological impact of a well-coordinated mechanized attack can be very great. But armor, to function optimally and without vulnerability, needs support from infantry. Against a well-prepared defender, tank formations lacking adequate infantry assistance can find themselves strikingly vulnerable – as the British discovered to their grief during the Goodwood operation in the summer of 1944, when General Bernard Montgomery sent attackers forward in massed, tank-pure formations without adequate infantry support. These formations were fatally vulnerable to dug-in German infantry and anti-tank guns, which the tank crews could neither see nor suppress. In general, though, mechanization changed the pace and nature of warfare in dramatic ways.

Forced – in a test of survival – to contend with the pointy end of the German spear, the Soviets rallied. Using geographical space, a large population, and material support from the Americans to keep themselves in the fight initially, the Soviets eventually developed a sophisticated army that was able, in time, to defeat the German army at its own game. The vast and complex combined arms contest fought out on the eastern front drained the fighting strength and endurance of the *Wehrmacht*, while the Anglo-Americans hammered the German home front by air, in a prelude to their own return to Europe with land armies in 1944.

Air Forces

The role of aircraft as weapons of war had engendered a great deal of speculation through the ages – indeed, such speculation had long predated the first successful flight of heavier-than-air craft in 1903. When World War I commenced, aircraft were still primitive machines; constructed of wood, and tied together with wire and baling twine, they evolved quickly and found their way to a variety of useful roles – from reconnaissance and artillery spotting to long-range bombing. Even the most conservative soldiers understood that aircraft would afford an unprecedented view of the battlefield. This they did, making the space above one's own troops – as well as the space above the enemy – a valuable and vital commodity. And this, in turn, led quickly to the development of purpose-built "fighter" aircraft designed to protect one's own skies and to penetrate the enemy's. Reconnaissance aircraft sought to determine the location of enemy troops, stores, and artillery pieces; they sought, as well, to chart enemy movement, including the deployment of reserves. Aircraft were used, in addition, to communicate with troops, and to batter enemy ground offensives through tactical bombing. Further from the battlefield they could interdict supplies and disrupt enemy transport and communications.[6]

Much of the speculation about aircraft in war, though, had centered on the potential of long-range or "strategic" bombers. This theorizing had been infused with drama and emotion. In the abstract, the prospect seemed daunting to say the least: aircraft might appear from anywhere, at any time, to rain down bombs that the people below would have no power to stop. The shielding effect of armies and navies would no longer be relevant, and there would be no adequate place for civilian populations to shelter or to hide. Some of those who focused on the prospect of such bombing found compelling the possibility that it might circumvent the ground war by going straight to a nation's "vital centers." In this way, bomber aircraft might – quickly and single-handedly – collapse the war-fighting infrastructure and will of an enemy state. The idea was both alluring and terrifying. Some hoped that the laws of war outlined at international conferences at The Hague in 1899 and 1907, and the attempts to stigmatize the bombing of "open cities" from the air, might provide a check on the use of aircraft in war. Such hopes proved overly optimistic.[7]

Popular speculation about the potential effectiveness of long-range bombing worked hand in hand with the idea that if war by-passed armies and was instead taken directly to civilians, those civilians might not be able to endure its demands and deprivations. In Britain, civil strife and industrial crises in the decades leading up to World War II helped to create a climate receptive to such speculation. How would industrial labor be carried out? How would order be maintained? Policy makers and government officials – already worried about the loyalty and stability of their working classes – had now to ponder the possibility that aerial bombardment of the home front might help trigger social upheaval in crowded, vulnerable cities. Military authorities expressed such concerns as well.

To a great extent, those who predicted vast results from long-range bombing were far ahead of available technology. It would take a long time before any state would develop the numbers of bombers with the necessary range and carrying capacity required to engage in sustained, effective strategic bombardment. At the end of World War I no combatant possessed the types or the numbers of bombers needed to create the kind of havoc and destruction envisioned by the prewar speculators. Nonetheless, even the very rudimentary trial afforded to this form of war was sufficient to prompt the development of a body of theory that would influence subsequent thinking.

Early in the war the Germans employed the great airships named for their inventor, Count Ferdinand von Zeppelin, in air strikes against targets in continental Europe and Britain.[8] Though the success of the German airship raids on Britain was circumscribed by limitations of range and bomb load (and was complicated by army–navy service rivalry), the zeppelins achieved some notable early successes, causing damage and disruption in a number of the places they attacked. Over time, British fighters increasingly were equipped with engines that could propel them up to the altitude of the zeppelins, while the development of incendiary and explosive-incendiary bullets made the hydrogen-filled dirigibles extremely vulnerable to attack. In addition, the British used signals intelligence successfully to identify and intercept airship flights. While intermittent airship raids continued throughout the war, the threat had largely abated by the end of 1916. The memory of the early raids, however, lingered uneasily in the public mind.

Early in the war the French were enthusiastic about the possibility of undermining the German war effort through aerial attacks. Perhaps this is not surprising in light of early French enthusiasm for aviation generally, but French bombing theory was pragmatic – oriented to providing maximum assistance to the ground war. Aircraft production problems and the increasingly urgent calls from the front lines for aerial support caused the French program to be scaled back by 1916. Nonetheless, the French would continue their efforts throughout the war, choosing their targets on the basis of feasibility and significance to the enemy war effort.[9]

The use of long-range bombers in 1917 and 1918 did not have an appreciable impact on the war's outcome: small numbers of fitful, sporadic, and often inaccurate long-range bombing raids inflicted only limited physical damage, and failed to speed the conclusion of the war through a psychological impact on the bombing victims. Nonetheless, these so-called "independent" operations affected the course of thinking about the potential of long-range bombardment in war, thus shaping perceptions about how bombers might be used, and what their effects might be, in the future.

In 1917 the Germans began to employ specially designed Gotha and Giant bombers against Britain. Both were technological marvels for their time; indeed, the Giant's 138-foot wing-span was scarcely shorter than that of a World War II-era B-29 bomber. The early attacks on London, carried out in daylight by a handful of bombers flying in formation and taking advantage of surprise, had an impact disproportionate to the bomb load they carried. The British fighters that sought to intercept the invaders had little success, causing an indignant public to recall the RNAS's failure against the early zeppelin raids.

The German raids had several immediate effects. First, they caused British fighters, badly needed in France, to be recalled to help defend the home island; second, they prompted Britain's war cabinet to give greater priority to aircraft production; and third, they set in motion a process which ultimately would result in the establishment of a separate and independent Royal Air Force.[10] In the meantime, however, British air defenses improved, and the Germans – frustrated with what were, ultimately, meager results from the long-range raids – refocused their bombers on more tactical roles in the European theater.

Major General Hugh Trenchard, formerly of the army's Royal Flying Corps, came to head the long-range bombing arm of the new service. Trenchard, who took up his duties officially in early June 1918, never had more than nine bombing squadrons available to him – less than a tenth of the total strength of the new RAF. He attempted genuine strategic bombing only on occasion, instead directing most of his effort to the interdiction of German rail traffic and strikes on German airfields. Trenchard realized, though, that he had popular pressure on him to achieve results. In his final war dispatch, he claimed that he had spread his attacks over as wide an area as possible, so as to maximize the "moral" (or psychological) effect of bombing, which he estimated to be twenty times the material effect. The British World War I postwar bombing survey emphasized the moral effect of bombing and the loss of production caused when workers were moved into air raid shelters. As the postwar chief of air staff, Trenchard fought for the RAF's continued independence, holding off army and navy attempts to regain their air arms.[11]

At the end of World War I no consensus on the record and the future of strategic bombing emerged and (as with land warfare) a running debate ensued between the advocates of change and the advocates of conservatism. But combat aviation had won a set of adherents who would, in the interwar years, warn repeatedly of its power and insist that their own nations maintain an air striking force in order both to deter war and serve as a first line of defense. These advocates found an audience among a generation of people who had witnessed the catastrophic impact of industrialized warfare and who looked forward with awe and trepidation to a future in which bombers would become larger, faster, and more capable.

During the interwar years flawed assumptions and mistaken projections about the future filtered and shaped memory. In Britain, for instance, what seemed to linger prominently in the public mind – and in the military mind as well – was the memory of the early zeppelin and Gotha–Giant raids; in contrast, the memory of the later raids – in which the defenders were dominant – seemed to fade. This effect was perhaps manifested most graphically when the former – and future – prime minister Stanley Baldwin proclaimed in the House of Commons in 1932 that the bomber "will always get through."

British politicians and military officers both had been troubled by the need to bring fighters back to Britain. After the war, RAF analyses and staff college lectures devoted much attention to the fact that the German strategic bombing offensives had, by the end of the war, demanded a significant defensive response in Great Britain. Trenchard ultimately used this idea as the main driver in his postwar rhetoric, arguing that, in the event of war, it would be essential to undertake an immediate, relentless aerial offensive which would cause enemy production losses and would create overwhelming public demands for protection. Once forced onto the defensive, the enemy would find himself on a slippery slope from which he would have no hope of recovery.[12]

Ironically, this strident declaratory policy did not keep Trenchard's RAF from making important strides in air defense – in essence it hedged its bets against its own public declarations. But those declarations in themselves had consequences that must not be overlooked. After the war the air staff's casualty estimates for future air war came to be based upon – and heavily skewed by – the first two Gotha raids against London, which alone had accounted for 40 percent of the total casualties suffered in Britain due to German bomber raids. These estimates, which were highly problematical for all sorts of statistical reasons, in turn formed the basis of ministry of health estimates (for hospital beds, etc.). These were adjusted to keep pace with the growth of the Luftwaffe, and so became increasingly frightening through the 1930s.

By 1935 a future prime minister, Clement Attlee, argued that another world war would mean the "end of civilization." And a few years later the former foreign secretary, Sir John Simon, predicted that in the first week or so of a war the Germans might be able to inflict damage on London to the tune of £5 million.[13] Noted military commentator Sir Basil Liddell Hart wrote in 1937 that the air raids of 1914–18 had had a profound and lingering effect on the public mind. And he added that from the apprehension of air war springs "a natural exaggeration." Liddell Hart himself had contributed to this in his 1925 book, *Paris, or the Future of War*, which focused on the possibilities of offensive air power.[14] Underlying these apocalyptic predictions was the notion that modern society was fragile as a result of its complexity and its density, and was thus particularly vulnerable to air raids. This notion had been furthered by the translated work of the Italian air theorist Guilio Douhet, who focused, in particular, on the prospect of gas being rained down on cities by long-range aircraft.[15]

In Britain casualty projections for an air war – should it come – were disquieting indeed. Based on air staff estimates that were recently scaled upward, government officials were predicting 30,000 casualties per day requiring hospital treatment, continuing over several weeks. Psychologists were predicting widespread neurosis and emotional instability. In April 1939 the ministry of health would issue a million burial forms to local authorities. In 1941, Prime Minister Winston Churchill would, in a fit of pique, charge the air staff with helping to paint a picture of air warfare that "depressed the statesmen responsible for the prewar policy, and played a definite part in the desertion of Czecho-Slovakia [the infamous Munich Agreement] in August 1938."[16]

In what would prove to be a welcome surprise to British planners in the early years of the war, however, actual casualties from air war proved only a small fraction of what had been feared and anticipated. Hospital admissions for neurosis declined, suicide rates fell, and incidents of drunkenness declined by half – relative to peacetime. To their credit, the psychologists admitted they were wrong. Writing in the *Lancet* in 1941, Dr Felix Brown explained: "The incidence of genuine psychiatric air-raid casualties has been much lower than might have been expected; the average previously healthy civilian has proved remarkably adjustable." He added that women had not been a "weakening element" in the general population – as it was expected they might be. In response to a Gallup poll asking what had made them most depressed that winter, Londoners early in 1941 ranked the weather over aerial bombing.[17]

The Germans, failing in their 1940 attempt to gain aerial supremacy over Britain, turned to attacking British cities, particularly London. The fact that the British people seemed to rally rather than falter under the strain might have given the British air staff pause with regard to their own plans for the strategic bombardment of Germany. But the air staff and the politicians guiding the war effort saw little alternative but to rely on the air arm against Germany. With the British army having been driven off the continent, there was no tool of offensive warfare to use against Hitler except for Bomber Command. Thus, great hopes and expectations were placed upon the shoulders of the Command – even though it was hardly in a position to bear them, early on.

Despite the emphasis on the central role of strategic bombing in a future war in their public declarations, the British had done little to prepare for it. When, in the late 1930s, the new head of Bomber Command, Sir Edgar Ludlow-Hewitt, surveyed the competencies of his force, he had found them sadly lacking.[18] Failure to attend to the technical details of strategic bombing had cost the British dearly; indeed, two years into the war, a thorough photo-reconnaissance evaluation would reveal that only one in five of Bomber Command's planes was getting within five miles of its target.[19] Flying at night to evade effective German defenses, the British were simply not hitting their targets with enough regularity to have any serious impact on the German war effort. Under the circumstances they made a formal change in tactics in 1942 – a change that had been in the offing for some time: instead of trying to discern specific points in the German war machine, the British would attack entire German cities, concentrating on areas of worker housing. Shortly after this directive took effect, a new head of Bomber Command, Sir Arthur Harris, was brought on board. He committed himself to the task, and implemented the kinds of technological and tactical changes that would eventually transform the Command into a force of great destructive power and technical competence.[20]

Though the Germans had maintained some interest in long-range bombing during the interwar years – and though Luftwaffe head Hermann Göring would boast in exaggerated terms about the power of his air force – the Germans had not managed, prior to 1939, to build a truly strategic air force. As a continental power they had to think, first, about the needs of their army. In addition, though, they made some weapons procurement choices that kept them from achieving their full potential in the air. Once the war had begun, both bureaucratic inefficiencies and the heavy demands of the ground war kept them from revisiting the issue of long-range bombing in a rational and sustained way. However, they did develop and use, first in 1944, the famous "V-weapons" that would rain down heavily on London, causing additional grief and war-weariness for the British. The Russians, fully occupied with a ground war that would decide their national survival, kept the bulk of their increasingly effective aircraft focused on, and in support of, the land battles.[21]

When the Americans entered the war in 1941, they set out to make a major contribution to the strategic bombing of Germany. Resisting British entreaties to join the nighttime area offensive against cities, they sought instead to fly their bombers against selected targets in the German war industry. They hoped that by striking "key node" targets in the enemy economy, they might manage to bring it crashing down like a house of cards. These hopes proved unfounded: the Americans also fell victim to the strong German defenses, and by late 1943 it was clear that their theory of air warfare had little in common with reality. But rather than change targets, as the British had, they brought fighter escorts into the war in large numbers. These planes protected the bombers and fought determined battles with German defenders. The resulting attrition of German aerial resources – skilled pilots in particular – provided for a more effective bombing campaign in the later part of the war and eroded the fighting strength of the Luftwaffe just prior to the return of Anglo-American and Canadian forces to the continent on D-Day, June 6, 1944.

By 1945 bombing was massive in scale. In March 1945, the peak month of the Anglo-American combined bomber offensive, the U.S. Army Air Forces and the RAF's Bomber Command together dropped more than 130,000 tons of bombs – well over the combined total they had dropped in the entire year of 1942, and just under the total dropped for 1943.[22] Though strategic bombing did not prove decisive on its own, or live up to the expectations of its most assertive interwar advocates, it did at least put a ceiling on Hitler's production during the war, and aided greatly in destroying the fighting power of the Luftwaffe – a crucial prerequisite for launching an amphibious assault on the beaches of Normandy in mid-1944. And strategic bombers would carry, in 1945, the most revolutionary and devastating weapons of the war: the atomic bombs dropped on the Japanese cities of Hiroshima and Nagasaki. If advances in nuclear physics in the 1930s were starting to lay bare the secrets of the atom, the work done in the United States under the secret name of the Manhattan Project would telescope that progress and create, in the space of a few short years, a destructive capability that would leave the world awed and anxious about the future.

Naval Warfare

In addition to ushering in sweeping changes in ground fighting and aviation, World War I saw major changes in naval warfare. In the early years of the twentieth century the British had responded to Germany's increased naval production by extending naval treaties to Japan, France, and Russia, and by building the *Dreadnought* – a new, super-sized battleship intended to outclass and outgun everything else on the high seas. The Germans, in addition to traditional construction, invested in mining and submarine assets designed to chip away at the British advantage – wearing down the Royal Navy prior to the major naval *Schlacht* (battle) that naval theorist Alfred Thayer Mahan had insisted was central and unavoidable in great power warfare.

Though the submarine had existed for some time, the Germans grasped it in an effort to exploit them against the larger British fleet. This effort ultimately caused disquiet among the British, as naval historian Geoffrey Till has pointed out: "After the disaster of the Broad Fourteens in September 1914, when one U-boat had sunk three antiquated cruisers as though potting ducks in a shooting gallery, the British swung from skepticism about the submarine to something approaching hysteria. The mere suspicion of a periscope caused several 'battles' at fleet anchorages, with destroyers rushing about dropping depth charges like confetti at a wedding."[23]

Early in the war, though, the Germans proved less than successful at draining strength from the Royal Navy. As in the other realms of warfare, new techniques were countered with defensive measures that tended to restore the state of affairs that existed at the beginning of the war. And, as in land warfare, underdeveloped communications limited capabilities and made the large fleets unwieldy; it was difficult for the two main navies simply to locate one another, even in confined waters. Naval gunnery, though ever more powerful, remained inaccurate.

Still, the Germans felt compelled to try to erode British dominance on the high seas, and it was Admiral Scheer's attempt to ambush the British fleet that led to the battle of Jutland on May 31, 1916. This inconclusive contest gave the Germans no strategic advantage in the end, and prompted Scheer to report to the Kaiser that the only sensible naval course thereafter would be a full-scale submarine assault on English commerce. This assault, commencing in the spring of 1917, was potent and daunting to the British, especially since they exacerbated its effect by their initial failure to convoy ships. But the German initiative had the effect of finally bringing the United States into the war, thus creating a whole new array of strategic problems for Germany. Eventually, the British and the Americans defeated the U-boat threat through improved tactics and superior equipment.

In the end, opinion was divided about whether the new developments in naval warfare had prompted the need for radical change. Interwar navies – like interwar land and air forces – waged ongoing and inconclusive debates over whether new technologies and tactics had been revolutionary enough to provoke a rethinking of the entire enterprise of war fighting.[24] Much of the naval debate focused on the future of the battleship, specifically its vulnerability to undersea and aerial attack. The issue was never settled entirely, and the British – as well as the Americans and the Japanese – would enter World War II with overconfidence about their ability to defeat the submarine threat. Most traditional naval officers failed to grasp, as well, the potency that aircraft would eventually display against ships. The Americans and the Japanese were, to a limited degree, exceptions to the latter; but they, too, had a great deal of rethinking and adapting to do once World War II commenced.[25] The Germans, who had held high expectations for their submarines during World War I (as they had for their bombers), emerged from the experience sobered and in some ways skeptical of panaceas outside the realm of the land army.

During the interwar years most naval officers assumed that the traditional battle fleet would perform the following functions in war: (1) find the enemy with light cruiser screens, submarine pickets, and reconnaissance aircraft; (2) fix the enemy and prevent him escaping; and (3) strike the enemy. Fleet submarines, aircraft, and destroyers would be used to prevent the enemy from concentrating his fire. The defeat of the enemy battle line would be effected through the volleys of the battleships' heavy guns, and then finished off via further submarine, aircraft, and destroyer attacks.[26]

Even if the Germans, by the commencement of World War II, were more sober in their expectations for submarines than they had been in the previous war, they did not hesitate to use them – and other weapons, such as magnetic mines – in an effort, once again, to chip away at British naval supremacy.[27] The Battle of the Atlantic, the German attempt to sever the sea link between the British and the Americans, was one of the most important of the war: failure of the Anglo-Americans to meet the challenge it posed would have caused their entire war effort to falter badly. The work of defeating the German submarine menace proved to be daunting: as historian John Keegan has written, "in mid-1942 the eventual outcome of the Battle of the Atlantic was evident to no one. The 'statistics, diagrams and curves' were pregnant with menace."[28]

Once France fell and the Germans acquired the use of the French Atlantic ports, they had clear access to the British maritime supply lines. Using "wolf pack" tactics to gang up on and assault convoys of ships, the German U-boats were able to hunt with daunting efficiency. When the Americans entered the war as combatants, the Germans placed a sizable portion of their subs off the American coast where they – for a time, at least – could attack Allied shipping almost at will. But the Americans introduced convoying in May 1942, and this, along with an accelerated ship-building program, began to reverse the trend that had seen 1.25 million tons of goods sunk between January and March.

The Battle of the Atlantic pitted navies against one another, but it was a contest, as well, of scientific and technical skill. The British made good use of their ability to decrypt material enciphered on Germany's Enigma machine, but they left themselves open to vulnerabilities in the intelligence war (including the use of a book code instead of a machine cipher). And inter-service fights between the admiralty and the Royal Air Force sometimes impeded progress. In the meantime, the Germans sought to extend the range of their boats by refueling at sea. But the increased use of long-range aircraft in an anti-submarine role eventually offset this German advance. In the back-and-forth of measure and counter-measure, the Allies suffered spikes in their tonnage losses in November 1942 and February–March 1943, but made steady progress despite these setbacks. By the end of 1943 new ship construction had made good the losses from earlier in the year, and improved tracking, positioning, and rerouting kept the new ships safer, as did "support group" escort tactics. Finally, the ever-expanding efforts of long-range anti-submarine aircraft continued to bear fruit, eventually sinking as many subs per month as Germany could manage to build: "The long-range aircraft, particularly the Liberator bomber, equipped with radar, Leigh light [searchlights], machine guns and depth charges, was flying death to a surfaced U-boat."[29]

Submarines were not the only vessels vulnerable to air power, however. Sea warfare around the globe proved the power of the airplane as a vital tool in naval striking power. Thus, the aircraft carrier and the carrier battle group came into their own, both for waging offensive strikes against the enemy and for defending one's own seaborne assets. This development was profound, and no nation wishing to possess a serious navy could afford to ignore its lessons. Both submarines and carriers would play central roles in the naval strategies of the major powers after 1945.

Conclusion

The first half of the twentieth century saw massive change in the nature of war fighting between the great powers. The industrial revolution had placed a great array of new capabilities and weapons systems on the battlefield, and these had their first tests between 1914 and 1918. Because many of these weapons were still in their infancy during World War I, and because the communications systems facilitating them and linking them remained primitive, these initial trials were only partial and inconclusive predictors of what the future might hold. They did, however, set up vigorous debates about the future of warfare, and these debates played themselves out against a background of unsettled and volatile politics during the interwar years.

Military professionals, finding themselves in an era of ongoing technological change, wrestled over the requirement for altering their fundamental assumptions, behaviors, and practices. Advocates of radical change sought to make their voices heard, and to move those who were comfortably ensconced in the familiar trappings of traditional means and methods. But military organizations went into World War II with many of these debates still unresolved: no great power reached an interwar consensus on the optimum employment of the weapons systems first tried during the Great War. Military doctrine for each combatant nation entering into World War II reflected the unfinished state of prevailing contests, discussions, and dilemmas stemming from vast technological and scientific change.

World War II proved that no combatant nation could afford to ignore the new technologies: the challenge of weapons such as submarines, aircraft, and tanks had to be met, not only with adaptation and doctrinal change, but also with innovation and a mustering of scientific and industrial skill. But predictions that any one weapon might prove "decisive" on its own were misguided. The battles fought during World War II revealed that the best adaptation to change came from integrating new technologies into established systems relying on the synergies of combined arms, and resting on sound doctrine, professionalism, and training.

NOTES

1   See Stephen Biddle, *Military Power: The Determinants of Victory and Defeat in Modern War* (Princeton NJ: Princeton University Press, 2004), p. 29.
2   See, in particular, Gary Sheffield, *Forgotten Victory* (London: Headline, 2001). Also: David G. Herrmann, *The Arming of Europe and the Making of the First World War* (Princeton NJ: Princeton University Press, 1996); Jonathan Bailey, *The First World War and the Birth of the Modern Style of Warfare* (Camberley: British Army Strategic and Combat Studies Institute, 1996), SCSI Occasional Paper no. 22; Robin Prior and Trevor Wilson, *Command on the Western Front* (Oxford: Blackwell, 1992); Gary Sheffield, "Blitzkrieg and Attrition: Land Operations in Europe, 1914–1945," in *Warfare in the Twentieth Century*, Colin McInnes and G. D. Sheffield, eds (London: Unwin Hyman, 1988), pp. 51–79; Timothy Travers, *The Killing Ground: The British Army, the Western Front, and the Emergence of Modern Warfare, 1900–1918* (London: Allen and Unwin, 1987); Shelford Bidwell and Dominick Graham, *Firepower: British Army Weapons and Theories of War, 1914–1945* (London: Allen and Unwin, 1985).
3   See Richard Preston, Alex Roland, and Sydney Wise, *Men in Arms*, 5th edn (Fort Worth TX: Harcourt, Brace, Jovanovich, 1991), p. 252.
4   On the evolution of European armies during the interwar years, see Sheffield, "Blitzkrieg and Attrition," pp. 64–7; also, generally, Hew Strachan, *European Armies and the Conduct of War* (London: Allen and Unwin, 1983); Larry H. Addington, *The Patterns of War Since the Eighteenth Century* (Bloomington: Indiana University Press, 1994); Colin McInnes, *Men, Machines and the Emergence of Modern Warfare* (Camberley: British Army Strategic and Combat Studies Institute, 1996), SCSI Occasional Paper no. 2; Shelford Bidwell and Dominick Graham, *Firepower: British Army Weapons and Theories of War, 1914–1945* (London: Allen and Unwin, 1945).
5   See James Corum, *The Roots of Blitzkrieg: Hans von Seeckt and German Military Reform* (Lawrence: University of Kansas Press, 1992); also, Robert Doughty et al., eds, *Warfare in the Western World*, vol. 2 (Lexington MA: D. C. Heath, 1996), pp. 639–40.
6   See Richard Muller, "Close Air Support: The German, British, and American Experiences, 1918–1941," in *Military Innovation in the Interwar Period*, Williamson Murray and Allan R. Millett, eds (Cambridge: Cambridge University Press, 1996), pp. 144–90; Tami Davis Biddle, "Learning in Real Time: The Development and Implementation of Air Power in

the First World War," in *Air Power History: Turning Points from Kitty Hawk to Kosovo*, Peter Gray and Sebastian Cox, eds (London: Frank Cass, 2002).

7 On air power and the law of war, see D. C. Watt, "Restraints on War in the Air Before 1945," in *Restraints on War: Studies in the Limitation of Armed Conflict*, Michael Howard, ed. (New York: Oxford University Press, 1979), pp. 57–77; Geoffrey Best, *Humanity in Warfare* (New York: Columbia University Press, 1980), pp. 262–85; W. Hays Parks, "Air War and the Law of War," *Air Force Law Review* 32/1 (1990): 1–225; and Tami Davis Biddle, "Air Power," in *The Laws of War*, Michael Howard, George Andreopoulos, and Mark Shulman, eds (New Haven CT: Yale University Press, 1994), pp. 140–59.

8 On the German zeppelin program, see Douglas Robinson, *The Zeppelin in Combat, 1912 to 1918* (London: G. T. Foulis, 1962); Peter Fritzsche, *A Nation of Flyers* (Cambridge MA: Harvard University Press, 1992).

9 On the French bombing program in the latter part of the war, see Tami Davis Biddle, *Rhetoric and Reality in Air Warfare: The Evolution of British and American Ideas about Strategic Bombing, 1914–1945* (Princeton NJ: Princeton University Press, 2002), pp. 25–9.

10 See Malcolm Cooper, *The Birth of Independent Air Power* (London: Allen and Unwin, 1986) and Neville Jones, *The Origins of Strategic Bombing* (London: William Kimber, 1973).

11 See Biddle, *Rhetoric and Reality in Air Warfare*, pp. 35–81.

12 1928 RAF Manual, Part I, Operations, Ministry of Defence, London.

13 Attlee and Simon quoted in *War Begins at Home* (Mass Observation), Tom Harrisson and Charles Madge, eds (London: Chatto and Windus, 1940), pp. 41–2.

14 Basil Liddell Hart, *Europe in Arms* (New York: Random House, 1937), p. 24; *Paris, or the Future of War* (New York: E. P. Dutton, 1925; reprint, New York: Garland, 1972), pp. 28–9.

15 Guilio Douhet, *Command of the Air* (Coward-McCann, 1942; reprint, Washington DC: Office of Air Force History, 1983); see also, for example, unsigned article, "The Air Doctrine of General Douhet," *Royal Air Force Quarterly* 4/2 (1933): 164–7.

16 Minute, Churchill to Portal, October 7, 1941, pp. 1–3, Papers of Sir Charles Portal, Christ Church, Oxford, folder 2C.

17 Felix Brown, "Civilian Psychiatric Air Raid Casualties," *The Lancet* May 31, 1941: 691; see also Biddle, *Rhetoric and Reality in Air Warfare*, pp. 190–1.

18 See Biddle, *Rhetoric and Reality in Air Warfare*, pp. 122–7.

19 For the report, see Appendix 13 in vol. 4 of Sir Charles Webster and Noble Frankland, *The Strategic Air Offensive against Germany* (London: HMSO, 1961), pp. 205–13.

20 See Tami Davis Biddle, "Bombing by the Square Yard: Sir Arthur Harris at War, 1942–1945," *International History Review* 21/3 (1999): 626–64.

21 On the Germans, see Richard Muller, *The German Air War in Russia* (Baltimore MD: Nautical and Aviation Publishing, 1992); Williamson Murray, *Luftwaffe* (Baltimore MD: Nautical and Aviation Publishing, 1985); R. J. Overy, *Goering: The Iron Man* (London: Routledge and Kegan Paul, 1984). On Russia, see Von Hardesty, *Red Phoenix: The Rise of Soviet Air Power, 1941–1945* (Washington DC: Smithsonian Institution Press, 1982), and Robert Kilmarx, *A History of Soviet Air Power* (New York: Praeger, 1962).

22 See Webster and Frankland, *Strategic Air Offensive*, vol. 3, p. 4.

23 Geoffrey Till, "Naval Power," in McInnes and Sheffield, *Warfare in the Twentieth Century*, p. 89.

24 See Holger Herwig, "Innovation Ignored: The Submarine Problem," and Geoffrey Till, "Adopting the Aircraft Carrier," in Murray and Millett, *Military Innovation*, pp. 227–64, 191–226.

25 On interwar and wartime sea power in the United States, see George Baer, *One Hundred Years of Sea Power: The US Navy, 1890–1990* (Stanford CA: Stanford University Press, 1994), pp. 119–247.
26 See Till, "Naval Power," p. 96.
27 See Preston, Roland, and Wise, *Men in Arms*, p. 272.
28 John Keegan, *The Second World War* (New York: Penguin, 1989), p. 106.
29 Keegan, *The Second World War*, pp. 116–20.

GUIDE TO FURTHER READING

Larry H. Addington, *The Patterns of War since the Eighteenth Century* (Bloomington: Indiana University Press, 1994). A useful overview of the history of modern warfare.

George W. Baer, *One Hundred Years of Sea Power* (Stanford CA: Stanford University Press, 1994). The main outlines of the evolution of naval thinking.

Jonathan Bailey, *The First World War and the Birth of the Modern Style of Warfare* (Camberley: British Army Strategic and Combat Studies Institute, 1996). An important study of the revolutionary nature of World War I.

Stephen Biddle, *Military Power: Explaining Victory and Defeat in Modern Battle* (Princeton NJ: Princeton University Press, 2004). An important analytical analysis of modern warfare.

Tami Davis Biddle, *Rhetoric and Reality in Air Warfare: The Evolution of British and American Ideas about Strategic Bombing, 1914–1945* (Princeton NJ: Princeton University Press, 2002). An intellectual and social history of the evolution of strategic bombing.

Shelford Bidwell and Dominick Graham, *Firepower: British Army Weapons and Theories of War, 1904–1945* (London: Allen and Unwin, 1982). A perceptive study of change and continuity in the British army in the first half of the twentieth century.

Bernard Brodie and Fawn Brodie, *From Crossbow to H-Bomb* (Bloomington: Indiana University Press, 1973). An influential overview of the history of warfare.

Robert Doughty and Ira Gruber, *Warfare in the Western World: Military Operations since 1871*, vol. 2 (Lexington MA: D. C. Heath, 1996). A recent history, with a focus on the operational and tactical levels of modern warfare.

Kenneth Hagan, *This People's Navy: The Making of American Sea Power* (New York: Free Press, 1991). A broad survey of modern sea power and naval thinking.

Colin McInnes, *Men, Machines, and the Emergence of Modern Warfare, 1914–1945* (Camberley: British Army Strategic and Combat Studies Institute, 1992). An important contribution on the evolution of technology and the nature of warfare.

Colin McInnes and G. D. Sheffield, eds, *Warfare in the Twentieth Century* (London: Unwin Hyman, 1988). An excellent series of essays on the evolution of the technology and tactics of modern warfare.

Williamson Murray and Allan R. Millett, eds, *Military Effectiveness*, 3 vols (Boston MA: Allen and Unwin, 1988). Three seminal volumes, with essays by expert contributors, on warfare during the first half of the twentieth century.

Williamson Murray and Allan R. Millett, eds, *Military Innovation in the Interwar Period* (Cambridge: Cambridge University Press, 1996). Specific case studies of important interwar innovations.

Richard Preston, Alex Roland, and Sidney Wise, *Men in Arms* (Fort Worth TX: Harcourt, Brace, Jovanovich, 1991). A sweeping but useful overview of the history of warfare.

Theodore Ropp, *War in the Modern World* (New York: Macmillan, 1962).

Stephen P. Rosen, *Winning the Next War: Innovation and the Modern Military* (Ithaca NY: Cornell University Press, 1991). An in-depth look at the determinants of interwar innovation.

Gary Sheffield, *Forgotten Victory* (London: Headline, 2001). An important reinterpretation of the British experience of World War I.

Timothy Travers, *The Killing Ground: The British Army, the Western Front, and the Emergence of Modern Warfare* (London: Allen and Unwin, 1987). A key contribution on the history of the British army during World War I.

Timothy Travers, *How the War Was Won: Command and Technology in the British Army on the Western Front* (London: Routledge, 1992). An important contribution by a leading scholar of the British army.

CHAPTER TWENTY-SIX

Hitler and the Origins of
World War II

ANITA J. PRAZMOWSKA

> The fact that a nation has acquired an enormous territorial area is not a reason why it should hold that territory perpetually. At most, the possession of such territory is a proof of the strength of the conqueror and the weakness of those who submit to them. And in this strength alone lives the right of possession. (Adolf Hitler, *Mein Kampf*)[1]

The enormity of the tragedy that was World War II created an emotional need after the war to show that what had overwhelmed Europe during the fateful years of 1939–45 was an aberration. Historians have battled not merely with the difficult question of why the war took place, but also with the issue of whether German political life during the interwar period had been rendered inherently unstable and thus prone to extremism as a result of the decisions made at the Paris peace conference. Although the role played by Hitler has been paramount in discussions of the war's origins, that played by Josef Stalin has also aroused considerable debate, while the policy of appeasement pursued by Neville Chamberlain has been interpreted by critics as encouraging Hitler's ambitions. These debates continue, though the earlier tendency to analyze the events leading to the outbreak of World War II in terms of a breakdown of the big power consensus has been enriched by an understanding of the role of the smaller, and not necessarily peripheral, players: Czechoslovakia, Poland, and the Balkan states. Finally, the end of the Cold War has created an environment in which historians no longer focus on the clash of the forces of evil (Nazism and communism) against the forces of good (democratic, liberal, republican ideals). The earlier quest to find guilty individuals has given way to inquiries into the context of interwar Europe that allowed aggressive nationalist ideologies to dominate. Earlier embarrassing revelations that neither France nor Britain was prepared to oppose Hitler's aspirations might, with time, lose their relevance and be replaced with debates on the economic and political life of the European democracies. Although archives continue to yield new evidence relating to the origins of the war, the most important elements of the story are well known. Future research will, however, continue to provide details and different approaches.[2]

When Hitler came to power in January 1933, the aims of the Nazi Party were well known, even if most European statesmen chose to believe that a distinction could be drawn between statements made for propaganda reasons and the way the new government would proceed once in power. Nevertheless, Hitler had already signaled in *Mein Kampf* that reversing the decisions of the Paris peace conference was not his main objective.[3] He linked the issue of control of territories to that of his racial theories.

Nazi Foreign Policy

In 1933 it was still impossible to judge whether the loose and rambling pronouncements made in *Mein Kampf* were likely to be pursued in practice. Nor was it clear whether Hitler's ambition to restore the German frontiers of 1914 could be restrained by governments opposed to such changes. These were dilemmas that confused contemporary politicians and have provoked extensive controversy ever since. Was Hitler driven by a vision, which he was determined to implement by any means possible? Or was he an opportunist who merely exploited situations as they arose?[4] While historians will continue to dispute this point, there can be little doubt that when Hitler came to power in March 1933 his stated aim of reversing the territorial decisions made at Versailles and flouting restrictions imposed on German military potential were supported by most political parties and individual German citizens. During the years that followed, Germany not merely embarked on a full program of remilitarization but successfully challenged the ban on union with Austria, destroyed Czechoslovakia, and attacked and defeated Poland. In the process the authority of the League of Nations was thoroughly undermined and France's system of continental alliances was ripped up. At the end of September 1939 European states were not able to prevent Hitler from pursuing further territorial conquests in Europe.

In 1933 Germany's economic plight preoccupied Hitler as much as his desire to see Germany powerful again. Thus, rearmament was not only a means of reaffirming Germany's position in Europe but also of revitalizing the economy and providing employment. Both would enable the Nazi Party to consolidate its authority and to extend its control over the state and the army. Conservative and nationalist elements in German political life supported Hitler because they were more anxious to destroy the Social Democratic Party and the trade unions than to uphold the democratic system. Further, they concurred in Hitler's objectives of challenging the European powers and reaffirming Germany's role in European politics. Since Hitler's expansionist plans focused on eastern Europe, neither the Nazis' political allies nor the army disagreed. Eastern Europe, the Baltic coast, and even the Balkans were traditionally seen as Germany's natural areas of economic development and within her sphere of influence. Nor did Hitler's racist policy of subjugating those peoples he believed to be racially inferior lead to disagreements. Racist theories were freely discussed – and not merely by German nationalists: they were common in France and Britain, in spite of their democratic traditions. Hitler's antisemitism may have been particularly virulent, but various forms of it had become the norm in Europe after World War I.

Hitler's role in the creation of the Nazi regime and in steering it towards a perpetually radical program is an issue which has preoccupied historians. Ian Kershaw and Wolfgang Mommsen have debated this point extensively, as have other eminent historians. There is no consensus as to whether Hitler played a critical role in defining the Nazi regime's character, or whether he was merely a catalyst, bringing together preexisting political ideas. Any attempt to understand the course of German foreign policy on the eve of World War II inevitably will include a debate on the role of the Nazi leadership, the army, and a number of ministries. Hitler's foreign policy initiatives and plans for war were pursued with the complicity of these powerful groups and, as they proved to be successful, they strengthened the Nazi Party's grip on power and enhanced his authority.

Hitler's first foreign policy initiatives were conventional rather than radical. The signing of a non-aggression pact with Poland followed Germany's withdrawal from the disarmament conference and the League of Nations. These decisions met with the approval of the German ministry for foreign affairs and the war ministry. In France and Britain, these moves elicited only muted responses, even when followed by the reoccupation of the Saarland and news of Hitler's rearmament program. The British government hoped that Germany would, once its main grievances had been dealt with, become a partner in the endeavors of the great powers to maintain stability in Europe. Even the surprising break with the earlier policy of isolating Poland was viewed merely as Germany's attempt to break with the post-Versailles order.

The period 1935–7 marked a new stage in Hitler's policy of probing the western democracies for signs of willingness to accept Germany's bid to dominate Europe. On the one hand, the signing of the Anglo-German naval agreement on June 17, 1935 indicated his willingness to conclude bilateral agreements with Britain. Nevertheless, when in February 1936 Hitler made an official claim for the restoration of German colonies taken away in 1919, this looked like a policy of confrontation. In reality, these apparently contradictory strands of German policy indicated divisions within the ruling elites. On the one hand, Schacht, minister for economics, in common with the conservatives and nationalists, thought of reclaiming the colonies and the development of foreign trade. Hitler, on the other hand, focused on Europe and merely used the colonial issue to test British willingness to compromise. In both cases, Britain's attitude was of critical importance. What Hitler ultimately sought was for Britain to turn a blind eye to Germany pursuing territorial conquests in eastern Europe. In return, he was willing to renounce Germany's colonial claims.[5] By 1936 Hitler decided that Germany could proceed without prior agreements with Britain: the remilitarization of the Rhineland in March, which elicited no military response from either France or Britain, increased Hitler's standing in Germany and whetted his appetite for more.

At the same time, Hitler was preparing extensive plans for the future. When Italy was condemned for launching a war in Abyssinia, Hitler was able to draw Italy into German plans, while at the same time seeking anti-Soviet unity with Japan. These moves culminated in the signing of the Anti-Comintern pact in November 1936, which suggested not merely that the three were united on ideological lines, but that a division of spoils would follow. Still, neither Britain nor France took action, which would have signaled to Germany their determination to put a stop to plans for a future redistribution of spheres of influence.

In 1936 the outbreak of a civil war in Spain gave Hitler a unique opportunity. During that year he had more openly asserted his control over the economy and foreign policy. The Four Year Program, announced in September 1936, focused on rearmament and heavy industry. State control over economic and financial activities was also increased. The Nazi leadership became bolder in its pursuit of foreign policy objectives, abandoning its earlier commitment to revision of the 1919 treaty settlement, and instead taking initiatives that were clearly aimed at France and Britain. After earlier hesitation, Hitler assisted the nationalist forces in Spain. This led to increased German and Italian influence in the region, while British and French influence in Iberia and the western Mediterranean was reduced.

Internally, the Nazi regime increased its authority. The staging of the Olympics in Berlin gave the party propagandists an opportunity to use the event as a platform for the glorification of racial ideas. The economy had benefited from the rearmament programs and, with the reduction of unemployment, support for the party increased. An eminent historian has stated that "at the beginning of 1937 Germany was unquestionably the most powerful country in Europe."[6]

The pursuit of an ideologically motivated policy of expansion was made possible by the gradual sidelining and removal of those very conservatives and nationalists who earlier supported Hitler on the assumption that the reversal of the Versailles decision was the aim of his policies. They had been willing to consider extending Germany's influence in the east, even by means of military conquest, though were not so comfortable about the possibility of a conflict with Britain and France. But by the beginning of 1938 Hitler no longer needed their support. The ministry for foreign affairs was purged and Joachim Ribbentrop was appointed to head it. Reliable party members replaced career diplomats, most notably, in London, Tokyo, and Rome. At the same time the foreign department of the Nazi Party became more active in pursuing what it considered to be true Nazi foreign policy. The proliferation of organizations with the authority to make decisions that affected relations with other states did not disguise the fact that Hitler had the ultimate authority in the Nazi state.[7] The power of the military leadership was likewise destroyed. Blomberg, minister of war, and Fritsch, commander-in-chief of the army, were both dismissed after being personally discredited. Hitler took over as head of the war ministry. The response of the officer ranks was muted.

The destruction of Czechoslovakia had been high on the list of Hitler's priorities. He saw the state, which enjoyed close political and economic ties with France, as the lynchpin of France's eastern policy. Furthermore, the fact that Czechoslovakia had in 1935 signed a treaty of mutual assistance with the Soviet Union increased Hitler's determination to destroy it. Nevertheless, at the end of 1937 events in Austria allowed Hitler to address that issue first.

When Hitler decided to take action to subjugate Austria, he was confident that Britain and France would do nothing in its defense and that Italy would acquiesce in his decisions. On November 19, 1937, only a few days after he had delivered a wide-ranging exposition to his party and military leaders in which he signaled his determination to pursue an aggressive policy towards eastern Europe irrespective of Britain's attitude, he met with Lord Halifax. Hitler's disdain for Britain was confirmed when Halifax indicated that as long as territorial revision was pursued by peaceful means Britain would not interfere. France, too, appeared no longer concerned with the fate of Austria. Italy, the only state that had shown a determination to uphold Austrian independence, had by 1937 become economically dependent on Germany.

When Mussolini visited Germany in September 1937 he was no longer able or willing to make Austrian independence a condition of good relations. On the contrary, Italy was by then only too happy to enter into close relations with Germany.[8] Thus Austria's fate was left in Hitler's hands.

Austrian–German unity was an issue which in any case was unlikely to cause the western democracies to take action against Germany. Even though the Treaty of Versailles forbade unity between the two, European statesmen and public opinion were ambivalent. At the end of 1937 Kurt von Schuschnigg, the Austrian chancellor, unhappy about the activities of the Austrian Nazis, sought to clarify relations with Germany. Hitler clarified by demanding, in February 1938, that the foreign policies of the two countries be coordinated and that the Austrian National Socialists be given a larger say in state matters. Schuschnigg's attempt to parry Hitler's demands by calling a referendum that was to exclude young Nazi supporters backfired, as did his belated request for British support. The British government refused to become involved, while the French government was in a crisis. The Italian government advised Schuschnigg not to provoke Hitler, and he was forced to accept the growing role of the National Socialist Party, which in turn was guided by Berlin. Hitler, who had planned to install Arthur Seyss-Inquart as his puppet in Austria, changed his mind and German troops marched into Austria in March. Western responses were muted, and the absence of military retaliation strengthened Hitler's arguments against his military leaders who had advised against sending troops into Austria. Britain and France were uneasy about the turn of events, but comforted themselves by choosing to view the event as an internal German matter. Absence of visible Austrian opposition to the *Anschluss* further validated their lack of action.

European statesmen immediately considered the implications of Germany's action. Few had doubts that Czechoslovakia was now more vulnerable to Hitler's ambitions. But it was a sovereign state on which Germany had no obvious territorial claim. Furthermore, its security was guaranteed by at least two important international treaties: the Franco-Czechoslovak alliance signed in 1924 and the more recent Czechoslovak-Soviet Treaty of Mutual Assistance of 1935, which was meant to complement the Franco-Soviet Pact of Mutual Assistance signed a week earlier. In all cases it was assumed that Germany was likely to be the aggressor. The Little Entente, which brought together Czechoslovakia, Yugoslavia, and Romania and which had France's full support, completed the appearance of perfect security. The reality was far from perfect. The French attitude towards the eastern allies was always ambivalent, as they regarded them as a poor substitute for the old alliance with Russia; thus, continuing negotiations with the Soviet Union indicated to Czechoslovakia and Poland a potential conflict of interest. The French agreements of 1935 were an illusion, as they lacked precision and even though many politicians and military leaders would have wanted to see the Soviet Union as France's ally, they worried about the impact of more binding agreements on France's internal conflicts. Poland, France's key eastern partner, pursued its own anti-Czechoslovak campaign, in the process allying itself more closely with Germany. The Little Entente had been formed from anxieties about Hungary and could not be converted into an anti-German pact.[9]

Czechoslovakia, the only politically stable and economically successful state in that region, had an Achilles heel in the form of 3 million Germans in the Sudetenland. Although German nationals constituted over 22 percent of Czechoslovakia's population, the Czechs were determined to prevent them from claiming autonomy within regions where they formed a majority. Both during the Weimar period and after Hitler came to power, a number of German organizations sought to maintain the national identity of the German community in Czechoslovakia, even though these were Germans from within the old Habsburg Empire. Hitler claimed the right to act as champion of German minorities, which was popular in Germany and justified interference in the internal affairs of states where there were German minorities: in Romania, Hungary, Yugoslavia, and the Baltic states. German borderland communities in Czechoslovakia and Poland had found themselves incorporated into the new states against their wishes. At times of crisis and economic difficulties the latter were only too willing for Germany to take up their grievances, and the local Nazi Party began to play an increasingly important role. When, in November 1937, Hitler decided to destroy Czechoslovakia by military means, the Sudeten Germans were instructed to put forward demands they knew the Czechs would not concede and foment a state of tension.[10]

Unlike the Austrian crisis, the simmering German–Czechoslovak crisis faced the European states with a profound dilemma. To ignore it would be tantamount to giving Hitler the green light. That course of action was difficult to justify, as Czechoslovakia was a sovereign state and an attack on it, even if provoked by alleged mistreatment of a minority, could precipitate a wider conflict. On the other hand, to take military action in defense of Czechoslovakia did not seem possible. Britain had signaled to Hitler that it considered his grievances justified. To Britain, the real issue was whether France and Russia would honor their commitments to Czechoslovakia and thus draw Britain into a war which it had no wish to fight. While the Nazi propaganda machine inflamed the situation by instructing the Sudeten Germans to increase their demands, the British and French governments sought to prevent the situation from escalating into an international crisis. On the personal initiative of Prime Minister Chamberlain, a minor politician, Lord Runciman, was dispatched to investigate, while the French government made it clear that it would welcome a diplomatic solution as it did not want to honor its commitment to defend Czechoslovakia. In September 1938 Chamberlain made two fateful visits to Germany to meet Hitler. This intervention allowed Hitler to present himself as the defender of a mistreated German minority. Chamberlain naively undertook to find a solution by arranging a conference that convened in Munich on September 30.[11] Germany and Italy saw the meeting as an opportunity to break up Czechoslovakia. The Czechoslovak government was not invited to make its case and under the threat of being left to face Germany alone, was forced to accept the Munich conference decisions. Germany was given the freedom to decide which areas of Czechoslovakia were to be incorporated into the Third Reich. The Soviet Union was kept out of the picture. At the same time, Polish and Hungarian claims to Czechoslovak territories, presented by Germany, were upheld in principle and Czechoslovakia ultimately lost areas to Germany, Poland, and Hungary.

Germany's political role among the east European states was henceforth enhanced. Hungary and Romania now looked to Berlin to resolve local conflicts. Poland, a state that since 1934 had enjoyed good relations with Germany, was likely to be the next victim of Hitler's desire to settle scores predating World War I. In the meantime, France appeared to abandon the idea of an eastern bloc against Germany, while

Britain reversed its traditional lack of interest in eastern Europe to become mediator of German grievances there.

Poland's relations with Germany during the interwar period had undergone a number of changes. Territorial decisions made after the war created problems not only between the Polish and German states but also had an impact on international relations. From the outset Germany resented the emergence of an independent Poland. The Versailles decision to award Poland access to the seacoast was seen by most Germans as unjust. The French desire to have a strong ally on Germany's eastern border exacerbated British distrust of France's European policy. The result was that while Poland's claim to part of Silesia, the Poznan district, and a strip of land which gave it direct access to the Baltic was upheld at Versailles, Poland was not given the port of Danzig. Its "Free City" status, guaranteed by the League of Nations, satisfied neither Poland nor Germany. During the 1920s Poland ostensibly remained in the French camp, benefiting from close political and military contacts. Nevertheless, the Poles distrusted the French. They were anxious that France might still ally itself with the Soviet Union, Poland's enemy. France's close relations with Czechoslovakia irritated the Poles to the same extent, as did France's willingness to go along with British security plans which aimed at drawing Germany into close cooperation with both European powers. In 1934 Poland appeared to score a diplomatic victory when it signed an agreement with Germany. The contentious issue of the Free City of Danzig was, by common agreement, excluded from the list of issues to be discussed by both sides. To the Poles, their newfound intimacy with Germany offered a way out of political dependence on France and increased the likelihood of foreign investment, earlier deterred by fear of a Polish–German conflict. There were, of course, more tangible advantages in developing better relations with Germany in the long term: Czechoslovak influence in the region might be reduced; Poland might succeed in reclaiming the coal-rich Teschen region grabbed by Czechoslovakia in 1919; they might even join Germany in a war against the Soviet Union in the foreseeable future. The Munich conference threw some of these plans into disarray. Poland's exclusion from it signaled the possibility that Germany would not treat Poland as a partner, but as a satellite. With that came the ominous prospect of Germany returning Danzig onto the agenda of issues to be resolved. In October 1938, while the Poles still thought they might persuade Germany not to raise this contentious issue, the international community generally perceived that Poland would be Germany's next victim.

The sense of anticipation and anxiety which characterized the last months of 1938 and the first months of 1939 was, by March 1939, made worse by rumors which were impossible to verify, but which, if true, would have required Britain and France to react. For the Chamberlain government, indications that Germany might strike west, possibly to extend its control over the Belgian coast and the Low Countries, were most worrying. French policy was in disarray: Mussolini, emboldened by Germany's victories and increasingly confident that Britain would not back France, laid claims to Nice and Corsica; Colonel Josef Beck, the Polish minister for foreign affairs, rejected French and British counsel during the Czechoslovak crisis; the Soviet Union remained an unknown dimension in the evolving European crisis.[12]

At the beginning of March two new potential flashpoints overwhelmed the British and French governments. The British government took the lead in trying to deal with them. Since this was done without being able to verify the facts, the response was muddled. The first was news that Germany had put pressure on Romania to coordinate its foreign and economic policies with Germany. This would have resulted in Romania's oil deposits being at Germany's disposal, a situation which would have made Germany immune to any attempts to reduce her preparations for war by means of an economic blockade. At the same time, British newspapers reported that Germany had presented Poland with an ultimatum, demanding the return of Danzig. Since neither the Romanian nor the Polish governments were willing to be absolutely truthful with the British, Chamberlain chose to believe the worst. As if to underline the need for the democracies to be seen to be responding to these rumors, Germany blatantly contravened the agreements made at Munich. On March 15 German troops occupied Prague. For the first time, German policies were not justified by any claim to revision of old borders, mistreatment of the German minority, or even provocation. Nazi Germany now began to appear simply as an aggressor.

The British and French leaders had hoped that the Munich agreement would, at worst, postpone the European conflict; at best, that it might persuade Hitler that cooperation rather than conflict would better serve Germany's interests. Hitler viewed the matter in an entirely different light. The conference had robbed him of an opportunity to wage a minor, local war, one that would have restored the pride of the German army. He therefore wanted to complete the destruction of the hated Czech state. His second objective was the defeat of France and Britain – in spite of their complicity during the Czechoslovak crisis. Ultimately, Hitler planned a war against the Soviet Union and the attainment of world domination.[13] But first Poland, a state that had refused to accept a subordinate role in Germany's plans, needed to be destroyed.[14]

The continuing British attempts to stave off the European conflict through negotiations were undoubtedly made more difficult by the conviction on the part of the Poles and Romanians that they were well placed to deal directly with Germany. Both states welcomed British concern about their security, though neither was willing to subordinate itself to British plans, which appeared vague. During the second half of March 1939 Chamberlain sought to forestall further German aggression by encouraging the east European states to form a diplomatic bloc. He hoped this would signal to Hitler their determination to stand united. All those approached knew that to go along with the British proposal risked provoking Germany – not least because in its first draft the plan was supposed to include the Soviet Union. The Poles noted that this broadly defined security bloc would not assure them of military assistance. Beck therefore put forward a counter-proposal for a bilateral agreement, which he believed would be less provocative to the Germans.[15] When, on March 31, Chamberlain announced to the House of Commons that Britain had undertaken to defend Polish security and the status of the Free City of Danzig, both sides knew the guarantee was a diplomatic gesture to forewarn Germany, as distinct from a statement to fight jointly. In fact, talks after March revealed that neither Britain nor France could provide military assistance to Poland in the event of a German attack.

Since the end of World War I France and Poland had maintained close relations, beginning with French military assistance to the Poles in their battles with the Red Army in 1919–21. France had since come to regard Poland as the lynchpin of its eastern policy, although this was tempered by the realization that Poland, on its own, could not stand up to Germany.[16] The alternative ally was the Soviet Union but, since Poland viewed its powerful neighbor with implacable hostility, the two options were mutually exclusive. Poland, lacking an absolute commitment of support from France, sought an alternative – signing a Declaration of Non-aggression with Germany in 1934 and cooperating closely with Germany during the Czechoslovak crisis. Poland had also claimed territories from Czechoslovakia in the wake of the Munich agreement. Thus in 1939, when it was generally perceived that Germany would lay claim to Danzig and a territorial link with eastern Prussia, it was unclear how the military regime in Warsaw would respond. The lingering suspicion that the Poles might choose to subordinate themselves to the Germans, though wholly unfounded, was anxiously considered in London and Paris. The Poles, though they welcomed British interest, which they hoped to convert into loans, credits, and military supplies, resolutely refused to allow France and Britain to negotiate on their behalf with Germany. They made it clear that if attacked or provoked by Germany they would fight. They also let it be known that any attempt to change the status of the Free City of Danzig would be seen as a provocation calling for a military response.[17] It was questionable though whether they had the military capacity to do so. Thus, in the months following the March crisis, as anticipation of a Polish–German conflict grew, France held back from confirming and strengthening its commitment to Poland, while Britain uneasily looked first to the other east European countries, then to France and, finally, to the Soviet Union, to ascertain whether anyone would do anything in the event of a German attack on Poland. When Germany did attack on the morning of September 1, these dilemmas were far from resolved. Poland was rich in paper commitments but lacked military support against Germany.[18]

During the months that followed the announcement that they would defend Poland, the British and the French failed to provide the concept of an eastern front with any substance. Neither was willing to fight in eastern Europe, nor were their military leaders willing to plan an attack on Germany. Meanwhile, Hitler decided to call Britain's bluff and denounced the Anglo-German naval agreement. The initiative was henceforth in Hitler's hands, with France and Britain trying to decide whether, and how, they could stop Germany. This raises the critical question of why did the British and French governments pursue such inept policies and whether, as asserted by the British historian A. J. P. Taylor, they might have encouraged German aggression.

Appeasement

It is debatable whether the policy of appeasement was one of ineptitude or of pragmatism. During the interwar period British military commitments were extensive, and continental policy was determined by what seemed to be rational considerations – in which financial concerns loomed large. Britain considered the extent of any commitment to the continental against the background of imperial priorities, which continued to be seen as the backbone of British economic wellbeing.[19] In 1919 financial restrictions based on the assumption that Britain and the empire were unlikely to be at war during the forthcoming years (the "Ten Year Rule") led to dramatic reductions in military expenditure. When, in 1932, these guidelines were set aside this was done as a result of growing anxiety about Japan. Cuts in funds for equipping infantry units designated for action in Europe continued to be made and, in 1935, the chancellor of the exchequer – Neville Chamberlain – confirmed this policy. In 1937, when he became prime minister, he continued reducing expenditure on units for continental action.[20] The neglect of the army's continental role was only reversed at the beginning of 1939. There was a rationale in Chamberlain's approach. In the first place, unemployment was viewed by the government as a priority, and the way to tackling it was seen through balanced budgets. It was believed that military expenditure would destroy that precarious economic recovery. The other factor determining Chamberlain's policies, one with which military leaders fully concurred, was a desire to learn lessons from World War I. Thus the general conviction was that any future war would once more be a long war of attrition in which economic strength would be as important as military power; hence the need to maintain economic links with the empire. The infantry's role in fighting in Europe was assigned a lower priority than the navy's in safeguarding sea routes to the empire. The highest priority was given to diplomacy, which was to defuse sources of tension in Europe and either avoid or postpone conflict there.

Chamberlain's limited political experience of foreign relations undoubtedly contributed to his conviction that personal diplomacy was the best way of resolving difficulties; hence his penchant for arranging meetings with Hitler. He rarely listened to the advice of those with whom he disagreed. A blinkered attitude towards Europe drove British policy towards Germany. Distrust of the French in general and of their policy towards the successor states in particular was a factor in Chamberlain's seeking an accommodation with Hitler. Finally, he intensely disliked the Soviets and felt there was no need to cooperate with them. In the circumstances it is possible to see how a well-intentioned desire to accommodate Germany's just grievances gave Hitler the impression of weakness.[21]

After March 1939 neither Chamberlain's ministers nor the military leaders were ever entirely sure that they were right in taking the initiative in relation to Germany. The need to conserve financial resources and to make supplies available only to those allies whose contribution to the war would count in the long term, clashed with attempts to do something about the imminence of the German attack on Poland. Thus, credits intended for the purchase of military equipment were not given to Poland, deemed unlikely to withstand a German attack for long. At the same time, supplies were offered to Iraq, whose oil supplies were vital if Britain were to fight a long war. Similarly, jointly with France, inconsistent efforts were made to retain Soviet good will. This nevertheless fell short of a full alliance, which is what the Soviet Union sought.

While the British government took the initiative during the closing months of 1938 and before September 1939, French policies have been unfairly characterized as falling in line with British actions. The image of France abdicating its European role is not correct. The French government did indeed scale down its commitment to the concept of an eastern front, but not because it was prepared to subordinate itself to Britain, but because French political and military leaders considered the immediate defense of French territory to be an absolute priority.[22] Critical to understanding France's response to Germany's belligerence is the role played by internal factors. In 1938 France was deeply polarized. The right wing, supported by the banks, proprietors of the most important daily newspapers, the Catholic church, and some military and political leaders, came to view the growing strength of the trade unions, the socialists, and the communists as the major threat to the French regime. The left wing, earlier strongly pacifist, had eventually mobilized around the call to fight the Nazis, and the right-wing Leagues in France, and to support the Spanish republican government. Military and political leaders were also divided on the question of which was France's major enemy: Italy or Germany. Those who supported an accommodation with Germany refer to the fact that Hitler made no reference to reclaiming Alsace and Lorraine, whereas Italy had decided to challenge France's Mediterranean position. Thus in 1938 the question of whether to support Czechoslovakia and, in 1939, what role to assume in relation to the Polish–German crisis, concerned both the advisability of seeking an accommodation with Germany in order to focus on the Italian threat, and the state of the French economy and the cost of remilitarization programs.

During the second half of the 1930s French military thinking had changed. In the 1920s France conceived of a security system that would constrain Germany's ability to attack either in the east or the west. Italy's aggression in Abyssinia, as well as economic difficulties and the falling French birth rate, influenced a change in strategy. Even then it was not entirely clear how a new strategy would work: would it defend only French territories, or would it include forward positions? Nowhere was this dilemma more obvious than in the building of the Maginot Line of fortifications on the Franco-German border, which left the Belgian–German border unprotected. Nothing could be done about the Belgian conviction that by assuming a non-belligerent status, they would be avoiding a German invasion. At the time of the German attack on Poland, General Gamelin had few illusions about the inadequacy of French defenses.[23] Nevertheless, since Munich, efforts had been made to improve France's military capability, with increased expenditure on armaments. Poland was once more elevated to the role of the key element in France's eastern front strategy. This dubious policy, which credited Poland with the capacity to withstand a German attack, suggests that the French military leadership, most notably Gamelin, were willfully avoiding the truth. The pretence of France and Poland united in planning for joint military action could not disguise the fact that all French military plans were confined to the defense of the French borders to the exclusion of any offensive action against Germany. Were the French to be more realistic they would have to reassess not only their eastern front strategy, but also possibly their main military doctrines. Thus the French pretended that they would assist Poland, and the Poles in turn pretended that they would be in a position to defend their own territory. Neither was the case.

Crucial to all considerations in the months preceding the outbreak of the war was the issue of the Soviet Union. British and French leaders would have preferred to leave Stalin out of the picture. This turned out not to be possible. Public opinion, as much as Soviet foreign policy initiatives, made it difficult to maintain that policy, without being accused of neglect. At the same time, Nazi Germany responded to Soviet feelers. Neither the democracies nor Germany knew what to expect from the Soviet Union. Both sides were unsure of the extent to which revolutionary ideals still determined the Soviet government's policies. At the same, in a war that was likely to be long and economically devastating, the economic wealth the Soviet Union might offer could not be overlooked.

The Soviet Dilemma

Soviet responses to the growth of German belligerence continue to be the subject of research, which makes it difficult to evaluate whether assessments made by the democracies on the one hand and the Nazis on the other, were correct. During the interwar period Soviet objectives continued to be an enigma. European states distrusted official pronouncements made by the Soviet government, most obviously because they were never entirely convinced of their truth. The October Revolution had given rise to a new government in Russia, one that claimed from the outset to be based on an entirely different set of political and ethical values. Furthermore, the desire to facilitate the spread of revolutionary ideas beyond Russian borders was an integral element of the new political creed. Some historians have argued that, notwithstanding the early revolutionary pronouncements, the regime had come to appreciate the value of diplomacy from the early days of its existence.[24] Nevertheless, to Britain and France, the Soviet Union remained an enigma – and one that they continued to distrust and fear. Industrial conflicts and political polarization in the immediate aftermath of the war and again during the Depression of the 1930s focused attention on fears of a Soviet-inspired revolution. Nor was it clear whether the Soviet government had succeeded in rebuilding its economy after the war, revolution, and the civil war. During the 1930s the Stalinist five-year plans promised to accelerate industrial takeoff, although, because of limited contacts between the capitalist and Soviet economies, little was known of their success. France's aim of establishing an eastern front against Germany was tempered by the dilemma of whether the Soviet Union was economically and militarily of any consequence. Polish hostility towards the Soviet Union suggested that France would have to make a choice between the smaller east European states or drawing the Soviet Union into closer military cooperation. Since this dilemma was insoluble, France's policy was inconclusive.

In 1932 the Soviet Union, anxious about Japanese belligerence and its own lack of military preparedness, moved to consider a policy of increased cooperation with the western democracies. In December 1933 this policy was approved by the Soviet Politburo. Maxim Litvinov, the new commissar for foreign affairs, came to be directly associated with that policy change. The Soviet Union joined the League of Nations and became its most vocal supporter. Collective security was advocated as a way of tackling the growing German threat. The Soviet Union was the main target of hostile Nazi propaganda statements after Hitler came to power. This, combined with anxiety about Japan, was the cause of Stalin's change of policy. The communist parties in Europe were instructed to abandon their previous policy of hostility to the socialist parties and instead to seek all opportunities for political collaboration with parties and trade unions on the basis of a common desire to combat fascism in Europe. The Seventh Congress of the Comintern approved this line and henceforth all communist parties were to support rearmament programs.

In spite of these gestures, cooperation between the Soviet Union and the western democracies continued to be fraught with distrust. In spite of signing a pact with the Soviet Union in 1935, the French did not want to open military talks. This played into the hands of sections of the Soviet leadership that felt it worth working towards improvement in Soviet–German relations.[25] This explains why Stalin was not willing to be seen supporting the republican side in the Spanish Civil War.[26] When the Soviet Union was not invited to the Munich conference, that group gained the upper hand. Litvinov's position became weaker; although he continued as commissar for foreign affairs until May 3, 1939, his policy of collective security was increasingly under attack. Earlier, on March 10, Stalin made a speech to the 18th Party Congress in which he indicated that the Soviet Union was willing to establish good relations with any state, which wanted to do the same. Although France and Britain hesitated, Berlin was responsive. Both sides were willing to overlook ideological differences. Stalin saw that time could be thus gained to improve the Soviet Union's military situation. Ribbentrop, the main German advocate of a rapprochement with the Soviet Union, pointed out to Hitler that it would assure Poland's defeat. From May onwards the Soviet Union toyed with the two options: a diplomatic front with France and Britain against Germany, or the offer of a non-aggression pact with Germany and territorial gains once Poland was defeated. Surprisingly, the Soviet leadership hoped that the British and French negotiators would come round to their point of view; they did not and, in August, the British–French–Soviet talks collapsed, ostensibly over Polish unwillingness to allow the entry of Soviet troops. Berlin had fewer qualms and, on August 23, Ribbentrop flew to the Soviet Union to sign a non-aggression pact. Poland's fate was thus sealed, as the Soviet Union undertook not to view the German attack on Poland as hostile. A secret annex to the agreement accorded the Soviet Union the right to claim Poland's eastern regions. Further economic and military talks followed, giving Germany the full benefit of Soviet resources.

The Outbreak of War

Since the initiative to attack Poland was Hitler's, the important question is why did he choose September 1939? Were domestic considerations possibly more important than the international dimension in determining the moment when the regime risked unleashing a world war? In spite of the strain that remilitarization had put on German society, neither this nor anxieties about internal opposition played a major role in Hitler's considerations.[27] His conviction that London and Paris had abandoned Poland and were unlikely to respond to German action in the east was clearly of greater importance. Furthermore, Hitler believed that an attack on Poland would lead to a war with Poland alone, not to a wider conflagration.

During the summer of 1939 Hitler had to make the decision to either proceed with attacking Poland by the beginning of September or to abandon the plan until late spring of 1940. In between these two dates, any military action in Poland, in particular one of a motorized character, would be at a disadvantage because Poland had few metallic roads: autumn rains, winter weather, and the spring thaw would make Poland impassable. During the last week of August, Germany made an alliance offer to Britain. At the same time, the Poles were instructed to send a negotiator to Berlin. Neither ruse worked. The British government only briefly considered the option of negotiations as a means of resolving the growing German–Polish crisis. Although the will to postpone war was there, the British cabinet no longer believed that Hitler was genuine. The Poles, having witnessed the destruction of Czechoslovakia, were not willing to accept the invitation to talks, and neither the British nor the French pressed them to do so.[28]

On the morning of September 1 a full-scale German aerial and land attack on Poland started World War II. Although Italy made diplomatic attempts to prevent the outbreak of the war, through continuing negotiations, this and initiatives taken by a number of individuals as well as the Vatican, came to nothing. In London, Chamberlain and his foreign secretary, Halifax, tried to define conditions on which Britain would be willing to resume negotiations with Hitler. A decision was made to issue an ultimatum to Hitler on September 3. When it appeared that the French might take action earlier, the British demanded that German troops withdraw from Poland and restore Danzig to its previous status by 11 a.m. When the Germans did not respond, Britain found itself at war. The French followed suit a few hours later. An air of unreality hung over both decisions. While German military action against Poland continued relentlessly and successfully, neither of Poland's two allies did anything to relieve Poland. Both governments had been forced to declare war by the logic of their own thinking. It would still be some time before they would actually wage war. In the meantime, attempts would be made to deny Germany economic resources needed for the continuation of war in Europe. The fate of Poland, sealed by the entry of the Red Army, was consigned to the final outcome of the long war.

NOTES

1   Adolf Hitler, *Mein Kampf* (London: Hurst and Blackett, 1939), p. 532.
2   For an interesting debate on the way the passage of time affected scholarship on the issue of responsibility for the outbreak of the war, see Williamson Murray, "Britain," in *The Origins of World War Two: The Debate Continues*, Robert Boyce and Joseph A. Maiolo, eds (Basingstoke: Palgrave, 2003), pp. 111–32. For a different view, see Richard J. Evans, in an edition of the *Journal of Contemporary History* 39/2 (2004): 163–7 dedicated to a review of recent research of the Nazi period in Germany.
3   Hitler, *Mein Kampf*, p. 524.
4   See Ian Kershaw, *The Nazi Dictatorship: Problems and Perspectives of Interpretation* (London: Edward Arnold, 1985), pp. 134–60.
5   See Klaus Hildebrand, *The Foreign Policy of the Third Reich* (London: B. T. Batsford, 1973), pp. 39–40.
6   Hildebrand, *Foreign Policy*, p. 1.
7   See Hans-Adolf Jacobson, "The Structure of Nazi Foreign Policy 1933–1945," in *The Third Reich*, Christian Leitz, ed. (Oxford: Blackwell, 1999), pp. 56–70.
8   See Gerhard L. Weinberg, *The Foreign Policy of Hitler's Germany: Starting World War II, 1937–1939* (Chicago: University of Chicago Press, 1980), pp. 28–81.
9   See Robert J. Young, *In Command of France: French Foreign Policy and Military Planning, 1933–1940* (Cambridge MA: Harvard University Press, 1978), pp. 122–9.
10 See Anthony Kojmathy and Rebecca Stockwell, *German Minorities and the Third Reich* (New York: Holmes and Meir, 1980), pp. 30–2.
11 See D. C. Watt, *How War Came: The Immediate Origins of the Second World War, 1938–1939* (London: Heinemann, 1989).
12 See Peter Jackson, "France," in Boyce and Maiolo, *Origins of World War Two*, pp. 99–101; Martin S. Alexander, *The Republic in Danger: General Maurice Gamelin and the Politics of French Defence, 1933–1940* (Cambridge: Cambridge University Press, 1992), pp. 302–5.
13 See Weinberg, *Hitler's Germany*, pp. 503–5.

14 See Hildebrand, *Foreign Policy*, p. 87.

15 Ibid, pp. 47–50.

16 See Piotr S. Wandycz, *The Twilight of French Eastern Alliances, 1926–1936: French–Czechoslovak–Polish Relations from Locarno to the Remilitarization of the Rhineland* (Princeton NJ: Princeton University Press, 1988), pp. 422–31.

17 See Anita Prazmowska, *Britain, Poland and the Eastern Front, 1939* (Cambridge: Cambridge University Press, 1987), pp. 7–74.

18 Ibid, pp. 173–4.

19 The most succinct analysis of Britain's military policies towards Europe is contained in Michael Howard's *The Continental Commitment: The Dilemma of British Defence Policy in the Era of Two World Wars* (London: Pelican, 1974).

20 See Brian Bond, *British Military Policy between the Two World Wars* (Oxford: Clarendon Press, 1980), pp. 248–52.

21 Chamberlain's role as the architect of the policy of appeasement has been the subject of numerous scholarly works. One of the more interesting continues to be Ian Colvin's *The Chamberlain Cabinet* (London: Victor Gollancz, 1971). More recent works are John Charmley, *Chamberlain and the Lost Peace* (London: Hodder and Stoughton, 1989) and R. A. C. Parker, *Chamberlain and Appeasement: British Policy and the Coming of the Second World War* (Basingstoke: Macmillan, 1993).

22 For a recent reassessment of debates concerning France's appeasement policy, see Peter Jackson, "France," in Boyce and Maiolo, *Origins of World War Two*, pp. 86–110.

23 See Alexander, *Republic in Danger*, pp. 207–9.

24 See Teddy J. Uldricks, *Diplomacy and Ideology: The Origins of Soviet Foreign Relations, 1917–1930* (London: Sage, 1979), pp. 27–9; Margot Light, *The Soviet Theory of International Relations* (Guildford: Wheatsheaf, 1988), pp. 27–31.

25 See Sylvio Pons, *Stalin and the Inevitable War, 1936–1941* (London: Frank Cass, 2002), pp. 17–26.

26 See Jonathan G. Haslam, "Soviet Russia and the Spanish Problem," in Boyce and Maiolo, *Origins of World War Two*, p. 75.

27 See Richard J. Overy, "Germany, 'Domestic Crisis' and the War in 1939," in Leitz, *The Third Reich*, pp. 125–6.

28 See Weinberg, *Hitler's Germany*, pp. 640–6.

GUIDE TO FURTHER READING

Martin S. Alexander, *The Republic in Danger: General Maurice Gamelin and the Politics of French Defence, 1933–1940* (Cambridge: Cambridge University Press, 1992). Detailed analysis of French military politics before World War II.

Brian Bond, *British Military Policy between the Two World Wars* (Oxford: Clarendon Press, 1980). One of the best monographs to explain the complexities of Britain's military situation during the interwar period.

Robert Boyce and Joseph A. Maiolo, eds, *The Origins of World War Two: The Debate Continues* (Basingstoke: Palgrave, 2003). Nineteen essayists reassess the controversies relating to the outbreak of the war.

Jonathan Haslam, *The Soviet Union and the Struggle for Collective Security in Europe, 1933–1939* (Basingstoke: Macmillan, 1984). The most thorough analysis of policy considerations and internal conflicts which determined Soviet responses to the growth of German belligerence.

Klaus Hildebrand, *The Foreign Policy of the Third Reich* (London: Batsford, 1973). Useful overview of the most important debates concerning German foreign policy.

Michael Howard, *The Continental Commitment: The Dilemma of British Defence Policy in the Era of Two World Wars* (London: Pelican, 1974). Essays that remain the best guide to the dilemma which bedeviled British military policy throughout the interwar period.

MacGregor Knox, *Mussolini Unleashed, 1939–1940: Politics and Strategy in Fascist Italy's Last War* (Cambridge: Cambridge University Press, 1982). Study of the internal working of the fascist regime.

Dov B. Lungu, *Romania and the Great Powers, 1933–1940* (Durham NC: Duke University Press, 1989). Only monograph that tackles the role played by Romania in the origins of the war; well researched and detailed.

R. A. C. Parker, *Chamberlain and Appeasement: British Policy and the Coming of the Second World War* (Basingstoke: Macmillan, 1993). Useful summary of Chamberlain's motives for pursuing appeasement of Germany.

Sylvio Pons, *Stalin and the Inevitable War, 1936–1941* (London: Cass, 2002). Wide-ranging study of Soviet foreign policy based on Soviet archives.

Anita J. Prazmowska, *Britain, Poland and the Eastern Front, 1939* (Cambridge: Cambridge University Press, 1987). Thorough analysis of British–Polish relations on the eve of the war.

Anita J. Prazmowska, *Eastern Europe and the Origins of the Second World War* (Basingstoke: Macmillan, 2000). Nine essays, each analyzing a different region and its response to the rise of tension in Europe during the 1930s.

M. Salerno Reynolds, *Vital Crossroads: Mediterranean Origins of the Second World War, 1935–1940* (Ithaca NY: Cornell University Press, 2002). Addresses British and French attempts to appease Italy when it was becoming dependent on Germany.

Piotr S. Wandycz, *The Twilight of French Eastern Alliances, 1926–1936: French–Czechoslovak–Polish Relations from Locarno to the Remilitarization of the Rhineland* (Princeton NJ: Princeton University Press, 1988). Invaluable contribution to understanding the apparent inconsistencies in French policy towards Germany.

Donald C. Watt, *How War Came: The Immediate Origins of the Second World War, 1938–1939* (London: Heinemann, 1989). Comprehensive and wide-ranging study.

Gerhard L. Weinberg, *The Foreign Policy of Hitler's Germany: Starting World War II, 1937–1939* (Chicago: University of Chicago Press, 1980). Well-researched and detailed study of Hitler's policy; strong analysis of the importance of ideology and the economy on the policies pursued by the regime.

Robert, J. Young, *In Command of France: French Foreign Policy and Military Planning, 1933–1940* (Cambridge MA: Harvard University Press, 1978). Fills gaps in our understanding of French military thinking before the war.

PART VI

World War II

CHAPTER TWENTY-SEVEN

Grand Strategy and Summit Diplomacy

MICHAEL JABARA CARLEY

The World War II alliance of Britain, the Soviet Union, and the United States and the strategies they devised to defeat Nazi Germany and Fascist Italy had their origins in the interwar years. During the 1930s a first grand alliance, which failed to materialize, aimed to contain Nazi Germany or to defeat it in war if containment failed. The main partners of this alliance should have been Britain, France, and the Soviet Union; in the 1930s the United States did not play a major role in European affairs.

The Grand Alliance that Never Was

What held the World War II alliance together was the indisputable perception of Nazi Germany as a mortal threat to the Big Three alliance partners. During the interwar years, however, clarity on this point was lacking. "Who is enemy no. 1?" was the question. "Germany or the Soviet Union?" Throughout these years a debate went on between "realists" who supported better relations with the Soviet Union and anti-communist ideologues who opposed them. The realists looked at the Soviet Union as a counterweight against a resurgent Germany. Anti-communists calculated that Germany was disarmed and not dangerous, while Bolshevik Russia was a plague house capable of spreading socialist revolution into Europe. During the 1920s anti-communism flourished: Britain broke off relations with the Soviet Union in 1927 and France nearly did so later that year. The United States only established diplomatic relations with Moscow in 1933. Bolshevik diplomats sought better relations with the west while Bolshevik revolutionaries meddled in revolution abroad. Both the western powers and the Soviet Union had their realists and ideologues. By the end of the 1920s the Soviet side appeared more effective in controlling its ideologues than were western governments in controlling theirs.[1]

Adolf Hitler's coming to power in January 1933 disrupted this pattern of hostility. Realists in France, Britain, and the Soviet Union argued that Nazi Germany posed such a threat to European security that ideological animosities must be subordinated to the greater need of containing an aggressive, rearming German state. Hitler's ideas about German world power were no secret; he had written about them in his *Mein*

Kampf, a book published in the 1920s. The Soviet Union had special reason to be concerned, for it was the principal target of German expansion. Incompetent Jewish Bolsheviks had taken over Russia, Hitler wrote. The Slavs were an "inferior race," and could not manage themselves. When Bolshevik domination was ended, Russia, as a state, would cease to exist. Then Germany would have *lebensraum,* lands to colonize. In Moscow, German diplomats protested Nazi good intentions, but M. M. Litvinov, commissar for foreign affairs, confronted them with *Mein Kampf.* Don't pay attention to that, the Germans replied: Hitler's book belongs to the past. In Berlin, Litvinov was that *grand crapule* "Funkelstein Litwinov," another disgusting Jew. The Soviet government began to call for collective security, which meant an anti-Nazi alliance. Britain, France, and the Soviet Union would serve as the strong nucleus; Czechoslovakia, Romania, Poland, and Yugoslavia would join a coalition sure to be able to contain Hitler.[2]

At first, Litvinov received a decent reception not only in Paris and London, but also in Washington, where Franklin D. Roosevelt had become president. Behind Soviet–American negotiations was the threat of Japan to both Soviet and American security.[3] In Paris, the French government concluded a non-aggression pact with Moscow in November 1932. A range of politicians from the right to the communist left supported closer Franco-Soviet relations, and between 1932 and 1934 Franco-Soviet relations improved. Hitlerite Germany was a threat which must be contained. In London, too, there was movement toward better Soviet relations. An Anglo-Soviet rapprochement began in 1934, led, not by politicians, but by an influential civil servant, Robert Vansittart, the permanent under-secretary in the foreign office. Like Litvinov, Vansittart saw Nazi Germany as a threat to European peace. He had no illusions about winning over a reasonable Hitler to new European security agreements. Winston Churchill, then an isolated Tory backbencher, agreed with Vansittart. Churchill had been a "die-hard" anti-communist during the 1920s, but he muted his anti-communism to advocate "a grand alliance" of Britain, France, and the Soviet Union. He had not gone soft on communism, but he thought, like Litvinov, that the only way to contain or if necessary defeat Nazi Germany in war was to create an Anglo-Franco-Soviet alliance. For a brief time an anti-German coalition seemed a possibility, but things went quickly wrong. First in Washington, then in Paris and London, interest in good relations cooled. In 1934 a possible Soviet–American economic settlement fell apart.[4] In May 1935 a Franco-Soviet pact of mutual assistance was signed, but within months the French foreign minister, Pierre Laval, wanted to wriggle out of it. Laval, a fervent anti-communist, preferred a general settlement with Nazi Germany. Soviet officials were dismayed by the French reversal.[5] In early 1936 the British government in turn cooled down ties with Moscow. The reasons were the usual ones about communist propaganda and the threat of socialist revolution. Obviously the proper place for an asp, a red one, was not the bosom.[6]

By early 1936 the basis for Churchill's grand alliance had been undermined, and just at the wrong time. In March 1936 German troops occupied the demilitarized Rhineland. In May a center-left coalition of radicals, socialists, and communists, the Popular Front, won French parliamentary elections. A Jewish socialist, Léon Blum, became premier. The British foreign office thought France was going red. In July civil war in Spain erupted, augmenting fears of socialist revolution in Europe. This was grist to the mill of Nazi propagandists who played upon the fears of communism in order to disrupt an anti-German coalition. Even Churchill was frightened by events in Spain. The Stalinist purges, which began in August 1936, were no help either, especially after Stalin turned on his high command the following year, executing many respected officers. In the west these executions mattered, for the Red Army was a potential weapon against Nazi Germany. Soviet diplomats could see the harm done.[7] The purges were not the cause of worsening western–Soviet relations, but they provided a convincing pretext for refusing intimacy with Moscow.

In London and Paris conservatives or "appeasers" thought Germany had legitimate grievances which should be met. Hitler was a rational statesman, nasty at the edges perhaps, but someone who could be brought around to new agreements once his demands had been met. There was no need for war: advocates of rapid rearmament, like Vansittart and Churchill, were exaggerating the German danger. Besides, war could spread revolution into the middle of Europe. In 1936 the British prime minister, Stanley Baldwin, opined that if war came, he should like to see the Bolshies and *Boches* doing the fighting.

At first, Hitler had a good sense of timing. In 1938 he struck at the moment of greatest weakness and division among the potential partners of a grand alliance. In March 1938 he annexed Austria and in September he negotiated the dismemberment of Czechoslovakia at Munich. These actions struck a blow against Anglo-French security. The French ambassador in Moscow, Robert Coulondre, warned that one more such defeat would mean the end of France, and he predicted that an alienated Soviet Union might abandon collective security for a deal with Nazi Germany. In Paris no one paid attention. Many French appeasers wanted to sever dangerous treaty relations with the Soviet Union. In London Prime Minister Neville Chamberlain, who succeeded Baldwin and was the broker of Munich, thought he had made an important step forward in securing European peace.

The false hopes of Munich lasted only a few months. In March 1939 Hitler occupied rump Czechoslovakia, and shortly thereafter he annexed Memel from Lithuania. Poland appeared to be Hitler's next target, and Britain and France quickly guaranteed its security. Churchill and other British politicians called for a tripartite alliance with the Soviet Union against Nazi Germany. The Soviet Union could mobilize 100 divisions at the outset, more than the French and British armies combined on the western front. Only the Soviet Union could anchor an eastern front and save Poland; only an Anglo-Franco-Soviet alliance could guarantee the success of an Allied blockade against Germany. French and British public opinion favored a grand alliance and expected it to be concluded quickly.

In April 1939 Litvinov offered Britain and France a full-fledged military alliance against Nazi Germany. Instead of seizing the offer with both hands, foreign office officials derided Litvinov and ridiculed his proposals. The French government responded more positively, but let the British take the lead. In early May Litvinov was sacked. A harder man was brought in to replace him. This was V. M. Molotov, Stalin's no. 2. Warning flags went up in London and Paris that Molotov's appointment could signal a change in Soviet policy away from collective security and toward agreement with Nazi Germany. This is what the Germans hoped, though Molotov assured the French and British that Soviet policy had not changed.

Litvinov's sacking failed to arouse Chamberlain's concern. He was a determined anti-Bolshevik, who resisted negotiations with Moscow. With public opinion moving, the British cabinet shifted to support a Soviet agreement, leaving Chamberlain isolated. In Paris the French government pushed the British forward, but only half-heartedly. At the end of July the would-be allies agreed to meet in Moscow to conclude a military alliance. The Anglo-French military mission took its time getting to Moscow. When it finally arrived, the British chief representative could not produce written powers authorizing him to negotiate with the Soviet government, while the French representative was scarcely better empowered. They can't be serious, concluded their Soviet interlocutors.

Hitler *was* serious. He wanted to break up the grand alliance before it formed. His diplomats began to court their Soviet counterparts in April. At first Molotov declined interest, and continued negotiations with the British and French. At the end of July, however, Molotov blinked; or, more likely, Stalin did. Enticing German offers had arrived in Moscow, which offered to improve relations at Polish expense. While the Germans talked to the Soviets, the British talked to the Germans. Information leaked out in the London press in July about discussions between German and British officials for a general settlement of differences. In the House of Commons Chamberlain had to admit it was true. In Moscow it looked like the British were fishing for an agreement with Germany, even as they sent a military mission to Moscow.

Stalin had few scruples. He liked to refer to Russian epigrams about wolves in the forest: if you live among wolves, you must behave like a wolf. If the British could negotiate with the Germans, so could the Soviet Union. In early August Soviet–German discussions got down to details. Poland was the principal medium of exchange, but the Germans were also willing to divide up the Baltic states on condition that the Soviet government did not interfere in a German war against Poland. In Moscow there was no love lost for the Polish government, which was anti-Russian and anti-communist. If Poland had to be the price of agreement with Germany, it was Poland's fault. Molotov and his German counterpart, Joachim von Ribbentrop, signed a non-aggression pact in the early hours of August 23. This agreement abruptly ended Churchill's hopes for a grand alliance.

The "Phoney War"

The French and British governments still sought a way out. Georges Bonnet, the French foreign minister and notorious appeaser, advocated a last minute settlement with Germany at Polish expense. From Bonnet's point of view France was in no position to wage war against Germany and would be defeated if it did. Earlier, he had supported an alliance with the Soviet Union because he reckoned that if war broke out, it would begin in the east. France and Britain could lie back until they were stronger. This was not what Stalin had in mind.

In the early morning of September 1, 1939 the German army invaded Poland. On September 2, Chamberlain spoke in the House of Commons about further negotiations in Berlin, which led the House and his cabinet to threaten revolt. The House would not tolerate further delay in confronting Nazi Germany. Britain thus declared war the next morning, September 3, and France followed later in the day.

None of this mattered to Poland, which was crushed in a fortnight by the German army. The Red Army then moved in from the east. Britain and France did little to help the Poles, settling back into what became known as the *drôle de guerre*, or "phoney war." The British and French governments intended to pursue a long war strategy, a *guerre de longue durée*: staying on the defensive, building up military strength, blockading Germany, and then – when Germany weakened – going on the offensive. The plan was good on paper. The British and French governments had started to rearm in the mid-1930s, but too slowly. Until 1939 Chamberlain had opposed all-out rearmament. After war began, the British centralized production, but not France. French industrialists wanted business as usual and no government interference. Hence, while British production increased, French production stalled or lost ground. Moreover, the blockade was less effective because the Soviet Union was neutral, as Molotov never tired of saying, and this left the back door open in eastern Europe. It looked like the long war strategy would not work. Germany was getting stronger, but not Britain and France. Some French senior officers believed that a long war would facilitate the spread of communism.[8]

While reflections about war strategy went on in Paris and London, Stalin, who thought he had played his hand well, made a grave mistake. He ordered an attack on Finland at the end of November in what became known as the Winter War. Stalin decided to take by force the security guarantees he could not obtain in negotiations with the Finns. The Red Army lost heavily before Finnish defenses. What was worse, the war unleashed an anti-communist tumult in France and Britain. Anti-communists had never been enthusiastic about fighting Nazi Germany or allying with the Soviet Union. Germany was the colossus, feared and admired at the same time. The Soviet Union looked like a pushover. For most of the right and center-right, especially in France, Germany was the wrong enemy, the Soviet Union, the real one. The French and British governments developed plans to bomb the Caucasian oil fields. These plans were "the product of a madhouse," A. J. P. Taylor commented: "the only charitable conclusion is to assume that the British and French governments had taken leave of their senses."[9]

The Fall of France

The French and British governments were saved from folly by the end of the Winter War in March 1940 and Hitler's offensive in the west in April. The *drôle de guerre* was over. The Germans overran Norway, Denmark, Holland, Luxembourg, Belgium, and, more spectacularly, France. The French army, which Churchill had considered the backbone of western defense, collapsed. Many French soldiers fought to the last, but the high command did not know what to do. The officer corps was largely anti-semitic, anti-republican, and anti-communist. If Litvinov was Funkelstein to the Nazis, the "Jew Blum" was Karfunkelstein to French antisemites. Only the Nazis seem largely to have escaped the loathing of the French high command. The generals did not anticipate a German offensive through the Ardennes forest, the center of the French line, and when they finally realized what was happening, it was "Goodnight France." The high command worried more about a communist rising in Paris than about how to make a fighting retreat.[10]

There has been much scholarly debate about the fall of France. Did it collapse because French society was rotten, "decadent," and bitterly divided between admirers of fascism and admirers of Soviet communism? Was the debacle the result of craven, incompetent French politicians and generals? Or did a strong, confident France embark upon a struggle against Nazi Germany, and tragically, accidentally falter despite the best that its leaders and the French army could give?

Few historians would dispute that France was a "decadent," troubled society until Munich. Then, say revisionist historians, the French government got hold of itself, recognized that war was inevitable, and began to prepare for it. Finances stabilized, rearmament surged, morale improved. Other historians counter that the turn-around was superficial, and that what appeared to be better morale was only resignation to the certainty of another war. In fact, one recent account holds that French recovery was anemic: war production did not meet targets and the treasury was running out of gold. If so, the long war strategy was indeed failing. France was doomed, and even a grand alliance might not have saved it.[11]

Keep Buggering On

Whether it was doom, decadence, or damnable luck, France capitulated in June 1940 and a collaborationist government was set up at Vichy. Only a little known Brigadier General, Charles de Gaulle, and a handful of followers continued the fight. They were no immediate help to Britain, which was left alone to face the Nazi juggernaut. The English Channel was all that saved Britain. Its main army, a meager 200,000 men, had been forced to evacuate from Dunkirk in May. The beaten French and the victorious Germans thought it was only a matter of time before the British asked for terms. Even some British cabinet ministers contemplated negotiations to end the war. Only one man was able to staunch British wounds, allay doubts, and rally morale.

This was Churchill, who became prime minister in May 1940. He maneuvered around the doubters in his cabinet and he adopted a policy which he called "KBO": keep buggering on. He did not know how he would get Britain out of the fix it was in. His hope was that eventually the United States and the Soviet Union would enter the war. He therefore assiduously courted Franklin Roosevelt and kept talking to Stalin and Molotov. In the meantime Britain had to hold out. Hitler ordered preparations for Operation Sea Lion, an invasion of Britain. He unleashed his air force in August, in what became known as the Battle of Britain, to establish air superiority in order to protect an invasion armada. The Battle of Britain was a near-run thing, but RAF pilots inflicted such losses upon the enemy that Hitler called off Sea Lion.

Hitler took this setback prosaically, for he had begun to think about "settling accounts" with the Soviet Union. Stalin, who was surprised by the French debacle and worried about Soviet security, annexed the Baltic states and Bessarabia and Bukovina in Romania. Hitler did not like to see the Soviet Union moving so close to Romanian oil fields. He started shifting divisions from France to the Soviet frontier. Soviet diplomatic and intelligence sources reported the build-up. During the summer of 1940 Hitler instructed his high command to start planning for an invasion of the Soviet Union: the Red Army was getting stronger and he feared that Stalin could come into the war on the British side. He wanted to crush the Red Army now, then turn back on Britain to compel its surrender. The risk of a long two-front war seemed minimal. The *Wehrmacht* was invincible. The Red Army had looked inept in defeating the insignificant Finns and would be destroyed before winter.

Hitler delayed before making a final decision. He invited Molotov to Berlin in November 1940. Hitler wanted to bring the Balkans under German control, and he offered to let the Soviet Union challenge Britain in central Asia and India. For Stalin, this was a fool's bargain. He had no intention of getting into a war with Britain, and wanted to secure Soviet interests in the Balkans. Molotov and German foreign minister von Ribbentrop negotiated in an underground shelter while British bombers hit Berlin. Ribbentrop told Molotov that Britain was beaten. Listening to the bombs exploding, Molotov said he did not think so. The meetings produced no deals. In December 1940 Hitler gave orders for an invasion of the Soviet Union in the spring of 1941: "Operation Barbarossa."[12]

In April 1941 Churchill warned Stalin that Hitler intended to invade the Soviet Union. Stalin was aware of the danger, having received countless intelligence reports on the German military build-up, but he did not think that Germany would attack before subduing Britain. The Red Army was in the middle of refitting and in no position to challenge the *Wehrmacht*. Interviewed long after events, Molotov remembered that the Soviet Union was not ready for war in 1941, and that even a few more months of peace mattered: What else could we do but stall?[13] Ironically, this was the same argument used by the French and British governments to explain their appeasement of Hitler. "Revisionist" historians justify Anglo-French appeasement on the grounds that France and Britain did not have the guns or gold to fight Nazi Germany, but many of the same historians would not explain with the same sympathy the Soviet policy of appeasement.

War in the East

Appeasement ended badly for the Soviet Union, just as it had for Britain and France. Hitler sent his forces forward on June 22, 1941: more than 3 million German soldiers in 150 divisions on a front reaching from the Baltic to the Black Sea. Churchill had quipped on the eve of the invasion that "if Hitler invaded Hell, he would at least make a favorable reference to the Devil!" He broke out cigars when news confirmed the actual German attack. Within 24 hours Churchill was on the BBC offering British support to the Soviet Union and welcoming it into that alliance which had failed to materialize in 1939. Churchill reminded his listeners that if Russia were defeated before winter, Hitler would turn back against Britain before the United States could bring its weight to bear. "The Russian danger is therefore our danger, and the danger of the United States."[14]

FDR had heard Churchill's arguments before. In March 1941 the US Congress approved Lend-Lease for Britain. Supplies began to flow freely for the British war effort. When Roosevelt heard of the Nazi invasion of the Soviet Union, he was less effusive, more cautious than Churchill, though he too said the United States would support Soviet resistance because it diverted Hitler's attention away from Britain.

Few gave the Red Army a chance against the *Wehrmacht*. After all, what army had been able to defeat the Germans? The British knew from cruel experience in France, Greece, Crete, and north Africa how tough they were. American and British intelligence services did not think the Red Army would hold out for more than a few weeks. In July the American military attaché in Moscow, a true blue anti-communist, burned his files, anticipating the imminent arrival of the Germans in the Russian capital.[15] Nevertheless, an Anglo-Soviet agreement of mutual assistance was signed on July 12. Soviet resistance of whatever duration had to be encouraged. Stalin, heretofore the cruel dictator, now became an ally, "Uncle Joe" (or "UJ" for short). On July 18, Stalin asked for the first time that a second front be established in northern France. In September, he asked again: we need a second front to draw off 30–40 German divisions; otherwise, we could be defeated or be so weakened as to be unable to help our allies.

As the summer unfolded and although the Soviet Union suffered frightful losses, resistance stiffened. "I am dying," an unknown Red Army soldier scrawled on a fortress wall, "but I am not surrendering!" At Smolensk the Red Army delayed the Nazi advance for more than a month, giving Moscow time to prepare its defenses. At Leningrad the city was surrounded, but held out. "Our cause is right," said one Soviet placard: "The enemy will be crushed. Victory will be ours!"[16]

The war became a great national cause. Even teenagers participated, fighting with Soviet partisans behind Nazi lines or working in munitions factories. "Mother Russia calls you" was a slogan on recruitment posters. This meant something, and most Russians responded. German military intelligence had expected to face 200 Red Army divisions; by August 1941 it had identified 360. In November the Germans thought Red Army reserves were exhausted.[17] In December the *Wehrmacht* offensive was stopped at the outskirts of Moscow, where a monument now marks the point of furthest advance near Sheremet'evo airport. On December 5 the Red Army launched a counter-offensive that threw back the Nazi armies in places more than 300 kilometers. During the first six months of war, 2.5 million soldiers were killed in action and 3.4 million taken prisoner. Uncounted millions of civilians died or disappeared. For Hitler, the Slavs were "sub-humans," *untermenschen*, to be exterminated or enslaved. German death squads, *SS Einsatzgruppen*, shot Bolsheviks, Jews, gypsies, or anyone who looked at them the wrong way. Occupied territories were to be stripped of foodstuffs and the local people left to starve. This is "total war," Hitler declared. If Hitler wants total war, Stalin replied, he will have it. The Red Army began to exact a price. For the first time the *Wehrmacht* suffered a strategic defeat. The aura of Nazi invincibility was broken; now Hitler and his armies began to get as good as they gave.[18]

"We're all in it now"

Two days after the beginning of the Moscow counter-offensive, on December 7, the Japanese attacked Pearl Harbor. On December 11 Germany and Italy declared war on the United States, a gesture which the American Congress immediately reciprocated. "We're all in it now," FDR told Churchill over the phone. "So we had won after all," Churchill later recalled in his history of World War II: "I went to bed and slept the sleep of the saved and thankful."[19]

KBO gave way to proactive Anglo-American strategic planning. In August 1941, even before the American entry into the war, Churchill and Roosevelt had met at Placentia Bay off Newfoundland to discuss war strategy. They agreed that the United States would give immediate aid to the Soviet Union and that jointly they would send an Anglo-American mission to Moscow to determine Soviet supply needs. But the United States did not plan to enter the war, unless attacked. Roosevelt told Churchill that "he would wage war, but not declare it." A few months later, in October 1941, the US Congress approved Lend-Lease for the Soviet Union.

A Europe first strategy was settled policy by the end of 1941. The Soviet Union had to be kept fighting, though Stalin was unhappy with the help he was getting from his American and British allies. While millions of men clashed in the Soviet Union, a mere handful of British divisions confronted small German and Italian forces in north Africa. Churchill did not like Stalin reminding him of what the Red Army needed. From Churchill's point of view, the Soviet Union had left Britain in the lurch in 1939; from UJ's point of view, Churchill sounded like the pot calling the kettle black. Even after the Soviet victory at Moscow, there were doubters, often unrepentant anti-communists, in London and Washington. In 1942 one of these asked Roosevelt what was the value of the Soviet contribution to the war. "The Russians," FDR replied, "are killing more Germans and destroying more German matériel than all other 25 United Nations put together."[20] What were the Allies doing in return? Stalin often asked, especially during the summer of 1942, when German forces launched a two-pronged offensive on the Caucasus oil fields and on Stalingrad.

Where is the Second Front?

Worried about Stalin's nagging questions, Churchill went to Moscow in August 1942 to say that there could be no second front that year. Stalin received the news badly, rounding on Churchill. The British, he said, were too afraid of fighting the Germans. "You will have to fight sooner or later," Stalin remarked. "You cannot win a war without fighting." Stalin complained that the British and Americans were not sending enough supplies. Churchill took umbrage, perhaps because he knew Stalin had a point. There were 280 Axis divisions in the Soviet Union, composed of Romanian, Finnish, Hungarian, Spanish, and Italian formations, as well as German. They totaled 3.65 million men. Many of these divisions were advancing toward Stalingrad and into the Caucasus toward Batum and Baku. Arrayed against them were 5.7 million Red Army soldiers. Stalin told Churchill that the situation was dangerous. "We are losing ten thousand men a day."[21]

Discussion turned to appeasement and the failed Anglo-Franco-Soviet negotiations in 1939. Churchill reminded Stalin that he had favored an alliance between Britain, the United States, and the Soviet Union before Munich. Churchill forgot to mention France, though in 1942 that was easy to do. Stalin indicated that he had always hoped for cooperation, but that under Chamberlain, an alliance was impossible. Stalin referred to the abortive military negotiations in Moscow in August 1939. These talks were a ruse to pressure Hitler into coming to terms with France and Britain.[22]

Churchill informed Stalin of plans for "Torch," the Anglo-American invasion of north Africa, which was the best the western Allies could do in 1942. Five British and seven American divisions would confront smaller German, Italian, and Vichy French forces. For Stalin, this was a sideshow, but he grudgingly accepted Churchill's argument that a landing in northern France in 1942 was impractical. The Soviet Union would have to hold out almost alone against the Axis. It did.

The Red Army launched a massive counter-offensive against German forces at Stalingrad. On November 23, 1942 the jaws of a great pincer movement closed around the German Sixth Army at Stalingrad. Hitler ordered his men to stand fast and tried to relieve them, but to no avail. What was left of the Sixth Army surrendered on February 2, 1943. Twenty-two divisions and 330,000 German soldiers were wiped from Hitler's order of battle, in addition to heavy Romanian and Italian losses. It was a turning point in the war. Other Soviet offensive operations compelled German forces in the Caucasus to withdraw. They only just escaped encirclement.

While these events took place in the east, Axis forces in north Africa were defeated. In June 1943 Sicily was invaded, but German losses were slight: a few thousand killed, 5,500 captured. The rest of the German force was evacuated. Another side-show, Stalin would have thought. His irritation showed during 1943 even though the tide of battle was turning to the Red Army. In June Churchill and Roosevelt decided that a second front in France would have to be put off for another year. "Your decision," Stalin cabled his allies, had been made without Soviet participation and will cause "exceptional difficulties for the Soviet Union." This was a heads-up to Churchill and Roosevelt on the eve of the great tank battle at Kursk. If Stalingrad turned the tide of battle against the *Wehrmacht*, the Red Army victory at Kursk sealed its fate. In the Kursk salient toward the southern end of the long eastern front, the Soviet high command concentrated 1,336,000 men, nearly 3,500 tanks, 19,000 guns, and 2,900 aircraft. They faced 900,000 German soldiers organized in 50 divisions with 2,700 tanks and 10,000 guns. On July 5 the Germans attacked the northern and southern waists of the Kursk salient. In a massive tank battle, the Germans were defeated, losing heavily in men and armor. There could be no doubt now about the ultimate outcome of the war. The Red Army launched a counter-offensive that reached the eastern banks of the Dnepr in early October. On November 6, 1943 Kiev was liberated.

Teheran

Alliance politics reflected battlefield realities. After Kursk, Roosevelt and Churchill had to pay more attention to Stalin's complaints about the absence of a second front, unless they were prepared to see the Red Army liberate all of Europe. The three leaders met in Teheran in late November 1943. Churchill tried to persuade Roosevelt and Stalin to support continued Allied operations in Italy. Churchill thought about getting into the Balkans before the Red Army and protecting British imperial interests in the Mediterranean. All to no avail, the balance of power had changed. The Big Three were now the Big Two-and-a-Half, according to one joker. Britain was the junior partner. If we help the Red Army, Roosevelt reasoned, we help ourselves. In 1943 massive Lend-Lease supplies arrived in the Soviet Union.[23]

In Teheran when Stalin insisted on Overlord, the code name given to the eventual Normandy invasion, Roosevelt backed him. For Stalin, the operations in Italy were another sideshow. The shortest way to the heart of Germany was through northern France, and so he pressed hard for a definite decision to invade France in the spring of 1944. Churchill still held out for the Mediterranean theater, but in the end he had to yield. Overlord was on.

Other issues were discussed at Teheran. These included the postwar status of Poland, unconditional German surrender, postwar European frontiers, and Soviet entry into the war against Japan. The mood at Teheran was good natured after business was settled. Winston drank to the health of the proletarian masses and Stalin to the Conservative Party.[24] Both leaders were laying it on. Teheran was the high point of Allied cooperation.

War, War, Not Jaw, Jaw

The war continued. Allied bombing of Germany intensified. The Allied advance up the Italian peninsula was slow and bloody, as Stalin had thought it would be. Instead of Allied forces tying down greater numbers of Germans, it was the other way round. In contrast, on the eastern front the Red Army advanced hundreds of kilometers toward Germany. By the end of 1943, the Red Army was a mighty force, directed by skilled commanders. Their success was based on combined operations of massed armor, artillery, and air power employed in rolling offensives carried out rapidly over broad fronts and covered by deception and concealment. The Soviet method was similar to that of Marshal Ferdinand Foch in the summer of 1918, but whereas Foch was happy with an advance of 15–20 kilometers a day on a much shorter front, the Red Army might advance 100 kilometers a day. Speed and space were the differences making possible vast encirclements and flanking movements in deep operations. Soviet tanks and Studebaker trucks carried the Red Army forward.[25] And to think that before the war almost no one in the west thought the Red Army could fight.

At the end of 1943, 3.2 million Axis troops in 177 divisions faced a Red Army of 6.4 million soldiers organized in 35 tank and mechanized corps and more than 480 division-sized forces. German commanders had no illusions about their prospects. Between December 1943 and May 1944 the Red Army launched two great offensives, the first in the north, which freed besieged Leningrad. In the south Soviet gains were spectacular, liberating all the Ukraine and Crimea and pushing up against the borders of Romania. The much greater sacrifices of the Red Army caused bitterness and skepticism in Moscow about the likelihood of a cross-Channel invasion. Second-front jokes were common: "What is an old believer?" was a question. "A person who still believes in a second front," came the reply. Another went: "They say that the second front will not open because Churchill is waiting until the last button has been sewn on the last greatcoat of the last English soldier."[26]

On June 6, 1944 American, British, and Canadian forces landed in Normandy. To resist the Allied invasion the German army had 58 divisions in the west of which only 15 were in the area of the initial fighting. In the east there were 228 Axis divisions to hold back the Red Army.[27] As Stalin promised at Teheran, the Red Army launched a massive June offensive. On June 23 the main assault began in the center of the German line. It collapsed at once. In June and July the Soviet offensive pushed back the *Wehrmacht* as much as 900 kilometers; this brought the Red Army to the outskirts of Warsaw. In the south beginning in August the advance carried into Romania, Bulgaria, Yugoslavia, and Hungary. In the west the second front also began to move. On July 25, as the Red Army approached Warsaw, the American army broke out of Normandy and advanced toward Paris.

Moscow and Yalta

Nazi Germany was doomed. Politics now became preeminent and began to weaken the grand alliance. Old anti-communist fears and prejudices reappeared. For Churchill, it was fear of the spread of communism into central Europe. For Stalin, it was fear of western intrigues. This was a war unlike others, Stalin said: "Whoever occupies a territory also imposes on it his own social system . . . It cannot be otherwise." The

Soviet Union did not feel secure in the interwar period; it would now create its own security through force of arms. The Allies needed to meet again to discuss the postwar world. Churchill went alone to Moscow in October 1944 to feel out Stalin's position. At their meeting in the Kremlin on October 9 Churchill handed Stalin a piece of paper on which he had written the names of five east European countries, parceling them out according to percentages in favor of the Soviet Union or Britain or sharing influence equally. Greece was to fall under British influence and Romania and Bulgaria under Soviet influence. Hungary and Yugoslavia were blessed with a 50–50 percentage arrangement. Stalin put a blue tick on the paper and handed it back to Churchill without saying a word.[28]

Peacemaking would not be so easy. Roosevelt did not put his blue tick on Churchill's paper. There had to be more negotiations. Another Allied conference took place at Yalta in February 1945. All the difficult issues were addressed. Poland was a bone of contention. Its eastern frontier was set on the so-called Curzon line, which ran more or less along the ethnographic frontier. Ukrainian and Byelorussian territories seized by Poland during the Russo-Polish war in 1919–20 reverted to the Soviet Union. As a *quid pro quo* Poland would absorb large areas of East Prussia and eastern Germany. Who was to govern Poland was also a matter of disagreement. Would it be the London Poles, the successors of interwar Poland, hostile to the Soviet Union, or the Lublin Poles, recognized by Stalin? At Yalta, Stalin made clear that Poland was an issue that would have to be settled his way.

Then there was the issue of postwar Germany. Was it to be dismembered, "pastoralized" to render it forever harmless; or was it to be rehabilitated according to Anglo-American standards? And would liberated France be recognized as an equal ally and given a zone of occupation in defeated Germany? De Gaulle now headed the French government, and he wanted to be involved in the postwar administration of Germany. Reparations were another bone of contention. Stalin insisted on $20 billion, of which half would go to the Soviet Union. Roosevelt was more flexible than Churchill with respect to Stalin's demands, no doubt because Stalin confirmed that the Soviet Union would enter the war against Japan after German surrender. Roosevelt was also thinking ahead to the postwar world, to the need to set up a new international organization, the United Nations, and for that he wanted Stalin's cooperation. For Roosevelt, there were still strong American interests in working with the Soviet Union. Not so for Churchill, who worried about an unstoppable Red Army advance into western Europe and who talked about arming a million German POWs to stem the tide. And the war was not yet over.

Potsdam and the End of the Grand Alliance

Unfortunately, Roosevelt died on April 12, 1945. FDR was succeeded by Harry S. Truman, an ordinary politician from the American midwest, who had outspoken anti-communist ideas. If the Russians did not want to cooperate, he told advisors shortly after he became president, "they can go to hell." Later, Molotov advised Stalin that the Americans were "trying to bid up." "Let them," Stalin replied, laughing.[29]

Roosevelt died two days before the start of the final Red Army advance into Berlin. For the Soviet Union, the seizure of Berlin was retributive justice. German frontiers were posted with placards: "Here is the lair of the fascist beast." German resistance was fierce but vain. On April 30 Hitler committed suicide and on the same day Red Army soldiers hoisted a Red flag over the Reichstag. On May 9 Soviet authorities accepted the German surrender. Henceforth, that day would be a major Soviet and then Russian holiday. Veterans would pin on their rows of jingling medals and join other younger citizens – literally the beneficiaries of these old soldiers' prodigious efforts – to celebrate Victory Day in the streets of Moscow and other cities.

The cost of victory was high: 10 million Red Army soldiers were killed or missing, 18 million were wounded or sick. No one knows how many civilians perished – estimates range between 12 and 40 million. These losses are so colossal that one wonders whether the term "Holocaust" should not be applied to the Soviet victims of Nazism. The memory of Soviet sacrifice was inconvenient during the Cold War, but surely it is not now. Few families escaped without loss, and many hundreds of thousands disappeared without a survivor to mourn them. Even for many Russians living in the twenty-first century the Great Patriotic War was about life or death. Revisionist historians may wish to consider whether their dispassionate World War II narratives would be recognizable to people who actually lived through those years.

The Red Army exacted a high price in return, inflicting 80 percent of all casualties on the *Wehrmacht*. Even after the Normandy invasion the Red Army held down two-thirds of German forces.[30] By June 1944 it was a matter of time before the Red Army crushed Nazi Germany. Stalin was in a strong position to secure what he regarded as Russian national interests.

The last meeting of the Allied wartime leaders took place in Potsdam in July–August 1945. Stalin and Truman were there, but Churchill would leave in mid-conference, having suffered electoral defeat at home. The Yalta issues remained unresolved. What were to be the new boundaries of Poland? Who would govern in Warsaw? How were reparations to be determined and exacted? Truman mentioned with feigned nonchalance that the United States had tested "a new weapon of unusual destructive force," that is, an atomic bomb, soon to be dropped on Japan.

Potsdam marked the beginning of the end of the grand alliance. As long as Nazi Germany was a threat, the alliance remained secure. As victory approached, the alliance disintegrated. With the German threat eliminated, ideology returned to the fore. The realists, who had tempered their anti-communism, no longer had to do so. Churchill was a good example: he reverted to die-hard positions and was relieved that the United States had the atomic bomb with which to threaten the Soviet Union. Stalin noticed: "Churchill did not trust us, and in consequence we could not fully trust him either." As for Truman, he abruptly stopped Lend-Lease to the Soviet Union, while senior American officials saw no grounds for long-term good relations with Moscow.[31] Each side reverted to prewar fear and aversion of the other. The big difference in 1945 was that the Soviet Union had become a world power. Stalin was no longer UJ; he was the bloody dictator again. A wolf after all cannot shed its skin.

The grand alliance was wrapped in irony. Stalin wanted to avoid carrying alone the burden of war against Nazi Germany. So did the French and British. In the end the Red Army had to carry the burden anyway, while the French collapsed and the British barely held out. They were all outsmarted. The French debacle left the Soviet Union, and not just Britain, alone against Nazi Germany. Neither Churchill nor Stalin had desired such an outcome, but it made them allies after June 22, 1941. After the American entry into the war the grand alliance was formed, though this outcome was less the result of deliberate policy than it was of good fortune.

Red Army sacrifices spared Anglo-American sacrifices. The British and American governments might have been more grateful. But sacrifices in blood, even immense sacrifices, counted for little in 1945. Western anti-communism trumped gratitude: the grand alliance proved to be merely an interregnum in a hostile western–Soviet relationship that began after the Bolshevik revolution in November 1917.

NOTES

1 See M. J. Carley, "Down a Blind-Alley: Anglo-Franco-Soviet Relations, 1920–1939," *Canadian Journal of History* 29/1 (1994): 147–72; M. J. Carley, "Episodes from the Early Cold War: Franco-Soviet Relations, 1917–1927," *Europe-Asia Studies* 52/7 (2000): 1275–1305; and Martin Gilbert, *Prophet of Truth: Winston S. Churchill, 1922–1939* (London: Minerva, 1976), pp. 47–9.

2 Adolf Hitler, *Mein Kampf*, Ralph Manheim, trans. (Boston MA: Houghton Mifflin, 1943), ch. 14; excerpt from Litvinov's journal, meetings with Rudolph Nadolny (German ambassador in Moscow), December 11 and 13, 1933, Arkhiv vneshnei politiki Rossiiskoi Federatsii, Moscow (hereafter AVPRF), fond 082, opis' 17, papka 77, delo 1, listy 6–2 (hereafter f., o., p., d., l[1].); and German antisemitic propaganda, January 1939, provided to the author by Professor Vicki Caron, Cornell University.

3 See I. N. Iakovlev et al., *Sovetsko-Amerikanskie Otnosheniia: Gody Nepriznaniia, 1927–1933* (Moscow: Rossiia XX Vek, 2002); and Iakovlev et al., *Sovetsko-Amerikanskie Otnosheniia, 1934–1939* (Moscow: Rossiia XX Vek. 2003).

4 See Iakovlev et al., *Sovetsko-Amerikanskie Otnosheniia, 1934–1939*, passim.

5 V. P. Potemkin, Soviet ambassador in Paris, to N. N. Krestinskii, deputy commissar for foreign affairs, no. 5346, secret, Nov. 26, 1935, AVPRF, f. 0136, o. 19, p. 814, ll. 119–22. For the wider story, see M. J. Carley, *1939: The Alliance that Never Was and the Coming of World War II* (Chicago: Ivan R. Dee, 1999).

6 See M. J. Carley, "'A Fearful Concatenation of Circumstances': The Anglo-Soviet Rapprochement, 1934–36," *Contemporary European History* 5/1 (1996): 29–69; and M. J. Carley, "Five Kopecks for Five Kopecks: Franco-Soviet Trade Relations, 1928–1939," *Cahiers du monde russe et soviétique* 33/1 (1992): 23–58.

7 Potemkin, then deputy commissar for foreign affairs, to I. Z. Surits, Soviet ambassador in Paris, no. 1181, secret, June 21, 1937, AVPRF, f. 05, o. 17, d. 109, p. 135, ll. 36–8.

8 See Talbot C. Imlay, *Facing the Second World War: Strategy, Politics, and Economics in Britain and France, 1938–1940* (New York: Oxford University Press, 2003).

9 A. J. P. Taylor, *English History, 1914–1945* (New York: Oxford University Press, 1965), p. 469, n. 1.

10 See Ernest R. May, *Strange Victory: Hitler's Conquest of France* (New York: Hill and Wang, 2000); Tony Judt, "Could the French Have Won?" *New York Review of Books* 43/3 (2001): 37–40.

11 See Peter Jackson, *France and the Nazi Menace: Intelligence and Policy Making, 1933–1939* (New York: Oxford University Press, 2000); Robert J. Young, *France and the Origins of the Second World War* (New York: St Martin's Press, 1996); and Imlay, *Facing the Second World War*.

12 See Gabriel Gorodetsky, *Grand Delusion: Stalin and the German Invasion of Russia* (New Haven CT: Yale University Press, 1999).

13 See Albert Resis, ed., *Molotov Remembers: Inside Kremlin Politics, Conversations with Felix Chuev* (Chicago: Ivan R. Dee, 1993), pp. 22–32.

14 See M. Gilbert, *Finest Hour: Winston S. Churchill, 1939–1941* (London: Minerva, 1989), pp. 1120–1.

15 See M. Gilbert, *Winston S. Churchill : "Never Despair," 1945–1965* (Boston MA: Houghton Mifflin, 1988), p. 550; Edward M. Bennett, *Franklin D. Roosevelt and the Search for Victory: American–Soviet Relations, 1939–1945* (Wilmington DE: SR Books), ch. 2; Bradley F. Smith, *Sharing Secrets with Stalin: How the Allies Traded Intelligence, 1941–1945* (Lawrence: University Press of Kansas, 1996), chs 1, 2; and David Carlton, *Churchill and the Soviet Union* (Manchester: Manchester University Press, 2000), pp. 83–6.

16 See V. A. Solotarev, G. N. Sevost'ianov et al., *Velikaia Otechestvennaia voina, 1941–1945*, 4 vols (Moscow: Nauka, 1998), vol. 1, photographs following p. 160.

17 See Smith, *Sharing Secrets*, p. 29; and Richard Overy, *Russia's War* (New York: Penguin, 1998), p. 116.

18 See Overy, *Russia's War*, pp. 84–5, 117, 139–42; and David M. Glantz and Jonathan M. House, *When Titans Clashed: How the Red Army Stopped Hitler* (Lawrence: University Press of Kansas, 1995), pp. 56–7.

19 See Martin, *Finest Hour*, pp. 1266–8; and W. S. Churchill, *The Second World War*, 6 vols (London: Cassell, 1948–53), vol. 3, pp. 538–9.

20 Smith, *Sharing Secrets*, p. 115.

21 Oleg A. Rzheshevskii, *Stalin i Cherchill'* (Moscow: Nauka, 2004), p. 353; Glantz and House, *When Titans Clashed*, p. 302.

22 See M. Gilbert, *Road to Victory: Winston S. Churchill, 1941–1945* (London: Minerva, 1989), p. 202.

23 See Smith, *Sharing Secrets*, pp. 166 and passim.

24 See Gilbert, *Road to Victory*, pp. 574, 586.

25 See Basil H. Liddell Hart, *History of the Second World War* (London: Papermac, 1992), pp. 503, 560–1.

26 Glantz and House, *When Titans Clashed*, p. 184; Overy, *Russia's War*, p. 240; and S. A. Shinkarchuk, *Istoriia Sovetskoi Rossii (1917–1953) v Anekdotakh* (St Petersburg: Nestor, 2000), p. 74.

27 See Overy, *Russia at War*, p. 240.

28 Rzheshevskii, *Stalin i Cherchill'*, p. 422.

29 Lloyd C. Gardner, *Spheres of Influence: The Great Powers Partition Europe, from Munich to Yalta* (Chicago: Ivan R. Dee, 1993), p. 256; Carlton, *Churchill and the Soviet Union*, p. 137; and Overy, *Russia at War*, p. 285.

30 See Overy, *Russia at War*, pp. 240, 288; Glantz and House, *When Titans Clashed*, p. 307.

31 See Robin Edmonds, "Churchill and Stalin," in Robert Blake and W. Roger Louis, *Churchill: A Major New Assessment of His Life in Peace and War* (New York: Norton, 1993), pp. 323, 325; Carlton, *Churchill and the Soviet Union*, ch. 6.

GUIDE TO FURTHER READING

Edward M. Bennett, *Franklin D. Roosevelt and the Search for Victory: American–Soviet Relations, 1939–1945* (Wilmington DE: SR Books, 1990). An account of American–Soviet relations from the American point of view.

Michael Jabara Carley, *1939: The Alliance that Never Was and the Coming of World War II* (Chicago: Ivan R. Dee, 1999). My view of western–Soviet relations during the interwar years and of the failure of the first grand alliance in 1939.

David Carlton, *Churchill and the Soviet Union* (Manchester: Manchester University Press, 2000). Focuses on Churchill's visceral anti-communism.

Lloyd C. Gardner, *Spheres of Influence: The Great Powers Partition Europe from Munich to Yalta* (Chicago: Ivan R. Dee, 1993). This study covers grand strategy and summit diplomacy from 1938 to 1945 from a left perspective.

Martin Gilbert, *Finest Hour: Winston S. Churchill, 1939–1941* (London: Minerva, 1989) and *Road to Victory: Winston S. Churchill, 1941–1945* (London: Minerva, 1989). An encyclopedic account of grand strategy and summit diplomacy from Churchill's point of view.

David M. Glantz and Jonathan M. House, *When Titans Clashed: How the Red Army Stopped Hitler* (Lawrence: University Press of Kansas, 1995). An account of Soviet military strategy on the eastern front, often drawing comparisons with military operations in north Africa and western Europe.

Gabriel Gorodetsky, *Grand Delusion: Stalin and the German Invasion of Russia* (New Haven CT: Yale University Press, 1999). The best account in English on the lead-up to the German invasion of the Soviet Union in June 1941.

Talbot C. Imlay, *Facing the Second World War: Strategy, Politics, and Economics in Britain and France, 1938–1940* (New York: Oxford University Press, 2003). The conclusions about France as basically doomed to defeat are interesting.

Peter Jackson, *France and the Nazi Menace: Intelligence and Policy Making, 1933–1939* (New York: Oxford University Press, 2000). This is an excellent revisionist study presenting France as resurgent and ready for the fight in 1939.

Ernest R. May, *Strange Victory: Hitler's Conquest of France* (New York: Hill and Wang, 2000). A revisionist account of the fall of France, holding that defeat was a tragic accident.

Hugh Ragsdale, *The Soviets, the Munich Crisis, and the Coming of World War II* (New York: Cambridge University Press, 2004). An excellent counter-revisionist look at the Munich crisis and its aftermath from an east European perspective.

Albert Resis, ed., *Molotov Remembers: Inside Kremlin Politics, Conversations with Felix Chuev* (Chicago: Ivan R. Dee, 1993). This is, among other things, Molotov's view of Soviet strategy and politics during World War II.

Bradley F. Smith, *Sharing Secrets with Stalin: How the Allies Traded Intelligence, 1941–1945* (Lawrence: University Press of Kansas, 1996). A highly interesting account of what worked and what did not work inside the grand alliance concerning the exchange of intelligence on Axis intentions, strategy, and armaments.

CHAPTER TWENTY-EIGHT

The Real War

DAVID FRENCH

Long periods of boredom were broken by short bursts of excitement. For the first time I had to learn to do nothing but wait – for me the most difficult lesson of all. To my great relief I found I did not get frightened in action – not that I enjoyed being shelled or dive-bombed any more than the next man; but fear never paralysed me or put me off my stroke. On the other hand I was never called on to show the sort of active courage which wins men the VC. A dumb, animal endurance is the sort of courage most men need in war. (Denis Healey, *The Time of My Life* (London, 1990), pp. 48–9)

Denis Healey's experiences as a soldier were typical of many men who served in uniform during World War II. For most soldiers World War II was a machine-age war. Employed in hauling the supplies or meeting the needs of the military bureaucracy, they rarely if ever fired a shot in anger. At one extreme by May 1945, for example, only 23 percent of personnel in the US army were assigned to the army's ground forces where they might actually have to fire rifles, drive tanks, or load artillery in action. Even in the German army, which managed to devote rather more of its manpower to front line units, by 1943 over one third of its men were still employed behind the line.[1] But essential as such soldiers were, no army could fight its battles without exposing some of its men to the dangers of front line service, and it is with their experiences that this chapter is chiefly concerned.

Casualties

To Anglophone readers born after 1945 no war can compare in its horror and enormity to World War I. The experience of war on the western front represents a historical and cultural discontinuity of enormous proportions. But the historical reality was different. By the end of World War I the German armed forces had lost just over 2 million dead, Russia 1.8 million, France and its empire 1.4 million, Britain and its empire 921,000, and the USA 114,000. The pattern of losses suffered by the belligerents during World War II was very different. British casualties were fewer than they were during World War I, the British army losing a total of 569,000 men, including 144,000 dead, 34,000 missing, 240,000 wounded, and 152,000 POWs. However, in Normandy the daily loss that the British suffered actually exceeded those for the third battle of Ypres. US ground forces suffered more heavily in World War II than they did in the earlier war. In the European theater alone they lost a total of 80,000 killed, 325,969 wounded, 40,000 POWs, and 10,000 missing between 1942 and 1945. But the losses of the western powers were low compared to those of the Germans, and more particularly, the Russians. The *Wehrmacht* lost 2 million men dead (of whom 1.78 million served in the army), 4.4 million wounded, and just under 2 million missing, probably half of whom were also dead. But German losses were dwarfed by those suffered by the Soviet Union. Recent research on Soviet losses suggests that Soviet forces suffered a staggering 8.7 million dead, and 18.3 million wounded or sick.

In all armies, however, losses were not evenly distributed. Some soldiers had a much greater chance of being killed or maimed than others. Men serving in the rear areas suffered the least; those unfortunate enough to be in the artillery, field engineers, or the armored corps suffered more heavily. Those doubly unfortunate to be serving in the infantry suffered the most. When the Red Army was on the offensive between 1943 and 1945, infantry casualties accounted for nearly 86 percent of all of its losses. In the British army in Normandy the infantry accounted for less than 25 percent of its strength, but they suffered about 71 percent of its casualties. In the US army the infantry represented only 14 percent of its strength, but they suffered 70 percent of its casualties. In the first two months of the Normandy campaign in the summer of 1944 the 90th US Infantry Division lost the equivalent of 100 percent of its riflemen. By contrast, the artillery accounted for 16 percent of a US infantry division's manpower, but accounted for an average of only 3 percent of its casualties.[2]

The result was much the same in all armies. By 1944–5 each of them was struggling to maintain the rifle strength of its divisions. In 1942 Soviet rifle divisions had a nominal strength of 10,566 men. By 1945 most divisions had shrunk to between 3,500 and 4,500 men. The British army in Italy was so short of infantrymen in the winter of 1944–5 that it reduced many battalions from four to only three rifle companies. The US army was chronically short of trained infantry replacements throughout the northwest European campaign and both the British and US armies had hastily to retrain men from other arms of the service in infantry skills to make good the shortfalls. Behind these gruesome statistics lay the human reality of battle. For the individual Tommy, GI, German *landsknecht*, or Soviet *frontoviki* caught up in the reality of battle at El Alamein, on Omaha Beach, or at Stalingrad, there was little to choose between his own experience of fear, fatigue, terror and, if he was lucky, comradeship, and his father's equally dreadful experiences at Verdun or Passchendaele. For those at the forward edge of the battlefield, war had lost none of its elemental character. It remained violent, brutal, and chaotic. Recalling a counter-attack that he participated in at Salerno in September 1943, Lieutenant Gerry Barnett remembered that it was complete confusion:

> The whole battle had been confused, but this was very confused. Anyway, we made the final walk up the hill. We got to the top of this "Pimple," it was a small summit sloping away on all sides and there must have been a group of Germans about 20 feet away. They were within grenade throwing range anyway. We could see the flashes coming from

their Schmeissers as they fired at us. There were about five of us at the most on our side on the top. There wasn't room for any more anyway! We were firing at them and throwing our grenades and they were firing back and throwing grenades. I was lying down between bursts of fire, then kneeling up so I could see just over the crown of the hill, see their flashes and then firing back with my Tommy gun – when it worked. The first time when I got up there I pressed the trigger and there was just a rough grating noise as the bolt slid forward because the dust was slowing the action. So I got back, lay down again, pulled the oil bottle out of the butt, oiled the bolt and like a good soldier put the oil bottle back in the butt. I got up and it worked, fortunately, it fired then.[3]

But if infantrymen were the main victims of the battlefield, they were not its most deadly killers. The majority of soldiers who became casualties were hit by men who were invisible to them. Although the statistics are imperfect, in the British army, for example, as many as three-quarters of men who were wounded were struck by weapons such as mortars, shells, or aerial bombs, which had been fired at such a distance that the soldiers operating them could not see their target. Only 10–20 percent of wounds were caused by direct-fire weapons such as rifles, machine guns, or anti-tank guns that had been fired by soldiers who could see their victims.

The most valuable characteristic that a front line soldier could possess was not dashing heroism, although that was never held in disdain, but stoical endurance, for without that he would not be able to withstand the multiple stresses that the experience of battle imposed upon him. Most men went into action tired, hungry, and overburdened by the weight of their equipment. In action they were deafened by the noise of exploding shells and the rattle of machine guns, and they might be paralyzed by the ever present fear that at any moment they might be wounded or killed. In earlier wars soldiers had fought in closely packed formations and could take comfort from the physical proximity of their comrades. The range and lethality of modern weapons made such tactics suicidal in World War II. If they were to survive, infantrymen had to advance in small groups and be widely dispersed. The characteristic activity of most infantrymen was not firing his rifle or bayoneting his opponent, it was burrowing underground. During training soldiers came to hate digging trenches. But once they had been shelled for the first time, they could not dig them fast enough. That was symptomatic of the one emotion that was common to almost every front line soldier. Once he came under fire he was frightened. Men who claimed that they were not afraid when they were being shot at were accounted liars or fools by the men who lived beside them. The fundamental problem that confronted every army was how to ensure that soldiers did not give way to their fears and run away from the firing line. Soldiers had to be taught to kill, but even more important, they had to be taught to be killed.

Personnel Selection

The attitude of recruits towards military service varied and consequently some armies had a more difficult task to perform in doing this than others. In the Soviet Union most recruits accepted conscription with dull resignation of the inevitable. By contrast the *Wehrmacht* had two great advantages; the German army had a prestige that predated Hitler's regime, and it existed in a society that was willing to glorify war as a positive experience that would bring the whole nation together. But in Britain and the USA military service was generally held in low public esteem. Armies had long been distrusted as economically wasteful institutions that posed a latent threat to civil liberties. In Britain regular army officers were often regarded as being inept and were blamed for the heavy losses of World War I. In the USA the dominant business culture rejected militarism as a leftover from the past. Some recruits happily embraced military service as a patriotic duty. Others accepted it as a necessary job that had to be done. Some saw it as a test of their manhood which they wanted to pass. Many were reluctant to leave their families, friends, and familiar surroundings for an unknown, uncomfortable, and probably dangerous future.

The German and Soviet armies also differed from the British and American in respect of whom they placed in the front line. The personnel policies of the contending armies were determined to a large extent by how they conceived war. All armies sought to employ modern weapons in the shape of tanks, artillery, and aircraft. But the Germans contended that weapons alone would not bring victory. To them war was a struggle that would ultimately be determined by the will to win of the leaders and men of the opposing armies. The Soviets expected to fight a prolonged and costly war of attrition involving both masses of men and machines, and were willing to pay the human cost. It therefore made sense for both the Germans and Soviets to ensure that their front line units received their fair share of the fittest and best educated men available.[4] But the Americans and the British, while never ignoring the importance of morale, gave much greater importance to the role of machinery in war fighting. The lesson they had learned from World War I was that fighting wars by relying on human will and manpower was likely to lead to excessive casualties, and that was no longer acceptable in a democracy. They had to find a cheaper way of winning battles and the course they chose was to generate the maximum amount of firepower and mobility by employing the largest possible number of the most sophisticated weapons. They did so in the expectation they could reduce to a minimum the number of men they exposed to the dangers of the front line.[5]

Consequently, in the first instance, both the British and American governments assigned their highest quality manpower to the air force and the navy. Their armies had to make do with what was left. Both armies then developed quasi-scientific tests to determine each recruit's physical and intellectual capabilities and occupational skills, so that they could be matched against detailed job descriptions for each military occupation. The US army had considered how to do this even before the war, and once the expansion of the US army commenced, it applied personnel selection tests across the board. The British were more cautious and did not adopt the full panoply of "scientific" personnel selection until 1942.[6] But the result was much the same as in the USA. Throughout the war the British army and, at least until 1944, the US army also, received less than their fair share of the highest quality manpower. And within that pool, the technical arms and rearward services received the fittest and most intelligent recruits. Front line infantry units found themselves assigned an unduly large proportion of the least well-educated and least fit, even though combat experience was to show that they needed men who were at least as intelligent and fit as an airman.[7] Front line combat became the preserve of the young, the ill-educated, and the socially disadvantaged. It was only in late 1943 that the US army began to realize its mistake and to place larger numbers of fit, young, and better-educated men into front line units.

However, it would be wrong to make too much of the fact that these policies gave the *Wehrmacht* a significant advantage over its enemies. It was denied this by a combination of heavy German casualties and the US army's ruthless rejection of men who could not fit its stringent medical and intellectual tests. In June 1944, at the start of the Normandy campaign, the average German soldier was over 31 years of age, or some 7 years older than his American counterpart. Many German soldiers were suffering from physical ailments that would have meant that the US army would have rejected them as unfit for service.

Training and Replacement Policies

The process of turning civilians into soldiers began during basic training. On their very first day in the army recruits were symbolically and literally shorn of their civilian identities when they shed their civilian clothes, donned uniform for the first time, had their hair cut very short in characteristic military fashion, and bedded-down for the night for the first time with the men who were to become their comrades. Basic training usually lasted for about 12–16 weeks, although when men were badly needed at the front the period was sometimes reduced. At other times it might be extended. Recruits became physically fit, familiar with the weapons they would use in combat and, above all, they lost many of their civilian preoccupations with rights and freedoms. In their place, the physical and mental hardships inherent in basic training made the individual soldier aware of just how dependent he was on the army for his comfort, and the close group of men around him for his survival. By setting recruits tough physical challenges, armies welded groups of individuals into teams. Ideally, the sense of comradeship bred during training became in most armies one of the foundation stones of battlefield discipline. The military authorities hoped that men would not run away under fire because if they did they would be letting down their friends.

Problems arose, however, when the primary groups so carefully nurtured during training began to break down on the battlefield as units were devastated by casualties. In the opening years of the war the Germans were perhaps the most successful at overcoming the inevitable degradation of the mutual ties between comrades that this entailed. The German army went to considerable lengths to sustain the morale of its front line troops by ensuring that when soldiers went into combat they did so among friends and under officers and NCOs they knew and trusted. Each corps at the front was attached to its own military district in Germany, and every division drew its replacements from a training unit in that district. Once recruits had completed their basic training they were posted as members of a march battalion to a field division where they received additional training, and got to know the officers and NCOs who would eventually lead them into combat. Divisions were usually kept in the line until they were exhausted, that is to say their infantry had been all but destroyed. Only then were they pulled out for a rest and reinforcements brought forward to fill up the gaps in their establishment. In theory this gave veterans and reinforcements the opportunity to train together and to form new primary groups before the division was once again thrown into battle. Whenever possible the army tried to maintain units which were nationally homogeneous, convinced that by ensuring that Prussians fought side by side with Prussians or Württembergers with Württembergers that they would enhance morale.

When the system worked it meant that men entered combat as part of a cohesive and well-integrated team. But the horrendous casualties that the *Wehrmacht* began to sustain in Russia from 1941 onwards steadily destroyed the German army's replacement system. The army could only reap the rewards of such a system if it had a manpower pool that was sufficiently deep to enable it to replace losses and the German replacement system began to show signs of overstretch as early as 1940. Within five months of the start of Operation Barbarossa the German army had exhausted its reserves of trained manpower and was 340,000 men below establishment. By April 1942 the deficit stood at 625,000. The only way it could begin to make good such a shortfall was by combing out rear area units of fit young men and, when that did not suffice, recruiting Russian POWs and civilians as support troops.

The Red Army adopted a similar system of replacing casualties. It too only withdrew divisions when their combat edge had become blunt because their front line units had run out of men. Soviet troops received their basic training in replacement training regiments well to the rear. At the end of their training the newly trained soldiers were posted to field replacement units attached to fronts and armies. Thence they were passed to divisional replacement battalions where they received, if they were fortunate, much badly needed further training before proceeding to their front line units. After March 1942, on Stalin's express order, replacements were no longer fed into Soviet divisions piecemeal. Henceforth, only when a division had been devastated in action was it withdrawn. It was then, if the exigencies of the battle allowed, given time to induct and train replacements before being put back into the line.[8]

Thus, both the Soviet and German armies at least tried to meet one of the most basic psychological needs of front line soldiers: the need to feel that they were fighting and suffering alongside men they knew and who would help them to bear the physical and psychological burdens of combat. By contrast, the US army placed far more emphasis on bureaucratic tidiness. In order to ensure that some units were not over-strength whereas others were under-strength, it treated replacements like so many spare parts in a vast machine. Units were kept in the front line for prolonged periods, and only rarely were they withdrawn for rest and refitting. Between D-Day and VE Day in Europe, half of all US infantry divisions in the theater spent 150 or more days in combat.[9] This bred an understandable bitterness among the survivors, who came to understand that their only way out of the front line was through being killed or wounded. After basic training, replacements were posted as individuals to a replacement depot, whence they were shipped overseas. There, in another replacement depot, they might (if they were lucky) receive several weeks of refresher training. If they were not, and if the need for men on the front line was pressing, they were quickly posted to a fighting unit. Wounded men were rarely returned to their original unit. When they were fit they were used to fill the first available slot in whichever unit needed them. Some men who were kept in replacement depots for too long actually went absent without leave in order to rejoin their old unit. It was not unusual for replacements to arrive at their new unit at night, to be posted to the front line immediately, and to be expected to fight and die alongside complete strangers. However, it would be wrong to assume that veterans cold-shouldered newcomers. If they had the opportunity they did try to integrate them into their unit, if only because a new pair of eyes and ears might relieve the survivors of another weary period of guard duty.

The British regimental system probably fell half way between the American and the German systems. In theory recruiting was done on a regional basis and men from a particular county or city were posted to their "local" regiment. When this system worked the army could rely on a primordial local attachment as one of the foundations for its morale. In practice, however, by 1942–3 the system was rapidly collapsing under the weight of casualties and a growing shortage of men of military age. It became increasingly common for men inducted into the army in one regiment to be posted on completion of their training into another and, if they were wounded and returned to duty, to find themselves serving in a third one.

Combat and Ideology

In the face of the rapid and heavy losses that many front line units sustained, any explanation of why men remained in combat that relies exclusively upon the notion that they did so because they did not want to let down their comrades is questionable. Primary group loyalty as an explanation of why men fought can only take us so far. There were many occasions when primary groups dissolved, but the survivors continued fighting. It is therefore necessary to examine the importance of two other factors that sustained front line troops: ideology and the system of formal discipline that armies adopted to deter men from leaving combat and to punish those who did so.

The importance of political indoctrination in motivating soldiers to fight has been much debated. It was once common for historians to dismiss its significance as at best marginal.[10] More recently, a better understanding of the effects of heavy casualties in undermining primary group loyalty has encouraged historians, particularly those analyzing the German army, to look afresh at its significance. All armies tried to indoctrinate their soldiers with notions about the righteousness of their cause, but the armies of the totalitarian regimes tried harder than those of the western liberal democracies. After Hitler's accession to power in 1933, the principles of the National Socialist state were inculcated into every budding German soldier at school, during his compulsory membership of the Hitler Youth, and once he was conscripted. They learned a dangerous combination of antisemitism, anti-Bolshevism, and racism. Radio broadcasts, films, and newspapers were all used from 1939 onwards to make the ordinary German soldier understand that the war, particularly on the eastern front, was an ideological conflict between good and evil. From the beginning of the invasion of Russia, front line troops were saturated by propaganda insisting that the war against the Soviet Union was a war of annihilation against "Jewish-Bolshevism." Alongside these negative notions there is also evidence that many ordinary German soldiers were committed to what they identified as the more positive aspects of Nazi ideology. The Landser saw the war on the eastern front as an ideological struggle because the enemy seemed to threaten the validity of the Nazi state, a state to which they were committed because it had apparently redeemed the failures of World War I and the Weimar republic. As late as 1944, when the war was clearly going against the Germans, officers reported that their soldiers were listening attentively to political lectures about the issues at stake, convinced that they had a right and duty to fight to protect Germany and European civilization from the threat of Bolshevism.[11]

The barbarous behavior of their enemies unsurprisingly provoked a fierce response from Soviet soldiers caught up in the war on the eastern front. They, too, were exposed to an onslaught of propaganda. It told them that they were engaged in a life and death struggle against the evils of fascism and militarism. In the initial phase of the German invasion Soviet propaganda emphasized traditional Russian patriotism. In an effort to highlight continuities between this campaign and earlier, successful efforts to expel invaders from Russian soil, Soviet propagandists initially labeled the conflict as the Great Patriotic War. Stalin was even prepared to compromise with the Orthodox church in order to unite all Soviet citizens against the invader. It was only after the tide had turned that the Soviet propaganda machine shifted some of its emphasis from the need to fight to defend traditional Russian values to emphasize the goal of supporting Soviet patriotism. But throughout the war the Soviet regime continued to harp on one common theme: the need to kill the invader.

Official propaganda in the western democracies also emphasized that they were fighting a war of good against evil. The western democracies insisted that they stood for what one historian has called "progressive, post-Enlightenment values," whereas their enemies were mired in barbarism.[12] However, overt political indoctrination in the British and US armies, compared to the *Wehrmacht* or the Red Army, was half-hearted. In both the British and American armies there was probably a widespread belief in the righteousness of their cause, but many soldiers would have been hard-put to express it. In 1940, when the British military authorities discovered that many recruits did not understand why Britain was at war and had little interest in the issues at stake, the war office established the Army Bureau of Current Affairs (ABCA) in an effort to enthuse and teach them.[13] It met with only limited success. After attending an ABCA session one paratrooper still opined that the average British soldier was concerned with only three things, "football, beer and crumpet."[14] One authority has asserted that patriotic appeals to American GIs on the eve of battle usually left them feeling disgusted and embarrassed. Growing up during the Depression had left them deeply suspicious of the Wilsonian idealism espoused by their father's generation at the end of World War I. They believed that they were fighting for a just cause, but they were deeply suspicious of anyone who talked about the war in terms of grand platitudes. Nearly all British and American soldiers hated Hitler and Nazism, but they also had a grudging respect for the ordinary *Wehrmacht* soldier – although not for members of the SS. Few British or US soldiers expressed any particular desire to kill Germans. The available evidence points squarely towards the fact that the war aims of most British and American soldiers focused not on exterminating their enemies, but on surviving, ending the war as quickly as possible, and returning to their family, a decent home, and a steady job after the war.[15]

Discipline, Psychiatry, and Punishments

Soldiers who performed up to or beyond the expectation of their superiors in combat were rewarded with medals and promotions. But soldiers who ran away presented armies with a stark problem which they tackled in widely different ways. During World War I the British army had maintained what was by contemporary standards a ferocious disciplinary system. It imposed over 3,000 death sentences, of which 346 were actually carried out, 266 of them for desertion. The suspicion that many men who were executed had been suffering from "shell shock" caused so much public and political disquiet that in 1930 parliament abolished the death penalty for desertion in the face of the enemy. During World War II the British army executed 40 soldiers, but none for desertion.

British soldiers who broke down when confronted by the horrors of the battlefield could expect to be disposed of in one of two ways. If they were known to their superior officers, and if the latter believed that they had made a genuine effort to overcome their fears, it was likely that they would be dealt with as a medical casualty and labeled as suffering from "battle exhaustion." In mid-1942 psychiatric casualties accounted for 7–10 percent of the total casualties suffered by the 8th Army in north Africa. In periods of intense fighting the proportion of exhaustion cases could rise even higher. Between late June and late July 1944 exhaustion cases accounted for nearly 24 percent of British casualties. They were treated at a forward psychiatric center, and either returned to their unit or posted to a job behind the line. However, if the soldier who broke down was a recent replacement whose record of previous service was unknown to his company or battalion commander, or if he was a known malcontent, he might be classified as a deserter and convicted by a court martial. Approximately 100,000 men deserted from the British army during World War II. On the battlefield infantrymen were far more likely to break down or desert than any other kind of soldier. When he was apprehended the typical deserter was awarded a prison sentence of 3–5 years. To avoid men deliberately committing offenses to exchange the dangers and discomforts of the front line for the relative comforts of a military prison, sentences for desertion were frequently suspended, and the guilty party was quickly returned to the front line where, if he behaved well, his sentence might in time be quashed. Some commanders – Gort in 1940, Auchinleck in 1942, and Alexander in 1944 – wanted the death penalty reinstated, but their political masters never thought the time was propitious.[16]

The US army did retain the death penalty for desertion, but it made little use of it. Of the 21,000 US soldiers court-martialed for desertion, only 162 were sentenced to death, and only one was executed. Like the British, the US army also suffered a high proportion of psychological casualties. In the first instance, nearly a million potential soldiers were rejected by the army on neuropsychiatric grounds and not even permitted to enlist, and about the same number who were enlisted were subsequently treated for psychiatric disorders. Even so nearly a quarter of US casualties in north Africa in 1942–3, and in northwest Europe in 1944–5, were caused by psychiatric breakdowns. Some senior US officers shared General Patton's low regard for such men, but others accepted that every soldier had his own personal breaking point, and that "combat exhaustion" was a medical, not a disciplinary problem. By 1944–5 both the British and US armies had developed similar methods for treating such men. Experience had taught them that if they were evacuated far to the rear, they were unlikely ever to return to front line duty. Exhaustion cases were therefore sent to rest stations only a short way behind the line, where mild cases recovered after being briefly sedated and then interviewed by a doctor who tried to assure them that their breakdown was only temporary and that they would soon be fit to return to front line duty. Between June and December 1944 over half of all combat exhaustion cases in the US 1st Army were returned to duty after only a brief respite, although it is likely that a considerable number of them suffered a relapse. More serious cases were evacuated further behind the line and if possible, eventually found a job on the lines of communication.[17]

The German and Soviet armies responded to this problem very differently. Soldiers in these armies knew that failure to endure the hardships and terrors of the battlefield would probably lead to a firing squad. During World War I the German military penal code was remarkably lax. Only 150 German soldiers were sentenced to death and only 48 were executed. The lesson that the German military authorities drew from the collapse of morale in their army in 1918 was that this had been a disastrous mistake. Only a draconian disciplinary system coupled with intensive political indoctrination could sustain their soldiers' will to fight. Following Hitler's accession to power, the military authorities took the opportunity to devise a new wartime military code that would ensure that the apparent mistakes of World War I would never be repeated. German soldiers knew that they could be executed not only for treason, mutiny, desertion, or striking a superior, but also for doing or saying something that undermined fighting power. German army doctors insisted that soldiers suffering from psychological disorders were the victims of lax discipline and poor morale, not of unbearable conditions at the front. Unlike their British or American counterparts they barely recognized the possibility that soldiers might be psychologically predisposed to breakdown in combat. Effectively forbidden to escape from the firing line by means of a psychological breakdown, German soldiers found other ways to quit. Some developed physical symptoms that might earn them a spell in hospital. Perhaps as many as 23,000 committed suicide. And others deserted, even though they knew that they risked being executed. By the end of the war German military courts had sentenced about 50,000 soldiers to death and executed about 33,000 of them. Between 16,000 and 18,000 of the soldiers who were executed had been found guilty of desertion.[18]

But it was the Soviet army that treated its own men most brutally. In August 1941 Stalin prescribed ruthless punishments for anyone guilty of desertion, surrender, or spreading panic. Behind the line the NKVD established "holding detachments" ready to shoot any Soviet soldier, be he private or general, who ran away. In August 1942 the Soviet Army introduced special punishment battalions. Life expectancy for the nearly 423,000 men who were drafted into them was normally very short, as they were frequently given near-suicidal missions to perform. Deserters could also face summary execution. As many as 13,500 Soviet soldiers are reported to have been executed by their own side during the battle of Stalingrad.[19]

The consequences of these differing disciplinary regimes were striking. Whereas in the German army an average of 7.9 soldiers per thousand deserted or went AWOL annually, by 1944, in the US army, the figure had reached 45.2 in the European theater. Some Soviet units did give way to panic and fled. But many others showed that they were determined to continue fighting even after the situation facing them was obviously hopeless. The unpalatable conclusion may be that draconian discipline worked, at least to the extent that it discouraged men from abandoning the front line.

Killing, Brutality, and Atrocities

The extent to which armies succeeded in persuading front line soldiers to kill their enemies with their own hand-held weapons is debatable. By developing doctrines that emphasized that battles were won by mobility and mechanically generated firepower, both the British and US armies minimized the need for their troops to do so. But no army could do without infantrymen who were willing to kill their enemies. Montgomery admitted privately shortly after El Alamein: "The trouble with our British lads is that they are not killers by nature." The attitudes and reactions of individual soldiers confronted by the apparent need to kill an enemy soldier defy easy generalization. During the war the US army deployed analysts in the front line to observe the behavior of men under fire. Their conclusions purported to show that only 15–25 percent of infantry soldiers ever fired their personal weapons at the enemy. More recently it has become clear that the apparent precision of their findings was based on what was at best only highly impressionistic evidence.[20] One major study of the attitude of British and American troops has recently tried to demonstrate that many actually enjoyed the act of killing. However, the author's use of sources has been criticized so roundly that the book's conclusions remain questionable. Soldiers penning letters at the front might be apt to exaggerate their propensity to kill in order to meet the expectations of their readers. The latter were not just the intended recipient, be they friends or relations at home, but also their military superiors, their platoon or company commander, who had the duty to censor their letters before they were posted. In either case the writer might have felt a compulsion to live up to an expected public image of the soldier as a loyal, patriotic, and willing killer. Furthermore, it is apparent that for every soldier who claimed at the time, or later, that he enjoyed killing, another claimed that he found the experience intensely painful, and that he acted under the pressing need of self-preservation, or revenge for a friend who had just been killed.[21]

British and American soldiers were usually quite content to spare the lives of any German who wanted to surrender, provided he was not so foolish as to have been firing on his would-be captors only moments earlier. Once captured, German prisoners in the hands of the British or Americans might be deprived of their watches and wallets, but they could otherwise expect to be treated broadly in accordance to the dictates of customary international law and the Geneva Convention. By contrast, prisoners taken on the eastern front, be they Germans who fell into Russian hands or Russians who had the misfortune to be captured by the Germans, could expect a much bleaker and more brutal future. All wars involve brutality, but the behavior of German forces on the eastern front after 1941 went beyond the limits of "normal brutality." The German political and military leadership were fighting a war to exterminate Bolshevism. Recent research has demonstrated that the defense offered by many German soldiers after 1945 that it was the SS, not the ordinary *Wehrmacht* soldiers, who were responsible for the atrocities committed by the Germans against Soviet prisoners and civilians is no longer tenable.[22] Of 5.7 million Soviet soldiers who fell into German hands, between 2.2 million and 3.3 million died before the end of the war. The precise number of German POWs captured by Soviet forces remains debatable and figures between 2.4 million and 3.2 million have been suggested. Early Soviet figures suggested that 352,000 of them died, but this is probably much too low and a figure closer to 1.2 million is more accurate.[23]

The barbarization of the war in the east began in Poland in 1939. Most members of the *Wehrmacht* regarded the indigenous Polish population with a mixture of distrust and racial arrogance. They were content to turn a blind eye to the murderous atrocities of the SS and *Einsatzgruppen*. Even officers and men who were not members of the Nazi Party accepted many of the key elements of its ideology, its antisemitism, anti-Slavism, and militant anti-Bolshevism. This helped to ensure the widespread acceptance of orders issued by Hitler on the eve of Operation Barbarossa that Soviet POWs would not be treated according to the Geneva Convention or customary international law, that Jews, Soviet commissars, and partisans were to be murdered, and that German soldiers would be exonerated from crimes they might commit against the Soviet people. After June 1941 senior army commanders endorsed these orders, insisting that as Jews might be both Bolsheviks and partisans, their mass murder was permissible as an essential measure to protect the lives of German soldiers. Other Soviet civilians were treated with equal brutality by the German occupying forces. From the outset the German army had expected to live off the land in Russia and the collapse of German logistical support in the first winter of the war made doing so an urgent necessity. It became common practice for German soldiers to steal whatever they wanted from each Soviet village through which they passed, be it food and livestock or warm winter clothing and fur-lined boots. Not all German soldiers on the eastern front took part in atrocities against civilians, Jews, and members of the Communist Party, but some did, and only a small minority of soldiers openly expressed their disquiet about the activities of the SS and *Einsatzgruppen*.[24] It was hardly surprising that when the Soviet army entered Germany, Soviet troops were bent on revenge and embarked upon an orgy of looting, raping, and murder. The Soviet authorities did not wage a deliberate policy of extermination against occupied enemy peoples, but they only acted to stop their troops from misbehaving when their behavior threatened military discipline.

Conclusion

There was no single reason why soldiers endured the awful experiences of war on the front line. For some, comradeship was the main reason. For others, it was ideological commitment to the cause for which they were fighting. For others, it was fear of the consequences if they deserted. For most men it was probably a combination of all three factors. But for all of them the war left poignant and often painful memories that they carried with them into the postwar world. Reflecting on his experiences in October 2002, one British 8th Army veteran concluded: "I'm 86 and have spent my whole life looking on the bright side. . . . For a lot of us the war was the biggest adventure of our entire lives. We're still talking about it, for heaven's sake. I can still remember the oranges we'd eat in Palestine . . . but what never leaves you are the memories of all the smashing blokes we lost."[25]

NOTES

1 See Alan R. Millet, "The US Armed Forces in the Second World War," in *Military Effectiveness*, vol. 3: *The Second World War*, A. R. Millet and Williamson Murray, eds (London: Allen and Unwin, 1988), p. 60; Jürgen E. Förster, "The Dynamics of Volksgemeinschaft: The Effectiveness of the German Military Establishment in the Second World War," in Millet and Murray, *Second World War*, p. 190.
2 See John Erickson, "Soviet War Losses: Calculations and Controversies," in *Barbarossa: The Axis and the Allies*, J. Erickson and David Dilks, eds (Edinburgh: Edinburgh University

Press, 1994), pp. 259–61; J. Erickson, "Red Army Battlefield Performance, 1941–45: The System and the Soldier," in *Time to Kill: The Soldiers' Experience of War in the West, 1939–1945*, Paul Addison and Angus Calder, eds (London: Pimlico, 1997), pp. 236, 241; John Ellis, *The Sharp End of War: The Fighting Man in World War Two* (London: David and Charles, 1982), p. 177; Reid Mitchell, "The GI in Europe and the American Military Tradition," in Addison and Calder, *Time to Kill*, pp. 306–7; Russell F. Weigley, *Eisenhower's Lieutenants: The Campaign of France and Germany, 1944–1945* (Bloomington: Indiana University Press, 1999), p. 370.

3   Imperial War Museum Sound Archive. Accession No. 12239. Gerry Barnett, Reel 6.

4   See Martin Van Creveld, *Fighting Power: German and US Army Performance, 1939–1945* (London: Arms and Armour Press, 1983), pp. 65–7; Albert Seaton, *The German Army, 1933–1945* (London: Weidenfeld and Nicolson, 1983), pp. 95–7; J. E. Förster, "Evolution and Development of German Doctrine 1914–45," in *The Origins of Contemporary Doctrine*, J. Gooch, ed. (London: Strategic and Combat Studies Institute, 1997), pp. 18–31; Earl F. Ziemke, "The Soviet Armed Forces in the Interwar Period," in *Military Effectiveness*, vol. 2: *The Interwar Period*, A. Millet and W. Murray, eds (London: Allen and Unwin, 1988), pp. 1–38.

5   See David French, "Doctrine and Organization in the British Army, 1919–1932," *Historical Journal* 43 (2001): 497–515; Michael D. Doubler, *Closing With the Enemy: How GI's Fought the War in Europe, 1944–45* (Lawrence: University Press of Kansas, 1994).

6   See Jeremy A. Crang, *The British Army and the People's War 1939–1945* (Manchester: Manchester University Press, 2000), pp. 5–20; John C. McManus, *The Deadly Brotherhood: The American Combat Soldier in World War II* (Novato CA: Presidio, 1998), pp. 8–11.

7   See David French, *Raising Churchill's Army: The British Army and the War against Germany, 1919–1945* (Oxford: Oxford University Press, 2000), pp. 65–6; Millet, "The US Armed Forces in the Second World War," pp. 60–1, 82; Trevor A. Wilson, "Who Fought and Why? The Assignment of American Soldiers to Combat," in Addison and Calder, *Time to Kill*, pp. 284–303.

8   See Erickson, "Red Army Battlefield Performance," p. 239.

9   See Doubler, *Closing with the Enemy*, p. 235.

10 See, for example, Edward Shils and Morris Janowitz, "Cohesion and Disintegration in the Wehrmacht," *Public Opinion Quarterly* 12 (1948): 280–315.

11 See Omer Bartov, *Hitler's Army: Soldiers, Nazis and War in the Third Reich* (Oxford: Oxford University Press, 1991); Omer Bartov, "Daily life and Motivation in War: The Wehrmacht in the Soviet Union," *Journal of Strategic Studies* 12 (1989): 200–14; Stephen G. Fritz, *Frontsoldaten: The German Soldier in World War Two* (Lexington: University Press of Kentucky, 1995); Stephen G. Fritz, "'We are trying to change the face of the world' – Ideology and Motivation in the Wehrmacht on the Eastern Front: The View from Below," *Journal of Military History* 60 (1996): 683–710; Gerd R. Ueberschär, "The Ideologically Motivated War of Annihilation in the East," in *Hitler's War in the East: A Critical Assessment*, Rolf-Dieter Müller and G. R. Ueberschär (Oxford: Oxford University Press, 2002), pp. 209–82 (provides a useful critical survey of the literature).

12 Richard Overy, *Why the Allies Won* (London: Jonathan Cape, 1995), p. 285.

13 See S. P. Mackenzie, *Politics and Military Morale: Current Affairs and Citizenship Education in the British Army 1914–1950* (Oxford: Oxford University Press, 1992).

14 David French, "'You can't hate the bastard who is trying to kill you . . .' Combat and Ideology in the British Army in the War Against Germany, 1939–1945," *Twentieth Century British History* 11 (2000): 6.

15 See Jeremy Crang, "The British Soldier on the Home Front: Army Morale Reports, 1940–45," in Addison and Calder, *Time to Kill*, pp. 60–74; R. Mitchell, "The GI in

Europe and the American Military Tradition," in Addison and Calder, *Time to Kill*, pp. 312–13; McManus, *Deadly Brotherhood*, pp. 182–3, 228–38.

16 See Robert H. Ahrenfeldt, *Psychiatry in the British Army in the Second World War* (London: Routledge and Kegan Paul, 1957); David French, "Discipline and the Death Penalty in the British Army in the War against Germany during the Second World War," *Journal of Contemporary History* 33 (1998): 531–46; David French, "'Tommy is no soldier': The Morale of the Second British Army in Normandy, June–August 1944," *Journal of Strategic Studies* 19 (1996): 154–78; Terry Copp and Bill McAndrew, *Battle Exhaustion: Soldiers and Psychiatrists in the Canadian Army, 1939–1945* (Montreal: McGill-Queen's University Press, 1990); Ben Shepherd, *A War of Nerves: Soldiers and Psychiatrists, 1914–1994* (London: Jonathan Cape, 2000), pp. 205–27.

17 See Van Creveld, *Fighting Power*, pp. 95–6; Overy, *Why the Allies Won*, pp. 293–4; Steven R. Welch, "'Harsh but just'? German Military Justice in the Second World War: A Comparative Study of the Court-Martialling of German and US Deserters," *German History* 17 (1999): 369–99.

18 See Bartov, *Hitler's Army*, pp. 22–4; Welch, "'Harsh but just'?" pp. 369–99; Omer Bartov, *The Eastern Front, 1941–1945: German Troops and the Barbarization of Warfare* (London: Macmillan, 2001), pp. 27–35; Shepherd, *A War of Nerves*, pp. 299–312; Jürgen E. Förster, "Luddendorff and Hitler in Perspective: The Battle for the German Soldier's Mind, 1917–1944," *War in History* 10 (2003): 321–34.

19 See Antony Beevor, *Stalingrad* (London: Viking, 1998), pp. 166–72.

20 See S. L. A. Marshal, *Men Against Fire: The Problem of Battle Command in Future War* (New York: William Morrow, 1947); Roger J. Spiller, "S. L. A. Marshall and the Ratio of Fire," *Journal of the Royal United Services Institute* 133 (1988): 63–71.

21 See Joanna Bourke, *An Intimate History of Killing: Face to Face Killing in Twentieth-Century Warfare* (London: Granta, 1999); French, "You can't hate the bastard who is trying to kill you," pp. 10–12.

22 This may be something that some older Germans still have some difficulty in accepting. See Hannes Heer, "The Difficulty of Ending a War: Reactions to the Exhibition 'War of Extermination: Crimes of the Wehrmacht 1941 to 1944'," *History Workshop* 46 (1998): 187–203.

23 See Overy, *Why the Allies Won*, pp. 281–3, 287–8, 291–2; Richard Overy, *Russia's War* (London: Allen Lane, 1997), pp. 260–2, 297–8; Beevor, *Stalingrad*, pp. 26–8, 125; Bartov, *Eastern Front*, p. 153.

24 See J. E. Förster, "Motivation and Indoctrination in the Wehrmacht, 1933–1945," in Addison and Calder, *Time to Kill*, pp. 263–73; T. J. Shute, "The German Soldier in Occupied Russia," in Addison and Calder, *Time to Kill*, pp. 275–83; A. Steim, "International Law and Soviet Prisoners of War," in *From Peace to War: Germany, Soviet Russia and the World, 1939–1941*, Bernd Wegner, ed. (Providence RI: Berg, 1997), pp. 293–308; Klaus-Jürgen Müller, "The Brutalisation of Warfare, Nazi Crimes and the Wehrmacht," in Erickson and Dilks, *Barbarossa*, pp. 229–37; H. Heer and Klaus Naumann, eds, *War of Extermination: The German Military in World War Two 1941–1944* (Oxford: Oxford University Press, 2000).

25 Helena Smith, "Last Post for Alamein and the Desert Rats," *Observer*, October 20, 2002.

GUIDE TO FURTHER READING

Paul Addison and Angus Calder, eds, *Time to Kill: The Soldiers' Experience of War in the West, 1939–1945* (London: Pimlico, 1997). An important collection of essays that examine the experience of ordinary soldiers in the Axis and Allied armies.

Omer Bartov, *Hitler's Army: Soldiers, Nazis and War in the Third Reich* (Oxford: Oxford University Press, 1991); *The Eastern Front, 1941–1945: German Troops and the Barbarization of Warfare* (London: Macmillan, 2001). Bartov's books are the essential starting point for understanding the conduct of German soldiers in Russia between 1941 and 1945.

Joanna Bourke, *An Intimate History of Killing: Face to Face Killing in Twentieth-Century Warfare* (London: Granta, 1999). Tackles a difficult and important subject, but the author's use of sources means that the book's conclusions should be treated with some reservations.

Jeremy A. Crang, *The British Army and the People's War 1939–1945* (Manchester: Manchester University Press, 2000). A good social history of the British army.

Michael D. Doubler, *Closing With the Enemy: How GI's Fought the War in Europe, 1944–45* (Lawrence: University Press of Kansas, 1994). Goes far towards rehabilitating the reputation of the US army in northwest Europe.

John Ellis, *The Sharp End of War: The Fighting Man in World War Two* (London: David and Charles, 1982). An early and still important study of the experience of frontline soldiers in the British and US armies.

David French, *Raising Churchill's Army: The British Army and the War against Germany, 1919–1945* (Oxford: Oxford University Press, 2000). Attempts to analyze the combat capability of the British army.

Steven G. Fritz, *Frontsoldaten: The German Soldier in World War Two* (Lexington: University Press of Kentucky, 1995). Examines the experience of German soldiers on the eastern front.

John C. McManus, *The Deadly Brotherhood: The American Combat Soldier in World War II* (Novato CA: Presidio, 1998). Makes use of oral history material to explore the behavior of GIs in battle.

S. L. A. Marshal, *Men Against Fire: The Problem of Battle Command in Future War* (New York: William Morrow, 1947). Although Marshall's methodology has been criticized, his book is still a landmark in the analysis of how soldiers behave on the battlefield.

Alan R. Millet and Williamson Murray, eds, *Military Effectiveness*, vol. 3: *The Second World War* (London: Allen and Unwin, 1988). A selection of essays that analyze the combat capabilities of the armed services of all of the major belligerents.

Ben Shepherd, *A War of Nerves: Soldiers and Psychiatrists, 1914–1994* (London: Jonathan Cape, 2000). An excellent account of how the British and US armies employed psychiatrists.

Edward Shils and Morris Janowitz, "Cohesion and Disintegration in the Wehrmacht," *Public Opinion Quarterly* 12 (1948): 280–315. A seminal article that suggested ideology was not important in motivating German soldiers on the battlefield. Much criticized by Bartov and Fritz.

Martin Van Creveld, *Fighting Power: German and US Army Performance, 1939–1945* (London: Arms and Armour Press, 1983). A comparative analysis of the combat capability of the US and German armies.

CHAPTER TWENTY-NINE

The Home Fronts: Europe at War, 1939–1945

NICHOLAS ATKIN

World War II, it is commonly said, was a war like no other. In the number of countries involved, in the diversity of fighting fronts, in the mobilization of populations and economies, in the extent of material devastation, in the numbers of lives lost, in the intensity of the struggle, and in the atrocities of slave labor and genocide, this conflict dwarfed all others. While historians dispute whether it constituted a "total war," there is consensus that the home fronts were so closely interconnected with the fighting fronts that the two became inseparable, a marked distinction with the past.[1] As Eric Hobsbawm notes, during the Revolutionary and Napoleonic era (1792–1815), states could still keep war and domestic affairs in "watertight compartments, as the ladies and gentlemen in Jane Austen's novels were just then doing in Britain."[2] During World War I such compartmentalization was no longer possible, but it would be a mistake to believe that war intruded into every walk of life. In his memoirs, *Goodbye to All That*, Robert Graves recalls how 20 miles beyond the trenches lay the tranquility of the French countryside, apparently oblivious to the horrors being perpetrated nearby. In 1939–45 such escape was not possible. In August 1940 Churchill declared: "The whole of the warring nations are engaged, not only soldiers, but the entire population, men, women and children. The fronts are everywhere."[3]

The nature of World War II has ensured that historians focus as much on propaganda, rationing, and the movement of populations as they do on weaponry, military campaigns, and logistics. There have, however, been remarkably few European-wide surveys of the home fronts, and most of them dwell on the sensationalist aspects of resistance and collaboration.[4] Although this situation is changing, the reasons for neglect are understandable.[5] Cross-national comparisons are difficult at the best of times, and especially so for Nazi Europe. As John Campbell observes, "For no two countries was the experience of German occupation identical, and in each country German rule was in a state of flux throughout."[6] Because of the importance of events, the literature on individual countries is also so vast that it would take several lifetimes to read, not to mention a command of several languages. Nevertheless, in the case of Hitler's Europe at least, historians possess a series of shared concerns: occupation, collaboration, and resistance. Several studies thus pursue a familiar path, focusing on what Germans call *Alltagsgeschichte* ("everyday life"). This usually involves analysis of defeat, the arrival of the occupier, the erection of a New Order, the material circumstances of wartime, and the impact shortages had on communities.[7] From a study of occupation, it is but a short step to look at collaboration and resistance. Here, historians have stressed the issue of choice: whether to collude with the occupier or to resist, or whether to wait on events (a phenomenon known as *attentisme*). Such choices were rarely straightforward, either for individuals or institutions or governments. It is in recognition of this ambiguity that historians have often preferred to investigate not a single country but a particular region, a trend noticeable in the cases of Italy and France, where there exists a tradition of local history.[8] Today, every Italian city of any size has its *Istituto nazionale per la storia del movimento di liberazione in Italia.*

European Geopolitics, 1939–1945

Any appreciation of the home fronts must begin with an awareness of the geopolitics of Hitler's Europe, which echoed Napoleon I's First Empire in its jumble of satellite states.[9] At the core, writes Henri Michel, was the greater Reich. This comprised Germany, as configured by the 1919 settlement, to which was added Austria, the Sudetenland, Alsace-Lorraine, Luxemburg, Eupen and Malmédy, Poznam, Upper Silesia, the Polish corridor, and Danzig. Here, continues Michel, German administration prevailed, and a process of Germanification introduced, to the cost of those peoples, notably Poles and Lorrainers, damned as racially inferior. Because of their strategic importance, military governors were imposed on Belgium, so-called "occupied France" (essentially the northern and western territories, significantly the wealthiest parts of the country), and those parts of the Soviet Union quickly surrendered by Moscow. In the course of 1940–1 puppet states were established in Serbia under Milan Nedić, in Croatia under Ante Pavelić, in Greece (under George Tsolakoglou, Constantine Lotothetopoulos, and Ioannis Rallis in turn), and in Slovakia under Josef Tiso. Because of their "Aryan" descent, explains Michael Burleigh, some autonomy was permitted in the following, although they were ultimately destined for absorption into the greater Germany: Holland (governed by the Dutch civil service, overseen by a civilian Reich commissioner); Norway (again governed by a civilian commissioner, periodically assisted by Vidkun Quisling); and Denmark (where national institutions, such as parliament, were uniquely allowed to survive, albeit under the watchful eye of the occupying forces).[10] Not wishing to inflame the country's revolutionary heritage and seeking a breathing space to prepare his invasion of Britain, Hitler left a third of France unoccupied under the Vichy regime of Marshal Pétain, although in the longer term he envisaged the disappearance of France altogether. Severest were the arrangements reached in Slav areas: a Protectorate was established over Bohemia-Moravia, while a "Government General" was imposed on what was left of Poland, where Hitler intended to offload what he called the "rubbish" – "Jews, the sick, slackers, etc." Among its allies, continues Michel, Germany counted Finland, Romania, Hungary, and Bulgaria (all minor but carefully watched by Berlin) and Fascist Italy, although Italian military shortcomings meant that Rome was soon Berlin's lackey. Switzerland, Sweden, Eire, Turkey, Spain, and Portugal proclaimed neutrality, yet the Iberian powers were ideologically aligned with Germany; the others volunteered material support.

The reshuffling of territories entailed the displacement of peoples on an unprecedented scale. This process had begun with the Nazi takeover of power which prompted 200,000 German Jews to flee abroad during the 1930s.[11] As Guderian's Panzers spearheaded the invasion of western Europe, in May–June 1940 anywhere in the region of 6–8 million civilians in France, Belgium, the Netherlands, and Luxemburg took to the roads, their harrowing experiences caught in such memoirs as Maurice Sachs' *La Chasse à courre*. Even though Britain had been preparing to welcome some 250,000 overseas refugees (in the event, only a tenth of that number arrived) should Germany have invaded, it is likely that the chaos in France would have been repeated across the Channel. Ian Beckett records that there were 60 million changes of address in Britain during the war years, this out of an overall population of 48 million.[12]

The scale of these displacements was as nothing compared to those in eastern Europe.[13] In 1939, 500,000 Finns headed westwards to avoid the Soviet advance, as did nearly 2 million Lithuanians, Estonians, Latvians, and Swedes. Thanks to the arrangements of the Nazi–Soviet pact (August 1939), approximately 750,000 Germans (located in Bessarabia, northern Bukovina, southern Bukovina, Dobrudga, and the Baltic) were expected to resettle in Greater Germany, although most ended up in transit camps. With the invasion of the Soviet Union (June 1941), possibly 16.5 million Poles, Russians, and Jews headed east to avoid the Nazis, while 1.75 million Lithuanians, Estonians, and Latvians fled the Red Army. Displacement did not end here: 8.5 million foreign workers were conscripted into Nazi factories; countless thousands were rounded up into ghettos (such as the 400,000 Jews in Warsaw); and approximately 6 million died in the Holocaust. While the Soviets did not systematically pursue genocide, a cruel fate awaited those 500,000 Germans, Bulgars, Poles, and Romanians who, following the successes of the Red Army in 1944–5, were deported to the USSR, often to Gulags where malnutrition, disease, and overwork claimed the lives of at least a million people for each of the war years. Anticipating what might await them, in 1945 7 million Germans retreated westwards. Overall, possibly 30 million Europeans were uprooted during World War II.[14]

With the reshuffling of peoples, Hitler's economic designs became apparent. His goal, writes Alan Milward, was to create an industrial dynamo within the Greater Germany which would draw on a steady supply of labor, goods, and raw materials from the conquered territories. As Jean Freymond adds, this was no more a blueprint for pan-European union than was Napoleon I's Continental System – German interests were overriding.[15] This vision explains why in the period since 1936 Hitler had been gearing the economy for war, notably through the Four Year Plan. Here is not the place to debate whether the war he really wanted was scheduled for the mid-1940s. It is agreed that he was keen to avoid the mistakes of 1914–18 when, he alleged, the army had been let down by a non-productive and demoralized home front. Some historians have since suggested that the strategy of blitzkrieg, the short lightning war used so effectively in Poland in 1939 and western Europe in 1940, was a deliberate ploy to cushion the home front from the insatiable demands of the military. Richard Overy has disputed this. Military expenditure, steadily rising since 1936, reached a high point in 1939–41 which, as one report acknowledged, required "a throttling of civilian consumption."[16] Additionally, the German economy was not sufficiently organized to permit any sudden shift from consumer and military spending, as implied by the theory of blitzkrieg. Typical of the topsy-turvy world of Nazi administration, there was not one but several bodies presiding over economic matters, including Göring's brief-lived Council of Ministers for Reich Defense. Some semblance of centralized control was achieved in February 1940 with the appointment of Fritz Todt as minister for weapons and munitions, yet the so-called "Organization Todt" still lacked the desired flexibility. After Todt's death in February 1942, Albert Speer was delegated extensive powers to "streamline" the "entire economy," which he did to great effect, yet, as Overy has again shown, he was undermined by military setbacks, rivalries between civilians, industrialists, and generals, and the inability to exploit occupied territories to the full. As the demands of total war rose, such exploitation lost rhyme and reason. In 1940 it was intended to develop Norway's hydroelectric power; by 1943, Germany was taking whatever Norway could supply, primarily lumber and manpower. The same process overcame France, the most economically precious of the occupied states. Short-term plunder gave the Germans what they needed, yet naturally discouraged the French from producing more.[17]

Because of the earlier drive towards collectivization, in 1941 the USSR already possessed the "command economy" which Nazi Germany lacked. Notwithstanding the debates over the effectiveness of planning and its interruption by the Terror, this had enabled the Soviets to make extensive military preparations. The Nazi–Soviet pact provided further respite, facilitating the stockpiling of goods in the east. When Germany eventually invaded, Stalin was quick to establish (June 1941) the Soviet State Defence Committee, empowered to direct all war production, which was soon coordinating the evacuation of both peoples and industrial plants. The German seizure of the Ukraine was an early setback, as it contained much of Soviet grain and livestock reserves, together with 66 percent of coal, iron, and aluminum production. Nonetheless, coercion and centralization enabled the Soviets to transform the remaining territories into an integrated economy. As Overy has shown in his book *The Dictators*, working conditions were "tough in the extreme," involving an extension of the working day, the wide-scale conscription of women and children, the setting up of makeshift factories, the imposition of draconian penalties for alleged slackers, and the abolition of holiday entitlements.[18] Such hardships enabled the production of weaponry on a formidable scale, far beyond what had been achieved under the five-year plans. Yet, as Overy concludes, the Soviets did not merely rely on intimidation. Apart from Allied assistance, consisting primarily of food, raw materials, and plant machinery as opposed to weapons, the people understood that their labor was the only way to scratch out an existence, an instinct hardened by the belief that civilians were just as important as soldiers in resisting the German menace. So evolved the legend of the Great Patriotic War and reawakening a Stalin personality cult, brilliantly depicted in Konstantin Simonov's novel *The Living and the Dead*.

Significantly, the home front which proved most efficient in responding to total war was that of the UK. Before April 1940, despite some key successes, the economy still seemed geared to peacetime, with unemployment running at unacceptable levels. It required the inspired leadership of Churchill and the recognition, painfully obvious after the fall of France, that the government was on its own in persuading the British people that tough measures were required if invasion and occupation were to be resisted. Thus, unlike the Soviet Union and Nazi Germany, Britain did not resort to coercion, but drew on public assent.[19] In a liberal democracy, the *Daily Telegraph* had declared presciently in April 1939, the "corporal's rule, brutality and slavery" were not required "to induce the country to make an effort." It further helped that, in the cabinet subcommittee created in spring 1940 by the lord president, Britain already had a central body with powers to synchronize production. This took on greater responsibilities the following year when it was fronted by the formidable Sir John Anderson. As mounting US aid arrived in Lend-Lease, planning was the trend, anticipating the nationalizations of 1945 and giving rise to the Beveridge Report of 1942, which founded the welfare state. The result was that the UK mobilized its citizens and resources more extensively than any other belligerent nation. By D-Day, records Angus Calder, 22 percent of the population was enrolled in one of the armed services, while 33 percent was engaged in civilian war work, a much higher figure if pensioners and part-timers in civil defense are included. Unemployment vanished, and women figured prominently in the workplace, although the USSR went further in their enlistment. Notions that the Nazis resisted female employment, on the grounds of misplaced gender assumptions, no longer hold good. By 1945 the "second sex" comprised half of Germany's workforce and two-thirds of its agricultural labor.[20]

Calder emphasizes that it would be erroneous to believe that the British war economy was the well-oiled machine it is occasionally portrayed. With the elimination of unemployment, trade union membership was enhanced, provoking several stoppages (technically illegal), although they tended to be short lived; the demands of wartime also artificially boosted heavy industries in need of streamlining before 1939; and outdated management and production processes persisted. Right-wing historians, most obviously Corelli Barnett, have subsequently suggested that war contributed to Britain's decline, saddling post-1945 governments with obsolescent management and labor practices, antiquated machinery, and an unsustainable welfare bill. For their part, left-wing historians have questioned whether war did enough to reshape class structures and institutions, perpetuating inequalities and sustaining division.[21] Whatever the truth, it cannot be denied that Britain's war economy was an achievement in itself, out-producing that of Nazi Germany.

The shift towards war production impacted on consumer consumption and heralded austerity measures in all belligerent nations, notably in Britain. As Calder has shown, the paradox was that, through egalitarian rationing and an emphasis on vital foodstuffs, elements of the working class were better nourished in terms of vitamins and calories than in the 1930s when Depression brought with it malnourishment. The same could not be said of the USSR which, in June 1941, initiated rationing on a calorie basis, with those employed in heavy industry being entitled to more. It was an unappetizing diet – mainly bread and potatoes. Those uninvolved in war work had no official ration entitlement, and it is believed significant numbers of the old and sick starved to death. Whereas the German workforce was better supplied, it is again misleading to assume that shortages only hit in 1943–4. Rationing for essential goods was introduced as early as 1939, and most people sustained themselves on a menu little different to that of Russians. At least Germany could call upon the resources of conquered territories, yet at the cost of the occupied peoples. Worst affected were east Europeans. In Warsaw, in 1941–2, individuals were entitled to 669 calories a day – Jews to only a third of that; people, in order to survive, resorted to begging, charity, and the black market. It was not uncommon to see the vulnerable, especially children, collapse with hunger.[22] Within western Europe, too, German plundering meant going without. As Richard Vinen records, in London the writer Simone Weil attempted to empathize with her compatriots by living off official French rations – she died of TB and anorexia.[23] By 1941, most French in the Vichy zone were surviving on less than 1,000 calories a day, although peasants squirreled away supplies with the result that death rates dropped for the war years in some rural areas. Before long, the food situation was desperate everywhere. In his moving account of the so-called "hunger winter" of 1943–4, Henri Van der Zee recalls how the Dutch survived on tulip bulbs and sugar beet.[24]

The greatest impact of shortages was on women. In wartime, women had traditionally kept the home fires burning, yet the scale of the 1939–45 conflict meant disruption to domestic life on an unprecedented scale. In his interviews with French women, Rod Kedward discovered the drudgery of everyday lives: the need to get up at an early hour to queue for scarce foodstuffs, the demands of balancing a small budget, and the chore of making the best of ersatz commodities. Many complained, for instance, of how inferior soap made washing-day unbearable.[25] Interestingly, within concentration camps, it was again women who seemed best suited to devising survival strategies, something highlighted by the Nazi segregation of sexes.[26] The traditional role of women on the home front was further emphasized by the absence of men, many of whom were either conscripted or held as POWs. In any case, for Nazi Germany, and for several states within the New Order, notably Fascist Italy and Vichy France, a woman's place was naturally in the home, resulting in pronatalist propaganda and punitive legislation directed against those who sought careers. The reality was that women had to work, even in Germany; and, as in World War I, they ended up doing "male" tasks. In Britain, first to conscript female labor, women thus moved from domestic service and textiles into desk jobs, munitions, civil defense, voluntary groups (such as the Women's Voluntary Service), and the Land Army. No European country, outside of the USSR, however, deployed women as fighting troops.

Gender historians disagree whether the years 1939–45 proved a liberating experience for women. It is only recently that women's lives, once dismissed as marginal, have been collated; for some countries, for instance Greece, that effort is only now being made; elsewhere, the material is contradictory. Within the world of work, in 1945 trade unions and employers, both in Britain and liberated Europe, were more accepting of female labor, yet equal pay and equal rights remained elusive. Within political life, women were at long last given the vote in France and Italy, in recognition of their contribution to resistance, although there remained formidable cultural and institutional obstacles to overcome. Within domestic life, the postwar years eventually brought with them in western Europe a new culture of labor-saving devices and fashion accessories, but these often reinforced traditional stereotypes. And within sexual relations, there was some relaxation of existing mores. Apart from the Freudian notion that war acts as an aphrodisiac, the bombing of civilians was a constant reminder of mortality – an injunction to enjoy life while one could, something made easier by the blackouts which, as Tom Driberg's memoirs *Ruling Passions* reveal, facilitated both heterosexual and homosexual behavior. Yet the rise in divorce rates, high among American servicemen who had married European brides, a hike in the numbers of illegitimate children, and the spread of venereal disease, common to many home fronts, prompted a moral backlash in which women were singled out for condemnation. Liberation, on any meaningful scale, would not happen until later in the century.

Collaboration

In uncovering the lives of women during wartime, historians have increasingly focused on *la collaboration horizontale*, that is sleeping with the enemy, a phenomenon highlighted at the Liberation when French women suspected of sexual relations with Germans were subjected to mob justice: around 10,000 had their heads shaved and were paraded naked, sometimes with swastikas daubed on their breasts.[27] Initially, however, historians of collaboration were preoccupied with the high politics of *collaboration d'état*, that is the relationships between Berlin and the subjugated countries, although it should not be overlooked that, following its invasion of the Baltic states, the communist puppet regimes colluded with their maker, in the shape of the USSR. As implied by the geopolitics of Hitler's Europe, these relationships varied from the relative freedoms permitted to the Aryan peoples of northern Europe, through the military administration placed on strategic areas such as Belgium, to the puppet regimes in the Balkans, to end with the repressive control exerted upon Poland and Slav territories. Race, strategic importance, and economic value, remarks Burleigh, thus determined the extent to which Berlin involved itself in the internal affairs of its possessions. Ultimately, Hitler had no intention of conceding anything worthwhile, although this did not deter subjected states from seeking collaboration. In the case of Vichy France – unique in Nazi Europe in that it was left unoccupied until November 1942 – the French fell over themselves to cooperate. As Robert Paxton famously suggested, the regime sought to avoid the fate of Poland, yet ended up "Polandizing" itself by facilitating the deportation of Jews, workers, and minorities.[28]

Beyond the high politics of *collaboration*, historians have focused on the *collaborationism* of individuals ideologically committed to Hitler's vision, although to believe that there is a marked division between the collaborators of puppet governments and the collaborationists of pro-fascist parties, as is sometimes implied, is misleading.[29] What is clear is that these Nazi sympathizers largely gravitated from the fascist movements of the 1930s: Léon Degrelle's Rexists in Belgium, Anton Mussert's *National Socialistische Beweging* in Holland, Quisling's *Nasjonal Samling* in Norway, Doriot's *Parti Populaire Français*, and Ferenc Szálasy's Arrow Cross (*Nyilas*) in Hungary. Ideologues, failed *hommes de lettres*, opportunists, criminals, and opportunists – they all sought to feather their own nests. Yet if fascist sympathizers thought that German victory would open the way to power, they were mistaken. At root, Berlin wanted compliant leaders who would not disrupt the war effort; men such as Admiral Horthy in Hungary, General Antonescu in Romania, and Pétain in France. Hitler knew full well, to use Paxton's phrase, that "playing second fiddle" fitted "badly with fascists' extravagant claims to transform their peoples and redirect history."[30] To allow Quisling and others to occupy real positions of authority was thus to invite a challenge to Nazi hegemony; and, on occasion, as with the Iron Guard in Romania, Berlin welcomed the suppression of extremists. Perhaps only in

Croatia, where the *Ustasha* ran amok, murdering its many ethnic enemies, did Germany fail to maintain tight discipline. Otherwise it was the task of Nazi authorities to play a game of "divide and rule" among collaborationists and, to use Laval's phrase, "what a lot of authorities" there were, a deliberate strategy to dissipate yet further the energies of occupied states. In this regard, it helped that the collaborationists themselves were at sixes and sevens. Prewar jealousies and ideological rivalries persisted during occupation. The only contribution Hitler really valued from collaborationists was their ability to recruit volunteers to fight on the eastern front, for instance the French *Légion des Volontaires contre le Bolschevisme*. Earlier, at the time of Operation Barbarossa, he had welcomed the support of those Ukrainians and Cossacks, victims of Soviet collectivization, who heralded the Nazis as liberators.

Notwithstanding the example of the Ukraine and those eastern states such as Hungary and Romania where the far right retained something of its prewar popularity, in western Europe, where the fascists had struggled to make much headway in the 1930s, a lack of popular appeal extended into occupation. In France, the collaborationist groupings never amassed more than 150,000 supporters (chiefly young, urban, middle-class males), whereas in Norway, says Hans F. Dahl, Quisling's party could not meet its own frugal membership targets.[31] This unpopularity is entirely understandable. As Burleigh writes, "German occupation was a rude intrusion into the lives of the peoples affected, exposing all of them to alien rule, and some to deportation, terror and mass murder. Very, very few people wanted the Germans there, regardless of how they conducted themselves."[32] It naturally followed that people had little time for the Nazis' satraps. As Mark Wheeler writes of the Balkans, "For the bulk of Slavs, Slovenes and Montenegrins, and eventually for the Croats and Macedonians" the Axis powers and their puppet regimes had "nothing positive to offer."[33]

It was not necessary to be ideologically committed to the New Order in order to engage in collaboration broadly defined. As Gerhard Hirschfeld reflects, "Whenever an army enters another country there is cooperation and a certain degree of fraternization between the occupied population and the occupier."[34] The nature of that collaboration was commonly defined by the spheres of activity in which people were engaged. For example, civil servants, who kept the wheels of local government turning, often discovered themselves working alongside the occupier. In so doing, several convinced themselves that they were pursuing – to borrow the Belgian phrase – *la politique du moindre mal*, a policy of doing the least harm. It proved increasingly hard to justify this position when the Holocaust required officials to hand over details of Jews and, on occasion, participate in the round-ups. After the war, bureaucrats put on trial for assisting genocide rehearsed a familiar defense: they were merely following orders; they knew little of the fate that awaited deportees; and, in their positions of authority, they disrupted the transportation process. Shameful was the way in which the Nazis established the *Judenräte*, councils of prominent Jewish leaders entrusted with caring for the welfare of fellow Jews destined for the camps. There was much debate, both at the time and after, as to whether such *prominenti*, caught in the maw of what might be called "administrative collaboration," had truly collaborated.[35] Others who had to justify their consciences included "economic" collaborators, especially Belgian, French, and Dutch industrial concerns obliged to contribute to the German war economy. Some cooperated all too willingly (e.g., Renault), whereas others (Rhône-Poulenc and Pechiney) objected that they had domestic markets to fulfill. Those demands were met by another type of "economic collaborator," the black-market racketeer who was frequently supplied by the Germans keen to exploit material shortages for their own ends. It was the Germans, too, who encouraged "cultural" collaborators – artists, writers, and musicians – who had to balance their commitment to writing and performance with the circumstances of occupation. Apart from those who nailed their colors to the Nazi mast, it was an impossible balancing act to maintain; for instance, the pro-Pétain but anti-Nazi singer Maurice Chevalier was appalled when a concert he gave for POWs was appropriated by collaborationists. As Julian Jackson writes, "The moral was that the only way to avoid compromising oneself was to abstain from any public gesture."[36] Although not in the spotlight, all the peoples of occupied Europe had to determine their behavior in respect of the occupier, the danger being that the slightest fraternization might lead to allegations of collaboration. As David Littlejohn suggests, "collaboration" ranged from volunteering for the SS to buying a postcard of Pétain.[37]

Resistance

The history of resistance is likewise riddled with ambiguity, something historians were initially reluctant to acknowledge for fear of denting the work of postwar reconstruction, which did not invite close examination of everyday behavior. Within Germany, both the FDR and the GDR made much of resistance to Hitlerism as the regimes sought to construct their competing political and economic systems. A similar process occurred elsewhere, notably in Italy and France, with the result that the history of resistance was often written in an uncritical manner, as an account of institutions which gallantly defied the occupier.[38] Only with the passing of time have more probing questions surfaced, including one obvious one: what was resistance?

In the simplest sense, as Michel wrote, it was a rejection of military defeat, a rejection of the occupier, but also a refutation of whatever administrative apparatus the Germans had erected. In those parts of the Greater Reich comprising large quantities of ethnic Germans – Austria, Sudetenland, Memelland, and Eupen-Malmédy – Bernard Kroener and others have shown that civilians did not view themselves as under subjugation, with the result that resistance was slow to evolve.[39] In those Aryan territories of northern Europe, rejection of Quisling and others was not difficult, but the relative freedoms permitted by the occupier diluted early attempts at protest. Interesting was the case of Vichy. In northern occupied France there was an immediate distaste for the Germans, although the military presence of the *Wehrmacht* impeded resistance. Within the southern unoccupied zone people had no difficulty in defying defeat and the armistice, but found it difficult to renounce Pétain. After the shock of military collapse and the *exode*, the marshal emerged as a symbol of security, an image enhanced by his reputation as one of the most humane generals of World War I. The fact that earlier in his career he had kept his reactionary political views to himself also meant people could read into him whatever they chose. As Kedward first stated, becoming a resister in France thus meant overcoming a loyalty to Pétain, who was often mistakenly credited with secretly working for liberation. Less ambiguity surrounded resistance in those countries immediately subject to the jackboot and, in the case of Poland, both Nazi and Soviet exploitation. Even before the Polish campaign had ended, partisan groups were forming, among them the Service for the Victory of Poland, which in early 1940 became part of the underground army, the Union for Armed Struggle, which liaised closely with Sikorski's government-in-exile in London.

In asking "what was resistance?" historians have uncovered three factors which determined its evolution: time, place, and tradition. As can be deduced from above, resistance was conditioned by where one lived and the speed with which the Nazis let slip the mask of civilization. Given these variables, it is small wonder that protest quickly developed in Poland, although it was hampered by Nazi brutality. In Denmark, resistance dawdled. The maintenance of national institutions and the relatively light touch of the occupier enabled people to wait on events. Increasingly, however, Germany reneged on earlier guarantees, conscripting workers and requisitioning foodstuffs. There was further disgust at Nazi plundering of the economy, an awareness, fueled by the BBC overseas broadcasts and agents belonging to the Special Operations Executive (SOE), that Germany was losing the war, and a repugnance at the rounding up of Jews. Resistance escalated in 1943, effectively forcing the Nazis to take full control.

To the variables of time and place may be added tradition. Resistance was concentrated in countries possessing a heritage of protest, such as Poland, which had been regularly partitioned by the great powers. "Poles had been in the Resistance since 1772," writes Michael Foot.[40] In Yugoslavia, too, memories of foreign intervention enhanced dissidence. In 1940–1 two groups appeared: the Četniks, the rump of the army and police force, under Milhailović, which sought a Serbian-dominated Yugoslavia under a restored monarchy, and who were not ashamed to do business with the Germans; and the Partisans (essentially the communists) under Josip Tito, who wanted revolution. As Wheeler observes, the result was that Yugoslavia became the location of Europe's "greatest resistance struggle," as Četniks and Partisans fought Germans, the puppet regimes set up in 1941, and one another.[41] Other areas of Europe, lacking legacies of defiance, proved less fertile ground, an obvious example being Germany itself, where a strong tradition of conformity prevailed, aided by the ruthlessness of the Nazi system which since 1933 had punished the slightest dissent. Finally, any discussion of traditions of protest must not neglect localities. In his pioneering study of France, Rod Kedward uncovered how, in the Protestant Cévennes, partisans drew inspiration from the dissidence of seventeenth-century Huguenot protests.[42] And, in Holland, one of the first resistance papers was significantly entitled *Action of the Gueux*, recalling the resistance of sixteenth-century Calvinist sea-beggars to the Spanish occupation of the Netherlands.

It is Kedward, too, who illustrated the diverse forms of resistance behavior. The most dramatic was, of course, military action. As noted, this was noticeable in countries with traditions of violent protest – Poland (scene of the 1944 Warsaw uprising), Yugoslavia, and Greece – and was less common in western Europe, at least in the early stages of the war, partly because German reprisals after the shooting of military personnel were ferocious. The involvement of communist parties in resistance further augmented the military dimensions, as did growing SOE operations. Beyond military resistance, there was industrial action. In the Nord-Pas-de-Calais, miners in 1941 undertook a gallant protest; in Denmark, an early sign of growing unease was an intensification of stoppages in 1942–3; in Turin and Milan, in March 1943, widespread strikes heralded the imminent collapse of the fascist state; and in Belgium, industrial life was peppered with go-slows. Belgium was home to another important type of resistance, the *réseaux*, which transferred intelligence information to London and aided the escape of Allied airmen shot down over Europe. Several hundreds of these lines existed, and secrecy was paramount as they could be easily disrupted by infiltrators. Networks were a further means of distributing clandestine tracts and newspapers. Such information was critical given Nazi censorship of the media. There were up to 300 different Norwegian resistance papers, many of which only lasted a few issues; a similar number existed in Belgium; in Poland, there may have been 1,400. Each major French organization had its own journal, some of which gravitated into dailies after the Liberation, for instance *Combat*, whose circulation rose from 40,000 in 1941 to 400,000 in 1944. To be caught reading such a newspaper during wartime could entail a stiff penalty, pointing to a category of resistance once thought inconsequential, that of "passive" resistance. This included such things as listening to the BBC, chalking V signs on the wall, giving wrong directions to German soldiers (a specialty in Amsterdam), and defacing notices, for instance scratching out letters in the sign *Raucher* (Smoking) in railway carriages to read *Rache* (revenge). Such actions were "pinpricks," writes Ralph White, yet they agitated the Germans.[43] For some historians, the "dignity" with which Jews and others faced deportation was an additional form of "passive" or "spiritual" resistance – a refusal to relinquish beliefs and traditions when confronted with the inhumanity of Nazism. The term "spiritual resistance" has also been applied to those Christians who struggled with their consciences when reconciling their hostility to Nazism with their duty to "render unto Caesar" and thus obey the state. In the event, Christians were evident in all types of resistance, although it could not be said that Catholics received clear guidance from their spiritual leader, Pius XII.[44]

Another question has preoccupied historians: who were the resisters? Apart from such figures as Tito and General de Gaulle, they were mainly ordinary civilians caught up in traumatic events, forced to undertake roles they would previously never have considered. Because of this, and because of the need to retain anonymity, it is virtually impossible to establish the numbers of resisters in any one country: 400,000 is the figure suggested for France, but this is guesswork. A series of other characterizations can be hazarded. First, resistance tended to grow out of existing networks of friends and colleagues. In Norway, veterans' associations, rifle clubs, and youth groups were especially crucial. Thanks to the attentions of the Gestapo, resistance cells in Germany were by necessity closely knit, for example the brief-lived *Weiße Rose* (White Rose) group, comprising students and academics from the University of Munich, which broadcast news of the exterminations. Second, communists were prominent although, as Tony Judt says, the timing of their entry into resistance depended on relationships with the USSR.[45] Within Greece and Yugoslavia communists paid little heed to Moscow and were quick to agitate; in France, the party slavishly followed Stalin's line and was held back by the Nazi–Soviet pact, though many resisted on an individual basis; and in Italy the party, exiled since Mussolini's coming to power in 1922, did not truly mobilize until the *Duce*'s fall in 1943. Yet because of their organizational skills, the communists often appeared the best prepared, and their involvement frequently masked the sizable contribution of other groups. Third, historians have gradually uncovered the role of women who, as Perry Wilson observes in the case of Italy, were hesitant to come forward "to claim the diplomas and medals later awarded to partisans."[46] Because of the absence of men in society, women could go about their business unnoticed. It further helped that, for some time, the Germans believed that women were naturally submissive and unlikely to act politically. While individuals in charge of resistance cells – for instance, Lucie Aubrac in France – were exceptional, it is now acknowledged that women generally made a significant contribution to resistance. Wilson records how in Italy women ferried propaganda, typed clandestine papers, collected clothes for partisans, and fronted food protests, a traditional form of discontent.

Nowhere in Europe was resistance united. Beyond the expulsion of the occupier, resisters were fighting for different ideological goals. Everywhere there was resentment at the ways in which communists attempted to dominate, often using resistance as an opportunity to eliminate their enemies. This gave rise to particular tensions in Greece, where internecine struggles and the wider context of the Cold War resulted in a bitter civil war which endured from 1946 until 1949. Personal rivalries further intruded. Resistance leaders often built up spheres of influence which they were reluctant to abandon, and they resented those who joined late in the day. Regionally, too, resistance was diverse. Much military activity was concentrated in mountainous areas where there was cover to engage in sabotage. It was the scrubland in France which, of course, provided the name for the *maquis*, comprising men avoiding compulsory work service in Germany. Organizationally, resistance movements frequently intruded on one another – within Norway, for instance, *Milorg* supposedly dealt with military matters and *Silorg* with civilian ones, yet the two often overlapped. Historians have been quick to criticize the splits within the resistance yet, as Kedward said, it is difficult to see how they could have functioned differently – the need for secrecy militated against there being single movements. Through counter-intelligences the Nazis devastated the Dutch networks in early 1944, for instance. That said, at least in France, resistance eventually achieved a remarkable degree of unity, something accomplished by de Gaulle and his emissaries to metropolitan territory, crucially Jean Moulin.

Because of these divisions, historians have questioned the overall contribution of resisters. In military terms, partisan units were more of a nuisance to the Germans than anything else, and tended only to be influential in liberating particular areas. In eastern and western Europe the Allies thought in conventional military terms and were reluctant to trust underground groups whose logistical strength and dependability were uncertain. It was perhaps only in Yugoslavia that Tito's supporters – maybe 200,000 strong in 1944 – caused the Germans real problems. However, this should not distort the wider picture. Historians agree that resistance maintained morale and gave people hope. It also bestowed a dignity on certain countries, most obviously France and Italy, enabling them to rejoin the war on the Allied side. They were thus able to play a role in the final defeat of Nazism and in the rebuilding of Europe. It is especially noticeable that leading proponents of European integration were often resistance veterans, several emanating from Catholic movements which evolved into Christian Democratic parties.

Historians stress that these achievements are all the more astonishing when it is recalled that most partisans originated from ordinary backgrounds, and it would be comforting to write the overall history of the home fronts as one of an emphatic

rejection of Nazism. This was not so. To become a resister – to become a collaborator – involved an issue of choice, often a brave one, occasionally an arbitrary one. In
his 1974 film *Lacombe Lucien* – a depiction of an adolescent boy in southern France
– the director Louis Malle portrayed the ambiguities in joining either the resistance
or collaborationist forces. A majority preferred to wait on events, yet occupation
meant that people increasingly had to take sides – a process which, as Rab Bennett
illustrates, involved agonizing dilemmas.[47] It is, though, hazardous to generalize
about the experience of the home fronts. Much depended on where one lived, on
one's race, on one's gender, on one's age, and on the extent of German economic
plunder, In Jiři Weil's semi-autobiographical novel *Life with a Star*, Czech rail trucks
laden with goods destined for Germany had the word "Stolen" chalked on them.
What might be safely said is that, throughout Europe, life became a matter of making
do, of keeping warm, of searching for food, processes which became incredibly inven-
tive and, just occasionally, fun.[48] It is also significant that social structures, at least
within western Europe, largely withstood this makeshift way of surviving. It can be
further said that nowhere in Europe was there liking for the Germans or the Soviets,
even if this discontent did not always equate with resistance. As the Nazi grip on
power began to loosen, as the round-ups, deportations, and arbitrary shootings
intensified, as the Soviet advances mounted, fear stalked Europe. Small wonder
people looked towards the end of the fighting. It lies beyond this chapter, but the
tragedy was that with liberation often came disappointment, as the hopes nurtured
on the home fronts for a better future were unrealized in the postwar world.

NOTES

1 See Peter Calvocoressi and Guy Wint, *Total War: Causes and Courses of the Second World War* (Harmondsworth: Allen Lane, 1972).
2 Eric Hobsbawm, *The Age of Revolution: Europe, 1789–1848* (London: Abacus, 1977), p. 88.
3 Winston Churchill, *Great War Speeches* (London: Corgi, 1965), p. 53.
4 See Gordon Wright, *The Ordeal of Total War* (New York: Harper, 1968); Enzo Collotti, ed., *L'occupazione nazista in Europa* (Rome: Editori Riuniti, 1964); Werner Röhr, ed., *Okkupation und Kollaboration, 1938–1945* (Berlin: Hüthig, 1994). On collaboration, see David Littlejohn, *The Patriotic Traitors* (London: Heinemann, 1972); Werner Rings, *Life with the Enemy* (New York: Doubleday, 1982); Rab Bennett, *Under the Shadow of the Swastika: The Moral Dilemmas of Resistance and Collaboration in Hitler's Europe* (Basingstoke: Macmillan, 1999). On resistance, see M. R. D. Foot, *Resistance: European Resistance to Nazism, 1940–45* (London: Methuen, 1976); Henri Michel, *Shadow War: Resistance in Europe, 1939–1945* (London: Deutsch, 1972); Stephen F. Hawes and Ralph T. White, eds, *Resistance in Europe, 1939–1945* (Harmondsworth: Penguin, 1975).
5 See the forthcoming volume by Robert Gildea and Olivier Wieviorka. Meanwhile, see part 9 of Jean-Pierre Azéma and François Bédarida, eds, *Le Régime de Vichy et les Français* (Paris: Fayard, 1992) and chs 29–33 in John Bourne, Peter Liddle, and Ian Whitehead, eds, *The Great World War, 1914–45*, vol. 1: *Lightning Strikes Twice* (London: Harper Collins, 2000).
6 John Campbell, ed., *The Experience of World War II* (London: Grange, 1989), p. 188.
7 Among studies on individual countries, see Ian Ousby, *Occupation: The Ordeal of France* (London: John Murray, 1997); Gerhard Hirschfeld, *Nazi Rule and Dutch Collaboration:*

The Netherlands under German Occupation, 1940–1945 (Oxford: Berg, 1988); Hagen Fleischer, *Im Kreuzschatten der Machte. Griechenland, 1941–1944 (Okkupupation, Resistance, Kollaboration)* (Frankfurt: Lang, 1986).

8   See especially Robert Gildea, *Marianne in Chains: In Search of the German Occupation, 1940–45* (London: Macmillan, 2002) and Camilla Cederna, Martina Lombardi, and Marilea Somaré, eds, Milano in guerra (Milan: Feltrinelli, 1979).

9   See Michel, *Shadow War*, pp. 21–2.

10 Michael Burleigh, *The Third Reich: A New History* (London: Pan, 2000), p. 408, who is good on the contours of Hitler's Europe.

11 See especially Tony Kushner and Katherine Knox, *Refugees in an Age of Genocide: Global, National and Local Perspectives during the Twentieth Century* (London: Cass, 1999).

12 Ian Beckett, "The Resilience of the Old Regime," in *Total War and Historical Change*, Arthur Marwick, Clive Emsley, and Wendy Simpson, eds (Buckingham: Open University Press, 2001).

13 Figures are from Calvocoressi and Wint, *Total War*, pp. 218–19, and Mark Harrison, *Soviet Planning in Peace and War, 1938–45* (Cambridge: Cambridge University Press, 1985), p. 71. See also John Lukacs, *The Last European War, September 1939–December 1941* (London: Routledge and Kegan Paul, 1977), pp. 239–40.

14 See Guy S. Goodwin-Gill, "The Experience of Displacement: Refugees and War," in Bourne, Liddle, and Whitehead, *Great World War*, p. 572.

15 See Alan Milward, *War, Economy and Society, 1939–1945* (London: Allen Lane, 1977); Mark Harrison, ed., *The Economics of World War II: Six Great Powers in International Comparison* (Cambridge: Cambridge University Press, 1998); Jean Freymond, *Le IIIe Reich et la réorganisation économique de l'Europe* (Leiden: Sijthoff, 1974); Brian Bond, *War and Society in Europe, 1870–1970* (London: Fontana, 1984).

16 Quoted in Richard Overy, *The Dictators: Hitler's Germany and Stalin's Russia* (London: Allen Lane, 2004), p. 504. See also his *War and Economy in the Third Reich* (Oxford: Clarendon Press, 1994).

17 See I. C. B. Dear and M. R. D. Foot, eds, *The Oxford Companion to World War II* (Oxford: Oxford University Press, 2001), pp. 744, 309.

18 Overy, *The Dictators*, pp. 504–11.

19 The classic work is Angus Calder, *The People's War: Britain 1939–1945* (London: Cape, 1969).

20 See Dörte Winkler, *Frauenarbeit im Dritten Reich* (Hamburg: Hoffman und Campe, 1977).

21 Corelli Barnett, *The Audit of War* (London: Macmillan, 1988). See also Peter Clarke and Clive Trebilcock, eds, *Understanding Decline: Perceptions and Realities of British Economic Performance* (Cambridge: Cambridge University Press, 1997).

22 See Michal Grynberg, ed., *Words to Outlive Us: Eyewitness Accounts from the Warsaw Ghetto* (London: Granta, 2003), pp. 35–6.

23 Richard Vinen, *France 1934–1979* (Basingstoke: Macmillan, 1996), p. 64.

24 Henri Van der Zee, *The Hunger Winter: Occupied Holland, 1944–1945* (Lincoln: University of Nebraska Press, 1998).

25 See H. Roderick Kedward, *Occupied France* (Oxford: Blackwell, 1985).

26 See Christian Bernadac, *Kommandos de Femmes. Ravensbück* (Paris: France-Empire, 1973).

27 See Fabrice Virgili, *La France "virile": des femmes tondues à la Libération* (Paris: Payot, 2001).

28 Robert O. Paxton, *Vichy France: Old Guard and New Order, 1940–1944* (New York: Knopf, 1972).

29 See Stanley Hoffmann, "Collaborationism in France," *Journal of Modern History* 40/3 (1968): 375–95.

30 Robert O. Paxton, *The Anatomy of Fascism* (London: Allen Lane, 2004), p. 111.

31 On France, see Philippe Burrin, *Living with Defeat: France under the German Occupation, 1940–1944* (London: Arnold, 1996); on Belgium, see Martin Conway, *Collaboration in Belgium: Léon Degrelle and the Rexist Movement* (New Haven CT: Yale University Press, 1993); on Norway, see Hans F. Dahl, *Quisling: A Study in Treachery* (Cambridge: Cambridge University Press, 1999), p. 336.

32 Burleigh, *Third Reich*, p. 410.

33 Mark Wheeler, "Pariahs to Partisans: The Communist Party of Yugoslavia," in *Resistance and Revolution in Mediterranean Europe, 1939–1948*, Tony Judt, ed. (London: Routledge, 1989), p. 125.

34 Gerhard Hirschfeld, "Collaboration in Nazi Occupied France: Some Introductory Remarks," in *Collaboration in France: Politics and Culture during the Nazi Occupation*, G. Hirschfeld and P. Marsh, eds (Oxford: Berg, 1989), p. 1.

35 A starting point is Yisrael Gutman and Cynthia J. Haft, eds, *Patterns of Jewish Leadership in Nazi Europe, 1933–1945* (Jerusalem: Yad Vashem, 1979).

36 Julian Jackson, *The Dark Years: France 1940–1944* (Oxford: Oxford University Press, 2002), p. 313.

37 Littlejohn, *Patriotic Traitors*, pp. 336–7.

38 On Italy, see Mario Isnenghi, ed., *I luoghi della memoria*, 3 vols (Rome: Laterza, 1997–8); on France, see Henri Rousso, *The Vichy Syndrome* (Cambridge MA: Harvard University Press, 1991).

39 Bernhard Kroener, Rolf-Dieter Müller, and Hans Umbreit, eds, *Germany and the Second World War* (Oxford: Oxford University Press, 2000), vol 5, part 1. For the experience of east Europeans, see Diemut Majer, *"Non-Germans" under the Third Reich* (Baltimore MD: Johns Hopkins University Press, 2003).

40 M. R. D. Foot, "What Good did Resistance Do?" in Hawes and White, *Resistance in Europe*, p. 215.

41 Wheeler, "Pariahs to Partisans," pp. 110–56. See also his entry in Dear and Foot, *Oxford Companion*, pp. 1015–16.

42 H. Roderick Kedward, *Resistance in Vichy France* (Oxford: Oxford University Press, 1978).

43 R. White, "Unity and Diversity of Resistance," in Hawes and White, *Resistance in Europe*, pp. 8–9.

44 Very judicious is Olivier Rota, "Les 'Silences' du Pape Pie XII," *Revue d'Histoire Ecclésiastique* 99/3–4 (2004): 758–66.

45 Introduction to Judt, *Resistance in Revolution*, pp. 4–5.

46 Perry Wilson, "Saints and Heroines: Rewriting the History of Italian Women in the Resistance," in *Opposing Fascism: Community, Authority and Resistance in Europe*, T. Kirk and A. McElligott, eds (Cambridge: Cambridge University Press, 1999), pp. 180–98.

47 Bennett, *Under the Shadow*, pp. 13–14.

48 This is the argument of Dominique Veillon, *Vivre et survivre en France, 1939–47* (Paris: Payot, 1995).

GUIDE TO FURTHER READING

Rab Bennett, *Under the Shadow of the Swastika: The Moral Dilemmas of Resistance and Collaboration in Hitler's Europe* (Basingstoke: Macmillan, 1999). Good on the ethical ambiguities of choices under occupation.

Joanna Bourke, *The Second World War: A People's History* (Oxford: Oxford University Press, 2003). Illustrates how fighting impacted on civilians.

John Bourne, Peter Liddle, and Ian Whitehead, eds, *The Great World War, 1914–45*, vol. 1: *Lightning Strikes Twice* (London: Harper Collins, 2000). An eclectic array of essays, several of which touch on the home fronts.

Michael Burleigh, *The Third Reich: A New History* (London: Pan, 2000). Excellent section on the high and low politics of collaboration.

Peter Calvocoressi and Guy Wint, *Total War: Causes and Courses of the Second World War* (Harmondsworth: Allen Lane, 1972). Good on context despite its age.

Józef Garlinski, *Poland in the Second World War* (London: Macmillan, 1985). Brings home the brutal reality of Nazi rule in eastern Europe.

Robert Gildea, *Marianne in Chains: In Search of the German Occupation, 1940–45* (London: Macmillan, 2002). An exemplary study which relates local conditions to the national picture.

Mark Harrison, ed., *The Economics of World War II: Six Great Powers in International Comparison* (Cambridge: Cambridge University Press, 1998). Examines the home fronts largely from an economist's standpoint.

Gerhard Hirschfeld, *Nazi Rule and Dutch Collaboration: The Netherlands under German Occupation, 1940–1945* (Oxford: Berg, 1988). Highlights the complexities of the Nazi presence.

Tony Judt, ed., *Resistance and Revolution in Mediterranean Europe, 1939–1948* (London: Routledge, 1989). An incisive collection that focuses on the communist contribution to resistance.

H. Roderick Kedward, *Resistance in Vichy France* (Oxford: Oxford University Press, 1978). Groundbreaking study whose lines of inquiry can be applied to other countries.

Bernard Kroener, Ralf-Dietrich Muller, and Hans Umbreit, eds, *Germany and the Second World War* (Oxford: Oxford University Press, 2000), vol. 5, part 1. Examines the nature of German rule in occupied countries.

Henri Michel, *Shadow War: Resistance in Europe, 1939–1945* (London: Deutsch, 1972). Full of ideas, albeit francocentric.

Sonya Rose, *Which People's War? National Identity and Citizenship in Britain, 1939–1945* (Oxford: Oxford University Press, 2003). One of many books on the British home front, arguing that divisions within society outweighed unity.

CHAPTER THIRTY

The Holocaust

DAVID ENGEL

What is the Holocaust?

History is not naturally divided into discrete sets of events. On the contrary, historical episodes are usually identified, named, and classified only after they occur. Moreover, the specific and generic names attached to past occurrences have great power to shape what people think about them. The evolution of the term "holocaust" since the Second World War and the ways in which it has framed discussion about one of that war's particularly frightening features are cases in point.

Into the 1950s "holocaust" served mainly as a workaday label for large-scale destruction and loss of life. In the English-speaking world the word was applied variously to the suppression of Italian nationalist activity by the Habsburg regime during the nineteenth century, the 1906 earthquake and fire in San Francisco, the devastation caused by Japanese air raids in China in 1938, the blaze that destroyed the Coconut Grove nightclub in Boston in 1942, and the sinking of the German battleship *Scharnhorst* in 1943. Often it was used to signify the carnage of war in general: among its most frequent referents were the American Civil War, the successive massacres of Armenians in the Ottoman Empire from 1894 to 1915 and, after 1945, the anticipated outcome of nuclear conflict. It was not until the 1960s that the catastrophic losses suffered by the Jews of Europe at the hands of the Nazi regime in Germany or its allies between 1933–45 – especially the death of some 5.8 million Jewish men, women, and children, who made up about two-thirds of Europe's Jewish population in 1939 – took on the status of a holocaust *par excellence*, to the point where the phrase "the Holocaust" (capitalized and preceded by the definite article) came in common parlance to designate that particular catastrophe.[1]

In fact, for 15–20 years after the end of World War II English speakers do not appear to have perceived any need to invent a special label to describe that instance of destruction, let alone to set it above any of the other events to which the word "holocaust" had been habitually applied. It hardly seemed that the persecution and mass death that befell European Jewry under Nazi impact should be regarded as anything more than a subset of the war's overall devastation or of the afflictions that were the lot of a host of casualties of Nazi brutality. Those victims included political dissenters (socialists, communists, and others with a record of anti-Nazi statements or activity in any of the countries under German occupation); so-called "asocials" (mostly vagrants, chronically unemployed persons, and repeat criminal offenders); male homosexuals from Germany and Austria; Jehovah's Witnesses (who refused military service and would not salute Hitler); slave laborers from many subjugated (mostly east European) populations; and members of groups targeted for wholesale killing, including the Sinti and Roma (Gypsies), Soviet prisoners of war, and the mentally and physically disabled. Many of these had been incarcerated in an extensive network of concentration, labor, prison, and transit camps notorious for their especially cruel regime and high mortality. When British and American armed forces entered those camps in April–May 1945 and first gained what would become lasting impressions of Nazi atrocities, they encountered a population of upwards of 700,000 inmates, of whom probably only about 100,000 were Jews. As a result, they and the journalists who followed close on their heels (recording the scenes of emaciated bodies and corpses stacked like cordwood that have served as symbols of twentieth-century barbarities, including "the Holocaust," ever since) were hard put to perceive that Jewish suffering bore any especially horrific features. On the contrary, most observers initially saw all those incarcerated in what a 1945 film newsreel called the "Nazi murder mills" simply as victims of a coercive and cruel dictatorship. As one editor of a major American newspaper explained, the prisoners had been deprived of their freedom because "they refused to accept the political philosophy of the Nazi party" or otherwise "refused to conform."[2] It took more than a decade until even the most sophisticated commentators understood that the Jews and certain other categories of victims (most prominently the Sinti and Roma and the disabled) were victimized without regard for what they believed or how they behaved, or that millions of Jews from throughout Europe died in far more lethal "murder mills" than the concentration camps that so shocked their liberators – in killing centers built especially to suffocate them *en masse* immediately upon arrival.

Most likely it was Israel's capture, trial, and execution in 1960–2 of Adolf Eichmann, a key engineer of the Third Reich's murderous anti-Jewish campaign, together with the animated discussion that accompanied and followed it in many countries, that catalyzed a new conceptualization of the similarities and differences between the experiences of Jews under Nazi rule and those of other victims of the Reich's savagery. The trial, widely covered in the mass media throughout Europe and the Americas, centered on the testimony of some 100 witnesses who described specific "crimes against the Jewish people" that prosecutors believed had not been afforded due attention at the Nuremberg trials 15 years before. The testimony of the witnesses and the accused together focused an international spotlight upon a Nazi program to kill each and every Jewish man, woman, and child within the Third Reich's reach; the thorough, systematic planning that underlay the program's conception and execution; the alarming degree to which the plan had succeeded in most German-occupied and allied countries; and the virtual impossibility for Jews to escape the death sentence that had been placed upon them, even through formal renunciation of any Jewish affiliation or active assistance to the German war effort. The sufferings of forced laborers, political prisoners, and other groups associated with the Nazi camp system now appeared mild compared to the horrors Jews had faced, which popular history writer Barbara Tuchman, writing under the trial's impact, labeled "the peak and apotheosis of [twentieth-century] violence."[3] Those horrors had earlier acquired a collective name in Israel: *sho'ah* – a biblical word suggesting utter, unprecedented devastation,[4] uncommon in modern Hebrew and thus appropriate to their exceptional magnitude in Jewish history. "The Holocaust" soon became the accepted English rendering of the Hebrew term, probably because "holocaust" also carried biblical associations and conveyed a sense of ruin beyond ordinary experience.

Of course, assigning the Jews' ordeal under the Third Reich its own special name raises the question of whether that ordeal was really fundamentally different from that of other victimized groups. After all, the Sinti and Roma also lost approximately two-thirds of their prewar populations in some parts of Europe, many in the same special killing centers and by the same methods used to murder Jews. Those methods were also employed against some 200,000 disabled persons and an equal or greater number of Soviet war prisoners, with 2.5 million more Soviet POWs dying from hunger, exposure, and abuse by their captors. Significant groups in other occupied countries, including a large segment of Poland's political, religious, and cultural elite, were marked for death, while much of the remainder of the Polish population was turned into a reservoir of helots whose individual lives were assigned minimal value. In all, close to 2 million Polish civilians (non-Jews) perished under German rule.

In 1944 the legal scholar Raphael Lemkin classified all of these murderous actions together under the rubric of "genocide," a term he coined to designate "a coordinated plan of different actions aiming at the destruction of essential foundations of the life of national groups, with the aim of annihilating the groups themselves."[5] For Lemkin, it made little difference whether the perpetrators of genocide sought to kill every individual member of the targeted group; genocidal policies were ultimately equally destructive of group life whether or not they displayed this one particular feature. In the late twentieth century, under the impact of the deadly intercommunal violence that accompanied the collapse of Yugoslavia, a similar behavior, often called "ethnic cleansing," was identified. That term has been employed to designate the forcible displacement or killing of large numbers of minority group members inhabiting a particular territory in order to create ethnically homogenous areas. Hence many people since have maintained that the encounter between the Third Reich and the Jews is most productively understood not as a phenomenon *sui generis* but as a specific variant of a more widespread crime committed repeatedly before and since.

Others have taken issue with this approach, arguing that the planned systematic total murder of European Jewry by the Nazi regime constitutes a historical *novum* that "reveals the dark, eccentric *essence* of Nazism . . . in a way that nothing else does."[6] In consequence they have advocated conceptualizing "genocide," "ethnic cleansing," and "the Holocaust" separately. Still others have accepted the distinction between "genocide," as defined by Lemkin, and "holocaust," by which they understand the planned killing of *all* members of a group; but they dispute the contention that "the [Jewish] Holocaust" was the first and only example of the latter. Some argue that the Sinti and Roma were indeed victims of a full-blown holocaust; others have identified a program to murder all individuals in the targeted group in the slaughter of Armenians by Turkish troops in 1915 or in the mass killings of certain native American populations by European settlers between the sixteenth and nineteenth centuries. The claims and counterclaims of proponents of the various competing conceptions have generated a rich literature analyzing the similarities and differences between the killing of Jews by the Third Reich and many other instances of mass death throughout human history. Nevertheless, popular usage in English and most European languages persists in equating "the Holocaust" primarily with the modern Hebrew *sho'ah*. The essay that follows conforms to popular usage insofar as it concentrates upon the encounter between the Third Reich and the Jews. It takes no position, however, about whether that encounter ought to be treated as one instance of a larger phenomenon or as a singularity. Precisely because history is not divided naturally into discrete sets of events, the identification, categorization, and naming of historical episodes is necessarily left to observers, who may choose for themselves whatever names, comparisons, and analytical rubrics best meet their particular needs.

Idea and Execution

Perhaps the most striking fact about the systematic mass murder of Jews during World War II is that, in the eyes of the leaders of the Third Reich, its ultimate justification lay in an idea about Jews that differed in at least two crucial respects from the stock anti-Jewish images that had permeated western culture since the middle ages. First, until the late nineteenth century even the most hostile depictions of Jews had located the source of their supposedly pernicious qualities in the religious system inculcated in them from childhood. As a result, it was generally accepted that Jews could be improved and redeemed through religious conversion or (in modern times) fundamental reform of their own traditions. Toward the end of the nineteenth century, however, some writers concluded that Jewish behavior was a function not of belief and education but of genetics (or, in the language of the time, "race"), which could never be altered. According to this notion, Jews who became Christians or otherwise assimilated into their surrounding societies were not to be welcomed but feared: even though they now appeared to be citizens of their countries like all others, they still supposedly bore injurious "Jewish" characteristics, making them an especially dangerous and invisible source of harm. The Nazi Party founded its approach to dealing with Jews upon this premise. Second, whereas earlier malevolent representations of Jews, even "racially" based ones, had been framed in language generally understood to be metaphorical, Adolf Hitler and some of his closest associates appear to have taken their own anti-Jewish images literally. In his two books, *Mein Kampf* (1924–6) and an unpublished work (1928), Hitler developed a theory of human history from which he inferred (under the influence of the occult racist circles from which he had learned during his youth in Vienna) that Jews were not human beings at all but actually noxious parasites in human bodies who could survive only by robbing other peoples of their food supply.[7] From this notion it followed that Jews were the inexorable mortal enemies not only of Germany but of all humanity; in principle, as long as a single Jew remained alive, all peoples faced potential ruin from them.

That Hitler personally held such beliefs does not mean, however, that a German effort to murder all Jews everywhere was inevitable once the Nazi Party assumed power in Germany in 1933; it means only that once the Nazi regime decided to undertake such an effort, that decision could be supported by reference to Hitler's worldview. As it happened, such a decision appears to have crystallized only in 1941.

Before that time the regime took a series of steps whose broad aim was to detach
Jews from German society and, once war began, to remove them from conquered
east European regions intended for German settlement. These measures included the
dismissal of Jews from the civil service, free professions, and cultural and educational
institutions; deprivation of Reich citizenship; a ban on marriages or extramarital
sexual relations between Jews and non-Jews; labeling Jews with special markings;
forced transfer of Jewish-owned businesses to non-Jewish owners; and restriction of
Jewish residences to specially designated buildings. Additionally, in 1933 and again
following the 1938 *Anschluss* with Austria, Jews were subjected to periodic physical
violence, culminating in the so-called *Kristallnacht* pogrom of November 9–10,
1938, in which 1,400 synagogues and 7,500 Jewish-owned shops were attacked and
91 Jews killed. The German foreign ministry explained in January 1939 that both
legislative and violent actions aimed at "a radical solution to the Jewish question"
through "the emigration of all Jews living in German territory."[8] Upon taking control
of Austria and Czechoslovakia in 1938–9, Reich authorities established special offices
in Vienna and Prague to enable the maximum number of Jews to leave those countries in the shortest possible time. After the outbreak of war, when some 2 million
Polish Jews fell under German rule (the remaining 1.5 million Jews in Poland inhabited territories occupied by the Soviet Union from September 1939 to June–July
1941), anti-Jewish measures were directed at transporting all Jews under the Reich's
control to a special Jewish "reservation," planned first for the area around Lublin,
later for the island of Madagascar, and later still for Siberia (in anticipation of the
eventual conquest of the USSR). Beginning in October 1939, Jews in a number of
Polish cities were concentrated in ghettos, from which they were to be removed to
the reservation once it could be established. Not until October 1941 were Jews forbidden to leave Reich-controlled territory; evidently only after that time did the
regime become fully committed to a program of continent-wide systematic mass
murder.

Several explanations of why Nazi leaders did not pursue such a program earlier
are possible. It may be that Hitler and his associates failed at first to draw the extreme
operative conclusion that his worldview seemingly required. It may also be that
although Hitler himself aspired to rid the entire world of all Jews eventually, he did
not believe such a goal was feasible in the short term – whether because until 1941
less than half of Europe's Jews, let alone the world's, were within Germany's reach,
or because few others in the Nazi regime shared his aspiration, and he was unable
to impose it by himself. Perhaps, realizing that they could not entirely eliminate the
putative danger to humanity posed by the existence of Jews anywhere in the world,
Nazi leaders concentrated initially on measures that would shield at least the *German*
people from the Jewish menace. Perhaps the technical means and organizational
infrastructure necessary for systematic mass killing throughout the continent were
not available from the outset. To be sure, some scholars have argued that all anti-
Jewish measures undertaken by the regime from the moment of its accession to power
(including, counterintuitively, encouragement of emigration) are best understood as
integral parts of a diabolical step-by-step plan conceived in advance to culminate in
total murder, but compelling evidence is lacking to sustain their view. Much the same
can be said, however, regarding virtually all other conjectures about long-range Nazi
plans for the Jews between 1933 and 1941. All that is certain is that large-scale

murders of Jews began only following Germany's invasion of the Soviet Union in 1941, that a mass killing program became systematized and extended throughout Europe only toward the end of that year, and that once the program began to be carried out, it was legitimized by the representation of Jews as incorrigibly noxious parasites rooted in Hitler's writings.

Much scholarly attention has thus been directed toward identifying what catalyzed the transition to murder. The search has been complicated by the absence of any written order directing mass killing to begin. Perhaps such an order was prepared but subsequently destroyed; perhaps it never existed at all. There is even a lack of unequivocal testimony about whether a specific *oral* order was ever given. Initially it was assumed that any order, written or oral, must have come from the highest levels of the Nazi hierarchy and been passed down the chain of command from Berlin outward. However, research accumulating since the 1990s has suggested that, although German troops invading the USSR carried orders to undertake *targeted* killings of Soviet Jewish state and Communist Party officials, intellectuals, communal leaders, and men of military age, it was actually local military personnel and commissioners in Balkan and east European areas conquered by Germany between April and October 1941 who ordered the first *wholesale* killing operations on their own initiative, then sought approval *up* the chain of command for a general policy of indiscriminate murder of Jews in the territories under their responsibility. Their requests were justified on the basis of wartime exigencies, as part of a campaign to eliminate partisan resistance or as a way to make certain that "useless" or "harmful" elements of the conquered population did not consume scarce food and supplies. Other local Nazi officials, evidently fearing that their bailiwicks might soon become a dumping ground for Jews deported from points west, appear to have concluded that the only truly effective way to prevent an unwanted increase in the Jewish population in their realms was to kill Jews *en masse*. These operations, undertaken in summer and early fall 1941, when thinking in Berlin still focused upon establishing a giant Jewish reservation in Siberia, gradually emerged in the final three months of the year as the preferred model for disposing of all Jews under Nazi rule once the invasion of the Soviet Union stalled and it became evident that a Siberian reservation would not be created as quickly as had been anticipated earlier.[9]

Recent studies also strongly suggest that the idea of systematic total killing may have recommended itself to its German initiators in the field at least partly through observation of the behavior of local non-Jews toward Jews in the Soviet, Polish, and Yugoslav territories occupied by Germany in 1941, as well as in Romania and the territories it reclaimed or conquered from the Soviet Union in the same year. All of these military actions brought in their immediate wake notable violence by Lithuanians, Estonians, Belorussians, Ukrainians, Romanians, Croats, and Poles against their Jewish neighbors in cities and small towns throughout the regions in question. Some of this violence appears to have been German-instigated or even German-organized, but much of it was evidently spontaneous, justified by no more than stereotypical identification of Jews with a hostile foreign power (usually Soviet or, in the case of Croatia, Serb). More often no overarching justification at all was sought: broadly aware that the new German occupiers were not likely to provide Jews any serious protection, murderous local mobs took advantage of the presence of the new regime to settle personal local grievances or to seize Jewish property. Yet although they lacked an ideological foundation legitimating the slaughter of entire populations, killings by these bands or by local police or collaborationist militias were often more extensive than German shootings of Soviet Jews. Many Jewish communities victimized by the local populace lost from a quarter to over half of their number in the space of a few days – far more than the proportional losses German forces were inflicting at the same time. On June 28–29, 1941, for example, Romanian (not German) police, soldiers, and townspeople in the Moldavian capital of Iaşi caused the deaths of more than 10,000 of the city's 34,000 Jewish residents. Around the same time Croatian forces deported perhaps a third of the 11,000 Jews of Zagreb and almost all Jews from Varaždin and other provincial towns and villages to specially constructed prison camps, where about 35,000 Jews were shot on arrival. In some cases, all Jews in a particular town who were unable to escape were killed by a portion of the town's non-Jewish residents, as at Jedwabne in north central Poland, where on July 10, 1941, a mob led by the local mayor and members of the town council herded at least 400 Jews (by some accounts many more) into a barn that was then doused with kerosene and burned.[10]

Nevertheless, it was ultimately the central Nazi hierarchy, in all likelihood under direct prodding from Hitler, that made the decision to turn mass killing from a local practice into a program for the entire area under German domination. Research indicates that a paramount factor in that decision was the progress of World War II. On January 30, 1939 Hitler had told the Reichstag that "if the international Jewish financiers . . . should succeed in plunging the nations . . . into a world war, the result will be . . . the annihilation of the Jewish race in Europe."[11] It was Hitler himself, of course, together with his regime, that was actually preparing for world war at the time, and each stage in German preparations and execution brought with it a concomitant radicalization of policy concerning Jews. The conquest of Poland in September 1939 was accompanied by a move from a program of coerced emigration to one of mass deportations and incarceration; the June 1941 invasion of the Soviet Union, which more than doubled the number of Jews living under Nazi rule, was quickly followed by extensive mass killings of Soviet Jews, including Polish Jews living in Soviet-occupied territory (about one half million between June and November 1941). Some Jews in other parts of eastern Europe (mainly Serbia and the western Polish Warthegau region that had been incorporated directly into the Reich in 1939) were also killed by German forces during fall 1941, and there is evidence that by October of that year plans had been formulated for the liquidation of all Polish Jewry. But documents uncovered since the mid-1990s point to Germany's entry into the war against the United States on December 11, 1941, which turned what had until then been a clash of European powers into a truly global conflict, as the trigger for extending the murder program systematically throughout Europe. The connection is consistent with Hitler's January 1939 statement.

Carrying out the liquidation of European Jewry on a continent-wide scale required extensive construction and organization. In eastern Europe, murders had been carried out by killing squads that moved from town to town, seizing local Jews, marching them to a nearby secluded location, and shooting them one by one. However, that method could not serve the needs of a more extensive program. Thus, when Reich leaders focused their attention on Polish Jewry, they determined to replace the mobile squads with centrally located killing centers, to which Jews would be transported from a distance, generally by rail. Construction of the first such center, Bełżec, in southeastern Poland, began in October 1941; exhaust from a diesel engine was fed into a sealed chamber, where all inside would be asphyxiated. The next month three specially equipped vans whose exhaust could be channeled back into the cargo area were sent to Chełmno in the Warthegau; in these vehicles Jews brought to the site would take their final ride. Construction of two additional centers similar to Bełżec – Sobibór, northeast of Lublin, and Treblinka, between Warsaw and Białystok – was begun in spring 1942 to assist in annihilating the Jews of Poland. Jews from the rest of Europe were slated to be killed at Birkenau, a branch of the Nazi prison and labor camp at Auschwitz, west of Kraków, where since September 1941 killing experiments using the fumes of evaporating prussic acid had been conducted on Soviet war prisoners and inmates too ill to work. In fall 1942 diesel exhaust gassing facilities were added to the labor camp at Majdanek near Lublin to relieve pressure on the other installations. These were the six so-called extermination camps, where the majority of Holocaust victims met their deaths (although for Bełżec, Chełmno, Sobibór, and Treblinka the name "camp" is misleading, because few victims remained there for more than the time required to unload them from the trains that brought them, strip them of their property, shave their heads, and herd them to the gas chambers). Contrary to a widespread belief, the concentration camps in Germany proper, like Dachau or Buchenwald, were not employed for the mass killing of Jews.

In order to make certain that the killing centers operated at maximum efficiency, transports from across Europe had to be scheduled precisely. The work of synchronization – clearing railroad tracks, allocating rolling stock, arranging with local police and military authorities to round up the victims – was one of the tasks of a meeting held in the Berlin suburb of Wannsee on January 20, 1942. Summoned by Reinhard Heydrich, head of the Reich's internal intelligence and secret police services, who earlier had been entrusted by top Nazi leaders Hermann Göring and Heinrich Himmler with coordinating the many government and party agencies who would play a role in what they called the "final solution of the Jewish problem," it brought together bureaucrats from 13 different offices, who developed a plan for "comb[ing] Europe from west to east," with a mind to ensnaring at least 11 million Jews in the killing mechanism.[12] In the end, somewhat more than half that number of Jews lost their lives. Success rates varied widely by country: in Germany, Austria, Poland, and the Baltic states some 90 percent of the prewar Jewish population perished; in Bulgaria, Denmark, Finland, Italy, and Luxembourg the killers reached only 2–20 percent of targeted Jewish victims. In Belgium, France, and Norway, death rates reached 25–50 percent; in Hungary, the Netherlands, Romania, Yugoslavia, and Soviet Belorussia and Ukraine, 50–75 percent; in Czechoslovakia and Greece, 75–90 percent. There were various reasons for these differences, including the attitudes of the occupied non-Jewish populations toward their Jewish neighbors, the degree to which local officials enjoyed freedom of action, and widely divergent political calculations by the rulers of Germany's independent allies (Bulgaria, Croatia, Hungary, Italy, Romania, Slovakia, and Vichy France) concerning the advisability of cooperating in the German murder scheme. Variations in Jewish responses to the threat of death, in contrast, appear to have affected the outcome of the killing program in different countries only marginally.

Fighting the Death Sentence

For several decades following World War II, common wisdom held that European Jews had been largely oblivious to the Nazi threat and had not shown much inclination to resist once it became manifest. By the 1980s, though, most scholars came to understand how immense the gap was between the resources Germans and Jews could marshal for achieving their respective goals. Jewish responses were encumbered especially by the fact that the Nazis never made their aims public. Jews had at all times to infer Nazi intentions indirectly on the basis of clues that were often muddled and inconsistent – sometimes deliberately so, as German occupation authorities frequently went to considerable lengths to camouflage their plans, which changed as the war progressed. Moreover, Jews could generally count on at most only limited assistance from the surrounding non-Jewish population, while in the areas of densest Jewish settlement significant segments of that population displayed murderous hostility toward them. Finally, as one perceptive historian has explained, "The post-Holocaust generation . . . already know[s] . . . that mass murder was possible; [Jews and non-Jews] who lived at the time did not. For them it was a totally new reality that was unfolding before their shocked eyes and paralyzed minds."[13] The thought that the government of a major European state with a long and distinguished cultural tradition – a state that many east European Jews recalled from World War I as an enlightened occupier who protected them from their neighbors' enmity – would now seek to kill each and every one of them, no matter what they thought or how they acted, merely because they happened to have been born Jews, was beyond belief.

Still, once they became aware that entire Jewish communities were being destroyed – a realization that dawned gradually in most places between late 1941 and mid-1942 – the great majority of Jewish leaders in the countries under direct German control understood that their charges were in immediate mortal danger and put their minds to the task of formulating an appropriate response to the new situation. They turned from the palliative and morale-building activities that had characterized earlier phases of Nazi rule to strategies for avoidance, escape, and direct resistance. To be sure, only a few leaders appear to have been persuaded that the annihilation of all of Jewry constituted a fundamental Nazi ideological goal from which the German regime could not be deterred. Hence the most common organized Jewish response to the Nazi murder campaign after 1941 involved efforts to convince German officials that it was in the Reich's interest to keep at least some Jews alive. That effort underlay the so-called "salvation through work" policies pursued by the Jewish leadership in many ghettos in Poland, including Łódż, Białystok, and Wilno: it was hoped that by demonstrating that the industrial capacity and available Jewish workforce in those cities offered a potential boon to the German war effort, German authorities would respond by protecting the workers and giving them adequate food, clothing, housing, and medical care. In the event, Jewish communities where such a program was implemented generally held out longer than those where it was not. Nevertheless, in the end the Germans would not be bargained with on such purely rational, economic grounds. The notion that Jews could be of value to them as laborers was not consistent with the fundamental Nazi representation of Jews as incorrigible parasites.

When the grounds for bargaining were not economic but diplomatic, in contrast, the situation proved somewhat different, as evidenced by negotiations to ransom large numbers of Jews in return for monetary payment, which took place in Slovakia in 1942–3 and in Hungary in 1944. Such ransom offers did not contradict Nazi stereotypes but actually built upon them, confirming in the minds of some German leaders that the highly successful Jewish parasites had succeeded in accumulating not only large sums of money and sources of income but also, even more importantly, powerful political influence outside the Nazi orbit. As it happened, Heinrich Himmler, who by some accounts was growing increasingly pessimistic about Germany's prospects on the battlefield, encouraged some of his subordinates to explore whether the Jews' supposed close contacts with British and American policy makers might perhaps be exploited to gain diplomatic advantage for the Reich in eventual negotiations with the Allies to end the war. Hence it appears that for a time, in 1943–4, Himmler might have been willing to sell, as it were, large numbers of east European Jews to a suitable buyer. From his perspective, though, the only suitable buyer was one or more of the Allied governments, not the Jews themselves. Once it became clear that the Allies were not interested in making a deal for Jewish lives, the possibility of rescue through ransom vanished; there was nothing Jews could do to resurrect it. Still, the Jewish–Nazi contacts that developed during ransom negotiations in Hungary appear to have played a role in the survival of significant portions of the Jewish populations of Budapest, Debrecen, Szeged, and several smaller Hungarian Jewish communities.[14]

Jews also continually sought ways to escape the Germans' grasp, whether by hiding, assuming a false identity as a non-Jew, or fleeing to a place not under Nazi occupation. Various Jewish organizations endeavored to help those who were able to do so. In particular, the so-called Working Group in Bratislava joined from 1942 with the Budapest-based Aid and Rescue Committee and a coalition of Zionist youth groups from the Zagłębie region in Poland to smuggle some 8,000 Jews from Slovakia, 4,000 from Germany, and 1,100 from Poland into Hungary, where until March 1944, when German troops occupied the country, Jews were relatively safe. Some 2,000 additional Jewish refugees from Nazi-occupied areas managed to make their way into Hungary on their own. Following the German occupation of Hungary the Aid and Rescue Committee and Hungarian Zionist youth movements turned their attention to moving Jews out of Hungary into unoccupied Romania. About 7,000 Jews were rescued in this fashion. In France, clandestine Jewish groups joined with non-Jewish anti-Nazi underground organizations to smuggle several thousand Jews into the neighboring neutral states, Switzerland and Spain. In contrast, the largest single Jewish mass escape, which brought 7,200 Danish Jews and some 700 of their non-Jewish relatives to safety in neutral Sweden on the night of September 30, 1943, was organized almost entirely by the Danish underground, with Jews providing partial financial support.

Rescue through flight across international boundaries within Europe could encompass only relatively small numbers of Jews, because it had to be accomplished without the knowledge of troops and officials guarding the borders. (In Denmark the large majority of Copenhagen's Jews could be spirited across the Øresund on a single night thanks largely to the uncommon reluctance of key figures within the German administration to carry out the mass deportations scheduled for the following day and their consequent willingness to look the other way.) It was also a realistic option only for Jews living in areas close to unoccupied territory. In contrast, for the large majority

of Jews, whose geographical situation was less favorable, the only ways to avoid falling
into Nazi hands were to hide or to live openly under false identity as a so-called
Aryan. Both strategies entailed severe risks that deterred most Jews from attempting
them: a study published in 2002 estimated that about 28,000 of the approximately
450,000 Jews who resided in Warsaw in 1941 tried either course. Of these, 11,500
remained alive at liberation.[15] Perhaps another 3,000–4,000 Jews survived in hiding
or in disguise in other parts of Poland. A joint Polish–Jewish underground organization called the Council for Aid to Jews, founded in December 1942 and known by
the code name Żegota, endeavored to locate safe shelter and provide sustenance for
concealed Jews and to prepare false identity documents and secure employment for
Jews seeking to pass as Poles; about 4,000 Jews benefited from its assistance. Little
is known to date about Jews in other countries who attempted similar survival
strategies.

   Armed resistance was an option available only in certain areas and to certain age
groups. Beginning in 1942, Jewish armed resistance units were organized in over
100 ghettos in Poland and the occupied Soviet territories. Some of these engaged
German forces in battle, others conducted sabotage operations. The most notable
armed engagement was the revolt in the Warsaw ghetto from April 19 to May 8,
1943, in which at most 1,250 poorly equipped young Jews held off double their
number of German soldiers armed with tanks and artillery. The activities of such units
were never conceived, however, as a means to dissuade the Germans from continuing
the murder campaign or to save large numbers of Jewish lives; their members sought
rather what they regarded as an honorable form of death. The leader of an underground Jewish fighting organization in the Kraków ghetto declared that his group
was "fighting for three lines in history," so that Jews would be remembered not as
pitiful, passive victims but as proud defenders of their integrity in the face of oblivion.[16] Prisoners in several killing centers and labor camps staged revolts in the hope
of escape, but only a few dozen survived, most of whom joined partisan units in
nearby forests. As many as 30,000 Jews served with the partisans in Poland and the
USSR, which included several dozen groups organized by Jews who identified themselves specifically as such. About 1,500–2,000 Slovakian Jews joined partisan forces
in that country; another 4,500 fought with the Tito movement in Yugoslavia. In
addition, Jews were highly visible in the general resistance movements in Italy, France,
Belgium, the Netherlands, and Greece; for example, three of the six founders of the
French resistance organization Libération were Jews.

   Survival rates among those who engaged in armed resistance were low, especially
in eastern Europe. In all likelihood, the number of Jews who survived the war thanks
to the organized efforts of other Jews to reduce the dimensions of the German
murder campaign did not amount to more than 5–6 percent of the total number of
potential victims in the countries within the Nazi orbit. Once the Nazi regime
decided to seek the death of all Jews within its reach, there was little the intended
targets could do to save themselves.

The Holocaust and the Modern Condition

In the end, the Holocaust's dimensions depended largely upon the action of
bystanders – local non-Jewish populations, their institutions and leaders, and the

governments of states beyond the Nazis' circle of influence. If they wished, local populations could choose to conceal the presence of Jews in their midst and otherwise encumber the German killers. Underground movements could organize escape mechanisms, supply arms to Jewish resistance groups, sabotage deportation trans- ports, convey information about mass killing, and exhort the people in whose name they fought actively to oppose the German murder scheme. Churches, too, could play an exhortatory role and offer refuge to Jews in hiding. Allied and neutral gov- ernments could provide a haven for Jews who escaped the area of Nazi control and offer diplomatic protection to those who remained. Countries at war with Germany could also warn Germans that the murder of Jews would be punished after the war; they could conduct reprisals, bomb rail lines leading to the killing centers, and offer ransom or return of interned German civilians or war prisoners in exchange for Jews slated for death. On the other hand, all of the various bystanders could choose not to do some or all of these things even when opportunities presented themselves. Some could even take actions that directly aided the Germans in carrying out their murderous plans.

Broadly speaking, the bystanders demonstrated the full gamut of possible responses, and the course taken by any particular bystander or group of bystanders in any given situation depended upon the complex interaction of an extensive number of variables. Among these variables, however, a central (though hardly exclusive) role appears to have been played by the place Jews occupied within the bystander's universe of obli- gation, defined by sociologist Helen Fein as "that circle of persons toward whom obligations are owed, to whom the rules apply, and whose injuries call for expiation by the community."[17] Where bystanders believed themselves unequivocally bound to assist threatened Jews, they tended actively to seek ways to do so; where they per- ceived their responsibilities toward those Jews as less than absolute, considerations of self-interest and historical memory played a greater role in their choices.

In twentieth-century Europe, universes of obligation were constructed primarily on the twin bases of citizenship and ethnicity. Between 1789 and 1917 Jews had become citizens of every European state, and they depended upon the legal protections that fact afforded to guarantee their physical security. That dependence was rendered problematic after World War I, however, by the principle, implicit in the postwar settlements for central and eastern Europe, that states might be obligated to foster the needs and interests of a particular ethnic or national group among its citizens more than those of its citizenry as a whole. The Nazi regime instituted that principle upon coming to power, effectively relegating Jews beyond the compass of those whose welfare the German state was bound to consider. In other countries, including Poland, Hungary, and Romania, that principle had been effectively in force during the interwar years, so that under Nazi impact (whether, like Poland, as an occupied country or, like Hungary and Romania, as Germany's allies) their governments (and in Poland's case its underground leadership as well) asked first how action on matters of Jewish concern might affect the ethnic communities to which they saw themselves as primarily responsible. Those ethnic communities, in turn, tended to view their own situation *vis-à-vis* the Nazis separately from that of their Jewish neighbors, even though they shared a common citizenship. In contrast, local populations and leaderships in states like Bulgaria, Denmark, and Italy, where tendencies toward ethnocracy were less pronounced, were inclined to a greater degree to view German attacks upon the Jews of their countries as violations of their own communities.

The protections of citizenship were also attenuated for Jews by the modern dogma of non-interference by one sovereign state (or the international community) in the internal affairs of another. As a result, when German Jews were stripped of their citizenship and its attendant guarantees of life, liberty, and property, no other state or international body was obligated or even permitted to intervene on their behalf. Similarly, the states fighting Germany could not be moved on any grounds other than moral ones to extricate Jews who were not their citizens from mortal danger. Doing so was the sole responsibility of the governments of the threatened Jews' countries of citizenship; if those governments chose not to fulfill their duty, their refusal was no other state's legal concern.

This failure of the modern institutions of citizenship and state sovereignty has been identified by some as but one way in which modernity as a whole is implicated in the Holocaust. In fact, it has been suggested that, far from constituting an atavistic outburst of barbarism that repudiated the civilizing values of the modern west, the Holocaust was actually a logical implementation of those values whose course and outcome were rooted in modernity's very premises. Sociologist Zygmunt Bauman has located the connection between the Holocaust and modern civilization in two of modernity's most essential characteristics: faith in the capacity of empirically based science to engineer a perfect society and the habit of assigning responsibility for implementing the engineers' blueprint to a bureaucracy trained to act according "to solely instrumental-rational criteria . . . dissociated from moral evaluation of the ends." In his view, such a quintessentially modern bureaucracy lacks an effective mechanism for preventing a situation in which "an ideologically obsessed power elite" committed to "a bold design of a better, more reasonable and rational social order . . . [such as] a racially uniform or a classless society" charges it with implementing that design in the most efficient way possible, even if that way is strewn with the corpses of those deviant human beings to whom the new rational order assigns no place. He has suggested that only by restoring the social system that modernity ostensibly destroyed, characterized by small, intimate communities whose members are bound to one another in "personal face-to-face relationships," can a future Holocaust be avoided.[18]

Bauman's characterization of the Holocaust as the product of deliberate social engineering implemented by a faceless, detached bureaucracy might well apply to that part of the Holocaust organized at Wannsee in January 1942. However, some 43 percent of the Jews who perished between 1941 and 1945 as a result of hostile actions by Germans or others died close to home, with little modern technology or administrative sophistication required to end their lives. Most of these were killed by shooting in encounters where they saw their killers face to face. Those who fell victim to the violence of local non-German populations often actually knew their killers personally; they had grown up with them in precisely the sort of premodern communities often supposed to be less amenable to murderous mass violence.

In the end, it may be that the diverse roads by which two-thirds of European Jewry met its death during World War II cast doubt upon whether it is possible to speak of a single "Holocaust" at all. Perhaps the fate of European Jewry during that period is better conceived as a composite of many small-scale, local "holocausts," complete or aborted, each demanding its own particular narrative and not easily congruent with a single hegemonic representation. Modernity may be implicated in some of these holocausts, but not in all.

NOTES

1   On the evolution of the term see, *inter alia*, Gerd Korman, "The Holocaust and American Historical Writing," *Societas* 1 (1972): 251–70; Jon Petrie, "The Secular Word HOLOCAUST: Scholarly Myths, History, and 20th Century Meanings," *Journal of Genocide Research* 2 (2000): 31–63.
2   Quoted in Deborah E. Lipstadt, *Beyond Belief: The American Press and the Coming of the Holocaust 1933–1945* (New York: Free Press, 1986), p. 255.
3   Barbara W. Tuchman, "Introduction," in Gideon Hausner, *Justice in Jerusalem*, 4th edn (New York: Schocken Books, 1977), p. xv.
4   See, for example, Isaiah 47:11: "and desolation [*sho'ah*] shall come upon thee suddenly, which thou shalt not know." The accent properly falls on the latter syllable (*sho'AH*).
5   Raphael Lemkin, *Axis Rule in Occupied Europe: Laws of Occupation, Analysis of Government Proposals for Redress* (Washington DC: Carnegie Endowment for International Peace, 1944), p. 79.
6   Steven T. Katz, *The Holocaust in Historical Context*, vol. 1 (New York: Oxford University Press, 1994), p. 3.
7   For a fuller explication of this theory, see Eberhard Jaeckel, *Hitler's World View: A Blueprint for Power* (Cambridge MA: Harvard University Press, 1981), pp. 47–66, 102–7.
8   Yitzhak Arad, Yisrael Gutman, and Abraham Margaliot, eds, *Documents on the Holocaust: Selected Sources on the Destruction of the Jews of Germany and Austria, Poland, and the Soviet Union* (Jerusalem: Yad Vashem, 1981), p. 127.
9   Some of this research has been collected and presented concisely in Ulrich Hebert, ed., *National Socialist Extermination Policies: Contemporary German Perspectives and Controversies* (New York: Berghahn Books, 2000).
10 For a detailed description of this incident, see Jan T. Gross, *Neighbors: The Destruction of the Jewish Community in Jedwabne, Poland* (Princeton NJ: Princeton University Press, 2001).
11 Arad, Gutman, and Margaliot, *Documents*, pp. 144–5.
12 The text of the conference protocol is reproduced in Arad, Gutman, and Margaliot, *Documents*, pp. 253ff. The figure of 11 million included Jews in European countries beyond the Nazi orbit – Ireland, Portugal, Spain, Sweden, Switzerland, (European) Turkey, and the United Kingdom.
13 Yehuda Bauer, *The Holocaust in Historical Perspective* (Seattle: University of Washington Press, 1978), p. 7.
14 For details of these and other negotiations, see Yehuda Bauer, *Jews for Sale? Nazi–Jewish Negotiations, 1933–1945* (New Haven CT: Yale University Press, 1994).
15 See Gunnar S. Paulsson, *Secret City: The Hidden Jews of Warsaw 1940–1945* (New Haven CT: Yale University Press, 2002).
16 Quoted in Y. Margolin (Peled), *Krakov haYehudit 1939–1943* (Tel Aviv: Hakibbutz Hameuchad, 1993), p. 163.
17 Helen Fein, *Accounting for Genocide: National Responses and Jewish Victimization during the Holocaust* (Chicago: University of Chicago Press, 1979), p. 33.
18 Zygmunt Bauman, *Modernity and the Holocaust* (Ithaca NY: Cornell University Press, 1989), pp. 85–116 passim.

GUIDE TO FURTHER READING

Omer Bartov, *Mirrors of Destruction: War, Genocide, and Modern Identity* (Oxford: Oxford University Press, 2000). A highly original analysis placing the Holocaust within the context of modern warfare and mass violence.

Yehuda Bauer, *Rethinking the Holocaust* (New Haven CT: Yale University Press, 2001). Empirical studies and essays summarizing four decades of research by an architect of the field of Holocaust studies.

Christopher R. Browning, *Ordinary Men: Reserve Police Battalion 101 and the Final Solution in Poland* (New York: Harper Perennial, 1993). Pathbreaking study of German soldiers who perpetrated mass shooting operations.

Christopher R. Browning, *The Origins of the Final Solution: The Evolution of Nazi Jewish Policy, September 1939–March 1942* (Lincoln: University of Nebraska Press, 2004). Comprehensive analysis and evaluation of the latest research concerning the decision to begin systematic mass killing (with contributions by Jürgen Matthäus).

Inga Clendinnen, *Reading the Holocaust* (Cambridge: Cambridge University Press, 1999). Thought-provoking reflections of an anthropologist confronting research and memoir literature on perpetrators and victims.

David Engel, *The Holocaust: The Third Reich and the Jews* (Harlow: Longman, 2000). Short, concise introduction to Holocaust history, including 28 key documents.

Barbara Engelking, *Holocaust and Memory* (New Haven CT: Yale University Press, 2001). Incisive study by a Polish social psychologist of how Jewish survivors still living in Poland lived through the war and came to grips with their experience afterwards.

Henry Friedlander, *The Origins of Nazi Genocide: From Euthanasia to the Final Solution* (Chapel Hill: University of North Carolina Press, 1995). Detailed, well-documented discussion of the connections between Nazi killings of Jews, Sinti and Roma, and the disabled.

Saul Friedländer, *Nazi Germany and the Jews*, vol. 1: *The Years of Persecution, 1933–1939* (New York: Harper Collins, 1997). First of a planned two volumes synthesizing the experiences of Germans and Jews during the Nazi years through a highly original narrative style.

François Furet, ed., *Unanswered Questions: Nazi Germany and the Genocide of the Jews* (New York: Schocken Books, 1989). Fifteen articles by leading scholars; still unsurpassed for its comprehensive scope and the fundamental issues it treats.

Israel Gutman, *The Jews of Warsaw: Ghetto, Underground, Revolt* (Bloomington: Indiana University Press, 1982). The standard history of the fate of Europe's largest Jewish community under Nazi rule.

Raul Hilberg, *The Destruction of the European Jews*, 3rd edn (New Haven CT: Yale University Press, 2003). Originally published in 1961, still the standard work detailing how the Nazi state organized the systematic mass killing of Jews.

Michael R. Marrus, *The Holocaust in History* (Hanover NH: University Press of New England, 1987). Survey of the development of historical thinking about the Holocaust to the mid-1980s.

Dan Michman, *Holocaust Historiography: A Jewish Perspective* (London: Valentine Mitchell, 2003). Stimulating essays critically examining the fundamental vocabulary of Holocaust research, emphasizing the experiences of Jewish victims.

CHAPTER THIRTY-ONE

Memories of World War II and the Holocaust in Europe

HAROLD MARCUSE

Since the late 1980s the study of "memory," of individual and group ideas about past events, has been a rapidly growing subfield of history. While the literature on memory is large and studies of specific events abound, there is still no common terminology or methods.[1] This essay thus begins by defining key concepts, and then reviews developments across Europe that illustrate key principles of the workings of memory.

"World War II," "the Holocaust," and "memory" may seem to be relatively clear concepts, but closer examination reveals a broad range of different meanings. Although September 1, 1939 is the official starting date of the war, in retrospect – especially for the affected populations – the Japanese invasion of China in 1937, the German occupation of the Sudetenland in 1938, or of Czechoslovakia in March 1939 might all be remembered as part of the war. Similarly, we must ask when "the war" ended in countries that either collaborated or were quickly conquered and then allied themselves with the conquerors, such as Vichy France, Norway, and Hungary. Do opposing groups within such countries, such as collaborators and persecutees, experience different terminal dates of war? Also, to what extent can memories of World War II include events during the global dates of the war, but before or after the cessation of military hostilities in a given place? For example, do US memories of the war include events before the attack on Pearl Harbor in 1941, and do European memories of the war include events between VE-Day in May 1945 and the Japanese surrender in August? Such questions show that memories of an event, especially of a complex event, depend to a large extent on who is doing the remembering. This insight applies not only to individuals but also to national and regional communities, and to different groups within those communities. Civilians, soldiers, collaborators, labor conscripts, prisoners of war, deserters, victims of persecution, and members of resistance organizations will all have different referents for their memories of "the war."

Since an analysis of memories of wartime requires a definition of "war" that goes beyond open military conflict, we should include the vast numbers of non-military persecutees and deaths, both intentional and unintentional. As David Engel's essay in this collection shows (chapter 30), the term "Holocaust" emerged during the decades after 1945 to denote the German attempt to systematically murder all Jews within its sphere of influence. It is thus itself a product of the ways individuals, groups, and societies have tried to express and share their mental images of the World War II era. Understandings of "Holocaust" range from narrower definitions encompassing the period of murder with exterminatory intent, from 1941 to 1945, to broader conceptions that include the period of isolation and persecution that led up to genocide, which are variously dated from 1933, 1935, or 1938. There is also a range of opinion about which groups should be included: whether only Jews (and perhaps Gypsies), or also groups with less fixed defining characteristics, such as political affiliation, religion, employment status, and sexual orientation. In this essay, "memories of World War II" includes events we now see as precursors of war, as well as experiences of occupation, and programs of persecution and genocide.

Just as "war" covers a range of events, "memory" is also a very elastic concept. It can denote what individuals remember about events they personally experienced, or what they recall to mind about events they learned about "secondhand" from eyewitnesses or news media, or through photographs, films, memoirs, scholarly histories, and historical novels. And, whether experienced firsthand or learned, individual memories are reinforced and modified by communication within and between social groups. Maurice Halbwachs, an early twentieth-century theorist of "collective memory," went so far as to argue that every individual memory exists only within the social context that shapes it. The dependence of individual memory on group context raises the question of how groups remember – be they smaller, more personally connected associations such as families and social networks, or larger social groups sharing little more than a common language or access to institutions of information such as schools, museums, and the same news and entertainment media.

Since analysis requires that we distinguish between individual, group, and collective memory processes, I offer the following conventions. *Remember* will denote the recalling to mind of lived and learned experiences by individuals, *memory work* the individual and group efforts to acquire and disseminate information about the past, and *recollect* the social process of sharing information about the past among members of a collectivity. Thus we can distinguish between more personal *memories* (experienced and learned), and more general *recollections*. While recollections are explicit and public, *collective memories* are more general feelings and attitudes about the past that may remain unarticulated. They usually originate in lived experience, but can shift according to subsequent experiences, including interpretations provided by public recollection. Discerning collective memories requires careful interpretations of a range of sources.

Collective memories are held in common by members of *memory groups*. A given individual is exposed to the recollective activities of multiple memory groups. These range from the people who experienced an event, to intimate groups including their family and friends, to closed private groups such as veterans' organizations, to open public associations and groups such as history workshops or political parties, to local, regional, and national governments, all the way to national and international publics that utilize the same information and entertainment media. Thus, collective memories arise from the interaction between individual experiences (some related to the events in question, others not), inchoate feelings about the past, accounts of historical events shared privately within memory groups, and the public circulation – recollection – of historical interpretations. Terms such as "official" and "public" commemoration and recollection indicate that such interpretations of the past are intentionally manufactured by governments, elites, and institutions to suit their goals.

When examining how past events influence people's thoughts and behaviors, we often find that unacknowledged and unarticulated feelings are important. In contrast to collective memories, such deeper feelings about historical events may be common across multiple memory groups, even though they are not explicitly shared. *Historical consciousness* can denote this hypothetical substrate of awareness about the past. It is useful when discussing the "return" of "repressed" or denied memories. In contrast to collective memories, historical consciousness can imply a hypothetical "truer" knowledge about the past that persists despite psychological needs and recollective attempts to change it. I say hypothetical because we do not know whether a more accurate version of any given past exists (either in the historical record or in individual or group consciousness), nor whether that version will ultimately emerge in the public sphere. However, some scholars of memory use psychological terms such as anamnesis (the recovery of buried memories) to describe situations where long-accepted recollections of the past are challenged by newer, presumably more accurate ones. Ultimately, this is a philosophical question of the existence of a single absolute truth, as opposed to multiple coexisting perceptions of reality. An examination of collective memories indicates that, with regard to the past, multiple perspectives coexist, although over time they may converge on common images.

How do individual remembering, group memory work, and public recollection interact? The public dissemination of visions of the past occurs through many channels: the mass media (television, radio, the internet, newspapers and magazines), films, memoirs, novels, scholarly works, textbooks, classroom instruction, museums, laws, and compensation schemes, as well as a host of explicitly commemorative activities such as the establishment of monuments and memorials, and the marking of anniversary dates with speeches and holidays. These disseminated visions both derive from and shape group memories. They provide the primary source material historians use to discern broadly shared collective memories. The relative importance of these different "vectors" of memory (a term coined by historian Henry Rousso) varies both over time and from country to country. For instance, in Soviet-bloc countries such as Poland and East Germany, some memory groups were quickly repressed so that government-organized commemorative activity would not be challenged. In contrast, private associations of former resistance fighters and concentration camp survivors necessitated compromises in Belgium and France. Commercially produced films and other media events were more important in West Germany, where the public activity of memory groups, from former persecutees to army and SS veterans, was monitored and often inhibited by governmental agencies.

The following country-by-country survey illustrates some of the important principles of collective remembering. West and East Germany, Austria, and Italy show how governments were able to reverse historical causality, as well as how memory events helped to precipitate change. The formerly German-occupied countries of western Europe show how the postwar goal of national unity shaped their recollection of the past, while Poland illustrates how memories repressed by Soviet control resurfaced decades later to challenge and change governmental recollective paradigms. In Britain and the Soviet Union, victorious powers with fewer uncomfortable events to exclude from recollection, the trajectory of recollection has been smoother. Ultimately, as time passes, across Europe we see a convergence of recollection around common meanings.

West and East Germany

The successor states of the obvious instigator of World War II had the most at stake in what events would be recollected.[2] After the war, the claims to compensation or political recognition of the many groups that had been repressed under Nazi rule depended upon clear memories of what had happened under Nazism. Conversely, those who had enjoyed wealth and power under Nazism knew that their continued status was predicated on the repression of those memories. At first, the victorious Allies exercised complete control of the public sphere, and they were determined to break the elite status of former Nazis. The International Military Tribunal at Nuremberg was to facilitate that break by establishing a common understanding of the causes and crimes of World War II. However, the Allies' competing visions of the postwar world order soon mushroomed into the Cold War, and the Soviet Union withdrew from the tribunal. Successor trials were conducted with diminishing public presence, and were wrapped up by 1949, when the two German states were established.

The western Allies were interested in a strong, autonomous West German state. The United States provided financial assistance to rebuild the economy, and yielded to German pressure to rehabilitate compromised elites to run it. In contrast, the Soviet Union was interested only in a loyal and subservient satellite state in the east. It forced East Germany to elevate the recollection of communist resistors far above all others. In both cases, after 1949 spontaneous early manifestations of group memories were excluded from public life. The western use of compromised Nazi elites to create a West German army and civil service necessitated the silencing of surviving persecutees' voices. To highlight the Cold War legitimation of this restoration, western recollection focused on the sufferings of POWs still being held by the Soviet Union. In East Germany the government's recollective efforts highlighted communist resistance against Nazism, while ignoring German suffering and pointing to West Germany as the home of all German perpetrators. Over the following decades each government pursued a different recollective strategy: the West worked indirectly by bestowing or withholding support from memory groups, while the East took direct control and created institutions of memory that explicitly pursued its formulated goals.

Within a decade of war's end in West Germany, the government strategy had succeeded. Nazi perpetrators, their victims, and even resistance against Nazism had disappeared from the public recollection of that era, leaving primarily long-suffering civilians as objects of commemoration. This situation did not last long, however. In the late 1950s and early 1960s the recollection of Germans as victims (of Nazi and then of postwar Soviet oppression) was challenged by the public reception of memory events from abroad that featured graphic evidence of German crimes. The West German release of the French concentration camp film *Night and Fog* in 1956 (which the West German government at first attempted to suppress), and prominent trials of Nazi perpetrators in the early 1960s, are examples of such events. The magnitude of the change in public interest is, however, most visible in the reception of Anne Frank's *Diary of a Young Girl*. The first German publication of 4,500 copies in 1950 did not reach a large audience. Then a new German paperback edition in 1955 immediately found a huge audience, selling 700,000 copies in 18 printings over the next five years. That was followed by the huge success of the German stage adaptation in 1957, with 2,150 performances for 1.75 million viewers by 1960. A 1959 film version of the play was seen by more than 4 million viewers in Germany within a year.

The *Diary*, featuring a presumptively non-German victim (Anne had emigrated from Germany at age four), in turn stimulated demand for recollective attention to aspects of the past that had been excluded from official recollection. By the early 1960s there was widespread interest in stories about Hitler's intended victims during the war, as the German and international success of publications by Bruno Apitz, Primo Levi, Leon Poliakov, and William Shirer attest.

Still, official West German recollection did not change until the student unrest of the late 1960s explicitly rejected this myth of Germans as victims. In 1969 Willy Brandt, who had opposed the Nazis since the early 1930s and agitated against them from exile in Scandinavia, was elected West German chancellor. One of his most famous actions, when international attention was focused on him for receiving the Nobel Peace Prize, was to kneel in front of the Warsaw ghetto memorial during a state visit to Poland in December 1970. This recognition of Nazi Germany's primary victims implicitly acknowledged German perpetration. Polls showed that the German public was evenly split over this symbolic act.

During the 1970s scholarly works and commemorative confessions, such as Chancellor Schmidt's 1978 admission that he had witnessed the anti-Jewish *Kristallnacht* rampages in 1938, undermined the basis of another West German recollective myth, namely that Germans had been ignorant of the persecution going on around them. It also challenged the myth of the victimization of "Aryan" German civilians. In 1979 the national broadcast of the US television miniseries *Holocaust* introduced a recollective paradigm in which Germans as victimizers figured prominently. Seen by almost half of the entire West German populace over 14 years of age, the broadcast catalyzed the formation of many local history workshops that researched the Nazi period, and prompted a series of Nazi-era themed history day competitions in West German schools. However, there was also a "boomerang effect" with renewed clamoring to view "Aryan" German civilians as the primary victims of World War II. A noteworthy example of this persistence was the 1983 West German television miniseries *Heimat* (Homeland), which was created explicitly as a response to *Holocaust*. It portrayed a German village with no victims of persecution, while sympathetically evoking the sufferings of the local populace. Such opposing responses are typical of memory events. They are attributable to divisions along generational and political lines, and work themselves out as generational shifts in powerholding elites take place.[3]

The ultimate demise of the myth of victimization in West German recollection began in 1985. Chancellor Kohl's attempt to have US President Reagan acknowledge German soldiers as victims at a military cemetery on the 40th anniversary of the end of the war backfired when the US and German publics responded with outrage. Additionally, in 1986–7, apologist agitation from members of the war-participant

and subsequent "white" (too young to have been drafted) generations fueled what
became known as the Historians' Debate. In that memory event most West German
daily and weekly newspapers and many German and international historical journals
published essays by prominent historians debating the pros and cons of Germany's
ongoing obligation to conduct its politics in the shadow of World War II. This give-
and-take had ended by 1988, when the leader of the West German parliament had
to resign after he invoked it during an official ceremony commemorating the
November 9, 1938 pogroms. With the unification of Germany in 1990 the present-
day basis for feelings of victimization – the postwar division of the country – disappeared, taking with it the utility of using recollection to shore them up. Although
the mythic victimization is still apparent in German popular culture, it is no longer
a part of official West German recollection.

Under the auspices of the Soviet Union in the tightly controlled public sphere of
East Germany, feelings of victimization were given no space and did not appear until
after the demise of the government in 1989. Instead, "anti-fascist" (namely communist) resistance was given center stage in public recollection from the early 1950s
on. Although the persecution of and even resistance by Jews did figure in official East
German recollection until the early 1950s, it was marginalized thereafter. Government
control of recollection was cemented after the 1953 uprisings, when the two major
associations of persecutees were brought firmly into line with the perceived needs of
state commemoration. Soon thereafter the ruling SED party began the construction
of national memorial sites, which were dedicated at Buchenwald in 1957, Ravensbrück
in 1959, and Sachsenhausen in 1961. From 1962 and 1968 a World War I memorial
in the center of Berlin was redesigned as a central "monument to the victims of
fascism and the two world wars." It featured side-by-side graves of an unknown
"anti-fascist resistance fighter" and an unknown soldier. The central sculpture in
Buchenwald also illustrates the state's recollective emphasis on resistance: it is a larger-
than-life sculpture depicting the heroic struggle and solidarity of camp inmates, but
not their persecution at the hands of fellow Germans.

Although there were some indications that East German recollection was becoming more pluralistic in the 1980s, there were no major challenges to the dominant
paradigm as in West Germany until the demise of the SED government in 1989.
After that, as elsewhere in the former eastern bloc, recollections of the Nazi period
were overshadowed by more immediate memories of the Soviet repression that followed it. In contrast to other countries in the former eastern bloc, however, East
Germany's 1990 annexation by West Germany placed it in a recollective sphere where
such recollection was inhibited. East Germans were forced to accept the recollective
agenda that had developed in the West. While individual memories of victimization
in the post-1945 period remain a strong element of historical consciousness in the
former East, they are excluded from public recollective activity, which is controlled
by the West.

Since 1990 recollection in Germany has been punctuated by a succession of
memory events, many of them focused on how the nation should balance recollections of the Nazi past between Germans as resistors, Germans as perpetrators, and
commemorations of the victims of Nazism. Vigorous public discussions of the 1993
Holocaust film *Schindler's List* (the story of a German businessman who rescued
Jews), Daniel Goldhagen's graphic indictment of Germans as vicious antisemites in

his 1995 book *Hitler's Willing Executioners*, and the 1995 publication of the diaries of Victor Klemperer, a German Jew who survived in Dresden, provide examples for each group.[4] Those discussions were less about the historical facts *per se*, than about the utility or detriment of certain interpretations of those facts for the present.

Austria and Italy

Since Austria had become part of Hitler's Germany with its overwhelming vote for annexation in March 1938, and Mussolini's Italy had been part of the Berlin–Rome "Axis" since 1936 and a full military ally since May 1939, once might expect that they would have faced the same Allied sanctions and existential memory questions after the war. However, before the war ended both managed to position themselves on the side of the victors, burying memories of their governments' and people's participation in war and genocide. While the recollective road in Italy has remained essentially uncontested until the present, Austria experienced vigorous memory events in the mid-1960s and 1970s before a radically new paradigm began to form in the 1980s.[5]

Although the historical record shows that Austrians overwhelmingly favored annexation by Nazi Germany, a recollective consensus quickly emerged among Austrian adherents and opponents of Nazism that Austria had been "Hitler's first victim." This view was endorsed by the Allies in their 1943 Moscow declaration and subsequently enshrined in the provisional government's April 1945 declaration of independence, which made the outlandish claim that Hitler's government

> had used the complete political, economic and cultural annexation of the country to lead the people of Austria, which had been rendered powerless and without its own will, into a senseless and hopeless war of conquest that no Austrian had ever wanted, nor had ever been able to anticipate or approve, in order to wage war on peoples against whom no true Austrian ever held feelings of enmity or hate.[6]

This historically one-sided but mutually beneficial recollective arrangement allowed both former opponents and former Nazis to participate in public life without coming to terms with the past. In spite of acrimonious public discussions when the Nazi allegiances of highly visible public figures were exposed in 1965 (when Nazi-friendly remarks by a professor triggered the lynching of a former anti-Nazi) and 1975 (when Chancellor Kreisky, a Jew, defended his coalition partner Friedrich Peter, a former SS man), the recollection of national victimization persisted essentially unchanged from the end of the Allied denazification program in 1948 to the international furor over former German army officer and UN secretary general Kurt Waldheim's presidential candidacy in 1986 (when he was elected and served out his six-year term). Although evidence about the extent of Waldheim's participation in a massacre perpetrated by his unit was not conclusive, the international outrage about it was sufficient to spark a national movement towards reexamining Austria's role as a perpetrator in World War II and the Holocaust. This historical reexamination was boosted by a number of publications at the time of the fiftieth anniversary of the annexation in 1988. Finally, under Chancellor Vranitzky in 1991, the Austrian government officially acknowledged Austria's role in the Holocaust.[7]

The late appearance in public recollection of the substantial Austrian participation in genocide illustrates what one might call the "time-lag principle" of recollection, namely that when significant historical experiences are excluded from public recollection, recollection may still be revised decades later to include them. This depends on the goals of those doing the remembering. As the generation of participants and eyewitnesses retires from the public arena, their grandchildren often develop an interest in reexamining inconsistencies in recollected history. This third generation's awareness of the past comes both from memories acquired in the private family sphere, and from information transmitted in schools and through other channels of public recollection. Thus the grandchildren are most apt to feel a need to reconcile discrepancies. Some evidence suggests that there is a "disparity principle" of recollection, whereby the magnitude of the gap between actual events and public recollections determines the virulence of the recovery of unrecollected experiences. The more measured discussion and relatively static forms of recollection in Italy, where wartime support for Nazism and genocide was more ambivalent, bears out this view.

In Italy as in Austria, public recollection of World War II has avoided an examination of Italy's alliance with Germany and its own role in genocide until recent years.[8] However, in contrast to Austria's unwavering participation in war and genocide, Italy's role in the unrecollected events was more ambivalent. On the one hand, Mussolini's Fascist Party inspired Hitler's organization of the Nazi Party, and, as noted, Italy was Germany's first military ally. Beginning already in 1938, Mussolini supported Hitler by passing discriminatory laws against Jews and interning non-Italian Jews in camps. On the other hand, Mussolini had shown clear hostility to Hitler's expansionist designs on Austria prior to their mutual support of Franco in the Spanish Civil War in 1936. Italians had never supported Mussolini as massively as Germans and Austrians followed Hitler, and even under Mussolini during the war Italy had been a relative haven for Jews fleeing from German-occupied countries. In July 1943, after numerous debacles in the war, including the Allied landing in Sicily, Mussolini's own government deposed and arrested him. Rescued by the Germans and reinstalled in German-occupied northern Italy, he was finally captured and executed by Italian partisans as the German occupation fell apart in April 1945. In the end, about 8,000 of Italy's 40,000 Jews were deported to Hitler's camps, most of them during the German occupation. This 80 percent survival rate was far higher than in most other European countries.

After the war the historical evidence of the Italian rejection of Mussolini was used to obscure Italy's own expansionist aspirations and collusion in genocide. In 1946 Minister of Justice Palmiro Togliatti, who was also head of the Italian Communist Party, decreed a general amnesty for wartime crimes. His reasoning, as outlandish as the Austrian declaration, neatly excised fascist collaboration from the national historical record: since fascism was not part of the "Italian cultural tradition," bureaucrats who served the fascist government bore no responsibility for its crimes. In the wake of such pronouncements Italian recollection focused exclusively on the partisan resistance against Italian fascism and German occupation, leaving all responsibility for war and genocide to the Germans. During the 1960s, especially after 1968, this interpretation of the past was challenged by a younger generation organized partially in Italy's communist party PCI, which opposed the ruling Christian Democrats in 1960, when they formed a coalition with the Mussolini-nostalgist *Movimento Sociale Italiano* party. However, the PCI's focus on war-era "red resistance" was delegitimized by the left-wing terrorism of the 1970s, and met its final demise with the fall of the Soviet bloc at the end of the 1980s. Since then Italian recollection has paid slightly more attention both to indigenous participation in war and genocide and to the experiences of Italians deported into the German extermination, concentration, and labor camp systems. With the passage of time, recollection of the war era in Italy seems to have lost both its unifying and dividing power. In recent years Italy has moved to a more Europeanized memory of the Holocaust. In 2001 Italy introduced January 27, the day of the liberation of Auschwitz, as a national holiday.

As the cases above show, the "objective" range of historical events and behaviors does not form the primary referent of recollection. The gap between the range of historical events and the spectrum of recollected events highlights that what is recollected depends on the goals of those who control recollection, not on what actually transpired. This principle is also illustrated by recollection in countries that had been occupied by Nazi Germany, where images of national resistance and suffering were invoked and memories of support for Nazism generally remained dormant.

Netherlands, Belgium, France, and Denmark

While memories of Nazism were potentially extremely detrimental for the governments of Nazi Germany's successor states and main ally, countries that had collaborated only after they had been conquered militarily had much more flexibility in choosing which memories they wished to foster, and which they wished to suppress. The Netherlands, Belgium, and France were all quickly conquered and occupied in May and June 1940. There was no experience of sustained military combat *per se*, and each country suffered a more or less harsh and humiliating occupation. Although there were also significant differences in the official and popular responses to German occupation in each country, these had little to do with the recollective strategies they pursued after the war. All three wished to rebuild a unifying national identity.

Occupied Belgium had been marked by a split between a vigorous left-wing (communist) resistance, and collaboration among both the Flemish, who, feeling excluded from power after World War I, were generally more supportive of the German occupiers, and the francophone Wallonian government, which with King Leopold III agreed to a "strategic" collaboration that would ostensibly preserve some Belgian autonomy.[9] In order to bridge the postwar division between these groups, Belgian recollection did not differentiate between underground resistance and collaborationist "patriotism," but focused instead on anyone who had suffered because of their patriotic goals. In 1946–7 a difficult compromise was reached regarding the compensation and recognition of survivors who had been arrested or deported from Belgium. Designed by a leader of the communist resistance who had become a government minister, it made persecution the only criterion for social aid, but vaguely defined "patriotic activity" the standard for honorary recognition. The ultimate effect was to exclude surviving Jews from the latter category. It took some time for this homogenizing paradigm to be established, as the controversy over the reinstatement of King Leopold shows. The public debate about whether he had been a traitor or a martyr came to a head with a referendum in March 1950, in which over 57 percent of the populace supported Leopold's return. This result belied deep internal divisions, however, with large majorities in the Flemish regions in favor of his patriotic position on collaboration, but only a minority in Brussels and Wallonia supporting his return. Public outcry – manifested in bloody riots and strikes – was so strong that within days Leopold transferred his royal powers to his son. The legacies of this delicate compromise are still evident today, in that the Jewish Holocaust is largely absent from Belgian recollection.

The Dutch government had refused to work with the Germans and gone into exile, so in spite of extensive popular collaboration there was no political split to be bridged as there was in Belgium. Rather, the belated liberation of the country had caused widespread starvation and devastation – while the Allies had liberated Belgium by October 1944, the Dutch suffered through the "hunger winter" of 1944–5 before the Germans were driven out in the spring. In this situation of postwar chaos the government discouraged the formation of groups of various kinds of resistors and persecutees, recollecting instead the solidarity and suffering of the entire nation. This was expressed in the iconic sculptures "Dockworker" (1952), which commemorates the February 1941 strike of Amsterdam municipal workers, and "Destroyed City" (1953) in Rotterdam.

In contrast to the decades of relatively static recollection in Belgium, the 1960s saw a shift in the Netherlands, whereby memories of the Jewish Holocaust came to play a major role. This change was heralded by the popularity of the television series *The Occupation*, broadcast in 21 installments from 1960 to 1965, and the success of Jacques Presser's comprehensive portrayal of the murder of Holland's Jews, *Downfall* (1965), which sold 100,000 copies within a year. It was at this time that the iconic figure of Anne Frank, reimported to Holland after her meteoric success abroad, established itself as the premier symbol of the Jewish Holocaust in the Netherlands.

In France the political division apparent in the low countries was expressed territorially: Germany occupied the northern part of the country, while a collaborationist government under Marshal Pétain was installed in Vichy to administer the southern part.[10] Those opposed to collaboration set up a government-in-exile in London under Charles de Gaulle. After the war a bloody purification (*épuration*) of collaborators swept the country, after which an uneasy truce between leftist-underground and conservative-exile resistance was formed. A national recollection not dissimilar to Belgium's emerged, forgetting collaboration, emphasizing resistance, equating the different groups that had been deported, and ignoring the Holocaust. As in Belgium, much commemorative ritual was based on forms developed for the veterans of World War I.

In contrast to Belgium, however, a major change in recollection took place a few years after de Gaulle's 1969 resignation in France. It was initiated by Marcel Ophüls' film *The Sorrow and the Pity* (1971), and Robert Paxton's book *Vichy France: Old Guard and New Order* (1972, France 1973), which sparked a reexamination of France's collaborationist past similar to what happened in West Germany after Brandt's election in 1969. In the 1970s France, like West Germany, embarked on an odyssey of historical reexamination that filled in numerous historical "white spots" and abandoned some of the distorting myths about popular and governmental resistance to Germany during the war. The arrests and trials of French collaborators Klaus Barbie

(1983–7), Paul Touvier (1989–1994), and Maurice Papon (1998) were further memory events that closed gaps in French recollection and continued this trend towards historical accuracy. In this case, as in West Germany, a generational shift coinciding with a major change of government transformed the dominant recollective paradigm.

Poland

In contrast to the Nazi-occupied countries of western and northern Europe, in Poland, due to the low status of Slavs in the Nazi racist worldview, there was little opportunity for collaboration. The two-year Soviet occupation of eastern Poland and the resulting political schism between nationalist and communist Poles prior to the German conquest resulted in Polish governments-in-exile in both London and Moscow. The majority nationalist Catholic populace experienced World War II as a victimization of the Polish Home Army by both the Soviets and the Germans. However, the postwar settlement that put Poland in the Soviet sphere of influence ensured that memories of persecution of Catholic Poles were subordinated to a government-dictated recollection in which communist anti-fascists (and initially also Jews) had resisted the German invaders. As Michael Steinlauf's 1997 book *Bondage to the Dead: Poland and the Memory of the Holocaust* makes clear, this has made the history of recollection in Poland quite complex.

Steinlauf uses two side-by-side posters in Warsaw in April 1945 to show how the communist leadership excluded the Polish army from public recollection. One read "Shame to the Fascist Flunkeys of the Home Army," while the other declared "Glory to the Heroic Defenders of the Ghetto." In fact, it was widely known in Poland that the Soviet army had not only perpetrated a massacre of over 4,000 Polish Home Army officers at Katyn in 1941, but had also stood by while the German army decimated the civilian population of Warsaw during the city's uprising in the summer of 1944.

This disjuncture between popular memories and official public recollection reinforced a strong undercurrent of antisemitic prejudices among the overwhelmingly Catholic populace, which identified the repressive communist leadership as Jewish or Jewish controlled. By 1947 Catholic Poles had murdered some 1,500–2,000 of the surviving Jewish Poles who had returned to their homes after the war. An uneasy truce of silence about the extent of popular antisemitism emerged that held through destalinization after 1956 until a younger, postwar generation of students challenged the government in 1968.

In this case the government bureaucracy, which had become more attuned to Polish historical consciousness, used recollection to deflect criticism away from itself. The government identified the student intelligentsia as Zionists, thereby unleashing a wave of popular violence that drove 20,000 of the remaining Jewish Poles out of the country. The communist Polish government's willingness to abandon its Jewish citizens in order to stymie a challenge from younger constituents indicates that its recollective policies were making expedient use of the historical consciousness of the antisemitic older populace.

Steinlauf titles the subsequent years from 1970 to 1989 as a new period of "memory reconstructed," although the evidence he presents instead demonstrates continuity with past views, punctuated in the 1980s by a scattering of historically reflective, anti-antisemitic publications, speeches, and films. These memory events were vehemently rejected by the populace at large. The most notable were the Polish television broadcast of Claude Lanzmann's nine hour documentary *Shoah* in 1985, and a 1987 article by literary critic Jan Błoński. These were followed in 1989 by a controversy about whether Carmelite nuns should be allowed to maintain a convent on the Auschwitz concentration camp grounds. The Catholic primate of Poland, Cardinal Glemp, concluded his defense of the nuns by blaming Jews for the international disapproval of the Polish Catholic recollective agenda: "If there is no antipolonism, there will be no antisemitism in us." It took a personal letter from the Vatican in 1993 to move the nuns to vacate the premises, on which they nevertheless left a 20-foot cross that still stands today, a monument to memory's disregard of history.

Still, these memory events did create an awareness of an alternative way of viewing the past, even if no group yet held it as their collective memory. Steinlauf adds a tentative question mark to his final period, 1989 to 1995: "Memory regained?" At the time of his book's publication in 1997, support for recollection of the brutal decimation of Poland's Jewish population was increasing, as evidenced by late 1990s pronouncements by prominent politicians, the staging of international commemorative anniversaries, and attempts to resurrect Jewish cultural life. However, a memory event beginning in 2000 offers more conclusive evidence: the Polish publication of Polish-US scholar Jan Gross's book *Neighbors*, about an especially horrific massacre perpetrated in 1941 by Polish villagers in Jedwabne on the village's Jewish population.[11] While rejection of the evidence that Jews were victims and some Poles perpetrators was still vehement among some memory groups, public recollection in Poland now clearly includes both prewar Jewish culture and its destruction during World War II. In the anniversary years 1995 and 2005, Poland hosted huge international commemorative ceremonies at Auschwitz.

Britain and the Soviet Union

If neither willing nor forced collaboration with Nazi Germany necessarily spawned memory events that changed the course of postwar recollection, the clear anti-German positions of Britain and the Soviet Union were all the more likely to experience smooth and celebratory recollective paths, and indeed they did (in the Soviet Union until the regime change of the 1980s). Although some emphases have shifted over the years, the basic icons of public and private memory have remained unchanged until the present.

In Britain World War II provided a series of unifying motifs: the Blitz on London, the home front, the BBC war reporting, cracking the Enigma code, the D-Day landing in Normandy, and the wartime conferences of the "big three" (Churchill, Roosevelt, and Stalin), in which Britain had again appeared as a premier world power.[12] An image of aristocrats and workers weathering the air raids side-by-side in underground shelters represented cross-class solidarity. Although historical research since the 1970s has called such images into question, they still dominate public recollection. Their functions have evolved from supporting economic pragmatism in the 1950s, to critiquing affluent society in the 1960s and 1970s, to supplying icons for the heritage industry of the Thatcherite 1980s. Since the 1990s memories of World War II in Britain have taken on a less heroic and more reflective "multicultural" character, with some attention paid to the contributions of women and soldiers from British colonies, and to the genocide of the Jews, with which Britain had little to do. The latter found its most potent expression in the June 2000 opening of a permanent "Holocaust exhibition" in the Imperial War Museum. Only since the turn of the millennium have some limited challenges arisen, such as questions regarding the unrestricted bombing of civilian targets in the later phase of the war, and the failure to act on intelligence about the mass slaughter of Jews in eastern Europe, but these issues show no sign of tarnishing the power of the established images.

In the Soviet Union the recollection of the "Great Patriotic War," as World War II is known there, was one of unabashed national heroism under Stalin's leadership.[13] Stalin excluded some events from public recollection, most notably his 1939 alliance with Germany and co-invasion of Poland, as well as his staggering military defeats, many of which were due to his own unpreparedness and misguided strategy. The trenchant defense of Moscow in the winter of 1941–2, the bitter "900-day" (a recollected, not an actual number) siege of Leningrad, and the heroic defense of Stalingrad in 1942–3 were given center stage in public recollection of the war. These leitmotifs of unitary Soviet recollection persisted unchallenged until the loosening of government control of the public sphere under Gorbachev's glasnost policy after 1985. The only notable shift prior to the 1980s came after Stalin's death in 1953, when his "cult of the Great Patriotic War," as Nina Tumarkin has called it, was destalinized. In his 1956 speech denouncing Stalin, Nikita Khrushchev shifted the recollective emphasis away from Stalin's leadership to the party and the people: "The main role and the main credit for the victorious ending of the war belongs to our Communist Party, to the armed forces of the Soviet Union, and to the tens of millions of Soviet people raised by the party." When this recollective paradigm was in turn "desacralized" under perestroika during the late 1980s, it was also displaced by more urgent memories of Stalinist repression both before and after World War II.

Since the May 9, 1985 celebration had been planned under Gorbachev's predecessor, it was not affected by Gorbachev's new course. In the following years a number of repressed films and literary works, such as Kuznezov's *Babi Yar*, were published. On May 8, 1990, the eve of the "Day of Victory," Gorbachev laid out the new paradigm of recollection in a speech he titled "Lessons of War and Victory."[14] He praised the "brotherhood of nations" that had made victory possible, and criticized Stalin for having punished some of those nations. He also mentioned for the first time the role of the western Allies and the extended illegal imprisonment of German POWs in the Soviet Union after the war.

When the Soviet Union broke apart in December 1991, Soviet recollection became Russian recollection (which has not changed significantly, although it has diminished in importance), and the various member states developed recollections according to their own needs and experiences, which deviated from those of Russia. In the Ukraine, for instance, memories of wartime atrocities committed under Stalin's policies are taking center stage.[15]

Conclusion

What general principles can we derive from this survey of countries? Most obvious is the lack of connection between the past events and the versions of them that come to be recollected. In case after case, those who controlled public discourse recollected interpretations of the past that bore little resemblance to what had actually transpired. In some cases these visions were contested by memory groups fighting for social recognition, but governments were able to meet their demands without yielding control of the past. Substantive change in recollection usually requires several factors. First would be a "memory event," some contested historical issue intruding on the present, such as a commemorative anniversary or other media event (a book publication, film release, or television broadcast), or a trial or revelations about the tainted past of a public figure. Rarely could such memory events alone change the course of recollection, however. Usually, a radical change in governmental orientation would have to coincide with one or more memory events before a major shift in popular consciousness began. And in most cases the passage of sufficient time to allow for changes in the generational composition of society was necessary as well.

The dynamics of governmental and generational change give rise to some commonalties with regard to periodization. In keeping with recollection's dependence on those who control remembrance in the present rather than what happened in the past, western and eastern Europe exhibit distinct temporal patterns. In western Europe the more open public sphere allowed private and semi-public memory groups to challenge official tropes of recollection. In eastern Europe ruling parties kept tight control of the public sphere and determined the acceptable images of the past. Thus while Western bloc countries' collective memories changed qualitatively several times from the mid-1950s to the late 1970s, in the eastern bloc the main emphases of recollection varied little until radical political change began in the 1980s.

In both west and east, from the immediate aftermath of the war until political stabilization was achieved five to ten years later, there was a period of indeterminacy, during which different memory groups competed to establish or repress recollection of certain aspects of the past. After political stability had been restored, a phase of what one might call expedient recollection emerged across Europe. Sometimes so far from the truth that they are referred to as myths, these recollective tropes focused on events and interpretations that served the purposes of governments and ruling parties. They stressed victimization or heroism, but not perpetration; they emphasized national unity and solidarity, not internal divisions. Expedient recollection magnified historically marginal phenomena, ignored huge collective traumas, distorted power relations, and even reversed the direction of causality. While these self-serving recollections persisted basically unchanged and unchallenged in eastern Europe until the political transitions of the late 1980s, in western Europe in the late 1950s and 1960s memory events gradually destabilized the established expedient paradigms. When coupled with governmental or generational changes, new paradigms emerged.

Since the late 1980s we can observe movement towards an international consensus in the recollection of World War II. In some countries (Germany, Austria, Italy, France) there has been a tendency towards the inclusion of memories of perpetration and collaboration in public recollection, and overall there is greater attention to the diverse groups of victims. One indication of this development was the January 2000 "Stockholm International Forum on the Holocaust," which was attended by more than a dozen heads of state and many prominent scholars and survivors from around the world.[16] The recent establishment of national Holocaust museums and exhibitions in Washington, London, and Berlin offers additional evidence of this trend, as does the creation of national memorial days on January 27 (the day the Soviet army entered the Auschwitz concentration camp) or some other nationally significant day (e.g., October 9 in Romania, the day in 1941 when deportations of Jews began) in Austria, Denmark, Estonia, Finland, Germany, Hungary, Italy, Romania, Sweden, and the United Kingdom. This internationalization of recollection both decontextualizes and universalizes the experience of World War II and the Holocaust. Decontextualization means that less attention is paid to unique features of historical developments in different countries. Universalization indicates that across many countries common understandings of the meanings of World War II are emerging. For instance, "the Holocaust" has come to stand for the ultimate crime against humanity, to serve as a referent for other genocides and state-implemented abuses of human rights occurring around the globe.

NOTES

1   In addition to the shorter discussions in most of the books listed in the guide to further reading, I recommend John Gillis's introduction to a collection of essays he edited: "Memory and Identity: The History of a Relationship," in *Commemorations: The Politics of National Identity* (Princeton NJ: Princeton University Press, 1994), pp. 3–24. An excellent overview of relevant social science research, which is little known among historians, is collected in James Pennebaker, Dario Paez, and Bernard Rimé, eds, *Collective Memory of Political Events: Social Psychological Perspectives* (Mahwah NJ: Lawrence Erlbaum, 1997). Finally, an excellent meta-discussion can be found in the contributions to a forum on "History and Memory" in the *American Historical Review* 102/5 (1997): 1372–403 – Susan Crane, "Writing the Individual Back into Collective Memory," and Alon Confino, "Collective Memory and Cultural History: Problems of Method." Although I disagree with some of its definitions and contentions, I nonetheless find extremely useful the historical and conceptual overview offered in the introductory chapter of Jay Winter and Emmanuel Sivan, eds, *War and Remembrance in the Twentieth Century* (New York: Cambridge University Press, 1999), pp. 6–39.

2   This section is based on the works by Marcuse and Herf, cited in the guide to further reading that follows.

3   For a detailed discussion of this dynamic, see Harold Marcuse, *Legacies of Dachau: The Uses and Abuses of a Concentration Camp, 1933–2001* (New York: Cambridge University Press, 2001), pp. 290–6.

4   See Yosefa Loshitzky, ed., *Spielberg's Holocaust: Critical Perspectives on Schindler's List* (Bloomington: Indiana University Press, 1997); and Geoff Eley, ed., *The "Goldhagen Effect": History, Memory, Nazism – Facing the German Past* (Ann Arbor: University of Michigan Press, 2000).

5   On Austria, see Peter Utgaard, *Remembering and Forgetting Nazism: Education, National Identity, and the Victim Myth in Postwar Austria* (New York: Berghahn, 2003).

6   See Utgaard, *Remembering*, p. 29. The original text is available at: www.nationalsozialismus.at/Themen/Umgang/opfermyt.htm.

7   The journalistic account by Hella Pick, *Guilty Victim: Austria from the Holocaust to Haider* (London: I. B. Tauris, 2000) discusses at length the inclusion of Nazi apologist Jörg Haider in the governing coalition in 2000.

8   Italian recollections of the war have received little scholarly attention. See Donald Sassoon, "Italy after Fascism: The Predicament of Dominant Narratives," in *Life after Death:*

Approaches to a Cultural and Social History of Europe during the 1940s and 1950s, Richard
Bessel and Dirk Schumann, eds (New York: Cambridge University Press, 2003), pp.
259–90. See also Pierluca Azzaro, "Italien: Kampf der Erinnerungen," in *Mythen der
Nationen: 1945, Arena der Erinnerungen*, Monika Flacke, ed. (Berlin: DHM, 2004), vol.
1, pp. 343–72.

9   See Pieter Lagrou, "Victims of Genocide and National Memory: Belgium, France and
the Netherlands, 1945–1965," in *The World War Two Reader*, Gordon Martel, ed. (New
York: Routledge, 2004), pp. 389–421; also the essays on Belgium and the Netherlands
in Flacke, *Mythen der Nation*, vol. 1.

10 On France, see Henry Rousso, *The Vichy Syndrome: History and Memory in France since
1944* (Cambridge MA: Harvard University Press, 1991).

11 For the reactions to Gross's publication, see Antony Polonsky and Joanna Michlic, eds,
The Neighbors Respond: The Controversy over the Jedwabne Massacre in Poland (Princeton
NJ: Princeton University Press, 2004). Another indication of a changing climate is the
Polish publication of Art Spiegelman's Holocaust memoir *Maus* in 2001.

12 See Athena Syriatou, "Grossbritannien: 'Der Krieg wird uns zusammenhalten,'" in Flacke,
Mythen der Nationen, vol. 1, pp. 285–307.

13 See Nina Tumarkin, *The Living and the Dead: The Rise and Fall of the Cult of World War
II in Russia* (New York: Basic Books, 1994). The Khrushchev quotation below is from
page 109.

14 Jutta Scherber, "Sowjetunion/Russland" in Flacke, *Mythen der Nationen*, vol. 2, esp. pp.
646ff.

15 See Amir Weiner, *Making Sense of War: The Second World War and the Fate of the Bolshevik
Revolution* (Princeton NJ: Princeton University Press, 2001).

16 See the official website: www.holocaustforum.gov.se.

GUIDE TO FURTHER READING

Ian Buruma, *The Wages of Guilt: Memories of War in Germany and Japan* (New York: Farrar,
    Straus, and Giroux, 1994). This well-researched and perceptive but non-scholarly compari-
    son of recollection in Germany and Japan provides historical context but focuses on the
    1980s.

Geoff Eley, ed., *The "Goldhagen Effect": History, Memory, Nazism – Facing the German Past*
    (Ann Arbor: University of Michigan Press, 2000). Essays that examine the national responses
    to the publication of a scathing indictment of German antisemitism published in 1996.

Monika Flacke, ed., *Mythen der Nationen: 1945, Arena der Erinnerungen* (Berlin: DHM,
    2004). This two-volume collection contains lavishly illustrated in-depth essays on memories
    of World War II in each of 30 European countries.

Norbert Frei, *Adenauer's Germany and the Nazi Past* (New York: Columbia University Press,
    2002). Detailed account of how recollections of the Nazi period were used for political ends
    in 1950s West Germany.

Jeffrey Herf, *Divided Memory: The Nazi Past in the Two Germanys* (Cambridge MA: Harvard
    University Press, 1997). An in-depth analysis of the 1945–65 period in East Germany based
    upon archival research.

Yosefa Loshitzky, ed., *Spielberg's Holocaust: Critical Perspectives on Schindler's List* (Bloomington:
    Indiana University Press, 1997). Essays that examine how this 1993 film affected recollec-
    tion in various countries.

Harold Marcuse, *Legacies of Dachau: The Uses and Abuses of a Concentration Camp, 1933–2001*
    (New York: Cambridge University Press, 2001). Based on a case study of the postwar history

of Dachau, this monograph offers an explanation for the shifting emphases of recollection in West Germany since 1945.

Judith Miller, *One, by One, by One: Facing the Holocaust* (New York: Simon and Schuster, 1990). Well-referenced analysis by a journalist offers a pan-European comparison of Holocaust recollection, focusing on the 1980s.

Peter Novick, *The Holocaust in American Life* (Boston MA: Houghton Mifflin, 1999). Sophisticated analysis of the reception of the Holocaust in the United States.

Henry Rousso, *The Vichy Syndrome: History and Memory in France since 1944* (Cambridge MA: Harvard University Press, 1991). Pathbreaking account of memories of World War II in France.

Michael Steinlauf, *Bondage to the Dead: Poland and the Memory of the Holocaust* (Syracuse NY: Syracuse University Press, 1997). Excellent account of the Polish recollection of World War II.

Nina Tumarkin, *The Living and the Dead: The Rise and Fall of the Cult of World War II in Russia* (New York: Basic Books, 1994). Insightful account of the recollection of World War II in Russia which combines personal and scholarly perspectives.

Peter Utgaard, *Remembering and Forgetting Nazism: Education, National Identity, and the Victim Myth in Postwar Austria* (New York: Berghahn, 2003). Although focusing on education, this dissertation offers an excellent overview of Austrian memory of the war years.

James Young, *The Texture of Memory: Holocaust Memorials and Meaning* (New Haven CT: Yale University Press, 1993). Collection of case studies of specific memorials in five countries, by a literary scholar.

Bibliography

Adams, Michael C. C., *The Great Adventure: Male Desire and the Coming of World War I*, Bloomington IN, 1990.

Adamthwaite, Anthony, *Grandeur and Misery; France's Bid for Power in Europe 1914–1940*, London, 1995.

Addington, Larry H., *The Patterns of War since the Eighteenth Century*, Bloomington IN, 1994.

Addison, Paul, and Angus Calder, eds, *Time to Kill: The Soldiers' Experience of War in the West, 1939–1945*, London, 1997.

Ahrenfeldt, Robert H., *Psychiatry in the British Army in the Second World War*, London, 1957.

Albertini, Luigi, *The Origins of the War of 1914*, 3 vols, Oxford, 1952–7.

Aldcroft, Derek H., *From Versailles to Wall Street*, London, 1977.

Alexander, Martin S., *The Republic in Danger: General Maurice Gamelin and the Politics of French Defence, 1933–1940*, Cambridge, 1992.

Alexander, Martin S., and Helen Graham, eds, *The French and Spanish Popular Fronts: Comparative Perspectives*, Cambridge, 1989.

Ambrosius, Lloyd, *Woodrow Wilson and the American Diplomatic Tradition*, Cambridge, 1990.

Anderson, Malcolm, *The Ascendancy of Europe, 1815–1914*, London, 1972.

Ansell, Christopher, *Schism and Solidarity in Social Movements: The Politics of Labor in the French Third Republic*, Cambridge, 2001.

Ascher, Abraham, *The Revolution of 1905*, 2 vols, Stanford CA, 1988 and 1992.

Ash, Mitchell G., *Gestalt Psychology in German Culture, 1890–1967: Holism and the Quest for Objectivity*, Cambridge, 1995.

Azéma, Jean-Pierre, and François Bédarida, eds, *Le Régime de Vichy et les Français*, Paris, 1992.

Azzaro, Pierluca, "Italien: Kampf der Erinnerungen," in *Mythen der Nationen: 1945, Arena der Erinnerungen*, Monika Flacke, ed., Berlin, 2004, pp. 343–72.

Baer, George, *One Hundred Years of Sea Power: The US Navy, 1890–1990*, Stanford CA, 1994.

Bailes, Kendall, *Technology and Society under Lenin and Stalin: Origins of the Soviet Technical Intelligentsia, 1917–1941*, Princeton NJ, 1978.

Bailey, Jonathan, *The First World War and the Birth of the Modern Style of Warfare*, Camberley, 1996.

Baldwin, Peter, *The Politics of Social Solidarity: Class Bases of the European Welfare State 1875–1975*, Cambridge, 1990.

Baldwin, Peter, *Contagion and the State in Europe, 1830–1940*, Cambridge, 1999.

Balfour-Paul, Glen, "Britain's Informal Empire in the Middle East," in *The Oxford History of the British Empire: The Twentieth Century*, Judith Brown and W. Roger Louis, eds, Oxford, 1999, pp. 490–514.

Banks, Olive, *Faces of Feminism: A Study of Feminism as a Social Movement*, Oxford, 1981.

Barnett, Corelli, *The Audit of War*, London, 1988.

Bartov, Omer, "Daily life and motivation in war: the Wehrmacht in the Soviet Union," *Journal of Strategic Studies* 12 (1989): 200–14.

Bartov, Omer, *Hitler's Army: Soldiers, Nazis and War in the Third Reich*, Oxford, 1991.

Bartov, Omer, *Mirrors of Destruction: War, Genocide, and Modern Identity*, Oxford, 2000.

Bartov, Omer, *The Eastern Front, 1941–1945: German Troops and the Barbarization of Warfare*, London, 2001.

Bauer, Yehuda, *The Holocaust in Historical Perspective*, Seattle WA, 1978.

Bauer, Yehuda, *Jews for Sale? Nazi–Jewish Negotiations, 1933–1945*, New Haven CT, 1994.

Bauer, Yehuda, *Rethinking the Holocaust*, New Haven CT, 2001.

Bauman, Zygmunt, *Modernity and the Holocaust*, Ithaca NY, 1989.

Baxell, Richard, *British Volunteers in the Spanish Civil War: The British Battalion in the International Brigades, 1936–1939*, London, 2004.

Beaumont, Caitriona, "Citizens not feminists: the boundary negotiated between citizenship and feminism by mainstream women's organizations in England, 1928–39," *Women's History Review* 9/2 (2000): 411–29.

Becker, Jean-Jacques, *1914: Comment les Français sont entrés dans la guerre: Contribution à l'étude de l'opinion publique, printemps-été 1914*, Paris, 1977/1983.

Becker, Jean-Jacques, *The Great War and the French People*, Providence RI, 1993.

Beckett, Ian F. W., ed., *The Army and the Curragh Incident 1914*, London, 1986.

Beckett, Ian F. W., *The Great War 1914–1918*, London, 2001.

Beckett, Ian F. W., "The Resilience of the Old Regime," in *Total War and Historical Change*, Arthur Marwick, Clive Emsley, and W. Simpson, eds, Buckingham, 2001.

Beetham, David, ed., *Marxists in Face of Fascism: Writings by Marxists on Fascism from the Inter-War Period*, Manchester, 1983.

Beevor, Antony, *Stalingrad*, London, 1998.

Beller, Steven, *Francis Joseph*, London, 1996.

Beloff, Max, *Imperial Sunset*, vol. 1: *Britain's Liberal Empire, 1897–1921*, 2nd edn, Basingstoke, 1987.

Bennett, Edward M., *Franklin D. Roosevelt and the Search for Victory: American–Soviet Relations, 1939–1945*, Wilmington DE, 1990.

Bennett, G. H., *British Foreign Policy during the Curzon Period, 1919–24*, New York, 1995.

Bennett, Rab, *Under the Shadow of the Swastika: The Moral Dilemmas of Resistance and Collaboration in Hitler's Europe*, Basingstoke, 1999.

Benninghaus, Christina, and Kerstin Kohtz, eds, *"Sag mir, wo die Mädchen sind . . .": Beiträge zur Geschlechtergeschichte der Jugend*, Cologne, 1999.

Berenbaum, Michael, ed., *Mosaic of Victims*, New York, 1990.

Berend, T. Iván, and G. Ránki, *Economic Development in East-Central Europe in the 19th and 20th Centuries*, New York, 1974.

Berger, Stefan, *Social Democracy and the Working Class in Nineteenth and Twentieth Century Germany*, London, 2000.

Berger, Stefan, "William Harbutt Dawson: The Career and Politics of an Historian of Germany," *English Historical Review* 116 (2001): 76–113.

Berghahn, Volker R., *Der Stahlhelm, Bund der Frontsoldaten, 1918–1935*, Düsseldorf, 1966.

Berghahn, Volker R., *The Americanisation of the German Economy*, Leamington Spa, 1986.

Berghahn, Volker R., *Germany and the Approach of War in 1914*, 2nd edn, Basingstoke, 1993.

Berghahn, Volker R., *Imperial Germany 1871–1914: Economy, Society, Culture and Politics*, Providence RI, 1994.

Berghaus, Gunter, *Futurism and Politics: Between Anarchist Rebellion and Fascist Reaction, 1909–1944*, Oxford, 1996.

Bernadac, Christian, *Kommandos de femmes. Ravensbrück*, Paris, 1973.

Berry, Sara S., *Cocoa, Custom, and Socio-Economic Change in Rural Western Nigeria*, London, 1975.

Bessel, Richard, "The Great War in German Memory: The Soldiers of the First World War, Demobilization, and Weimar Political Culture," *German History* 6/1 (1988): 20–34.

Bessel, Richard, *Germany after the First World War*, Oxford, 1993.

Bessel, Richard, ed., *Fascist Italy and Nazi Germany*, Cambridge, 1996.

Best, Geoffrey, *Humanity in Warfare*, New York, 1980.

Betts, Raymond, *Assimilation and Association in French Colonial Theory, 1890–1914*, New York, 1961.

Betts, Raymond, *Tricolour*, London, 1978.

Betts, Raymond, *Uncertain Dimensions: Western Overseas Empires in the Twentieth Century*, Minneapolis MN, 1985.

Beyerchen, Alan, *Scientists under Hitler: Politics and the Physics Community in the Third Reich*, New Haven CT, 1977.

Beyerchen, Alan, "On the Stimulation of Excellence in Wilhelmian Science," in *Another Germany: A Reconsideration of the Imperial Era*, Jack R. Dukes and Joachim Remak, eds, Boulder CO, 1988.

Biddle, Stephen, *Military Power: Explaining Victory and Defeat in Modern Battle*, Princeton NJ, 2004.

Biddle, Tami Davis, "Air Power," in *The Laws of War*, Michael Howard, George Andreopoulos, and Mark Shulman, eds, New Haven CT, 1994, pp. 140–59.

Biddle, Tami Davis, "Bombing by the Square Yard: Sir Arthur Harris at War, 1942–1945," *International History Review* 21/3 (1999): 626–64.

Biddle, Tami Davis, "Learning in Real Time: The Development and Implementation of Air Power in the First World War," in *Air Power History: Turning Points from Kitty Hawk to Kosovo*, Peter Gray and Sebastian Cox, eds, London, 2002.

Biddle, Tami Davis, *Rhetoric and Reality in Air Warfare: The Evolution of British and American Ideas about Strategic Bombing, 1914–1945*, Princeton NJ, 2002.

Bidwell, Shelford, and Dominick Graham, *Firepower: British Army Weapons and Theories of War, 1904–1945*, London, 1982.

Biezunski, Michel, *Einstein à Paris: Le temps n'est plus*, Saint-Denis, 1991.

Blake, Jody, *Le Tumulte noir: Modernist Art and Popular Entertainment in Jazz-Age Paris, 1900–1930*, University Park MD, 1999.

Blewett, Neal, "The franchise in the United Kingdom, 1885–1918," *Past & Present* 32 (1965): 27–56.

Blinkhorn, Martin, ed., *Fascists and Conservatives: The Radical Right and the Establishment in Twentieth-Century Europe*, London, 1990.

Blinkhorn, Martin, ed., *Fascism and the Right in Europe, 1919–1945*, London, 2000.

Blinkhorn, Martin, ed., "Afterthoughts, Route Maps and Landscapes: Historians, 'Fascist Studies' and the Study of Fascism," *Totalitarian Movements and Political Religions* 5/3 (2004): 507–26.

Bock, Gisela, *Women in European History*, Oxford, 2002.

Boemeke, Manfred, Gerald Feldman, and Eisabeth Glaser, eds, *The Treaty of Versailles: A Reassessment after 75 Years*, Cambridge, 1998.

Bond, Brian, *British Military Policy between the Two World Wars*, Oxford, 1980.

Bond, Brian, *War and Society in Europe, 1870–1970*, London, 1984.

Bosworth, R. J. B., *The Italian Dictatorship: Problems and Perspectives in the Interpretation of Mussolini and Fascism*, London, 1998.

Bosworth, R. J. B., *Mussolini*, London, 2002.

Bourke, Joanna, *Dismembering the Male: Men's Bodies, Britain, and the Great War*, Chicago IL, 1996.

Bourke, Joanna, *An Intimate History of Killing: Face to Face Killing in Twentieth-Century Warfare*, London, 1999.

Bourke, Joanna, *The Second World War: A People's History*, Oxford, 2003.

Bourne, John M., *Britain and the Great War*, London, 1989.

Bourne, John M., Peter Lidddle, and Ian Whitehead, eds, *The Great World War, 1914–45*, vol. 1: *Lightning Strikes Twice*, London, 2000.

Boyer, John W., and Jan Goldstein, *Twentieth-Century Europe*, vol. 9, University of Chicago Readings in Western Civilization, Chicago IL, 1987.

Bradbury, Malcolm, and James McFarlane, eds, *Modernism: A Guide to European Literature 1890–1930*, revd edn, London, 1991.

Braunthal, Julius, *History of the International*, vol. I, London, 1966.

Braybon, Gail, and Penny Summerfield, *Out of the Cage: Women's Experiences in Two World Wars*, London, 1987.

Braybon, Gail, and Penny Summerfield, "Women, War, and Work," in *The Oxford Illustrated History of the First World War*, Hew Strachan, ed., Oxford, 1998, pp. 149–62.

Brecher, Edward M., *The Sex Researchers*, London, 1970.

Bridenthal, Renate, Anita Grossmann, and Marion Kaplan, eds, *When Biology Became Destiny*, New York, 1984.

Brittain, Vera, *Chronicle of Youth: War Diary 1913–1917*, Alan Bishop and Terry Smart, eds, London, 1981.

Brodie, Bernard, and Fawn Brodie, *From Crossbow to H-Bomb*, Bloomingtron IN, 1973.

Brown, Judith, and W. Roger Louis, eds, *The Oxford History of the British Empire: The Twentieth Century*, Oxford, 1999.

Browning, Christopher R., *Ordinary Men: Reserve Police Battalion 101 and the Final Solution in Poland*, New York, 1993.

Browning, Christopher R., *The Origins of the Final Solution: The Evolution of Nazi Jewish Policy, September 1939–March 1942*, Lincoln NB, 2004.

Bry, Gerhard, *Wages in Germany*, Princeton NJ, 1966.

Bullock, Alan, "The Double Image," in *Modernism: A Guide to European Literature 1890–1930*, Malcolm Bradbury and James McFarlane, eds, London, 1991.

Bullough, Vern L., *Science in the Bedroom: A History of Sex Research*, New York, 1994.

Burch, Noel, *Life to those Shadows*, London, 1990.

Bürger, Peter, *Theory of the Avant-Garde*, Michael Shaw, trans., Minneapolis MN, 1984.

Burleigh, Michael, and Wolfgang Wippermann, *The Racial State*, Cambridge, 1993.

Burleigh, Michael, and Wolfgang Wippermann, *Death and Deliverance*, Cambridge, 1994.

Burleigh, Michael, and Wolfgang Wippermann, *The Third Reich: A New History*, London, 2000.

Burrin, Philippe, *Living with Defeat: France under the German Occupation, 1940–1944*, London, 1996.

Buruma, Ian, *The Wages of Guilt: Memories of War in Germany and Japan*, New York, 1994.

Butler, Christopher, *Early Modernism: Literature, Music and Painting in Europe 1900–1916*, Oxford, 1994.

Cain, P. J., and A. G. Hopkins, *British Imperialism*, 2 vols, London, 1993.

Caine, Barbara, *English Feminism, 1780–1980*, Oxford, 1997.

Calder, Angus, *The People's War: Britain 1939–1945*, London, 1969.

Calder, K. J., *Britain and the Origins of the New Europe, 1914–1918*, Cambridge, 1976.

Calinescu, Matei, *Five Faces of Modernity: Modernism, Avant-Garde, Decadence, Kitsch, Postmodernism*, Durham NC, 1987.

Calvocoressi, Peter, and Guy Wint, *Total War: Causes and Courses of the Second World War*, Harmondsworth, 1972.

Campbell, John, ed., *The Experience of World War II*, London, 1989.

Canning, Kathleen, "Gender and the Politics of Class Formation: Rethinking German Labor History," in *Society, Culture, and the State in Germany, 1870–1930*, Geoff Eley, ed., Ann Arbor MI, 1996, pp. 105–41.

Carley, Michael J., "Five Kopecks for Five Kopecks: Franco-Soviet Trade Relations, 1928–1939," *Cahiers du monde russe et soviétique* 33/1 (1992): 23–58.

Carley, Michael J., "Down a Blind-Alley: Anglo-Franco-Soviet Relations, 1920–1939," *Canadian Journal of History* 29/1 (1994): 147–72.

Carley, Michael J., "'A Fearful Concatenation of Circumstances': The Anglo-Soviet Rapprochement, 1934–36," *Contemporary European History* 5/1 (March 1996): 29–69.

Carley, Michael J., *1939: The Alliance That Never Was and the Coming of World War II*, Chicago IL, 1999.

Carley, Michael J., "Episodes from the Early Cold War: Franco-Soviet Relations, 1917–1927," *Europe–Asia Studies* 52/7 (2000): 1275–305.

Carlton, David, *Churchill and the Soviet Union*, Manchester, 2000.

Carr, Edward H., *International Relations Between the Two World Wars, 1919–1939*, London, 1947.

Carr, Edward H., *The Twilight of Comintern, 1930–1935*, London, 1982.

Carr, Edward H., *German–Soviet Relations Between the two World Wars, 1919–1939*, Westport CT, 1983.

Carsten, F. L., *Revolution in Central Europe, 1918–1919*, Berkeley CA, 1972.

Carsten, F. L., *War Against War: British and German Radical Movements in the First World War*, London, 1982.

Cassis, Youssef, *Big Business: The European Experience in the Twentieth Century*, Oxford, 1997.

Castellan, Georges, *L'Allemagne de Weimar, 1918–1933*, Paris, 1969.

Castle, Kathryn, *Britannia's Children: Reading Colonialism through Children's Books and Magazines*, Manchester, 1996.

Cecil, Hugh, and Peter Liddle, eds, *Facing Armageddon: The First World Experienced*, London, 1996.

Cederna, Camilla, Martina Lombardi, and Marilea Somaré, eds, *Milano in guerra*, Milan, 1979.

Cell, John, "Colonial Rule," in *The Oxford History of the British Empire: The Twentieth Century*, Judith Brown and W. Roger Louis, eds, Oxford, 1999, pp. 232–54.

Chandler, Alfred, *Strategy and Structure: Chapters in the History of the American Industrial Enterprise*, Cambridge MA, 1962.

Chandler, Alfred, *The Visible Hand: The Managerial Revolution in American Business*, Cambridge MA, 1977.

Chandler, Alfred, *Scale and Scope: The Dynamics of Industrial Capitalism*, Cambridge MA, 1990.

Charmley, John, *Chamberlain and the Lost Peace*, London, 1989.

Chase, William J., *Workers, Society, and the Soviet State: Labor and Life in Moscow, 1918–1929*, Champaign-Urbana IL, 1987.

Chase, William J., *Enemies Within the Gates? The Comintern and the Stalinist Repression, 1934–1939*, New Haven CT, 2001.

Chickering, Roger, *Imperial Germany and the Great War, 1914–1918*, Cambridge, 1998.

Childs, Peter, *Modernism*, London, 2000.

Chipp, Herschel B., ed., *Theories of Modern Art*, Berkeley CA, 1968.

Churchill, Winston, *Great War Speeches*, London, 1965.

Clancy-Smith, Julia, and Frances Gouda, eds, *Domesticating the Empire: Race, Gender and Family Life in French and Dutch Colonialism*, Charlottesville VA, 1998.

Clark, Chris M., *Kaiser Wilhelm II*, London, 2000.

Clark, Colin, *The Conditions of Economic Progress*, London, 1940.

Clarke, Peter, and Clive Trebilcock, eds, *Understanding Decline: Perceptions and Realities of British Economic Performance*, Cambridge, 1997.

Clendinnen, Inga, *Reading the Holocaust*, Cambridge MA, 1999.

Cline, Catherine Anne, "British Historians and the Treaty of Versailles," *Albion* 20 (1988): 43–58.

Cohen, Deborah, *The War Come Home: Disabled Veterans in Britain and Germany, 1914–1939*, Berkeley CA, 2001.

Cohen, Gary B., "Neither absolutism nor anarchy: new narratives on society and government in late imperial Austria," *Austrian History Yearbook* 29 (1998): 37–61.

Collotti, Enzo, ed., *L'occupazione nazista in Europa*, Rome, 1964.

Colton, Joel, and Léon Blum, *Humanist in Politics*, Cambridge MA, 1974.

Colvin, Ian, *The Chamberlain Cabinet*, London, 1971.

Confino, Alon, "Collective memory and cultural history: problems of method," *American Historical Review* 102/5 (1997): 1386–403.

Conklin, Alice L., "Redefining 'Frenchness': Citizenship, Race Regeneration, and Imperial Motherhood in France and West Africa, 1914–40," in *Domesticating the Empire: Race, Gender, and Family Life in French and Dutch Colonialism*, Julia Clancy-Smith and Francis Gouda, eds, Charlottesville VA, 1998, pp. 65–83.

Connelly, Mark, "'Never such innocence again': Grossbritannien und das Jahr 1914," *Aus Politik und Zeitgeschichte* 29–30 (2004): 13–20.

Conquest, Robert, *The Great Terror: A Reassessment*, New York, 1990.

Conrad, Sebastian, and Jürgen Osterhammel, eds, *Das Kaiserreich transnational. Deutschland in der Welt 1871–1914*, Göttingen, 2004.

Conway, Martin, *Collaboration in Belgium: Léon Degrelle and the Rexist Movement*, New Haven CT, 1993.

Cook, Hera, *The Long Sexual Revolution: English Women, Sex, and Contraception 1800–1975*, Oxford, 2004.

Cooper, Frederick, and Ann Laura Stoler, eds, *Tensions of Empire: Colonial Cultures in a Bourgeois World*, Berkeley CA, 1997.

Cooper, Malcolm, *The Birth of Independent Air Power*, London, 1986.

Copp, Terry, and Bill McAndrew, *Battle Exhaustion: Soldiers and Psychiatrists in the Canadian Army, 1939–1945*, Montreal, 1990.

Corner, Paul, and Giovanna Proacacci, "The Italian Experience of 'Total' Mobilization, 1915–1920," in *State, Society and Mobilization in Europe during the First World War*, John Horne, ed., Cambridge, 2002, pp. 223–40.

Corni, Gustavo, *Hitler and the Peasants*, Oxford, 1990.

Cornwall, Mark, "News, rumour and the control of information in Austria-Hungary, 1914–1918," *History* 77/249 (1992): 50–64.

Cornwall, Mark, ed., *The Last Years of Austria-Hungary: A Multi-National Experiment in Early Twentieth-Century Europe*, revd edn, Exeter, 2002.

Corum, James, *The Roots of Blitzkrieg: Hans von Seeckt and German Military Reform*, Lawrence KS, 1992.

Cosner, Sharon, and Victoria Cosner, *Women under the Third Reich*, Westport CT, 1997.

Cottaar, Annemarie, and Wim Willems, "Justice or injustice? A survey of government policy towards gypsies and caravan dwellers in Western Europe in the 19th and 20th centuries," *Immigrants and Minorities* 11/1 (1992): 42–66.

Cowman, Krista, "Crossing the Great Divide: Inter-Organisational Suffrage Relationships on Merseyside, 1895–1914," in *A Suffrage Reader: Charting Directions in British Suffrage History*, Claire Eustance, Joan Ryan, and Laura Ugolini, eds, London, 2000, pp. 37–52.

Crane, Susan, "Writing the individual back into collective memory," *American Historical Review* 102/5 (1997): 1372–85.

Crang, Jeremy A., "The British Soldier on the Home Front: Army Morale Reports, 1940–45," in *Time to Kill: The Soldiers' Experience of War in the West, 1939–1945*, P. Addison and A. Calder, eds, London, 1997, pp. 60–74.

Crang, Jeremy A., *The British Army and the People's War 1939–1945*, Manchester, 2000.

Crawford, Elisabeth, *Nationalism and Internationalism in Science, 1880–1939: Four Studies of the Nobel Population*, Cambridge, 1992.

Crew, David, ed., *Nazism and German Society*, London, 1994.

Cunningham, Andrew, and Perry Williams, eds, *The Laboratory Revolution in Medicine*, New York, 1992.

Cunningham, Valentine, *British Writers of the Thirties*, Oxford, 1989.

Czarnowski, Gabriele, "The Value of Marriage for the *Volksgemeinschaft*," in *Fascist Italy and Nazi Germany*, Richard Bessel, ed., Cambridge, 1996, pp. 94–112.

Dahl, Hans F., *Quisling: A Study in Treachery*, Cambridge, 1999.

Dahrendorf, Ralf, *Society and Democracy in Germany*, London, 1966.

Daley, Caroline, and Melanie Nolan, eds, *Suffrage and Beyond: International Feminist Perspectives*, Auckland, 1994.

Dangerfield, George, *The Strange Death of Liberal England 1910–1914*, London, 1936.

Darrow, Margaret H., "French volunteer nursing and the myth of war experience in World War I," *American Historical Review* 101/1 (1996): 80–106.

Dauncey, Hugh, and Geoff Hare, eds, *Tour de France, 1903–2003*, London, 2003.

Davidson, Roger, *Dangerous Liaisons: A Social History of Venereal Disease in Twentieth-Century Scotland*, Amsterdam, 2000.

Davidson, Roger, and Lesley Hall, *Sex, Sin and Suffering: Venereal Disease and European Society since 1870*, London, 2001.

Davies, R. W., *The Socialist Offensive: The Collectivization of Soviet Agriculture, 1929–1930*, Cambridge MA, 1980.

Davison, Peter, ed., *Orwell in Spain*, London, 2001.

De Groot, Gerard J., *Blighty: British Society in the Era of the Great War*, London, 1996.

Dean, Carolyn J., *Sexuality and Modern Western Culture*, New York, 1996.

Dear, Ian C. B., and M. R. D. Foot, eds, *The Oxford Companion to World War II*, Oxford, 1995; pbk edn, 2001.

Debo, Richard, *Survival and Consolidation: The Foreign Policy of Soviet Russia, 1918–1921*, Montreal, 1992.

DeGrazia, Victoria, *How Fascism Ruled Women: Italy, 1922–1945*, Berkeley CA, 1992.

Deist, Wilhelm, "The military collapse of the German empire: the reality behind the stab-in-the-back myth," E. J. Feuchtwanger, trans., *War in History* 3/2 (1996): 186–207.

Diehl, James M., "Germany: Veterans' Politics under Three Flags," in *The War Generation: Veterans of the First World War*, Stephen R. Ward, ed., Port Washington NY, 1975, pp. 135–86.

Diehl, James M., *Paramilitary Politics in Weimar Germany*, Bloomingtron IN, 1978.

Dobson, Sean, *Authority and Upheaval in Leipzig, 1910–1920: The Story of a Relationship*, New York, 2001.

Dockrill, Michael, and J. Douglas Goold, *Peace Without Promise: Britain and the Peace Conferences 1919–1923*, London, 1981.

Dockrill, Michael, J. Douglas Goold, and John Fisher, eds, *The Paris Peace Conference 1919: Peace Without Victory?* Basingstoke, 2001.

Dose, Ralf, "The World League for Sexual Reform: Some Possible Approaches," in *Sexual Cultures in Europe: National Histories*, Franz Eder, Lesley Hall, and Gert Hekma, eds, Manchester, 1999, pp. 242–59.

Doubler, Michael D., *Closing With the Enemy: How GI's Fought the War in Europe, 1944–45*, Lawrence KS, 1994.

Doughty, Robert, and Ira Gruber, *Warfare in the Western World: Military Operations since 1871*, vol. 2, Lexington MA, 1996.

Dowe, Dieter, ed., *Jugendprotest und Generationenkonflikt in Europa im 20. Jahrhundert: Deutschland, England, Frankreich und Italien im Vergleich*, Bonn, 1986.

DuBois, Ellen C., "Woman suffrage and the Left: An international socialist feminist perspective," *New Left Review* 186 (1991): 20–45.

Dunn, Seamus, and T. G. Fraser, eds, *Europe and Ethnicity: World War I and Contemporary Ethnic Conflict*, London, 1996.

Dunnage, Jonathan, *Twentieth-Century Italy: A Social History*, London, 2002.

Eckardt, Wolf von, and Sander Gilman, *Bertolt Brecht's Berlin: A Scrapbook of the Twenties*, Lincoln NB, 1993.

Edelmann, Robert, *Serious Fun: A History of Spectator Sports in the USSR*, New York, 1993.

Eder, Franz, Lesley Hall, and Gert Hekma, *Sexual Cultures in Europe: National Histories*, Manchester, 1999.

Eder, Franz, Lesley Hall, and Gert Hekma, *Sexual Cultures in Europe: Themes in Sexuality*, Manchester, 1999.

Edmonds, Robin, "Churchill and Stalin," in *Churchill: A Major New Assessment of His Life in Peace and War*, Robert Blake and W. Roger Louis, eds, New York, 1993.

Eksteins, Modris, *Rites of Spring: The Great War and the Birth of the Modern Age*, Toronto, 1989.

Eley, Geoff, ed., *Society, Culture, and the State in Germany, 1870–1930*, Ann Arbor MI, 1996.

Eley, Geoff, ed., *The "Goldhagen Effect": History, Memory, Nazism – Facing the German Past*, Ann Arbor MI, 2000.

Eley, Geoff, ed., *Forging Democracy: The History of the Left in Europe, 1850–2000*, Oxford, 2002.

Ellis, John, *The Sharp End of War: The Fighting Man in World War Two*, London, 1982.

Emsley, Clive, *Total War and Social Change 1914–1955*, Milton Keynes, 2000.

Emsley, Clive, Eric Johnson, and Pieter Spierenburg, *Social Control in Europe 1800–2000*, Columbus OH, 2004.

Emy, Hugh V., *Liberals, Radicals and Social Politics, 1892–1914*, Cambridge, 1973.

Engel, David, *The Holocaust: The Third Reich and the Jews*, Harlow, 2000.

Engelking, Barbara, *Holocaust and Memory*, New Haven CT, 2001.

Erickson, John, "Soviet War Losses: Calculations and Controversies," in *Barbarossa: The Axis and the Allies*, J. Erickson and David Dilks, eds, Edinburgh, 1994.

Erickson, John, "Red Army Battlefield Performance, 1941–45: The System and the Soldier," in *Time to Kill: The Soldiers' Experience of War in the West, 1939–1945*, P. Addison and A. Calder, eds, London, 1997, pp. 233–48.

Eubank, Keith, *The Summit Conferences 1919–1969*, Oklahoma, 1966.

Eubank, Keith, *The Origins of World War II*, 3rd edn, Wheeling IL, 2004.

Evans, Richard, ed., *Proletarians and Politics: Socialism, Protest and the Working Class in Germany Before the First World War*, London, 1990.

Evans, Richard, ed., *The Coming of the Third Reich*, London, 2003.

Everdell, William R., *The First Moderns: Profiles in the Origins of Twentieth-Century Thought*, Chicago IL, 1997.

Eysteinsson, Astradur, *The Concept of Modernism*, Ithaca NY, 1990.

Fahey, Tony, "Religion and Sexual Culture in Ireland," in *Sexual Cultures in Europe: National Histories, Franz Eder, Lesley Hall, and Gert Hekma*, eds, Manchester, 1999, pp. 53–70.

Farquharson, John G., *The Plough and the Swastika*, London, 1976.

Farrar Jr, Lancelot L., *Divide and Conquer: German Efforts to Conclude a Separate Peace, 1914–1918*, London, 1978.

Farrar Jr, Lancelot L., "Reluctant warriors: public opinion on war during the July crisis, 1914," *Eastern European Quarterly* 16 (1983): 417–46

Farrar Jr, Lancelot L., "Nationalism in Wartime: Critiquing the Conventional Wisdom," in *Authority, Identity and the Social History of the Great War*, Frans Coetzee and Marilyn Shevin-Coetzee, eds, Oxford, 1995, pp. 133–52.

Faulkner, Peter, ed., *A Modernist Reader*, London, 1986.

Fein, Helen, *Accounting for Genocide: National Responses and Jewish Victimization during the Holocaust*, Chicago IL, 1979.

Feinstein, Charles H., Peter Temin, and Gianni Toniolo, *The European Economy Between the Wars*, Oxford, 1997.

Feldman, Gerald D., *The Great Disorder: Politics, Economics, and Society in the German Inflation, 1914–1924*, New York, 1997.

Fellner, Fritz, "Austria-Hungary," in *Decisions for War*, K. Wilson, ed., London, 1995, pp. 9–25.

Ferguson, Niall, "Germany and the origins of the First World War: new perspectives," *Historical Journal* 35 (1992): 734–42.

Ferguson, Niall, "Keynes and the German inflation," *English Historical Review* 110 (1995): 368–91.

Ferguson, Niall, *The Pity of War*, London, 1998.

Ferguson, Niall, *Empire: The Rise and Demise of the British World Order and the Lessons for Global Power*, New York, 2003.

Ferguson, Niall, "Prisoner taking and prisoner killing in the age of total war: towards a political economy of military defeat," *War in History* 11 (2004): 148–92.

Ferris, John R., *Men, Money and Diplomacy: The Evolution of British Strategic Policy, 1919–26* Ithaca NY, 1989.

Ferro, Marc, *The Great War 1914–1918*, London, 1973.

Figes, Orlando, *A People's Tragedy: The Russian Revolution: 1891–1924*, London, 1996.

Fink, Carole, *Marc Bloch: A Life in History*, Cambridge, 1989.

Fink, Carole, *The Genoa Conference: European Diplomacy, 1921–1922*, revd pbk edn, Syracuse NY, 1993.

Fink, Carole, *Defending the Rights of Others: The Jews, the Great Powers, and International Minority Protection, 1878–1938*, Cambridge, 2004.

Fischer, Fritz, *Germany's Aims in the First World War*, London, 1967.

Fischer, Fritz, *War of Illusions: German Policies from 1911–1914*, London, 1975.

Fitzpatrick, Sheila, "Cultural Revolution as Class War," in *Cultural Revolution in Russia, 1928–1932*, Sheila Fitzpatrick, ed., Bloomingtron IN, 1978, pp. 8–40.

Fitzpatrick, Sheila, ed., *Cultural Revolution in Russia, 1928–1932*, Bloomingtron IN, 1978.

Fitzpatrick, Sheila, ed., *Education and Social Mobility in the Soviet Union, 1921–1934*, Cambridge, 1979.

Fitzpatrick, Sheila, ed., *The Russian Revolution*, 2nd edn, Oxford, 2001.

Flacke, Monika, ed., *Mythen der Nationen: 1945, Arena der Erinnerungen*, Berlin, 2004.

Fleischer, Hagen, *Im Kreuzschatten der Machte. Griechenland, 1941–1944, Okkupupation, Resistance, Kollaboration*, Frankfurt, 1986.

Fletcher, Ian C., Laura E. Nym Mayhall, and Philippa Levine, eds, *Women's Suffrage in the British Empire: Citizenship, Nation and Race*, London, 2002.

Flood, P. J., *France 1914–18: Public Opinion and the War Effort*, London, 1990.

Foot, M. R. D., "What good did Resistance do?" in *Resistance in Europe, 1939–1945*, Stephen F. Hawes and Ralph T. White, eds, Harmondsworth, 1975.

Foot, M. R. D., *Resistance: European Resistance to Nazism, 1940–45*, London, 1976.

Foreman-Peck, James, *A History of the World Economy: International Economic Relations since 1850*, 2nd edn, Brighton, 1994.

Forman, Paul, "Weimar culture, causality, and quantum theory, 1918–1927: adaptation by German physicists and mathematicians to a hostile intellectual environment," *Historical Studies in the Physical Sciences* 3 (1971): 1–115.

Forman, Paul, John L. Heilbron, and Spencer Weart, "Physics circa 1900: personnel, funding, and productivity of the academic establishments," *Historical Studies in the Physical Sciences* 5 (1975): 12.

Forner, Sean A., "War commemoration and the republic in crisis: Weimar Germany and the *Neue Wache*," *Central European History* 35/4 (2002): 513–49.

Förster, Jürgen E., "The Dynamics of Volksgemeinschaft: The Effectiveness of the German Military Establishment in the Second World War," in *Military Effectiveness*, vol. 3: *The Second World War*, A. R. Millet and W. Murray, eds, London, 1988, pp. 204–8.

Förster, Jürgen E., "Motivation and Indoctrination in the Wehrmacht, 1933–1945," in *Time to Kill: The Soldiers' Experience of War in the West, 1939–1945*, P. Addison and A. Calder, eds, London, 1997, pp. 263–73.

Förster, Jürgen E., "Evolution and Development of German Doctrine 1914–45," in *The Origins of Contemporary Doctrine*, John Gooch, ed., London, 1997, pp. 18–31.

Förster, Jürgen E., "Luddendorff and Hitler in perspective: the battle for the German soldier's mind, 1917–1944," *War in History* 10 (2003): 321–34.

Fox, Robert, and Anna Guagnini, *Laboratories, Workshops, and Sites: Concepts and Practices of Research in Industrial Europe, 1800–1914*, Berkeley CA, 1999.

Freese, Matthias, *Betriebspolitik im Dritten Reich*, Paderborn, 1991.

Frei, Norbert, *Adenauer's Germany and the Nazi Past*, New York, 2002.

French, David, "The Edwardian crisis and the origins of the First World War," *International History Review* 4 (1982): 207–21.

French, David, "'Tommy is no soldier': the morale of the Second British Army in Normandy, June–August 1944," *Journal of Strategic Studies* 19 (1996): 154–78.

French, David, "Discipline and the death penalty in the British Army in the war against Germany during the Second World War," *Journal of Contemporary History* 33 (1998): 531–46.

French, David, *Raising Churchill's Army: The British Army and the War against Germany, 1919–1945*, Oxford, 2000.

French, David, "'You can't hate the bastard who is trying to kill you . . .' Combat and ideology in the British Army in the war against Germany, 1939–1945," *Twentieth Century British History* 11 (2000): 1–22.

French, David, "Doctrine and organization in the British Army, 1919–1932," *Historical Journal* 43 (2001): 497–515.

Freymond, Jacques, *Le IIIe Reich et la réorganisation économique de l'Europe*, Leiden, 1974.

Fridenson, Patrick, ed., *The French Home Front 1914–1918*, Oxford, 1992.

Friedlander, Henry, *The Origins of Nazi Genocide: From Euthanasia to the Final Solution*, Chapel Hill NC, 1995.

Friedländer, Saul, *Nazi Germany and the Jews*, vol. 1: *The Years of Persecution, 1933–1939*, New York, 1997.

Fritz, Stephen G., *Frontsoldaten: The German Soldier in World War Two*, Lexington KY, 1995.

Fritz, Stephen G., " 'We are trying to change the face of the world' – ideology and motivation in the Wehrmacht on the Eastern Front: the view from below," *Journal of Military History* 60 (1996): 683–710.

Fritzsche, Peter, *A Nation of Flyers*, Cambridge MA, 1992.

Führer, Karl C., "A medium of modernity? Broadcasting in Weimar Germany, 1923–32," *Journal of Modern History* 69 (1997): 722–53.

Furet, François, ed., *Unanswered Questions: Nazi Germany and the Genocide of the Jews*, New York, 1989.

Fussell, Paul, *The Great War and Modern Memory*, New York, 1975.

Gardner, Lloyd C., *Spheres of Influence: The Great Powers Partition Europe, from Munich to Yalta*, Chicago IL, 1993.

Garland, David, "The criminal and his science," *British Journal of Criminology* 25/2 (1985): 109–37.

Garlinski, Józef, *Poland in the Second World War*, London, 1985.

Gatrell, Peter, *The Tsarist Economy 1850–1917*, London, 1986.

Gatrell, Peter, *Government, Industry and Rearmament in Russia, 1900–1914: The Last Argument of Tsarism*, Cambridge, 1994.

Gatrell, V. A. C., "Crime, Authority and the Policeman-State," in *The Cambridge Social History of Britain 1750–1950*, vol. 3, F. M. L. Thompson, ed., Cambridge, 1990.

Gatzke, Hans, ed., *European Diplomacy between Two Wars, 1919–1939*, Chicago IL, 1972.

Gay, Peter, *Schnitzler's Century: The Making of Middle-Class Culture 1815–1914*, New York, 2001.

Geary, Dick, "Working-class identities in Europe, 1850s–1930s," *Australian Journal of Politics and History* 45 (1999): 20–34.

Geary, Dick, *Hitler and Nazism*, 2nd edn, London, 2000.

Geary, Dick, "Social Protest in the Ruhr, 1945–49," in *A Social History of Central European Politics, 1945–52*, Eleonore Breuning, Jill Lewis, and Gareth Pritchard, eds, Manchester, 2005.

Geary, Dick, "Working-Class Identities in the Third Reich," in *Nazism, War and Genocide: Essays in Honour of Jeremy Noakes*, Neil Gregor, ed., Exteter, 2005.

Geldern, James von, and Richard Stites, eds, *Mass Culture in Soviet Russia*, Bloomington IN, 1995.

Gellately, Robert, *Backing Hitler: Consent and Coercion in Nazi Germany*, Oxford, 2001.

Gellately, Robert, and Nathan Stolzfuss, eds, *Social Outsiders in Nazi Germany*, Princeton NJ, 2002.

Gerber, David, A., ed., *Disabled Veterans in History*, Ann Arbor MI, 2000.

Gerschenkron, Alexander, *Economic Backwardness in Historical Perspective*, Cambridge MA, 1966.

Getty, J. Arch, *Origins of the Great Purges: The Soviet Communist Party Reconsidered, 1933–1938*, New York, 1985.

Getty, J. Arch, Gabor T. Rittersporn, and V. N. Zemskov, "Victims of the Soviet penal system in the pre-war years: a first approach on the basis of archival evidence," *American Historical Review* 98/4 (1993): 1017–49.

Getty, J. Arch, and Oleg V. Naumov, *The Road to Terror: Stalin and the Self-Destruction of the Bolsheviks, 1932–1939*, New Haven CT, 1999.

Geyer, Michael, "Ein Vorbot des Wohlfahrsstaates. Die Kriegsopferversorgung in Frankreich, Deutschland und Grossbritannien nach dem Ersten Weltkrieges," *Geschichte und Gesllschaaft* 9/2 (1983): 230–77.

Geyer, Michael, "Restorative Elites, German Society and the Nazi Pursuit of War," in *Fascist Italy and Nazi Germany*, Richard Bessel, ed., Cambridge, 1996, pp. 134–64.

Gilbert, Martin, *Winston S. Churchill*, vols 5–8, London, 1976–88.

Gilbert, Sandra M., "Soldier's Heart: Literary Men, Literary Women and the Great War," in *Behind the Lines: Gender and the Two World Wars*, Margaret Randolph Higonnet et al., eds, New Haven CT, 1987, pp. 197–226.

Gildea, Robert, *France 1870–1914*, London, 1994.

Gildea, Robert, *Marianne in Chains: In Search of the German Occupation, 1940–45*, London, 2002.

Gildea, Robert, *Barricades and Borders: Europe, 1800–1914*, 2nd edn, Oxford, 2003.

Gillingham, John R., *Industry and Politics in the Third Reich*, London, 1985.

Gillis, John R., *Youth and History: Tradition and Change in European Age Relations, 1770–Present*, New York, 1981.

Gillis, John R., ed., *Commemorations: The Politics of National Identity*, Princeton NJ, 1994.

Gillis, John R., Louise A. Tilly, and David Levine, *The European Experience of Declining Fertility, 1850–1970: The Quiet Revolution*, Cambridge, 1992.

Glantz, David M., and Jonathan M. House, *When Titans Clashed: How the Red Army Stopped Hitler*, Lawrence KS, 1995.

Gleason, Abbot, Peter Kenez, and Richard Stites, eds, *Bolshevik Culture: Experiment and Order in the Russian Revolution*, Bloomingtron IN, 1985.

Glick, Thomas, *Einstein in Spain: Relativity and the Recovery of Science*, Princeton NJ, 1998.

Goddard, Chris, *Jazz Away from Home*, New York, 1979.

Goldman, Wendy Z., *Women, the State, and Revolution: Soviet Family Policy and Social Life, 1917–1936*, New York, 1993.

Goldman, Wendy Z., *Women at the Gates: Gender and Industry in Stalin's Russia*, New York, 2002.

Goldstein, Erik, *Winning the Peace: British Diplomatic Strategy, Peace Planning and the Paris Peace Conference 1916–1920*, Oxford, 1991.

Gooch, G. P., *History of Modern Europe, 1873–1919*, New York, 1923.

Gooch, G. P., *Recent Revelations in European Diplomacy*, London, 1927.

Goodwin-Gill, Guy S., "The Experience of Displacement: Refugees and War," in *The Great World War*, vol. 1: *Lightning Strikes Twice*, John Bourne, Peter Lidddle, and Ian Whitehead, eds, London, 2000, 566–79.

Gordon, Michael, "Domestic conflict and the origins of the First World War: The British and German cases," *Journal of Modern History* 46 (1974): 191–226.

Gorodetsky, Gabriel, *Grand Delusion: Stalin and the German Invasion of Russia*, New Haven CT, 1999.

Gorsuch, Anne E., *Youth in Revolutionary Russia*, Bloomingtron IN, 2000.

Graham, Helen, and Paul Preston, eds, *The Popular Front in Europe*, London, 1987.

Graham, Helen, and Paul Preston, eds, *The Spanish Republic at War, 1936–1939*, Cambridge, 2002.

Graham, Loren, *Science in Russia and the Soviet Union: A Short History*, Cambridge, 1993.

Grand, Alexander De, *The Italian Nationalist Association and the Rise of Fascism*, Lincoln NE, 1978.

Grayson, Richard S., *Austen Chamberlain and the Commitment to Europe: British Foreign Policy, 1924–29*, London, 1997.

Grayzel, Susan, *Women's Identities at War: Gender, Motherhood and Politics in Britain and France during the First World War*, Chapel Hill NC, 1999.

Grayzel, Susan, *Women and the First World War*, London, 2002.

Grazia, Victoria de, "Mass culture and sovereignty: the American challenge to European cinemas, 1920–1960," *Journal of Modern History* 61 (1989): 53–87.

Grazia, Victoria de, *How Fascism Ruled Women: Italy 1922–1945*, Berkeley CA, 1992.

Gregor, Neil, *Daimler Benz in the Third Reich*, New Haven CT, 1998.

Gregory, Adrian, *The Silence of Memory: Armistice Day, 1919–1946*, Providence RI, 1994.

Gregory, Paul R., *Russian National Income 1885–1913*, Cambridge, 1982.

Griffin, Gabrielle, and Rosie Braidotti, eds, *Thinking Differently: A Reader in European Women's Studies*, London, 2002.

Griffin, Roger, *The Nature of Fascism*, London, 1991.

Griffiths, Paul, *Modern Music: A Concise History*, London, 1994.

Gronow, Pekka, "The record industry: the growth of a mass medium," *Popular Music* 3 (1983): 53–75.

Gronow, Pekka, and Ilpo Saunio, *An International History of the Recording Industry*, Christopher Moseley, trans., London, 1998.

Gross, Jan T., *Neighbors: The Destruction of the Jewish Community in Jedwabne, Poland*, Princeton NJ, 2001.

Grosse, Pascal, *Kolonialismus, Eugenik und bürgerliche Gesellschaft in Deutschland 1850–1918*, Frankfurt, 2000.

Grossmann, Anita, "Feminist debates about women and National Socialism," *Gender and History* 3 (1991): 350–8.

Grossmann, Anita, *Reforming Sex: The German Movement for Birth Control and Abortion Reform, 1920–1950*, New York, 1995.

Gruber, Helmut, and Pamela Graves, eds, *Women and Socialism, Socialism and Women: Europe Between the Two World Wars*, Oxford, 1998.

Grynberg, Michal, ed., *Words to Outlive Us: Eyewitness Accounts from the Warsaw Ghetto*, London, 2003.

Gumbrecht, Hans, *In 1926: Living at the Edge of Time*, Cambridge MA, 1997.

Gutman, Yisrael, and Cynthia J. Haft, eds, *Patterns of Jewish Leadership in Nazi Europe, 1933–1945*, Jerusalem, 1979.

Gutman, Yisrael, and Cynthia J. Haft, eds, *The Jews of Warsaw: Ghetto, Underground, Revolt*, Bloomingtron IN, 1982.

Hachtmann, Rüdiger, *Industriearbeit im Dritten Reich*, Göttingen, 1989.

Hagan, Kenneth, *This People's Navy: The Making of American Sea Power*, New York, 1991.

Hagemann, Karen, and Stefanie Schüler Springorum, *Home/Front: The Military, War and Gender in Twentieth-Century Germany*, Oxford, 2002.

Haimson, Leopold, "The problem of social stability in Urban Russia, 1905–1917," *Slavic Review* (part 1) 23/4 (1964): 618–42; (part 2) 24/1 (1965): 1–22.

Hale, Oron J., *The Great Illusion, 1900–1914*, New York, 1971.

Halévy, Elie, *The Era of Tyrannies*, New York, 1965.

Hall, Lesley A., *Hidden Anxieties: Male Sexuality, 1900–1950*, Oxford, 1991.

Hall, Lesley A., "Eyes Tightly Shut, Lying Rigidly Still and Thinking of England? British Women and Sex from Marie Stopes to Hite," in *Sexual Pedagogies: Teaching Sex in America, Britain, and Australia, 1879–2000*, Michelle Martin and Claudia Nelson, eds, Basingstoke, 2003, pp. 53–71.

Hall, Lesley A., "Hauling down the double standard: feminism, social purity and sexual science in late nineteenth-century Britain," *Gender and History* 16 (2004): 36–56.

Hall, Peter, *The World Cities*, London, 1966.

Hamilton, Alastair, *The Appeal of Fascism: A Study of Intellectuals and Fascism, 1919–1945*, London, 1971.

Hamilton, Richard F., and Holger H. Herwig, eds, *The Origins of World War I*, Cambridge, 2003.

Hannam, June, and Karen Hunt, *Socialist Women: Britain, 1880s to 1920s*, London, 2001.

Hardesty, Von, *Red Phoenix: The Rise of Soviet Air Power, 1941–1945*, Washington DC, 1982.

Hare, Geoff, *Football in France: A Cultural History*, Oxford, 2003.

Harrington, Anne, *Reenchanted Science: Holism in German Culture from Wilhelm II to Hitler*, Princeton NJ, 1996.

Harris, James R., *The Great Urals: Regionalism and the Evolution of the Soviet System*, Ithaca NY, 1999.

Harrison, Mark, *Soviet Planning in Peace and War, 1938–45*, Cambridge, 1985.

Harrison, Mark, ed., *The Economics of World War II: Six Great Powers in International Comparison*, Cambridge, 1998.

Harwood, Jonathan, *Styles of Scientific Thought: The German Genetics Community, 1900–1933*, Chicago IL, 1993.

Hasegawa, Tsuyoshi, *The February Revolution: Petrograd 1917*, Seattle WA, 1981.

Haselsteiner, Horst, "The Habsburg Empire in World War I: Mobilization of Food Supplies," in *East Central European Society in World War I*, Béla K. Király and Nándor F. Dreisziger, eds, Boulder CO, 1985, pp. 73–86.

Haslam, Jonathan, *The Soviet Union and the Struggle for Collective Security in Europe, 1933–1939*, London, 1984.

Haslam, Jonathan, "Soviet Russia and the Spanish Problem," in *The Origins of World War Two: The Debate Continues*, Robert Boyce and Joseph A. Maiolo, eds, Basingstoke, 2003, pp. 70–85.

Hausner, Gideon, *Justice in Jerusalem*, 4th edn, New York, 1977.

Havinden, Michael, and David Meredith, *Colonialism and Development: Britain and Its Tropical Colonies, 1850–1960*, London, 1993.

Hawes, Stephen F., and Ralph T. White, eds, *Resistance in Europe, 1939–1945*, Harmondsworth, 1975.

Hayes, Carlton J. H., *A Generation of Materialism 1871–1900*, New York, 1941.

Heater, Derek, *National Self-Determination: Woodrow Wilson and His Legacy*, Basingstoke, 1994.

Hebert, Ulrich, ed., *National Socialist Extermination Policies: Contemporary German Perspectives and Controversies*, New York, 2000.

Heer, Hannes, "The difficulty of ending a war: reactions to the exhibition 'War of extermination: crimes of the Wehrmacht 1941 to 1944,'" *History Workshop* 46 (1998): 187–203.

Heer, Hannes, and Klaus Naumann, eds, *War of Extermination: The German Military in World War Two 1941–1944*, Oxford, 2000.

Heilbron, John L., editor-in-chief, *The Oxford Companion to the History of Modern Science*, New York, 2003.

Heinemann, Elizabeth, *What Difference Does a Husband Make?* Oxford, 2003.

Heinemann, Ulrich, *Die verdrängte Niederlage. Politische Öffentlichkeit und Kriegsschuldfrage in der Weimarer Republik*, Göttingen, 1983.

Hekma, Gert, "Same-sex relations among men in Europe, 1700–1990," in *Sexual Cultures in Europe: Themes in Sexuality*, Franz Eder, Lesley Hall, and Gert Hekma, eds, Manchester, 1999, pp. 79–103.

Henig, Ruth, *Versailles and After, 1919–1933*, 2nd edn, London, 1995.

Herbert, Ulrich, *Hitler's Foreign Workers*, Cambridge, 1998.

Herf, Jeffrey, *Divided Memory: The Nazi Past in the Two Germanys*, Cambridge MA, 1997.

Herrmann, David G., *The Arming of Europe and the Making of the First World War*, Princeton NJ, 1996.

Herwig, Holger H., "Admirals versus generals: the war aims of the Imperial German Navy, 1914–1918," *Central European History* 5 (1972): 208–33.

Herwig, Holger H., "Innovation Ignored: The Submarine Problem," in *Military Innovation in the Interwar Period*, Williamson Murray and Allan R. Millett, eds, Cambridge, 1996, pp. 227–64.

Herwig, Holger H., *The First World War: Germany and Austria-Hungary, 1914–1918*, London, 1997.

Hessenbruch, Arne, *Reader's Guide to the History of Science*, London, 2000.

Hiden, John, *Germany and Europe, 1919–1939*, 2nd edn, London, 1993.

Hilberg, Raul, *The Destruction of the European Jews*, 3rd edn, New Haven CT, 2003.

Hildebrand, Klaus, *The Foreign Policy of the Third Reich*, London 1973.

Hill, Polly, *The Migrant Cocoa-Farmers of Southern Ghana*, Oxford, 2nd edn, 1997.

Hinsley, F. H., ed., *British Foreign Policy under Sir Edward Grey*, Cambridge, 1997.

Hirschfeld, G., *Nazi Rule and Dutch Collaboration: The Netherlands under German Occupation, 1940–1945*, Oxford, 1988.

Hirschfeld, G., Gerd Krumeich, and Irina Renz, eds, *Enzyklopädie Erster Weltkrieg*, Paderborn, 2003.

Hirschfeld, G., and P. Marsh, eds, *Collaboration in France: Politics and Culture during the Nazi Occupation*, Oxford, 1989.

Hobsbawm, Eric, *The Age of Revolution: Europe, 1789–1848*, London, 1977.

Hobsbawm, Eric, *The Age of Empire, 1875–1914*, Cambridge MA, 1987.

Hobsbawm, Eric, *Echoes of the Marseillaise: Two Centuries Look Back on the French Revolution*, New Brunswick NJ, 1990.

Hochschild, Adam, *King Leopold's Ghost: A Story of Greed, Terror, and Heroism in Colonial Africa*, Boston MA, 1999.

Hoffmann, Stanley, "Collaborationism in France," *Journal of Modern History* 40/3 (1968): 375–95.

Hohenberg, Paul, and Lynn Hollen Lees, *The Making of Urban Europe, 1000–1994*, Cambridge MA, 1995.

Holmes, Richard, *Tommy: The British Soldier on the Western Front, 1914–1918*, London, 2004.

Holquist, Peter, *Making War, Forging Revolution: Russia's Continuum of Crisis, 1914–1921*, Cambridge MA, 2002.

Holt, Richard, *Sport and Society in Modern France*, London, 1981.

Holton, Sandra S., *Feminism and Democracy: Women's Suffrage and Reform Politics in Britain, 1900–1918*, Cambridge, 1986.

Holton, Sandra S., "Women and the Vote," in *Women's History: Britain, 1850–1945*, June Purvis, ed., London, 1995.

Holton, Sandra S., *Suffrage Days: Stories from the Women's Suffrage Movement*, London, 1996.

Horn, Daniel, *The German Naval Mutinies of World War I*, New Brunswick NJ, 1969.

Horne, Janet R., "In Pursuit of Greater France: Visions of Empire among Musée Social Reformers, 1894–1931," in *Domesticating the Empire: Race, Gender, and Family Life in French and Dutch Colonialism*, Julia Clancy-Smith and Francis Gouda, eds, Charlottesville VA, 1998, pp. 21–42.

Horne, John, and Alan Kramer, *German Atrocities 1914: A History of Denial*, London, 2001.

Horne, John, and Alan Kramer, "Introduction: Mobilizing for 'Total War,' 1914–1918," in *State, Society and Mobilization in Europe during the First World War*, John Horne, ed., Cambridge, 2002, pp. 1–17.

Horwood, Catherine, "'Girls who arouse dangerous passions': women and bathing, 1900–1939," *Women's History Review* 9/4 (2000): 653–73.

Howard, Michael, *The Continental Commitment: The Dilemma of British Defence Policy in the Era of Two World Wars*, London, 1974.

Huelsenbeck, Richard, ed., *The Dada Almanach*, Malcolm Green, trans., London, 1993 [Berlin, 1920].

Hughes, Robert, *The Shock of the New*, revd edn, New York, 1991.

Hyam, Ronald, "The British Empire in the Edwardian Era," in *The Oxford History of the British Empire: The Twentieth Century*, Judith Brown and W. Roger Louis, eds, Oxford, 1999, pp. 47–63.

Iakovlev, I. N., et al., *Sovetsko-Amerikanskie Otnosheniia: Gody Nepriznaniia, 1927–1933*, Moscow, 2002.

Iakovlev, I. N., et al., *Sovetsko-Amerikanskie Otnosheniia, 1934–1939*, Moscow, 2003.

Imlay, Talbot C., *Facing the Second World War: Strategy, Politics, and Economics in Britain and France, 1938–1940*, New York, 2003.

Innes, Christopher, "Modernism in Drama," in *The Cambridge Companion to Modernism*, Michael Levenson, ed., Cambridge, 1999.

Isnenghi, Mario, ed., *I luoghi della memoria*, 3 vols, Rome, 1997–8.

Jackson, Julian, *The Popular Front in France: Defending Democracy, 1934–38*, Cambridge, 1988.

Jackson, Julian, *The Dark Years: France 1940–1944*, Oxford, 2002.

Jackson, Julian, ed., *Europe, 1900–1945*, Oxford, 2002.

Jackson, Peter, *France and the Nazi Menace: Intelligence and Policy Making, 1933–1939*, New York, 2000.

Jackson, Peter, "France," in *The Origins of World War Two: The Debate Continues*, Robert Boyce and Joseph A. Maiolo, eds, Basingstoke, 2003, pp. 86–110.

Jacobson, Hans-Adolf , "The Structure of Nazi Foreign Policy 1933–1945," in *The Third Reich*, Christian Leitz, ed., Oxford, 1999, pp. 51–94.

Jacobson, Jon, *Locarno Diplomacy: Germany and the West, 1925–1929*, Princeton NJ, 1972.

Jacobson, Jon, *When the Soviet Union Entered World Politics*, Berkeley CA, 1994.

Jaeckel, Eberhard, *Hitler's World View: A Blueprint for Power*, Cambridge MA, 1981.

James, Harold, *The German Slump*, Oxford, 1986.

Jeal, Tim, *Baden-Powell*, New Haven CT, 1989.

Jelavich, Peter, *Berlin Cabaret*, Cambridge MA, 1993.

Jenkins, Roy, *Mr Balfour's Poodle: An Account of the Struggle Between the House of Lords and the Government of Mr Asquith*, London, 1954.

Johnson, Eric, *The Nazi Terror*, New York, 1999.

Johnson, Martin P., *The Dreyfus Affair*, Basingstoke, 1999.

Joll, James, *Europe Since 1870: An International History*, New York, 1973.

Joll, James, *The Second International 1889–1914*, London, 1974.

Joll, James, *The Origins of the First World War*, 2nd edn, London, 1992.

Jones, Neville, *The Origins of Strategic Bombing*, London, 1973.

Jones, Peter, ed., *Imagist Poetry*, London, 1972.

Joyce, Patrick, *Visions of the People: Industrial England and the Question of Class, 1848–1914*, Cambridge, 1991.

Judt, Tony, ed., *Resistance and Revolution in Mediterranean Europe, 1939–1948*, London, 1989.

Juliá, Santos, *Orígenes del Frente Popular en España (1934–1936)*, Madrid, 1979.

Juliá, Santos, "The Origins of the Spanish Popular Front," in *The French and Spanish Popular Fronts: Comparative Perspectives*, M. Alexander and H. Graham, eds, Cambridge, 1989.

Kann, Robert A., *A History of the Habsburg Empire, 1526–1918*, Berkeley CA, 1974.

Kaplan, Alice Yeager, *Reproductions of Banality: Fascism, Literature, and French Intellectual Life*, Minneapolis MN, 1986.

Kater, Michael, *Different Drummers: Jazz in the Culture of Nazi Germany*, New York, 1992.

Katz, Steven T., *The Holocaust in Historical Context*, vol. 1, New York, 1994.

Kean, Hilda, "'Searching for the past in present defeat': the construction of historical and political identity in British feminism in the 1920s and 1930s," *Women's History Review* 3/1 (1994): 57–80.

Kedward, H. Roderick, *Resistance in Vichy France*, Oxford, 1978.

Kedward, H. Roderick, *Occupied France*, Oxford, 1985.

Keegan, John, *The Second World War*, New York, 1989.

Keegan, John, *The First World War*, London, 1998.

Keiger, John F. V., *France and the Origins of the First World War*, London, 1983.

Keiger, John F. V., "France," in *Decisions for War*, K. Wilson, ed., London, 1995, pp. 121–49.

Kennedy, Paul, ed., *The War Plans of the Great Powers, 1880–1914*, Boston MA, 1979.

Kennedy, Paul, ed., "The Development of German Naval Operations Plans against England, 1896–1914," in *The War Plans of the Great Powers, 1880–1914*, Paul Kennedy, ed., Boston MA, 1979.

Kennedy, Paul, ed., *The Realities Behind Diplomacy: Background Influences on British External Policy, 1865–1980*, London, 1981.

Kennedy, Paul, ed., *The Rise of Anglo-German Antagonism*, London, 1982.

Kent, Bruce, *The Spoils of War: The Politics, Economics and Diplomacy of Reparations, 1918–1932*, Oxford, 1991.

Kent, Marian, ed., *The Great Powers and the End of Ottoman Empire*, 2nd edn, London, 1996.

Kent, Susan K., *Making Peace: The Reconstruction of Gender in Interwar Britain*, Princeton NJ, 1993.

Kenwood, A. G., and A. L. Lougheed, *The Growth of the International Economy, 1820–1990: An Introductory Text*, 4th edn, London, 1992.

Kern, Stephen, *The Culture of Time and Space 1880–1918*, 2nd edn, Cambridge MA, 2000.

Kershaw, Ian, *Popular Opinion and Political Dissent in the Third Reich*, Oxford, 1983.

Kershaw, Ian, *Hitler*, 2 vols, London, 1998/2000.

Kershaw, Ian, *The Nazi Dictatorship*, 4th edn, London, 2000.

Kilmarx, Robert, *A History of Soviet Air Power*, New York, 1962.

Kindleberger, Charles P., *The World in Depression 1929–1939*, 2nd edn, London, 1987.

King, Lynda J., *Best-Sellers by Design: Vicki Baum and the House of Ullstein*, Detroit MI, 1988.

Király, Bela, and László Vezprémy, eds, *Trianon and East Central Europe: Antecedents and Repercussions*, Boulder CO, 1995.

Kitchen, Martin, *Europe Between the Wars: A Political History*, London, 1988.

Kitching, Carolyn, *Britain and the Problem of International Disarmament, 1919–1934*, London, 1999.

Kocka, Jürgen, *Facing Total War: German Society 1914–1918*, Barbara Weinberger, trans., Cambridge MA, 1984.

Koebner, Thomas, Rolf-Peter Janz, and Frank Trommler, eds, *"Mit uns zieht die neue Zeit": Der Mythos Jugend*, Frankfurt am Main, 1985.

Kojmathy, Anthony, and Rebecca Stockwell, *German Minorities and the Third Reich*, New York, 1980.

Kolakowski, Leszek, *Main Currents of Marxism*, Oxford, 1981.

Komlos, John, *The Habsburg Monarchy as a Customs Union: Economic Development in Austria-Hungary in the Nineteenth Century*, Princeton NJ, 1983.

Konirsch, S., "Constitutional struggles between Czechs and Germans in the Habsburg monarchy," *Journal of Modern History* 27 (1955): 231–61.

Koon, Tracy, *Believe, Obey, Fight: Political Socialization of Youth in Fascist Italy*, Chapel Hill NC, 1985.

Koonz, Claudia, *Mothers in the Fatherland*, New York, 1987.

Kopp, Anatole, *Town and Revolution: Soviet Architecture and City Planning, 1917–1935*, Thomas E. Burton, trans., New York, 1970.

Koralka, Jiri, "Spontaneity and organization in Czech youth movements," in *La Jeunesse et ses Mouvements*, Paris, 1992.

Korman, Gerd, "The Holocaust and American historical writing," *Societas* 1 (1972): 251–70.

Koshar, Rudy, *Splintered Classes: Politics and the Lower Middle Classes in Interwar Europe*, New York, 1990.

Kotkin, Stephen, *Magnetic Mountain: Stalinism as a Civilization*, Berkeley CA, 1995.

Krementsov, Nikolai, *Stalinist Science*, Princeton NJ, 1997.

Krige, John, and Dominique Pestre, eds, *Science in the Twentieth Century*, Amsterdam, 1997.

Kroener, Bernard, Ralf-Dietrich Müller, and Hans Umbreit, eds, *Germany and the Second World War*, vol. 5, part 1, Oxford, 2000.

Krumeich, Gerhard, *Armaments and Politics in France on the Eve of the First World War*, Leamington Spa, 1984.

Kuromiya, Hiroaki, *Stalin's Industrial Revolution: Politics and Workers, 1928–1932*, New York, 1998.

Kushner, Tony, and Katherine Knox, *Refugees in an Age of Genocide: Global, National and Local Perspectives during the Twentieth Century*, London, 1999.

Kuznets, Simon S., *Modern Economic Growth*, New Haven CT, 1966.

Kuznets, Simon S., *Economic Growth of Nations: Total Output and Production Stucture*, Cambridge MA, 1971.

Lagrou, Pieter, "Victims of Genocide and National Memory: Belgium, France and the Netherlands, 1945–1965," in *The World War Two Reader*, Gordon Martel, ed., New York, 2004.

Langdon, John W., *July 1914: The Long Debate 1918–1990*, New York, 1991.

Langhamer, Claire, *Women's Leisure in England 1920–1960*, Manchester, 2000.

Langhorne, R. T. B., "Great Britain and Germany, 1911–1914," in *British Foreign Policy under Sir Edward Grey*, F. H. Hinsley, ed., Cambridge, 1997, pp. 288–314.

Laqueur, Walter, *Young Germany: A History of the German Youth Movement*, London, 1962.

Larkin, Maurice, *Church and State after the Dreyfus Affair: The Separation Issue in France*, London, 1974.

Lawrence, Paul, "Images of Poverty and Crime: Police Memoirs in England and France," *Crime, History and Societies* 3/1 (2000): 63–82.

Leaska, Mitchell A., ed., *The Virginia Woolf Reader*, New York, 1984.

Ledeen, Michael A., "Italy: War as a Style of Life," in *The War Generation: Veterans of the First World War*, Stephen R. Ward, ed., Port Washington NY, 1975, pp. 104–34.

Lee, Marshall M., and Wolfgang Michalka, *German Foreign Policy, 1917–1933: Continuity or Break?* Leamington Spa, 1987.

Leed, Eric J., "Class and disillusionment in World War I," *Journal of Modern History* 50/4 (1978): 680–99.

Leed, Eric J., *No Man's Land: Combat and Identity in World War I*, Cambridge, 1979.

Lees, Andrew, *Cities Perceived: Urban Society in European and American Thought, 1820–1940*, Manchester, 1995.

Leese, Peter, *Shell-Shock: Traumatic Neurosis and the British Soldiers of the First World War*, Basingstoke, 2002.

Legates, Marlene, *In Their Time: A History of Feminism in Western Society*, London, 2001.

Leitz, Christian, ed., *The Third Reich*, Oxford, 1999.

Lemkin, Raphael, *Axis Rule in Occupied Europe: Laws of Occupation, Analysis of Government Proposals for Redress*, Washington DC, 1944.

Lentin, Antony, *Guilt at Versailles: Lloyd George and the Pre-History of Appeasement*, London, 1985.

Lentin, Antony, "Decline and fall of the Versailles settlement," *Diplomacy and Statecraft* 4/2 (1993): 358–75.

Lentin, Antony, *Lloyd George and the Lost Peace: From Versailles to Hitler, 1919–1940*, Basingstoke, 2001.

Lentin, Antony, "Maynard Keynes and the 'bamboozlement' of Woodrow Wilson: what really happened at Paris? (Wilson, Lloyd George, pensions and pre-armistice agreement)," *Diplomacy and Statecraft* 15/4 (2004): 725–63.

Lerman, Katharine, *Bismarck*, London, 2004.

Leslie, John, "Österreich-Ungarn vor dem Kriegsausbruch. Der Ballhausplatz in Wien im Juli 1914 aus der Sicht eines österreichisches Diplomaten," in *Deutschland und Europa in der Neuzeit. Festschrift für Karl Otmar v. Aretin*, vol. 2, R. Melville, ed., Stuttgart, 1988, pp. 661–84.

Levenson, Michael, ed., *The Cambridge Companion to Modernism*, Cambridge, 1999.

Levi, Giovanni, and Jean-Claude Schmitt, eds, *A History of Young People in the West*, vol. 2: *Stormy Evolution to Modern Times*, Cambridge MA, 1997.

Lewis, Jill, "Conservatives and Fascists in Austria, 1918–34," in *Fascists and Conservatives: The Establishment and the Radical Right in Twentieth-Century Europe*, Martin Blinkhorn, ed., London, 1990, pp. 98–117.

Lichtheim, George, *Marxism: An Historical and Critical Study*, New York, 1982.

Liddell Hart, Basil H., *History of the Second World War*, London, 1992.

Lidtke, Vernon, *The Alternative Culture: Socialist Labor in Imperial Germany*, Oxford, 1985.

Lieven, D. C. B., *Russia and the Origins of the First World War*, London, 1983.

Lieven, D. C. B., *Nicholas II: Emperor of all the Russias*, London, 1993.

Light, Margot, *The Soviet Theory of International Relations*, Guildford, 1988.

Linke, Horst Günther, *Das zarische Rußland und der Erste Weltkrieg. Diplomatie und Kriegsziele, 1914–1917*, Munich, 1982.

Lipstadt, Deborah E., *Beyond Belief: The American Press and the Coming of the Holocaust 1933–1945*, New York, 1986.

Littlejohn, David, *The Patriotic Traitors*, London, 1972.

Loriga, Sabina, "The Military Experience," in *A History of Young People*, vol. 2: *Stormy Evolution to Modern Times*, Giovanni Levi and Jean-Claude Schmitt, eds, Cambridge MA, 1997, pp. 11–36.

Loshitzky, Yosefa, ed., *Spielberg's Holocaust: Critical Perspectives on Schindler's List*, Bloomington IN, 1997.

Louis, W. Roger, *Imperialism at Bay: The United States and the Decolonization of the British Empire, 1941–1945*, New York, 1978.

Lowe, C. J., and M. L. Dockrill, *The Mirage of Power: British Foreign Policy, 1914–22*, London, 1972.

Lowe, Donald M., *History of Bourgeois Perception*, Chicago IL, 1982.

Lüdtke, Alf, "The 'Honour of Labour,'" in *Nazism and German Society*, David Crew, ed., London, 1984.

Lüdtke, Alf, ed., *The History of Everyday Life*, Princeton NJ, 1995.

Lüdtke, Alf, ed., "The Appeal of Exterminating Others," in *The Third Reich*, Christian Leitz, ed., Oxford, 1999, pp. 153–78.

Luebbert, Gregory M., *Liberalism, Fascism, or Social Democracy: Social Classes and the Political Origins of Regimes in Interwar Europe*, New York, 1991.

Lukacs, John, *The Last European War, September 1939–December 1941*, London, 1977.

Lunn, Eugene, *Marxism and Modernism: An Historical Study of Lukács, Brecht, Benjamin, and Adorno*, Berkeley CA, 1984.

Lutz, Ralph. H., ed., *Fall of the German Empire, 1914–1918*, vol. 1, Palo Alto CA, 1932.

Lyttelton, Adrian, *The Seizure of Power: Fascism in Italy, 1919–1929*, 2nd edn, London, 1987.

Macartney, C. A., *The Habsburg Empire, 1790–1918*, New York, 1969.

McCormick, Richard W., *Gender and Sexuality in Weimar Modernity*, New York, 2001.

McDermott, Kevin, and Jeremy Agnew, *The Comintern: A History of International Communism from Lenin to Stalin*, London, 1996.

McDonald, David M., *United Government and Foreign Policy in Russia, 1900–1914*, Cambridge MA, 1992.

MacDonald, Stephen C., *A German Revolution: Local Change and Continuity in Prussia, 1918–1920*, New York, 1991.

MacDonogh, Giles, *The Last Kaiser: The Life of Wilhelm II*, New York, 2000.

McElligott, Anthony, *The German Urban Experience, 1900–1945: Modernity and Crisis*, London, 2001.

MacFadyen, David, *Songs for Fat People: Affect, Emotion and Celebrity in the Russian Popular Song, 1900–1955*, Montreal, 2002.

McInnes, Colin, and Gary D. Sheffield, eds, *Warfare in the Twentieth Century*, London, 1988.

McInnes, Colin, and Gary D. Sheffield, eds, *Men, Machines, and the Emergence of Modern Warfare, 1914–1945*, Camberley, 1992.

McKean, Robert B., *St Petersburg Between the Revolutions: Workers and Revolutionaries June 1907–February 1917*, New Haven CT, 1990.

MacKenzie, John M., *Propaganda and Empire: The Manipulation of British Public Opinion, 1880–1960*, Manchester, 1984.

MacKenzie, John M., "Empire and Metropolitan Cultures," in *The Oxford History of the British Empire: The Nineteenth Century*, A. Porter, ed., Oxford, 1999, pp. 270–93.

Mackenzie, S. P., *Politics and Military Morale: Current Affairs and Citizenship Education in the British Army 1914–1950*, Oxford, 1992.

McKercher, B. J. C, ed., *Anglo-American Relations in the 1920s: The Struggle for Supremacy*, Basingstoke, 1991.

McLaren, Angus, *Twentieth-Century Sexuality: A History*, Oxford, 1999.

MacLeod, Roy M., and E. Kay Andrews, "The origins of the D.S.I.R.: reflections on ideas and men, 1915–1916," *Public Administration* 48 (1970): 23–48.

MacLeod, Roy M., and E. Kay Andrews, "The chemists go to war: the mobilization of civilian chemists and the British war effort, 1914–1918," *Annals of Science* 50 (1993): 455–81.

McManus, John C., *The Deadly Brotherhood: The American Combat Soldier in World War II*, Novato CA, 1998.

MacMillan, Margaret, *Paris 1919: Six Months that Changed the World*, New York, 2001.

Macnicol, John, "In pursuit of the underclass," *Journal of Social Policy* 16/3 (1987): 293–318.

Maddison, Angus, *Phases of Capitalist Development*, Oxford, 1982.

Maddison, Angus, *Monitoring the World Economy*, Paris, 1995.

Maddison, Angus, *The World Economy: A Millennial Perspective*, Paris, 2001.

Magee, Frank, "Limited liability? Britain and the Treaty of Locarno," *Twentieth Century British History* 6/1 (1995): 1–22.

Maier, Charles S., *Recasting Bourgeois Europe: Stabilization in France, Germany, and Italy in the Decade after World War I*, Princeton NJ, 1975; revd edn, 1988.

Maisel, Ephraim, *The Foreign Office and Foreign Policy, 1919–1926*, Brighton, 1994.

Majer, Diemut, *"Non-Germans" under the Third Reich*, Baltimore MD, 2003.

Maltby, Richard, ed., *Dreams for Sale: Popular Culture in the 20th Century*, London, 1989.

Marcus, Geoffrey, *Before the Lamps Went Out*, London, 1965.

Marcuse, Harold, *Legacies of Dachau: The Uses and Abuses of a Concentration Camp, 1933–2001*, New York, 2001.

Marks, Sally, *The Illusion of Peace: International Relations in Europe, 1918–1933*, 2nd edn, Basingstoke, 2003.

Marrus, Michael R., *The Holocaust in History*, Hanover MA, 1987.

Marsch, Ulrich, *Zwischen Wissenschaft und Wirtschaft: Industrieforschung in Deutschland und Großbritannien 1880–1936*, Paderborn, 2000.

Marshal, S. L. A., *Men Against Fire: The Problem of Battle Command in Future War*, Gloucester MA, 1947.

Marsollek, Inge, and René Ott, *Bremen im Dritten Reich*, Bremen, 1986.

Martel, Gordon, *Modern Germany Reconsidered*, London, 1992.

Martel, Gordon, *The Origins of the Second World War Reconsidered: The Debate Continues*, London, 1999.

Martel, Gordon, "Military Planning and the Origins of the Second World War," in *Military Planning and the Origins of the Second World War*, Brian McKercher and Michael Hennessy, eds, New York, 2000, pp. 11–34.

Martel, Gordon, *The Origins of the First World War*, 3rd edn, London, 2003.

Martin, Benjamin F., *France and the Apres Guerre, 1918–1924*, Baton Rouge LA, 1999.

Martin, Terry, *The Affirmative Action Empire: Nations and Nationalism in the Soviet Union, 1923–1939*, Ithaca NY, 2001.

Marwick, Arthur, Clive Emsley, and Wendy Simpson, eds, *Total War and Historical Change*, Buckingham, 2001.

Mason, Tim, *Arbeiterklasse und Volksgemeinschaft*, Opladen, 1975.

Mason, Tim, *Social Policy in the Third Reich*, Oxford, 1993.

Mason, Tim, *Nazism, Fascism and the Working Class*, Cambridge, 1995.

Matz, Jesse, *Literary Impressionism and Modernist Aesthetics*, Cambridge, 2001.

Mawdsley, Evan, *The Russian Civil War*, Boston MA, 1987.

May, Ernest R., *The World War and American Isolation, 1914–1917*, Cambridge MA, 1959.

May, Ernest R., *Strange Victory: Hitler's Conquest of France*, New York, 2000.

Mayer, Arno J., "Causes and purposes of war in Europe, 1870–1956: a research assignment," *Journal of Modern History* 41 (1969): 291–303.

Mayer, Arno J., *Political Origins of the New Diplomacy*, New York, 1970.

Mayhall, Laura E. Nym, "Creating the 'suffragette' spirit: British feminism and the historical imagination," *Women's History Review* 4/3 (1995): 319–44.

Mayhall, Laura E. Nym, *The Militant Suffrage Movement: Citizenship and Resistance in Britain, 1860–1930*, Oxford, 2003.

Maynes, Mary Jo, *Taking the Hard Road: Life Course in French and German Workers' Autobiographies in the Era of Industrialization*, Raleigh NC, 1995.

Mazower, Mark, *Dark Continent: Europe's Twentieth Century*, New York, 1998.

Mazower, Mark, "Two Cheers for Versailles," *History Today* 49 (1999): 8–14.

Méadel, Cécile, "Programmes en masse, programmes de masse?" in *Masses et culture de masse dans les années 30*, Régine Robin, ed., Paris, 1991, pp. 51–68.

Medvedev, Roy, *Let History Judge: The Origins and Consequences of Stalinism*, New York, 1989.

Melman, Billie, *Women and the Popular Imagination in the Twenties: Flappers and Nymphs*, Basingstoke, 1988.

Merridale, Catherine, "War, Death, and Remembrance in Soviet Russia," in *War and Remembrance in the Twentieth Century*, Jay Winter and Emmanuel Sivan, eds, Cambridge, 1999, pp. 61–83.

Merridale, Catherine, *Night of Stone: Death and Memory in Twentieth Century Russia*, New York, 2001.

Michael-Mallmann, Klaus, and Gerhard Paul, *Herrschaft und Alltag*, Bonn, 1991.

Michalka, Wolfgang, ed., *Der Erste Weltkrieg. Wirkung, Wahrnehmung, Analyse*, Munich, 1994.

Michel, Henri, *Shadow War: Resistance in Europe, 1939–1945*, London, 1972.

Michman, Dan, *Holocaust Historiography: A Jewish Perspective*, London, 2003.

Miliukov, P. N., *Vospominaniia, Tom vtoroi (1859–1917)*, Moscow, 1990.

Miller, Judith, *One, by One, by One: Facing the Holocaust*, New York, 1990.

Millet, Allan R., and Williamson Murray, eds, *Military Effectiveness*, vol. 3: *The Second World War*, London, 1988.

Millet, Allan R., and Williamson Murray, eds, "The US Armed Forces in the Second World War," in A. R. Millet and W. Murray, eds, *Military Effectiveness*, vol. 3: *The Second World War*, London, 1988.

Milward, Alan, *War, Economy and Society, 1939–1945*, London, 1977.

Mitchell, Brian R., *International Historical Statistics*, 5th edn, London, 2003.

Mitchell, Reid, "The GI in Europe and the American Military Tradition," in P. Addison and A. Calder, eds, *Time to Kill*, London, 1997, pp. 304–18.

Mombauer, Annika, *Helmuth von Moltke and the Origins of the First World War*, Cambridge, 2001.

Mombauer, Annika, *The Origins of the First World War: Controversies and Consensus*, London, 2002.

Mommsen, Wolfgang J., "The German Revolution 1918–1920: Political Revolution and Social Protest Movement," Jane Williams, trans., in *Social Change and Political Development in Weimar Germany*, R. Bessel and E. J. Feuchtwanger, eds, London, 1981, pp. 21–54.

Mommsen, Wolfgang J., *Imperial Germany 1867–1918: Politics, Culture and Society in an Authoritarian State*, London, 1995.

Moore, Barrington, *Injustice: The Social Basis of Obedience and Revolt*, White Plains NY, 1978.

Morgan, Robert P., ed., *Modern Times*, Basingstoke, 1993.

Morrison, Mark S., *The Public Face of Modernism*, Madison WI, 2001.

Morsch, Günther, *Arbeit und Brot*, Frankfurt am Main, 1993.

Morton, Desmond, *When Your Number's Up*, Toronto, 1993.

Mosse, George L., *Fallen Soldiers: Reshaping the Memory of the World Wars*, New York, 1990.

Motherwell, Robert, ed., *The Dada Painters and Poets: An Anthology*, 2nd edn, trans. Ralph Manheim, Cambridge MA, 1988.

Müller, Klaus-Jürgen, "The Brutalisation of Warfare, Nazi Crimes and the Wehrmacht," in *Barbarossa: The Axis and the Allies*, J. Erickson and D. Dilks, eds, Edinburgh, 1994, pp. 229–37.

Muller, Richard, *The German Air War in Russia*, Baltimore MD, 1992.

Muller, Richard, "Close Air Support: The German, British, and American Experiences, 1918–1941," in *Military Innovation in the Interwar Period*, Williamson Murray and Allan R. Millett, eds, Cambridge, 1996.

Murray, Williamson, *Luftwaffe*, Baltimore MD, 1985.

Murray, Williamson, and Allan R. Millett, eds, *Military Effectiveness*, 3 vols, Boston MA, 1988.

Murray, Williamson, and Allan R. Millett, eds, *Military Innovation in the Interwar Period*, Cambridge, 1996.

Murray, Williamson, and Allan R. Millett, eds, "Britain," in *The Origins of World War Two: The Debate Continues*, Robert Boyce and Joseph A. Maiolo, eds, Basingstoke, 2003, pp. 111–32.

Myers, Charles, *Shell-Shock in France*, Cambridge, 1940.

Nadeau, Maurice, *The History of Surrealism*, revd edn, Richard Howard, trans., Cambridge MA, 1989.

Nagy-Talavera, Nicholas M., *The Green Shirts and the Others: A History of Fascism in Hungary and Romania*, 2nd edn, Portland OR, 2001.

Neitzel, Sönke, *Kriegsausbruch. Deutschlands Weg in die Katastroph*, Munich, 2002.

Neufeld, Michael, *The Rocket and the Reich: Peenemünde and the Coming of the Ballistic Missile Era*, New York, 1995.

Neville, Peter, *Neville Chamberlain: A Study in Failure?* London, 1992.

Nichols, Peter, *Modernisms: A Literary Guide*, Berkeley CA, 1995.

Nicolson, I. F., *The Administration of Nigeria: Men, Methods and Myths*, Oxford, 1969.

Noakes, Jeremy, and Geoffrey Pridham, eds, *Nazism: A Documentary Collection*, 4 vols, Exeter, 1983–98.

Noakes, Jeremy, and Geoffrey Pridham, eds, "Social Outcasts in the Third Reich," in *Life in the Third Reich*, Richard Bessel, ed., Oxford, 1987, pp. 83–96.

Nolan, Mary, "Work, Gender and Everyday Life," in *Nazism and German Society*, David Crew, ed., London, 1994, pp. 311–42.

Nolte, Hans-Heinrich, "Stalinism as Total Social War," in Roger Chickering and Stig Förster, eds, *The Shadows of Total War*, Cambridge, 2003, pp. 295–311.

Northedge, F. S., *The League of Nations: Its Life and Times 1920–1946*, Leicester, 1986.

Nott, James J., *Music for the People: Popular Music and Dance in Interwar Britain*, Oxford, 2002.

Nove, Alec, *An Economic History of the USSR*, London, 1969.

Novick, Peter, *The Holocaust in American Life*, Boston MA, 1999.

Nye, Mary Jo, ed., *The Cambridge History of Science*, vol. 5: *The Modern Physical and Mathematical Sciences*, Cambridge, 2003.

Nye, Robert A., *Crime, Madness and Degeneration in Modern France*, Princeton NJ, 1984.

O'Riordan, Elspeth Y., *Britain and the Ruhr Crisis*, Basingstoke, 2001.

Offen, Karen, *European Feminisms, 1700–1950: A Political History*, Stanford CA, 2000.

Ogren, Kathy J., *The Jazz Revolution: Twenties America and the Meaning of Jazz*, New York, 1989.

Okey, Robin, *The Habsburg Monarchy: From Enlightenment to Eclipse*, New York, 2001.

Olby, Robert C., G. N. Cantor, J. R. R. Christie, and M. J. S. Hodge, eds, *Companion to the History of Modern Science*, London, 1990.

Oosterhuis, Harry, "The Netherlands: Neither Prudish Nor Hedonistic," in *Sexual Cultures in Europe: National Histories*, Franz Eder, Lesley Hall, and Gert Hekma, eds, Manchester, 1999, pp. 71–90.

Oosterhuis, Harry, *Stepchildren of Nature: Krafft-Ebing, Psychiatry and the Making of Sexual Identity*, Chicago IL, 2000.

Oram, Gerard, ed., *Conflict and Legality: Policing Mid-Twentieth Century Europe*, London, 2003.

Orde, Anne, *Great Britain and International Security, 1920–26*, London, 1978.

Osterhammel, Jürgen, *Colonialism: A Theoretical Overview*, Princeton NJ, 1997.

Ousby, Ian, *Occupation: The Ordeal of France*, London, 1997.

Overy, Richard J., *Goering: The Iron Man*, London, 1984.

Overy, Richard J., *War and Economy in the Third Reich*, Oxford, 1994.

Overy, Richard J., *Why the Allies Won*, London, 1995.

Overy, Richard J., *The Nazi Economic Recovery*, 2nd edn, London, 1996.

Overy, Richard J., *Russia's War*, London, 1997; New York, 1998.

Overy, Richard J., "Germany, 'Domestic Crisis' and the War in 1939," in *The Third Reich*, Christian Leitz, ed., Oxford, 1999, pp. 97–128.

Overy, Richard J., *The Dictators: Hitler's Germany and Stalin's Russia*, London, 2004.

Parker, R. A. C., *Chamberlain and Appeasement: British Policy and the Coming of the Second World War*, Basingstoke, 1993.

Parkins, Wendy, ed., *Fashioning the Body Politic: Dress, Gender, Citizenship*, Oxford, 2002.

Parks, W. Hays, "Air war and the law of war," *Air Force Law Review* 32/1 (1990): 1–225.

Paul, Harry W., *From Knowledge to Power: The Rise of the Science Empire in France, 1860–1939*, Cambridge, 1985.

Paulicelli, Eugenia, *Fashion under Fascism: Beyond the Black Shirt*, New York, 2004.

Paulsson, Gunnar S., *Secret City: The Hidden Jews of Warsaw 1940–1945*, New Haven CT, 2002.

Paxton, Robert O., *Vichy France: Old Guard and New Order, 1940–1944*, New York, 1972.

Paxton, Robert O., *The Anatomy of Fascism*, London, 2004.

Payne, Matthew, *Stalin's Railroad: Turksib and the Building of Socialism*, Pittsburgh PA, 2001.

Payne, Stanley G., *A History of Fascism, 1914–1945*, Madison WI, 1995.

Payne, Stanley G., *Fascism in Spain, 1923–1977*, Madison WI, 1999.

Pearsall, Ronald, *Popular Music of the Twenties*, London, 1976.

Pennebaker, James, Dario Paez, and Bernard Rimé, eds, *Collective Memory of Political Events: Social Psychological Perspectives*, Mahwah NJ, 1997.

Pereboom, Maarten L., *Democracies at the Turning Point: Britain, France, and the End of the Postwar Order, 1928–1933*, New York, 1995.

Perloff, Nancy L., *Art and the Everyday: Popular Entertainment and the Circle of Erik Satie*, Oxford, 1991.

Perman, David, *The Shaping of the Czechoslovak State*, Leiden, 1962.

Péter, Lázló, "Montesquieu's paradox on freedom and Hungary's constitutions 1790–1990," *History of Political Thought* 16 (1995): 77–121.

Petersen, Jens, "Jugend und Jugendprotest im faschistischen Italien," in *Jugendprotest und Generationenkonflikt in Europa im 20. Jahrhundert: Deutschland, England, Frankreich und Italien im Vergleich*, Dieter Dowe, ed., Bonn, 1986, pp. 199–208.

Petrie, Jon, "The secular word HOLOCAUST: Scholarly myths, history, and 20th-century meanings," *Journal of Genocide Research* 2 (2000): 31–63.

Peukert, Detlev, *Inside the Third Reich*, London, 1987.

Pick, Daniel, *Faces of Degeneration: A European Disorder, c. 1848–c. 1918*, Cambridge, 1989.

Pick, Hella, *Guilty Victim: Austria from the Holocaust to Haider*, London, 2000.

Pine, Lisa, *Nazi Family Policy*, Oxford, 1997.

Pinto, Antonio Costa, *The Blue Shirts: Portuguese Fascism in Interwar Europe*, New York, 2000.

Playne, Caroline E., *The Pre-War Mind in Britain*, London, 1928.

Poggioli, Renato, *The Theory of the Avant-Garde*, Gerald Fitzgerald, trans., New York, 1971.

Pollard, Sidney, *Peaceful Conquest: The Industrialisation of Europe 1760–1970*, Oxford, 1981.

Polonsky, Antony, and Joanna Michlic, eds, *The Neighbors Respond: The Controversy over the Jedwabne Massacre in Poland*, Princeton NJ, 2004.

Pons, Sylvio, *Stalin and the Inevitable War, 1936–1941*, London, 2002.

Porter, Andrew, ed., *The Oxford History of the British Empire: The Nineteenth Century*, Oxford, 1999.

Post, Ken, *Revolution and the European Experience, 1800–1914*, London, 1999.

Pramowska, Anita, *Britain, Poland and the Eastern Front, 1939*, Cambridge, 1987.

Preston, Paul, *The Coming of the Spanish Civil War: Reform, Reaction and Revolution in the Second Republic*, London, 1983.

Preston, Paul, "The Creation of the Popular Front in Spain," in *The Popular Front in Europe*, H. Graham and P. Preston, eds, London, 1987.

Preston, Paul, "The Great Civil War: European Politics, 1914–1945," in *The Oxford Illustrated History of Modern Europe*, T. C. W. Blanning, ed., Oxford, 1998, pp. 148–81.

Preston, Richard, Alex Roland, and Sidney Wise, *Men in Arms*, 5th edn, Fort Worth TX, 1991.

Prinz, Michael, *Vom neuen Mittelstand zum Volksgenossen*, Munich, 1986.

Prinz, Michael, and Rainer Zitelmann, eds, *Nationalsozialismus und Modernisierung*, Darmstadt, 1991.

Prior, Robin, and Trevor Wilson, *Command on the Western Front*, Oxford, 1992.

Procacci, Giovanna, "A 'Latecomer' in War: The Case of Italy," in *Authority, Identity and the Social History of the Great War*, Frans Coetzee and Marilyn Shevin-Coetzee, eds, Providence RI, 1995, pp. 3–27.

Proctor, Robert, *Racial Hygiene: Medicine under the Nazis*, Cambridge MA, 1988.

Proctor, Tammy M., "Scouts, Guides, and the Fashioning of Empire, 1919–1939," in *Fashioning the Body Politic*, Wendy Parkins, ed., Oxford, 2002.

Prost, Antoine, *In the Wake of War: "Les Anciens Combattants" and French Society, 1914–1939*, Providence RI, 1992.

Purvis, June, ed., *Women's History: Britain, 1850–1945*, London, 1995.

Purvis, June, ed., *Emmeline Pankhurst: A Biography*, London, 2002.

Putkowski, Julian, *Shot at Dawn: Executions in World War One by Authority of the British Army Act*, Barnsley, 1996.

Quine, Maria, *Population Politics in Twentieth-Century Europe*, London, 1996.

Quinn, Susan, *Marie Curie: A Life*, New York, 1995.

Ragsdale, Hugh, *The Soviets, the Munich Crisis, and the Coming of World War II*, New York, 2004.

Rauchensteiner, M., *Der Tod des Doppeladlers, Österreich-Ungarn und der Erste Weltkrieg*, Graz, 1993.

Rearick, Charles, *The French in Love and War: Popular Culture in the Era of the World Wars*, New Haven CT, 1997.

Reddy, William, *Money and Liberty in Modern Europe: A Critique of Historical Understanding*, Cambridge, 1987.

Reese, Dagmar, et al., eds, *Rationale Beziehungen? Geschlectsverhältnisse im Rationalisierungs prozess*, Frankfurt am Main, 1993.

Reese, Dagmar, et al., eds, "Emancipation or Social Incorporation: Girls in the Bund Deutscher Mädel," in *Education and Fascism: Political Identity and Social Education in Nazi Germany*, Heinz Sünker and Hans-Uwe Otto, eds, London, 1997.

Reich, Jacqueline, and Piero Garofalo, eds, *Re-viewing Fascism: Italian Cinema, 1922–1943*, Blooomington IN, 2002.

Reichardt, Sven, *Faschistische Kampfbünde. Gewalt und Gemeinschaft im italienischen Squadrismus und in der deutschen SA*, Cologne, 2002.

Rendall, Jane, *The Origins of Modern Feminism: Women in Britain, France and the United States, 1780–1860*, Basingstoke, 1985.

Rentschler, Eric, *The Ministry of Illusion: Nazi Cinema and its Afterlife*, Cambridge MA, 1996.

Resis, Albert, ed., *Molotov Remembers, Inside Kremlin Politics, Conversations with Felix Chuev*, Chicago IL, 1993.

Reynolds, Sian, *France Between the Wars: Gender and Politics*, London, 1996.

Riley, Denise, *"Am I That Name?" Feminism and the Category of "Women" in History*, Basingstoke, 1988.

Rings, Werner, *Life with the Enemy*, New York, 1982.

Riordan, James, and Pierre Arnaud, eds, *Sport and International Politics*, London, 1998.

Robb, George, and Nancy Erber, eds, *Disorder in the Court: Trials and Sexual Conflict at the Turn of the Century*, Basingstoke, 1999.

Roberts, Mary L., *Civilization Without Sexes: Reconstructing Gender in Postwar France, 1917–1927*, Chicago IL, 1994.

Robin, Régine, ed., *Masses et culture de masse dans les années 30*, Paris, 1991.

Robinson, Douglas, *The Zeppelin in Combat, 1912 to 1918*, London, 1962.

Rohe, Karl, *Das Reichsbanner Schwartz Rot Gold: Ein Beitrag zur Geschichte und Struktur der politischen Kampfverbände zur Zeit der Weimarer Republik*, Düsseldorf, 1966.

Röhl, John C. G., ed., *1914: Delusion or Design? The Testimony of Two German Diplomats*, London, 1973.

Röhl, John C. G., and N. Sombart, eds, *Kaiser Wilhelm II: New Interpretations*, Cambridge, 1982.

Röhl, John C. G., "The Emperor's New Clothes: A Character Sketch of Kaiser Wilhelm II," in *Kaiser Wilhelm II: New Interpretations*, J. C. G. Röhl and N. Sombart, eds, Cambridge, 1982, pp. 23–61.

Röhl, John C. G., "Germany," in *Decisions for War*, K. Wilson, ed., London, 1995, pp. 27–54.

Röhl, John C. G., *The Kaiser and His Court*, Cambridge, 1995.

Röhr, Werner, ed., *Okkupation und Kollaboration, 1938–1945*, Berlin, 1994.

Ropp, Theodore, *War in the Modern World*, New York, 1962.

Rosario, Vernon, *Science and Homosexualities*, London, 1997.

Rose, Phyllis, *Jazz Cleopatra: Josephine Baker in her Time*, London, 1989.

Rose, Sonya, *Which People's War? National Identity and Citizenship in Britain, 1939–1945*, Oxford, 2003.

Roseman, Mark, ed., *Generations in Conflict: Youth Revolt and Generation Formation in Germany 1770–1968*, Cambridge, 1995.

Roseman, Mark, ed., "National Socialism and Modernisation," in *Fascist Italy and Nazi Germany*, Richard Bessel, ed., Cambridge, 1996, pp. 196–229.

Rosen, Stephen P., *Winning the Next War: Innovation and the Modern Military*, Ithaca NY, 1991.

Rosenberg, Arthur, *A History of the German Republic*, Ian F. D. Morrow and L. Marie Sieveking, trans., London, 1936.

Rosenhaft, Eve, *Beating the Fascists: The German Communists and Political Violence 1929–1933*, Cambridge, 1983.

Ross, Dorothy, ed., *Modernist Impulses in the Human Sciences, 1870–1930*, Baltimore MD, 1994.

Rostow, Walt W., ed., *The Economics of Take-Off into Sustained Growth*, London, 1963.

Rostow, Walt W., *The Stages of Economic Growth*, 2nd edn, London, 1971.

Rota, Olivier, "Les 'Silences' du Pape Pie XII," *Revue d'Histoire Ecclésiastique* 99/3–4 (2004): 758–66.

Rothstein, Andrew, *The Soldiers' Strikes of 1919*, London, 1980.

Rothwell, Victor H., *British War Aims and Peace Diplomacy, 1914–1918*, Oxford, 1971.

Rousso, Henry, *The Vichy Syndrome: History and Memory in France since 1944*, Cambridge MA, 1991.

Rupp, Leila, *Worlds of Women: The Making of an International Women's Movement*, Princeton NJ, 1997.

Rzheshevskii, O. A., *Stalin i Cherchill'*, Moscow, 2004.

Sachse, Carola, et al., eds, *Angst, Belohnung, Zucht und Ordnung*, Opladen, 1982.

Sachse, Carola, et al., eds, *Betriebliche Sozialpolitik als Familienpolitik*, Hamburg, 1987.

Sachse, Carola, et al., eds, *Siemens, Nationalsozialismus und die moderne Familie*, Hamburg, 1990.

Saldern, Adelheid von, "Victims or Perpetrators," in *Nazism and German Society*, David Crew, ed., London, 1994, pp. 141–65.

Saler, Michael T., *The Avant-Garde in Interwar England: Medieval Modernism and the London Underground*, Oxford, 1999.

Salter, Stephen, "Structures of Consent and Coercion," in *Nazi Propaganda*, David Welch, ed., Beckenham, 1983.

Salzmann, Stephanie, *Great Britain, Germany, and the Soviet Union: Rapallo and After, 1922–1934*, London, 2003.

Sanborn, Joshua, "The mobilization of 1914 and the question of the Russian nation: a reexamination," *Slavic Review* 59 (2000): 267–89.

Sassoon, Donald, "Italy after Fascism: The Predicament of Dominant Narratives," in *Life after Death: Approaches to a Cultural and Social History of Europe during the 1940s and 1950s*, Richard Bessel and Dirk Schumann, eds, New York, 2003, pp. 259–90.

Saunders, Tom, *Hollywood in Berlin: American Cinema and Weimar Germany*, Berkeley CA, 1994.

Schädlich, K.-H., "Der 'Unabhängige Ausschuß für einen deutschen Frieden' als Zentrum der Annexionspropaganda im Ersten Weltkrieg," in *Politik im Krieg. Studien zur Politik der deutschen herrschenden Klassen im Ersten Weltkrieg*, Fritz Klein et al., eds, East Berlin, 1964, pp. 50–65.

Schleifer, Ronald, *Modernism and Time: The Logic of Abundance in Literature, Science, and Culture, 1880–1930*, Cambridge, 2000.

Schlör, Joachim, *Nights in the Big City*, London, 1998.

Schnieder, William H., *Quality and Quantity: The Quest for Biological Regeneration in Twentieth-Century France*, Cambridge, 1990.

Schoenbaum, David, *Hitler's Social Revolution*, London, 1964.

Schöllgen, Gregor, ed., *Escape into War? The Foreign Policy of Imperial Germany*, Oxford, 1990.

Schöllgen, Gregor, ed., "Germany's Foreign Policy in the Age of Imperialism: A Vicious Circle?" in *Escape into War? The Foreign Policy of Imperial Germany*, G. Schöllgen, ed., Oxford, 1990.

Schuker, Stephen A., *The End of French Predominance in Europe: The Financial Crisis of 1924 and the Adoption of the Dawes Plan*, Chapel Hill NC, 1976.

Schuster, Kurt G. P., *Der Rote Frontkämpferbund 1924–1929: Beiträge zur Geschichte und Organisationsstruktur eines politischen Kampfbundes*, Düsseldorf, 1975.

Schwabe, Klaus, *Woodrow Wilson, Revolutionary Germany, and Peacemaking 1918–1919*, Chapel Hill NC, 1985.

Schweitzer, Arthur, *Big Business in the Third Reich*, London, 1964.

Scott, Joan, "On language, gender, and working-class history," *International Labor and Working Class History* 31 (1987): 1–13.

Scott, Joan, ed., *Gender and the Politics of History*, New York, 1988.

Scott, John, *Behind the Urals: An American Worker in Russia's City of Steel*, Bloomington IN, 1989.

Searle, G. R., *The Quest for National Efficiency: A Study of British Politics and Political Thought, 1895–1914*, London, 1971.

Seaton, Albert, *The German Army, 1933–1945*, London, 1983.

Segré, Claudio G., *Fourth Shore: The Italian Colonization of Libya*, Chicago IL, 1974.

Seligmann, Matthew S., and Roderick R. McLean, *Germany from Reich to Republic 1871–1918*, Basingstoke, 2000.

Sengoopta, Chandak, and Otto Weininger, *Sex, Science and Self in Imperial Vienna*, Chicago IL, 2000.

Sewell Jr, William H., *Work and Revolution in France: The Language of Labor from the Old Regime to 1848*, Cambridge, 1980.

Sharp, Alan, *The Versailles Settlement: Peacemaking in Paris, 1919*, Basingstoke, 1991.

Sheffield, Gary D., "Blitzkrieg and Attrition: Land Operations in Europe, 1914–1945," in *Warfare in the Twentieth Century*, Colin McInnes and G. D. Sheffield, eds, London, 1988.

Sheffield, Gary D., *Forgotten Victory*, London, 2001.

Shepherd, Ben, *A War of Nerves: Soldiers and Psychiatrists, 1914–1994*, London, 2000.

Sherman, Daniel J., "Bodies and names: the emergence of commemoration in interwar France," *American Historical Review* 103/2 (1998): 443–66.

Sherman, Daniel J., *The Construction of Memory in Interwar France*, Chicago IL, 1999.

Shils, Edward, and Morris Janowitz, "Cohesion and disintegration in the Wehrmacht," *Public Opinion Quarterly* 12 (1948): 280–315.

Shinkarchuk, S. A., *Istoriia Sovetskoi Rossii (1917–1953) v Anekdotakh*, St. Petersburg, 2000.

Showalter, Dennis, *The Wars of German Unification*, London, 2004.

Shute, T. J., "The German soldier in occupied Russia," in *Time to Kill*, P. Addison and A. Calder, eds, London, 1997, pp. 274–83.

Siegel, Tilla, and Thomas von Freyberg, *Leistung und Lohn in der nationalsozialistischen "Ordnung der Arbeit"*, Opladen, 1989.

Siegel, Tilla, and Thomas von Freyberg, *Industrielle Rationalisierung unter dem Nationalsozialismus*, Frankfurt am Main, 1991.

Siegel, Tilla, and Thomas von Freyberg, "Rationalizing Industrial Relations," in *Reevaluating the Third Reich*, Thomas Childers and Jane Kaplan, eds, New York, 1993.

Siegelbaum, Lewis H., *The Politics of Industrial Mobilization in Russia, 1914–17: A Study of the War-Industries Committees*, London, 1983.

Silverman, Daniel P., *Hitler's Economy*, London, 1998.

Siriani, Carmen, *Workers Control and Socialist Democracy: The Soviet Experience*, London, 1982.

Sked, Alan, *The Decline and Fall of the Habsburg Empire 1815–1918*, 2nd edn, London, 2001.

Smith, Bradley F., *Sharing Secrets with Stalin: How the Allies Traded Intelligence, 1941–1945*, Lawrence KS, 1996.

Smith, Harold L., *British Feminism in the Twentieth Century*, Aldershot, 1990.

Smith, Harold L., *The British Women's Suffrage Campaign, 1866–1928*, London, 1998.

Smith, Leonard V., *Between Mutiny and Obedience: The Case of the French Fifth Infantry during World War I*, Princeton NJ, 1994.

Smith, Leonard V., et al., *France and the Great War, 1914–1918*, Cambridge, 2003.

Smith, Woodruff D., *The Ideological Origins of Nazi Imperialism*, New York, 1986.

Sohn, Anne-Marie, "French Catholics Between Abstinence and 'Appeasement Of Lust', 1930–1950," in *Sexual Cultures in Europe: Themes in Sexuality*, Franz Eder, Lesley Hall, and Gert Hekma, eds, Manchester, 1999, pp. 233–54.

Solotarev, V. A., G. N. Sevost'ianov, et al., *Velikaia Otechestvennaia voina, 1941–1945*, 4 vols, Moscow, 1998.

Sontag, Raymond J., *A Broken World, 1919–1939*, New York, 1971.

Soucy, Robert, "France: Veterans' Politics Between the Wars," in *The War Generation: Veterans of the First World War*, Stephen R. Ward, ed., Port Washington NY, 1975, pp. 59–103.

Soucy, Robert, *French Fascism: The First Wave, 1924–1933*, New Haven CT, 1986.

Soucy, Robert, *French Fascism: The Second Wave, 1933–1939*, New Haven CT, 1995.

Souto Kustrin, Sandra, "Taking the street: Workers: youth organizations and political conflict in the Spanish second republic," *European History Quarterly* 34/2 (2004): 131–56.

Spiller, Roger J., "S. L. A. Marshall and the ratio of fire," *Journal of the Royal United Services Institute* 133 (1988): 63–71.

Spohn, Wilfred, "Religion and Working-Class Formation in Imperial Germany, 1871–1914," in *Society, Culture, and the State in Germany*, G. Eley, ed., Ann Arbor MI, 1996, pp. 163–87.

Spring, Derek W., "Russia and the Coming of War," in *The Coming of the First World War*, R. J. W. Evans and H. Pogge von Strandmann, eds, Oxford, 1988, pp. 57–86.

Springhall, John, *Coming of Age: Adolescence in Britain 1860–1960*, Dublin, 1986.

Springhall, John, "'Young England, Rise UP, and Listen!' The Political Dimensions of Youth Protest and Generation Conflict in Britain, 1919–1939," in *Jugendprotest und Generationenkonflikt in Europa im 20. Jahrhundert: Deutschland, England, Frankreich und Italien im Vergleich*, Dieter Dowe, ed., Bonn, 1986, pp. 151–63.

Starr, S. Frederick, *Red and Hot: The Fate of Jazz in the Soviet Union, 1917–1980*, New York, 1983.

Steadman-Jones, Gareth, *Languages of Class: Studies in English Working Class History, 1832–1982*, Cambridge, 1983.

Steele, Valerie, *Paris Fashion: A Cultural History*, Oxford, 1999.

Steenson, Gary P., *After Marx, Before Lenin: Marxism and Socialist Working-Class Parties in Europe, 1884–1914*, Pittsburgh PA, 1991.

Steim, Alfred, "International Law and Soviet Prisoners of War," in *From Peace to War: Germany, Soviet Russia and the World, 1939–1941*, Bernd Wegner, ed., Providence RI, 1997, pp. 293–308.

Steiner, Zara, *Britain and the Origins of the First World War*, London, 1977.

Steiner, Zara, "The Treaty of Versailles Revisited," in *The Paris Peace Conference 1919: Peace without Victory?* Michael Dockrill and John Fisher, eds, Basingstoke, 2001.

Steiner, Zara, and Keith Neilson, *Britain and the Origins of the First World War*, London, 2003.

Steinlauf, Michael, *Bondage to the Dead: Poland and the Memory of the Holocaust*, Syracuse NY, 1997.

Stephenson, Jill, *The Nazi Organization of Women*, London, 1981.

Stephenson, Jill, *Women in Nazi Germany*, London, 2001.

Stevenson, David, *French War Aims Against Germany, 1914–1919*, Oxford, 1982.

Stevenson, David, *The First World War and International Politics*, Oxford, 1988.

Stevenson, David, *Armaments and the Coming of War: Europe 1904–1914*, Oxford, 1996.

Stevenson, David, "War Aims and Peace Negotiations," in *World War I: A History*, Hew Strachan, ed., Oxford, 1998.

Stevenson, David, *1914–1918: The History of the First World War*, London, 2004; published in the USA as *Cataclysm: The First World War as Political Tragedy*, New York, 2004.

Stevenson, Randall, *Modernist Fiction*, London, 1992.

Stewart, A. T. Q., *The Ulster Crisis*, London, 1967.

Stibbe, Matthew, *German Anglophobia and the Great War, 1914–1918*, Cambridge, 2001.

Stibbe, Matthew, *Women in the Third Reich*, Oxford, 2003.

Stites, Richard, *Russian Popular Culture: Entertainment and Society since 1900*, Cambridge, 1992.

Stöcker, Michael, *Augusterlebnis 1914 in Darmstadt: Legende und Wirklichkeit*, Darmstadt, 1994.

Stoecker, Helmut, ed., *German Imperialism in Africa*, London, 1986.

Stoff, Heiko, *Ewige Jugend. Konzepte der Verjüngung vom späten 19. Jahrhundert bis ins Dritte Reich*, Cologne, 2004.

Stone, Dan, *Breeding Superman: Nietzsche, Race and Eugenics in Edwardian and Interwar Britain*, Liverpool, 2002.

Stone, Norman, *Europe Transformed, 1878–1919*, Cambridge MA, 1984.

Stourzh, Gerald, "The multinational empire revisited: reflections on late imperial Austria," *Austrian History Yearbook* 23 (1992): 1–22.

Strachan, Hew, *European Armies and the Conduct of War*, London, 1983.

Strachan, Hew, ed., *The Oxford Illustrated History of the First World War*, Oxford, 1998.

Stuart, Robert C., *Marxism at Work: Ideology, Class and French Socialism, 1882–1905*, Cambridge, 1992.

Summerfield, Penny, "Women and War in the Twentieth Century," in *Women's History: Britain, 1850–1945*, June Purvis, ed., London, 1995.

Suny, Ronald G., "Toward a social history of the October Revolution," *American Historical Review* 88 (1983): 31–52.

Suny, Ronald G., "Revision and retreat in the historiography of 1917: social history and its critics," *Russian Review* 53 (1994): 165–82.

Sutcliffe, Anthony, ed., *Metropolis 1890–1940*, London, 1984.

Swanson, John C., *The Remnants of the Habsburg Monarchy: The Shaping of Modern Austria and Hungary, 1918–1922*, Boulder CO, 2001.

Sweeney, Regina M., *Singing Our Way to Victory: French Cultural Politics and Music during the Great War*, Middletown, 2001.

Syriatou, Athena, "Grossbritannien: 'Der Krieg wird uns zusammenhalten'," in *Mythen der Nationen: 1945, Arena der Erinnerungen*, Monika Flacke, ed., Berlin, 2004, pp. 285–307.

Szöllosi-Janze, Margit, ed., *Science in the Third Reich*, Oxford, 2001.

Szreter, Simon, "Falling Fertilities and Changing Sexualities," in *Sexual Cultures in Europe: Themes in Sexuality*, Franz Eder, Lesley Hall, and Gert Hekma, eds, Manchester, 1999, pp. 159–94.

Taylor, A. J. P., *The Struggle for Mastery in Europe, 1848–1918*, Oxford, 1954.

Taylor, A. J. P., *The Origins of the Second World War*, London, 1964.

Taylor, A. J. P., *English History, 1914–1945*, New York, 1965.

Terraine, John, *To Win a War: 1918, The Year of Victory*, London, 1978.

Thane, Pat, *The Foundations of the Welfare State*, Harlow, 1982.

Theweleit, Klaus, *Male Fantasies*, vol. 1: *Women, Floods, Bodies, History*, vol. 2: *Male Bodies: Psychoanalyzing the White Terror*, Oxford, 1987 and 1989.

Thimme, Annelise, *Flucht in den Mythos. Die Deutschnationale Volkspartei und die Niederlage von 1918*, Göttingen, 1969.

Thompson, Christopher, "The Tour in the Inter-War Years: Political Ideology, Athletic Excess and Industrial Modernity," in *Tour de France, 1903–2003*, Hugh Dauncey and Geoff Hare, eds, London, 2003, pp. 79–102.

Thompson, F. M. L., ed., *The Cambridge Social History of Britain 1750–1950*, vol. 3, Cambridge, 1990.

Thurschwell, Pamela, *Sigmund Freud*, London, 2000.

Tickner, Lisa, *The Spectacle of Women: Imagery of the Suffrage Campaign, 1907–1914*, London, 1987.

Tidrick, Kathryn, *Empire and the English Character*, London, 1990.

Till, Geoffrey, "Naval Power," in *Warfare in the Twentieth Century*, Colin McInnes and G. D. Sheffield, eds, London, 1988.

Tidrick, Kathryn, "Adopting the Aircraft Carrier," in *Military Innovation in the Interwar Period*, Williamson Murray and Allan R. Millett, eds, Cambridge, 1996.

Tortella, Gabriel, *The Development of Modern Spain: An Economic History of the Nineteenth and Twentieth Century*, Cambridge MA, 2000.

Trachtenberg, Marc, *Reparation in World Politics: France and European Economic Diplomacy, 1916–1923*, New York, 1980.

Travers, Tim, *The Killing Ground: The British Army, the Western Front, and the Emergence of Modern Warfare, 1900–1918*, London, 1987.

Travers, Tim, *How the War Was Won: Command and Technology in the British Army on the Western Front*, London, 1992.

Travers, Tim, *Gallipoli 1915*, Stroud, 2001.

Trommler, Frank, "Mission ohne Ziel. Über den Kult der Jugend im modernen Deutschland," in *"Mit uns zieht die neue Zeit": Mythos Jugend*, Thomas Koebner, Rolf-Peter Janz, and F. Trommler, eds, Frankfurt am Main, 1985.

Trumpener, Ulrich, *Germany and the Ottoman Empire, 1914–1918*, Princeton NJ, 1968.

Tuchman, Barbara, *The Zimmermann Telegram*, London, 1959.

Tumarkin, Nina, *The Living and the Dead: The Rise and Fall of the Cult of World War II in Russia*, New York, 1994.

Turner, Arthur, *The Cost of War: British Policy on French War Debts 1918–1932*, Brighton, 1998.

Turner, Henry Ashby, "Continuity in German foreign policy? The case of Stresemann," *International History Review* 1/4 (1979): 509–21.

Turner, Henry Ashby, *Big Business and the Rise of Hitler*, Oxford, 1985.

Ueberschär, Gerd R., "The Ideologically Motivated War of Annihilation in the East," in *Hitler's War in the East: A Critical Assessment*, Rolf-Dieter Müller and G. R. Ueberschär, eds, Oxford, 2002, pp. 209–82.

Uldricks, Teddy J., *Diplomacy and Ideology: The Origins of Soviet Foreign Relations, 1917–1930*, London, 1979.

Usborne, Cornelie, " 'Pregnancy is the woman's active service:' Pronatalism in Germany during the First World War," in *The Upheaval of War: Family, Work and Welfare in Europe 1914–1918*, Richard Wall and Jay Winter, eds, Cambridge, 1988, pp. 389–416.

Utgaard, Peter, *Remembering and Forgetting Nazism: Education, National Identity, and the Victim Myth in Postwar Austria*, New York, 2003.

Van Creveld, Martin, *Fighting Power: German and US Army Performance, 1939–1945*, London, 1983.

Van der Zee, Henri A., *The Hunger Winter: Occupied Holland, 1944–1945*, Lincoln NE, 1998.

Varcoe, Ian, "Scientists, government and organised research in Great Britain 1914–1916: the early history of the DSIR," *Minerva* 8 (1970): 192–216.

Veillon, Dominique, *Vivre et survivre en France, 1939–47*, Paris, 1995.

Veitch, Colin, " 'Play up! Play up! And win the war!' Football, the nation and the First World War 1914–15," *Journal of Contemporary History* 20 (1985): 363–78.

Verhey, Jeffrey, *The Spirit of 1914: Militarism, Myth, and Mobilization in Germany*, Cambridge, 2000.

Vierhaus, Rudolf, and Bernhard vom Brocke, eds, *Forschung im Spannungsfeld von Politik und Gesellschaft: Geschichte und Struktur der Kaiser-Wilhelm-/Max-Planck-Gesellschaft*, Stuttgart, 1990.

Vinen, Richard, *France 1934–1979*, Basingstoke, 1996.

Viola, Lynne, *Peasant Rebels under Stalin: Collectivization and the Culture of Peasant Resistance*, New York, 1996.

Viola, Lynne, ed., *Contending with Stalinism: Soviet Power and Popular Resistance in the 1930s*, New York, 2002.

Virgili, Fabrice, *La France "virile": des femmes tondues à la Libération*, Paris, 2001.

Wade, Rex A., *The Russian Revolution, 1917*, Cambridge, 2000.

Waldron, Peter, *Between Two Revolutions: Stolypin and the Politics of Renewal in Russia*, London, 1998.

Walker, Mark, *German National Socialism and the Quest for Nuclear Power, 1939–1949*, Cambridge, 1989.

Wall, Richard, and Jay Winter, eds, *The Upheaval of War: Family, Work and Welfare in Europe 1914–1918*, Cambridge, 1988.

Walther, Daniel J., *Creating Germans Abroad: Cultural Policies and National Identity in Namibia*, Athens OH, 2002.

Walworth, Arthur, *Wilson and His Peacemakers: American Diplomacy at the Paris Peace Conference, 1919*, New York, 1986.

Wandycz, Piotr S., *The Twilight of French Eastern Alliances, 1926–1936: French–Czechoslovak–Polish Relations from Locarno to the Remilitarization of the Rhineland*, Princeton NJ, 1988.

Wanrooij, Bruno P. F., "Italy: Sexuality, Morality and Public Authority," in *Sexual Cultures in Europe: National Histories*, Franz Eder, Lesley Hall, and Gert Hekma, eds, Manchester, 1999, pp. 114–37.

Ward, Stephen R., "Great Britain: Land Fit for Heroes Lost," in *The War Generation: Veterans of the First World War*, Stephen R. Ward, ed., Port Washington NY, 1975, pp. 10–37.

Wardley, Peter, "The commercial banking industry and its part in the emergence and consolidation of the corporate economy in Britain before 1940," *Journal of Industrial History* 3 (2000): 71–96.

Watt, D. C., "Restraints on War in the Air Before 1945," in *Restraints on War: Studies in the Limitation of Armed Conflict*, Michael Howard, ed., New York, 1979.

Watt, D. C., *How War Came: The Immediate Origins of the Second World War, 1938–1939*, London, 1989.

Wawro, Geoffrey, *The Franco-Prussian War: The German Conquest of France in 1870–1871*, Cambridge, 2003.

Webster, Richard A., *Industrial Imperialism in Italy, 1908–1915*, Berkeley CA, 1975.

Weigley, R. F., *Eisenhower's Lieutenants: The Campaign of France and Germany, 1944–1945*, Bloomington IN, 1999.

Weinberg, Gerhard L., *The Foreign Policy of Hitler's Germany: Starting World War II, 1937–1939*, Chicago IL, 1980.

Weindling, Paul, *Health, Race and German Politics between National Unification and Nazism, 1870–1945*, Cambridge, 1989.

Weiner, Amir, *Making Sense of War: The Second World War and the Fate of the Bolshevik Revolution*, Princeton NJ, 2001.

Welch, David, *Modern European History 1871–2000: A Documentary Reader*, London, 2000.

Welch, David, *Germany, Propaganda and Total War 1914–1918: The Sins of Omission*, London, 2000.

Welch, Steven R., "'Harsh but just'? German military justice in the Second World War: a comparative study of the court-martialling of German and US deserters," *German History* 17 (1999): 369–99.

Whalen, Robert W., *Bitter Wounds: German Victims of the Great War, 1914–1939*, Ithaca NY, 1984.

Wheeler, Mark C., "Pariahs to Partisans: The Communist Party of Yugolsavia," in *Resistance and Revolution in Mediterranean Europe, 1939–1948*, Tony Judt, ed., London, 1989.

White, Dan S., *Lost Comrades: Socialists of the Front Generation 1918–1945*, Cambridge MA, 1992.

White, Ralph, "Unity and Diversity of Resistance," in *Resistance in Europe, 1939–1945*, Stephen F. Hawes and Ralph T. White, eds, Harmondsworth, 1975, pp. 7–23.

Wildenthal, Lora, *German Women for Empire, 1884–1945*, Durham NC, 2001.

Wildman, Allan K., *The End of the Russian Imperial Army: The Old Army and the Soldiers' Revolt (March–April 1917)*, Princeton NJ, 1980.

Williamson, Samuel R., *Austria-Hungary and the Origins of the First World War*, New York, 1991.

Williamson, Samuel R., and Russel Van Wyk, *July 1914: Soldiers, Statesmen, and the Coming of the Great War: A Brief Documentary History*, Boston MA, 2003.

Willitt, John, *Art and Politics in the Weimar Period: The New Sobriety 1917–1933*, New York, 1978.

Wilson, Keith M., *The Policy of the Entente: Essays on the Determinants of British Foreign Policy 1904–1914*, Cambridge, 1985.

Wilson, Keith M., ed., *Decisions for War, 1914*, London, 1995.

Wilson, Perry R., "Saints and Heroines: Rewriting the History of Italian Women in the Resistance," in *Opposing Fascism: Community, Authority and Resistance in Europe*, T. Kirk and A. McElligott, eds, Cambridge, 1999, pp. 180–98.

Wilson, T. A., *The Downfall of the Liberal Party*, London, 1966.

Wilson, T. A., "Who Fought and Why? The Assignment of American Soldiers to Combat," in *Time to Kill: The Soldiers' Experience of War in the West, 1939–1945*, Paul Addison and Angus Calder, eds, London, 1997, pp. 284–303.

Winkler, Dörte, *Frauenarbeit im Dritten Reich*, Hamburg, 1977.

Winter, Denis, *Death's Men: Soldiers of the Great War*, London, 1978.

Winter, Jay M., *The Experience of World War I*, New York, 1989.

Winter, Jay M., *Sites of Memory, Sites of Mourning: The Great War in European Cultural History*, Cambridge, 1995.

Winter, Jay M., and Blaine Baggett, *1914–1918: The Great War and the Shaping of the Twentieth Century*, London, 1996.

Winter, Jay M., and Emmanuel Sivan, eds, *War and Remembrance in the Twentieth Century*, New York, 1999.

Wittgens, Herman J., "War Guilt Propaganda Conducted by the German Foreign Ministry During the 1920s," in *Historical Papers/Communications Historiques*, Canadian Historical Association, Montreal, 1980, pp. 228–47.

Wohl, Robert, *The Generation of 1914*, Cambridge MA, 1979.

Wolff, Kurt H., ed., *The Sociology of Georg Simmel*, Glencoe IL, 1950.

Wootton, Graham, *The Politics of Influence: British Ex-Servicemen, Cabinet Decisions, and Cultural Change, 1917–57*, London, 1963.

Wouters, Cas, *Sex and Manners: Female Emancipation in the West 1890–2000*, London, 2004.

Wright, Gordon, *The Ordeal of Total War*, New York, 1968.

Wright, Jonathan, "Stresemann and Locarno," *Contemporary European History* 4/2 (1995): 109–31.

Young, James, *The Texture of Memory: Holocaust Memorials and Meaning*, New Haven CT, 1993.

Young, Robert J., *In Command of France: French Foreign Policy and Military Planning, 1933–1940*, Cambridge MA, 1978.

Young, Robert J., *France and the Origins of the Second World War*, New York, 1996.

Youngblood, Denise J., *Movies for the Masses: Popular Cinema and Soviet Society in the 1920s*, Cambridge, 1992.

Zamagni, Vera, *The Economic History of Italy 1860–1990: Recovery after Decline*, Oxford, 1982.

Zantop, Susanne, *Colonial Fantasies: Conquest, Family and Nation in Pre-colonial Germany,*
      1770–1870, Durham NC, 1997.
Ziemke, Earl F., "The Soviet Armed Forces in the Inter-War Period," in *Military Effectiveness,*
      vol. 2: *The Interwar Period*, A. Millet and W. Murray, eds, London, 1988, pp. 1–38.
Zitelmann, Rainer, *Hitler: Selbstverständnis eines Revolutionärs*, Hamburg, 1987.
Zitelmann, Rainer, *Hitler: The Politics of Seduction*, London, 1998.
Zuber, Terence, "The Schlieffen Plan reconsidered," *War in History* 6/3 (1999): 262–305.
Zuber, Terence, *Inventing the Schlieffen Plan*, Oxford, 2003.
Zweig, Stefan, *World of Yesterday: An Autobiography*, Lincoln NE, 1964.

Index